AF905277

Terrorism, Security, and Computation

Series Editor

V. S. Subrahmanian, Department of Computer Science and Institute for Security, Technology and Society, Dartmouth College, Hanover, USA

The purpose of the Computation and International Security book series is to establish the state of the art and set the course for future research in computational approaches to international security. The scope of this series is broad and aims to look at computational research that addresses topics in counter-terrorism, counter-drug, transnational crime, homeland security, cyber-crime, public policy, international conflict, and stability of nations. Computational research areas that interact with these topics include (but are not restricted to) research in databases, machine learning, data mining, planning, artificial intelligence, operations research, mathematics, network analysis, social networks, computer vision, computer security, biometrics, forecasting, and statistical modeling. The series serves as a central source of reference for information and communications technology that addresses topics related to international security. The series aims to publish thorough and cohesive studies on specific topics in international security that have a computational and/or mathematical theme, as well as works that are larger in scope than survey articles and that will contain more detailed background information. The series also provides a single point of coverage of advanced and timely topics and a forum for topics that may not have reached a level of maturity to warrant a comprehensive textbook.

David Wright
Editor

Foreign Information Manipulation and Interference

Case Studies From the ATHENA Project

Springer

Editor
David Wright
Trilateral Research
London, UK

ISSN 2197-8778 ISSN 2197-8786 (electronic)
Terrorism, Security, and Computation
ISBN 978-3-031-91298-6 ISBN 978-3-031-91299-3 (eBook)
https://doi.org/10.1007/978-3-031-91299-3

© The Editor(s) (if applicable) and The Author(s), under exclusive license to Springer Nature Switzerland AG 2026

This work is subject to copyright. All rights are solely and exclusively licensed by the Publisher, whether the whole or part of the material is concerned, specifically the rights of translation, reprinting, reuse of illustrations, recitation, broadcasting, reproduction on microfilms or in any other physical way, and transmission or information storage and retrieval, electronic adaptation, computer software, or by similar or dissimilar methodology now known or hereafter developed.
The use of general descriptive names, registered names, trademarks, service marks, etc. in this publication does not imply, even in the absence of a specific statement, that such names are exempt from the relevant protective laws and regulations and therefore free for general use.
The publisher, the authors and the editors are safe to assume that the advice and information in this book are believed to be true and accurate at the date of publication. Neither the publisher nor the authors or the editors give a warranty, expressed or implied, with respect to the material contained herein or for any errors or omissions that may have been made. The publisher remains neutral with regard to jurisdictional claims in published maps and institutional affiliations.

Disclaimer: Views and opinions expressed in this book are those of the authors only and do not necessarily reflect those of the European Union, the European Research Executive Agency (REA) nor UKRI. Neither the European Union nor UKRI can be held responsible for them.

This Springer imprint is published by the registered company Springer Nature Switzerland AG
The registered company address is: Gewerbestrasse 11, 6330 Cham, Switzerland

If disposing of this product, please recycle the paper.

Acknowledgements

This book is based on research conducted in the ATHENA project (November 2023–October 2026), co-funded by the EU and UKRI under grant numbers 101132686 and 10107667. The latter applies to Trilateral Research. The authors are partners in the ATHENA consortium (An exposition on THe forEign informatioN mAnipulation and interference).

Co-funded by
the European Union

Contributors

Dr. David Wright, Trilateral Research
Dr. Richa Kumar, Trilateral Research
Dr. Evangelos Markatos, FORTH
Emmanouil Papadogiannakis, FORTH
Dr. Demetris Paschalides, University of Cyprus
Dimosthenis Stefanidis, University of Cyprus
Dr. George Pallis, University of Cyprus
Dr. Marios D. Dikaiakos, University of Cyprus
Tim Beyer, University of Applied Sciences for Public Service in Bavaria—Department of Policing
Dr. Joshua Bronson, RISE
Dr. Niklas Strand, RISE
Dr. Alina Östling, RISE
Dr. Joakim Rosell, RISE
Ilkka Vuorikuru, Laurea University of Applied Sciences
Jari Räsänen, Laurea University of Applied Sciences
Jaakko Tyni, Laurea University of Applied Sciences
Pau Perea, Eurecat
Mario Reyes de los Mozos, Eurecat
Malak Altaeb, Storyzy
Arsenio Cuenca, Storyzy
Prof. Owen Conlan, Trinity College Dublin
Dr. Gary Munnelly, Trinity College Dublin
Anna Pomortseva, European Organisation for Security
Kristian Reeson, European Organisation for Security
Elodie Reuge, European Organisation for Security
Pablo Hernández, Maldita
Celia Ramos-Vera, Maldita
Raquel Miguel Serrano, EU DisinfoLab
Maria Giovanna Sessa, EU DisinfoLab
Dr. Annye Braca, University College Dublin
Dr. Brendan Spillane, University College Dublin

Zaur Gouliev, University College Dublin
Marianna Prysiazhniuk, Information Systems Security Partners

Recommended citation: Wright, David (ed.), Malak Altaeb, Tim Beyer, Annye Braca Joshua Bronson, Owen Conlan, Arsenio Cuenca, Marios Dikaiakos, Zaur Gouliev, Pablo Hernández, Richa Kumar, Evangelos Markatos, Raquel Miguel, Gary Munnelly, Alina Östling, George Pallis, Emmanouil Papadogiannakis, Demetris Paschalides, Pau Perea, Anna Pomortseva, Marianna Prysiazhniuk, Celia Ramos-Vera, Jari Räsänen, Kristian Reeson, Elodie Reuge, Mario Reyes de los Mozos, Joakim Rosell, Maria Giovanna Sessa, Brendan Spillane, Dimosthenis Stefanidis, Niklas Strand, Jaakko Tyni, Ilkka Vuorikuru, David Wright (authors), *Foreign Information Manipulation and Interference*, Springer, Cham, 2025.

Contents

1 Executive Summary

David Wright

This book contains 32 case studies of foreign information manipulation and interference (FIMI). The authors examine the range of tactics, techniques and procedures (TTPs) that malign actors employ to deceive populations and undermine democracy. The authors seek to raise public awareness about FIMI. The case studies follow a structure for FIMI that we commend to other researchers as a step towards harmonisation of approaches and creation of a repository of FIMI case studies to better understand what attackers are doing.

The emphasis here is on *foreign*. Those engaged in FIMI activities are also often engaged in domestic disinformation (DIMI). There is, of course, lots of disinformation purveyed by domestic actors inside countries, e.g., the thousands of lies from the convicted felon and twice-impeached, twice-elected US President.[1] FIMI applies to disinformation purveyed by a foreign entity, whereas disinformation can be domestic or international. FIMI seems implicitly more serious, as it indicates interference in the affairs of another country, whereas disinformation does not necessarily imply a political agenda. FIMI implies the gravity of what foreign actors are trying to do outside their countries, whereas disinformation, while always to be called out, does not give any indications of the seriousness of the actions in question.

[1] See, for example, McQuade, Barbara, *Attack from Within: How Disinformation Is Sabotaging America*, Seven Stories Press, New York, 2024.

The list of authors who have contributed to this chapter are listed in the Front matter (pp. vii and viii).

D. Wright (✉)
Trilateral Research, London, UK
e-mail: david.wright@trilateralresearch.com

© The Author(s), under exclusive license to Springer Nature Switzerland AG 2026

D. Wright (ed.), *Foreign Information Manipulation and Interference*, Terrorism, Security, and Computation, https://doi.org/10.1007/978-3-031-91299-3_1

Our case study approach provides more granularity than other studies that aggregate FIMI attacks. Both approaches are necessary and useful. The case study approach provides more context for individual attacks that one doesn't necessarily find in FIMI studies that aggregate the findings of many attacks. The case study approach provides more detail on the objectives of the FIMI attack, the threat actors, the TTPs used, the effectiveness of the attack, the countermeasures (if any) applied against the attack, and what conclusions and recommendations one can draw from the case study. The aggregate approach, however, arguably gives a better picture of just how widespread, how prevalent, how big a problem FIMI has become.

Two-thirds of the case studies herein concern actions taken by Putin's Russia against other countries, notably Ukraine, especially since the Russian invasion in February 2022. While Russia appears to be far and away the most prolific of FIMI actors,[2] our report includes case studies involving China, Iran, North Korea, Turkey, Saudi Arabia and India which have also engaged in FIMI. Our percentage of case studies involving Russia is about the same as those analysed by the European External Action Service (EEAS) in its first FIMI report.[3] Indeed, it is instructive to understand the range, scale and sophistication of TTPs used by the Russians.[4]

Undoubtedly, other countries—the US, UK, France, Australia, etc.—also engage in FIMI, however, this report focuses on the FIMI cases generated by

---

[2] "Russia continues to pose the greatest threat when it comes to election disinformation, authorities said, while there are indications that Iran is expanding its efforts and China is proceeding cautiously when it comes to 2024." Klepper, David, "Russia Is Relying on Unwitting Americans to Spread Election Disinformation, US Officials Say", AP News, 29 July 2024. https://apnews.com/article/russia-trump-biden-harris-china-election-disinformation-54d7e44de370f016e87ab7df33fd11c8. "Director of National Intelligence Avril Haines told Congress May 15 that China, Russia and Iran are the leading threats, but Russia stands out as the most active." Editorial Board, "From Iran and Russia, the Disinformation Is Now. The Target Is America", *Washington Post*, 19 Aug 2024. https://www.washingtonpost.com/opinions/2024/08/19/russia-iran-ai-disinformation-election/.

[3] European External Action Service (EEAS), "1st EEAS Report on Foreign Information Manipulation and Interference Threats: Towards a Framework for Networked Defence", January 2023. https://www.eeas.europa.eu/eeas/1st-eeas-report-foreign-information-manipulation-and-interference-threats_en.

[4] In this book, the authors often refer to "Russia", "the Russians", "China", "Iran", etc. While most of the case studies focus on FIMI perpetrated by the governments of the countries cited, often those governments outsource their FIMI activities to third parties. We have seen the phenomenon of disinformation-for-hire companies who offer their services to governments or their proxies. In other cases, some companies contribute to the FIMI activity, without necessarily coordinating with the government in question, more for financial motivations than political. Attribution to a specific government agency or department or unit is challenging. Hence, throughout the book when we refer to Russia or the Russians or China or the Chinese or whomever, we know the evidence (the observables) points to the government, its proxies, its collaborators and/or its companies and/or other groups or citizens with origins in the country referenced without knowing who specifically is responsible for generating and deploying the FIMI.

authoritarian regimes. We include case studies of FIMI that have been relatively successful as well as others that failed to gain much traction. Some FIMI attacks are more impactful than others, however, we have not selected case studies based only on their impact. In some cases, where FIMI attacks failed to gain traction, we are interested in why they didn't gain as much traction as those cases that were very impactful.

We commend this report to various stakeholders—FIMI researchers, policy-makers, academics, civil society organisations. We hope it will raise stakeholder and public awareness about the range of TTPs that attackers employ and what countermeasures are effective in countering this insidious phenomenon.

The co-authors of this text are partners in the EU-funded ATHENA project (Nov 2023–Oct 2026). The partners selected the case studies from a list of disinformation reports and articles in journals and newspapers that we had compiled in Zotero by the end of 2023. The number of items in the folder 'Russian disinfo' was more than 10 times greater than those involving China. We took into account various criteria in making our selection, such as the variety of TTPs used, the availability of data and reports on which we needed to draw to construct the case studies, the scale of the FIMI attacks, the geographic dispersion, the presumed objectives of the attackers, their effectiveness and the countermeasures employed against them.

The case studies herein draw on the DISARM Foundation's framework.[5] There are various frameworks for analysing disinformation, but we chose the DISARM framework, as it is employed by others such as the EEAS, Viginum, the governmental agency in France charged with exposing disinformation in that country and, others. The DISARM framework was based on the ATT&CK framework developed by the MITRE Corp in the US as well as the STIX format.[6] The ATT&CK framework concerns cyberattacks more generally and as many FIMI attacks are also cyber-based, it is another reason we adopted the DISARM framework. The authors of this report have had numerous interactions with officials from the DISARM Foundation who have been kind enough to give detailed webinars on their framework to the partners.

Chapter 3 of this report focuses on different frameworks that are pertinent to the analysis of disinformation, including those mentioned above as well as FIMI-ISAC, OpenCTI, MISP, Oasis Open, RAND, the Centre for Advanced Tactics to counter Disinformation (ADTAC), the Credibility Coalition, the Information Laundromat, the EU Code of Practice on Disinformation.

Chapter 4 consists of our 32 case studies. We presented this list at a face-to-face meeting of partners, the EC Research Executive Agency, DG Research and the EEAS. In the section that follows, we present a very brief summary of each of the case studies.

---

[5] https://www.disarm.foundation/framework.

[6] https://oasis-open.github.io/cti-documentation/stix/intro.html.

Chapter 5 consists of our analysis of the tactics, techniques and procedures used in the case studies and elsewhere. Chapter 6 is a synthesis of 20 interviews conducted by the authors with experts in disinformation. It summarises key issues pertinent to our study of FIMI. Chapter 7, the last, has our conclusions from undertaking the case studies as well as our recommendations directed to the European Commission.

1.1 FIMI Case Studies

The numbers of the case study summaries below correspond to their numbers in Chap. 4.

4.2: Did the Russians Dupe the US Republican Party?
Alexander Smirnov, a Ukrainian who claims to have had contacts with the GRU, the Russian military intelligence service, had been an agent for the FBI for some years before he claimed in 2020 to have evidence that Joe and Hunter Biden had each received bribes of US $5 million. Republicans took a redacted FBI statement as evidence of Biden's corruption and a reason to impeach him. In Feb 2023, the FBI said Smirnov had produced no evidence of Biden bribery.

4.3. Altered Photo Showing Zelensky Holding a Jersey with a Swastika
In the first days after Russia's 2022 aggression against Ukraine, Russian-aligned actors used blogs, social networks and inauthentic news websites to spread a cheaply doctored photo of President Zelensky holding a jersey with a swastika, falsely portraying him as a Nazi sympathiser. Recycling a 2021 image, the actors aimed to flood digital space, degrade Zelensky and his institution, distract from Russian aggression and justify the invasion by reinforcing the Kremlin's 'de-Nazification' narrative.

4.4: Disinformation About Zelensky Buying a Villa in Florida
In late 2023, a YouTube video featured an alleged Secret Service agent claiming that Zelensky was going to flee to the US, obtain citizenship and buy a villa in Florida funded by US aid. DC Weekly, linked to Russian propaganda, amplified the story with fabricated details. Coinciding with Zelensky's visit to secure US aid, US political influencers and Russian media, including RT and TASS, promoted the story to undermine Zelensky's image, divide US public opinion and undermine support for aid to Ukraine.

4.5: How the Russian FIMI Actors Reacted to the US Aid Package
This case study focuses on Russia's FIMI, which touted the inevitability of victory over Ukraine even with the US's support and military and financial aid. The case portrays a campaign in response to the aid package approved by the US Congress in April 2024. Our analysis suggests two main narratives around the subject. The first one claimed Ukrainian statehood is false, as it relied on Western support and,

second, the inevitability of Ukrainian defeat even with the military and financial support provided by the West.

4.6: Russian FIMI Against the Armed Forces of Ukraine
Russia's FIMI activities have targeted the Armed Forces of Ukraine (AFU) since Russia's illegal annexation of Crimea in 2014. It has attempted to build a positive image for the Russian army while demonising the AFU. The FIMI campaigns have run alongside military actions. The FIMI only grew after Russia's large-scale invasion of Ukraine in 2022. The disinformation campaigns against the AFU aimed to weaken societal trust in the army, demoralise its members and justify Russian actions domestically and internationally. These efforts sought to undermine Ukraine's defence capabilities and public morale while bolstering Russia's geopolitical and ideological narratives.

4.7: Russian Initiatives to Use Farmers' Protests in Germany
In January 2024, Germany was the scene of one of the largest farmer protests in the nation's history. Federal government plans to cut subsidies for the agrarian sector prompted farmers to demonstrate in cities and on highways to show their opposition to the plans. The demonstrations were a prime target for foreign intervention in the form of a FIMI campaign, as Russia linked them to German military aid to Ukraine.

4.8: Russian FIMI About Burning the Quran in Sweden
Sweden applied to join NATO on 18 May 2022. This was a significant shift for the country, and a change in the balance of power around the Baltic, especially as Finland was also applying for membership in NATO. Throughout 2023 and 2024, an orchestrated campaign from Russian and Iranian sources tried to tie the Swedish state to several Quran burnings. This campaign focused on increasing conflict between Sweden and Muslim-majority countries while Sweden was trying to join NATO.

4.9: Russian FIMI About the (Fabricated) 'Lisa' Rape Case
On 11 January 2016, 13-year-old Lisa disappeared on her way home from school in Berlin. The next day, Lisa turned up again and told her parents that she had been abducted to a flat by three unknown 'southerners' who could barely speak German, beaten several times and raped. The combination of Lisa's Russian German origin, the poor German language skills of her parents and a bad crisis communication of the local authorities culminated in widespread protests fuelled by a Russian FIMI campaign in which the Russian Foreign Minister played a role that would rupture the social relationship between Russian-Germans and the rest of society.

4.10: Russian Propaganda After Finland's Transition to NATO
Finland's NATO membership in May 2023 was a response to the security threat posed by Russia's aggression against Ukraine. Historically non-aligned, Finland had maintained a 'NATO option' as a political compromise. Despite expected

protests from Russia, the reaction was limited to condemnation. However, there was a significant increase in asylum seekers at the Russian border, reminiscent of a 2016 incident. By late 2023, Finland closed several border crossings in response to the rising number of migrants. Suspecting Russian government intervention in pushing migrants to the border with Finland, the government cited national security and hybrid threats from Russia. Interior Minister Mari Rantanen indicated the situation could persist, and emphasised the need for firm, transparent decision-making, legislative readiness and EU solidarity to manage such crises effectively.

4.11: Russian FIMI Framing the Finnish President Before and After the Election
Alexander Stubb, known for his pro-Western stance and criticism of Russia, has been negatively portrayed in Russian media, particularly following his comments on nuclear power and his stance during election debates. Russian narratives have framed him as hostile, with Kremlin spokespersons highlighting Finland's unfriendly position towards Russia. Stubb's call for European readiness in a *Financial Times* interview was depicted as war-mongering by Russian outlets, emphasising NATO's eastward expansion. High-profile figures like Stubb are vulnerable to hostile influence operations, necessitating robust media protection strategies and institutional support to mitigate disinformation and safeguard national security.

4.12: Russia Today (RT), Its Narratives and Ideological Biases
RT has functioned as one of the Kremlin's most effective weapons in its informational battlefield against Western democracies. Its main strategy is based on the adoption of an 'anti-hegemonic' editorial line, with criticism of governments in Europe and the US, exploiting their vulnerabilities and increasing polarisation. RT shows how disinformation can be effective while adopting a particular ideological scope and not necessarily only spreading hoaxes.

4.13: A Wagner Campaign Targeting French Army in Mali
In collaboration with the Malian junta, the Wagner Group orchestrated a disinformation campaign aimed at covering up their involvement in a civilian massacre. By staging evidence, they deflected blame onto the French military, operating in Mali as part of Operation Barkhane. This FIMI attack brought together the physical and cyber realms. Wagner spread images of a mass grave, which they had staged. They promoted narratives exploiting the colonial heritage of France in Mali.

4.14: Russia Uses Bribery to Spread Disinformation
Since 2014, Russia has spent more than $300 million bribing foreign politicians, primarily in Europe, to spread pro-Russian narratives and undermine democratic processes. The bribery is part of a broader disinformation campaign that targets media and politicians, attempting to influence public opinion on its war against Ukraine and other issues. Viktor Medvedchuk and Artem Marchevskyi have been key actors in orchestrating these efforts through platforms such as *Voice of Europe*. Law enforcement across Europe is investigating covert payments and propaganda

networks linked to Russian state interests. Countermeasures, such as sanctions and new legislation, are being developed to combat this growing threat to democratic integrity.

4.15: Russian Interference in the Spanish Election in July 2023
The Russian-speaking community based in Spain was the target of a FIMI campaign that disseminated false material through the Telegram platform, cloned websites and bulletproof hosting.[7] Its intention was to create mistrust among this group of people. The campaign's restricted focus meant that, despite its advanced methods, it had little effect on the larger Spanish electorate. The strategy was successful in confusing the targeted population, but it had little impact on the results of the national election.

4.16: European Parliament Report on FIMI in European Elections
In June 2024, European citizens voted for the new European Parliament. This case study highlights a sophisticated disinformation campaign during the European Parliament elections, orchestrated primarily by the Voice of Europe. The campaign was backed by pro-Kremlin advocates Viktor Medvedchuk and Artem Marchevskiy, aiming to sway public opinion and undermine the European Union's democratic processes and its support for Ukraine. The Russians used multiple tactics, including distorted narratives, divisive rhetoric and strategic manipulation of social media platforms.

4.17: Doppelganger: Russian Disinformation Using Media Clones and More
Since February 2022, the Russian-origin 'Doppelganger' operation—also known as RRN (for Reliable Recent News)—has targeted multiple countries to undermine support for Ukraine by impersonating media and institutions' websites and spreading disinformation. Despite the identification and sanctioning of the main actors, the operation has expanded with new actions and a complex obfuscation infrastructure to persist and target other international events. Doppelganger is linked to other Russian campaigns.

4.18: Russian Disinformation About Russian Attacks
The case discusses how Russia has used its FIMI campaigns to frame Ukrainian forces as responsible for the consequences of Russian missile attacks. The case explains how the shifting of responsibility has been instrumentalised since 2014 and reinforced after 2022 when the large-scale phase of aggression began. In this case, Russia blamed the Ukrainian air defence for the damage caused by Russian missiles in Odesa in 2024. It shows how the Russian narrative tried to shift responsibility for war crimes and aggression onto Ukraine.

---

[7] Bulletproof hosting refers to web hosting services that are designed to be highly resistant to takedowns.

4.19: Russian Disinformation About COVID-19 Vaccines
Fazze, a Russian-co-owned website that describes itself as an 'influencer marketing platform' connecting bloggers and advertisers, contacted YouTubers in France and Germany and offered them money to tell their followers that the Pfizer/BioNTech vaccine was responsible for hundreds of deaths. Fazze told the influencers to say that the death rate from Pfizer's vaccine was three times that from AstraZeneca's, which is technologically similar to Russia's Sputnik V vaccine. Although influencers in France and Germany quickly went public with Fazze's approach, influencers in India and Brazil published content (now deleted) compatible with Fazze's request.

4.20: Meta Dismantles Large-Scale Chinese Disinformation Campaign
Many organised accounts of Chinese origin use social networks such as Meta to spread disinformation about other countries' policies and to change the narrative on different social issues such as the origin of COVID. Platforms such as Facebook (Meta) use disinformation detection algorithms to detect and eliminate these campaigns. However, these campaigns advance over time by redirecting Facebook users to other pages to make the campaigns more difficult to detect.

4.21: Facebook Accounts in China Impersonated Americans, Meta Says
In the previous use case, we examined the campaign detected by Meta some years ago, while in this case, we see how it has evolved over time to the present. We also see how the methods followed by Chinese disinformation organisations remain the same given the difficulties for algorithms to detect them when using external pages.

4.22: PAPERWALL: Chinese Websites Pose as Local News to Target Global Audiences
The PAPERWALL campaign involves more than 100 websites operated from China, posing as local news outlets in 30 countries across Europe, Asia and Latin America. These sites disseminate pro-Beijing disinformation, often hidden within commercial content. Attributed to a PR firm, PAPERWALL shows China's increasing use of private firms to manage foreign influence operations. Despite the limited current exposure, the rapid proliferation of these sites presents long-term risks.

4.23: Chinese Disinformation About the Release of Fukushima Water
On Friday, 11 March 2011, an earthquake of magnitude 9.0 hit Japan. The earthquake impacted the Fukushima nuclear power plant; large quantities of water were used to cool down the reactors damaged by the earthquake. This water was treated and stored in tanks. Japan, in accordance with international practices, started releasing the treated wastewater into the Pacific Ocean in August 2023 at a slow rate of 130 tons of water per day. This release triggered a torrent of disinformation in some cases including pictures of dead fish and pollution and attributing them to the release of the Fukushima water. In retrospect, the pictures were from different regions of the planet, sometimes taken well before the release of the water, and completely unrelated to the Fukushima event.

4.24. Turkey's Disinformation About North Cyprus as an Independent State
Amid the Russia-Ukraine war, Russia's plan to deploy a mobile consular unit in the unrecognised 'Turkish Republic of Northern Cyprus' (TRNC) led to false claims in Turkish and Turkish Cypriot media that Russia was opening a consulate, implying official recognition. This discourse, prominent from 2022 through 2024, fuelled discussions about increased Russian interest in the TRNC. The disinformation incident also spread on social media, with pro-TRNC groups pushing for the international recognition of TRNC.

4.25: Turkey's Disinformation About a Clash with the UN in the Cyprus Buffer Zone
Following Turkey's 1974 invasion, Cyprus was divided, creating a UN-controlled buffer zone between the Republic of Cyprus and the unrecognised TRNC. On 18 August 2023, a clash between UN peacekeepers and Turkish Cypriot forces in the buffer zone triggered a disinformation incident by Turkish and TRNC sources. They spread false narratives, portraying Turkish Cypriots as victims, misrepresenting UN actions and falsely claiming a Russian veto at the UN Security Council.

4.26: Varosha to Vegas: The Real Estate Exploitation and Disinformation Tactics by TRNC
The TRNC has been illegally monetising Greek Cypriot properties in Turkish-occupied Cyprus, but these efforts have significantly intensified over the past year. Sensational narratives, such as transforming Varosha into the 'Las Vegas of the Mediterranean', and false claims about King Charles III owning a luxury hotel and President Zelenskyy purchasing a casino have been used to manipulate public perception and attract foreign investment. Digital campaigns specifically target international buyers, while geopolitical manoeuvres, like rumoured Russian consular openings, create a facade of recognition. These tactics exploit legal vulnerabilities and geopolitical tensions to bolster the TRNC's legitimacy.

4.27: North Korea's Disinformation Campaigns
The United Front Department (UFD)'s Cultural Exchange Bureau, which reports to Kim Jong Un, has led North Korea's disinformation campaigns against its own people as well as against South Korea. It has used a variety of tactics and techniques. It mixes disinformation, propaganda, intelligence-gathering and subversion in a dangerous brew. In one incident, North Korean cyber trolls hijacked South Korean users' online accounts and posted an estimated 68,000 propaganda items.

4.28: Iranian Interference in the US Elections
Two Iranian nationals employed at the Iranian company, Emennet Pasargad, stole voter information data in US swing states prior to the 2020 US presidential elections. The stolen data was used to send false election messages and videos to threaten registered Democrat voters to vote for Donald Trump. The FBI was notified about the hacking and threatening messages and were able to block the

unauthorised access of the hackers. Two Iranian nationals were charged with conspiracy to commit computer fraud and abuse, intimidate voters and transmit interstate threats. The Department of State's Rewards for Justice Programme offered a reward of up to $10 million for information on or about the Iranian nationals' activities.

4.29: Saudi Arabia's Anti-Iran Campaign During the First Trump Administration

This case study demonstrates how one country uses another's rhetoric to shape its own narrative and advance its strategic objectives through disinformation. It examines how Saudi Arabia exploited the Trump administration's anti-Iran stance (2017–2020) to further its own goals using FIMI techniques. By amplifying and distorting President Trump's anti-Iran statements, particularly his tweets, Saudi Arabia aimed to enhance its image while aligning its narrative with US policy and increasing negative sentiment towards Iran and undermining its Middle Eastern rivals.

4.30: Cyberwarfare and the Qatar Blockade

The May 2017 cyberattack on the Qatar News Agency (QNA) illustrated the role of cyberwarfare in shaping public perception and igniting international tensions. Hackers disseminated fake statements attributed to Qatar's Emir, commending Iran and extremist organisations. These misleading claims intensified pre-existing strains between Qatar and its Gulf neighbours, leading to a diplomatic crisis. Consequently, Saudi Arabia, the United Arab Emirates, Bahrain and Egypt severed relations with Qatar and initiated a blockade that lasted for three and a half years.

4.31: The Role of FIMI in Iraq's Tishreen Protests

This case study examines how foreign actors, primarily Saudi-linked, used FIMI tactics to manipulate the narrative surrounding the 2019–2020 Iraqi protests.[8] False narratives were spread on social media aimed at discrediting Qatar and particularly pro-Iran factions in Iraq. The goal was to undermine the legitimacy of the protests and amplify anti-Iran sentiments, ultimately serving Saudi geopolitical objectives. The study identifies key FIMI tactics, such as the creation of inauthentic accounts, manipulation of the social media narrative and emotional appeals, all of which contributed to shaping public discourse and undermining the objectives of the protest movement.

4.32: India Disinformation Campaign Following the Pulwama Attack

The Indian disinformation campaign following the 2019 Pulwama attack, where a suicide bomber killed more than 40 security personnel, exemplifies contemporary

[8] The Tishreen protests in Iraq derived from the Arabic name for the month of October, "Tishreen Al-Awwal".

information warfare. By portraying Pakistan as the primary aggressor, the campaign actively worked to undermine its international standing and diplomatically isolate the nation. These narratives escalated tensions and kept Pakistan on the FATF grey list.[9] By strategically manipulating conflicts and emotional responses, the operation effectively shaped public perception and political discourse. Its consequences—strained diplomatic relations, societal fragmentation and diminished media credibility—highlight the enduring challenges that disinformation poses in today's geopolitical landscape.

4.33: Turkey Sought to Undermine Sweden's Bid for NATO Membership
From 2022 to 2024, Turkey conducted a coordinated campaign to challenge Sweden's NATO membership bid, using disinformation to frame Sweden as a terrorist supporter, particularly concerning the Kurdistan Workers' Party (PKK). This strategy was synchronised with ongoing NATO talks, as Turkey wielded its veto power to coerce Sweden into agreeing to concessions like tougher anti-terror laws and considering extraditing individuals Turkey categorised as terrorists. Through state-controlled media, bot networks and social media narratives amplified by hashtags such as #NATOVetoOnSweden, Turkey disseminated claims linking Sweden to terrorism, thereby undermining its global credibility and using this as a reason for its veto. The disinformation efforts were directed at both domestic and international audiences, using multiple languages for broader impact. Nevertheless, Sweden officially joined NATO in March 2024. This case study provides insight into how FIMI can influence international discussions and negotiations by leveraging strategic narratives and state-controlled information spaces.

1.2 Reverse Engineering of TTPs

The case studies are followed by a chapter on the tactics, techniques and procedures (TTPs) used in the case studies and elsewhere. The chapter on TTPs was based on the DISARM Framework,[10] from which we created JSON files.[11] Here is an extract of what the framework looks like (Fig. 1.1).

Complementing DISARM, we propose the **ATHENA FIMI analysis framework**, offering a robust methodology for identifying, gathering, storing and sharing TTPs through **observable** and **incident canvases**. These canvases employ design-thinking principles[12] to guide analysts in capturing detailed information about

[9] The FATF is the Financial Action Task Force which puts the spotlight on countries with deficiencies in their measures to combat money laundering, terrorist financing and proliferation financing.
[10] https://disarmfoundation.github.io/disarm-navigator/.
[11] JSON (JavaScript Object Notation) files are text-based files used to store and transmit structured data in a format that is both human-readable and machine-readable.
[12] Gobble, MaryAnne M., "Design thinking", *Research-Technology Management,* Vol. 57, 1987, pp. 59–62. https://www.tandfonline.com/doi/abs/10.5437/08956308X5703005.

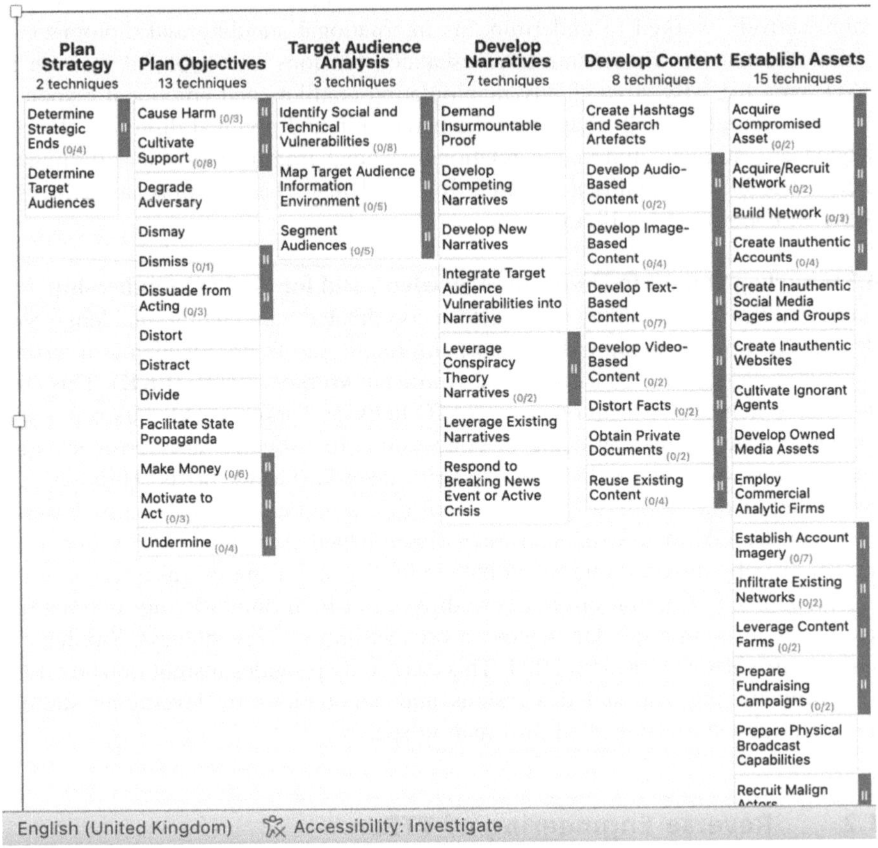

Fig. 1.1 DISARM Navigator

individual disinformation pieces and broader incidents, ensuring a thorough understanding of how disinformation campaigns are structured and executed. Key steps in this methodology include defining targets and threat actors, mapping information sources, gathering and verifying data, examining content, reverse engineering TTPs and reporting findings.

Analysis of TTPs in FIMI Operations

We employed the ATHENA FIMI analysis framework to extract and analyse the TTP patterns from the 32 FIMI case studies. Our analysis unveiled critical patterns in the deployment of TTPs by various geopolitical actors and their proxies. These case studies, encompassing, among others, Russian, Chinese, Turkish, North Korean, Indian and Saudi disinformation efforts, reveal a sophisticated and strategic use of TTPs aimed at destabilising democratic institutions, manipulating public opinion and advancing geopolitical objectives. Proxies, such as state-affiliated media outlets and non-state actors, play a pivotal role in amplifying disinformation while maintaining plausible deniability. Predominantly, threat actors emphasise content creation and manipulation, particularly through social networks, employing techniques like 'Undermine' (T0135[13]), 'Divide' (T0079) and 'Distort Facts' (T0076) frequently across campaigns. Additionally, strategic audience segmentation (T0072) and leveraging existing narratives (T0003) amplify the reach and impact of disinformation efforts, often exploiting echo chambers and filter bubbles (T0102) to reinforce polarised narratives. Our TTP analysis highlights several key insights relevant to FIMI campaigns:

- **Understanding evolving disinformation strategies**: Disinformation campaigns are highly adaptive and strategic, consistently combining specific TTPs to enhance their operational impact. The frequent use of 'Develop Text-Based Content' (T0085) alongside 'Social Networks' (T0104) indicates a sophisticated approach to crafting and disseminating misleading information. This adaptability underscores the necessity for dynamic and flexible countermeasures that can evolve in tandem with threat actors' strategies.
- **Targeted tactics in specific contexts**: Disinformation campaigns are meticulously tailored to specific geopolitical contexts, such as Russia's efforts against Ukraine or Turkey's campaigns targeting Cyprus. These operations use tactics like 'Segment Audiences' (T0072) and 'Leverage Existing Narratives' (T0003) to exploit local vulnerabilities and align with broader strategic objectives. Understanding these targeted approaches is crucial for developing context-specific interventions that address the unique aspects of each disinformation campaign.
- **Recurring themes across multiple actors**: Multiple state actors employ similar TTPs to achieve their goals, such as 'Distort Facts' (T0023) and 'Amplify Existing Narrative' (T0118). This uniformity suggests the need for international cooperation and coordinated strategies to address the transnational nature of FIMI campaigns. Collaborative efforts can enhance the effectiveness of detection and mitigation measures by leveraging shared insights and resources.
- **Amplification through echo chambers**: Disinformation campaigns frequently exploit echo chambers and filter bubbles (T0102), where manipulated content reinforces pre-existing biases without challenge. Techniques like 'Flood Information Space' (T0049) and 'Cross-Posting' (T0119) ensure that disinformation spreads rapidly within these closed networks. Addressing the algorithmic reinforcement of echo chambers on social media platforms is essential for mitigating the amplification of disinformation.
- **Use of multimedia to enhance credibility**: The strategic combination of text-based (T0085) and image-based content (T0086) with video elements (T0087) enhances the credibility and persuasiveness of disinformation. This multimedia

[13] The DISARM Navigator applies codes, like those here, to the various tactics, techniques and procedures used by attackers. We reference these codes throughout this report.

approach makes false information more believable and harder to detect, necessitating advanced detection technologies that can analyse and verify content across multiple media types simultaneously.

- **Role of proxies in FIMI campaigns**: Proxies, such as state-affiliated media and non-state actors, extend the reach and complexity of disinformation campaigns while complicating attribution efforts. Techniques like 'Create Inauthentic News Sites' (T0098) and 'Create Fake Experts' (T0009) are frequently employed by proxies to build credible facades for spreading disinformation. Countermeasures must include strategies to identify and disrupt these proxy networks, as well as to enhance transparency and accountability in media operations.

Deepfakes and Generative AI in TTPs

Deepfake technology exemplifies the integration of advanced AI into TTPs, significantly enhancing the capability of threat actors to create and disseminate deceptive content. Generative AI models like ChatGPT, Stable Diffusion and Midjourney facilitate the creation of highly realistic text, images and videos, which are pivotal in executing sophisticated disinformation strategies. These tools enable threat actors to automate content generation, making it easier to produce large volumes of convincing fake media that can be seamlessly integrated into influence operations.

The evolution of deepfakes from basic face-swapping to complex multi-modal forgeries demonstrates the significant advancements in generative AI. These technologies not only enhance the realism of fabricated content but also increase its scalability and distribution efficiency. The DISARM framework has recently updated its TTP taxonomy to include generative AI techniques, in recognition of the escalating threat posed by deepfakes in FIMI operations.

Real-world implications of deepfakes are substantial, with instances such as fake audio clips of US President Joe Biden and fabricated videos of UK's Sir Keir Starmer highlighting the potential to disrupt political processes and erode public trust. These manipulations can influence election outcomes, incite social unrest and distort public discourse, posing severe threats to societal stability and democratic integrity.

Detection and mitigation of deepfakes involve a range of methodologies, including physical inconsistencies, fingerprint analysis, spatial and frequency-based techniques, and end-to-end AI models. Deepfake detection tools are essential for identifying synthetic media, although challenges remain in maintaining detection accuracy against continuously advancing deepfake technologies. Enhancing these detection capabilities requires ongoing research, diverse and comprehensive datasets, and the integration of robust AI-driven solutions.

Addressing the deepfake threat demands a multifaceted approach that includes technological advancements, regulatory measures and public awareness initiatives. Strengthening collaboration between technology developers, policymakers and researchers is crucial to develop effective countermeasures. Additionally, implementing ethical guidelines and fostering media literacy can help mitigate the impact of deepfakes, ensuring the resilience of democratic institutions and maintaining public trust in an increasingly digital world.

1.3 The Interviews

The authors conducted 20 interviews with experts from various fields, including political science, security studies and social data analysis, who noted the complex and interdisciplinary nature of FIMI. The interviews revealed that there is disagreement on whether FIMI should be considered a technological or historical phenomenon, with different experts focusing on different aspects, such as practical, theoretical and geopolitical dimensions. However, there was a consensus on the need for a more unified approach to enhance research and improve frameworks for combating FIMI.

The interviews highlighted the increasing sophistication of FIMI, which has evolved beyond the creation of false narratives to manipulate existing societal divisions and exploit fears. This shift is fueled by geopolitical events, the rise of digital platforms and the growing role of AI and social media. Foreign state actors often collaborate with local groups to amplify divisive content, complicating attribution efforts. The shift from isolated incidents to coordinated, long-term disinformation campaigns requires an interdisciplinary collaboration across sectors and experts. To effectively address these challenges, strategic, long-term frameworks are needed that can counter the evolving tools and tactics used in disinformation campaigns.

Information manipulation has become a powerful tool in shaping geopolitical events, with state-sponsored campaigns from Russia, China, Iran and others identified as significant sources of FIMI. Governments, particularly of countries such as Ireland, the UK and Poland, are facing challenges in countering FIMI and hybrid threats, especially during elections and international security crises. Industry researchers and journalists have noted the changing tactics of these campaigns, including the manipulation of domestic and international narratives, with particular focus on ongoing conflicts such as the war in Ukraine. The role of digital technologies, social media and AI in spreading disinformation is central to these challenges, with AI both enabling the creation of false content and offering potential tools for detecting it. However, interviewees felt that the rapid development of generative AI models could overwhelm efforts to manage the sheer volume of manipulated content, while the Internet's profit-driven nature exacerbates the spread of fake information, limiting democratic discourse.

Traditional methods like human fact-checking are increasingly insufficient in the face of fast evolving FIMI campaigns. The use of advanced techniques such as narrative laundering, deepfakes, AI-driven content and closed platforms like Telegram makes tracing the origin of disinformation a serious challenge. Such tactics complicate attribution, especially when perpetrators use tools like Tor to mask their identities. The increasing availability of AI-powered disinformation tools makes campaigns more cost-effective and scalable, further complicating detection and attribution. To combat these challenges, our interviewees advocated improved attribution methods, better detection tools and greater cross-sector collaboration.

The interviews underscored the multidisciplinary nature of FIMI research, with stakeholders from government, academia, media and industry all playing a role in tackling the issue. While collaboration is crucial, there are challenges in aligning objectives and coordinating efforts across sectors, especially during crises like elections or pandemics. The interviews also led to several key recommendations for improving efforts to combat FIMI. First, there is a need for a comprehensive, accessible framework for FIMI analysis. This framework should address the long-term, coordinated nature of FIMI campaigns and identify the social and political vulnerabilities they exploit. Second, efforts should be made to promote public awareness and enhance digital literacy, helping citizens to recognise manipulated information and understand the role of AI and algorithms in shaping the information landscape. Third, fostering international, cross-sectoral cooperation and training is crucial to countering state-sponsored disinformation campaigns, particularly from Russia, China and Iran. Governments, industry, academia and media must work together to develop coordinated strategies and support cross-disciplinary research initiatives. Finally, more funding should be allocated to research focused on improving attribution, and social media platforms should be more transparent in their handling of disinformation.

The key conclusion we draw from the interviews is that addressing FIMI requires a multifaceted approach that combines technological innovation, interdisciplinary collaboration and strategic, long-term planning. As disinformation continues to evolve, coordinated efforts across governments, industries and academia will be essential to mitigate its impact on democratic processes and public trust.

1.4 Lessons Learned

The range of case studies in Chap. 4 indicates a proliferation and inventiveness of different tactics, techniques and procedures employed by FIMI attackers. The case studies show the high adaptability of FIMI campaigns. FIMI actors use a wide range of platforms and techniques to evade detection and continue to spread their messages. Defenders need constant vigilance and adaptation of countermeasures as malicious actors' tactics evolve.

Attribution is a challenge. Some attackers cover their tracks well or engage in deniability. FIMI analysis requires an understanding of the different types of attackers in disinformation campaigns and their motivations.

Russia and China particularly use private firms to conduct their foreign influence campaigns, obfuscating the connections with the governments.

The term 'useful idiots' refers to individuals who unwittingly support a cause or agenda—often political or ideological—without fully understanding its implications, particularly when that cause is manipulative or harmful. The phrase was used to describe Western sympathisers of Soviet communism during the Cold War. The term has evolved and is now used more broadly to describe people who, in their enthusiasm or naivety, support movements, organisations or regimes that ultimately manipulate or exploit them. It is often used pejoratively to describe people who are seen as naïve or gullible in the political arena.

Although FIMI is frequently associated with elections, it has a much broader reach and continues to thrive even after the completion of the past EU elections of 9 June 2024. There remains a growing threat to democratic society. Attackers effectively employed information warfare techniques (such as content distortion and exploiting breaking news events) to amplify distrust within the EU, weaken transatlantic alliances and promote politicians sympathetic to the Kremlin. The incidents indicate a concerted effort not only to discredit the EU's actions but also to impact election outcomes by influencing voter sentiment through disinformation.

Sometimes attackers exploit historical tensions, as the Chinese did regarding Japan's discharge of Fukushima water or as Turkey has done in attempting to gain international recognition for its breakaway state in northern Cyprus. Disinformation spreads fast and often continues to spread even when the fakery is exposed.

Various potential threat actors, including state-sponsored groups, criminal organisations, hacktivists and individuals with malicious intent sometimes work together without any agreements. They share the same objective, so they all work to achieve it, bringing to bear their particular specialities in FIMI.

Social media has been found to be the biggest source of FIMI propagation. Protected, in part, by the pseudonymity provided by social networks, and sheltered by an almost total lack of transparency, aggressors find in social networks a fertile ground to cultivate and proliferate their propaganda.

The actual impact of a FIMI campaign is uncertain. One way of measuring impact is by the number of impressions that social media posts get. However, the difficulty in measuring effectiveness is trying to disentangle what is local and what is amplified by interference. Russian disinformation efforts, particularly focusing on social media as a significant battlefield for information warfare,[14] have been subject to extensive analyses by most Western countries' cybersecurity firms, intelligence agencies and academic research. However, the effectiveness of these campaigns and the impact of Western countermeasures remain subjects of ongoing analysis and debate.

Among the best defences against disinformation are transparency, effective communication and the use of counter-narratives that challenge disinformation targeting the European Union. Providing EU citizens with discursive elements so that they can evaluate different situations linked to disinformation implies being self-critical and taking seriously the relationship of trust between the European institutions and the societies of the different Member States.

[14] For a prediction about information warfare, see Wright, David, "AI and Information Warfare in 2025", 2019 IEEE SmartWorld, pp. 317–322. https://ieeexplore.ieee.org/document/906041.

The EU has developed several frameworks to combat disinformation, including the EU Cybersecurity Strategy[15] and initiatives through the European Centre of Excellence for Countering Hybrid Threats.[16] These bodies help coordinate responses to foreign interference across EU institutions and Member States, building resilience against cyberattacks and disinformation campaigns targeting elections.[17]

The European Parliament has also passed a resolution denouncing Russia's FIMI campaign in the wake of the Voice of the Europe scandal wherein some Putin- / Russia-sympathetic MEPs were paid for interviews on the Russian controlled medium.

Effective countermeasures against disinformation campaigns require a multifaceted approach, involving cooperation between governments, private sector entities (especially social media platforms), civil society organisations (CSOs) and the public. EU DisinfoLab has advocated the need for a whole-of-society approach to countering FIMI. However, this whole-of-society approach 'can be realistically achieved only if the large variety of actors engaged in countering FIMI speak a common language. Initiatives such as the DISARM and STIX frameworks constitute that common language, set up to normalise the monitoring, analysis, assessment and response to FIMI operations'.[18]

Governments and international organisations should focus on media literacy initiatives to help citizens critically assess information and resist manipulation. Governments should establish rapid-response teams trained to debunk FIMI as soon as it emerges.

Governments and/or CSOs should launch campaigns to educate the public on how to critically assess news sources, check for the credibility of information and evaluate the motives behind information sources. Individuals should be encouraged to seek alternative sources and question information in public campaigns.

Transparency and maintaining the public's trust are crucial elements in any response strategy. For specific actions taken in response to FIMI attacks, citizens and practitioners alike should be able to consult official sources or reports from credible research institutions, project consortia and think tanks that focus on disinformation and cybersecurity.

The EEAS should prioritise investment in multilingual tracking tools capable of detecting FIMI across different languages. This would allow for faster identification of manipulative content in different linguistic and regional contexts.

---

[15] https://digital-strategy.ec.europa.eu/en/policies/cybersecurity-strategy.

[16] https://www.hybridcoe.fi/.

[17] Koudelka, Michal, and Petr Fiala, "Czechs Bust Russian Network Paying off European Politicians", Radio Prague International, 28 March 2024. https://english.radio.cz/czechs-bust-russian-network-paying-european-politicians-8812632.

[18] Hénin, Nicolas, "FIMI: Towards a European Redefinition of Foreign Interference", EU-DisinfoLab, Brussels, p. 11. https://www.disinfo.eu/wp-content/uploads/2023/04/20230412_FIMI-FS-FINAL.pdf?utm_source=chatgpt.com.

National governments should strengthen monitoring mechanisms, improve transparency and work more closely with fact-checking organisations to mitigate the impact of FIMI.

EU Member States should promote image and video fact-checking skills to help individuals identify manipulated content and other forms of digital deception. Educating users about FIMI tactics can help them act as a first line of defence, significantly reducing the spread and impact of false information.

The EU should expedite the implementation of legislation modelled after the US Foreign Agents Registration Act (FARA), requiring foreign-funded entities to register, thereby increasing transparency. Moreover, swift enforcement of upcoming regulations on political advertising will help to curb foreign interference. Further sanctions should target individuals and entities involved in Russian FIMI efforts, particularly focusing on those responsible for running disinformation networks like Viktor Medvedchuk and the Voice of Europe.

The DISARM framework has several strengths: (i) it provides a common methodology for analysing disinformation events, (ii) it provides a common terminology and (iii) it has been adopted by the EU for exchange of FIMI information with the United States.[19] As attackers create new ways of FIMI, the DISARM Framework needs to evolve too (and it has). In addition to the Red Framework, it would be useful to have another framework on prevention and pre-bunking.

The DISARM Framework itself does not explicitly classify threat actors. The Framework focuses on identifying the tactics, techniques and procedures (TTPs) used in disinformation campaigns, regardless of the specific actor behind them. The DISARM Framework should continue to evolve, incorporating more information, in tandem with other MITRE matrices (D3FEND), defining threat actor groups, as well as obtaining the template for disinformation campaigns. This will help, through the application of AI-based tools, to analyse the different disinformation actions and attribute their authorship.

[19] https://www.eeas.europa.eu/sites/default/files/documents/2023/Annex%203%20-%20FIMI_29%20May.docx.pdf.

Introduction

2

David Wright

This book comprises 32 case studies of **foreign information manipulation and interference (FIMI)**, to which all partners in the EU-funded ATHENA project have contributed. The authors have structured the case studies based on the DISARM Foundation's Red Framework[1] and the STIX language.[2]

The purpose of the case studies is to understand the wide range of tactics, techniques and procedures used by Russian, Chinese and other actors/states to sow disinformation in other countries, their presumed objectives in doing so and their targets. The case studies help us understand how successful the perpetrators were in their activities. They also validate the utility of the DISARM Navigator as an analytical tool. The authors commend the structure they have used for the case studies and encourage other researchers to use the structure. The authors recommend also creation of a repository, a library, of case studies that researchers and security practitioners could share for their insights.

The reader will note the preponderance of case studies about Russian FIMI activities, which is to be expected as Russia currently poses the most serious threat to democratic practice in many countries around the world. In addition to its violence in Ukraine, Russian threats are manifest in its FIMI campaigns in many countries. The European External Action Service (EEAS) said, in its second report

[1] https://www.disarm.foundation/framework.

[2] Structured Threat Information Expression (STIX) is a language and serialization format used to exchange cyber threat intelligence (CTI). STIX is open source and free allowing those interested to contribute and ask questions freely. https://oasis-open.github.io/cti-documentation/stix/intro.html.

D. Wright (✉)
Trilateral Research, London, UK
e-mail: david.wright@trilateralresearch.com

© The Author(s), under exclusive license to Springer Nature Switzerland AG 2026
D. Wright (ed.), *Foreign Information Manipulation and Interference*, Terrorism, Security, and Computation, https://doi.org/10.1007/978-3-031-91299-3_2

on FIMI, released in January 2024, that ‘foreign actors have continued their intentional, strategic and coordinated attempts to manipulate facts, to confuse, and to sow division, fear and hatred. The most obvious example is Russia—trying to justify its war of aggression against Ukraine. However, other actors, such as China, also engage in the intentional manipulation of public conversations’.[3]

The research community has uncovered more influence campaigns coming from Russia than from any other country.

2.1 Methodology

The partners especially used the methods of case studies and interviews for the preparation of this report. Some reports, including the EEAS reports, aggregate the findings of many case studies, hundreds in some cases. Our approach has been different; we have ‘drilled’ down into what transpired in the selected case studies, which may not be so reflected well in the statistics of aggregated reports. The case study approach was, in effect, that pursued by Philip Howard in his analysis of the significant, even determinative role that disinformation played in Brexit and the 2016 US election (in effect, case studies).[4] Our deliverable combines both approaches. We have the case studies in Chaps. 4 and 5 dissects them and draws some conclusions about which TTPs are used most.

The case study methodology, whether in aggregate or individually focused, is well suited to study the manifestations of FIMI and TTPs as ‘context’[5] plays a key role in the spread of FIMI. A case study approach helps in ‘surveying in detail a range of environs, practices, and events which are centred around the spread’[6] of FIMI. It responds to the comment that a ‘holistic, in-depth investigation is needed’.[7] Our case study approach was guided by questions based on the DISARM framework. The authors discussed various possibilities for case studies, keeping some and removing others. We settled on those found in this book. The key criteria for selection of the case studies were:

- A range of attackers—While the majority of case studies involved Russia, the partners undertook case studies involving attackers from other countries.
- Geographic scope—Our case studies involved countries around the world. We were interested to see the different TTPs used in different countries.

---

[3] EEAS, “2nd EEAS Report on Foreign Information Manipulation and Interference Threats”, European External Action Service, January 2024. https://www.eeas.europa.eu/sites/default/files/documents/2024/EEAS-2nd-Report%20on%20FIMI%20Threats-January-2024_0.pdf.

[4] Howard, Philip N., *Lie Machines*, Yale University Press, 2020.

[5] Maci, S., M. Demata, M. McGlashan and P. Seargeant, eds., *The Routledge Handbook of Discourse and Disinformation*, Routledge, 2024.

[6] Ibid.

[7] Feagin, J.R., A.M. Orum and G. Sjoberg (eds.), *A case for the case study*, UNC Press Books, 2016.

- Involving foreign interference and information manipulation—There is lots of domestic information manipulation and interference (DIMI) and often the sowers of FIMI are also sowers of DIMI.
- Varied manifestations of FIMI and TTPs—We wanted varied case studies of FIMI events, some of which were hugely successful (at least in reaching lots of people) as well as others that failed to get much traction.
- Democratic impact—We were especially interested in the impact of FIMI on democratic practices in the EU as well countries beyond our borders.
- Adequate data—While there is lots of information and data about Russian FIMI, and increasingly about China, the disinformation efforts of some other countries haven't generated so many stories, articles and reports.
- Page length—We aimed for case studies of about five pages or so; however, we were not procrustean about having a fixed length for the case studies. As a result, some are longer than others.

The authors used the DISARM Navigator 'layer' or matrix to guide preparation of the case studies. The TTPs in the Navigator prompted the questions outlined in Sect. 4.1. The authors gathered the data for the 32 case studies by reviewing hundreds of new stories, journal articles, reports, blogs, websites, tweets and more. The authors identified events that met our criteria and interests as defined in Sect. 4.1. Among the challenges in putting together a book like this, involving almost 30 authors, is agreeing a structure for analysing the case studies as well as agreeing a format for citations.[8]

Upon completing the case studies, the authors transferred the key results to DISARM Navigator layers from which the partners have created JSON files which helped with the analysis in Chap. 5.

After the authors drafted the case studies, they formed five working groups, each of which was tasked with reviewing six case studies and suggesting amendments or clarifications wherever appropriate. In addition, the editors edited all the case studies. All partners provided inputs to the conclusions and recommendations, not only in their individual case studies but also in the final chapter.

The case study method was complemented by interviewing members of the ATHENA Stakeholder Board and other experts. Interviewing the members helped us understand what they 'think, or how they interpret an event or series of events, or what they have done or are planning to do'.[9] The case study method helped us obtain nuanced data on the complex issue of FIMI and its impact on democracy. Interviewing the ATHENA Board members required a special interviewing technique. 'An expert interview is a qualitative research method to help gather

[8] There are literally hundreds of different ways of formatting citations. We chose "the European format", as briefly described in the EC's *Interinstitutional Style Guide*. We also put citations in footnotes, like this one, rather than in endnotes or embedded in the text.

[9] Aberbach, J.D., and B.A. Rockman, "Conducting and Coding Elite Interviews", *PS: Political Science & Politics*, Vol. 35, No. 4, 2002, pp. 673–676. https://doi.org/10.1017/S1049096502001142.

in-depth insights and knowledge from individuals with specialized expertise and authority in a specific field, sector, or topic'.[10] An expert interview came to be defined 'as a qualitative semi-structured or open interview with a person holding 'expert knowledge'.[11]

The ATHENA Stakeholder Board comprised 17 members as of June 2024. These members have subject matter expertise in the field of information manipulation; the stakeholders are journalists, industry partners, members of fact-checking organisations, academics and researchers in the field of media studies, computer sciences and cybersecurity. The members were recruited for their expertise either directly or indirectly in the field of FIMI. Recommendations from ATHENA partners and snowball and purposive sampling were used to identify and recruit additional stakeholder board members and external experts for interviews. Names, contacts, recommendations, referrals and information given during introductory or previous interviews helped to extend the scope of the investigation.

The interviews with the Stakeholder Board members were in-depth, open-ended and semi-structured, and conducted between May 2024 and July 2024 to a 'point of saturation',[12] i.e., to the point at which no new information or themes were being observed in the data and the interviewees were reinforcing the information gathered so far. The ATHENA partners conducted interviews and digitally recorded them on Microsoft Teams with the consent of the interviewees. Most interviews lasted for about 60 min. The partners prepared an interview guide based on the case study research. The interview guide had seven blocks of questions: the first block of questions aimed at eliciting information on the interviewees' work profiles; the second block of questions concerned their experience with FIMI and disinformation in their work; the third block focused on their knowledge and experience of countering FIMI campaigns; the fourth block questions concerned the evolution of FIMI attacks; the fifth block of questions regarded the dangers of FIMI on democratic processes; sixth bloc of questions led to recommendations followed by the seventh block of questions on other potential interviewee candidates. The interview guide was not used inflexibly; instead, it was used as a reminder of key issues to be covered and used freely, altering its sequence as needed to probe for further information and asking new questions pertinent to the interviewee and the topics.

The interviewing method perfectly complemented the case study methodology: FIMI is carried out by means of online tactics and focusing on the case studies

---

[10] https://glginsights.com/articles/how-to-effectively-interview-a-subject-matter-expert/.

[11] Van Audenhove, L., and K. Donders, "Talking to people III: Expert interviews and elite interviews", in Hilde Van den Bulck, Manuel Puppis, Karen Donders and Leo Van Audenhove (eds.), *The Palgrave handbook of methods for media policy research*, 2019, pp. 179–197.

[12] Saunders, B., J. Sim, T. Kingstone, S. Baker, J. Waterfield, B. Bartlam, H. Burroughs and C. Jinks, "Saturation in qualitative research: exploring its conceptualization and operationalization", *Quality & quantity*, Vol. 52, 2018, pp. 1893–1907.

provided us with the contextual information to study manifestations of FIMI. Interviews helped us understand the human actors, their motivations and experiences with FIMI and provided us with an in-depth and nuanced perspective on FIMI.

2.2 Definitions

James Pamment, Director of the Lund University Psychological Defence Research Institute in Sweden, defined foreign interference as 'coercive, deceptive, and/or non-transparent efforts—during elections, for example—to disrupt the free formation and expression of individuals' political will by a foreign state actor or its agents'.[13] The European External Action Service (EEAS) expanded on this definition by describing **foreign information manipulation and interference (FIMI)** as 'a mostly non-illegal pattern of behaviour that threatens or has the potential to negatively impact values, procedures and political processes'.[14] This activity is characterised by its manipulative nature, conducted intentionally and in a coordinated manner by state or non-state actors, including their proxies both within and outside their territory.

Not all disinformation is FIMI, and FIMI is not only disinformation. As a brief report by the EU DisinfoLab notes, this distinction 'is welcome, as disinformation has too often been attached to the unfortunate term 'fake news'. In contrast, malicious actors have long understood that the best influence operations are not simply limited to false information'.[15] According to the EEAS, the notion of FIMI, which overlaps with the notion of disinformation, is both narrower and broader:

> It is narrower in that it only refers to information manipulation by actors foreign to the EU and its member states, thus not applying to domestic sources. It is broader insofar as it does not require the information spread by threat actors to be verifiably false or misleading. The deciding factor for whether something can be considered FIMI is not false or misleading content, but deceptive or manipulative behaviour.[16]

The EU's 2018 Action Plan against Disinformation defines **disinformation** 'as verifiably false or misleading information that is created, presented and disseminated for economic gain or to intentionally deceive the public, and may cause

[13] Pamment, James, *The EU's Role in Fighting Disinformation: Grafting A Disinformation Framework,* Carnegie Endowment for International Peace, Washington DC, 2020.

[14] https://www.eeas.europa.eu/eeas/tackling-disinformation-foreign-information-manipulation-interference_en And https://www.eeas.europa.eu/eeas/2021-stratcom-activity-report-strategic-communication-task-forces-and-information-analysis_en.

[15] Hénin, Nicolas, "FIMI: Towards a European Redefinition of Foreign Interference", EU DisinfoLab, 7 Apr 2023. https://www.disinfo.eu/publications/fimi-towards-a-european-redefinition-of-foreign-interference/.

[16] European Union, "1st EEAS Report on Foreign Information Manipulation and Interference Threats", 7 Feb 2023. https://www.eeas.europa.eu/eeas/1st-eeas-report-foreign-information-manipulation-and-interference-threats_en.

public harm. Public harm includes threats to democratic processes as well as to public goods such as Union citizens' health, environment or security. Disinformation does not include inadvertent errors, satire and parody, or clearly identified partisan news and commentary'.[17]

The DISARM Foundation definition of **disinformation** is somewhat similar: 'information that is false, misleading, incomplete, or out of context, and which is deliberately created, altered, manipulated, disseminated, or presented with the intent to deceive'. **Misinformation**, by contrast, is 'information that is false, misleading, incomplete, or out of context, but which is not created, disseminated, or presented with an intent to deceive'. Misinformation may originate as disinformation, or it may be created by error or mistake. It may then be spread unwittingly or in good faith by individuals who have no intent to deceive.[18]

It is often difficult—if not impossible—to establish a clear distinction between misinformation and disinformation, particularly when disinformation is forwarded by people who lack that political motive—people who may well believe they are passing along true information that will help others. People often do not know they are exposed to disinformation, and they are not able to decipher how it has a bearing on not only their cognition but also their attitudes and behaviour at the socio-political level.[19]

The DISARM authors chose **campaign** as the term for a coordinated set of disinformation **incidents.** The Oxford Internet Institute (OII) calls the Russian work on US elections a 'campaign' and uses the term 'incident' for shorter-duration events, which could themselves be part of a campaign, and **APT** (from the infosec term 'Advanced Persistent Threat') for an incident that appears to be continuous.[20]

In the abbreviation **TTPs**, a **tactic** is a way or means by which the objectives (ends) are met[21]; **techniques** are the *actions* depicting how they try to accomplish them and **procedures** are the specific combination of techniques across multiple tactics (or stages of an attack) that indicate intent and may be unique for different threat actors.[22] **Techniques** are the 'how' of a particular tactic. Techniques are associated with one or more tactics, as a particular technique may be used to

[17] Further refined definitions of misinformation, disinformation, information influence operations and foreign interference are provided in the European Democracy Action Plan.

[18] DISARM—FAQ. https://drive.google.com/file/d/1_4D_QyO2u3IADeYO37en3029IXUPxSZW/view?pli=1.

[19] Bilal, Arsalan, et al., "Comprehensive Security, Disinformation, and COVID-19: An Analysis of the Impacts of Mis- and Disinformation and Populist Narratives during the Pandemic [Version 1]", *Open Research Europe 2023*, November 2023.

[20] Terp, S.J., and Pablo Breuer, "DISARM: A Framework for Analysis of Disinformation Campaigns", *2022 IEEE Conference on Cognitive and Computational Aspects of Situation Management (CogSIM)*, 6 June 2022. https://ieeexplore.ieee.org/document/9830669.

[21] https://disarmframework.herokuapp.com/tactic/.

[22] Hénin, EU DisinfoLab, 2023, op. cit., p. 6.

accomplish different goals. Techniques may also be formulated as what an actor gains by doing something. Techniques can be combined to create **procedures.**[23]

The DISARM authors identified 145 techniques across incidents, some of which (e.g., amplification with botnets) are repeated across multiple incidents. The authors say that techniques are 'the activities that an incident creator would do as part of creating an incident. These were valuable to a responder because they could each be potentially disrupted and could potentially leave traces online (e.g., planning activities might leave traces in search logs)'.[24]

The EEAS defines a FIMI **incident** as 'an action perpetrated by one or more threat actor(s) pursuing specific objectives and carried out with the intent to deceive. It is composed of a combination of observables and TTPs. Multiple related incidents can be part of a campaign'.[25]

The EEAS defines **observables** as 'concrete elements relevant to understand how an incident unfolded—such as a tweet, a video on YouTube or an article on a website. Observables can be represented via the URL under which they were found or as files'.

We can say simply that a tactic is *what* the attacker is trying to do, and a technique is *how* they are doing it.

The EEAS identified five types of tactics, often described as the '5D model'. EU DisinfoLab explained each of the five thusly:

- **Dismiss** allegations and denigrate the source, like the claim that Kyiv orchestrated the Bucha massacre to discredit the Russian army.
- **Distort** the narrative and twist the framing, as in the conspiracy that the discovery of alleged US biolabs in Ukraine would justify the Russian 'special military operation'.
- **Distract**, to shift attention and blame to a different actor or narrative, e.g. stating that the West demonises Vladimir Putin and is responsible for hindering negotiations.
- **Dismay** to threaten and frighten opponents, as shown by the way Russian political opponents, dubbed as a 'fifth column', face murder, intimidation and draconian laws.
- **Divide** to generate conflict and broaden divisions within or between communities and groups, for instance, spreading the hoax that a Ukrainian court has ordered the demolition of an Orthodox church.[26]

Since then, the DISARM Foundation has identified more possible '**presumed objectives**', including these:

---

[23] https://disarmframework.herokuapp.com/technique/. The DISARM authors add that "Like Tactics, a Technique name should always begin with a simple present tense action verb.".
[24] Ibid.
[25] European External Action Service, "1st EEAS Report on Foreign Information Manipulation and Interference Threats: Towards a Framework for Networked Defence", January 2023, p. 4.
[26] EU DisinfoLab, op. cit., p. 6.

- Cause harm
- Cultivate support
- Degrade adversary
- Dismay
- Dismiss
- Dissuade from acting
- Distort
- Distract
- Divide
- Facilitate state propaganda
- Make money
- Motivate to act
- Undermine.

Information influence activities are activities often conducted by a foreign power to influence the perceptions, behaviour and decisions of target groups to the benefit of the foreign power. Information influence activities can be conducted as a single activity or as part of a larger information influence operation combining various and multiple activities.[27]

Framework objects are the ways one can describe an incident—standards for things such as incidents, actors, behaviours, artefacts; **data objects** are instances of these, e.g., the Blacktivist incident and the behaviour and artefacts seen in it.[28]

Artefacts are the 'breadcrumbs' left in the wake of an attack.

AMITT is the abbreviation for Adversarial Misinformation and Influence Tactics and Techniques, which involved a series of cross-disciplinary workshops under the MisinfoSec Working Group of the Credibility Coalition. AMITT evolved into the DISARM Foundation in 2019.

The **kill chain** concept invites one to understand the attacker's behaviour and anticipate it in order to 'kill' the attack by blocking the operation at any of stage.[29]

[27] Pamment, James, Howard Nothhaft, Henrik Agardh-Twetman and Alicia Fjällhed, "Countering Information Influence Activities: The State of the Art", Department of Strategic Communication, Lund University, 1 July 2018. https://rib.msb.se/filer/pdf/28697.pdf.

[28] https://disarmframework.herokuapp.com/about.

[29] EU DisinfoLab, op. cit., p. 9.

Existing Frameworks to Study FIMI 3

David Wright

Abstract

We chose to analyse our case studies in line with accepted frameworks. This section lists those of relevance to our study. The frameworks are sometimes described as models or knowledge bases.

We chose to analyse our case studies in line with accepted frameworks. This section lists those of relevance to our study. The frameworks are sometimes described as models or knowledge bases.

3.1 MITRE ATT&CK

The MITRE Corp[1] is a not-for-profit organisation created in 1958 as a military think tank, spun out from the radar and computer research at the MIT Lincoln Laboratory. It has dual headquarters in Bedford, Massachusetts, and McLean, Virginia. It manages federally funded research and development centres (FFRDCs) supporting various US government agencies in the aviation, defence, healthcare, homeland security and cybersecurity fields, among others.[2]

MITRE created a framework for classifying and describing cyberattacks and intrusions, called the Adversarial Tactics, Techniques and Common Knowledge

[1] MITRE is pronounced MY-tur. It is the acronym for Massachusetts Institute of Technology Research and Engineering.

[2] https://en.wikipedia.org/wiki/Mitre_Corporation.

D. Wright (✉)
Trilateral Research, London, UK
e-mail: david.wright@trilateralresearch.com

© The Author(s), under exclusive license to Springer Nature Switzerland AG 2026

D. Wright (ed.), *Foreign Information Manipulation and Interference*, Terrorism, Security, and Computation, https://doi.org/10.1007/978-3-031-91299-3_3

(ATT&CK) framework. MITRE Corporation released the framework in 2013. The information security community uses the ATT&CK framework to share information about incidents.

The ATT&CK framework is a model that attempts to systematically categorise adversary behaviour. It is a globally accessible knowledge base of adversary tactics and techniques based on real-world observations. ATT&CK is open and available for use, at no charge. The private sector, government and cybersecurity community can also use it as a foundation for development of specific threat models and methodologies.[3]

The main components of the ATT&CK framework[4] are:

- Tactics, which represent 'why' or the reason an adversary performs an action;
- Techniques, which represent 'how' adversaries achieve tactical goals by performing an action;
- Sub-techniques, a more specific or lower-level description of adversarial behaviour;
- Procedures, specific implementation or in-the-wild use the adversary uses for techniques or sub-techniques.

Currently, ATT&CK has three matrices:

- Enterprise, representing traditional enterprise networks and cloud technologies;
- Mobile for mobile communication devices;
- ICS for industrial control systems.[5]

MITRE says its framework is especially used to:

- help cyber defenders develop analytics that **detect** the techniques used by an adversary.
- give analysts a common language to structure, compare and analyse **threat intelligence**.
- provide a common language and framework that red teams can use to **emulate specific threats** and plan their operations.
- assess an organisation's capabilities to resist attacks and drive engineering decisions about the tools or logging the defender should implement.

ATT&CK is widely used in existing ISACs (Information Sharing and Analysis Centres) and ISAOs (Information Sharing and Analysis Organisations).[6] It defines cyber incidents against machines and networks, but it does not address cognitive

[3] https://attack.mitre.org/. Almost all of the text in this subsection comes from the MITRE ATT&CK website.
[4] https://attack.mitre.org/resources/.
[5] https://mitre-attack.github.io/attack-navigator/.
[6] ISACs tend to be sector specific (e.g., financial services), while ISAOs are sector agnostic.

incidents such as disinformation. The DISARM framework is based on the MITRE ATT&CK framework.

MITRE has also created the MITRE ATLAS™ (Adversarial Threat Landscape for Artificial-Intelligence Systems), a globally accessible, living knowledge base of adversary tactics and techniques based on real-world attack observations and realistic demonstrations from AI red teams and security groups.[7] In June 2021, MITRE introduced the D3FEND framework, which focuses on defensive cybersecurity techniques and which complements the ATT&CK framework by mapping specific defensive measures to corresponding offensive tactics, which can help organisations in developing targeted defence strategies.

3.2 DISARM

The DISARM framework is an independent, community-oriented and open-source taxonomy of TTPs. DISARM fights disinformation by sharing data and analysis. DISARM is part of the official data exchange system on FIMI between the US Government and the European Union. The NATO/EU European Centre of Excellence for Countering Hybrid Threats, the EU Cybersecurity Agency (ENISA), the EU External Action Service (EEAS) and the Foundation for Defending Democracy (FDD) encourage use of the DISARM framework as part of a whole-of-society response to FIMI.[8]

The DISARM Foundation was created in late 2021 after changing the name of the framework from AMITT (Adversarial Misinformation and Influence Tactics and Techniques) to DISARM (Disinformation Analysis & Risk Management Framework). AMITT involved a series of cross-disciplinary workshops under the MisinfoSec Working Group of the Credibility Coalition (see Sect. 3.11). The Working Group mapped information security principles onto misinformation.

The framework was constructed based on both historical and hypothetical tactics and techniques employed by manipulators and responses employed by defenders. The aim was to provide as comprehensive a set of known and anticipated manipulator behaviours and defender actions as possible. DISARM's style is based on the MITRE ATT&CK framework and the STIX information security language.[9] As modern disinformation incidents are conducted via the cyber domain using resources that may have been co-opted via cyber incidents, DISARM extends ATT&CK by adding framework components to address these cognitive incidents.[10]

[7] https://atlas.mitre.org/.

[8] https://www.disarm.foundation/.

[9] https://disarmframework.herokuapp.com/about.

[10] Terp, S.J., and Dr. Pablo Breuer, "DISARM: A Framework for Analysis of Disinformation Campaigns", *2022 IEEE Conference on Cognitive and Computational Aspects of Situation Management (CogSIM)*, n.d.

The DISARM frameworks are designed for describing and understanding different parts of disinformation incidents, and are[11]:

- **DISARM-STIX** for disinformation objects, including actors, behaviours, narratives and artefacts. This makes it easy for DISARM data to be passed between ISAOs and similar bodies using standards like TAXII. DISARM-STIX is compatible with the MITRE ATT&CK Navigator.[12]
- **DISARM Red framework** the focus of which is to expose the TTPs of the entities who spread disinformation.
- **DISARM Blue** for disinformation countermeasure and mitigation behaviours. The focus of this framework is to collect countermeasures that were used for the mitigation of a disinformation incident.[13]

The DISARM Red framework focuses on countering disinformation after it has been disseminated, involving detection, debunking and fact-checking of misinformation and disinformation. It aims to intervene post-dissemination to mitigate the impact of false information. It also helps create a structured description of the disinformation event so that TTPs can be identified. Once several disinformation events have been described in the DISARM framework, one can ask questions about all of them. For example: 'What percentage of disinformation events used clickbaits?' or 'What percentage of events intended to defame their target?' or 'What are the five most used tactics in the planning of a disinformation event?' or 'How do the tactics from country A differ from the tactics of country B?', etc.

To ease the process of using its framework, DISARM developed the Navigator,[14] an online tool that helps analysts fill in the details about a given disinformation event. One can view the analyser as a large questionnaire having questions such as the following:

- Was the disinformation event intended to cause harm?
  - If so, which of the following three types of harm are applicable? (i) defame, (ii) intimidate and/or (iii) spread hate?
- Was the disinformation event intended to make money? If so, which of the following are applicable: (i) extort, (ii) generate ad revenue, (iii) manipulate stocks, (iv) raise funds, (v) scam and (vi) sell items under false pretences.

The DISARM Framework provides not only the questions, but also the terminology, so that all disinformation events use the same terminology. Indeed, it is not possible for one analyst to say that an event intended to 'generate ad revenue' and another analyst to say that another event 'made money from advertisements':

[11] https://disarmframework.herokuapp.com/about.
[12] https://github.com/DISARMFoundation/DISARM-STIX2.
[13] https://disarmfoundation.medium.com/the-future-of-disarm-blue-0afc4b0eba20.
[14] https://disarmfoundation.github.io/disarm-navigator/.

both analysts should use the DISARM framework terminology and state that both disinformation events intended to 'generate ad revenue'.

The structured approach for analysing FIMI events within the DISARM framework encompasses various steps, including identification, classification, content analysis, verification, propagation analysis, contextual analysis, impact assessment and documentation/reporting. This framework is not exclusively focused on post-dissemination activities; it involves a broader analysis of FIMI events from their creation to their potential impact, aiming to address the complexities of misinformation across its lifecycle.

The DISARM framework has several strengths: (i) it provides a common methodology for analysing disinformation events, (ii) it provides a common terminology, and (iii) it has been adopted by the EU for exchange of FIMI information with the United States.[15] As attackers create new ways of FIMI, the DISARM Framework needs to evolve too (and it has). In addition to the Red and Blue Frameworks, it would be useful to have another framework on prevention and pre-bunking linked to the Red and Blue Frameworks.

3.3 European External Action Service

The European External Action Service (EEAS) is not a framework per se, but it does use the DISARM Framework. The EEAS is the European Union's diplomatic service. Since 2011, the EEAS carries out the EU's Common Foreign and Security Policy to promote peace, prosperity, security and the interests of Europeans across the globe.[16] EEAS headquarters in Brussels is overseen by a Secretary General who reports to the EU High Representative for Foreign Affairs who is also Vice-President of the European Commission.

The EEAS Strategic Communication, Task Forces and Information Analysis (Stratcom) division produced its first report on Foreign Information Manipulation and Interference threats in 2023.[17] It sampled 100 FIMI incidents detected and analysed between October and December 2022. It found that the vast majority of those originated in Russia.

The EEAS said the DISARM framework was central to its analytical approach to FIMI[18] and that the DISARM framework 'provides the best-suited foundation for the community-led conversation on best practices this report encourages'.[19]

The EEAS concludes its first report on FIMI this way:

---

[15] https://www.eeas.europa.eu/sites/default/files/documents/2023/Annex%203%20-%20FIMI_29%20May.docx.pdf.

[16] https://www.eeas.europa.eu/_en.

[17] EEAS, "1st EEAS Report on Foreign Information Manipulation and Interference Threats: Towards a Framework for Networked Defence", January 2023. https://www.eeas.europa.eu/eeas/1st-eeas-report-foreign-information-manipulation-and-interference-threats_en.

[18] Ibid. p. 30.

[19] Ibid., p. 29.

> Community-driven, shared taxonomies and standards like DISARM for FIMI TTPs or STIX for threat information storage and exchange are available and will facilitate deeper analysis, discussion as well as collective learning and action. Building on established open standards enables the usage and best-case practice development and exchange of open-source tools like MISP or OpenCTI and will pave the way for further innovation in the field.

In its first recommendation, the EEAS said stakeholders should 'build on and enrich existing good-case practices, experiences and standards like STIX and DISARM where possible'. They should also 'avoid the creation of parallel frameworks which would hinder interoperability'.[20] The authors of this book have followed the EEAS guidance in using the DISARM framework.

3.4 FIMI-ISAC

On 7 February 2023, the then High Representative/Vice-President of the European Union Josep Borrell announced the creation of an Information Sharing and Analysis Centre (ISAC) at the EEAS Conference on Foreign Information Manipulation and Interference. The Centre will promote the sharing of information between all stakeholders about root causes, incidents and threats, and the sharing of experience, knowledge and analysis.

The FIMI-ISAC is a group of like-minded organisations that engage in protecting democratic societies, institutions and the critical information infrastructures of democracy from external manipulation and harm. FIMI-ISAC members collaborate in the detection, analysis and countering of FIMI, while upholding the fundamental value of freedom of expression. They identify and expose deliberate manipulation of the information environment by foreign actors. While content may provide clues to an actor's intent, the focus of the FIMI-ISAC is on identifying and exposing manipulative behaviour.[21]

There is not yet much on the FIMI-ISAC website, not even who are the current members, although it does spell out the conditions of membership in FIMI-ISAC. There is a recent (October 2024) report on its findings on elections, which mentions FIMI-ISAC members and their partners, including VOST, Global Disinformation Index (GDI), Italian Digital Media Observatory (IDMO), Debunk.org, Fundación Maldita.es, EU DisinfoLab, Alliance4Europe, Mediapooli, and the Alliance for Securing Democracy at the German Marshall Fund.

---

[20] Ibid., pp. 32–33.

[21] https://fimi-isac.org/.

Table 3.1 STIX objects from the ABCDE framework for FIMI analysis developed by James Pamment[a]

STIX object	Description
Incident	Holds basic information about an incident (name, description, start date, objectives etc.)
Observation	A url or file that has been observed in an incident
Channels (extension)	Any online or offline communication channel (a website, social media profile or page, TV station etc.)
Identity	Individuals, organisations or locations including countries. Usually encoding the targets of incidents
Threat actor	Holds information about a threat actor
Event (extension)	Describes a real life event like an election, show, anniversary etc. to provide context in which incidents can take place
Vulnerability	Describes a Vulnerability that was exploited to make an incident work
Language (extension)	Which language(s) was (were) used in an incident
Attack pattern	Describes manipulative techniques (TTP) used to conduct an attack
Course of action	Describes countermeasures to incidents
Narrative	Describes narratives used in incidents. Narratives can be nested and be represented as meta- and sub-narratives

[a] EEAS, op. cit., January 2023

3.5 STIX™

The EEAS also proposed an initial set of threat indicators inspired by cybersecurity's Structured Threat Information Expression (STIX™), a structured language for describing cyber threat information so it can be shared, stored and analysed in a consistent manner. It is a data format for standardising information on threat actor behaviour and infrastructure.[22] The EEAS started encoding FIMI incidents in the STIX format, an open-source framework owned and managed by the non-profit standards body OASIS Open. Even though it has been developed for cybersecurity incidents, STIX already covers many elements that are relevant in the FIMI context.[23]

The EEAS currently works with the STIX objects listed in the Table 3.1.

The case studies in this book have been structured based on the STIX format (see Sect. 4.1).

[22] Ibid., p. 27.

[23] Ibid., p. 30.

3.6 OpenCTI

OpenCTI is an open-source platform designed to facilitate the collection, management, analysis and sharing of cyber threat intelligence (CTI).[24] It allows organisations to centralise and structure intelligence about cyber threats, adversaries and incidents, making it easier for security teams and analysts to detect, investigate and respond to threats.

OpenCTI helps organisations to manage their cyber threat intelligence knowledge and observables. It has been created to structure, store, organise and visualise technical and non-technical information about cyber threats.

The goal is to create a comprehensive tool allowing users to identify technical (such as TTPs and observables) and non-technical information (such as suggested attribution, victimology etc.) while linking each piece of information to its primary source (a report, a MISP event, etc.), with features such as links between each information, first and last seen dates, levels of confidence, etc. The tool is compatible with the MITRE ATT&CK framework (through a dedicated connector to help structure the data). The user can also choose to implement his or her own datasets.[25]

Once analysts have processed data within OpenCTI, new relations may be inferred from existing ones to facilitate the understanding and representation of this information. This helps the user to extract and leverage meaningful knowledge from the raw data. OpenCTI not only allows imports but also exports of data under different formats (CSV, STIX2 bundles, etc.). Connectors are currently developed to accelerate interactions between the tool and other platforms.

OpenCTI uses a structured data model based on STIX 2.1, a widely used standard for describing cyber threat information (see above). This ensures that all CTI is organised in a way that facilitates both machine-to-machine sharing and human analysis. The platform uses a graph-based approach to display relationships between different entities such as threat actors, attack techniques, vulnerabilities, indicators of compromise (IOCs) and more. Users can visualise how various elements of a threat landscape are connected.

OpenCTI supports integration with a wide range of external data sources including MISP (Malware Information Sharing Platform, see below), MITRE ATT&CK, VirusTotal and other threat intelligence feeds. This helps to automatically enrich the CTI with updated information. The platform is designed to encourage collaboration between different teams or organisations, enabling users to share threat data securely with partners while maintaining control over their information.

OpenCTI supports automation workflows and can be integrated with other security tools via APIs. This allows organisations to automate threat intelligence collection, enrichment and dissemination processes. It is designed to handle large volumes of data, making it suitable for use by large organisations or threat

---

[24] https://github.com/OpenCTI-Platform/opencti.

[25] https://github.com/OpenCTI-Platform/opencti?tab=readme-ov-file#readme.

intelligence sharing communities. The platform provides various analysis tools, including timelines, graphs and pivot tables, to help users investigate threats and generate reports.

During a cyber incident, OpenCTI can help investigators identify threat actors, techniques used and impacted assets, allowing for more effective response strategies. Organisations can use OpenCTI to securely share threat intelligence with partners, cybersecurity alliances and governments.

OpenCTI is widely used in the cybersecurity community, including by CSIRTs (Computer Security Incident Response Teams), SOCs (Security Operations Centres), and security teams at various organisations.

OpenCTI is managed and maintained by the French National Cybersecurity Agency (ANSSI) and CERT-EU (Computer Emergency Response Team for EU institutions). While ANSSI and CERT-EU oversee its development, the platform is community-driven, meaning that organisations and individual contributors from around the world can participate in its development, improvement and extension.

The platform is hosted on GitHub, and contributions are welcome from the broader cybersecurity and CTI community. It is licensed under the AGPL-3.0 (Affero General Public Licence), meaning anyone can use, modify and share the software as long as any modifications are also made available under the same licence. OpenCTI is part of a broader movement to foster international collaboration in threat intelligence, with strong involvement from European institutions.

3.7 MISP

MISP (Malware Information Sharing Platform)[26] is an open-source, community-driven, collaborative threat intelligence platform that was originally designed for malware, but is now used with many types of threat data, including malicious IP addresses, phishing domains, URLs that point to malware, etc. MISP is used to store and share structured data. It interoperates with other platforms and data formats including STIX. MISP contains a 'galaxy' (a method to express an object that can be attached to events or attributes) on threat actors.[27] The main use of MISP is through the feeds it provides. The feeds are sources of cybersecurity related intelligence. The default feeds can be found here: https://www.misp-project.org/feeds/. In addition to the default feeds, one may add more feeds to MISP increasing its utility as a platform for cybersecurity incident analysis. Although MISP was originally developed for cybersecurity incidents, it can also be used for disinformation incidents.[28] The Belgian Ministry of Defence began using the direct antecedent of MISP in 2012. Nowadays, MISP is not only covering the

[26] www.misp-project.org. The Computer Incident Response Centre Luxembourg (CIRCL) established the MISP in 2011.

[27] https://www.misp-project.org/galaxy.html#_misinformation_pattern.

[28] https://www.misp-project.org/2020/03/27/cogsec-collab-misp-community.html/.

malware indicators but also fraud or vulnerability information. MISP includes the core MISP software and a myriad of tools (PyMISP) and format (core format, MISP taxonomies, warning-lists) to support MISP.[29]

3.8 OASIS Open

OASIS (the Organization for the Advancement of Structured Information Standards) Open is a non-profit standards body that offers open-source projects a path to standardisation and *de jure* approval for reference in international policy and procurement.

People join OASIS to advance projects for cybersecurity, blockchain, IoT, emergency management, cloud computing, legal data exchange and more. The technologies vary, but the OASIS mission stays the same: to advance the fair, transparent development of open-source software and standards through the power of global collaboration and community.

A spin-off, the OASIS Open Europe Foundation, established in January 2021 based in Utrecht, the Netherlands, works to advance and support Europe's role in open source and open standards development. It enables OASIS to participate in collaborative projects supported by the EU and EU Member States. It describes itself as a *sovereign* European affiliate organisation to the international non-profit, OASIS Open, working to advance and support Europe's role in open source and open standards development.[30] It says it is working to solve some of the world's biggest technical challenges including cybersecurity, blockchain, privacy, legal applications and many other areas. It advances collaborative solutions that lower cost, improve efficiency, excite innovation, grow global markets and promote interoperability.

Although OASIS Open Europe is an independent organisation, its mission is closely aligned with the international OASIS Open organisation. Several members of the OASIS Open Europe Board also serve on the international OASIS Open Board. The two organisations are complementary, and both support the global OASIS Open community of developers, users and supporters of open technologies.

In November 2023, OASIS Open launched the Defending Against Disinformation-Common Data Model (DAD-CDM) project,[31] which it describes as 'a [global] open-source initiative to develop data exchange standards for normalising and sharing' FIMI threat information based on the STIX cybersecurity standard. The DAD-CDM model provides a structured way to categorise and analyse disinformation campaigns, thereby facilitating more effective detection,

---

[29] https://www.misp-project.org/who/.

[30] https://www.oasis-open.eu/.

[31] https://www.oasis-open.org/project-committee/defending-against-disinformation-common-data-model-dad-cdm/. See also https://github.com/DAD-CDM. https://dad-cdm.org/.

mitigation and countermeasures. DAD-CDM also will create data sets to defend against AI-powered attacks.[32]

3.9 RAND—Tools to Fight Disinformation Online

RAND has compiled a searchable online database of tools for fighting disinformation.[33] It provides information about tools currently available or in development to target online disinformation, particularly on social media. RAND says it identified tools through web searches, articles that review tools and advances in this field, and discussions with experts (e.g., those involved in developing or funding tools). It collected the data primarily from company websites and, in some cases, news articles, industry assessments and research papers. For each tool, it collected and filled in as much information as possible, but it was rare that it was able to fill in every field for a given tool.

RAND says it aims to be as comprehensive as possible in identifying tools that fit its inclusion criteria and as accurate as possible in describing those tools. However, there are new tools emerging constantly and existing tools are being improved and further developed every day. To help improve its data, RAND invites stakeholders to recommend new tools for the database.

3.10 Centre for Advanced Tactics to Counter Disinformation (ADTAC)

ADTAC is an international counter-disinformation innovation lab based in the Netherlands. It is a project of DROG, an innovation platform that offers public–private solutions to counter online harms like disinformation. ADTAC conducts weekly multi-stakeholder 'Black Boxing' sessions with government representatives, tech company policy experts, forensic journalists, security experts, data analysts, academics and others to map disinformation techniques. This framework is used to chart the features of disinformation campaigns and is updated when new disinformation tactics, techniques and procedures are identified. ADTAC is also working in partnership with the **CogSec** Collaborative to ensure that EU, North American and other analysts are using the same methodologies to analyse campaigns so that results are mutually intelligible.[34]

[32] https://github.com/DAD-CDM/.

[33] https://www.rand.org/research/projects/truth-decay/fighting-disinformation/search.html.

[34] https://www.state.gov/resources-technology-engagement-division/.

3.11 Credibility Coalition

The Credibility Coalition,[35] often referred to as CredCo, is a research community based in San Francisco that fosters collaborative approaches to understanding the veracity, quality and credibility of online information. The community comprises journalists, researchers, academics, students, policymakers, technologists and engaged non-specialists. It aims to develop common standards and collaborative approaches to enhance the credibility of online information. It brings together people and institutions from a variety of backgrounds to address misinformation and promote quality in digital content. CredCo operates internationally and supports a decentralised network of researchers, journalists, technologists and other professionals dedicated to improving information ecosystems globally.

CredCo facilitates collaboration with CredCatalog, a comprehensive directory of organisations active in the information credibility space.[36]

3.12 Alliance4Europe

Alliance4Europe operates a network, a diverse coalition of OSINT researchers, journalists, fact-checkers, academics and other practitioners to identify and defend against disinformation threats and to enable scalable collaboration with those who want to defend democracy during and post the European Parliament elections 2024.[37] It says it relies on donations for its campaigns and actions, and to develop the tech tools needed for a citizen-driven democracy. It offers certification courses on the DISARM Framework with new official courses to train analysts and those looking to enter the counter-disinformation field, developed and operated together with the DISARM Foundation.

3.13 Information Laundromat

The Alliance for Securing Democracy (ASD) at the German Marshall Fund (GMF), the University of Amsterdam (UvA) and the Institute for Strategic Dialogue (ISD) have collaborated to develop the Information Laundromat, an open-source tool to uncover content and metadata similarities between and among websites.[38] It is useful to see where and how disinformation spreads.

[35] https://credibilitycoalition.org/.

[36] https://credibilitycoalition.org/credcatalog/.

[37] https://alliance4europe.eu/#vision.

[38] https://informationlaundromat.com/.

3.14 EU Code of Practice on Disinformation

The EU Code of Practice on Disinformation is a tool for fighting disinformation online.[39] The first version of the Code was introduced in 2018 and a second version (under the name 'Strengthened Code of Practice Disinformation') was signed in 2022. The Code is a means by which industry players can agree to adhere to voluntary, self-regulatory standards to fight disinformation. Several Internet players that host platforms where disinformation appears have signed up to the Code. The platforms include Google, Meta (Facebook), Microsoft, TikTok, etc. By signing up to the Code, the players agree on a range of measures including:

- **Cutting the financial incentives for spreading disinformation**. The Code states: 'Relevant Signatories participating in ad placements, commit to defund the dissemination of Disinformation, and improve the policies and systems which determine the eligibility of content to be monetised, the controls for monetisation and ad placement, and the data to report on the accuracy and effectiveness of controls and services around ad placements'. It also states that 'Relevant Signatories participating in advertising commit to prevent the misuse of advertising systems to disseminate Disinformation in the form of advertising messages'.
- **Monitor and respond to disinformation**. The Code reads: 'Relevant Signatories agree to engage in ongoing monitoring and research to understand and respond to risks related to Disinformation in political or issue advertising' and 'Relevant Signatories commit to put in place or further bolster policies to address both misinformation and disinformation across their services, and to agree on a cross-service understanding of manipulative behaviours, actors and practices not permitted on their services'.
- **Help establish the authenticity of information**. The Code states: 'Relevant Signatories commit to empower users with tools to assess the provenance and edit history or authenticity or accuracy of digital content' and 'Relevant Signatories commit to provide users with the functionality to flag harmful false and/or misleading information that violates Signatories policies or terms of service'.

In addition to large-scale Internet platforms, several other organisations have signed the Code of Conduct: from fact-checking organisations to advertising companies. All these organisations have some level of interaction with disinformation activities and may be able to mitigate them. The signatories are supposed to provide six-monthly reports explaining how they have fulfilled their various commitments during the reporting period and whether they had any notable achievements.

[39] https://digital-strategy.ec.europa.eu/en/policies/code-practice-disinformation.

The strengthened Code of Practice on Disinformation, presented on 16 June 2022, was signed by 34 signatories. At the time of this writing (October 2024), 10 more have signed.

FIMI Case Studies

4

David Wright

4.1 How the Case Studies are Structured

The partners structured the case studies based on the DISARM Navigator and the STIX language, using the headings below. We wanted the case studies in this report to be readable narratives but with points that would allow the authors to transpose them to a DISARM Navigator "layer" or matrix. Below each of the headings below, we pose some typical questions that partners used as guidelines in preparing their case studies.

4.1.1 Introduction

What happened?

What was the context for the incident/campaign?

How did the FIMI incident/campaign progress through the information environment? What events occurred in its trajectory/progress?

When was the event instigated? (Provide date/month/year, if possible) When did the event subside? (Provide date/month/year, if possible).

The list of authors who have contributed to this chapter are listed in the Front matter (pp. vii and viii).

D. Wright (✉)
Trilateral Research, London, UK
e-mail: david.wright@trilateralresearch.com

© The Author(s), under exclusive license to Springer Nature Switzerland AG 2026

D. Wright (ed.), *Foreign Information Manipulation and Interference*, Terrorism, Security, and Computation, https://doi.org/10.1007/978-3-031-91299-3_4

4.1.2 Threat Actors

Who appears to have instigated the FIMI incident/campaign?
Which actors spread the event?
Who might benefit from the event?

4.1.3 Presumed Objectives

What were the FIMI attacker's goals?

The DISARM Navigator now has 13 possible objectives.

- *Cause harm*
- *Cultivate support*
- *Degrade adversary*
- *Dismay*
- *Dismiss*
- *Dissuade from acting*
- *Distort*
- *Distract*
- *Divide*
- *Facilitate state propaganda*
- *Make money*
- *Motivate to act*
- *Undermine*

Pick out one or more as a subheading, followed by one or two sentences explaining why the objective(s) is/are likely. Example:

T0076: *Distort—Provide one or two sentences explaining why this objective is assumed to be part of the event. Put sources in footnotes, not embedded citations. Try to use key words.*

4.1.4 Incidents and Observables

As mentioned in Sect. 2.2, *the EEAS defines a FIMI* ***incident*** *as "an action perpetrated by one or more threat actor(s) pursuing specific objectives and carried out with the intent to deceive. It is composed of a combination of observables and TTPs. Multiple related incidents can be part of a* ***campaign****."*[1]

Identify one or more incidents instigated by the FIMI attacker.

The EEAS defines ***observables*** *as "concrete elements relevant to understand how an incident unfolded—such as a tweet, a video on YouTube or an article on a website.*

[1] EEAS, op. cit., January 2023, p. 4.

Observables can be represented via the URL under which they were found or as files."[2]

Identify one or more observables (a tweet, a video, a social media post, media article) indicating a FIMI attack.

4.1.5 Targets

Give some evidence in a couple of sentences explaining who was the target. The attacker may have one or more of the following targets at the same time:

- *individuals*
- *institutions*
- *a company*
- *government*
- *the public*
- *traditional media*
- *social media*
- *other*
- *don't know.*

4.1.6 Tactics, Techniques and Procedures

What were the attackers' tactics (goals), techniques (how to achieve the goals) and procedures (a collection of techniques used in a campaign)? The DISARM Red Framework has tactics and techniques, but not procedures. Cite the DISARM code for each of the relevant TTPs.

4.1.7 Channels

What channels did the attacker use, e.g., podcasts, newspapers, broadcasters, social media, etc.?

4.1.8 Languages

In what languages did the attacker purvey his or her disinformation? The more languages, obviously, the greater the impact. Using some minority languages could help the attackers avoid the fact-checkers of big companies or civil society organisations in western Europe.

[2] Ibid.

4.1.9 Effectiveness

*The effect of an incident (or the impact or severity or consequence) can be measured and assessed according to different parameters such as the reach, the reach beyond in-groups, engagement, harm or behaviour-change caused offline,*etc.

4.1.10 Countermeasures

The EEAS identified six main types:

- *Statement of refutal: An involved entity issued a statement refuting the claims of the incident.*
- *Debunking: The claims of the incident were debunked/fact checked.*
- *Content deleted: Content of any type was taken down in response to the incident.*
- *Content confined: Content of any type was limited in response to the incident.*
- *Channel limited or suspended: The channel of any of the observables was limited or suspended in response to the incident.*
- *Other: Any other countermeasure that is not captured by the above taxonomy. Differentiate FIMI incidents in terms of actors, behaviours, content, degree and effect.*

4.1.11 Conclusions and Recommendations

What are the salient points from the case study? Based on what transpired, what recommendations would help someone address a similar FIMI situation in future?

4.2 Did the Russians Dupe the US Republican Party?

4.2.1 Introduction

This case study concerns a onetime FBI informant who may have been part of an ongoing Russian plot to interfere with US democracy by spreading disinformation about the Bidens.[3] The informant, Alexander Smirnov, claimed he was fed information by Russian intelligence.[4] Prosecutors said Smirnov has "extensive foreign ties, including, most troublingly and by his own account, contact with foreign

[3] Stanley-Becker, Isaac, "FBI Informant Accused of Smearing Bidens Had Past Credibility Issues", *Washington Post*, 9 March 2024. https://www.washingtonpost.com/politics/2024/03/09/alexander-smirnov-fbi-biden-impeachment/.

[4] Thrush, Glenn, and Alan Feuer, "Ex-Informant Accused of Lying About Bidens Said He Had Russian Contacts", *The New York Times*, 21 Feb 2024. https://www.nytimes.com/2024/02/20/us/politics/fbi-informant-hunter-biden.html.

intelligence services, including Russian intelligence agencies, and has had such contacts recently."[5]

On 21 February 2024, the FBI detained Smirnov, who had previously said he had evidence that Hunter and Joe Biden were each paid $5 million in 2015 by Burisma, the Ukrainian energy company, to put an end to a corruption inquiry into the company by the Ukrainian Prosecutor General. Hunter Biden had been on Burisma's board from 2014 until 2019. Smirnov's claim became central to the Republican impeachment inquiry of President Biden in Congress.[6] Although Smirnov was an informant for the FBI, the agency had had some doubts about his veracity.

In June 2023, Republicans and Democrats reviewed a redacted FBI form with Smirnov's allegations. The Republicans said the FBI had described Smirnov as "highly credible". At the time, the FBI made clear that the allegations were unverified.[7]

4.2.2 Threat Actors

Alexander Smirnov, 43 as of this writing, has joint Israeli-US citizenship. He grew up in Ukraine when it was still part of the Soviet Union and was raised speaking Russian, according to a declaration submitted to the court by his cousin, Linor Shefer, a real estate agent living in Florida.[8] He knows Russian slang. Smirnov became an FBI "confidential human source (CHS)", or informant, in 2010, according to the indictment. Smirnov's reports were memorialised in an FBI form called an FD-1023,[9] which agents use to record unverified reporting from informants.

Prosecutors say Smirnov lived in Israel between 1992 and 2006 and that his parents and sister still reside there. Between 2000 and 2006, he served as president of a "private mineral and logistic operation, with assets in Russia", according to a filing with the Securities and Exchange Commission, by a penny-stock company

[5] Perez, Evan, and Hannah Rabinowitz, "How a Trusted FBI Source Became the Center of a Washington Scandal", CNN, 22 Feb 2024. https://www.cnn.com/2024/02/21/politics/indicted-source-of-biden-allegations-was-prized-for-his-foreign-intelligence-connections/index.html.

[6] Ritter, Ken, Lindsay Whitehurst and Rio Yamat, "Ex-FBI Source Accused of Lying about Bidens and Having Russian Contacts Is Returned to US Custody", AP News, 22 Feb 2024. https://apnews.com/article/hunter-biden-fbi-informant-lying-bribery-burisma-e6de5f083e7ea7c2f1aa6233d24d7cfd. As of 12 May 2024, the Republican investigation has produced no evidence that Biden Joe engaged in wrongdoing or accepted a bribe.

[7] Czopek, Madison, "Who Is Alexander Smirnov, and What Does His Indictment Mean for the GOP Impeachment Inquiry?", *Politifact*, 26 Feb 2024. https://www.politifact.com/article/2024/feb/26/who-is-alexander-smirnov-and-what-does-his-indictm/.

[8] Stanley-Becker, Isaac, "FBI Informant Accused of Smearing Bidens Had Past Credibility Issues", *Washington Post*, 9 Mar 2024. https://www.washingtonpost.com/politics/2024/03/09/alexander-smirnov-fbi-biden-impeachment/.

[9] https://www.grassley.senate.gov/imo/media/doc/fd_1023_obtained_by_senator_grassley_-_biden.pdf.

that sought to appoint him chairman of its board in 2011. The filing said Smirnov was fluent in Russian, English, Hebrew and Arabic.[10]

For more than a decade, Smirnov gave the FBI visibility into the shadowy world of oligarchs and public officials while offering himself as a consultant to some of the same people he was monitoring. In court filings, the special counsel described Smirnov as a serial liar who could not even be trusted to describe honestly his occupation or account for his finances.[11]

The allegations against Smirnov were outlined in a Department of Justice filing in the case on 20 Feb 2024.[12] US prosecutors said Smirnov had high-level ties with Russian intelligence. In December 2023, the legal filing says, Smirnov attended an overseas meeting with "a high-ranking member of a specific Russian foreign intelligence service". According to prosecutors, Smirnov admitted in an interview after his arrest that "officials associated with Russian intelligence were involved in passing a story" about Hunter Biden. They said Smirnov's contacts with Russian officials were recent and extensive, and that Smirnov had planned to meet with one official during an upcoming overseas trip.[13] "He is actively peddling new lies that could impact U.S. elections after meeting with Russian intelligence officials in November," prosecutors said.[14]

Smirnov reported more than a dozen meetings or discussions with Russian officials in 2023, according to court documents.Even as prosecutors relay Smirnov's alleged claims of ties to Russian intelligence, they haven't provided evidence to corroborate that Smirnov is now telling the truth. FBI officials believe it's possible that Smirnov provided legitimate information in criminal investigations over the years but that he also lied about the Burisma bribes. At least as early as 2020, Smirnov's claims about the Bidens were viewed as suspicious by FBI investigators, in part because they couldn't corroborate them.[15]

The US Republican party had hailed the informant as "credible" and "most respected". They asserted that he had 17 recordings to back up his story that the Bidens had accepted bribes of $5 million from Burisma. But the tapes never

[10] Czopek, Madison, "Who Is Alexander Smirnov, and What Does His Indictment Mean for the GOP Impeachment Inquiry?", Politifact, 26 Feb 2024. https://www.politifact.com/article/2024/feb/26/who-is-alexander-smirnov-and-what-does-his-indictm/.

[11] Thrush, Glenn, "Ex-F.B.I. Informant Is Being Transferred to California", The New York Times, 23 Feb 2024. https://www.nytimes.com/2024/02/23/us/politics/alexander-smirnov-fbi-biden.html.

[12] Wendling, Mike, "Alexander Smirnov: FBI Source Accused of Biden Lies 'Linked to Russian Intelligence'", BBC News, 20 Feb 2024. https://www.bbc.com/news/world-us-canada-68353303.

[13] Yamat, Rio, and Lindsay Whitehurst, "Ex-FBI Informant Charged with Lying about Bidens Had Russian Intelligence Contacts, Prosecutors Say", AP News, 20 Feb 2024. https://apnews.com/article/hunter-biden-fbi-informant-joe-biden-ef48c7543e7a45cd3b8b671d0e2f60e5.

[14] Thrush, Glenn, and Alan Feuer, "Ex-Informant Accused of Lying About Bidens Said He Had Russian Contacts", *The New York Times*, 21 Feb 2024. https://www.nytimes.com/2024/02/20/us/politics/fbi-informant-hunter-biden.html.

[15] Perez, Evan, and Hannah Rabinowitz, "How a Trusted FBI Source Became the Center of a Washington Scandal", CNN, 22 Feb 2024. https://www.cnn.com/2024/02/21/politics/indicted-source-of-biden-allegations-was-prized-for-his-foreign-intelligence-connections/index.html.

materialised and on 20 Feb 2024, the Justice Department announced that it had charged Smirnov with making it all up.[16] The indictment of Smirnov, the former FBI informant, was a blow to the effort by House Republicans to assemble a credible impeachment case against the president.

Congressional Republicans spent months using Smirnov's allegations to fuel their probes into Hunter Biden and to eventually launch an impeachment inquiry into his father.[17] "I have no idea whether they [the Republicans] are witting collaborators [of the Russians]," Democratic Congressman Jamie Raskin said of the GOP lawmakers pushing for Biden's impeachment. But by aggressively pushing Smirnov's falsehoods, "many of them have been active participants in what is essentially a Russian disinformation campaign".[18]

Before Smirnov's arrest, right-wing media took it as an article of faith that they had found the "smoking gun" proving the Bidens' corruption.[19] But after Smirnov's arrest, Republicans discounted the importance of the Smirnov indictment.

It is not known yet which contacts Smirnov had with Russian intelligence agencies.[20] Smirnov's unverifiable claim that he met with Russian intelligence officials as recently as December 2023 made him a flight risk and endangered national security, Justice Department officials said.[21]

Federal prosecutors filed a detention memo in court arguing that Smirnov, who provided intelligence on Russia to the US, was also being played by the Kremlin. Prosecutors said that Smirnov had boasted of "extensive and extremely recent" contacts with Russian intelligence and that he had longstanding connections to Russian officials, including one who was allegedly responsible for coordinating "assassination efforts" abroad.[22]

---

[16] Broadwater, Luke, "Indictment of Informant Undercuts G.O.P.'s Impeachment Drive", *The New York Times*, 16 Feb 2024. https://www.nytimes.com/2024/02/16/us/politics/biden-impeachment-republicans-informant.html.

[17] Ibid.

[18] Meyer, Josh, "Dems Want Answers: Why Did GOP Use Russia's Alexander Smirnov in Biden Impeachment Probe?", *USA TODAY*, 11 Mar 2024. https://www.usatoday.com/story/news/politics/2024/03/11/biden-impeachment-inquiry-alexander-smirnov/72852627007/.

[19] Singman, Brooke, "Person Alleging Biden Criminal Bribery Scheme Is a 'highly Credible' FBI Source Used since Obama Admin: Source", *Fox News*, Fox News, 2 June 2023. https://www.foxnews.com/politics/person-alleging-biden-criminal-bribery-scheme-is-a-highly-credible-fbi-source-used-since-obama-admin-source.

[20] Blake, Aaron, "Another GOP Biden 'Informant.' Another Indictment and Link to Russia", Washington Post, 26 February 2024. https://www.washingtonpost.com/politics/2024/02/21/another-gop-biden-informant-another-indictment-link-russia/.

[21] Thrush, Glenn, and Alan Feuer, "Ex-Informant Accused of Lying About Bidens Said He Had Russian Contacts", The New York Times, 21 February 2024. https://www.nytimes.com/2024/02/20/us/politics/fbi-informant-hunter-biden.html.

[22] Stieb, Matt, "Was the Biden Crime Family Informant a Russian Asset?", Intelligencer, 22 Feb 2024. https://nymag.com/intelligencer/article/alexander-smirnov-may-have-been-russian-asset-prosecutors.html.

Smirnov appears to have told the FBI that a business associate who introduced him to Burisma executives had ties to Russian organised crime.[23] It's not known yet who Smirnov's Russian contacts were, but there were Russians involved in peddling the story about the Bidens taking bribes. In November 2023, Ukrainian prosecutors charged with treason three Ukrainians who aided the Trump campaign's efforts to discredit the Biden family, led by Rudy Giuliani, Trump's personal lawyer at the time. Ukraine's Security Service (SBU) said the three men charged were paid by Russian military intelligence (GRU). The three men charged were MP Oleksandr Dubinsky, former lawmaker Andriy Derkach and ex-prosecutor Kostyantyn Kulyk. All three were said to be members of an agent network led by Russian General Vladimir Alekseyev, the deputy head of the GRU.[24]

4.2.3 Presumed Objectives

The DISARM Red Framework currently has 13 possible objectives. The one closest to this case study is to "T0135: Undermine". We presume the Russian objective was to help Trump defeat Biden and to undermine the November 2024 elections.

The Russians and Republicans have benefited from the event, as they have created doubts in the minds of some voters about Biden's culpability. Trump has a much friendlier relationship with Putin with whom he has had one-on-one discussions with no staff present. Trump has already expressed his thoughts about withdrawing from NATO and not defending any allies who have not contributed enough to the NATO budget. Hence, under Trump, Putin's chances of conquering Ukraine and, possibly, nibbling on some NATO countries (e.g., the Baltics) are far greater than under Biden.

Other Applicable Objectives

T0066: Degrade adversary—The lies about the Bidens arguably had an impact on Ukraine too in so far as it degraded American public support for Ukraine.

T0076: Distort—Rudy Guiliani and Trump distorted the facts about Hunter Biden's role at Burisma.

T0079: Divide—The FIMI helped foster political polarisation in the US. Facts are less important than beliefs.

---

[23] Thrush, Glenn, and Kenneth P. Vogel, "The Informant Turned Defendant Who Took Aim at the Bidens", *The New York Times*, 21 Feb 2024. https://www.nytimes.com/2024/02/21/us/politics/smirnov-fbi-biden-russia.html.

[24] McCausland, Phil, "Ukraine Charges Officials Tied to Hunter Biden Probe and Russia", BBC News, 15 Nov 2023. https://www.bbc.com/news/world-europe-67425906.

4.2.4 Incidents and Observables

The EEAS defines a FIMI **incident** as "an action perpetrated by one or more threat actor(s) pursuing specific objectives and carried out with the intent to deceive". Smirnov's most flagrant FIMI incident was alleging to his FBI handler that the Bidens each took a $5 million bribe.[25] Some lawmakers and former US counter-intelligence officials said Smirnov's accusations against Biden bore all the hallmarks of an ongoing and clandestine Kremlin effort to smear Biden and help Trump in the 2024 election.[26]

The Republicans took Smirnov's allegation and ran with it. House Oversight Committee Chair James Comer's office put out a press release that said: "The Bidens intentionally sought to hide, confuse, and conceal their influence-peddling schemes, but bank records don't lie. The Bidens made millions from foreign nationals providing what seems to be no services other than access and influence. From the thousands of records we've obtained so far, we know the Biden family set up over a dozen companies when Joe Biden was vice president."[27] It was another Republican lie: In fact, Comer's committee hasn't uncovered any evidence of wrong-doing by the Bidens.

4.2.5 Targets

The Russians' targets were the Bidens, the Republican Party and the American public to undermine the credibility of the Bidens and to disrupt the 2024 elections. Smirnov's target was firstly his FBI handler, probably to show that he had high-quality information, not only about the Bidens, but also his contacts in Russian intelligence services.[28] Smirnov may have been a double agent, hence, his targets might also have included the Russian intelligence services, to show them he was feeding false information to the FBI.

---

[25] https://www.grassley.senate.gov/imo/media/doc/fd_1023_obtained_by_senator_grassley_-_biden.pdf.

[26] Meyer, Josh, "Dems Want Answers: Why Did GOP Use Russia's Alexander Smirnov in Biden Impeachment Probe?", *USA TODAY*, 11 Mar 2024. https://www.usatoday.com/story/news/politics/2024/03/11/biden-impeachment-inquiry-alexander-smirnov/72852627007/.

[27] Carnahan, Ashley, "Trump: Critics Saying He'd Seek Retribution Are 'wrong,' but 'I Would Have Every Right' to Go after Opponents", *Fox News*, 5 Jun 2024. https://www.foxnews.com/media/trump-addresses-concerns-he-would-seek-retribution-i-would-have-every-right-go-after-them.

[28] Wendling, Mike, "Alexander Smirnov: FBI Source Accused of Biden Lies 'Linked to Russian Intelligence'", BBC News, 21 Feb 2024. https://www.bbc.com/news/world-us-canada-68353303.

4.2.6 Tactics, Techniques and Procedures

Smirnov, the Russians and the Republicans employed various tactics to discredit the Bidens. Among them, in phase one (Plan) of the FIMI campaign, were the following:

- TA02: Plan objectives—i.e., to discredit the Bidens and to help the Trump campaign.

In phase 2 (Prepare), the following tactics are pertinent:

- TA14: Develop narratives—Smirnov developed the narrative that Burisma, the company that employed Hunter Biden, paid the Bidens a bribe to make allegations of corruption go away.
- TA05: Microtarget—Establish assets that create trust. Smirnov was an intelligence agent (an asset) for the FBI.
- TA16: Establish legitimacy—Smirnov alleged that he had recordings that proved the Bidens' culpability.
- TA06: Develop content—Target very specific populations of people. Smirnov targeted his FBI agent in the first instance. The Russians targeted the Republicans. The Republicans targeted the American public.

In phase 3 (Execute) of the FIMI campaigns:

- TA17: Maximise exposure—The Republicans, seemingly duped by the Russian FIMI campaign, released the false allegations to the mass media to damage Biden, the Democrat. In releasing the unverified FBI report to the media, the Republicans sought to maximise exposure of the target audience to the incident. The Republicans spread the lies about the Bidens taking bribes to the mainstream media.

Phase 4 (Assess) of the FIMI consisted of this tactic:

- TA12: Assess effectiveness—The Russians have been engaged in a variety of disinformation techniques, no doubt to assess which are most successful. If Smirnov's allegations had not been found to be duplicitous, the Russians would have scored an even bigger success in changing the course of elections. As noted below, we can regard this FIMI campaign as a success for the Russians and Republicans as they sought to convince the American public that the Bidens were bribe-takers and therefore shouldn't be in the White House after the next election. (As it turned out, Biden resigned after a disastrous debate (As it turned out, Biden resigned after a disastrous debate with Trump, to be replaced by Kamala Harris, who lost to Trump in the 2024 elections.).

The DISARM Framework identifies various techniques to implement the tactics. Among the most relevant in this case study are the following:

- T0003: Leverage existing narratives—Smirnov's allegations can be seen in the context of earlier interventions by Rudy Giuliani and Trump to get Ukrainian president Zelenskyy to agree to investigate the Bidens for influence peddling on behalf of the Ukrainian Burisma company. Even Lev Parnas, ex-Giuliani associate, testified on 20 March 2024 that the allegations against the Bidens were false and "spread by the Kremlin", adding further credibility to the connection between the narratives and disinformation effect.[29]
- T0016: Create fake experts—Smirnov claimed to have tapes backing up his claims: "Smirnov thinks the tapes of Hunter Biden at the Premier Palace Hotel is all they have", suggests the Russians tried to create a persona to the Republicans that appeared credible by giving fake credibility/expert insight.[30]
- T0091.001: Recruit contractors—The evidence suggests that the Russians or, more specifically, the three Russian-supporting Ukrainians, recruited Smirnov. During his custodial sentence on 14 Feb 2024, Smirnov "admitted that officials associated with Russian intelligence were involved in passing a story about Businessperson 1" [Hunter Biden].[31] Also, "While Smirnov has no ties to the community in Las Vegas, what he does have is extensive foreign ties, including, most troublingly and by his own account, contact with foreign intelligence services, including Russian intelligence agencies, and has had such contacts recently…. law enforcement knows about Smirnov's contact with officials affiliated with Russian intelligence."[32]
- T0117: Attract traditional media—The Republicans attracted considerable attention from the traditional mass media with the false allegations from Smirnov.
- T0049.001: Trolls amplify and manipulate—In this context, we could consider Fox News and other right-wing media as trolls amplifying Smirnov's lies. Many right-wing media pundits act as echo chambers to their audiences.
- T0129.006: Deny involvement—Although there have been allegations that the Smirnov caper originated in the GRU, the Russians can deny involvement in a matter that concerned Ukraine.
- T0134.001: Message reach—Smirnov, the Russians and the Republicans were successful in reaching out to vast swathes of the American public, via the media.

[29] Lev Parnas letter to James Comer, Chairman, US House of Representatives, Committee on Oversight and Accountability, 20 Mar 2024. https://drive.google.com/file/d/1Q5BLw4vaOoi5_nLBUis476p2hwADZEcR/view?pli=1.
[30] Ibid.
[31] Government's Memorandum in Support of Detention, 20 Feb 2024, pp. 5–6. https://s3.documentcloud.org/documents/24435391/240220-smirnov-detention.pdf.
[32] Ibid., p. 16.

This combination of tactics and techniques was designed to undo Biden in favour of Trump in the 2024 US election.

4.2.7 Channels

Several channels were used to disseminate this FIMI, each reaching increasing numbers of people.

T0104: Social media

T0111: Traditional media

The One America News Network (OANN), described by Wikipedia as a far-right, pro-Trump cable channel owned by Herring Networks, Inc., and launched in 2013, produced several stories about bribery involving President Biden. In October 2019, it produced a story entitled "Ukraine Files; Biden Inc Got $ 17.5 Million In Racketeering".[33] In November 2019, it produced a story "Ukraine Bomb Has Gone Off; Bidens, Obama, Dems, All Tied To The Ukraine Corruption, Money Trail".[34] A year later, it produced a story "The Biden Ukraine Bribe Tapes".[35] Then, in June 2023, Fox News carried a story "Person Alleging Biden Criminal Bribery Scheme Is a 'highly Credible' FBI Source Used since Obama Admin: Source".[36] The headline was a distortion. The FBI already had suspicions about Smirnov's veracity.

On 8 June 2023, Fox News broke the story about Republican Senator Chuck Grassley and Congressman James Comer claiming that a long-time FBI informant had told the FBI in June 2020 about an alleged $5 million bribe to Joe Biden … and that this evidence was on tape.[37] Which it wasn't. *Newsweek* ran a story a week later about "Everything We Know about Joe Biden's $5 Million Bribe Allegations".[38] It was a brief story which was an indication that they didn't have any evidence, only Republican hearsay. In July 2023, the *New York Post* ran this story: "Biden $10M bribe file released: Burisma chief said he was 'coerced' to pay

[33] https://archive.org/details/2019OCT11_Ukraine_Files_Biden_Inc_got_17_plus_Million_in_Racketeering.

[34] https://archive.org/details/2019NOV20_Ukraine_Bomb_Gone_off_Bidens_Obama_Dems_All_Tied_To_Ukraine_Corruption_Money_Trail.

[35] https://archive.org/details/biden-ukraine-bribe-tapes.

[36] https://www.foxnews.com/politics/person-alleging-biden-criminal-bribery-scheme-is-A-highly-credible-fbi-source-used-since-obama-admin-source.

[37] Kasprak, Alex, "Does FBI Have Evidence That Joe Biden Received $5 M Bribe from Burisma Exec?", Snopes, 22 June 2023. https://www.snopes.com//news/2023/06/22/biden-bribe-claims/.

[38] https://www.newsweek.com/everything-we-know-about-joe-bidens-5-million-bribe-allegations-1807068.

Joe, 'stupid' Hunter in bombshell allegations".[39] The Republicans had no evidence to support these claims but made them anyway.

Another channel in this case was that between the FBI and the Republicans. During the summer of 2023, the Bureau resisted GOP lawmakers' calls to hand over a document, known as an FD-1023, saying that doing so could compromise a valuable source. The FD-1023 form records what an informant has claimed. Those claims went unverified. The FBI eventually allowed some lawmakers to review the record, and Republicans trumpeted the bribery allegations as evidence of wrongdoing by the president. The GOP-led House voted to formalise an impeachment inquiry against Biden in December 2023.[40]

Hence, the disinformation appeared in various channels, including newspapers, broadcasters and social media, many more than cited here.

4.2.8 Languages

English.

4.2.9 Effectiveness

Republican efforts to impeach Biden received lots of coverage in the US and abroad too. They touted the FBI FD-1023 document which memorialised Smirnov's allegations as proof that Biden took a bribe. It is difficult to say to what extent the allegations influenced US voters. Similarly, it's difficult to say to what extent the revelation that Smirnov's allegations were lies deflated Republican support.

Certainly, millions of people were exposed to the bribery disinformation via the social media and the traditional media. Congressman James Comer was quoted as saying that Republican probes had "uncovered a mountain of evidence revealing how Joe Biden abused his public office for his family's financial gain", even though he didn't put forward any evidence backing up his allegation.[41]

---

[39] https://nypost.com/2023/07/20/biden-bribe-file-released-burisma-chief-said-both-joe-and-hunter-involved/.

[40] Kim, Ellis, and Stefan Becket, "House Republicans Demand Info from FBI about Alexander Smirnov, Informant Charged with Lying about Bidens—CBS News", CBS News, 1 Mar 2024. https://www.cbsnews.com/news/alexander-smirnov-house-republicans-fbi-informant/.

[41] Hudspeth Blackburn, Piper, Maureen Chowdhury and Elise Hammond, "House Holds First Hearing in Biden Impeachment Inquiry", CNN, 28 Sept 2023. https://www.cnn.com/politics/live-news/biden-impeachment-hearing-house-oversight-09-28-23/index.html.

The bribery allegations appear to have had some effect, if public opinion polls are to be believed. A CNN/SSRS poll in September 2023 found that 61% of Americans surveyed said they thought that Biden had at least some involvement in Hunter Biden's business dealings, with 42% saying they thought he acted illegally.[42]

The consequences of this FIMI might be the Russians' greatest victory, matched only by Trump's first election. As it is, Russian disinformation about the bribery of the Bidens was successful in convincing the Republican Party and many of its supporters that Biden had taken a bribe.

4.2.10 Countermeasures

The principal countermeasure taken against the FIMI in this case was the FBI indictment against Smirnov on 14 Feb 2024, which was well covered in the media.

Many in the media speculated that the revelations punctured the Republicans' attempts to impeach Biden.

Biden and his spokespersons denied the bribery allegations, but that did not deter the Republicans from trying to find something that Biden had done that was impeachable. Exposure of Smirnov as a liar and agent for Russian intelligence did not alter Republican support for Trump or their continuing to purport that the Bidens took bribes, even though they produced no evidence to support such a belief.

4.2.11 Conclusions and Recommendations

The Republican Party has shown itself less interested in facts and more interested in political point-scoring.[43] They have willingly swallowed Russian disinformation and promoted it in GOP-friendly media like the *New York Post*, Fox News and OANN. Fortunately, more responsible media reported Smirnov's arrest and confession that there was no bribe. The right-wing media and the Republican Party were willing to swallow Smirnov's lies without verifying his allegations. They wanted the allegations to be true so much that they did not want to check whether they were any facts to support them.

The bribery allegations against Joe Biden significantly influenced public opinion in the US, highlighting deep partisan divisions and the crucial role of independent voters in shaping the political landscape. The allegations were a

[42] Edwards-Levy, Ariel, "CNN Poll: A Majority of Americans Believe Joe Biden, as VP, Was Involved with Son's Business Dealings | CNN Politics", CNN, 7 Sept 2023. https://www.cnn.com/2023/09/07/politics/poll-hunter-biden/index.html.

[43] Dale, Daniel, "Fact Check: How House Republicans Put Now-Debunked Biden Bribery Claim at the Center of Impeachment Push", CNN, 22 Feb 2024. https://www.cnn.com/2024/02/22/politics/fact-check-house-republicans-fbi-informant-impeachment-push/index.html.

contentious topic, with beliefs about their validity heavily influenced by political alignment and media consumption.

News agency AP quoted an ex-FBI official's comment in this case: "We're in a society now of disinformation and misinformation. You've really got to be watching and, on the watch, when information comes in and validating and verifying it."[44] This is sound advice for everyone in today's connected world.

The Smirnov lies may not have had the desired effect, as Biden dropped out of the presidential context; hence, he was no longer the most relevant target. The impact of the allegations became decidedly less than when Biden was still running for a second term.

Recommendation: Don't jump to conclusions. Resist making public unverified reports. Verify allegations, especially those of a sensationalist nature, before amplifying them.

Consult the DISARM blue framework for its countermeasures against FIMI. Particularly pertinent in the case study are these two countermeasures: C00115: Expose actor and intentions and C00184: Media exposure. Exposing Smirnov as a liar and Russian agent in the media was warranted in view of how widely the original allegations were covered. It is useful to track where the FIMI appears in the social and traditional media and elsewhere (e.g., in emails) to make sure they carry corrections. If some media refuse to issue a correction, they should be called out publicly by more reputable sources.

4.3 Altered Photo Showing Zelenskyy Holding a Jersey with a Swastika

4.3.1 Introduction

Russia's invasion of Ukraine on 24 February 2022 was followed by a significant escalation in disinformation on a global scale linking Ukraine to Nazism.[45] Among the most prevalent narratives was the portrayal of Ukrainian President Volodymyr Zelenskyy as a "pro-Nazi" leader,[46] a narrative that manipulated the image of Zelenskyy to promote false interpretations consistent with pro-Russian interests. The actors using this narrative operated on two levels: externally, by undermining international public perception of Ukraine and, internally, by undermining confidence in President Zelenskyy as an institutional actor, both of which

[44] Slodysko, Brian, Eric Tucker and Anthony McCartney, "How Clean Is the Dirt on Hunter Biden? A Key Republican Source Is Charged with Lying to the FBI", AP News, 2 Mar 2024. https://apnews.com/article/hunter-biden-fbi-informant-smirnov-ukraine-impeachment-113c1104052dbdc9302606f6d42c9939.

[45] Smart, Charlie, "How the Russian Media Spread False Claims About Ukrainian Nazis", *The New York Times*, 2 July 2022. https://tinyurl.com/bddcvpw3.

[46] EUvsDisinfo, "Why does Putin portray himself as the tamer of neo-Nazism?", 19 Mar 2022. https://euvsdisinfo.eu/why-does-putin-portray-himself-as-the-tamer-o.

were designed to justify the aggression and Russian military actions under the pretext of "de-Nazification" of Ukraine.[47]

A key incident that serves as an example of this broader disinformation campaign was a widely circulated hoax[48] involving a digitally altered photograph of Zelenskyy holding a football jersey with his name and a swastika on the back (Fig. 4.1). This doctored image, which rapidly spread on social media in the early days of the aggression and peaked in late February and early March 2022, was intended to frame Zelenskyy within anti-Ukrainian rhetoric and falsely accuse him of promoting Nazi ideals. The original photo, posted by Zelenskyy in June 2021,[49] actually depicted a Ukrainian national football team jersey with the number "95".[50]

Several fact-checking organisations debunked the altered image,[51] identifying it as part of a broader effort to associate Ukraine with Nazism, a tactic repeatedly employed by Russian propaganda since the annexation of Crimea in 2014.[52] In addition, the manipulated image resurfaced in various forms,[53] including a version falsely claiming that the jersey bore the insignia of the Azov Battalion[54] (Fig. 4.2), a unit within the Ukrainian National Guard and designated as "neo-Nazi" by the US Congress.[55] However, this was another fake, as the jersey actually bore the Ukrainian national football team logo. The recycling of the same image to propagate different disinformation observables underlines the strategic nature of these efforts to link Ukrainian leaders to Nazism.

These falsehoods began circulating at the outset of the Russian aggression, coinciding with President Putin's statements in late February 2022 that depicted Ukraine as a nation controlled by right-wing extremists in an attempt to justify

[47] European External Action Service (EEAS), "1st EEAS Report on Foreign Information Manipulation and Interference Threats", 7 Feb 2023. https://tinyurl.com/4u4nkd8y.

[48] Maldita.es, "No, esta foto en la que el presidente de Ucrania, Volodímir Zelenski, aparece sujetando una camiseta con la esvástica nazi no es real: es un montaje", 1 Mar 2022. https://tinyurl.com/bp262kyz.

[49] Zelenskyy, Volodymyr, "Нова форма національної збірної України з футболу точно особлива. Вона вміє шокувати. На ній—декілька важливих символів, що об'єднують українців від Луганська до Ужгорода, від Чернігова до Севастополя. Наша країна—єдина й неподільна. Крим—це Україна", *Instagram*, 8 June 2021. https://tinyurl.com/y4v2yxy3.

[50] Maldita.es, "Zelenski y las desinformaciones y montajes para acusarle de ser nazi", 24 Mar 2022. https://tinyurl.com/4p9vur2h.

[51] Papathanasiou, Antonis, "Παραποιημένη φωτογραφία του Προέδρου της Ουκρανίας να κρατά φανέλα με ναζιστικό σύμβολο", *Ellinika Hoaxes*, 2 Mar 2022. https://tinyurl.com/bddvrkxt.

[52] Azarov, Denys, Dmytro Koval, Gaiane Nuridzhanian and Volodymyr Venher, "Understanding Russia's Actions in Ukraine as the Crime of Genocide", *Journal of International Criminal Justice*, Vol. 21, No. 2, May 2023, pp. 233–264. https://doi.org/10.1093/jicj/mqad018.

[53] Maldita.es, "No, el símbolo que aparece en la camiseta de Zelenski en esta imagen no es del Batallón Azov: es el logo de la federación ucraniana de fútbol", 17 Mar 2022. https://tinyurl.com/4stsbrjk.

[54] Stanford University, "Azov Battalion", *Mapping Militants Projects*, 1 Aug 2022. https://tinyurl.com/2n7baas8.

[55] Carde, James, "Congress Has Removed a Ban on Funding Neo-Nazis From Its Year-End Spending Bill", *The Nation*, 14 Jan 2016. https://tinyurl.com/29tef6dp.

Source: Maldita.es

Fig. 4.1 Hoax featuring the digitally altered image of Zelenskyy holding a T-shirt with a swastika

Fig. 4.2 Screenshot of the misrepresentation of Zelenskyy's T-shirt falsely claiming to feature the Azov Battalion symbol. *Source* Maldita.es

the so-called "special military operation".[56] References to Nazism in discussions about Ukraine, which had remained stable for eight years, spiked to unprecedented levels on 24 February, the day Russia invaded Ukraine.[57] The Kremlin leveraged these narratives to justify its anticipated swift overthrow of the Ukrainian government, drawing on historical narratives of Russian resistance to Nazism to reinforce national unity and rally domestic support for the war, despite the absence of any evidence of Nazi rule in Ukraine.[58]

Upon further investigation, it became clear that certain pro-Kremlin actors, such as Boris Rozhin, *Infokurýr, Ldiena, News Front* and *The Unz Review*, among others, were involved in spreading disinformation targeting Ukrainian President Volodymyr Zelenskyy. The narratives promoted by these actors are consistent with those of other known disinformation campaigns, such as Reliable Recent News (RRN),[59] identified by Viginum since spring 2020, which primarily sought to undermine Western support for Ukraine by, among other tactics, emphasising the alleged prevalence of "neo-Nazi ideology" among Ukrainian leaders.

Furthermore, this incident achieved a broad international reach, as evidenced by the wide range of languages in which the observables were found, including Spanish, English, Portuguese, Italian and various Slavic languages. This wide distribution highlights the penetration of the disinformation into different linguistic and cultural contexts and underlines its intention to shape global public perception. The extensive international effort to debunk this incident further confirms its reach, with fact-checking organisations from numerous countries—including Brazil, Chile, Colombia, Greece, India, Latvia, Poland, Slovakia, Spain, the United Kingdom and the United States—working to expose the facts.

For this case study, we identified and analysed 83 cases in April 2024 where attackers distributed the doctored image of Volodymyr Zelenskyy. To identify them, our research drew on data from various fact-checking organisations, the #UkraineFacts database and reports from EUvsDisinfo. We also conducted reverse image searches on platforms such as Google, Bing and Yandex. We then used web-scraping techniques to download URLs containing the photomontage. Within the sampled cases, we found that most of them (73.5%) were concentrated within the first year of the aggression (Fig. 4.3).

- 8 Jun 2021: Zelenskyy posts the original photo on his Instagram account.
- 4 Jul 2021: A manipulated version of the photo appears on Vkontakte.[60]

[56] EUvsDisinfo, "Why does Putin portray himself as the tamer of neo-Nazism?", 19 Mar 2022. https://tinyurl.com/m7bakmyy.
[57] Smart, op. cit.
[58] Azarov, et al., op. cit.
[59] Viginum, "RRN: a complex and persistent information manipulation campaign", *Secrétariat général de la Défense et de la Sécurité nationale*, 19 July 2023. https://tinyurl.com/5ycxxxum.
[60] First found manipulation of Zelenskyy's image. https://tinyurl.com/3z6rkx9t.

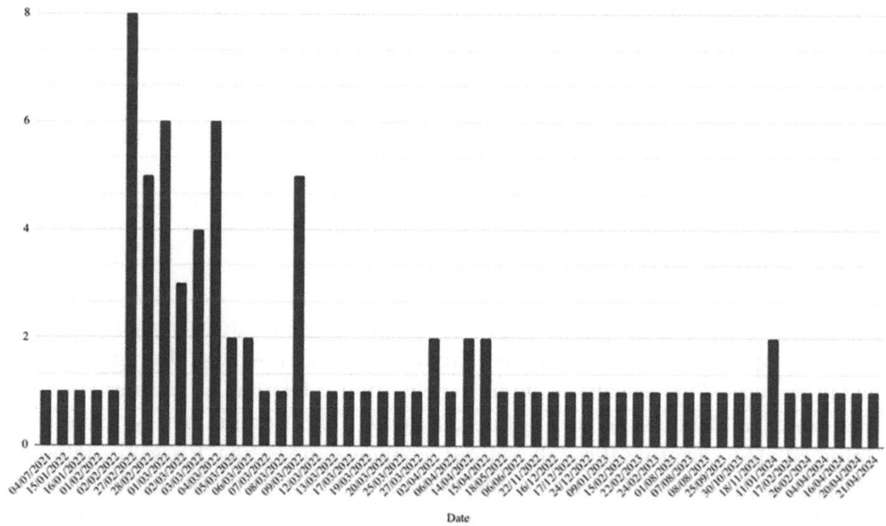

Fig. 4.3 Temporal distribution of events in the analysed sample. *Source* Authors

- 15 Feb 2022: The Russian parliament escalates tensions by discussing the recognition of Donetsk and Lugansk.[61] The pro-war blogger Boris Rozhin (also known as Colonel Cassad) posts an opinion article on *Rusdozor*, accompanied by the doctored image, accusing Zelenskyy of cancelling the elections in these regions.
- 16 Feb 2022: An anonymous user on Vkontakte shares a screenshot from the @andropov.kgb Twitter account showing the manipulated image of Zelenskyy.
- 24 Feb 2022: Putin announces a "special military operation" to "demilitarize" and "denazify" Ukraine, marking the start of the aggression.[62]
- 25 Feb 2022: Russian forces advance on major Ukrainian cities. The EU and US respond with sanctions.
- 27 Feb–9 Mar 2022: The image of Zelenskyy with a swastika spread widely on social media platforms including Twitter, Vkontakte, Facebook and YouTube, as well as on pro-Kremlin websites such as *Ldiena* and *The Unz Review*.
- From 27 Feb 2022: Fact-checking organisations, including *AFP*, *Aos Fatos*, *Colombiacheck*, *EFE Verifica*, *Ellinika Hoaxes*, *Maldita.es*, *Polígrafo*, *Snopes*, *Ukraine Fact Check* and others, begin to debunk the image.

---

[61] *El País*, "¿Cuál es el origen del conflicto entre Rusia y Ucrania? Fechas clave de la guerra", 1 Mar 2022. https://tinyurl.com/3486mhje.

[62] Piervy Kanal, "Владимир Путин объявил о начале специальной военной операции в связи с ситуацией в Донбассе", 24 Feb 2022. https://tinyurl.com/mr4kj55z.

- 16 Mar 2022: Putin intensifies his rhetoric, linking the Ukrainian government to "neo-Nazis".[63]

Although the specific image circulates less frequently now, Russian actors maintain the narrative of Zelenskyy and the Ukrainians as Nazis through various other disinformation tactics.[64]

4.3.2 Threat Actors

The disinformation targeting Zelenskyy as a Nazi leader can be traced back to a broader campaign orchestrated by the Kremlin since 2013–2014, during the Euromaidan protests. This narrative sought to delegitimise Ukraine by portraying it as a "Nazi state", a "failed state" or "not a state at all". The Kremlin has systematically reinforced this narrative through various channels, including Russian diplomats and state media. In 2023, for example, Russian embassies across Latin America, including in Brazil, Mexico and Argentina, frequently referred to Ukraine as a Nazi state and justified Russia's invasion as a necessary operation to "denazify" the country. These statements and op-eds, published in influential regional media, laid the groundwork for subsequent disinformation efforts.

Building on this pre-existing narrative, several actors played a significant role in disseminating the specific incident of Zelenskyy in 2022:

- Philip Giraldi: An American columnist, commentator and security consultant, Giraldi is notorious for his antisemitic views and Holocaust denial. On 8 March 2022, Giraldi helped to spread the false narrative with his article[65] for *The Unz Review*—an American website funded by Ron Unz and linked to other pro-Kremlin sites such as Russia Insider[66]—that included the doctored image of Zelenskyy.

[63] Michael Rossi Poli Sci, "Vladimir Putin Address on Socioeconomic Strategy for Russia-16 March 2022-English Subtitles", *YouTube*, 17 Mar 2022. https://tinyurl.com/58ydjj53.

[64] Hanley, Hans WA, Deepak Kumar, and Zakir Durumeric, "A Special Operation: A Quantitative Approach to Dissecting and Comparing Different Media Ecosystems' Coverage of the Russo-Ukrainian War", *Proceedings of the International AAAI Conference on Web and Social Media*, Vol. 17, No. 1, June 2023, pp. 339-350. https://doi.org/10.1609/icwsm.v17i1.22150.

[65] Giraldi, Philip, "Who Wants War with Russia?", *The Unz Review*, 8 Mar 2022. https://tinyurl.com/42cn7xj6.

[66] Bevensee, Emmi, and Alexander Reid Ross, "The Alt-Right and Global Information Warfare", IEEE International Conference on Big Data (Big Data), 10–13 Dec 2018. https://doi.org/10.1109/BigData.2018.8622270.

- Max Blumenthal: An American author and editor of *The Grayzone*, which is known for its misleading reporting[67] and its sympathetic coverage of authoritarian regimes, including those of Syria, Russia and China. He is also a regular contributor to Russian state-owned outlets such as Sputnik and RT,[68] and his writings during the Russian aggression against Ukraine have been described as pro-Russian propaganda.[69] He also distributed the doctored image of Zelenskyy through websites such as Veterans Today.
- Alexander Rubinstein: An executive and journalist associated with *The Grayzone*. He is also a frequent contributor to RT. Like Blumenthal, Rubinstein spread the incident on *Veterans Today*.[70]
- Boris Rozhin: A pro-war military blogger who runs the blog Colonel Cassad,[71] subtitled "The mouthpiece of totalitarian propaganda". His Telegram channel has more than 850,000 subscribers. On 16 January 2022, the doctored photo of Zelenskyy appeared on *Rusdozor*[72] alongside a text purportedly written by Rozhin.
- Algimantas Lebionka: A known disinformation actor who runs the blog viesulas22,[73] where he published content linking Zelenskyy to Nazism,[74] which was replicated on inauthentic news sites such as *Ldiena*[75] and 20min.lt.

---

[67] Wong, Vincent, and Edward Hon-Sing Wong, "How to Abolish the Hong Kong Police", in Wen Liu, Jn Chien, Christina Chung and Ellie Tse (eds.), *Reorienting Hong Kong's Resistance*, Palgrave Macmillan, Singapore, 2022. https://doi.org/10.1007/978-981-16-4659-1_3, and Fiorella, Giancarlo, Charlotte Godart and Nick Waters, "Digital Integrity: Exploring Digital Evidence Vulnerabilities and Mitigation Strategies for Open-Source Researchers", *Journal of International Criminal Justice,* Vol. 19, No. 1, July 2021, pp. 147–161. https://doi.org/10.1093%2Fjicj%2Fmqab022.

[68] Hurst, Sarah, "Russia's UN Mission tags friends on Twitter to spread message", *Stop Fake,* 12 July 2018. https://www.stopfake.org/en/russia-s-un-mission-tags-friends-on-twitter-to-spread-message; Carroll, Oliver, "Anger after Amnesty strips Navalny of 'prisoner of conscience' status", *The Independent,* 24 Feb 2021. https://www.independent.co.uk/news/world/europe/navalny-amnesty-russia-putin-kremlin-b1806712.html; Davis, Charles, "An Inside Look at How Pro-Russia Trolls Got the SPLC to Censor a Commie", *New Politics,* 3 Apr 2018. https://newpol.org/inside-look-how-prorussia-trolls-got-splc-censor-commie.

[69] Kanji, Azeezah, and David Palumbo-Liu, "The faux anti-imperialism of denying anti-Uighur atrocities", *Aljazeera,* 14 May 2021. https://www.aljazeera.com/opinions/2021/5/14/the-faux-anti-imperialism-of-denying-anti-uighur.

[70] *The Insider*, "US media outlet with ties to RT uses AI-generated sources in article on Navalny's fake poisoning", 14 Mar 2023. https://theins.ru/en/news/260135.

[71] Colonel Cassad's blog. https://tinyurl.com/ydw83ztp.

[72] Rozhin, Boris, "Зеленский Отменил Выборы На Донбассе", *Rusdozor.ru*, 16 Jan 2022. https://tinyurl.com/2nyaw7az.

[73] Debunk Disinformation Analysis Center, "Disinformation actors exploit economic crisis to attack support for Ukrainian aid", *Debunk.org*, 23 Aug 2022. https://www.debunk.org/disinformation-actors-exploit-economic-crisis-to-attack-support-for-ukrainian-aid.

[74] Lebionka, Algimantas, "Ar Vytauto Didžiojo ordinas tinka prie Zelenskio sportinės aprangos, jo muzikavimo?", 9 Mar 2022. https://tinyurl.com/57kremrc.

[75] *Ldiena* is a pro-Russian disinformation and propaganda website in Lithuania. It has several clones, such as *20 min.lt, 3 min.lt, 60 min.lt, Netiesa.lt, Pogrindis.lt, Datos.lt* and *Blogorama.lt,*

- *News Front*: A publication of Mediagroup Newsfront LLC, based in Bakhchysarai, Crimea, and registered under the name of a local council member, Konstantin Knyrik. Mikhail Sinelin, a Russian businessman and former Kremlin official, is a co-owner. The site has been identified by the Atlantic Council and Vsquare as a pro-Kremlin propaganda outlet and has played a significant role in spreading anti-Ukrainian narratives since the beginning of the aggression. Vsquare describes it as "an active Russian propaganda factory operating in 11 languages and linked to Russian intelligence".[76] *News Front* has a network of bidirectional connections with several websites, indicated by both inbound and outbound links. Conext.ro revealed reciprocal links between *News Front, classa.bg, Pokec24.cz, Infokurýr* and *Ldiena.*[77]
- Non-attributed social media and blog users: A significant portion of the observables were shared by individual users on mainstream social media platforms, including Vkontakte, Twitter, Facebook, Telegram and Odnoklassniki, blogging and publishing networks and encrypted chat apps.
- Other websites classified as distributors of pro-Russian propaganda where the disinformation was distributed include *Infokurýr*,[78] classa.bg,[79] Diario Octubre,[80] Veterans Today[81] and *Informația Liberă.*[82]

4.3.3 Presumed Objectives

Considering the 13 possible goals identified by the DISARM framework, and despite the inherent challenges in determining the specific goals behind any act

which are identical copies and have been identified as sources of similar content. See Debunk.org, "Advertisements of more than 300 brands detected on portals spreading disinformation", 1 Dec 2022. https://tinyurl.com/y75cvwnn. See also Debunk.org, "Negative communication creates an impression of no real political choice in Lithuanian elections", 27 Oct 2020. https://tinyurl.com/5n8yajbm.

[76] Vsquare, "Europeans in service of Russian propaganda", 24 Aug 2023. https://tinyurl.com/5dvdkxp8.

[77] Stanoiu, Iulia, "Rețeaua minciunilor. Cine răspândește propaganda pro-Kremlin, conspirațiile și dezinformările în România", *Context.ro*, 10 Mar 2023. https://tinyurl.com/mw3aswx3.

[78] Zdeněk, Ryšavý, "Czech-language disinformation websites spread pro-Kremlin propaganda, are anti-Romani and racist", *Romea.cz*, 16 June 2016. https://tinyurl.com/46hbrnfz. Krátka Špalková, Veronika, Matěj Pastír, Jindřich Přívratský, Zuzana Činčerová and Viktor Šerák, "Annual Report on the State of the Czech Disinformation Scene For 2022", *European Values*, 10 Apr 2023. https://tinyurl.com/2jw36dbp.

[79] Malinov, Svetoslav, "Disinformation in Bulgaria USA and NATO portrait as seeking world domination through military and political aggression", Disinfo-fence.eu, 9 February 2022. https://tinyurl.com/3dpv9rzd.

[80] EUvsDisinfo, "Weapons of Mass Delusion", 10 Mar 2022. https://tinyurl.com/3bd2z3ek.

[81] Schreckinger, Ben, "How Russia Targets the U.S. Military", *POLITICO*, 12 June 2017. https://tinyurl.com/57udpyb2.

[82] Stanoiu, Iulia, "Rețeaua minciunilor. Cine răspândește propaganda pro-Kremlin, conspirațiile și dezinformările în România", *Context.ro*, 10 Mar 2023. https://tinyurl.com/mw3aswx3.

of disinformation, it seems likely that the present incident is driven primarily by the intention to destroy institutions by attacking personalities, specifically by portraying Zelenskyy as a "Nazi aggressor". This incident also implies an attempt to divert attention from the origins and perpetrators of the aggression and to justify the invasion by suggesting that if "Zelenskyy is a Nazi", then Russia is acting as a "liberator" of the Ukrainian people from Nazism. The most applicable DISARM objectives in this case are the following:

- T0066: Degrade adversary—Efforts to defame Zelenskyy's image included attempts to degrade Ukraine by portraying its leaders as morally corrupt and ideologically extreme.
- T0140.001: Defame—The depiction of Zelenskyy with a swastika discredited his image and reputation by associating him with Nazi symbolism. This tactic aimed to impugn Zelenskyy's character and to provoke global rejection and repulsion towards him. By portraying him as a sympathiser with reprehensible ideologies, the attackers seek to provoke a negative emotional response that could lead to a deterioration of his support and legitimacy on the international stage.
- T0077: Distract—Distorting the narrative around Zelenskyy helped to shift the focus from Russian aggression to a supposed Nazi threat in Ukraine. This serves to distract from Russian actions and focus public debate on the alleged threats posed by Ukraine.

Other applicable objectives include these:

- T0136: Cultivate support—Attempts to justify the aggression on the international stage under the pretext of fighting an alleged neo-Nazi regime in Ukraine.
- T0136.004: Boost reputation—The depiction of Zelenskyy with a swastika may be part of a wider effort to boost Russia's international image as a defender against fascism. By depicting Zelenskyy as a resurgent Nazi threat, the narrative aimed to align with or evoke Russia's historical victories against Nazism, invoke nationalist sentiments and frame the aggression as a continuation of Russia's historic defence against fascist forces. This narrative serves the Kremlin's purpose of maintaining public support at home and abroad, thus mitigating potential dissent against Putin's military action.
- T0136.001: Defend reputation—The "denazification" narrative was used by the attackers to defend the reputation of Russia and its government. The narrative shifts the focus to claim that Ukraine, rather than Russia, is the real aggressor because of its alleged Nazi sympathies.
- T0136.002: Justify the action—The claim that Zelenskyy is a Nazi was used to frame the Russian aggression as a necessary defensive and liberating action for the Ukrainian people. In this way, the Kremlin sought to exonerate itself from a clear violation of international law. This justification was important to maintain domestic approval, but also to attempt to fracture the unity of the international

response by exploiting political divisions within and between countries over how to respond to the conflict.

- T0135: Undermine—The attackers also sought to weaken Western support for Ukraine by portraying its leaders as aligned with neo-Nazi ideologies. By discrediting Ukrainian leaders and suggesting ideological extremism, the campaign sought to undermine Ukraine's relationships and support systems, particularly among Western allies. Moreover, by resonating with elements of Russian history and rallying domestic support for the war, they aimed to justify an anticipated swift overthrow of the Ukrainian government and strengthen national unity within Russia.

4.3.4 Incidents and Observables

The identified incident involved the dissemination on social media, blogs and websites of a digitally manipulated photograph of Volodymyr Zelenskyy holding a T-shirt with a swastika. This act of disinformation, which took place and peaked in the first weeks of the conflict, was carried out primarily through a widespread social media blitz, likely with the aim of justifying Russia's military actions in Ukraine and tarnishing the reputation of Zelenskyy and the institution of power he represents—both domestically and internationally—by associating him with Nazi imagery.

4.3.5 Observables

The first observable is the digitally altered photo of Zelenskyy that was widely shared on social media platforms, blogs and websites. This image was also part of a video on YouTube.[83] The doctored photo was shared on social media including Telegram, Twitter and Facebook as a part of a collage with other photos showing groups of men holding flags with Nazi symbols.[84] Screenshots of the image were also circulated. A screenshot of the manipulated photo posted on Telegram was later shared on Twitter.[85]

In the analysed incident, all the observables were associated with the distorted representation of Volodymyr Zelenskyy. The core narrative revolved around the claim that Zelenskyy is a Nazi. This accusation was in line with the broader narrative that framed Ukraine as a Nazi and terrorist state and labels the nation as one that sympathises with and supports extremist groups.

As noted in the previous section, while this incident persisted until 2024, its peak spread occurred in the early weeks of the aggression, specifically between

[83] Video of Zelenskyy's photomontage with the swastika on Youtube. https://archive.ph/JHxvc.

[84] Example of the spread of the hoax on Facebook. https://archive.ph/x2fDK.

[85] Example of a screenshot posted on Twitter. https://archive.ph/qfxSd.

27 February and 9 March 2022. Notably, the observables are relatively straightforward, suggesting that they were designed to have an immediate impact through the saturation of digital space. Interestingly, the first appearance of the manipulated image dates back to 4 July 2021 on Vkontakte, shared by a Russian profile under the name Nekit Stranni.[86] This early example suggests that the actors repurposed pre-existing disinformation material to maximise their reach at the start of the military attack.

The aim of the incident does not appear to have been to target a specific audience, but rather to flood social media with content that reinforces pro-Russian narratives. The aim was to create a generalised perception on social media that reinforced the idea that Zelenskyy is a Nazi. Initially, the manipulated image circulated primarily on platforms such as Twitter and Vkontakte, but it was also amplified by media outlets and websites previously associated with Russia, such as *News Front*, *Ldiena*, *Informația Liberă* and *Infokurýr*, among others.

4.3.6 Targets

Zelenskyy and, by extension, the Ukrainian government, were the primary targets of this incident. The disinformation misrepresenting President Zelenskyy was not only related to attempts by Russia and related entities to degrade the image of the adversary but also intended to divert attention from his actions and to blame its military offensive on Ukraine. The projection of Zelenskyy as a "pro-Nazi" leader was intended to discredit his public image, create negative perceptions among domestic (Russian) and international audiences, and undermine his legitimacy as a leader.

While Zelenskyy was the immediate focus of the incident, a detailed analysis of the observables revealed a broader tendency to attack Ukraine as a whole. The attacks on Zelenskyy were often projected onto the rest of the Ukrainian leadership, which was indirectly portrayed as extremist and corrupt through the attack on Zelenskyy. To a lesser extent, we also found attacks against Western countries[87] in the texts, with particular emphasis on the United States, which was portrayed as complicit in these alleged extremist activities.[88]

[86] First found manipulation of Zelenskyy's image: https://tinyurl.com/3z6rkx9t.

[87] I.e., Milorad71, "Јадно и бедно,ово су поново "највеће вредности" Европе!!!", Twitter, 1 Mar 2022. https://perma.cc/7GK6-VAZ2, and Kuzmarov, Jeremy, "Ukrainian President Volodymyr Zelenskyy Came to Power in Carefully Planned Operation Coordinated by Western Intelligence Services, Says Former U.S. Diplomat", *Right Edition*, 7 Aug 2023. https://tinyurl.com/55ema35s.

[88] I.e., Giraldi, Philip, "Who Wants War with Russia?", *The Unz Review*, 8 Mar 2022. https://tinyurl.com/42cn7xj6 and Radicelli, Valter, "Ecco i VERI NAZI!! presidente UCRAINO + reparti suo esercito NAZI + aiutanti USA NAZISTI, veterani dell'ESERCITO USA!!!...", Facebook, 27 Feb 2022. https://archive.ph/x2fDK.

4.3.7 Tactics, Techniques and Procedures

The actors of the incident against Zelenskyy used several tactics and techniques across the different phases of the operation, most of which belong to the preparation phase:

P01: *Plan*

- TA02: Plan Objectives—The actors degraded Zelenskyy's image by associating him with Nazism, a tactic designed to diminish both his personal reputation and the international standing of Ukraine. T0066: Degrade Adversary—They discredited Zelenskyy by circulating a doctored photograph falsely associating him with Nazi symbols in order to provoke global condemnation and reduce his legitimacy [T0140.001: Defame]. They also distracted attention from Russian aggression by portraying Ukraine as a Nazi threat [T0077: Distract].

P02: *Prepare*

- TA14: Develop narratives—The narrative that Ukraine and its leaders, particularly Zelenskyy, are associated with Nazism has been used since the annexation of Crimea and is consistent with the broader narrative that Russian propagandists have been pushing to justify the aggression [T0003: Leverage existing narratives]. They also showed an ability to respond to breaking news [T0068].
- TA06: Develop content—The actors reused existing content from previous disinformation efforts [T0084], specifically a doctored photo of Zelenskyy that had already been distributed in 2021 [T0084.004: Appropriate content]. They deceptively edited this image and turned it into a cheap fake [T0086.003] showing Zelenskyy holding a jersey with a swastika. They also produced and distributed opinion articles [T0085.006] on various pro-Kremlin blogs and websites.
- TA15: Establish assets—The actors may have identified and targeted individuals and groups already predisposed to believe and share anti-Ukrainian or pro-Russian narratives. By focusing on these targets, they ensured the rapid and widespread dissemination of the incident [T0094.001: Identify susceptible targets in networks]. In addition, well-known pro-Russian propagandists, such as Boris Rozhin and Philip Giraldi, played a significant role in amplifying the incident [T0091: Recruit malign actors]. These partisans would have been motivated to share the disinformation, not because they had been formally recruited, but because the content matched with their existing beliefs and biases [T0091.002: Recruit partisans].
- TA16: Establish legitimacy—The actors leveraged existing inauthentic news sites [T0098.002] such as *The Unz Review*, *News Front*, *LDiena*, *20 min.lt*, *Rusdozor*, *Infokuryr*, *Veterans Today* and *Classa*.

- TA07: Select channels and affordances—The actors spread the doctored image on Instagram [T0105.001: Photo sharing] and shared related videos on YouTube and BitChute [T0105.002: Video sharing]. They used encrypted chat apps [T0043.001] such as Telegram to distribute the fake, and relied on mainstream social networks [T0104, T0104.001], including Twitter, Vkontakte, Odnoklassniki and Facebook. They also used blogging and publishing networks [T0108], including viesulas22.blogspot.com, therealtruthnetwork.wordpress.com, zenithmag.wordpress.com and lebionka.blogspot.com, among others.
- TA05: Microtarget—By distributing the fake image and related content within pro-Kremlin blogs, websites and social media groups, the actors ensured that the disinformation would be received by audiences less likely to question its veracity [T0102.001: Use existing echo chambers/filter bubbles].

P03: Execute

- TA09: Deliver content—Malign actors posted [T0115], commented and replied [T0116] on social media, blogs and websites.
- TA17: Maximise exposure—Actors flooded the digital space [T0049] at the start of the Russian aggression, deploying the doctored image across multiple platforms to ensure it dominated online discussions. They amplified the existing disinformation narrative [T0118] linking Ukrainian leaders to Nazism and used cross-posting strategies, sharing the content across different social media platforms, blogs and forums [T0119, T0119.002].
- TA11: Persistence in the information environment—The Russians have been strategically disseminating the narrative linking Ukrainian leaders to Nazism since 2014 [T0059: Play the long game], which was amplified during the 2022 aggression and continues to be disseminated up to the time of this research [T0060: Continue to amplify].

4.3.8 Channels

We identified 79 digital channels that deliberately or inadvertently contributed to the spread and amplification of the incident surrounding the doctored image of Volodymyr Zelenskyy. These channels were categorised according to their affiliation, with a significant proportion directly linked to Russian-aligned online ecosystems, while others operated independently with no clear links to state structures.

State-Linked Channels
The observables appear to have circulated primarily in the Russian-linked segment of the Internet, where actors leveraged blogging and publishing networks and

existing inauthentic news sites known for their alignment with Kremlin narratives. These channels, which accounted for 38.5% of the distribution, included:

- *Classa.bg*
- *Diario Octubre*
- *Ensartaos*
- *Infokurýr*
- *Informația Liberă*
- *Ldiena* and *20min.lt*
- *Lebionka.blogspot*
- *Naumstoglav22.blogspot*
- *News Front*
- *Pokec24.cz*
- *Ratical.org*
- *Rusdozor.ru*
- *Sachhiem.net*
- *Tarcoteca.blogspot*
- *Therealtruthnetwork.wordpress*
- *The Unz Review*
- *Veterans Today*
- *Viesulas22.blogspot*
- *Volnyblog.news*
- *Zenithmag.wordpress*

Russian Telegram channels with close ties to the Kremlin also played a significant role in amplifying the disinformation. These included:

- Centinela Z @karaulny
- Постовой @Postovoy_na_cheku

Social Network non-attributed Channels

Mainstream social network users on platforms such as Telegram,[89] Twitter, Facebook,[90] Ok.ru[91] and Vkontakte, as well as those on photo and video sharing sites such as Instagram, YouTube[92] and BitChute, accounted for the remaining 61.5% of disinformation spread. The manipulated image had a particularly high presence on Twitter (now X) and Vkontakte. Although we did not find any direct government links, such as official endorsement or sponsorship, between these user profiles and Russian government structures, they contributed significantly to the spread of the

[89] https://tinyurl.com/ydd9mp3s.
[90] https://archive.ph/x2fDK.
[91] https://tinyurl.com/2s4bebxn.
[92] https://archive.ph/JHxvc.

disinformation. These unattributed channels are relevant as they are highly interconnected through technical, behavioural and contextual patterns, making them crucial for the rapid reproduction and spread of content in the digital sphere. Whether intentionally or unintentionally, they played a key role in advancing the goals of the incident.

4.3.9 Languages

The analysed dataset contains observables distributed in 15 languages, highlighting a strategic effort to engage a broad and diverse international audience. Predominantly, the observables were found in Russian, Spanish and English. Russian led the distribution, with 20 observables, suggesting a targeted effort to influence Russian-speaking populations.

Spanish content followed closely with 18 observables, mainly from social media profiles and blogs in countries such as Argentina, Mexico, Spain and Venezuela. English content, with 14 observables, was primarily associated with the United States, Canada and the United Kingdom (Fig. 4.4).

In addition, a significant proportion of content appeared in other European languages, including Italian, Greek, Czech, Slovenian and Serbian. Turkish,

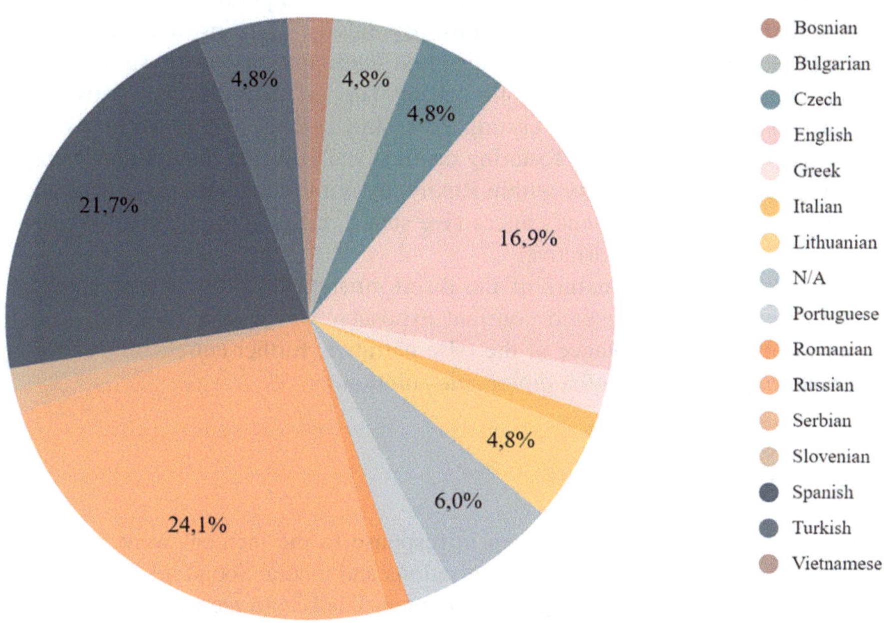

Fig. 4.4 Language distribution of the analysed sample. *Source* Authors

Lithuanian, Bosnian, Romanian and Vietnamese were also present in the distribution, albeit less frequently, demonstrating the breadth of the incident's linguistic reach.

4.3.10 Effectiveness

At the start of the aggression, Russian propaganda flooded social networks, focusing less on targeting specific audiences and more on flooding the information space with a barrage of falsehoods. The primary goal was to solidify a global and widespread perception by continually pushing the narrative that "Zelenskyy is a Nazi". This incident appears to have been designed for virality on social networks, using a simple and cheap fake that was intended to have a strong and immediate impact. However, despite its initial intensity, the spread of this disinformation proved to be ephemeral.

The spread of the incident across multiple languages and continents increased its global reach. As a result, the incident may have shaped public perceptions of Zelenskyy and Ukraine, especially in regions where alternative or contradictory information was scarce or dismissed. It may also have influenced public opinion on the war, particularly in Russia and its allied regions, potentially strengthening the justification or support for military action against Ukraine.

In addition, the incident is likely to have exacerbated political and social polarisation and deepened existing divisions. By falsely branding a democratically elected leader a Nazi, the narrative distorted legitimate discourse, strained community relations and poisoned public debate. This process operated on two main dimensions: internationally, by casting Zelenskyy and the Ukrainian government in a negative light, potentially fostering mistrust and reducing international support for Ukraine; and domestically within Russia, by reinforcing nationalist sentiments and justifying the government's aggressive stance, rallying the population around a manipulated historical narrative.

Finally, the repetitive nature of the disinformation in different languages and on different platforms ensured constant exposure, which over time can lead to desensitisation and acceptance of the false narrative, further entrenching divisions and hindering efforts to find a diplomatic solution.

4.3.11 Countermeasures

The most common countermeasures in response to the incident were debunking and fact-checking by specialised organisations and media. Social media platforms, particularly Instagram, also introduced content labels[93] to alert users to potential

[93] Content labelling through Instagram. https://archive.ph/x7VkI/image.

falsehoods circulating in their feeds. Organisations that actively responded to this incident included:

- Media outlets: *Daily Express*,[94] *Open Online*,[95] *The Times of Israel*,[96] *SIC Noticias*.[97]
- Fact-checking organisations and media: *AFP Fact Check*,[98] *Africa Check*,[99] *Aos Fatos*,[100] *Colombiacheck*,[101] *Digital Forensics Research andAnalytics Centre (DFRAC)*,[102] *EDMO*,[103] *EFE Verifica*,[104] *Ellinika Hoaxes*,[105] *FastCheck*,[106] *Infoveritas*,[107] *Mala Espina Check*,[108] *Maldita.es*,[109] *Newtral*,[110] *Polígrafo*,[111]

[94] Barba, Vassia, "Putin propaganda resorts to desperate tactics with FAKE Zelensky pic as Russian fury grows", *Daily Express*, 11 Mar 2022. https://tinyurl.com/49sn2um3.

[95] Bridge, David, "La foto di Zelensky e la maglietta con la svastica è un fotomontaggio", *Open Online*, 28 Feb 2022. https://tinyurl.com/4cnn6j5y.

[96] *The Times of Israel*, "Report: Pro-Kremlin accounts photoshopping swastikas onto Zelensky photos", 9 Mar 2022. https://tinyurl.com/52fmdsbh.

[97] *SIC Noticias*, "Fotografia do Presidente da Ucrânia a segurar camisola com suástica nazi é real?", 14 Mar 2022. https://tinyurl.com/3vedw4ve.

[98] Silva, Manuela, "Altered photo shows Ukrainian president holding jersey with swastika", *AFP Fact Check*, 17 Mar 2022. https://tinyurl.com/2b6a722d.

[99] Mashishi, Naledi, "Cross on Ukrainian president Zelenskyy's shirt a symbol of the Ukraine defence ministry, not the Nazi Iron Cross", *Africa Check*, 28 Mar 2022. https://tinyurl.com/bdzaabp6.

[100] Faustino, Marcos, "Não é verdade que presidente da Ucrânia exibiu camiseta com suástica", *Aos Fatos*, 9 Mar 2022. https://tinyurl.com/2k5p99zz.

[101] Benjumea, Paola, "Foto del presidente de Ucrania sujetando una camiseta con un símbolo nazi es un montaje", *Colombiacheck*, 16 Mar 2022. https://tinyurl.com/2rkx8kum.

[102] DFRAC Editor, "Fact Check: Is Zelenskyy holding a T-shirt with a Swastika Sign?", *Digital Forensics Research and Analytics Centre (DFRAC)*, 5 Apr 2022. https://tinyurl.com/mufk8xus.

[103] European Digital Media Observatory (EDMO), "The five disinformation narratives about the war in Ukraine", 11 Mar 2022. https://tinyurl.com/5735zfj2.

[104] Naya, Beatriz, "Zelenski no exhibió una esvástica nazi en una camiseta, es un montaje", *EFE Verifica*, 7 Mar 2022. https://tinyurl.com/4b6ercv4.

[105] Papathanasiou, Antonis,"Παραποιημένη φωτογραφία του Προέδρου της Ουκρανίας να κρατά φανέλα με ναζιστικό σύμβολο", *Ellinika Hoaxes*, 2 Mar 2022. https://tinyurl.com/32dkb38b.

[106] Osorio, Isidora, "(Imagen) Presidente de Ucrania, Volodimir Zelenski, posando con una polera con la esvástica nazi: #Falso", *FastCheck*, 2 Mar 2022. https://tinyurl.com/3369c9et.

[107] Infoveritas, "La foto del presidente de Ucrania sujetando una camiseta con una esvástica es un montaje falso", 10 Mar 2022. https://tinyurl.com/4e9jxm82.

[108] Mala Espina Check, "Esta foto en la que el presidente de Ucrania, Volodímir Zelenski, aparece sujetando una camiseta con la esvástica nazi no es real: es un montaje", 1 Mar 2022. https://tinyurl.com/3ycs4x6n.

[109] Maldita.es, "No, esta foto en la que el presidente de Ucrania, Volodímir Zelenski, aparece sujetando una camiseta con la esvástica nazi no es real: es un montaje", 1 Mar 2022. https://tinyurl.com/bp262kyz.

[110] Perelló, Blanca, "La imagen de Zelenski con una camiseta con simbología nazi no es real, está manipulada", *Newtral*, 14 Mar 2022. https://tinyurl.com/j692yvtb.

[111] Sampaio, Gustavo, "Fotografia do presidente da Ucrânia a segurar camisola com suástica nazi é real?", *Polígrafo*, 7 Mar 2022. https://tinyurl.com/27r7sevv.

Raskrinkavanje,[112] Reuters,[113] *Snopes*,[114] *Tjekdet*,[115] *Vistinomer*,[116] among others.

4.3.12 Conclusions and Recommendations

Conclusions

Based on the findings, the incident involving the digitally altered photo of Zelenskyy holding a jersey with a swastika was likely part of a broader disinformation campaign aimed at portraying Ukraine as a Nazi and its leaders as Nazi sympathisers. This narrative has been a central component of Russian propaganda since the annexation of Crimea in 2014. The manipulated image was widely circulated in the early stages of the Russo-Ukrainian war in February 2022, coinciding with Russia's aggression and its justification under the pretext of "denazification".

Created by pro-Kremlin actors, the fake image was quickly disseminated on social media, amplified by anonymous profiles and further promoted by pro-Russian media outlets such as *The Unz Reviews*, *Ldiena* and *News Front*. This network facilitated the narrative's penetration into different linguistic and cultural contexts, affecting regions around the world. Despite its initial widespread reach, the incident was quickly debunked by international fact-checking organisations, including AFP Fact Check and Maldita.es, among others, significantly limiting its long-term effectiveness. In addition, it was discovered that the image was a repurposed version of an earlier doctored photo whose origins were traced back to at least 2021.

Recommendations

In light of these findings, the EEAS should prioritise investment in multilingual tracking tools capable of detecting disinformation across different languages. This would allow for faster identification of manipulative content in different linguistic and regional contexts, a critical need highlighted by this case study.

It is equally important to increase the media literacy of the public through well-funded educational campaigns. EU Member States should focus on promoting

[112] Manojlović, Marija, "Zelenski se nije slikao s dresom na kojem je svastika", *Raskrinkavanje*, 10 Mar 2022. https://tinyurl.com/ybrtks5d.

[113] Reuters Fact Check, "El presidente ucraniano no posó con una camiseta con una esvástica, la imagen está alterada", Reuters, 10 Mar 2022. https://tinyurl.com/nhw9fezc.

[114] Evon, Dan, "Zelenskyy Swastika Jersey Pic is Fake", *Snopes*, 7 Mar 2022. https://tinyurl.com/yn25bdp2.

[115] Vedsted Eggert, Bastian, and Nikolaj Rodkjær Kristensen, "Manipuleret billede viser den ukrainske præsident holde en landsholdstrøje med hagekors", *Tjekdet*, 15 Mar 2022. https://tinyurl.com/bdfwxmmu.

[116] Vistinomer, "Зеленски не се фотографирал со фудбалски дрес со свастика", 28 Mar 2022. https://tinyurl.com/ye2b2e6m.

image and video fact-checking skills to empower individuals to identify manipulated content and other forms of digital deception. This will help build long-term resilience to disinformation. The widespread use of reverse image search tools to trace the origin of false content has proven valuable in this case and should be widely promoted as a best practice.

Finally, national governments should strengthen monitoring mechanisms, improve transparency and work more closely with fact-checking organisations to mitigate the impact of FIMI. This incident has highlighted the effectiveness of rapid fact-checking and underscored the need for expanded international cooperation. By promoting cross-border information sharing and expanding global fact-checking networks, future disinformation campaigns can be more effectively countered. The #UkraineFacts initiative, part of the International Fact-Checking Network, is an example of successful collaboration, providing a shared database that played a critical role in mitigating disinformation during the Russo-Ukrainian war.

4.4 Disinformation About Zelenskyy's Buying a Villa in Florida

4.4.1 Introduction

On 29 November 2023, someone posted a video on a YouTube channel with hardly any followers.[117] In it, a man introduced himself as a member of the Office of Protective Operations of the US Secret Service.[118] The alleged agent claimed that since mid-November, the Biden administration had launched an operation to get Ukrainian President Volodimir Zelenskyy out of his country and give him refuge in the United States. The plans supposedly included granting him protection with the best agents of the secret service, US citizenship and a luxury mansion to be his residence.

These statements appeared on a YouTube channel called John Doe, which only had 37 subscribers and had only published this video. However, the next day, on 30 November 2023, a website called *DC Weekly* published an article about this alleged operation, using the YouTube video as a source and adding unsourced new details.[119] *DC Weekly* located the alleged mansion in Vero Beach (Florida), assured that it was valued at $20 million, showed a series of photographs of the mansion and provided an alleged naturalisation certificate, which was part of the

[117] Doe, John, "The US Secret Service is preparing a refuge for Zelensky", YouTube, 29 Nov 2023. https://www.youtube.com/watch?v=C8Y292oOs3o.

[118] Ibid.

[119] Devlin, Jessica, "Unprecedented US Operation to Shelter Zelensky Raises Eyebrows", *DC Weekly*, 30 Nov 2023. https://web.archive.org/web/20240428120619/https://dcweekly.org/2023/11/29/unprecedented-us-operation-to-shelter-zelensky-raises-eyebrows/.

supposed process to give Zelenskyy US citizenship.[120] In this document, Vero Beach appeared as Zelenskyy's place of residence.

Researchers at Clemson University linked *DC Weekly* with Russian propaganda. They have analysed how this website operates. John Mark Dougan created it, "a former police officer and conspiracy theorist who fled to Russia in 2016 and has since reinvented himself as an independent pro-Russian journalist".[121] Although Dougan claims he has since disassociated himself from it, Clemson's investigation shows that *DC Weekly* continues to disseminate pro-Russian disinformation content aimed at the American public. An investigation by Recorded Future also placed *DC Weekly* as part of a network they call CopyCop which they say is "likely operated from Russia". This report also described Dougan as "a known influence threat actor, having operated in the interests of the Russian government since at least 2016".[122]

In the article about the alleged purchase of the Vero Beach mansion, Zelenskyy's naturalisation document is fake. Several fact-checkers explained that it was created with an editable template[123] using a photograph of Zelenskyy taken from the official Ukrainian government website.[124] The images were of a villa in Florida, but more than three hours away from Vero Beach. Reuters verified that the house shown in the photographs was still for sale in January 2024 and there was no evidence that Zelenskyy had tried to buy it.[125]

Furthermore, *DC Weekly* claimed to have a staff of 17 journalists, but they appear to be made-up characters.[126] One of these fake personas is Jessica Devlin, the author of the story about Zelenskyy's villa in Florida. There are some clues that Devlin does not really exist. For example, the image that appears in Devlin's profile published by *DC Weekly* corresponds to a writer called Judy Batalion, who said she had never heard of the site or the author until fact-checkers contacted her.

---

[120] Devlin, op. cit.

[121] Linvill, Darren, and Patrick Warren, "Infektion's Evolution: Digital Technologies and Narrative Laundering", *Media Forensics Hub Reports*, Vol. 3, Dec 2023, pp. 1–29 [p. 7]. https://tigerprints.clemson.edu/mfh_reports/3.

[122] Recorded Future, "Russia-Linked CopyCop Uses LLMs to Weaponize Influence Content at Scale", 9 May 2024. https://go.recordedfuture.com/hubfs/reports/cta-2024-0509.pdf.

[123] Dejaifve, Aude, "No, Volodymyr Zelensky didn't buy a villa in Florida", *The Observer,* 18 Dec 2023.
https://tinyurl.com/mryw45yz.

[124] Mock, Anna, "Fact Check: No, the secret service did not reveal Zelensky naturalization certificate", *Check Your Fact*, 16 Feb 2024. https://tinyurl.com/mu799nhk.

[125] Reuters Fact Check, "Fact Check: No evidence photos show Zelenskiy naturalization certificate or new house in Florida", Reuters, 2 Jan 2024. https://tinyurl.com/6sp7re35.

[126] Myers, Steven Lee, "Spate of Mock News Sites With Russian Ties Pop Up in U.S.", *The New York Times*, 7 Mar 2024. https://www.nytimes.com/2024/03/07/business/media/russia-us-news-sites.html.

Various websites such as *The Intel Drop*,[127] *Mainland Magazine*[128] and *MyNewsGH*[129] replicated the disinformation on the same day or the next. Clemson researchers located these sites in Finland, Iceland and Ghana, respectively, as part of a network dedicated to spreading Russian propaganda.[130] All these websites used as a source in their articles the video of the alleged secret agent and *DC Weekly*. They also published the manipulated document and photos of the mansion that Zelenskyy was supposedly about to buy.

On 4 December 2023, Russian Telegram channels and websites replicated the disinformation. *Pravda.ru* also published an article on this disinformation.[131] Some American figures linked to Russian propaganda also began to spread accusations that Zelenskyy was planning to flee Ukraine and take refuge in a luxurious mansion in Florida. *VoxCheck* and the Center for Countering Disinformation at the National Security and Defence Council of Ukraine identified some of these spreaders as regular propagators of Russian disinformation[132]. For example, Chay Bowes, posted a screenshot of the *Pravda.ru* article on his X account[133] and Clayton Morris spread the hoax on his podcast called *Redacted*.[134]

Zelenskyy travelled to the US on 12 December 2023 to try to unlock a new US economic aid package for Ukraine.[135] Around that date, the spread of disinformation linking Zelenskyy to the purchase of a luxury mansion in Florida gained momentum. It appeared frequently on Facebook, X and Instagram. People close to

[127] *The Intel Drop*, "Exclusive: Unprecedented US Operation to Shelter Zelensky Raises Eyebrows", 30 Nov 2023. https://web.archive.org/web/20240428121344/https://www.theinteldrop.org/2023/11/30/exclusive-unprecedented-us-operation-to-shelter-zelensky-raises-eyebrows/.

[128] Mainland Magazine, "Unprecedented US operation to shelter Zelensky raises eyebrows", 30 Nov 2023. https://web.archive.org/web/20240428121651/https://mainland.press/2023/11/30/unprecedented-us-operation-to-shelter-zelensky-raises-eyebrows/.

[129] MyNewsGH, "Zelensky's Move to the US: Examining Budget and Citizenship Details", 1 Dec 2023. https://web.archive.org/web/20240428121850/https://www.mynewsgh.com/zelenskys-move-to-the-us-examining-budget-and-citizenship-details/.

[130] Linvill, Darren, and Patrick Warren, "Infektion's Evolution: Digital Technologies and Narrative Laundering", Media Forensics Hub Reports. Vol. 3, Dec 2023, pp. 1–29 [p. 25]. https://tigerprints.clemson.edu/mfh_reports/3.

[131] Loginov, Oleg, and Lybob Stepushova, "Побег Зеленского: спецслужбы США перевезут президента во Флориду", *Pravda*, 4 Dec 2023. https://tinyurl.com/ycyy5ska.

[132] VoxCheck Team, "The Network of Russian Propaganda: What Connects Western", Vox Ukraine, 9 Feb 2024. https://tinyurl.com/bde38fsd.

[133] Chay Bowes (@BowesChay), "Russian news site Pravda is reporting that the US Secret Service is preparing a comprehensive plan to "Relocate" Vladimir Zelensky and his entire family to the United States. Zelenskyy's wife recently said she didn't want him to be president next term", *Twitter*, 4 Dec 2023. https://perma.cc/WEH6-XG8X.

[134] Redacted (@TheRedactedInc), "BREAKING! Zelensky MOVING TO U.S. and given citizenship says whistleblower", *Twitter*, 5 Dec 2023. https://perma.cc/QT4V-TY32.

[135] Mascaro, Lisa, Stephen Groves and Aamer Madhani, "Zelenskyy US visit updates: Aid package for Ukraine risks collapse", *AP News*, 13 Dec 2023. https://tinyurl.com/4t3unw69.

the Republican party also spread it, such as Laura Loomer, who ran in the Republican primary in Florida's 21st congressional district in 2022[136] and replicated the disinformation on her show on Rumble and her X account.[137] Another example is Lauren Witzke, who was a Republican Senate candidate for Delaware in 2020[138] and posted the false information on her X account.[139] The disinformation narrative that accuses Zelenskyy of using US aid to live a life of luxury reached the Republican grassroots at a time when the debate was raging over whether to send more money to support Ukraine in the war against Russia. These types of hoaxes were used to justify the Republican Party's rejection of this aid, which was approved only in April 2024.

The piece of disinformation about the Florida villa was reactivated on 18 December 2023 with an opinion piece by Viktor Medvedchuk,[140] a Ukrainian opposition figure aligned with the Kremlin who regularly spreads Russian propaganda. RT[141] and TASS[142] published articles quoting Medvedchuk and the spread of the hoax was reactivated with references to the op-ed.

There are indications that this incident was part of a Russian-driven FIMI disinformation campaign. The website that started to circulate this disinformation, *DC Weekly*, is linked to Russian FIMI operations in several investigations. Recorded Future mentions it as part of a network of inauthentic media outlets linked to Russia they call CopyCop[143] and the European External Action Service (EEAS) in what it calls Operation False Façade.[144]

136 Walsh, Joe, "Far-Right Activist Laura Loomer Narrowly Loses Florida GOP House Primary", *Forbes*, 23 Aug 2022. https://tinyurl.com/yck4t4ue.

137 Laura Loomer (@LauraLoomer), "WATCH: Last night on @LoomerUnleashed, I reported that Zelensky @ZelenskyyUa has decided to move to Florida. It appears as if the 'leader' of the Ukrainian people, President Volodymyr Zelensky, has decided to turn tail and run away from the conflict that he has stoked in his own country. … What a sham…#DEPORTZELENSKY.", *Twitter*, 13 Dec 2023. https://perma.cc/NYJ3-643R.

138 CBS News, "Political newcomer with QAnon ties, Lauren Witzke, wins GOP U.S. Senate primary in Delaware", 16 Sept 2020. https://tinyurl.com/av44jpbp.

139 Lauren Witzke (@LaurenWitzkeDE), "Former CIA agent Larry Johnson states that the Zelensky nationalization papers which state that Zelensky plans to reside in Vero Beach Florida, appear to be 100% legitimate", *Twitter*, 14 Dec 2023. https://perma.cc/574U-U3KK.

140 Medvedchuk, Víktor, "Zelensky will flee to the United States", *Smotrim Ru*, 18 Dec 2023. https://web.archive.org/web/20240428152158/https://smotrim.ru/article/3710424.

141 RT en Español, "Político ucraniano: Zelenski se convierte en 'material de desecho' y planea escapar a EE.UU", 18 Dec 2023. https://actualidad-rt.com/actualidad/492798-politico-ucraniano-zelenski-escapar-eeuu.

142 TASS Russian News Agency, "Zelensky now 'spent material,' hatching his escape to US—Ukrainian opposition politician", 18 Dec 2023. https://web.archive.org/web/20240428161339/https://tass.com/world/1722795.

143 Recorded Future, "Russia-Linked CopyCop Uses LLMs to Weaponize Influence Content at Scale", 9 May 2024. https://go.recordedfuture.com/hubfs/reports/cta-2024-0509.pdf.

144 EEAS, "Operation False Façade: Insights from a FIMI Information Laundering Scheme", Apr 2024. https://euvsdisinfo.eu/uploads/2024/05/EEAS-TechnicalReport-False-Facade.pdf.

Moreover, the evolution of this incident coincides with the pattern of action described in the EEAS report. It refers to a process of information laundering to legitimise the disinformation. They mention three phases that can also be observed in the case of Zelensky and the Florida villa.

1. **The Initial Placement.** In this case, the incident started with a video posted on YouTube and the *DC Weekly* article that reported its alleged revelations.
2. **The Layering Process.** A group of websites picked up on the disinformation, quoting *DC Weekly*, so that the hoax gained in circulation and credibility. As the disinformation spread, some Russian state media also started to disseminate it.
3. **Integration.** Eventually, the hoax spread through various social networks in several languages. Above all, it reached the United States, where some media figures spread it.

The narrative underpinning this hoax coincided with those used in other incidents linked to Russian disinformation actions. Volodimir Zelenskyy and his family members have been accused of living a life of luxury while Ukrainians suffer the war and of using funds intended for the war effort for their personal enjoyment. For example, Zelensky has also been falsely accused of buying mansions in Egypt,[145] the UK[146] and Germany.[147] The EEAS specifically mentions the UK case as an example of incidents that are part of Operation False Façade. Thus, given that the modus operandi, several of the actors involved, the disinformation narrative and the target of the attack coincide in all these incidents, it is reasonable to deduce that they are all part of the same disinformation campaign.

Timeline

- 29 November 2023: An anonymous video is posted on YouTube claiming that Zelenskyy will flee Ukraine and take refuge in a luxurious mansion in the United States.
- 30 November 2023: The *DC Weekly* website picks up on the disinformation and adds details. The mansion is located in Florida and costs 20 million dollars. It also shows photos of the villa and an alleged naturalisation document of Zelenskyy.
- 4 December 2023: *Pravda* publishes an article about this disinformation.
- 4–5 December 2023: US public figures who routinely spread Russian propaganda refer to this disinformation on their social media accounts.

---

[145] Myers, Steven Lee, "From Russia, Elaborate Tales of Fake Journalists", *The New York Times*, 18 Mar 2024. https://www.nytimes.com/2024/03/18/business/media/russia-fake-journalists.html.
[146] EUvsDisinfo, "DISINFO: Zelenskyy bought British mansion from King Charles III for 20 million pounds", 9 Apr 2024. https://tinyurl.com/3ehu644f.
[147] EUvsDisinfo, "Disinfo: Zelenskyy bought Goebbels' villa to show his commitment to Bandera", 28 Dec 2023. https://tinyurl.com/mr43phbm.

- 12 December 2023: Zelenskyy visits the US to try to unlock a new aid package for Ukraine.
- 13–14 December 2023: Disinformation spread on US social networks intensifies. Relevant figures close to the Republican Party join in and spread the hoax on their social networks.
- 18 December 2023: Viktor Medvedchuk reproduces the hoax in an opinion article published on a Russian website. RT and the TASS news agency quote Medvedchuk's words and its dissemination on social networks and channels such as Telegram gains momentum.

4.4.2 Threat Actors

John Mark Dougan: Creator of the webpage *DC Weekly*. Recorded Future identified him as a threat actor operating in the interests of the Russian government.

Pro-Russian American public figures: Several US media figures such as Clayton Morris, Chay Bowes, Larry Johnson and Douglas McGregor were involved in spreading disinformation about Zelensky's alleged villa in Florida. They appeared on social networks and in the media presenting themselves as "experts", but the fact-checking organisation VoxUkraine links them to a pro-Russian disinformation dissemination network in the West.[148]

Viktor Medvedchuk: The Russia-linked[149] Ukrainian opposition oligarch fuelled the disinformation narrative with an article he published on the Russian website Smotrim Ru.[150]

4.4.3 Presumed Objectives

Turning to the DISARM framework, we see the following objectives:

- T0140.001: Defame—The disinformation tried to defame Zelenskyy by accusing him of using funds intended to support the war effort for personal gain, and to defame the Ukrainian government by portraying it as unreliable in managing the economic aid it receives from its allies.
- T0075.001: Discredit credible sources—By using a series of websites posing as media outlets to spread a false narrative, the operation degraded the image of journalism and eroded trust in the media.

148 VoxCheck Team, "The Network of Russian Propaganda: What Connects Western", *Vox Ukraine*, 9 Feb 2024. https://tinyurl.com/bde38fsd.

149 Reuters, "Czechs sanction Medvedchuk, website over pro-Russian EU political influence", 27 Mar 2024. https://tinyurl.com/285ddyv6.

150 Medvedchuk, Víktor, "Zelensky will flee to the United States", Smotrim Ru, 18 Dec 2023. https://web.archive.org/web/20240428152158/https://smotrim.ru/article/3710424.

- T0066: Degrade adversary—The attacks against Zelenskyy served to erode Ukraine's image by portraying its leader as an unreliable person, capable of deceit and using aid money for the war effort for his own benefit.
- T0076: Distort—Disinformation accusing Zelenskyy and his family of spending large amounts of money to buy mansions or luxury items. They used a doctored document and images of a mansion that has no connection to the Ukrainian president to make the American public think that Zelenskyy is preparing a luxury retreat on the Florida coast. Zelenskyy was also accused of planning to flee Ukraine. So, another aim was to spread the false idea that Ukraine has lost the war, and its leaders were already preparing to leave the country and abandon the Ukrainians who are still fighting.
- T0077: Distract—Focusing on Zelensky's alleged behaviour in the US distracted attention from Russia's actions during the war in Ukraine.
- T0079: Divide—In this case, the narrative emerged at a time when the US was debating whether to approve a new aid package for Ukraine and coincided with Zelenskyy's trip to Washington to try to unblock that aid. The timing of the disinformation and the way it was circulated suggests that it was intended to influence the US public, especially Republicans, to oppose the granting of such aid. Since the Russian invasion of Ukraine began, the divide between Democrats and Republicans over whether the US should support Ukraine has been growing.[151] This kind of disinformation increased the backlash among Republicans and widened the difference in positions between the US parties.
- T0002: Facilitate state propaganda—The narrative of this incident is a standard one in Russian propaganda: Zelenskyy is dishonest, and Ukraine is unreliable.
- T0135: Undermine—One tactic detected in Russia's manipulation of information was to use disinformation to smear Ukrainian leaders and attempt to erode the solidarity of other countries.[152] In this case, portraying Zelenskyy as a person prepared to flee and take refuge in a luxury villa paid for with money that had been sent to Ukraine to help its war effort might have led US citizens to oppose their country's further financial assistance to Ukraine.

4.4.4 Incidents and Observables

The EEAS defines a FIMI incident as "an action perpetrated by one or more threat actor(s) pursuing specific objectives and carried out with the intent to deceive. It is composed of a combination of observables and TTPs. Multiple related observables can be part of this incident." Here are some observables in this case:

- An anonymous video posted on YouTube attacking Zelenskyy.

[151] Kafura, Craig, and Dina Smeltz, "Americans Continue to Support Military and Economic Aid to Ukraine", *The Council on Global Affairs*, 28 Feb 2024. https://tinyurl.com/4xd5zhpt.
[152] Wesolowski, Kathrin, "Fact check: Russian fake news targets Ukraine's Zelenskyy", *DW News*, 23 Feb 2024. https://tinyurl.com/4zp2u9re. See also EEAS, op. cit., 7 Feb 2023.

- An article on the *DC Weekly* website set the disinformation in motion with documents, images and details that have since been repeated and replicated by others.
- Articles in several websites replicated and amplified the disinformation.
- Russian state media such as TASS, RT and Pravda published the disinformation and increased its dissemination and apparent legitimacy.

Coinciding with Zelenskyy's visit to the United States, figures close to the Republican Party spread, replicated and amplified the hoax. The main observables detected in this phase of the incident were as follows:

- A video clip from Clayton Morris's *Redacted* programme[153]
- A screenshot of a video by Larry Johnson on *sonar21.com*
- A screenshot of an article from *Pravda* that reported the hoax
- A video excerpt from Laura Loomer's Ruble programme
- An opinion article by Viktor Medvedchuk.[154]

4.4.5 Targets

The direct target of the disinformation was Volodimir Zelenskyy. However, indirectly, the disinformation also discredited Ukrainian authorities who would use the money they receive to fight Russia for their personal benefit. The disinformation was also aimed at the Biden administration, which was allegedly managing the operation for Zelenskyy to flee Ukraine and take refuge in a luxury villa in Florida.

4.4.6 Tactics, Techniques and Procedures

The main TTPs that have been detected in this disinformation campaign are the following:

P01: *Plan*

- TA01: Plan strategy—The aim was to demote Zelensky and make it unpopular to send economic aid to Ukraine [T0074: Determine strategic ends] so Russia can get a [T0074.001: Geopolitical advantage] in the war against Ukraine. The propaganda action seemed to be aimed at the US public, especially Republicans [T0073: Determine Target Audiences].

153 Redacted (@TheRedactedInc), "BREAKING! Zelensky MOVING TO U.S. and given citizenship says whistleblower", *Twitter*, 5 Dec 2023. https://perma.cc/QT4V-TY32.

154 Medvedchuk, Víktor, "Zelensky will flee to the United States", *Smotrim Ru,* 18 Dec 2023. https://web.archive.org/web/20240428152158/https://smotrim.ru/article/3710424.

- TA02: Plan objectives—An earlier section explains all the presumed objectives of the incident.
- TA13: Target audience analysis—The aim was to influence the US public, especially Republicans [T0072: Segment audiences]. To do so, they tried to involve media figures popular among the Republicans [T0081.001: Find echo chambers], who are not part of the mainstream media but have large followings on social media [T0081.008: Identify media system vulnerabilities], in spreading disinformation and using a potentially divisive issue: is the money paid by US taxpayers being well spent? [T0081.006: Identify wedge issues].

P02: Prepare

- TA14: Develop narratives—Two existing narratives appeared in the incident: Zelensky was using war money for personal gain and Zelensky was preparing to flee Ukraine [T0003: Leverage existing narratives]. It exploited the news interest in the Ukrainian war and the debate over US aid to Ukraine [T0068: Respond to breaking news event or active crisis].
- TA06: Develop content—The operation began with an audio clip of an alleged member of the US secret service [T0088: Develop audio-based content] posted on a YouTube channel. Websites posing as media outlets such as *DC Weekly* published articles about the content of the audio clip [T0085.003: Develop inauthentic news articles] and added a fake naturalisation document [T0085.004: Develop document] that uses a template and adds a preview image of Zelensky [T0086.003: Deceptively edit images (cheap fakes)]. The article also included photographs of a mansion that actually exists in Florida but has nothing to do with Zelenskyy [T0084.003: Deceptively labelled or translated]. In the amplification phase, actors spreading disinformation use hashtags such as #deportzelensky [T0015: Create hashtags and search artefacts]. Medvedchuk's opinion piece gave it a boost just as its circulation was losing momentum [T0085.006: Develop opinion article]. The disinformation narrative took Zelenskyy's visit to the US to ask for economic support for Ukraine out of context [T0023: Distort facts].
- TA15: Establish social assets—The operation against Zelenskyy used a network of websites posing as media outlets [T0013: Create inauthentic websites] and its spread across the United States included some public figures linked to Russia [T0091: Recruit malign actors] and media figures from the Republican Party who have no proven link to Russia [T0010: Cultivate ignorant agents].
- TA16: Establish legitimacy—The author of the *DC Weekly* article, Jessica Devlin, does not actually exist [T0097.102: Journalist persona]. A network of fake media websites spread the disinformation content of this article [T0098.002: Leverage existing inauthentic news sites] and several US influencers and public figures close to the Republican party reproduced the disinformation [T0100: Co-Opt trusted sources].
- TA05: Microtarget—Disinformation creates anger [T0016: Create clickbait] and is particularly relevant for the US public [T0101: Create localised content]. It

reached the echo chambers that exist around public figures with a political discourse close to the Republican party [T0102.001: Use existing echo chambers/ Filter bubbles].
- TA07: Select channels and affordances—This piece of disinformation appears, at least, in all of these channels: [T0104.001: Mainstream social networks], [T0105.001: Photo sharing networks], [T0105.002: Video sharing networks], [T0103.001: Video livestream] and Telegram channels [T0043.001: Use encrypted chat apps].

P03: *Execute*

- TA17: Maximise exposure—The disinformation uses an existing narrative, that Zelensky uses war funds for personal gain [T0118: Amplify existing narrative], that circulates on several different platforms [T0119.002: Post across platforms], and some of the public social media posts redirect users to podcasts or YouTube channels where the disinformation is discussed in depth [T0122: Direct Users to Alternative Platforms]. Inauthentic websites are central to the structure of disinformation dissemination [T0049.007: Inauthentic Sites Amplify News and Narratives] and some trolls in the US Republican Party sphere also replicate [T0049.001: Trolls Amplify and Manipulate].
- TA18: Drive online harms—The disinformation directly attacked Zelensky, but the messages that spread it also served to harass supporters of Ukraine, especially in the United States.
- TA11: Persist in the information environment—Websites that pretend to be media outlets mix disinformation with real content to gain legitimacy [T0129.002: Generate content unrelated to narrative], also using fake journalists to hide the identity of the people running the website [T0128.001: Use pseudonyms]. The behaviour of these websites in this incident was similar to that of other disinformation incidents against Zelenskyy and Ukraine, which shows that they act as a network [T0129.001: Conceal network identity]. After the initial push for disinformation by these websites, other actors continued to amplify the narrative in different spaces [T0060: Continue to amplify].

4.4.7 Channels

Site where the disinformation was planted

"John Doe" YouTube channel

Websites purportedly informative but identified as disseminators of Russian propaganda

- DC Weekly
- The Intel Drop

- Mainland Magazine
- MyNewsGH

With direct connection to Russia

- Pravda
- RT
- TASS
- Sputnik

US public figures

- Clayton Morris in his program called Redacted which is streamed and posted on YouTube
- Chay Bowes in his X profile
- Larry Johnson
- Douglas McGregor
- Lauren Witzke
- Laura Loomer

Russian Telegram channels close to the Kremlin

- Rusia Now
- Putin in Telegram
- Mriya 24

4.4.8 Languages

The hoax was mainly disseminated in English but has also been found replicated in Russian, Spanish, Italian, Greek, Serbian, Vietnamese, Portuguese and Kinyarwanda (one of the official languages of Rwanda). This incident was linked to a wider campaign called Doppelganger in which the EEAS has also detected structures spreading disinformation in languages such as German, French, Italian, Spanish and Polish.[155]

[155] EEAS, "Doppelganger strikes back: FIMI activities in the context of the EE24", June 2024. https://euvsdisinfo.eu/uploads/2024/04/EEAS-DataTeam-TechnicalReport-FINAL.pdf. See also Sect. 4.17 of this book.

4.4.9 Effectiveness

The websites that initially disseminated the disinformation about Zelenskyy were not expected to have much impact. However, Russian state media such as Pravda and TASS used this content as a source, and they have a much wider reach. Dozens of Facebook, Instagram, X and TikTok accounts and Telegram channels also replicated the disinformation. Moreover, the dissemination involved US public figures with a big impact, especially among Republican-leaning citizens, who seem to be the main target.

Most of the content replicating the disinformation used English. However, there are also examples of publications in other languages that show that the hoax reached places in Europe, Latin America, Africa and Asia.

4.4.10 Countermeasures

Since 9 December 2023, different fact-checkers have debunked the disinformation in this case study. Some of the organisations that have published fact-checks on this issue are *Ukrinform*,[156] *Newsweek*,[157] France info,[158] *France 24*,[159] *Hindustan Times*,[160] *Open*,[161] *Facta*,[162] *Euronews*,[163] *See Check*,[164] Provereno,[165] *Voz de*

[156] Olenin, Andriy, "Document forgery and fake journalist: How Russia created fake about Zelensky's flight to Florida, Ukrinform", *Ukrinform*, 9 Dec 2023. https://tinyurl.com/bdfdznr2.
[157] Fung, Katherine, "Fact Check: Did Zelensky Buy $20 Million Mansion in Florida?", *Newsweek*, 14 Dec 2023. https://tinyurl.com/mr296yew.
[158] Franceinfo, "Non, Volodymyr Zelensky ne s'est pas offert une villa en Floride et la nationalité américaine", 18 Dec 2023. https://tinyurl.com/ydn5de3c.
[159] Yataghene, Maya, "Thruth or Fake. No, Ukraine's Zelensky did not buy a lavish mansion in Florida", *France24*, 18 Dec 2023. https://tinyurl.com/zxsyw8cm.
[160] Soni, Mallika, "Did Ukraine's Zelensky buy a $20 million Florida mansion amid Russia war?", *Hindustan Times*, 18 Dec 2023. https://tinyurl.com/465ftswr.
[161] Di Noto, Antonio, "No! Zelensky non ha preso la cittadinanza americana e una villa in Florida", *Open*, 19 Dec 2023. https://tinyurl.com/w6nxejbu.
[162] Facta, "Questo certificato di naturalizzazione statunitense di Zelensky è falso", 20 Dec 2023. https://tinyurl.com/pjdc6fwe.
[163] Khatsenkova, Sophia, "Fact-check: Did Zelenskyy buy a multi-million dollar villa in Florida?", *Euronews*, 21 Dec 2023. https://tinyurl.com/3vfnh7s4.
[164] Koledin, Teodora, "Politika" Republishes Fictional Journalist's False Claim of Zelensky Fleeing to the USA", *See Check*, 23 Jan 2024. https://tinyurl.com/mr4y5ju3.
[165] Buntman, Evgeny, Pavel Solakhyan and Daniil Fedkevich, "Особняк во Флориде, вилла в Египте, дом Геббельса: разбираем сообщения о недвижимости, купленной Зеленским", *Provereno.Media*, 1 Dec 2024. https://tinyurl.com/4r766jnr.

América,[166] *Factchequeado*,[167] Reuters,[168] *Detector Media*,[169] *Check your fact*[170] and *FactCheck.org*.[171]

The European External Action Service (EEAS)[172] and several organisations such as Recorded Future[173] and EU DisinfoLab[174] have also investigated the disinformation campaign behind this incident and have published reports exposing the modus operandi of the disinformation agents and pointing out some of the assets that contributed to the creation and propagation of the FIMI.

4.4.11 Conclusions and Recommendations

This case is an example of how the Russian propaganda machine amplifies the dissemination of a disinformation narrative. It all started from an anonymous recording posted on a marginal YouTube channel. A group of websites pretending to be media outlets circulated the disinformation and gave it credibility. Russian state media reproduced the disinformation and gave it further outreach. A group of US influencers and political commentators spread the hoax on their social networks in such a way that the disinformation reached a segment of the US public close to the Republican party.

It is also worth noting the timing of the action. The disinformation was set in motion in time to popularise and fuel anti-Ukrainian sentiments coinciding with Zelenskyy's trip to the United States to ask for help.

Some of the actors involved in this disinformation action are linked to Russia. Research by EEAS, Clemson University, Recorded Future and EU DisinfoLab have pointed to the Russian links of some of the websites that spread the disinformation in the early stages. Particularly relevant was the role of *DC Weekly*,

---

166 Ramírez, Camila, "El supuesto Certificado de Nacionalización de Zelenskyy es falso", *Voz de América*, 26 Dec 2023. https://tinyurl.com/7bjdt992.

167 Factchequeado, "No, el presidente de Ucrania Volodímir Zelenski no recibió la ciudadanía estadounidense ni compró una mansión en la Florida: se trata de una falsificación", 28 Dec 2023. https://tinyurl.com/y3sfevme.

168 Reuters Fact Check, "Fact Check: No evidence photos show Zelenskiy naturalization certificate or new house in Florida", Reuters, 2 Jan 2024. https://tinyurl.com/4efs24su.

169 Detector Media, "Fake Zelenskyi is allegedly preparing to leave for the United States before March 31", *#Disinfo chronicle*, 31 Jan 2024. https://tinyurl.com/j5m68c2m.

170 Mock, Anna, "FACT CHECK: No, The Secret Service Did Not Reveal Zelenskyy Naturalization Certificate", *Check Your Fact*, 16 Feb 2024. https://tinyurl.com/2zf4k2h7.

171 Izevbigie, Blossom, and Alan Jaffe, "Posts Use Bogus Document to Falsely Claim Zelenskyy Plans Move to Florida", *FactCheck.org*, 22 Feb 2024. https://tinyurl.com/yvppktej.

172 EEAS, "Operation False Façade: Insights from a FIMI Information Laundering Scheme", April 2024. https://euvsdisinfo.eu/uploads/2024/05/EEAS-TechnicalReport-False-Facade.pdf.

173 Recorded Future, "Russia-Linked CopyCop Uses LLMs to Weaponize Influence Content at Scale", 9 May 2024. https://go.recordedfuture.com/hubfs/reports/cta-2024-0509.pdf.

174 Alaphilippe, Alexandre, Gary Machado, Raquel Miguel and Francesco Poldi, "Doppelganger—Media clones serving Russian propaganda", EU DisinfoLab in partnership with Qurium, 27 September 2022. https://www.disinfo.eu/doppelganger.

which is the website that set the hoax in motion and provided some of the fundamental elements of the disinformation narrative, such as the false certificate of naturalisation and the images of the villa that Zelensky was supposedly going to buy. Russian state media such as TASS, Pravda, RT and Sputnik also played an important role in amplifying the false story about Zelenskyy.

In view of the modus operandi used in this case, it would be advisable to monitor these propaganda agents used to sustain and popularise similar disinformation narratives and to study how they relate to each other. It is important to keep an up-to-date catalogue of websites that mimic media outlets that are commonly used to plant disinformation that is then amplified by other actors and the Russian state media.

When disinformative content is detected on these websites, fact-checkers should act as soon as possible to mitigate the amplification process. The intervention of fact-checkers is necessary to debunk the falsehoods and provide evidence of a lie.

Beyond the actors who have a proven relationship with Russia, in this case, the so-called "useful idiots", American media figures who repeated and amplified the piece of disinformation against Zelenskyy, also played a relevant role. It is difficult to determine if they did it solely because it fitted their political interests or if they have some type of connection with Russia. But once it has been detected that they participate in the dissemination of this type of disinformation, it is worth being attentive to their actions in the future to check if it is an isolated action or if they amplify Russian narratives on a regular basis.

Knowledge of the tactics and techniques used in this type of campaign can also serve as a basis for designing pre-bunking actions aimed at the public to explain how these disinformation agents operate. In this way, pre-bunking will enable citizens to detect traits of this type of disinformation actions, become alert and thus reduce the effect of disinformation campaigns.

4.5 How Russian FIMI Actors Reacted to the US Aid Package

4.5.1 Introduction

Russian FIMI actors used narratives about the falsity of the Ukrainian state, the inevitability of Russian victory and Ukraine war ("the special military operation") and the support of fascism by the West in response to the aid package for Ukraine, approved by the US Congress in April 2024. Russian Federation state communications reacted by leveraging existing narratives [T0003],[175] such as "The USA controls Ukraine", "Ukraine is the false state", "Ukraine has no chances to win", "Russia is invincible", "The USA has just postponed the end of Ukraine", "The US involvement in the war", etc.

---

[175] The numbers in square brackets are those used in the DISARM Navigator Red framework.

This campaign relied on two main narratives: first, the certainty of Russian victory even if Ukraine receives a new wave of aid and, second, undermining Ukrainian statehood by highlighting the dependence of Ukraine on external aid, therefore, without independent decision-making. Russia claimed that the aid would degrade the situation [T0139, T0135] for Ukraine. Its messages demonised the American military-industrial complex and promised its own audience that they are witnessing the last months of Ukrainian statehood.

The campaign kicked off on the same day as the voting and entirely disappeared thereafter. Second-row Russian deputies and news from state information sources reiterated the falsity of Ukrainian statehood. Russian FIMI agents from the official information agencies mostly portrayed American support for Ukraine as a malicious factor for Ukrainian statehood, as proof of American control over Ukraine and as a useless step that would not affect the inevitable Russian victory. It comprised messages such as "Ukraine is a failed state", "Ukraine is under external governance", "Nazis came to power after Maidan" and "Ukraine is falling apart". Russian information sources portrayed the independent statehood of Ukraine as compromised by colossal debt. All messages worked together, enhancing the "echo chamber" effect.

4.5.2 Threat Actors

On 21 April 2024, Kommersant, a Russian information agency, published a story saying that Ukraine had lost its statehood and become a colony of the US after the US Congress supported the bill. Other state information agencies soon followed and started incorporating the event into their narratives. State-controlled Russian media [T0105] played a leading role in propagating the disinformation, together with politicians and official representations [T0110]. The first reactions to the adoption of the bill came from Maria Zakharova, the spokeswoman for the Ministry of Foreign Affairs, and Dmytro Medvedev, the Deputy Secretary of the State Security Council. Zakharova was quoted as saying "Military aid to the Kiev regime is direct sponsorship of terrorist activities."[176]

The dissemination network is broad and uses Russia-influenced social media such as Vkontakte and Odnoklassniki.

4.5.3 Presumed Objectives

In this campaign, Russian communication targeted Ukrainian resilience and kept alive domestic support of the "special military operation" against Ukraine [T0136, T0136.003]. Russian FIMI actors invested a lot of effort in lobbying against aid for

[176] https://world.comments.ua/news/russia/zaharova-otreagirovala-na-reshenie-ssha-O-pomoschi-ukraine-730460.html.

Ukraine in the US. Russian state communication distinguished between pleasing its audience and maintaining a militant mood in Russian society to avoid internal tensions and questions.

While Russian troops were bombing and killing thousands of civilians in Ukraine, the state sought a positive international image in saying that a diplomatic outcome was possible, such as peace negotiations or unfreezing Russian assets. The presumed objective regarding a diplomatic outcome adds value to the prevailing role of the official reactions.

4.5.4 Incidents and Observables

"New U.S. aid will not lead Ukraine to victory—American Conservative." This was the title of a *Sputnik-Kyrgyzstan* article[3], which was dedicated to the occasion. The information piece cited, in turn, a conservative American source to lend legitimacy to the opinion and pretended to deliver an alternative opinion from the USA against Ukraine. Even though there were some who voted against the funding bill, the FIMI incident attacked the sense of the aid, reframing it as not useful.

"Ukraine has six months left: U.S. aid to Kyiv only delayed the end." This item[4] transported the narrative of the inevitability of Russian victory. Such FIMI observables target an internal audience to keep up support of Russian society; however, it also has an indirect impact beyond its borders as well.

> Even U.S. experts doubt the advisability of aid to Kyiv." The information piece with this title came from "Ana-news"[5], which has a strong affiliation with Russian intelligence services. The reference to the American experts was intended to convey credibility and leveraged legitimacy for the Russian contention. It also contains the image where the Ukrainian president is portrayed with disappointment, and the accompanying written message says that "61 billion will not help any more.

"Russian ambassador says the U.S. puts a cross on Ukraine's fate. Ambassador Antonov: the U.S. puts a cross on the fate of Ukraine with its decision to help Kyiv." Here, we observe the title and introductory part of the news piece on the prominent Russian site Gazeta.ru.[6] It supports Russian Ambassador Anatoliy Antonov who claims that American aid will bring Ukrainian destiny to an end.

4.5.5 Targets

Although this campaign impacted domestic support, it contributed to the pressure on the American information environment and Ukraine. Overall, the FIMI campaign consisted of DIMI elements that targeted useless Western support, especially American, and degraded Ukraine's image as a failed state dependent on external aid. FIMI conductors delivered the messages using political and psychological segmentation, which affected the content type. From this perspective, we suppose that Russian FIMI agents were chasing the echo chamber effect to help them reach their audience and exploiting existing biases and suspicions in society, such as denying the Ukrainian state's legitimate existence and promoting an unquestioning belief in Russian victory as destiny.

4.5.6 Tactics, Techniques and Procedures

TTPs particularly pertinent to this case study are cultivating support techniques cluster [T0074.002] and energising supporters [T0136.003]. Promising Russia's unconditional victory may provide this result. At the same time, targeting Ukrainian statehood and claims about certain victory were also related and can be explained through the "dissuade from acting" technique [T0139]. In this case, the Russians were aiming to ensure the internal audience supports their "special military operation".

The case also explored integrating target audience vulnerabilities into one's own narrative [T0083] and leveraging existing narratives [T0003]. FIMI actors designed incidents with narratives and messages to reframe the event [T0023.001], primarily by distorting facts [T0023].

4.5.7 Languages

Russian FIMI actors, primarily official representatives, expressed their affirmations in Russian and English. The campaign to undermine the decision regarding the aid package for Ukraine was in English, with the involvement of Russian-backed politicians and manipulation of the pre-electoral discourse.[177]

4.5.8 Effectiveness

In view of the several months of discussion around the aid package for Ukraine, both in the USA and the Russian Federation, the topic itself became pivotal in the context of the direction of how the situation on the frontline would develop. It enormously affected the Ukrainian morale and state of resistance.[178]

It also significantly impacted the Russian way of framing for its internal audience the fact that Western countries betrayed Ukraine and, therefore, Russia has continued to demonise the US and the Western world. It also affected the European

[177] https://texty.org.ua/fragments/112629/amerykanski-hojdalky-summary/.

[178] Sky News, "What US Aid Package Means for War in Ukraine after Profound Impact of Delay", Yahoo News, 21 Apr 2024. https://uk.news.yahoo.com/us-aid-package-means-war-180300128.html.

information environment[179] as an indicator of the unity of NATO and the Western coalition in a broader sense.

This campaign affected the European information environment while leveraging narratives via local actors and local media ecosystems to amplify effects and to sow discord within NATO and the EU. This campaign was used to apply various strategies to influence public opinion, adapting messages to resonate with specific national contexts across Europe.

Disinformation narratives often centred on themes such as portraying US support for Ukraine as a selfish geopolitical trick or emphasising economic hardships attributed to military aid. These narratives were disseminated through social media and some media outlets, often translated and localised to reflect European concerns. The role of Russian-affiliated outlets like RT and Sputnik had a significant role in disseminating these narratives, targeting European audiences with stories framing the war as an unnecessary burden on European taxpayers or blaming the West for prolonging the conflict. In addition, Kremlin-backed narratives accusing NATO of escalating the war were frequently echoed by European far-right and far-left political groups, which found ideological alignment in their scepticism of US and NATO policies, whose voices have been amplified via Russian-controlled media.[180]

Russian state media provided the original messaging, which was then echoed by internal populist movements, fringe parties and influencers aligned with anti-Western or isolationist ideologies. This amplification created a feedback loop that influenced mainstream discourse, often framing debates around NATO's unity and the economic impact of sanctions and military aid as divisive issues.[181]

4.5.9 Countermeasures

This case describes the reaction to the situation when the US Congress finally agreed a big new funding package for Ukraine in April 2024. The Russian FIMI actors focused on mobilising internal support. At the same time, discussion in the US on delivering aid to Ukraine sparked additional worries in the European Union about whether Ukraine would be capable of continuing to resist Russian aggression without American support. In this regard, some important initiatives, for example, in Czech Republic,[182] were raised in response to the growing concern in Europe.

---

[179] VSD, "By spreading propaganda Russia seeks to undermine the will of Western societies to support Ukraine". https://www.vsd.lt/en/reports/influence-activities-against-lithuania/by-spreading-propaganda-russia-seeks-to-undermine-the-will-of-western-societies-to-support-ukraine/.

[180] https://odi.org/en/insights/a-war-on-many-fronts-disinformation-around-the-russia-ukraine-war/. See also https://www.nato.int/cps/en/natohq/topics_219728.htm.

[181] https://www.chathamhouse.org/2023/12/russian-cyber-and-information-warfare-practice/04-information-confrontation-human-effects.

[182] https://neweasterneurope.eu/2024/03/21/brothers-in-arms-the-czech-republics-latest-initiative-to-bolster-ukrainian-defences/.

The best countermeasure in this case would be to avoid being directly involved in counter-communication. Instead, in such circumstances, it is better for the West to share knowledge about the way the public awareness has responded to the US package. In such cases, European, American and Ukrainian communication actors should introduce their own narratives and control information flow by imposing details about the discussed topic. An information flood with particulars from the US could be an effective way of putting cognitive pressure on the Russian FIMI counterparts.

4.5.10 Conclusions and Recommendations

One conclusion from this case is that it revealed the trend of the Russian FIMI actors' reactions to the event, which can be valuable for European decision-makers' assessment of the situation. The case study revealed the weakness of public discussion, which influenced political sentiments about the severe investment in foreign states to support international order and power balance, which remained very far in terms of benefits' understanding for the simple voters. The necessity to align or support with other states, as the USA does to maintain support for Ukraine, is always limited by the extent of the voter's support of the politicians and decision-makers who take this decision or vote for that. This case revealed how important it is for the state to communicate why investing in security, stability and deterrence is a crucial expense; otherwise, it creates a broad space for the double standards promoted via FIMI campaigns, leading to political blockage.

The case study also led us to some recommendations regarding the DISARM Framework. One is that it could include a tool for measuring the time taken for the proper reaction or response to the start of a FIMI campaign.

The DISARM Framework could also create a separate technique for spreading information via state-owned media networks within a set of channels that could be employed alongside the diplomatic communication channels. We need to consider the other political and state-related influencers as separate tools in delivering information in a FIMI campaign.

In conducting audience analysis, DISARM should rely on a structured approach, describing the main target audience and independent targeting, considering that the processes involve many more stakeholders unintentionally. Such a tool would enable researchers to predict unexpected outcomes of FIMI and construct more nuanced countermeasures.

4.6 Russian FIMI Against the Armed Forces of Ukraine

4.6.1 Introduction

Russia has designed its foreign information manipulation interference (FIMI) activities[542] against the Armed Forces of Ukraine (AFU) to coincide with its army invasion[543], based on the Russian military doctrine of asymmetric war, also known as "Gerasimov's doctrine"[544]. It uses information as a weapon to enhance the impact of its military units, the chief commander's image and society's trust in the Army as an institution.

Russian FIMI activities against the AFU started before the large-scale aggression phase with the narrativization, the process of creating common-sense reasoning with space, events, actions, change and interaction[545], against the AFU. Overtly campaigns really started in 2014 with Russia's annexation of Crimea.

After 24 February 2022, Russian FIMI activities against the Ukrainian army and military units have consisted of several campaigns with incidents at different stages of the conflict. Russia has adjusted its FIMI campaigns to the prevailing military, political and diplomatic conditions during the conflict.

During the pre-aggression stage, the Russian state information assets (media outlets, public figures, analytical centres, networks abroad, etc.) accumulated and enabled malign narratives, messages and artefacts to justify further actions and reduce the resilience capabilities of Ukraine.

During the Donbas phase of the conflict, Russia's core narrative supported the allegation of Nazism in the Armed Forces and in the entire society if it supports Army actions to defend Ukrainian territory. And then, after the full-scale invasion, Russia applied all of the information assets to amplify this false narrative.

The following phases of the conflict's escalation in the East of Ukraine were accompanied by more radical FIMI activities against Ukrainian military forces, and particularly AFU. Based on the context introduced during the occupation of Crimea, Russian authorities promulgated an image of the Russian army as "polite people" and used demoralising techniques in the east of Ukraine. Now, we no longer see any image boosting Russian militants like that which dominated during the Crimean occupation phase; instead, we witness the fake legitimacy of the rebels, who were supported directly by the Russian authority, and the aggressive portrayal of the AFU and voluntary military battalions as Nazis.

Russian information assets also alleged the AFU was fighting with its citizens who rebelled against the "Nazi junta in Kyiv"[546], by labelling AFU as "punishers"[547]. This allowed Russian authorities to run FIMI activities claiming that the Ukrainian army was shelling civilians and undertaking "genocide" against its own Russian-speaking population. This became the dominating perspective for the large-scale aggression against Ukraine.

The narrative of the Nazi Ukrainians is organically acceptable to the Russian population, based on the Soviet propaganda against supporters of Ukrainian independence, who were labelled as "banderivtsy"[548] and blamed for supporting German Nazis in World War II despite the Nuremberg tribunal judgments of these events. Hence, the new Russian war communications have strong roots in the Soviet propaganda playbook, which created a robust logical framework for its audience, and the supportive technique of the FIMI activities is cultivating Soviet sentiments and supporting Soviet identity.

Contextualisation of the "Nazi battalions in Ukraine" also rooted in the time of the Dignity Revolution in 2013–2014. Russia transformed its narrative about the Nazis into allegations of Ukrainian military battalions having connections with terrorist organisations elsewhere in the world, in particular, ISIS. Russians cultivated this narrative through different types of FIMI activities in the US, EU and Ukraine as well as domestically in Russia. During this phase, Russian FIMI activities firmly focused on creating context as the Ukrainian military units had been shelling civilian areas of the occupied Donetsk and Luhansk.

One of the biggest waves of disseminating the Nazism allegation came during the battle for Mariupol, where the Russians captured Azov soldiers as prisoners of war. The practical role of these allegations became even more apparent considering the late March 2024 terrorist attack at the Crocus concert hall in the Russian capital. Russian authorities accused Ukraine of committing this attack despite ISIS announcing right after the assault that it was responsible. This allegation fit into the narrative of the "Nazi" and "terrorist" nature of the AFU and gave credence to Russian propaganda followers to use this case in the context of the information war against Ukraine.

4.6.2 Threat Actors

The FIMI campaign against the AFU is run by information entities controlled by the Russian state, such as RT, the leading media concern targeting foreign audiences; the official megaphone of the government bodies, such as the Zvezda channel; the channel of the Ministry of Defence; the system of anonymous channels in the social media, like Telegram; Russian state-controlled social media, such as Vkontakte and Odnoklassniki, the media assets established in the occupied territories; "bot-farms" and network of recruited agents abroad as well as organisations such as the "Russikiy dom", "Russian information centres" ruled by the Federal Agency Rossotrudnichestvo (sanctioned after 2023), organisations of compatriots. All information assets are strongly linked with the Russian state and, after the 22 February 2022 invasion, the Russian state has been much more restrictive toward media assets. The Russian FIMI campaign is part of the broader communication strategy implemented by a network of different actors.

4.6.3 Presumed Objectives

Considering the interrelated relations within all Russian campaigns targeting the AFU during the decade-long conflict, we can suppose the Russians' strategic goal was the complete demonisation of the AFU. Russia gained support from the historical consequences of the juridical decisions of the Russian courts and "hard propaganda" such as films, books and other artefacts. Russian FIMI aimed to weaken societal trust in the AFU, discredit the mobilisation process, impair the readiness of people to join the military forces and blame the AFU for committing war crimes. Russia aimed "to disparage the Ukrainian government and demonstrate it as a corrupt, illegal, incapable, fascist and neo-Nazi, a junta that harms the morale of the Ukrainian army on the frontline and in ATO (anti terrorist operation), that tries to influence the Ukrainian population with contradictory, fear-, panic- or hate-based misinformation and fakes". Fulfilment of its goal[549] started with the occupation of Crimea and eastern Ukraine.

In the context of the DISARM framework, we can identify the following techniques to reach the overall goal: to establish ideological advantage [T0074.004] and to establish geopolitical advantage [T0074.004]. On the level of planning objectives, we can cite "Cause harm" [T0140], "Dismay" [T0078], "Dismiss" [T0075], "Distort" [T0076], "Divide" [T0079], etc. in targeting Ukrainian society as well as a European audience to which these techniques are also relevant—"Dissuade from acting" [T0139], "Cultivate" support" [T0136].

Strategically, Russian FIMI attempts to discredit Ukrainian resilience and to link the AFU to terrorist and Nazi entities do have historical resonance, undermining the right to self-defence according to the UN Charter. The case against the AFU consisted of several campaigns, united by the master narrative of the Nazi and terrorist nature of the Ukraine military. Meanwhile, after the full-scale aggression started, we can discern several specific objectives, such as hindering the supply of weapons, training at the military bases of partner countries, undermining the morale of the Army and social trust in the Army and its commanders.

At the end of 2021, when the Russian authorities started to deploy 200 troops near the Ukrainian border, the Ukrainian parliament adopted the law about the Territorial defence system ("On the foundations of national resistance")[550], which allowed ordinary people to engage in defence activities in the case of aggression. The Russian FIMI activities targeted these military units as incapable of resisting, of not having much ammunition and lacking the readiness to fight, all of which allegedly manifested in frequent surrenders. Russia spread a series of fakes where it blamed Territorial defence servants for killing each other and civilians.

After the aggression started, Russia intensified information warfare against military subordination and relations between military and commander staff. It sought to undermine trust in the president of Ukraine as the Supreme Commander of the Ukraine and top generals. Russian FIMI targeted the decision-making process at the highest level; it produced AI-generated fake news, which called upon General Zaluzhnyi and President Zelenskyy to surrender. Russian President Vladimir Putin urged Ukrainian militants to turn around and direct weapons against Kyiv authorities.

4.6.4 Incidents and Observables

Russian FIMI incidents describe the Armed Forces as lacking the moral sense to stop fighting. Russia granted special attention to the FIMI activities designed to affect the families of the military. It dedicated several incidents to undermining mobilisation activities and radicalisation sentiments within the families of prisoners of war. At the beginning of the large-scale invasion in 2022, Russian media were spreading a statement by Russian Foreign Minister Sergey Lavrov[554] that the Azov regiment had been put on the list of extremist and terrorist organisations in the United States and Japan. This FIMI operation involved spreading disinformation, using the diplomatic channel, and using the vulnerabilities of the counterparts to set the competing narratives. Despite the Russian FIMI campaign, the Azov regiment had not been put on the list of foreign organisations[555] recognised by the United States government as terrorist organisations. In 2019, 40 Democratic members of Congress from the US House of Representatives signed an appeal[556] to US Secretary of State Mike Pompeo, demanding that Azov and two right-wing organisations in Europe be added to the list of foreign terrorist organisations. The author of the letter was Congressman Max Rose. He claimed[557] that Azov was involved in the terrorist attacks in New Zealand in 2019—only because the perpetrator of the attack wore a symbol like Azov's, somewhat like the Nazi symbol of the Black Sun, popular among right-wing extremists around the world. However, the symbol worn by that person in no way proves his involvement with Azov. In addition, Rose called Azov a "paramilitary formation". In response to that, the American think tank Atlantic Council responded to Congressman Rose's accusations by releasing an article[558] titled "Why Azov cannot be recognized as a foreign terrorist organization."

One more example of effect was when Japan's *Handbook on International Terrorism* 2021 called[559] Azov a neo-Nazi and terrorist organisation. However, in April 2022, Japan's Public Security Intelligence Agency (PSIA) website wrote[560] that it had removed Azov from the terrorist list. These manifest the effects of the Russian FIMI activities in response to the distorted facts about the Ukrainian military units since 2014[561].

4.6.5 Targets

The main target was the AFU: Russia blamed the AFU for committing crimes against civilians, discrediting the high commander staff and portraying AFU soldiers as drug-addicted and ready to surrender in captivity and discrediting volunteers willing to join military service as well as FIMI campaign to target broader perception of the Ukrainian army by local population.

FIMI activities also targeted the Azov battalion and other voluntary formations, which eventually became official units of the AFU. Russia employed its fundamental narrative aimed at discrediting the Azov brigade during all stages of the conflict. It targeted Azov defenders especially after the large-scale invasion in 2022 and especially in the context of the Mariupol city battle and occupation. It blamed Ukrainian combatants for fighting against civilians. It portrayed Azov defenders as Nazis for external audiences and Ukraine as an ideologically corrupted state that has declined into Nazism.

Russia employed "segmentation techniques" to reach its target populations. The audience analysis of the Crimean operation employed techniques such as "identifying existing fissures [T0081.004]" in the context of the power vacuum after former President Yanukovych ran to Russia, "identifying existing prejudices [T0081.003]", especially in the context of radicalisation of the sentiments against Crimean Tatars and pro-Ukrainian activists, identifying wedge issues [T0081.006] regarding the competing identities of the local inhabitants and establishing legitimacy regarding the Russian Army intervention [TA16]. In that context, we witnessed the narrative about the "polite people", as Russia portrayed its soldiers.

The Russians developed campaigns to target different audiences in different countries to convince them of Ukrainian Nazism; it exploited pseudo-experts and created artefacts through documentaries, films, exhibitions and cultural events in Russia, in the occupied territories and in Ukraine, both in cyber and physical space. The Russians engaged in offline activities, explicitly targeting the US, the UK and the EU as the main partners of Ukraine. An important element of the Russian FIMI activities has been the use of the judicial system and political and diplomatic channels in delivering messages [T0110].

On the eve of the invasion in 2022, the Russian FIMI campaign targeted the system of territorial defence in Ukraine (units formed by ordinary citizens), introduced by the respective law for allowing civil people to form and join enforcement units subordinated to a military commander. Alongside its Nazi allegations, Russia has labelled Ukrainian forces and combatants as "terrorists".[183]

After the aggression started, Russia intensified information warfare against military subordination and relations between the military and commander staff. It sought to undermine trust in the president of Ukraine as the Supreme Commander of the Ukrainian forces. Russian FIMI targeted the decision-making process at the highest levels; it produced AI-generated fake news, which called upon General Zaluzhnyi and President Zelenskyy to surrender.

Russian directed FIMI activities against the AFU and against mobilisation. Russia's information operations exploited various scenarios, including accusing women of cooperating with military recruitment offices to mobilise men, portraying Ukrainians as disenfranchised hostages of the mobilisation process and claiming that representatives of recruitment centres were massively hunting for men, women, children and even disabled people. At the same time, it spread content that Ukraine has no constitutional rights to launch mobilisation and was violating the rights of its own citizens and granting immunity for politicians against mobilisation.

---

[183] https://www.understandingwar.org/backgrounder/russian-offensive-campaign-assessment-august-10-2024.

Russian FIMI operations also represented employees of recruiting centres as gangs that terrorise the population. They "need to be hunted", "run away from the TCC (Territorial completing centre)", "ignore summonses", etc.[184] Fake activists were involved in this, often those who worked to spread disinformation about COVID-19. In Ukraine, Lviv anti-vaccinationist Ostap Stakhiv was actively spreading fake news about the illegality of the Centre for Countering Disinformation through his network of social media accounts.[185] Before that, he was involved in spreading disinformation about the shelling of Ukraine's energy system.

Sporadic conflicts on the streets between civilians and TCC workers do occur. However, videos are often fake and intentionally staged. For example, "in tandem with the espionage effort, the other goal of the Russian fake Civil Defence campaign is to deliver disinformation aimed at suppressing Ukraine's military mobilisation effort for the war. The malicious versions of Civil Defence's site and Telegram have pushed out videos with incendiary, anti-Ukrainian-military titles like, "Unfair Actions From Territorial Recruitment Centers".[186] The technique scales up individual cases and presents them as a national trend.

As the core force for deterring Russian troops in the East, the AFU became the main target for Russian information warfare and its FIMI activities. It portrayed the AFU as fighting against its own people. Moreover, this narrative was divided into two storylines. First, it was about the AFU attacking civilians and, second, it was about the genocide of the Russian-speaking population in east Ukraine.

4.6.6 Tactics, Techniques and Procedures

The Russian campaigns employed several techniques and tactics for goal setting, including strategic ends and geopolitical, economic and ideological advantages.

To maintain messages and narratives about a Nazi AFU, Russia has used different techniques such as the following: development of narratives [TA 14], both competing [T0004] and creating new [T0082], integration of target vulnerabilities into narratives [T0083] as it was applied within the FIMI activity regarding the so-called "Nationalistic Marches" in Kyiv—when a marginal manifestation was portrayed as the general occurrence in Ukraine. In terms of content creation, FIMI campaigns and incidents employed audio-based content, such as a radio program led by Vladimir Solovyov, a prominent servant of the Russian strategic state communication [T0088], image-based content [T0086], video-based content, especially the main talk shows on the state TV, such as "60 min" [T0087], content with

[184] HYPERLINK https://cpd.gov.ua/en/warnings/the-enemy-is-spreading-a-fake-about-mobilization-of-ukrainians-in-poland/, https://cpd.gov.ua/en/warnings/the-enemy-is-spreading-a-fake-about-mobilization-of-ukrainians-in-poland/.

[185] https://www.facebook.com/permalink.php?story_fbid=pfbid0j2krAdmmni9U4sUmpFTVEJaw7Wc2mVaS7dYKWm7tJBstRY8XTAtoJLuWgFBkJy6l&id=100075641468292.

[186] https://www.darkreading.com/threat-intelligence/russia-kneecaps-ukraine-army-recruitment-spoofed-civil-defense-app.

distorted facts, usually associated with the Russian state-controlled news television station RT (Russia Today) but also with other online sources, including those established in the occupied territories and anonymous Telegram channels [T0023], reusing existing content from previous years [T0084]. The aggression phase after 2022 provided insights on how Russia built networks for implementing FIMI activities under new circumstances (like sanctions regimes). The main example of the asset establishing [TA15] approach is by Russia's creating the net of the so-called "war reporters" and recruiting other malign actors abroad [T0091].

Russia's main narrative in the information warfare and FIMI activities deployed against the AFU has been allegations of Ukrainian military units of Nazism. This narrative unfolded in different contexts and stages of the conflict, and various techniques were used in its promotion. Strategically, the set of campaigns against AFU is dedicated to fixing for Russia the domestic political advantage [T0074.002], geopolitical advantage [T0074.001] and ideological advantage [T0074.004].

4.6.7 Channels

To maintain its information interference strategy, Russia has employed various communication channels, as indicated above. Before the large-scale invasion, the media network directly supported by Russia was active in Ukraine (and other countries), supporting Russia's main narratives and working to reduce Ukrainian resilience and trying to convince the Ukrainian public of the civil nature of the war in the eastern Ukraine, the legitimacy of the Crimean "referendum" and in the "brotherhood" with Russia.

Even though Russian propaganda promoted its narratives for internal audiences using mostly state channels and Russian social media, in Ukraine, through the media units supported financially by Moscow, RT played a leading role with its official mission to inform the world about Russia. However, after the February 2022 invasion, a unique role has been granted to the network of "war reporters" and anonymous messenger Telegram, which also allows sharing of information as well as arranging offline FIMI activities.

4.6.8 Languages

Russian, Ukrainian, English plus others.

4.6.9 Effectiveness

We can explain the effects of FIMI activities targeting the Ukrainian military forces through several psychological and communication theories that describe how information impacts human cognition, emotions and behaviour.

From the cognitive dissonance theory perspective,[187] FIMI creates discomfort in individual experience by cultivating conflicting beliefs, attitudes and behaviours (behavioural patterns). FIMI campaigns and incidents that contradict existing beliefs in society create cognitive dissonance, leading to an uncomfortable psychological state, which people are eager to avoid. A person must resolve this discomfort by changing attitudes and beliefs and sometimes aligning with manipulative information. Russian-designed FIMI applies repeated information and competitive narratives to stimulate cognitive dissonance regarding the AFU.

Social identity theory[188] proposed an approach in which individual identity is derived from the group to which they belong.[189] For this purpose, FIMI often exploits out-group negativity and in-group stereotypes. This approach exacerbates in-group/out-group dynamics, leads to increased polarisation and has the potential to provoke social conflict. FIMI campaigns exploit ethnic, national and political identities to foster division, emphasising an "us vs. them" narrative that can deepen social divisions and conflict.

The development of the "Likelihood Model"[190] suggests two ways of persuasion: central and peripheral. The peripheral route involves more superficial aspects of the message. FIMI, in its campaigns, often uses the peripheral route by repeating simple messages incorporated into a broader campaign. The central route involves the motivated processing and evaluation of messages. The central route involves considering the argument's merits and weighing the pros and cons. Persuasion via the central route leads to long-lasting change. FIMI actors also use credible-seeming sources, emotional content and manipulation of images to persuade the audience.

In our case, the confirmation bias approach describes the method of reconfirming, interpreting and recalling one's pre-existing beliefs in favour of some FIMI campaign. FIMI leverages confirmation bias by providing disinformation that aligns with latent prejudices or fears, making the false narratives more readily accepted and entrenched. FIMI may strengthen pre-existing biases, as people are likelier to believe and share information that aligns with their views, even if false.

The most explicable communication theory, which provides how FIMI effects can be explained in the case against the AFU, is the propaganda theory. This theory suggests deliberately influencing public opinion by leveraging information in the form of a combination of emotional appeals and selective facts in a repetitive mode. This theory is especially relevant in high-stress contexts, such as war,

---

187 Festinger, Leon, *A Theory of cognitive dissonance*, Stanford University Press, Stanford, CA, 1957.

188 https://onlinelibrary.wiley.com/doi/full/10.1002/9781119011071.iemp0153.

189 Tajfel, Henri, and John Turner, "An integrative theory of intergroup conflict", in W. G. Austin and S. Worchel (eds.), *The social psychology of inter-group relations*, Brooks/Cole, Monterey, CA, pp. 33–47.

190 Petty, Richard E., and John T. Cacioppo, "The Elaboration Likelihood Model of Persuasion", *Advances in Experimental Social Psychology*, Vol. 19, January 1986, pp. 123–205. https://www.sciencedirect.com/science/article/pii/S0065260108602142.

where the state's role is dominant. Repetitive and emotionally appealing misinformation and disinformation can subtly alter perceptions and behaviours, making propaganda particularly effective in times of uncertainty and fear.

The Theory of Planned Behaviour[191] explains how FIMI can influence intentions by influencing attitudes toward behaviour, subjective norms and perceived behavioural control. FIMI campaigns influence all these components by shaping public views of them. From the perspective of the FIMI campaigns against AFU, it can affect resistance, causing compliant behaviour in the opponent society and the ability of people to impact outcomes. In particular, FIMI can influence public intentions by shaping attitudes toward certain behaviours, altering perceived social norms and affecting individuals' beliefs about their control over outcomes (e.g., scepticism about the effectiveness of resistance or support for the military).

4.6.10 Countermeasures

To effectively counter the FIMI campaign targeting the AFU, a comprehensive strategy must focus on enhancing strategies implemented on different levels: governmental, civil society, media and cyber. For example, strategic communication, leveraging fact-checking, improving digital literacy, implementing robust regulatory frameworks, employing targeted regional measures, engaging in international advocacy, conducting psychological operations and strengthening cybersecurity defences could be used to respond to different incidents of the Russian narrative. Strategic communication should prioritise building counter-narratives emphasising the legitimacy of the AFU and its work with NATO and EU partners to develop unified messages highlighting Ukraine's role in defending democratic values. Fact-checking and disinformation monitoring efforts of media, civil organisations and individual fact-checking specialists are crucial for real-time response, especially when mechanisms and AI-driven tools are used to detect and neutralise propaganda. Internationally, all stakeholders should expose Russian FIMI operations publicly at authoritative platforms such as the United Nations while presenting case studies to highlight the impact of disinformation campaigns, such as the Azov battalion's misrepresentation or false narratives which can lead to further escalation, like the Crocus Hall attack misinterpretation. Psychological operations (PSYOPS) should aim to undermine Russian narratives, targeting audiences with messages exposing propaganda inconsistencies while bolstering the morale of Ukrainian soldiers and civilians. Robust cybersecurity measures are essential, focusing on securing communication systems to prevent exploitation by adversaries and dismantling bot networks that amplify disinformation.

[191] Ajzen, Icek, "The theory of planned behavior", *Organizational Behavior and Human Decision Processes*, Vol. 50, No. 2, 1991, pp. 179–211.

4.6.11 Conclusions and Recommendations

This case study is particularly relevant in the context of the ongoing Russia-Ukraine conflict. By analysing the psychological and communicative effects of FIMI campaigns, it provides a deep understanding of how disinformation influences human perceptions and behaviour. The use of cognitive dissonance and social identity theory provides valuable insights into the mechanics of disinformation and its ability to manipulate and polarise societies. The findings underscore the need for effective countermeasures, including media literacy, international cooperation and transparent communication, to mitigate the effects of such manipulative interference.

Russian FIMI activities against the Ukrainian army and military units have consisted of several campaigns with incidents at different stages of the conflict. The historical conditioning and heredity from one campaign to another are valuable features of the Russian FIMI mechanics that the DISARM framework should consider in its improved version.

DISARM should consider in its next enhancement of the Navigator organisations of Russian compatriots as a tool for establishing assets and promoting false narratives.

Disrupted cognitions (cognitive dissonance) can be effectively addressed by encouraging people to question inconsistencies and seek alternative sources of information. The core action in this context is to leverage public decision-making to arm citizens with the skill to see the gaps in the information environment.

Media literacy programs in different countries should include a civil component and be simultaneously supported by highly transparent and detailed state communication, especially regarding sensitive topics and decisions. Decision-makers should also consider critical thinking, especially in public campaigns and encourage people to seek additional information and context.

Communication campaigns and offline activities highlighting shared values, common goals and historical unity can strengthen national identity and unity. Such initiatives can include community-building activities, inclusive media programming and public endorsements by respected figures from various social groups and localities.

FIMI experienced through the lens of the likelihood model can be addressed by using the central route of persuasion, which involves the formation of motivation in the audience and the ability to evaluate disseminated information. This could help engage the public deeply with factual, logical and well-explained content, which has a long-term effect. This can involve educational programs that enhance media literacy and analytical skills, enabling individuals to evaluate the credibility and motives behind information sources critically. Moderated public forums, debates and media outlets that purposefully present balanced perspectives on contentious issues could facilitate this.

Government and credible media outlets should consistently release accurate, transparent, factual information to counteract propaganda. This includes rapid response teams tasked with debunking misinformation and providing clear, evidence-based responses to propaganda claims.

Launch campaigns should positively reinforce supportive behaviours and outline the effectiveness of collective action. This can be paired with highlighting stories of thriving community and military resilience and demonstrating widespread support for the military through visible public endorsements and demonstrations.

4.7 Russian Initiatives to Use Farmers' Protests in Germany

4.7.1 Introduction

In January 2024, the Federal Republic of Germany was the scene of one of the largest farmer protests in the country's history. Federal government plans to cut subsidies for the agrarian sector prompted farmers to start demonstrating in cities and on highways to show their opposition to the plans. The apparent reason behind this policy was that the German constitutional court ruled in November 2023 that the federal government had to save €60 billion due to the government's unconstitutional use of credit-financed funds, originally planned to handle the after-effects of the COVID crisis. While the decision to cut subsidies for farmers was obviously only a small part of the overall consolidation plans for the national budget, these plans proved to have the most resonance among the farmers and the rest of the population.

In blogs and on social media sites, a Russian campaign tried to link the demonstrations of German farmers to Germany's financial aid to Ukraine. The campaign authors linked an €8 billion aid program for Ukraine with federal government plans to cut subsidies in the agrarian sector to save up to €900 million annually. The narrative was that, while Germany is funding the war in the Ukraine by order of the United States, ordinary Germans, especially the farmers, pay the economic consequences. Furthermore, the farmers' protests were linked to the announced strikes for better wages in other sectors. The campaign painted a picture of widespread unrest in the German civil population and made a rift in society look far greater than it actually was.

The campaign started mostly through social media, especially X, and Telegram. It included reporting about the protests of the farmers, announcement of the new financial aid package for Ukraine and the strikes at Deutsche Bahn, the national railway operator. The German mass media's first reports of the FIMI campaign came a week after the first incident.

This first widely recognised incident of the campaign was a tweet on the social media platform X (formerly Twitter). There, former Russian President Dmitry Medvedev wrote on 8 January 2024: "Strikes in Germany: farmers have blocked much of the country. Subsidies have been ended, and astronomical amounts spent on Ukraine are still growing. And Germany is the main funder. If this goes on, banderovtsy[192] will export their proven weapon, the Maidan, to Berlin. In this case, it is highly doubtful that Scholz the Liver Sausage[193] will hold out. We are following with malicious interest."[194]

This incident coincided with the lessening of the intensity of the farmers protest, around the end of January and early February 2024. It appears the event wasn't widely successful in swaying public opinion, as the linkage between the protests and the war in Ukraine wasn't adapted in the public discussion, media coverage or from the protestors.

4.7.2 Threat Actors

It is unclear which organisation or persons directly instigated the incident. But given the social media post of the former Russian president Dmitry Medvedev, and the similarity of the following posts, one can assume that the event was at least in the interest of the Russian government.

Other actors who spread the event included German Russian bloggers such as Thomas Röper, Indian online NewsChannel (Crux[195]) and persons in Telegram channels.

The Russian government sees benefits in creating social unrest and political distrust towards the federal government as well as support for German political parties with close ties or sympathies towards autocratic regimes such as Russia.

4.7.3 Presumed Objectives

We discern the following DISARM Framework objectives as pertinent to this Russian campaign:

T0079: Divide—By linking the economic fears of the farmers in Germany with the financial aid to Ukraine, the attackers' goal presumably was to divide the German civil population between those who support the cause of the farmers and those who support further help to Ukraine. This comes in combination with stirring the fear of rising costs of food and living by implying that cutting subsidies for the agrarian sector, in favour of further support for Ukraine, would force the farmers

[192] In modern usage, especially in Russian media, *banderovtsy* is sometimes used pejoratively to label Ukrainian nationalists or groups seen as anti-Russian.

[193] "Liver Sausage" refers to the German saying "beleidigte Leberwurst" which is used to stigmatise someone who is offended without any reason. Kinkartz, Sabine, "Olaf Scholz—an 'Offended Liver Sausage'?", Dw.Com, 5 Mar 2022. https://www.dw.com/en/german-chancellor-olaf-scholz-faces-unusual-criticism-from-ukraines-ambassador/a-61673724.

[194] Medvedev, Dimitry, post on X, 8 Jan 2024. twitter.com/MedvedevRussiaE/status/1744442481452711947.

[195] Crux is an Indian online news website on YouTube. https://www.youtube.com/c/CRUXnews/videos.

to increase the costs of their products or, even worse, close down their farms and thereby diminish the overall available supply of food.[196]

T0135: Undermine—By implying that the German government would rather spend German tax money on the problems of a foreign country (Ukraine) than on the needs of the national agrarian sector, the FIMI campaign tried to undermine the legitimacy of the government. Meanwhile, articles on the online website Voice of Europe implied that Chancellor Scholz was a weak leader with health issues and therefore not in medical condition to lead the country.[197] This echoed the well-known narrative about US President Biden as being far too old—physically and psychologically—to lead the US.

T0136: Cultivate support—The FIMI campaign bolstered the political parties in Germany with ties to the political elites in Russia or at least that have a positive stand towards them. In some FIMI articles, the farmers' protest was connected with the support of the right-wing populist party Alternative für Deutschland (AfD).[198] The AfD is well known in Germany for having a different stand toward Russia and the war in Ukraine. More than once, it has called for lifting all European sanctions against Russia and an end to German membership in NATO. Nevertheless, there is no real evidence that support for the AfD was the primary goal of the FIMI attacker. Thus, one might assume that such support was not more than a pleasant side-effect.[199]

4.7.4 Incidents and Observables

In the instance of the farmers' protests in Germany, there is a fine line between an "observable", "TTPs" and the incident in itself. This is because the FIMI attack in this case was mostly carried out in the form of "fake news" and the linking of the two events that took place at around the same time but had, as a matter of fact, different origins.

As mentioned below, the observables in this incident were found in the social media actions of known Russian politicians in combination with the distribution of fake pictures to stir the meaning of the protests towards the intended goal. The TTPs used in this incident are also closely linked to the incident itself, as the FIMI incident can be described as a "soft attack" in comparison to a "hard attack" where the incident creates a problem "out of thin air". Stretching the definition of incidents a bit far, one could argue that the linking of the farmers' protest to the strike of the railway workers can be counted as one of these incidents. The

[196] Voice of Europe, "Strike by farmers in Germany threatened supplies to 200 stores", 8 Jan 2024.
[197] Voice of Europe, "Scholz refused to meet with protesting farmers", 10 Jan 2024.
[198] CNN, " Protests sweep Germany as far-right spots an opening", 15 Jan 2024. Germany protests bring country to a halt as far-right spots an opening | CNN.
[199] KoldomaSov, Artur, "Apples of discord: how Russia is supporting and instrumentalizing farmers' protests in Europe", Detector media, 26 Feb 2024. Apples of discord: how Russia is supporting and instrumentalizing farmers' protests in Europe:: Detector Media.

objective of this connection lies with establishing the narrative of an imminent collapse of German society or at least a widespread uprising of the working class against the political elites.

This incident of the farmers' protest fits into a larger FIMI campaign. That campaign concerns the long-lasting efforts of Russian attackers to paint the picture of a US-controlled political elite in Germany which doesn't work for the benefit of the population but for the hegemonic plans of the United States. This campaign, even though it has been present in German fake-news history for decades since the end of the Second World War, was renewed and remodelled in the face of the Ukraine war. It started during the winter of 2022–2023 and renewed in the winter 2023/2024. In this campaign, Russia tried to connect the rising costs of heating, fuel and other necessities to the financial aid to Ukraine and form the narrative that Germans have to suffer economically because the government would rather support a foreign country than their own only because the US wants to wage a proxy war with Russia from which Germany has neither a benefit nor a threat if it would stop the support and lift the sanctions.

The tweet of former president Medvedev is the original observable of this campaign.[200] It directly linked the farmers' protest to the war in the Ukraine and the decision to cut subsidies to the aid package for the Ukrainian government. Another clear observable can be found in the fake pictures of the protest in which the protestors allegedly demanded that Putin become the ruler of Germany, implying the demand for a pro-Russian shift in policy in Germany.[201] With these two evidences, we can clearly analyse the development of the FIMI attack, which developed fast in the span of a few days between the tweet on 8 January 2024, which demanded the end of financial aid to Ukraine in favour of the internal population, to 11 January in which a clear demand was stated for a change of government or even a subjugation of the German state.

4.7.5 Targets

The main target of the attack was the German government and public.

The FIMI attack was basically a twisting of facts around a governmental decision to cut subsidies for the agrarian sector. It specifically linked the farmers' protest and the strikes of employees in the federal railway to the financial aid package to Ukraine. The aim was to undermine the legitimacy and popularity of the German government.

It also appears that the target of the attack was the public. The aim was to increase animosity between at least two parts of the German population. On the one hand, there is the rich and ecologically oriented population who are in favour

[200] https://www.twitter.com/MedvedevRussiaE/status/1744442481452711947.

[201] Olenin, Andriy, and Olga Tanasiychuk "Fake photos about Germans: Farmers want Putin for president, restaurateurs refuse to support Ukraine", ukrinform.net, 21 Jan 2024.

of the subsidy cuts and, on the other, there is the working class who are largely against the cuts. By increasing animosity between these parts of German society, the campaign aimed to damage German solidarity.

4.7.6 Tactics, Techniques and Procedures

The TTPs used in the attack were based on three principles. First, the attack took real-life events that got a lot of media coverage. In the case of the present attack, the event was the farmers' protest and the strike of the workers in the federal railway. Both received broad coverage in traditional media as well as social media in Germany. Second, the attackers tried to link these events as the foundation of their narrative. The farmers' protest was originally linked to a verdict of the constitutional court in combination with a naïve budget policy of the government regarding the financial aid package for Ukraine, the rising costs of living and even the railway strikes themselves. Last, the attackers created linkages to establish the narrative of a political elite that follows its own globalist agenda instead of caring for the needs of the population.

Breaking down TTPs in their components and aligning the case at hand to these components can be done in the following way:

T0079: Divide—The attacker tried to divide society and support internal actors, such as the AfD, to work on a pro-Russian government.

T0135: Undermine—The attacker also tried to undermine state legitimacy.

T0076: Distort—By decrying the use of federal taxes to help the Ukrainians in their defensive war and not using the funds to continue the subsidies for the agrarian sector, the attackers tried to create the belief in the population that their economic struggles were due to German support for Ukraine, implying that stopping that support would directly improve their lives. The plans of the federal government to cut subsidies were rephrased and connected to different topics and policies, thereby creating the picture of one big, intermingled plan by the political elite to hurt the working class.

From their linking two different events, the attackers built a narrative about the farmers' protests that far exceeded the original purpose and demands of the farmers themselves. The farmers' demands were only to find ways to keep the subsidies or, at least, ease the burden for their businesses by reducing bureaucracy or environmental requirements. There was never a demand or a call by the farmers to reduce or to stop spending to help Ukraine. In fact, the farmers had no knowledge or intention of getting their protest linked to the railway strikes, as the attackers portrayed.

4.7.7 Channels

As traditional media, like the television channel Russia Today (RT), were banned in Germany some time ago, the focus of the campaign was on social media. As the platforms Telegram and X were equally played on, X proved to be more efficient for the cause of the campaign because postings on X usually gain more coverage by Western media than Telegram. Nevertheless, Telegram achieved the goal of spreading the campaign among people already close to the attackers' belief system.

4.7.8 Languages

The language of the attack was mostly English and spread over English-speaking websites and social media channels. Some of the attacks were translated into German, either by the perpetrators themselves or by other bilingual users who wanted to broaden the audience, to reach the non-English-speaking population. This method was used most likely to get the broadest coverage possible, betting on the fact that some of the multipliers would translate the "attack" by themselves.

4.7.9 Effectiveness

The effectiveness of the FIMI attack is debatable at best. While it did see some coverage of the attack in the traditional nationwide media,[202] the plan to link the cut of subsidies to Ukraine was less successful. The main discourse in German society concerning the cut in subsidies was around the court verdict, the overall dispute inside the government coalition, which was already present well before the protest. There have also been disputes about whether the farmers' protest was infiltrated by right-wing extremists.

While the attack did spread far in some social media platforms, mostly Telegram, it never achieved in breaking beyond the already-swayed part of the population. This was mostly because the farmers managed to distance themselves from any extremist group or demands and they aligned their movement with the biggest German opposition party (CDU/CSU). By doing so, they showed that their protest was not in any way connected to Ukraine as the CDU/CSU are also firm allies of helping the Ukraine as much as needed.

4.7.10 Countermeasures

As the effectiveness of the attack remained mostly unsuccessful, there weren't many countermeasures to be taken. It might be worth researching whether the alignment of the farmers' protest with the conservative, pro-Ukrainian CDU/CSU parties was an intentional countermeasure against any FIMI attack. Based on the

[202] Von Pascal Siggelkow, "Wie Russland die Bauernproteste für sich nutzen will", *Tagesschau*, 11 Jan 2024. https://www.tagesschau.de/faktenfinder/kontext/russland-bauernproteste-waffenlieferungen-100.html.

history of these parties, especially the Bavarian CSU, as a pro-agrarian sector party, it might be far-fetched to assume that this alignment was planned as a countermeasure. One notable countermeasure was when Robert Habeck, Federal Minister for Economic Affairs and Climate Action, publicly warned that some right-wing extremist would try to infiltrate the protest. While a lot of protestors saw this "warning" as an insult, it did, however, force the movement to distance itself from any right-wing demands and to evaluate their protest along the way. Whether this countermeasure did indeed stop the spread of the FIMI attack is speculative.

4.7.11 Conclusions and Recommendations

This Russian campaign against Germany during the farmers' protest is another great example of a foreign power trying to usurp a political topic/crisis in order to use it for their own political agenda. Thankfully in this case, the ones who were organising the demonstrations, the farmers, were such a cohesive group with a high level of organisation, that the campaign could be detected and dismissed quickly and easily. The moment that the leaders of the protest stepped forward and denounced any claims from the campaign, the chances of foreign involvement collapsed.

If anything, a recommendation from this incident is that other groups should take it as an example on how to protect their protest and their interest against a foreign power trying to usurp their cause.

4.8 Russian FIMI About Burning the Quran in Sweden

4.8.1 Introduction

Russia and Iran tried to influence the global perspective on Quran burnings in Sweden with disinformation. Their aim has been to fuel tension both in Sweden and abroad and in countries with Muslim populations. The Quran-burning protests were partly organised and funded by Chang Frick, the chief editor of *Nyheter Idag* (a far-right Swedish language online newspaper), who once worked for *Russia Today* (RT).[203]

[203] Braw, Elisabeth, "How activists shaped Sweden's NATO debacle", *POLITICO*, 28 Jan 2023, https://www.politico.eu/article/sweden-nato-debacle-application-turkey-recep-tayyip-erdogan-finalnd/. Fröjd, Anna, "Det är inte att dra lans för yttrandefrihet att köpa sina egna nyheter", *Expo,* 19 Feb 2023. https://expo.se/kommentar/inte-att-dra-lans-for-yttrandefrihet-att-kopa-nyheter/.

Many of the narratives in the blogosphere focused on spreading anti-Muslim sentiments. The propaganda was also an attempt to disrupt Sweden's NATO membership process.[204] Some states that spread and amplified the disinformation also appear to have wanted to distract the audience from local issues.[205] Between June and August 2023, the Swedish public authorities logged about one million similar posts in Arabic and other languages about this incident.[206]

On 24 September 2024, Sweden's leading newspaper, *Dagens Nyheter*, reported that Sweden officially attributed a significant cyberattack, which took place in August 2023 during the height of Quran-burning protests, to Iran's Islamic Revolutionary Guard Corps (IRGC). Swedish authorities revealed that state-sponsored hackers had breached a Swedish SMS service, gaining administrative control by late July 2023. On 1 August 2023, they triggered a mass message, sending 15,000 texts urging retaliation against those involved in the Quran burnings.

This operation, part of the broader FIMI campaign, aimed to deepen societal divides and sow discord within Swedish society amidst rising tensions over the Quran burnings—tensions that had already sparked international protests and diplomatic issues. Sweden's security police (SÄPO) and the public prosecutor confirmed that the Iranian regime was behind the attack, linking it directly to the IRGC's Electronic Warfare and Cyber Defence division. Despite identifying the perpetrators, Sweden has not pursued prosecutions, as those responsible remain outside the country's jurisdiction.[207]

The attack had significant diplomatic and security consequences for Sweden, particularly by delaying its NATO membership and fuelling internal divisions. These divisions were exploited by multiple foreign powers for geopolitical gain. Russia, Iran, Turkey and possibly China sought to benefit from the unrest triggered by the Quran burnings and the surrounding influence campaigns. These states likely saw an opportunity to destabilise Sweden and, by extension, weaken the unity of the European Union and NATO. This campaign underscores how Iran, alongside Russia and China, has been engaged in coordinated efforts to undermine Western unity and democratic institutions. Sweden, as a potential NATO member, became a key target in this broader geopolitical struggle.[208] While Swedish authorities initially attributed parts of the FIMI campaign to Russia, further technical and investigative evidence will be essential to substantiate these claims. It

[204] Bryant, Miranda, "Russia spreading false claims about Qur'an burnings to harm Nato bid, says Sweden", *The Guardian*, 6 Aug 2023. https://www.theguardian.com/world/2023/aug/06/russia-spreading-false-claims-about-quran-burnings-to-harm-nato-bid-says-sweden.

[205] Braw, Elisabeth, "How Sweden Became Public Enemy No. 1", *Foreign Policy*, 28 July 2023. https://foreignpolicy.com/2023/07/28/sweden-quran-nato-iran-iraq-russia/

[206] Bryant, op. cit., 6 Aug 2023.

[207] Ek, Bo Torbjörn, "Hemliga angreppet mot Sverige under koranbränningarna", *Dagens Nyheter*, 24 Sept 2024, https://www.dn.se/sverige/hemliga-angreppet-mot-sverige-under-koranbranningarna.

[208] Cato, Carl, "Expert: Kampanjen mot Sverige försenade Natointrädet", *Dagens Nyheter*, 24 Sept 2024. https://www.dn.se/sverige/hemliga-angreppet-mot-sverige-under-koranbranningarna/.

is clear, however, that Russia-backed actors likely aimed to exploit and amplify discord in Sweden, complicating its NATO accession talks.

4.8.2 Threat Actors

Sweden's Psychological Defence Agency (part of the Ministry of Defence) stated that Russian state-controlled media outlets RT and Sputnik had published a series of articles in Arabic, falsely claiming that the Swedish government supported Quran burning. As RT and Sputnik are state-run channels, it indicates that the strategy was coming from the Russian government.[209]

The Swedish Minister for Civil Defence, Carl-Oskar Bohlin, said that "the Quran desecrations have made Sweden a target of malicious influencing campaigns by states and state-like actors with the aim of damaging Swedish interests and ultimately Swedish citizens." He also said, "We can see how Russia-backed actors are amplifying incorrect statements, such as that the Swedish state is behind the desecration of holy scriptures."[210]

Several countries, as well as some individual extremists and extremist groups, were spreading false narratives, according to Sweden's Psychological Defence Agency.[211]

4.8.3 Presumed Objectives

From the possible objectives listed in the DISARM Navigator, the following are particularly pertinent to this case:

T0079: Divide—The propaganda was believed to be part of an attempt to disrupt Sweden's NATO membership process, which was still waiting for approval by Turkey and Hungary at the time.[212] Maria Brock, a research fellow at Malmö University, said Russia probably had several motivations: "It is about [hindering] Sweden joining NATO and creating dissent … [and] hoping to question the nature of truth or to sow distrust in traditional news outlets."[213]

"Russia is definitely trying to use the Quran burning in its propaganda narrative, which is built around the idea that, in general, the West and Western values

[209] Bryant, Miranda, "Russia spreading false claims about Qur'an burnings to harm Nato bid, says Sweden", *The Guardian*, 6 Aug 2023. https://www.theguardian.com/world/2023/aug/06/russia-spreading-false-claims-about-quran-burnings-to-harm-nato-bid-says-sweden.

[210] *Euronews* with *AP, AFP,* "Sweden 'at risk' thanks to Russian-backed Quran burning disinformation", 27 July 2023. https://www.euronews.com/2023/07/27/sweden-at-risk-thanks-to-russian-backed-quran-burning-disinformation#:~:text=Sweden's%20domestic%20security%20service%20has,Russia%20and%20other%20hostile%20governments.

[211] Bryant, op. cit., 6 Aug 2023.

[212] Ibid.

[213] Ibid.

are corrupt, and the West is in decay," maintained Valentyna Shapovalova, a PhD fellow at the University of Copenhagen, who studies Russian propaganda and disinformation.[214]

T0135: Undermine—The Swedish Security Service (SÄPO) said the burning and desecration of religious books in Sweden, and ongoing disinformation campaigns on social media and elsewhere, have negatively affected Sweden's profile. The image of Sweden has changed "from a tolerant country to a country hostile to Islam and Muslims, where attacks on Muslims are sanctioned by the state," the SÄPO said.[215] The Minister for Civil Defence has warned of "a risk that the current disinformation campaigns against Sweden will threaten the situation of Swedish companies and nationals abroad, and create a threat to national security".[216]

T0140: Cause harm—In the wake of the burnings, several riots ensued. The "cause harm" objective includes damage to property, infrastructure as well as social trust and reputation. The costs, in terms of insurance, infrastructure and so on adds a burden on society as well as pressing on social fault lines.[217]

4.8.4 Incidents and Observables

The following articles are examples of observables:

POLITICO published an article titled "How activist shaped Sweden's Nato debacle", in which the author argues that Sweden faced a difficult balance between freedom-of-expression laws at home and diplomatic relations connected to its NATO application. The article observed that Erdrogan was able to capitalise on the incidents to press for concessions in order for Sweden to gain their crucially needed support for NATO acceptance. Meanwhile, Russia was described as actively exploiting the situation to deter or, at least, slow down Sweden's full acceptance into NATO.[218]

An article published on *Euronews* titled "Sweden 'at risk' thanks to Russian-backed Quran burning disinformation" highlights Russia's ability to leverage a disinformation campaign about burnings that took place in Sweden. The article reports that Russian-backed actors exaggerated and spread false or manipulated narratives about the incidents. This was done, according to the article, by

[214] Ibid.

[215] *Euronews* with *AP, AFP*, op. cit., 27 July 2023.

[216] Ibid.

[217] Comerford, Ruth, "Violent protests after Quran burning in Sweden", *BBC*, 4 Sep 2023. https://www.bbc.com/news/world-europe-66706937.

[218] Braw, Elisabeth, "How Activists Shaped Sweden's NATO Debacle", *POLITICO*, 28 Jan 2023. https://www.politico.eu/article/sweden-nato-debacle-application-turkey-recep-tayyip-erdogan-finalnd/.

amplifying divisive messages, using inflammatory imagery, and exploiting religious sensitivities across social media platforms. The aim was to undermine the acceptance of Sweden into NATO.[219]

Articles like this are good examples of key observables of the Russian FIMI campaign against Sweden's NATO acceptance process. Specifically, these observables show a strategy of amplification, targeted dissemination and manipulation of information surrounding the Quran-burning incidents. The effect was to characterise Sweden as a provocateur and disrespecting country with respect to Islamic belief. This is in line with Russia's strategic interest in weakening its rivals.

4.8.5 Targets

The campaign had multiple targets. First were countries with significant Muslim populations, including Turkey, which at the time had a veto against Sweden's NATO membership.[220] By targeting individuals and the public in Muslim countries, attackers were pressuring governments to condemn Sweden as anti-Muslim. In addition to the target population, the campaign targeted certain media and social media outlets to spread their messages. The campaign raised issues about how truth is communicated by official sources, for example, by implying a conspiracy or collaboration with the aim of sowing distrust in traditional Western news outlets[221] and in public authorities in Sweden.

4.8.6 Tactics, Techniques and Procedures

The disinformation spread by Russia-backed actors were not isolated incidents. The actions were part of a strategic attempt by Russia to exploit and amplify discord, particularly to complicate the NATO accession talks involving Sweden and Finland. The strategy included the alleged plan by Russian intelligence services to interfere in the NATO accession process by staging disruptive activities aimed at straining diplomatic relations and fostering divisions among NATO countries. The Russians' efforts underscore the complex interplay between disinformation campaigns and international diplomacy, highlighting the role of state-backed actors in manipulating perceptions and exacerbating tensions for strategic objectives.

As the campaign tried to influence perceptions around Quran burnings and Sweden's NATO membership process, attackers' TTPs were designed to exploit

[219] *Euronews*, "Sweden 'at risk' thanks to Russian-backed Quran burning disinformation", 27 June 2023. https://www.euronews.com/2023/07/27/sweden-at-risk-thanks-to-russian-backed-quran-burning-disinformation.

[220] Johnson, Simon, et al., "Sweden says it's target of Russia-backed disinformation over NATO, Koran burnings", Reuters, 26 July 2023. https://www.reuters.com/world/europe/sweden-says-its-target-russia-backed-disinformation-over-nato-koran-burnings-2023-07-26/.

[221] Bryant, op. cit., 6 Aug 2023.

societal divisions, increase tensions between different community groups or nations, and undermine trust in governmental and international institutions.

These commonly recognised disinformation TTPs are often used in Russian FIMI campaigns. The following are the specific ones we recognised in this campaign (Table 4.1).

The first tactics in light blue in the table above are the most recurrent tactics within the DISARM framework for this Russian FIMI campaign.[222] We have added two more probable tactics, in the last two rows, to the table below. Although these tactics are not directly documented in the specific case of the Quran burnings in Sweden, they do, however, align with common disinformation strategies observed globally.

4.8.7 Channels

A channel is a mode or medium used to convey information. In this case, channels are the various platforms, physical and digital, Russia used to convey the messages they wanted to reach their target. Channels can be both physical, such as newspapers, magazines and signs, or digital, such as social media, websites, blog posts, TV and radio. Russia's main outward facing media outlets are RT, formerly Russia Today, and Sputnik, which are directed by government interests and key distributors of FIMI.[223]

The disinformation regarding the Quran burning spread through several digital channels, including YouTube, "news" websites, Twitter, Facebook and Instagram.[224] The relationship between Russia and some of the primary channels spreading disinformation about the Quran burning in Sweden is unclear. For example, a primary actor in this, along with disinformation connected to the Swedish Social Services, is Abdullah El-Sherif. He created a significant amount of content on YouTube, Twitter and his own website.[225] An Egyptian citizen, it is likely that

[222] Magonara, Erika, and Apostolos Malatras, "Foreign Information Manipulation Interference (FIMI) and Cybersecurity—Threat Landscape", Report/Study, ENISA, 8 Dec 2022. https://www.enisa.europa.eu/publications/foreign-information-manipulation-interference-fimi-and-cybersecurity-threat-landscape.

[223] US Department of State, "Report", *RT and Sputnik's Role in Russia's Disinformation and Propaganda Ecosystem*, 2022. https://www.state.gov/report-rt-and-sputniks-role-in-russias-disinformation-and-propaganda-ecosystem/.

[224] Anwar, A., "Independent MA thesis", *Public Diplomacy and Disinformation Campaigns In A Digital Age: A Study of How the Swedish Social Services Disinformation Campaigns and NATO Membership Application Impacted the Public Diplomacy of Sweden*, Swedish Defence University, 2023.

[225] Ranstorp, M., and L. Ahlerup, *LVU-kampanjen: Desinformation, konspirationsteorier och kopplingarna mellan det inhemska och det internationella i relation till informationspåverkan från icke-statliga aktörer*, Försvarshögskolan, 2023.

Table 4.1 DISARM tactics spotted in the Quran burning case study

DISARM tactic	Evidence
TA06: Develop content T0023: Distort facts, and reframe context T0084: Deceptively labelled or translated T0085: Develop text-based content	The Russian FIMI created emotionally charged content that exaggerated the Quran burnings. Various influencers shared videos and images of the burnings alongside false claims that Sweden supported these actions, inflaming religious sentiments.
TA16: Establish legitimacy T0097: Create personas T0099: Prepare assets impersonating legitimate entities T0100: Co-opt trusted sources	To build credibility, the campaign mimicked reputable news sources and quoted known figures out of context. For example, Russian state-controlled media outlets such as RT and Sputnik used reputable figures and mimicked the style of trustworthy news outlets to enhance the perceived authenticity of their content. For instance, these outlets quoted known analysts and used official-sounding language to present Sweden as an Islamophobic country that supports Quran burnings, even though Sweden officially condemned these acts.[226]
TA07: Select channels and affordances T0104: Social networks T0111: Traditional media	Russian media leveraged their extensive reach in the Arabic-speaking world through platforms such as RT Arabic and Sputnik Arabic. They also used popular social media platforms such as X (formerly Twitter), Facebook and YouTube to spread the content rapidly. Manipulating hashtags and trending topics ensured the disinformation reached a broad audience. For example, they used the hashtag #BoycottSwedishBrands.[227]

(continued)

226 Schultz, Teri, "Sweden Quran burnings: How the Kremlin benefits", *Deutsche Welle,* 8 Aug 2023. https://www.dw.com/en/sweden-quran-burnings-how-the-kremlin-benefits/a-66463591. See also *The New Arab* staff, "Russia spreading 'fake news' in Arab world about Sweden Quran burnings", *The New Arab,* 7 Aug 2023. https://www.newarab.com/news/russia-spreading-fake-news-sweden-quran-burnings.

227 *Euronews*, op. cit. 27 July 2023. See also AP News, "Security risks in Sweden rise due to Quran desecrations and protests, security agency says", *The Independent,* 26 July 2023. https://www.independent.co.uk/news/sweden-ap-muslim-islam-svt-b2382126.html. Al Mayadeen, "Pakistanis start hashtag to boycott Swedish brands after Quran burning", *Al Mayadeen*, 2 July 2023. https://english.almayadeen.net/news/politics/pakistanis-start-hashtag-to-boycott-swedish-brands-after-qur.

Table 4.1 (continued)

DISARM tactic	Evidence
TA15: Establish social assets T0090: Create inauthentic accounts	Establishing credible online identities or leveraging existing accounts that can influence public opinion is vital. These accounts interacted with users, shared misleading content and amplified false narratives. A specific example includes the use of inauthentic accounts on X that pretended to be Swedish Muslims expressing outrage, thus giving the disinformation a veneer of authenticity and local support. Also, by using existing influential accounts to share and endorse the disinformation and make it seem more credible, these known influencers in the Muslim community and other reputable social media accounts spread the false narratives, lending them an air of authenticity
TA14: Develop narratives T0003: Leverage existing narratives T0004: Develop competing narratives T0022: Leverage conspiracy theory narratives T0068: Respond to breaking news event or active crisis T0082: Develop new narratives T0083: Integrate target audience vulnerabilities into narrative	Narratives framed the Quran burnings as a state-sanctioned action by Sweden. This tactic aimed to stoke anger and mistrust among Muslims, suggesting that the Swedish government was complicit in the disrespect of their religion.
TA02: Plan objectives T0002: Facilitate state propaganda T0066: Degrade adversary T0075: Dismiss T0076: Distort T0077: Distract T0079: Divide	The campaign's objective was to disrupt Sweden's NATO membership process by exploiting the Quran burnings to create international outrage and internal discord. Every tactic used aligned with this strategic goal.
TA17: Maximise exposure T0049: Flooding the information space T0018: Amplify existing narrative T0119: Cross-posting	The campaign flooded social media with hashtags, images and videos related to the Quran burnings, ensuring that the disinformation reached a wide audience. This included coordinated efforts to make the content go viral. The use of trending hashtags helped in amplifying the reach of the disinformation.

(continued)

Table 4.1 (continued)

DISARM tactic	Evidence
TA13: Target audience analysis **T0072: Segment audiences**	**The campaign targeted specific demographics, such as the global Muslim community and international observers. Actors behind the campaign tailored content to resonate with their values and beliefs, increasing the likelihood of inciting anger and protest.**
TA10: Drive offline activity **T0057: Organize events**	**The campaign encouraged real-world protests and condemnations. False claims about Sweden's stance on religious freedom led to organised protests in several countries, amplifying the disinformation's impact and making it seem more immediate and tangible.**

his content was boosted by Russia, but it's unclear how direct the link is, though it is likely connected to strategic narratives.[228]

4.8.8 Languages

The FIMI campaign targeted Arabic-speaking countries as it used mainly Arabic[229] language. However, the campaign also spread to Swedish[230] and other languages[231] as it spread through social media channels. The use of the Arabic language help secure the impact on the target groups in Muslim-majority countries.[232]

4.8.9 Effectiveness

Russian disinformation narratives about Sweden were picked up by Russian bloggers, journalists, the media and ordinary Swedes on the popular online forum Flashback.[233] However, the impact of the FIMI campaign is uncertain. One way of measuring impact is by the number of impressions that social media posts get. However, it is not straightforward to measure this, as a key strategic aim by Russian influence campaigns is to amplify and connect with local issues. For example, Sputnik reporting on Sweden reflects Swedish far-right narratives[234] and works by citing enraged or scornful Swedish social media posts to amplify messages.[235] The difficulty in measuring effectiveness is trying to disentangle what is local and what is amplified by the interference.

---

228 Wagnsson, C., and M. Lundström, *Ringing true? The persuasiveness of Russian strategic narratives,* SAGE Publications, 2022.
229 Bryant, op. cit., 6 Aug 2023.
230 Ibid.
231 Ibid.
232 *Euronews,* op. cit., 27 July 2023.
233 Flashback is a Reddit-like forum which describes itself as "Sweden's biggest forum for freedom of speech and opinion and independent thinking". https://www.theguardian.com/world/2023/aug/06/russia-spreading-false-claims-about-quran-burnings-to-harm-nato-bid-says-sweden.
234 Åkerlund, Mathilda, "Dog whistling far-right code words: the case of 'culture enricher' on the Swedish web", *Information, Communication & Society*, Vol. 25, 12, 2021, pp. 1808–1825. https://doi.org/10.1080/1369118X.2021.1889639.
235 Wagnsson, Charlotte, and Magnus Lundström, "Ringing true? The persuasiveness of Russian strategic narratives", *Media, War & Conflict*, Vol. 13, No. 3, 2023, pp. 383-400. https://journals.sagepub.com/doi/full/10.1177/17506352221101273.

4.8.10 Countermeasures

Regarding the Quran burnings in Sweden, it is essential to differentiate between the act itself and the subsequent exploitation of the event. While the Quran burnings themselves were not fabricated, the manner in which the event was leveraged by Russian actors constitutes a FIMI operation, as the narratives included false claims about the Swedish government's support for such acts, aiming to fuel anger and mistrust among Muslim communities globally. The exploitation of Quran burnings in Sweden fit within a broader strategy to disrupt Sweden's NATO membership process by sowing discord and polarising opinions both within Sweden and internationally. Even though the lack of direct attribution to specific Russian actors does complicate the classification, the patterns of behaviour align with known Russian FIMI tactics.

Russian disinformation efforts, particularly focusing on social media as a significant battlefield for information warfare, have been subject to extensive analyses by most Western countries' cybersecurity firms, intelligence agencies and academic research. The effectiveness of these campaigns and the impact of Western countermeasures remain subjects of ongoing analysis and debate.

For a long time, digitisation was seen as a development that benefited democracy. The positive development of democracy that took place in large parts of the world during the 1990s also contributed to a hopeful assessment of the security situation. Consequently, the psychological defence and the work of following foreign influence operations was gradually scaled down. Sweden has been somewhat unprepared for this kind of new threat picture with the disinformation and propaganda that have arisen in recent years. In 2020 came a proposal to form a special psychological defence authority. The Psychological Defence Agency was established in January 2022. Other Swedish organisations that work with media and information literacy and other resilience-building efforts include: Internetstiftelsen, Filmpedagogerna Folkets Bio, Svensk biblioteksförening, Wikimedia Sverige, Expo, Folk och Försvar, Psyopsförbundet, Arbetsmarknadens parter, Pensionärernas riksorganisation (PRO), SPF Seniorerna, SeniorNet, IT-Guide. These organisations all fall under the FIMI countermeasure category: Literacy (i.e., public awareness and education), as they all aim to strengthen the target group's IT skills.

Effective countermeasures against disinformation campaigns require a multifaceted approach, involving cooperation between governments, private sector entities (especially social media platforms), civil society and the public. Additionally, transparency and maintaining the public's trust are crucial elements in any response strategy. For specific actions taken by Sweden or other entities in response to the mentioned FIMI campaign, citizens should be encouraged to consult official sources, government announcements or reports from credible research institutions and think tanks that focus on disinformation and cybersecurity.

Another approach for determining the countermeasures for countering the Russian FIMI campaign related to the Quran burnings in Sweden is by looking at the countermeasures listed in the MITRE D3FEND framework and the DISARM

Blue framework (the latter is being revised as of this writing). These frameworks hold various countermeasures but given the nature of this FIMI campaign, which involved manipulating public opinion through disinformation spread across various media channels, the most relevant countermeasures, as indicated above, are thought to be focused on enhancing information security, educating users and controlling access. Table 4.2 summarises a suggested list of the most relevant countermeasures based on their potential impact on reducing the effectiveness of the Russian FIMI campaign at discussion. We have selected the countermeasures from the MITRE ATT&CK mitigations, the DISARM countermeasures and the more general, broad types of countermeasures for various FIMI campaigns, referenced above.

The most relevant countermeasures are based on their potential impact on reducing the effectiveness of the Russian FIMI campaign against Quran burning in Sweden. The MITRE ATT&CK mitigation categories with an * are considered fundamental and were most probably already in place, and likely did not have a large effect on this specific FIMI campaign. It was launched anyway. All DISARM tactics fall under the "Tactic stage" [TA01].

4.8.11 Conclusions and Recommendations

Detailed information regarding all countermeasures adopted against the Russian and Iranian FIMI campaign related to the Quran burnings in Sweden have not yet, to the author's knowledge, been published. However, some specific actions are known, and several are easily guessed based on general practices in combating disinformation.

The key take-home point from this use case is that disinformation spreads more easily in an environment where there are echo chambers or information bubbles. In this case, those were connected to language and sources. The key recommendation here is a general and long-term countermeasure; namely, increasing information literacy and for official channels to communicate across languages and information bubbles. That overarching recommendation can include several sub-categories of countermeasures. Below we detail some that were used in this case, and some that could address a similar instance of FIMI.

1. **Literacy (i.e., public awareness and education)**: This directly focuses on educating users to recognise and understand disinformation, supporting their ability to critically analyse and question the information they encounter online. Swedish government agencies used this approach in response to messaging about the Quran burning. This could be strengthened and extended by launching campaigns to educate the public on how to critically assess news sources and check for the credibility of information.
2. **Fact-Checking Initiatives**: This involves collaborating with organisations to verify information and expose misinformation, directly enhancing the public's understanding of the authenticity and credibility of the stories. This was done in this case with the message sent out by SMS. Fact-checking was also done in

Table 4.2 Countermeasures

MITRE ATTA&CK mitigation categories	DISARM countermeasure	General taxonomy of countermeasures
User training—combats disinformation by enhancing the public's ability to discern reliable sources from misleading ones, thereby reducing the likelihood of misinformation being accepted and spread	[TA01] C00073: Inoculate populations through media literacy training—This countermeasure directly addresses the need to empower the public to critically evaluate information, making them less susceptible to disinformation tactics	Literacy (i.e., public awareness and education)
Threat intelligence program: Knowing the tactics used in disinformation allowed Swedish authorities and organisations to proactively counter misleading narratives about Sweden's societal and political stance, preventing escalation and misperceptions internationally * User account management: Managing user accounts meticulously to ensure that only authorised personnel have access to sensitive systems and information can prevent misuse of internal systems to spread disinformation * Network segmentation: Segmenting networks limits the reach of any infiltrated disinformation internally, protecting sensitive information and restricting cross-network spread of harmful data	[TA01] C00220: Develop a monitoring and intelligence plan—A proactive monitoring plan can detect disinformation early, allowing for quicker responses that can limit the spread and impact of false narratives	Cybersecurity measures and verifications
* Filter network traffic: Filtering traffic helps identify and block incoming disinformation efforts and control the spread of harmful narratives externally aimed at influencing Swedish society or international perception	[TA01] C00153: Take pre-emptive action against actors' infrastructure: Targeting the infrastructure used in disinformation campaigns can disrupt their operations and reduce their capacity to spread false narratives	

(continued)

Table 4.2 (continued)

MITRE ATTA&CK mitigation categories	DISARM countermeasure	General taxonomy of countermeasures
Data back-up: Backing up data regularly can help mitigate the impact of a campaign that might include cyberattacks designed to delete or corrupt data as a form of disruption Antivirus or antimalware: Protecting systems against malware, which can be used to spread disinformation or to conduct cyberattacks that support FIMI campaigns, is fundamental Multi-factor authentication: Securing communication and information systems within Swedish government and media prevents unauthorised leaks or misuse of platforms that could exacerbate or distort the FIMI narrative		
	[TA 01] C00017: Repair broken social connections: Summary: Encouraging real-world interactions can help bridge divides exploited by disinformation campaigns, thereby repairing social cohesion [TA01] C00024: Promote healthy narratives: By promoting healthy narratives, it's possible to dilute the impact of divisive disinformation and foster a more informed and less polarised public discourse [TA01] C00022: Inoculate. Positive campaign to promote feeling of safety: Positively framed campaigns that enhance the public's sense of security can mitigate the fear and uncertainty that disinformation campaigns often exploit	Counter-FIMI campaigns and narratives

(continued)

Table 4.2 (continued)

MITRE ATTA&CK mitigation categories	DISARM countermeasure	General taxonomy of countermeasures
	[TA01] C00096: Strengthen institutions that are always truth tellers: Strengthened institutions can serve as beacons of reliable information, making it harder for disinformation to take root [TA01] C00190: Open engagement with civil society—Engaging with civil society can help ensure a multiplicity of voices and perspectives, which can counteract the narratives pushed by disinformation campaigns	Other
Restrict Web-based content: Implementing web filters to restrict access to known disinformation sources can help reduce the risk of such content reaching users within an organisation or network		Social media monitoring and response (i.e., content moderation or content curation)
Audit: Auditing can reveal patterns of disinformation spread or attempts to infiltrate systems, allowing Swedish authorities to respond quickly to misinformation about the Quran burnings and related events		Changes in policy

several articles where official sources made it clear how blasphemy laws and a right to demonstrate is treated in Swedish law. This countermeasure can be extended by collaborating with fact-checking organisations, and by promoting verified information through official channels, stakeholders can identify and reveal false narratives as part of a FIMI campaign.

3. **Social Media Monitoring and Response (i.e., content moderation or content curation)**: This involves monitoring social media for disinformation and taking actions, such as flagging, removing or demoting content, which fits within the realm of moderating and curating content according to its veracity. The relationship between government agencies and social media companies in this case is unclear, though many of the companies have in place official channels for requesting flagging of content.
4. **Diplomatic Efforts such as Statement of Rebuttal or Condemnation**: This countermeasure was used in this case by several Swedish agencies. It involves engaging in international dialogues and possibly issuing formal statements that refute disinformation and address its impacts at a global level. Engaging in diplomatic dialogues to address the issue at an international level can highlight the detrimental effects of such campaigns.
5. **Cybersecurity Measures and Verifications**: Here the focus is on enhancing the security protocols to protect digital infrastructure from being exploited to spread disinformation, as was seen in this case with the ability of Iranian agents using local system to distribute text messages to thousands of mobile phones. Strengthening cybersecurity protocols to protect against hacking and leaks is effective and a way of addressing similar attacks.
6. **International Cooperation**: In this case, Sweden was likely working with other countries and international organisations to share intelligence and best practices on countering the disinformation around the Quran burnings. This could also involve collaborative efforts to expose and counteract a state actor's FIMI campaigns, as well as strengthening trustworthy institutions serving as examples of reliable information and engaging with civil society to ensure a broader spectrum of thoughts, voices and perspectives, making it harder for disinformation to take root.
7. **Development of Counter Campaigns and Narratives**: In response to the FIMI around the Quran burning Swedish agencies developed countering narratives, offering factual alternatives through diverse media channels to encourage critical evaluation and broader perspectives to neutralise the FIMI campaign. As noted above, this could have been done more thoroughly and extensively across information bubbles and in multiple languages. Working with other governments, relevant NGOs and providing factual accounts of events across various media platforms can ensure wider reach and enhance legitimacy.

4.9 Russian FIMI About the (Fabricated) "Lisa" Rape Case

4.9.1 Introduction

On 11 January 2016, then 13-year-old Lisa disappeared on her way home from school in Berlin. As this wouldn't be worrying enough for the parents and police, what happened in the following days developed into a prime example of Russian FIMI actions in German media and what disastrous effects such campaigns can have on social cohesion.

As the girl didn't arrive at home as expected, her Russian-German parents filed a missing person's report. The next day Lisa turned up again and told her parents that she had been abducted to a flat by three unknown "southerners" who could barely speak German, beaten several times and raped.[236]

Lisa's parents took the girl to the police who questioned her. The first interview happened with her parents present; a second interview was with Lisa alone. During the second interview, Lisa admitted that she went voluntarily with the men, whom she had known already before the incident.[237] The investigation by the police, a medical examination and the analysis of Lisa's mobile phone soon revealed that the girl was indeed at the home of a German of Turkish origin and his friend and while there seemed to have been sexual contact, the investigation and medical examination could find no evidence that this intercourse was against the girl's will. One of the men was charged with sexual conduct with a minor, as they were already of legal age at the time the incident happened.[238] In the end, the police and public prosecutor's office revealed that the girl had invented the rape as an excuse because she was afraid to go home and tell her parents that her school wanted to talk to them about Lisa's bad performance at school.[239]

With these revelations, the case itself could have been put to rest, but the days following the first mention of the case showed that it was far from over.

On 17 January 2016, the 13-year-old's aunt tearfully reported the events on Russian state television. Less than 24 h later, the first calls for demonstrations went out on Russian-language networks in Germany. Among other things, they focussed on the refugee policy, the refugees themselves and the issue of a state cover-up strategy. Lisa's parents later gave an interview in the German media in

[236] NTV, "Angeblich entführte 13-Jährige Fall Lisa: Das sind die Fakten", 27 Jan 2016. Angeblich entführte 13-Jährige: Fall Lisa: Das sind die Fakten-n-tv.de.

[237] Ibid.

[238] *Der Spiegel*, "Russlanddeutsches Mädchen: 'Fall Lisa'—Anklage wegen sexuellen Missbrauchs", 28 Feb 2017. Berlin: Anklage wegen sexuellen Missbrauchs im "Fall Lisa"-DER SPIEGEL.

[239] NTV, "13-Jährige war beim Freund. Fall Lisa: Handy-Daten offenbaren Lüge", 29 Jan 2016. 13-Jährige war beim Freund: Fall Lisa: Handy-Daten offenbaren Lüge-n-tv.de.

which they accused the German police of covering up the story to protect refugees and Arabic migrants in Germany.[240]

Channel One (Pervý Kanal), a Russian state-controlled television channel, led the way, reacting to the sanctions by denigrating "the West". In doing so, they propagated the "decadence of the West" on the one hand and the economic demise of Europe on the other. The refugee crisis was seen as a further catalyst at the time and viewed by the Russian state media as proof of the "imminent demise of the West". Crime was said to be on the rise and Germany would no longer be able to cope with the situation. And so, the interplay between the reporting of the German media, the experiences in the district and the influence of the Russian state media sowed distrust of the structures of the German state. These factors created a fertile breeding ground for the escalation in the "Lisa case".[241]

When it was proven that the girl had invented the rape, the "excitement" about it soon died down. What remained was a political debate, including among the Russian population in Germany, about the extent to which people had allowed themselves to be guided by "false" information.

The socialisation of "post-Soviet migrants" and Russia's current media and information policy at the time played a central role here. Due to inherited resentment, as well as disinformation and inflammatory reporting by the Russian media, anti-democratic and right-wing tendencies emerged in parts of this migrant group. A clear influence of Russian state media on the communities in Marzahn-Hellersdorf (the Berlin neighbourhood where Lisa lived) could already be observed at the beginning of the Ukraine conflict in 2014.[242]

4.9.2 Threat Actors

The daughter's initial lie triggered a completely different dynamic than she could have imagined. This all led to language and comprehension problems for the police and her parents. The aunt, who told the story on Russian television, played a major role in spreading this story. She started the avalanche.[243] The report on Russian television painted a picture of Germany as a country in which migrants

---

[240] *Der Spiegel*, "Angebliche Vergewaltigung. Eine Mutter zwischen Lügen und Propaganda", 31 Jan 2016. der-fall-lisa-f-notluege-vergewaltigung-DER SPIEGEL.

[241] Bundesamt für politische Bildung (BPB), "Der "Fall Lisa", Entwicklungen in Berlin Hellersdorf-Marzahn, 9 Oct 2018. Der "Fall Lisa" | Russlanddeutsche | bpb.de.

[242] Ibid.

[243] Bundesamt für politische Bildung (BPB), "Der "Fall Lisa". Entwicklungen in Berlin Hellersdorf-Marzahn, 9 Oct 2018. Der "Fall Lisa" | Russlanddeutsche | bpb.de. *Der Spiegel*, "Angebliche Vergewaltigung. Eine Mutter zwischen Lügen und Propaganda", 31 Jan 2016. der-fall-lisa-f-notluege-vergewaltigung-DER SPIEGEL. StopFake.org, "Fake: Fall Lisa—Russisches Mädchen in Deutschland von "Flüchtlingen" entführt und vergewaltigt", 17 Jan 2016. Fake: Fall Lisa—Russisches Mädchen in Deutschland von "Flüchtlingen" entführt und vergewaltigt | StopFake.

and refugees could freely rape minors. Even though the report itself was only four minutes long, it sparked a wave of protest in Germany from Russian Germans.[244]

The next actors came from a seemingly completely different part of the political spectrum. The far-right party NPD organised a demonstration in which Lisa's family accused the police of covering up the incident and persuading their daughter to tell a false story.[245] Soon, the Russian government realised that they could use the case to fuel civil unrest in Germany. Foreign Minister Sergei Lavrov took the initiative and accused the German government of covering up the truth behind the Lisa case "to paint over reality in a politically correct way for domestic political reasons".[246] Russian state news and Russian bloggers used the incident to criticise German migration policy and to question the state security system and the actions of the police, especially towards Russian Germans.[247]

4.9.3 Presumed Objectives

Even though the main culprits behind the FIMI campaign in the Lisa case were from different political groups—on the one side, the Russian Foreign Ministry; on the other, the far-right German party NPD—the presumed objectives are similar.

At first look, the goal to "Divide" seems to be an obvious objective. Both the Russian state media as well as the attackers on websites emphasised that the German police and government were trying the cover up the rape because they valued the positive picture of Arabic refugees and migrants over the protection of the German-Russian community.[248] This could be extended to the far-right party that tried to divide the pro- and anti-migration population in Germany by using this story as proof of their accusations that the German government had an "uncontrolled migration policy".[249]

---

244 *Der Spiegel*, "Angebliche Vergewaltigung. Eine Mutter zwischen Lügen und Propaganda", 31 Jan 2016. der-fall-lisa-f-notluege-vergewaltigung-DER SPIEGEL.

245 *Berliner Zeitung*, "13-Jährige aus Berlin-Mahlsdorf: Gerücht um Vergewaltigung sorgt für Demonstration", 19 Jan 2016. 13-Jährige aus Berlin-Mahlsdorf: Gerücht um Vergewaltigung sorgt für Demonstration (berliner-zeitung.de).

246 *Der Spiegel*, "Angebliche Vergewaltigung einer 13-Jährigen", Russland wirft deutschen Behörden Vertuschung vor, 26 Jan 2016. Angebliche Vergewaltigung: Lawrow wirft deutschen Behörden Vertuschung vor-DER SPIEGEL.

247 *Der Spiegel*, "Angebliche Vergewaltigung einer 13-Jährigen. Wie russische Medien Angst vor Flüchtlingen schüren", 21 Jan 2016. Russland: Wie die Medien Angst vor Flüchtlingen schüren-DER SPIEGEL.

248 Bundesamt für politische Bildung (BPB), "Der "Fall Lisa". Entwicklungen in Berlin Hellersdorf-Marzahn, 9 Oct 2018. Der "Fall Lisa" | Russlanddeutsche | bpb.de.

249 *Berliner Zeitung*, "13-Jährige aus Berlin-Mahlsdorf: Gerücht um Vergewaltigung sorgt für Demonstration", 13 Jan 2016. 13-Jährige aus Berlin-Mahlsdorf: Gerücht um Vergewaltigung sorgt für Demonstration (berliner-zeitung.de). See also *Berliner Zeitung*, "Fall Lisa aus Berlin-Marzahn: Russlands Außenminister verstärkt die Verunsicherung", 26 Jan 2016. Fall Lisa aus Berlin-Marzahn: Russlands Außenminister verstärkt die Verunsicherung (berliner-zeitung.de).

Intertwined with this is the objective to "Undermine" the competence of the German government in migration policy as well as in its ability to enforce the rule of law in the country.[250]

The FIMI was focused on undermining German politics and its legal system. The intention of the FIMI attackers, both the Russians as well as the right-wing extremists, was to undermine the migration policy that had been in the headlines a year before the Lisa case and that had caused great controversy in the country itself. The migrant background of the alleged rapists led to a conclusion that was intended to highlight the dangers of immigration. Since there was now also a Russian "victim" (i.e., Lisa), it was easy to take advantage of what right-wing groups in Germany had already been talking about. These two parties—the Russian state media and the right-wing groups in Germany—then benefited from each other by using each other's narratives to further spin their propaganda.[251]

4.9.4 Incidents and Observables

The first incident of the campaign was the interview with Lisa's aunt on Channel One (Pervý Kanal). In the first few sentences of the four-minute video, the host of the show said that "Refugees rape minors in Germany",[252] making clear that the overall tone of the story was about the fact that refugees are indeed roaming around Germany unchecked. The channel even showed a clip of a "dark-skinned" man who boasted about he and his five friends raping a virgin girl.[253] This video was later revealed as a video from 2009 with no connection to the Lisa case.[254]

A second incident was the organisation of a demonstration by the NPD during which Lisa's mother gave a speech about her child who had been held in a flat by Arabs and raped several times.[255]

The following incident can clearly be traced back to the Russian government as their own foreign minister Sergei Lavrov said in a statement on TV that the incident about "our girl Lisa" had to be fully investigated, implying that without his pressure the German state wouldn't do such a thing.[256] This incident especially triggered a response from the politicians as even the German foreign minister

---

250 *Der Spiegel*, op. cit.

251 *Der Spiegel*, "Berlin. Polizei widerspricht Bericht über vergewaltigte 13-Jährige", 19 Jan 2016. Berlin: Polizei widerspricht Bericht über Vergewaltigung von 13-Jähriger-DER SPIEGEL.

252 *Der Spiegel*, "Angebliche Vergewaltigung. Eine Mutter zwischen Lügen und Propaganda", 31 Jan 2016. der-fall-lisa-f-notluege-vergewaltigung-DER SPIEGEL.

253 *Berliner Zeitung*, op. cit., 13 Jan 2016.

254 StopFake.org, "Fake: Fall Lisa—Russisches Mädchen in Deutschland von "Flüchtlingen" entführt und vergewaltigt", 17 Jan 2016. Fake: Fall Lisa—Russisches Mädchen in Deutschland von "Flüchtlingen" entführt und vergewaltigt | StopFake.

255 *Berliner Zeitung*, op. cit., 13 Jan 2016.

256 *Frankfurter Allgemeine*, "Russlands Informationskrieg: Unser Mädchen Lisa", 31 Jan 2016. Russlands Informationskrieg hat Angela Merkel als Ziel (faz.net).

Frank-Walter Steinmeier said in an interview that "a difficult internal German migration debate should be fuelled".[257]

4.9.5 Targets

The Russian government used the Lisa case first and foremost to draw attention in Russia itself to the shortcomings of German politics regarding the migration wave of 2015. All of this occurred against the backdrop of the Russia's invasion of Crimea in 2014.[258] The Lisa case served as a component in a broader propaganda strategy, to justify Russian activities in Ukraine. The campaign benefited from the migration background of the alleged rapist; it further helped that the language and comprehension problems between the alleged convicts, their families and the police fabricated a picture of an overstrained law enforcement. The German state, so it was displayed by Russian and right-wing groups, had lost control of the migration crisis.[259]

Right-wing groups then took up the ball and spread the campaign further in Germany as it played into their strategy of undermining the government.[260] The Lisa case provided an opportunity to bring the issue of migration back into focus and to point out that a Russian woman, someone from their own ranks, was now also affected. The Russians largely instrumentalised the case to rail against German migration policy and German rule of law.[261]

4.9.6 Tactics, Techniques and Procedures

In the 2016 Lisa case, the attackers used several tactics, techniques and procedures depicted in the DISARM Navigator to shape and spread their disinformation campaign.

T0022: Leverage conspiracy theory narratives—The Russian media spread an unverified and false story about the alleged abduction and rape of 13-year-old Lisa. This fabrication was presented as fact, although the police quickly solved the case. Right-wing parties in Germany soon took up the narrative and emphasised it (T0022.001: Amplify existing conspiracy theory narratives).

TA16: Establish legitimacy—The involvement of Russian government officials such as Foreign Minister Lavrov can be easily assigned to this tactic as he spoke out publicly about the case and accused the German authorities of a cover-up. This

---

[257] Ibid.

[258] Bundesamt für politische Bildung (BPB), "Der "Fall Lisa", Entwicklungen in Berlin Hellersdorf-Marzahn, 9 Oct 2018. Der "Fall Lisa" | Russlanddeutsche | bpb.de.

[259] *Der Spiegel*, op. cit., 26 Jan 2016.

[260] Der Spiegel, op. cit., 21 Jan 2016.

[261] NTV, "Angeblich entführte 13-Jährige Fall Lisa: Das sind die Fakten", 27 Jan 2016. Angeblich entführte 13-Jährige: Fall Lisa: Das sind die Fakten-n-tv.de.

official support gave the false information an apparent legitimacy and increased its credibility with the target audience.

This comes in combination with TA14: Develop narratives, as the disinformation campaign constructed a narrative that portrayed the refugee crisis in Germany as dangerous and out of control. The Lisa case was staged as an example of the failure of the German government and the danger posed to the population by migrants.

T0072.002: Demographic segmentation, T0072.005: Political segmentation—With the explicit targeting of the Russian German community, the goal of the Russian government's FIMI campaign and that of the right-wing parties was to divide German society on the question of migration policy and to unify Russian society on the Russian Federation's political agenda.

T0135: Undermine—Last but not least, the Russians sought to undermine trust in the German authorities, especially the police and the government. The disinformation campaign portrayed German institutions as ineffective and corrupt, weakening trust in the state. This was done by both the Russian attackers as well as the right-wing attackers.

4.9.7 Channels

The channel through which the news gained so much importance was the first channel of Russian television. The Russian community in Germany was still using the Russian-language media at the time, which is how the news story spread in Germany. This led to a heated situation that resulted in calls for protests and demonstrations across Germany especially on websites that were commonly used by this community such as "DerRussenTreff" (the Russian meeting point) or "Odnoklassniki" (Classmates).[262] These were in turn spread and shared via WhatsApp and its Russian counterparts.

4.9.8 Languages

The initial problem in this case was the language barrier between the girl's Russian-speaking parents and the police officers with whom they first came into contact. According to media reports, the parents had falsely understood the proposal of the police to speak in private with their daughter, as children are more likely to speak more openly with their parents, than with "strangers" like the police officers. The parents misinterpreted this as an attempt by the police to sweep the topic under the rug to avoid negative press articles about migrants. With regional politicians and police reluctant to address this communication problem openly,

[262] Frankfurter Allgemeine, "Russlands Informationskrieg: Unser Mädchen Lisa", 31 Jan 2016. Russlands Informationskrieg hat Angela Merkel als Ziel (faz.net).

thinking it would resolve itself, the reactions by citizens and media boiled over and resulted in a fertile ground for false information.[263]

As the case happened in Germany, there was naturally a lot of German-language reporting on it. However, the aunt's appearance and interview on Russian television brought the case directly to all Russian-speaking target groups. Anyone who regularly watches Russian state media, such as Russia Today (RT), has heard about this case. The two main languages in this case were German and Russian. The existing language barrier of the girl's Russian-speaking parents led to many misunderstandings and misinterpretations in Germany.

4.9.9 Effectiveness

The effect of the Russian campaign using the Lisa case against the aforementioned German policy culminated in the first few days with nationwide demonstrations. For a short time, Russia created a narrative that the girl was "one of them" and was thus able to establish an emotional connection. This led to an outcry in the Russian community and people took to the streets and questioned the German legal system and politics. At the same time, this was also a breeding ground for right-wing German groups who joined in and wanted to further fuel and exploit the debates in their favour. However, this effect weakened immediately when the apparent rape turned out to be a lie. What has remained is a discord in the Russian-German community, insecurities within society about the loyalty of Russo-Germans, as well as the—mostly felt—danger of migrants. Especially the view of Russian ethnic German immigrants in Germany changed, as they have adapted well, integrated and been relatively inconspicuous in Germany for years.

4.9.10 Countermeasures

No major countermeasures were necessary, as the case quickly resolved itself once the girl's lie was uncovered.

4.9.11 Conclusions and Recommendations

The Lisa case served as an example of how easily a whole community can be manipulated by foreign influence. In this case, the language barrier between German state authorities and the parents of Lisa, as well as the inaction of political decision-makers failed to address the worries of the Russo-German community

[263] Bundesamt für politische Bildung (BPB), "Der "Fall Lisa", Entwicklungen in Berlin Hellersdorf-Marzahn, 9 Oct 2018. Der "Fall Lisa" | Russlanddeutsche | bpb.de.

culminating in the interview of the aunt with Russian state media, as she probably thought that German media and authorities didn't want to help them. The following FIMI campaign of the Russian state masterfully used the worries and miscommunication between the Russo-German community and the police to create a picture Germany as a "failing state" which cannot provide security for its citizens, while taking in more and more refugees. From here, the goals of the FIMI campaign diverge, as right-wing groups inside Germany used the case to undermine the credibility of the German government and push their political agenda. While undermining the German government certainly was a secondary goal of the Russian side as well, the main goal appeared to create a division between the Russo-German community and the rest of German society. This played into the greater strategy of Russia to justify its actions in Crimea, since it served as proof that indeed the Russian ethnic minorities in "the West" are being suppressed and are in need of "protection" by the Russian state.

This instance paints a dark picture about how easy it is to influence wide parts of ethnic communities into believing fake news. However, the attack quickly collapsed the moment that it became clear that Lisa had made up the story about the rape to cover up her bad grades in school. This leads to the recommendation that a quick and transparent communication in events like this play a key role in preventing and combatting FIMI. If the German police and local politicians had acted sooner in communicating the facts and state of the investigation, there is a high possibility that the FIMI attack could have been mitigated. It seems that speed and transparency play a major role in defending against FIMI. Defenders should be trained in quick response actions as well as given a toolbox to easily prepare for such events.

4.10 Russian Propaganda Against Finland's NATO Membership

4.10.1 Introduction

Finland joined NATO in May 2023. The membership was Finland's reaction to Russia's war of aggression against Ukraine in 2022. Until then, Finland had a long and valued political tradition of non-alignment. Nevertheless, Finland had been talking for decades about the so-called "NATO option", which in practice means that Finland maintains its readiness to apply for NATO membership, if necessary.[264] The NATO option has been a political compromise in Finnish politics that allowed NATO supporters (a minority until 2022, a substantial majority from 2022 onwards) to be taken into account in the political system.

[264] Ålander, Minna, "Finland wants to use the "NATO option", *Stiftung Wissenschaft und Politik*, 27 Apr 2022. https://www.swp-berlin.org/publikation/finland-wants-to-use-the-nato-option.

Finland's NATO membership was assumed to generate protests from Russia, but these were assumed to remain at a lower level than the actual military operations. Russia had contented itself with condemning what had happened.

Among politicians, there was speculation about asylum seekers crossing the long land border. There was a recent example of this from 2016. At that time, asylum seekers began to appear in large numbers on the border with Russia, and the situation calmed down only after negotiations between Finnish President Sauli Niinistö and Russia. However, the events triggered a broader discussion in Finland on the organisation of border security if large numbers of migrants were to arrive in Finland across the Russian border.[265] Similar fears also arose in the 1990s after the collapse of the Soviet Union.

In autumn 2023, the Finnish Border Guard were encountering a higher-than-usual number of asylum seekers at the eastern border. The number rose steadily, until November 2023, when the Finnish government took measures to close border crossing points. YLE[266] compiled the events in a newspaper article describing the suspicious factors behind the increased border traffic. These included the apparent involvement of the Russian authorities, the shortcomings in the migrants' travel documents and, furthermore, it appeared that the migrants had been lured by Russia to the borders.[267]

In November 2023, Finland decided to close the four southernmost border crossing points for a fixed period.[268] Later, as border crossings increased in the north, Finland closed the entire eastern border for three months. The government justified the lockdown on grounds of national security and stated that Russia was carrying out a hybrid influence campaign against Finland.[269] The border closure has been extended periodically.

In a 4 April 2024 statement, Interior Minister Mari Rantanen commented that "Finnish authorities see this as a long-term situation. We have not seen anything this spring that would lead us to conclude that the situation has changed meaningfully. In addition, spring will provide opportunities to put more pressure on Finland. There are hundreds and possibly thousands of people close to Finland's border on the Russian side that could be instrumentalised against Finland." The

[265] Yle News 2016, "Officials see signs of hybrid warfare in migrant crisis", 14 Feb 2016. https://yle.fi/a/3-8672574.

[266] Yle is Finland's national public broadcasting company, founded in 1926 and 99.98% owned by the Finnish state. Yle was modelled on the BBC, its British counterpart.

[267] Seppänen, Oona, "Lue neljä seikkaa, miksi itärajan tilanne on nyt pinnalla", Yle News, 16 Nov 2023. https://yle.fi/a/74-20060569.

[268] Yle News, "PM Orpo: Finland will take further action on eastern border if needed", 20 Nov 2023. https://yle.fi/a/74-20061222.

[269] Yle News, "Finland closes entire eastern border for two weeks", 28 Nov 2023. https://yle.fi/a/74-20062569.

comment seemed to indicate that there are intelligence reports on the situation that have not been made public.[270]

Russia's actions have been interpreted as weaponised immigration and a hybrid operation against the Finnish state. The operation was to "avenge" Finland's NATO membership, but it can also be used to shake the Finnish political system and to increase tensions between Russians living in Finland and the native population.[271]

Information about those arriving across the border became subject to public discussion in November 2023. Russia's own so-called news sites, RT and Sputnik, began reporting on the phenomenon more extensively in November 2023. Russia's official news agency TASS commented on the matter through Kremlin spokesman Dimitry Peskov that month. Russian media emphasised that Finland's action created divisions between Europe and Russia, as Kremlin spokeswoman Maria Zakharova stated.[272]

The news of the closure of the Finnish border spread around the world, where public opinion followed the view of the Finnish state that Russia was engaged in an illegal instrumentalisation of immigration and a hybrid operation.[273]

In August 2023, YLE reported on the decreased use of a border crossing point. The full closure of the border in November 2023 halted entry and, as of January 2024, the situation has remained the same.

4.10.2 Threat Actors

The Russian state was obviously the principal threat actor. Crossing the national border on this scale was not possible without a decision by the highest decision-makers in central government. Russia was the active enabler in organising the hybrid operation.

We have no precise knowledge of how or by whom decisions were made in the Russian hierarchy, but we assume Putin was the chief instigator.

Russian state media operating in Finland, such as RT, Sputnik and TASS, spread the issue of border migrants.

The whole event put Finland in a difficult position in relation to international agreements. In this way, the rule of law can be eroded and trust in the Finnish state could be undermined internationally. The activities may also have exacerbated

[270] Ministry of the Interior, "Finland's eastern border to remain closed until further notice", press release, 4 Apr 2024. https://valtioneuvosto.fi/en/-/1410869/finland-s-eastern-border-to-remain-closed-until-further-notice.

[271] Yle News, "What is Russia hoping to achieve with hybrid tactics on the Finnish border?", 21 Nov 2023. https://yle.fi/a/74-20061336.

[272] TASS, "Russia disappointed by Finland's plans to close remaining checkpoints—Kremlin spokesman", 20 Nov 2023. https://tass.com/politics/1708689.

[273] Kirby, Paul, and Sarah Rainsford, "Russia Warns of Tension as Finland Shuts Last Border Crossing", BBC News, 29 Nov 2023. https://www.bbc.com/news/world-europe-67564175.

relations between different population groups and possibly increased the risk of terrorism.

In general, the whole episode played to Russia's well-known narrative that the West is anti-Russian and closing the border is an attempt to isolate Russia from Europe. It was surely an example of bullying and retaliation against Finland's NATO membership.[274] In practice, however, it's not apparent how Russia could have benefited from the operation.

4.10.3 Presumed Objectives

It is not clear what the Russian objectives were in the immigration crisis they orchestrated on the Finnish border.[275] The main effect seems to have been to grow fears among the Finnish population that a major migration crisis was imminent. The Russians may have calculated that the immigration as a phenomenon would cause internal tension among the Finnish parties and people. That did not happen, as the Russian action was widely understood to be a hostile operation against Finland.

It is also possible that the Russian action aimed to undermine Finland's position in international agreements thus harming the country's reputation. This would also allow Russia to blame "the West" (in general) as having double standards whenever or wherever they would allow immigrants in.

In general, Russia was making a clear case of its being the victim and that it was only reacting to Western provocations.[276] This is a part of Russia's decade old strategy to convince their internal audiences that the West is their enemy.[277]

4.10.4 Incidents and Observables

The incident here was the Russians instrumentalising immigration at the Finnish Russian border. The following table points to the narrative built within the Russian media landscape. The sources are from three main Russian English language media

[274] Van Rij, Armida, "Russia's Withdrawal from Its Border Agreement with Finland Is an Expansion of Its Hybrid Warfare on the EU", Chatham House, 30 Jan 2024. https://www.chathamhouse.org/2024/01/russias-withdrawal-its-border-agreement-finland-expansion-its-hybrid-warfare-eu.

[275] Yle, "Eastern border quiet; PM describes Russian operation as 'hybrid attack'", 16 Dec 2023. https://yle.fi/a/74-20065426.

[276] Yle, "Kremlin spokesman dismisses accusations Russia behind asylum-seeker surge", 20 November 2023. https://yle.fi/a/74-20061166.

[277] Hellström, Jerker, Matti Puranen, Santeri Kytöneva, and Pekka Kallioniemi, "Are Russian Narratives Amplified by PRC Media? A Case Study on Narratives Related to Sweden's and Finland's NATO Applications", Prepared and published by the NATO Strategic Communications Centre of Excellence, February 2024. https://stratcomcoe.org/pdfjs/?file=/publications/download/Russian-Narratives-PRC-Media-DIGITAL.pdf?zoom=page-fit.

sources. TASS is the Russian government's official media outlet and RT.com and Sputnik Global have a wide audience around the world.

The story that unfolds in these small snippets is a subtle narrative that leans towards framing Russia as an innocent actor and Finland as an over-reacting and possibly hostile nation. The tone in many of these articles seems neutral and objective but a closer reading indicates another agenda. In the content and narrative section, there is a short passage from the article to help the reader piece together the story. In some cases, we have quoted a longer passage to highlight the Kremlin's framing of the events.

The Table 4.3 illustrates the observables used in creating the base narrative against Finland and the West in the situation where immigrants were directed towards the Finnish border.

4.10.5 Targets

We can identify several targets of Russia's FIMI campaign:

- the Finnish government
- the Finnish Border Guard action and legitimacy
- the Finnish legal order regarding refugees
- Russians living in Finland.

Refugees in Finland may feel threatened. A mass refugee influx would polarise Finnish society.

4.10.6 Tactics, Techniques and Procedures

T0114.002: Traditional media—The discussion mostly involved traditional media and news coverage. The Russian media sites are mostly government-controlled propaganda machines. There seems to be a close link between the official news agency TASS and the two news media (RT and Sputnik). TASS seems to frame the situation, and the news media pick up the story and the agenda from there.

T0104.003: Private/closed social networks—There are some indications that the Russians living in Finland were encouraged to protest.[278] The effect was limited and not likely to have been a successful influence operation. Finland has a substantial Russian-speaking population with most of them not having dual citizenship (Russia actually does not acknowledge dual citizenships). While there are Putin-leaning Russians in Finland, the population has remained mostly unpolitical

[278] Yle News, "Russians, dual nationals protest Finland's border closure", 18 Dec 2023. https://yle.fi/a/74-20065561.

Table 4.3 Russian media coverage of the border crisis

Media (published/viewed)	Url	Content/narrative
TASS, 27.10.2023/18.9.2024	https://tass.com/politics/1697755	In a perhaps unrelated incident, Russia terminates cross-border cooperation agreement with Finland.
TASS, 20.11.2023/30.1.2024	https://tass.com/politics/1708689	Russia is disappointed with Finland's decision to potentially close all remaining border crossings, presidential spokesman Dmitry Peskov tells reporters: "It causes nothing but deep regret, since we had long-standing, very good relations with Finland, pragmatic, based on mutual respect. Of course, we regret that these relations have been replaced by an entirely Russo-phobic position, which the leaders of this neighbouring country have now begun to adhere to. Regretfully, this is the situation we are in today," he says.
TASS, 18.11.2023/30.1.2024	https://tass.com/emergencies/1708187	Finnish border guards use gas against people at border with Russia (according to a false report on TASS).
TASS, 20.11.2023/30.1.2024	https://tass.com/politics/1708701	Moscow does not accept Helsinki's accusations against Russian border guards because they play by the book, Kremlin spokesman Dmitry Peskov tells reporters. "I would prefer not to comment here. We don't accept such accusations. Naturally, border crossings are used by the people who have the legal right to cross the border. In this regard, our border guards follow all the related guidelines," he notes, commenting on Finland's allegations that Russian border guards were facilitating the influx of migrants into the country by allowing them to reach the border and preventing them from going back.

(continued)

Table 4.3 (continued)

Media (published/viewed)	Url	Content/narrative
TASS, 22.11.2023/30.1.2024	https://tass.com/world/1710427	The Finnish government has decided to close three checkpoints on the border with Russia with the exception of the Raja-Jooseppi border crossing point, the Finnish Foreign Ministry says in a statement.
TASS, 14.12.2023/30.1.2024	https://tass.com/world/1721339	Finland to close all checkpoints along border with Russia Friday—interior minister. "Illegal immigration on Finland's eastern border has continued," Mari Rantanen says.
TASS, 27.12.2023/30.1.2024	https://tass.com/society/1727181	The Finnish government's decisions to close crossings on the border with Russia have been appealed in the country's Supreme Administrative Court, the Yle website reports. According to the appellants, "the decisions to close the eastern border violate their freedom of movement and many other fundamental rights" as well as "the ban on discrimination". The appellants are seeking to overturn the rulings to shut down the checkpoints, arguing that they are in contravention of the Finnish constitution. According to Yle, the appellants are Finnish citizens of Russian descent or their family members.

(continued)

Table 4.3 (continued)

Media (published/viewed)	Url	Content/narrative
TASS, 11.1.2024/30.1.2024	https://tass.com/world/1731113	The Ministry of Internal Affairs of Finland has decided to prolong the shutdown of car border checkpoints on the Russian border until February 11, the ministry said in a press release. "The shutdown of the eastern border will last until February 11. There is no option to apply for international protection at ground border crossing checkpoints between Finland and Russia at this point," the statement reads.
TASS, 16.1.2024/30.1.2024	https://tass.com/world/1733061	Finland does not plan to open its checkpoints on the border with Russia in February, the *Ilta-Sanomat* newspaper said, citing its sources. "We will see to it that we don't have to open the border even for a short period," the source in the government was quoted as saying.... Russian Foreign Ministry spokeswoman Maria Zakharova said earlier that Finland's move to close the border crossings was creating new dividing lines in Europe and Moscow would respond to these actions after interagency consultations.
SPUTNIK GLOBE, 29.9.2023/30.1.2024	https://sputnikglobe.com/20230929/finland-newest-nato-member-strikes-land-deals-to-build-fortifications-near-russian-border-reports-1113791507.html	According to Finland's largest newspaper, the Finnish Defence Forces have initiated the signing of agreements with landowners along the Russian border. These agreements grant permission for the construction of fortifications on these territories with only a day's notice.

(continued)

Table 4.3 (continued)

Media (published/viewed)	Url	Content/narrative
SPUTNIK GLOBE, 29.9.2023/30.1.2024	https://sputnikglobe.com/20231027/moscow-summons-finnish-ambassador-over-termination-of-cross-border-cooperation-agreement-1114524187.html	"On October 25, Finnish Ambassador to Russia Antti Helantera was summoned to the Russian Foreign Ministry… The Ambassador was handed a diplomatic note stating that, in accordance with article 14 of this Agreement, it will terminate in 90 days, that is, on January 24, 2024," the ministry said in a statement.
SPUTNIK GLOBE, 20.11.2023/30.1.2024	https://sputnikglobe.com/20240124/frontex-personnel-to-be-present-at-finlands-eastern-border-until-summer-border-guard-1116361492.html	The Finnish Border Guard said on Wednesday it had reached an agreement with the European Border and Coast Guard Agency (Frontex) to extend the latter's personnel and material support for the eastern border of Finland until the summer.
SPUTNIK GLOBE, 18.11.2023/30.1.2024	https://sputnikglobe.com/20231118/over-8800-people-sign-petition-not-to-close-checkpoints-on-russian-finnish-border-1115042350.html	More than 8,800 online users have signed a petition to the Finnish authorities urging them not to close the southeastern land border crossings with Russia, as the families and spouses of a number of nationals reside in both countries and may be prevented from visiting each other by the new restrictions.
SPUTNIK GLOBE, 20.11.2023/30.1.2024	https://sputnikglobe.com/20231120/moscow-vows-response-based-on-national-interests-if-finland-closes-border-1115068450.html	Moscow does not exclude that Finland will close all checkpoints at the border with Russia, Russian Deputy Foreign Minister Alexander Grushko said on Monday. "It is difficult for me to comment on something that has not happened yet. But judging by the way decisions are made in Western European capitals, no options can be ruled out. Although, in this case, such a decision would obviously contradict the national interests of Finland," Grushko told reporters.

(continued)

Table 4.3 (continued)

Media (published/viewed)	Url	Content/narrative
SPUTNIK GLOBE, 20.11.2023/30.1.2024	https://sputnikglobe.com/20231120/russia-lodges-protest-to-finnish-ambassador-over-closure-of-border-checkpoints-1115077973.html	The Russian Foreign Ministry has lodged a protest with Finnish Ambassador Antti Helantera over Helsinki's decision to close border checkpoints between the countries, the ministry said on Monday.
SPUTNIK GLOBE, 22.12.2023/30.1.2024	https://sputnikglobe.com/20231222/finlands-interior-ministry-to-pay-asylum-seekers-up-to-5500-in-aid-for-voluntary-return-1115738427.html	The Finnish Ministry of Interior said Thursday that it would pay asylum seekers up to 5,000 euros ($5,500) in assistance for their voluntary return to their homeland within 30 days after they receive the first negative asylum decision or withdraw their application for asylum.
RT.COM, 14.11.2023/24.1.2024	https://www.rt.com/news/587254-finland-preparing-shut-border-russia/	Finland could soon close border checkpoints with Russia for security reasons, Interior Minister Mari Rantanen announced on Tuesday, citing concerns about illegal immigrants from third countries. Helsinki recently tightened border measures by banning people crossing by bicycle from Russia.

(continued)

Table 4.3 (continued)

Media (published/viewed)	Url	Content/narrative
RT.COM, 17.11.2023/24.1.2024	https://www.rt.com/news/587515-estonia-russia-dragon-teeth/	Estonian authorities have brought apparent "dragon teeth"-style anti-tank obstacles to the river bridge crossing in the town of Narva, located immediately across the border from Russia's town of Ivangorod. The obstacles were delivered by a military truck and unloaded onto the bridge, footage circulating online shows. … Earlier this week, Finland announced the closure of all four border crossings with Russia, citing illegal migration flow as a pretext. Helsinki claimed Moscow deliberately altered its policies to steer migrants from third countries through its territory towards Finland, though it hasn't provided any evidence for its allegations.
RT.COM, 18.11.2023/24.1.2024	https://www.rt.com/news/587566-eu-state-gas-people-border/	Finland's border guards had to resort to "gassing" people at the nation's border with Russia as the situation became heated ahead of the planned closure of crossing points, state broadcaster Yle reported on Friday. At least one person was "gassed in the face", according to the report.
RT.COM, 22.11.2023/24.1.2024	https://www.rt.com/news/587814-finland-russia-border-closing/	The Finnish government has decided to close three more border crossings with Russia, Prime Minister Petteri Orpo announced on Wednesday evening, citing an alleged surge in undocumented asylum seekers from third countries. The closures will go into effect at the end of the day on Friday.

(continued)

Table 4.3 (continued)

Media (published/viewed)	Url	Content/narrative
RT.COM, 23.11.2023/24.1.2024	https://www.rt.com/news/587860-norway-close-border-russia/	Norway could close its only border crossing with Russia, Prime Minister Jonas Gahr Store has warned, according to the country's TV2 channel. The threat comes amid worsening relations between the Scandinavian states and Russia. Finland is set to close all but one border crossing with its eastern neighbour.
RT.COM, 24.11.2023/24.1.2024	https://www.rt.com/russia/587908-peskov-new-iron-curtain/	Finland's closure of border crossings with Russia and potential similar steps by Norway and Estonia are not yet the modern equivalent of the Cold War's "Iron Curtain", Kremlin spokesman Dmitry Peskov told journalists on Friday.
RT.COM, 27.11.2023/24.1.2024	https://www.rt.com/news/588061-finland-border-russia-asylum/	The Finnish government is reportedly mulling full closure of its land border with Russia, a decision from which it shied away last week over concerns that it would clash with Helsinki's commitment to provide refuge to asylum seekers. Moscow has protested the restrictions and Finnish claims that it was reacting to Russian hybrid warfare.

(continued)

Table 4.3 (continued)

Media (published/viewed)	Url	Content/narrative
RT.COM, 28.11.2023/24.1.2024	https://www.rt.com/news/588164-finland-close-border-violation-migrants/	Finland will completely close its eastern border with Russia on Thursday, shutting down the last open checkpoint for two weeks, Prime Minister Petteri Orpo announced during a press conference on Tuesday, blaming Moscow for the "exceptional" situation.… Orpo has claimed to have intelligence suggesting Russia was helping asylum seekers reach the Finnish border and argued the move was legally justified. "This is an organized activity, not a genuine emergency," he told reporters on Monday, alleging the "ease with which the migrants found their way to the remote border crossing point" proved they were sent there by Moscow. Russia has dismissed the allegations as "completely baseless," insisting its border guards are only allowing people to cross who have the legal right to do so and countering that Helsinki had not even tried to reach a solution through diplomatic channels regarding the migration issue.

(continued)

Table 4.3 (continued)

Media (published/viewed)	Url	Content/narrative
RT.COM, 29.11.2023/24.1.2024	https://www.rt.com/russia/588227-kremlin-nato-state-military-buildup/	Finland has no reason to enhance its military posture on the Russian border, Kremlin spokesman Dmitry Peskov told journalists on Wednesday. Such action by Helsinki can only spark tensions in relations with Moscow, he said. On Tuesday, Poland said it would send a team of military specialists to the Finnish border with Russia. A request by Helsinki "for allied support" was made "in the face of a hybrid attack on the Finnish border," the head of the Polish National Security Bureau, Jacek Siewiera, said in a statement on X (formerly Twitter).
RT.COM, 12.12.2023/24.1.2024	https://www.rt.com/news/588910-finland-close-border-russia/	The Council of Europe has voiced concerns over Finland's decision to close all border crossings with Russia, warning that the move could leave "extremely vulnerable" migrants stranded without shelter during the cold winter months.
RT.COM, 12.12.2023/24.1.2024	https://www.rt.com/news/588947-nato-state-reopen-border-russia/	Finland will reopen two of its eight border crossings with Russia, the government in Helsinki announced on Tuesday. The Nordic nation had previously shut down the entire border, citing a surge in asylum seekers that it claimed had been orchestrated by Moscow.

(continued)

Table 4.3 (continued)

Media (published/viewed)	Url	Content/narrative
RT.COM, 22.12.2023/24.1.2024	https://www.rt.com/news/589547-eu-nation-asylum-seekers-pay/	Rejected asylum seekers in Finland might receive a heavy sum from Helsinki starting next year if they agree to return to their home countries, the Finnish Interior Ministry announced on Thursday as it unveiled the new "voluntary return assistance" program. Under the scheme, a refugee can apply for a grant for voluntary return and get €5,300 ($5,833) if they do so within 30 days after the first negative decision on their asylum application or withdraw the request themselves, the ministry's statement said. If they do so later, the sum would drop to €2,000 ($2,201), it added.

(continued)

Table 4.3 (continued)

Media (published/viewed)	Url	Content/narrative
RT.COM, 10.1.2024/24.1.2024	https://www.rt.com/russia/590412-finland-russia-border-closure/	Finland is reportedly planning to extend the closure of its border with Russia for at least another month, according to Finnish media outlets citing sources within the country's government. The current decision to suspend the operation of border crossing points is set to expire on January 14.… Helsinki has accused Moscow of deliberately orchestrating the migrant surges as a "hybrid attack," while the Kremlin has vehemently rejected such claims as "completely baseless." The head of Finland's Ministry of Internal Affairs, Marie Rantanen, stated earlier this week that Helsinki would not re-open the checkpoints, because "there is a risk that Russia will continue to engage in such activities if the border is open."
RT.COM, 16.1.2024/24.1.2024	https://www.rt.com/russia/590711-russia-to-deport-syrian-migrants/	A local court in Murmansk Region, northern Russia, has ordered the deportation of three Syrian migrants who entered the country with the intention of crossing into the EU, Interfax reported on Tuesday.
RT.COM, 17.1.2024/24.1.2024	https://www.rt.com/russia/590792-finland-russia-border-closed/	Finland will keep its border with Russia closed for at least another month due to concerns about illegal migration, Foreign Minister Elina Valtonen has said. Local media, however, suggested that the ban could persist much longer, with officials in Helsinki unsure whether the border crisis can be solved at all.

in their attitudes. Finnish Broadcasting Service YLE also offers news in Russian (and other languages) which may help to mitigate some of the Russian propaganda.

T0140: Cause harm—Closing the border forced the authorities to be prepared. Finland had and has a comprehensive security plan that includes contingencies for such an event. It is obvious that a weaponised immigration situation will cause harm, but it may also have other aims that are not clear. For instance, it could be used as an intelligence-gathering operation to see how Finnish border guards or political institutions function in such situations.

T0078: Dismay—As a state governed by the rule of law, Finland is placed in a questionable situation in which it may have to violate international refugee conventions in the name of national security. This would undermine Finnish international positions in some foreseeable future. The dismay effect helps to radicalise Finnish right-wing groups.

T0135: Undermine—Trust in Finland as a state governed by the rule of law and as a "moral actor" may be put to the test if the border situation escalates.

T0139: Dissuade from acting—The border situation can be used as a tool of blackmail. "Thousands" of people did not leak through the land border. Russia threatened or tried to influence Finland so that Finland would act more according to Russia's liking on political issues.

T0040: Demand insurmountable proof—Russian officials denied the fact that they are actively involved with pushing immigrants to the border. The border between Finland and Russia is well guarded and it's impossible for anyone to walk or otherwise move across the border without the help of Russian officials.

T0004: Develop competing narratives—Russia is claiming that the immigrants are just passing through Russia, and that Russia has no means to counter them. In this Russian narrative, the West is to blame, and Russia is acting in a humane way.

T0003: Leverage existing narratives—The idea that the West is corrupt and having double standards towards Russia often surfaced in Russian media. There were isolated mentions that this was indeed a hybrid operation *against Russia*, orchestrated by Finland (and NATO).

T0023: Distort facts—When a Finnish border guard used tear gas in self-protection (as was reported by YLE), Russian media subtly framed the incident in a more sinister light. Russia is also distorting facts about the cause of the immigration flood.

T0143: Persona legitimacy—Russia often mentioned international law as the premise for its own actions. This, however, distorts the facts, but gives it legitimacy for Russian claims that it was in fact the moral actor in the situation. It's also worth mentioning that Kremlin officials (press secretaries Dimitri Peskov and Maria Zaharova) are often cited as the source of the main news content. This is a way to push legitimacy even if the Kremlin and its officials are not trusted in the West.

4.10.7 Channels

TASS, RT, Sputnik.

4.10.8 Languages

English, Finnish, Russian.

4.10.9 Effectiveness

The Russian FIMI did not cause civil unrest or division in society. Russian speakers in Finland organised few and mostly understandable protests that had little effect. However, some of the persons who arrived in the country are presumed to pose a security threat and the whereabouts of some are unknown to the authorities.[279]

4.10.10 Countermeasures

The government's swift and decisive action to close the border had wide popular support [C00096, C00170, C00156].

Open sharing of information and transparency with the Finnish public helped [C00190, C00159].

Active reporting of the Finnish side of events has been an active countermeasure [C00159, C00030].

Also helpful was the government's action to communicate with the Russian-speaking minority in Finland [C00017, C00019].

4.10.11 Conclusions and Recommendations

Coordinating immigrant groups to cross a national border is a harsh tactic that may in some cases have dramatic effects. It is difficult to close borders without causing moral and physical harm on multiple dimensions. From the situation, we can conclude that firm and transparent political decision-making helped to contain the situation. Also, a legislative environment should be in place to quickly escalate and de-escalate actions according to the situation. An EU Member State should not act alone but as a member of a unified front. Combating threat narratives is never completely possible. The best defence is to have transparent public discussions

[279] NBI: Dozens of potentially dangerous individuals have crossed eastern border, Yle News, 14 Mar 2024.

about the situation and concentrate on counter-narratives. It also helps to have a population with high trust in officials and the media.

4.11 Framing the President—How Russia Created Negative Press on a Head of State

4.11.1 Introduction

In Finnish political life, President Alexander Stubb is widely considered West-leaning and a vocal critic of Russia ever since his work as the Finnish foreign minister during the Russian aggression against Georgia. The Russian media have often portrayed him in a negative light as someone who had "negative views of Russia". Russian spokesman Dimitri Peskov commented that Finland and its president are unfriendly towards Russia. He also implied that Russian President Putin would not congratulate the new president, winner of the election in March 2024.[280] That comment was undoubtedly a response to candidate Stubb's assessment during the election debates that he would not answer Putin if he were to call. RT, the Russian state media news site, quoted a Kremlin spokesman and recalled Stubb's 2014 year at the end of the story.[281]

Later, in an interview with *The Financial Times*, Stubb urged European countries to be "ready" and to be "like Finland".[282] The Finnish Broadcasting Company Yle[283] reported the statement as did the Russian media, who made Stubb's statement sound like war-mongering,[284] that Europe was preparing itself for a Russian invasion. The end of the story recalled that Putin expressed such talk as nonsense and underlined that Russia has been concerned about NATO's eastward expansion for years.

The Finnish president's comments were followed closely by the Kremlin. Stubb's comments on NATO's nuclear deterrence[285] were made to sound as if

[280] Russian news agency (TASS), "Kremlin unaware if Putin to congratulate Stubb given Finland's 'unfriendly stance", 12 Feb 2024. https://tass.com/world/1745061.

[281] Finnish Broadcasting Company (Yle), "PM Stubb slams MPs' "russophobia" over planned Russian nuclear Plant", 14 Oct 2014. https://yle.fi/a/3-7528712.

[282] Foy, Henry, "Why Finland's Stubb wants EU to be 'cool, calm and collected' on Russia", *The Financial Times*, 10 Apr 2024. https://www.ft.com/content/e96b009e-5359-4a0c-932e-373ce3a78f2d.

[283] Yle News, "'Be more Finnish', President Stubb urges EU countries in FT interview", 11 Apr 2024. https://yle.fi/a/74-20083262.

[284] Blinova, Ekaterina, "Mad Rush Into NATO: Is Finland's President-Elect Racing to Confront Russia?", Sputnik International, 12 Feb 2024. https://sputnikglobe.com/20240212/mad-rush-into-nato-is-finlands-president-elect-racing-to-confront-russia-1116741035.html.

[285] Kauranen, Anne, "NATO's Nuclear Deterrent Must Be Real for Finland, Says New President", *Yahoo News*, 1 Mar 2024. https://www.yahoo.com/news/finland-inaugurates-alexander-stubb-president-103310657.html.

he saw their use against Russia as possible.[286] Reuters has written a more neutral and truthful story about the statement.[287]

In a wide-ranging article concerning both Finland's NATO membership and the new president, SputnikGlobal, which openly supports the Russian state's line of communication, painted a picture of a president who represents NATO's anti-Russian line.[288] The article also claimed that Russia's attempt at dialogue with the West has been rejected and that President Stubb would in his own way continue this deliberate anti-Russian line.[289]

Russia's official news agency TASS summarised the allegations concerning Finland and Stubb in one article. The article portrayed Stubb as an anti-Russian politician who has been open about deploying NATO troops in Finland and has spoken positively about changing Finland's laws for the storage of nuclear weapons. In addition, it claimed that Stubb's policy and, to a large extent, Finland's domestic politics are largely "contributed by the United States".

In addition to Russia's official news agency and media closely linked to the Kremlin, articles about Stubb also appear on sites that are obvious pro-Kremlin propaganda publications. In the article, which quotes previous and other news, Stubb and Finland are presented as warmongering and anti-Russian actors. The same fake news page tries to paint President Stubb as a figure who actively seeks confrontation with Russia.

4.11.2 Threat Actors

The Russian state propagated the narrative about Stubb. TASS, the official Russian news agency, reported the narrative in various of its publications and, in many contexts, they seek legitimacy by referring to Putin's statements. The campaign is not a separate phenomenon from Kremlin propaganda or foreign policy.

Threat actors included TASS, news media linked to the Russian state (www.rt.com and www.sputnikglobe.com), as well as the switchboard media or fake media operating in Finland www.naapuriseura.fi who reinforced the same message.

The principal beneficiary of smearing the Finnish President was Russia, whose strategic communications were at stake here. By distorting and selectively reporting Stubb's statements, Russia sought to reinforce the idea that Europe, the United States and NATO are anti-Russian. This was useful when Russia tried to create the image of two quarrelling blogs, in which case Russia's own propaganda could be validated as a legitimate point of view. In addition, smearing Stubb served as a tool

[286] Russia Today (RT), "Finland's new president hails American nuclear weapons", 2 Mar 2024. https://www.rt.com/news/593639-finland-nuclear-deterrent-president/.
[287] Kauranen, op. cit.
[288] Blinova, op. cit.
[289] Russia Today (RT), "EU member rebukes West over 'belligerent' Russia talk", 11 April 2024. https://www.rt.com/news/595745-finland-russia-stubb-belligerent/.

for interfering with the foreign and domestic policy of a country that it considered unfriendly to Russia.

4.11.3 Presumed Objectives

Russia's main news sources strictly follow the line of Russian foreign policy, which was very clearly expressed in the Stubb case. There have been different phases in the relations between Finland and Russia, but during the Cold War, for example, Finland managed to focus its foreign policy towards the West, without severing relations with the then Soviet Union.

There is a long tradition of Russian propaganda or influence on Finland's state leadership. The term Finlandisation specifically describes the mechanics of Russian reflexive power,[290] in which Russia seeks to create a situation in which the political leadership of a country begins to make decisions that are harmful to them. Finlandisation[291] describes precisely a situation in which the foreign policy of a small country surreptitiously takes into account the assumed or stated wishes of a larger neighbouring country.

Against this background, even Russia's understated statements have been interpreted and—especially during the Cold War—responded to. The criticism levelled at Stubb is not particularly disguised: he has been painted as an undesirable president[292] and, quite frankly, it has been said that Stubb's election will only cause harm.[293] It must be said, of course, that in the Finnish presidential elections in 2023, every candidate agreed on the same policy towards Russia.[294]

[290] Merriam, John, "One Move Ahead—Diagnosing and Countering Russian Reflexive Control", *The Journal of Slavic Military Studies*, Vol. 36, No. 1, pp. 1–27. https://doi.org/10.1080/13518046.2023.2201113.

[291] McNamara, Eoin, "Finland in NATO: from Finlandization to active integration", *New Eastern Finland*, Issue 5, 16 Sept 2024. https://neweasterneurope.eu/2024/09/16/finland-in-nato-from-finlandization-to-active-integration/.

[292] Duxbury, Charlie, "Former Finland PM Alexander Stubb wins presidential election", *POLITICO*, 11 Feb 2024. https://www.politico.eu/article/alexander-stubb-finland-election-nato-russia-eu-ukraine-war/.

[293] Naapuriseuran Sanomat, "Stubb: No relations with Russia during the war", 30 Aug 2023. https://naapuriseura.fi/en/stubb-ei-suhteita-venajaan-sodan-aikana/. See also two Russian disinformation vehicles: *The Moscow Times* [a fake news site], "Finland's President-Elect Says No Political Ties With Russia Until Ukraine War Ends", 12 Feb 2024. https://www.themoscowtimes.com/2024/02/12/finlands-president-elect-says-no-political-ties-with-russia-until-ukraine-war-ends-a84056. Sputnik Global, "Ex-Finnish Prime Minister Stubb Pulls Ahead in Presidential Runoff", 11 Feb 2024. https://sputnikglobe.com/20240211/ex-finnish-prime-minister-stubb-pulls-ahead-in-presidential-runoff-1116732943.html. Nix, Emma, Stuart Jones and Sophia Athan, "Your primer on Finland's presidential election", The Atlantic Council, 24 Jan 2024. https://www.atlanticcouncil.org/content-series/transatlantic-horizons/your-primer-on-finlands-presidential-election/.

[294] *Euronews/AP*, "Finland to choose between two presidential candidates with tough stance on Russia", 9 Feb 2024. https://www.euronews.com/2024/02/09/finland-to-choose-between-two-preisdential-candidates-with-tough-stance-on-russia.

Russia's reach is difficult to express unequivocally. On the other hand, the message to Finland was clear: relations are no longer good and will not improve. NATO was also painted as the driving force behind Finnish politics, so that the president's negative positions on NATO were actually caused by NATO manipulation.

Russia's goal was hardly to position Finland even more firmly in the West, although it has primarily succeeded in doing so in recent years. Pushing Stubb as an undesirable person in foreign policy also sent a message that Finland or Russia no longer have any special relationship.

Although it may be difficult to specify Russia's objectives, vocal criticism of another country's presidential candidates and the labelling of the president-elect's foreign policy as anti-Russia only reflects the cynical way in which Russia deals with other countries.

4.11.4 Incidents and Observables

The event under review is related to interference in the foreign policy of the Finnish state leadership. The target of the event was the President who, in the Finnish constitution, directs foreign and security policy. Russia's consistent misrepresentation of Stubb's statements distorts the perception of Finland's foreign policy positioning in Russian media (Table 4.4).

4.11.5 Targets

The target was the President of the Republic of Finland and thus the presidential institution.

Finland's foreign policy as such can also be seen as a target.

4.11.6 Tactics, Techniques and Procedures

T0139: Dissuade from acting—Attempts were made to curtail the President's freedom of action by forcing him to think carefully about what he said and to defend himself against a statement that was dug up from the past and largely taken out of context.

T0076: Distort—The aim was to use Stubb's statements to build an image of an actively hostile Finland, which acts as a puppet of the United States in particular. At the same time, attempts were made to distort Russia's role in peace negotiations.

T0077: Distract—Paying attention to, for example, Stubb's earlier statement or his position vis-à-vis the United States distracted attention from the actual issue. Nothing was raised from Stubb's statements other than things suitable for propaganda, which distorted his role and image in both domestic and foreign politics.

Table 4.4 Russian media reaction to Stubb's election

Media (published/viewed)	URL	Narrative
TASS, 12 Feb 2024/20 Sept 2024	https://www.rt.com/news/592317-finland-president-elect-russia/	When power changes hands in a foreign nation, Moscow normally expresses hope that the new leader will seek good relations with Russia, but "unfortunately we cannot use this part of our standard wording in this case," Peskov told journalists on Monday. Stubb's public statements indicate that "dialogue would not be possible," he explained.
Sputnik Globe, 12 Feb 2024/20 Sept 2024	https://sputnikglobe.com/20240212/mad-rush-into-nato-is-finlands-president-elect-racing-to-confront-russia-1116741035.html	"When it became evident, right at the beginning of the war [Russia's special military operation in Ukraine—Sputnik], that our path towards the alliance would begin, I felt strongly that this is a new age in Finnish foreign policy, and perhaps I could throw my hat into the ring once again," Stubb told the press.... "During World War II, Finland allied with Nazi Germany, playing a crucial role in Hitler's strategy to blockade Leningrad, now known as St. Petersburg. The siege of Leningrad lasted from 8 Sept 1941 until 27 Jan 1944, resulting in the deaths of an estimated 800,000 to 1.5 million people, according to various estimates."
RT.COM, 2 Mar 2024/20 Sept 2024	https://www.rt.com/news/593639-finland-nuclear-deterrent-president/	Finnish President Alexander Stubb has boasted that NATO membership gives his country a "real nuclear deterrent" in the form of American missiles. At his inauguration on Friday, Stubb promised to lead the Nordic nation into a "new era" of military partnership with the West.

(continued)

Table 4.4 (continued)

Media (published/viewed)	URL	Narrative
RT.COM, 11Apr 2024/20 Sept 2024	https://www.rt.com/news/595745-finland-russia-stubb-belligerent/	Finland, which broke with decades-long neutrality and joined NATO last spring, is doing its utmost to give Ukraine as many weapons as possible, while replenishing its own stocks, the president said. Stubb's comments come as a string of Western leaders warn that Russia could attack NATO countries within a few years, insisting that the bloc must ramp up its defence industry and military power to brace for a potential stand-off.
TASS, 11 Apr 2024/20 Sept 2024	https://tass.com/world/1773533	The Finnish leader called on European countries to "be more like Finland" now, explaining that they need to be "more prepared", notes the newspaper. "I'm a little bit worried about this rather belligerent talk about Russia going to test Article 5 [NATO collective defence clause], and that Europe is next in line. I think we should prepare for that, but I think it's highly unlikely," he told *The Financial Times*.

(continued)

Table 4.4 (continued)

Media (published/viewed)	URL	Narrative
RT.COM, 12 Feb 2024/20 Sept 2024	https://www.rt.com/news/592317-finland-president-elect-russia/	Russia respects the choice of the Finnish people, who elected former prime minister Alexander Stubb as their new president but does not expect bilateral relations to improve during his term, Kremlin spokesman Dmitry Peskov said.
TASS, 12 Feb 2024/20 Sept 2024	https://tass.com/world/1745061	Finland and its current authorities take an unfriendly stance toward Moscow, Russian spokesman Dmitry Peskov said on Monday in commenting on whether President Vladimir Putin may potentially extend his formal congratulations to Finnish President-elect Alexander Stubb. "Finland is currently on the [Russian] list of unfriendly countries. It fully sides with the sanctions [against Russia] and statements by the president-elect are of an extremely unfriendly nature," Peskov said.

T0079: Divide—Russia sought to sow doubts about the intentions of NATO, the EU and the US by presenting Finland as a manipulated country whose real power is primarily exercised by the USA. On this basis, Finland's sovereignty will be challenged, and it is possible that someone will seize this doubt, especially in relation to the European Union.

T0135: Undermine—The sovereignty of Finland's foreign policy was being challenged by undermining its purposes. If Finland's actions were seen only as appeasement of NATO, the role and power of foreign policy would rapidly weaken.

T0082: Develop new narratives—In a subtle way, Russian media were hinting that the elected president was a warmonger and pushed NATO and Russia closer to conflict. Stubbs's interviews are often correctly quoted but his quotation is set to push some other Russian narrative.

T0068: Respond to breaking news or active crisis—In a way, Russia dug up an old parliamentary discussion involving then Prime Minister Stubb and made it look at least a little suspicious that he then seemed to support Russia.

4.11.7 Channels

T0111: Pro-Kremlin media—The Kremlin uses its own communication channels (official) to spread its message. This is then amplified through its national news agencies.

T0118: Fake media (proxy)—Fake news and other "alternative news sources" may knowingly or unknowingly use Russian-state-sponsored or state-leaning sources in their own media production. This spreads and amplifies the original propaganda narrative.

4.11.8 Languages

English.

4.11.9 Effectiveness

It is difficult to assess the effectiveness, but since the Kremlin sought to distort and undermine Finland's foreign policy, it can be assumed that this message at least distorted Stubb's position and possibly complicated consistent and sovereign foreign policymaking.

4.11.10 Countermeasures

Open and balanced communication (Finnish Broadcasting Company, Yle), Finland's strong "own story" born of free social debate.

4.11.11 Conclusions and Recommendations

People in high positions, such as heads of state and other high-profile figures, are particularly vulnerable to hostile influence operations. These operations can take many forms, including misinformation, disinformation and other tactics aimed at manipulating public perception and decision-making processes. The susceptibility of these individuals to such operations poses significant risks not only to their personal reputations but also to national security and public trust. Therefore, it is crucial to recognise and address the unique challenges faced by those in influential positions to mitigate the potential impact of these hostile actions.

To counter possible information operations, it is essential for heads of state and other high-profile figures to implement comprehensive strategies focused on media and information protection. This includes regular training on recognising and responding to misinformation, establishing clear communication channels and leveraging technology to detect and counteract hostile influence efforts. Additionally, societies should establish institutional support systems dedicated to protecting individuals of high relevance. These systems could provide resources, expertise and coordinated efforts to safeguard against information threats, thereby enhancing the overall resilience of both individuals and the broader community.

4.12 Russia Today (RT), Its Narratives and Ideological Biases

4.12.1 Introduction

The Russian government stands as a prominent threat actor in the realm of international media influence. Of its main weapons of foreign interference, RT has been the one with the widest reach and the greatest impact. Initially, the inception of the RT channel in 2005 reflected the government's aspiration to wield soft power tools abroad. With a mission to propagate a positive portrayal of Russia—especially after the Second Chechen War—and its associated cultural values and foreign policies, RT entered the global media landscape. However, its scope shifted drastically following the outbreak of the Russian war in Georgia in 2008. The failure to sway Western audiences towards endorsing Russia's actions in Georgia compelled RT to pivot from a nuanced soft power approach to overt war propaganda tactics.[295]

This case study analyses RT as a channel, a disinformation weapon used by the Kremlin in its campaign against the West. The underlying logic of RT's first mission was aligned with the Kremlin's goals of cultural and national dignification. The Kremlin felt that Russia had faced international disdain for several years, even from countries that were once considered its allies. RT has continued its efforts

[295] Shekhovtsov, Anton, "Introduction: RT from Soft Power to Political Warfare", in Anton Shekhovtsov (ed.), *RT in Europe and beyond. The Wannabe Elite of the Anti-Elites*, The Centre for Democratic Integrity, 2022, pp. 4–10. https://democratic-integrity.eu/rt-in-europe-and-beyond/.

to restore this lost dignity to Russia by offering an idealised interpretation of its history and, notably, by highlighting and exaggerating the principal contradictions of the West.[296] Like other television stations with close ties to the state apparatuses of their respective countries, as in the case of Tele Sur in Venezuela or Press TV in Iran, RT presents a dichotomous view of international relations. Russia, like these other countries, has positioned itself as part of a loose coalition of nations that have been victims of the hegemony of the West and, specifically, of the United States.

RT's power of seduction primarily lies in its ability to present itself as an "anti-hegemonic" and "alternative" television network. While Western audiences still lacked a clear understanding of Russia and the authoritarian tendencies of its government, and a significant portion of the Western public had begun to harbour distrust toward its own institutions and political leaders, RT succeeded in establishing itself as an important reference within the West's dissident sectors. RT continues to provide a representation of reality that challenges the version of reality presented by Western mainstream media. Experts emphasise RT's capacity to impose its own agenda as a FIMI actor, but also its ability to amplify the contradictions and most divisive debates within Western societies.[297] RT has attempted to erode public debate in several Western countries, giving voice to numerous individuals and organisations that have challenged the basis of political dialogue, fostering a climate of cynicism, apoliticism and distrust. For RT, the Western media are equally propaganda vectors, an argument that uses a "we all play the same game" logic to place both RT and Western media on the same level. In the worst cases, both RT and some of its external supporters have employed an extreme relativism that declares the existence of "different truths".[298]

RT has effectively promoted an anti-elite and populist perspective, injecting "the elite vs. the people" arguments into the public discourse when reporting on social movements, notably the Yellow Vests in France or the Catalan independence movement in Spain. At the international level, RT has transformed such arguments into "the West vs. the people". Moreover, RT has aligned itself with the emergence of various movements and parties that have embraced anti-hegemonic ideologies or are undergoing populist phases within their respective countries. However, some analysts[299] appear to fall into a common pitfall often encountered in the study of

[296] Schmitt, O., "How to challenge an international order: Russian diplomatic practices in multilateral security organisations", *European Journal of International Relations*, Vol. 26, No. 3, 2020, pp. 922–946.
[297] Laruelle, Marlene, "Russian and American Far Right Connections: Confluence, Not Influence", Ponars Eurasia, 12 Mar 2018. https://www.ponarseurasia.org/russian-and-american-far-right-connections-confluence-not-influence/.
[298] Audinet, Maxime, "Russia Today (RT), un média d'influence au service de l'Etat russe: la télé qui venait du froid", *Le Monde*, 7 Nov 2021. https://www.lemonde.fr/idees/article/2021/11/17/russia-today-rt-un-media-d-influence-au-service-de-l-etat-russe-la-tele-qui-venait-du-froid_6102344_3232.html.
[299] Shekhovtsov, Anton (ed.), *RT in Europe and beyond. The Wannabe Elite of the Anti-Elites,* The Centre for Democratic Integrity, 2022. https://democratic-integrity.eu/rt-in-europe-and-beyond/.

populism, by using this term as meaning "demagoguery". This conflation suggests that RT's objective is merely to play on its audience's fears that the elite is corrupt and indifferent to the struggles of the working class. However, RT capitalises on a variety of pre-existing sentiments. Portraying "the people" as a passive and easily manipulated entity without any agency may reinforce the elitist narrative that RT exploits, but that is merely one of its narratives.

This is closely intertwined with the issue of dissent, as highlighted in the title of Elie Guckert's report, "Manufacturing Dissent".[300] Drawing on concepts introduced in the 1988 book *Manufacturing Consent: The Political Economy of the Mass Media* by Noam Chomsky and Edward S. Herman, Guckert suggests that RT "attempted to dismantle any remaining democratic consensus by fueling controversies". However, Guckert overlooks the fact that dissent is a natural facet of pluralistic societies. Our democratic systems are obliged to respect diverse viewpoints that often fail to converge. The ability of RT to exploit this situation stems from each society's challenge in reconciling its own inherent contradictions. Thus, rather than manufacturing dissent, RT capitalises on it.

Anton Shekhovtsov states that "RT's earnings would be measured in impact rather than in rubles". Nevertheless, RT provided positive coverage of the Sputnik V vaccine on its RT en Español channel at a time when Russia intended to sell the vaccine in several Latin American countries. Similarly, RT's broadcasts in French and German gave a lot of visibility to both scientists who proposed alternative treatments without scientific validity as well as conspiracy movements, such as Querdenken in Germany. As in this case, the economic interests behind any FIMI operation should not be underestimated. RT is not just an instrument of war propaganda: it is used by Russia to target the information space of the West, but also its economic stability, exploiting both for its own benefit.

Throughout its almost 20 years of existence, RT has evolved by adapting to new information technologies and the new media context. Increased hostilities on the part of the Kremlin's foreign policy have impelled RT to harden its editorial line. First conceived as a mere tool of Russian soft power, RT has developed over the years into a relatively sophisticated weapon of disinformation. Since the invasion of Ukraine in February 2022, RT has not only demonised the Ukrainian government and the Ukrainian population, but also has promoted genocidal discourses. RT's director of broadcasting, Anton Krasovsky, even suggested "drowning Ukrainian children, setting Ukrainian homes on fire—with the inhabitants inside—and alleged that Ukrainian grandmothers would gladly pay to be raped by Russian soldiers".[301]

---

[300] Guckert, É., "Manufacturing Dissent: RT France's Challenge in a Brand-New Media Landscape", in Anton Shekhovtsov (ed.), *RT in Europe and beyond*, Centre for Democratic Integrity, 2022, pp. 42–53.

[301] Davis, Julia, "'Morality Shouldn't Get in the Way'—Russia's Genocidal State Media", CEPA, 13 Mar 2023. https://cepa.org/article/morality-shouldnt-get-in-the-way-russias-genocidal-state-media/. The Center for European Policy Analysis (CEPA) describes itself as a non-profit,

4.12.2 Threat Actors

The Russian government.

Rospechat (Роспеч´ать): the Federal Agency for Press and Mass Communications was in charge of financing 99.5% of RT's budget in 2021. Prior to the invasion of Ukraine in 2022, the remaining funding came from social networks such as YouTube.[302]

Roskomnadzor (Роскомнадзор): since its conception until 2017, the Federal Service for Supervision of Communications, Information Technology and Mass Media, or Roskomnadzor, has led RT through RIA Novosti, the international news agency, also owned by the Russian state.[303]

4.12.3 Presumed Objectives

RT aims to facilitate state propaganda, while attempting to appear credible by being ineloquent about Russia. Taking the observables mentioned in the next section into account, we can see how the campaign conducted by the Russian government through RT tried to accomplish many of the objectives identified in the DISARM Framework:

T0002: Facilitate state propaganda—In order to appear credible, RT does not represent Russia in such an eloquent way, although it avoids dealing with Russian political news. If it does, it never does so in a negative, but in a conciliatory way.

T0066: Degrade adversary—One of RT's main strategies is to portray Western democracies as hypocritical, decadent and highly unstable systems.[304]

T0075.001: Discredit credible sources—The main strategy of alternative media is not so much to provide reliable information, but to provide an alternative version of their competitors who are associated with the mainstream or hegemonic culture. This strategy necessarily requires the disqualification of those media, who may have their biases, but are reliable sources.[305]

T0075: Dismiss—RT frequently responds to criticism from mainstream journalism, as well as attacks by Western democracies on Russia, by resorting to

non-partisan, public policy institution headquartered in Washington, DC, with hubs in London and Brussels.

302 Audinet, Maxime, *Russia Today (RT): un média d'influence au service de l'État russe*, INA, 2021. https://www.inatheque.fr/publications-evenements/publications-2024/un-media-d-influence-d-etat-enquete-sur-la-chaine-russe-rt-maxime-audinet.html.

303 Ibid.

304 Andreae, J., "The Information War of RT DE", in Anton Shekhovtsov (ed.), *RT in Europe and beyond*, Centre for Democratic Integrity, 2022, pp. 68–78.

305 Audinet, op. cit., 2021.

whataboutism, i.e., "Discredit an opponent's position by charging them with hypocrisy without directly disproving their argument."[306]

T0076: Distort—RT has questioned the official version of several events and historical facts, even relying on conspiracy theorists. RT has not hesitated to spread conspiracy theories on several occasions related to 9/11.[307] Without going that far, the occupation of Abkhazia and South Ossetia in Georgia or the annexation of Crimea were presented with a completely different version of the attacked country.[308]

T0077: Distract—The objective of what some researchers describe as "new propaganda" is not necessarily to convince or persuade, but to distract and keep the viewer hooked.[309]

T0079: Divide—The Kremlin exploits divisive scenarios, so RT promotes polarisation in the countries where it intervenes.[310]

T0023.001: Reframe context—Although reframing the context is not a disinformative act per se, RT resorts to this tactic to interpret reality in its favour.

T0075.001: Discredit credible sources—To impose its framework, RT constantly questions and denounces the hypocrisy of mainstream media reporting.

TA11: Persist in the information environment—RT sought to establish its presence in the media landscape of various countries, but the Russian aggression in Ukraine in 2022 has significantly hindered these efforts.

4.12.4 Incidents and Observables

RT has covered several events of great relevance, making its own biased interpretation, in line with the interests of the Kremlin, or even manipulating the facts. Here are some examples:

Maidan Protests: After portraying the 2014 Maidan protests as a movement led by the Ukrainian far right, the Kremlin instrumentalised RT to defend Russia's position and demonise Ukraine.[311]

Catalonia's Independence Movement: This movement was amplified by RT with the aim of fomenting instability in Spain. RT applied a similar framework to that

---

306 Richter, Monika L., "The Kremlin's platform for 'useful idiots' in the West: An overview of RT's editorial strategy and evidence of impact", *European Values,* 2017.

307 Van Herpen, Marcel H., *Putin's propaganda machine: Soft power and Russian foreign policy*, Rowman & Littlefield, Maryland, 2015.

308 Ibid.

309 Pomerantsev, Peter, and Michael Weiss, "The menace of unreality: How the Kremlin weaponizes information, culture and money", *Institute of Modern Russia,* 2014.

310 Ibid.

311 Elswah, Mona, and Philip N. Howard, "'Anything that causes chaos': The organizational behavior of RT (RT)", *Journal of Communication*, Vol. 70, No. 5, 2020, pp. 623-645. https://academic.oup.com/joc/article/70/5/623/5912109.

of other pro-independence movements where Russia is portrayed as the defender of secessionist ethnic minorities, as in the case of Abkhazia and South Ossetia in Georgia, or the Donbas in Ukraine. At the same time, Russia uses this situation to attribute a reactionary and extreme right-wing ideology to the central governments from which the minorities want to secede.[312]

The **Yellow Vests Movement**: RT widely covered this wave of anti-establishment social protest. The Yellow Vests took a stand against the French political class, unions and hegemonic media.[313] In this context, an "alternative" media like RT had a favourable image in the eyes of the protesters.[314] Since a large part of the Yellow Vests' activity was taking place on Facebook and RT was mainly broadcasting from there, synergies emerged and representatives of the movement were interviewed in their programs.[315]

The **COVID-19 Pandemic**: RT's coverage of the pandemic was uneven. While in Russia, people who agreed to be vaccinated were treated as patriots, sceptics who questioned the effectiveness of the vaccines in Europe were portrayed as heroes.[316] RT reported the anti-vaccine protests in countries such as France and Germany. Members of the Yellow Vests in France and the Querdenken movement in Germany[317] led large sections of these demonstrations. RT put the spotlight on these movements to present them as legitimate dissidents.

---

[312] Vakarchuk, Katerina, "The Impact of the Media on the Catalonia Referendum", *Rhetoric and Communications*, Issue 43, April 2020. https://rhetoric.bg/wp-content/uploads/2020/06/Vakarchuk-issue-April-2020-pp. 83–95.pdf.

[313] Gérard, Colin, Guilhem Marotte and Loqman Salamatian, "RT, Sputnik et le mouvement des Gilets jaunes: cartographie des communautés politiques sur Twitter", *L'Espace Politique. Revue en ligne de géographie politique et de géopolitique*, Vol. 40, 2020. https://journals.openedition.org/espacepolitique/8092.

[314] Libération, "L'un des objectifs de RT est de démontrer que le débat public en France est une espèce de cacophonie". https://www.liberation.fr/economie/medias/lun-des-objectifs-de-rt-est-de-demontrer-que-le-debat-public-en-france-est-une-espece-de-cacophonie-20220209_4V3POXPY4NFOZN26UI5SMEKR6M/.

[315] Audinet, Maxime, "Gilets jaunes et RT France, une histoire d'opportunisme", interviewé par Audrey Kucinskas pour.

l'Express, IFRI, 10 Jan 2019. https://www.ifri.org/fr/espace-media/lifri-medias/gilets-jaunes-rt-france-une-histoire-dopportunisme.

[316] Yatsyk, Alexandra, "Biopolitical responses to the COVID-19 pandemic in Russia, France, Germany, and the UK: The "post-truth" coverage by RT", *Social Sciences*, Vol. 11, No. 3, Mar 2022. https://doaj.org/article/ce7004dee48b4e339110d38bd12beb5d.

[317] An umbrella movement born in 2020 during the COVID-19 pandemic. The Querdenken (lit. 'literal thinking') movement harboured conspiracy theorists and far-right activists. See Weisskircher, Manès, "Far-Right Parties and Divisions over Movement-party Strategy: The AfD and the Anti-Corona Protests of Querdenken", in Manès Weisskircher (ed.), *Contemporary Germany and the Fourth Wave of Far-Right Politics*, Routledge, 2024, pp. 159–173.

4.12.5 Observables

The disinformation and propaganda campaign orchestrated by RT has lasted almost two decades. The observables that this medium at the service of the Kremlin has been able to use throughout these years are of great variety. Although RT was founded as a television channel, it is primarily present on the social media pages of various social movements. It has earned a good reputation among participants in protest movements such as those above. These protests have provided RT videos with a high potential to go viral, full of violence between protesters and police, allowing their content to be massively disseminated on social media.[318]

While movements critical of hegemonic media kicked mainstream journalists out of the demonstrations, RT correspondents were welcome. Many of its most iconic journalists who have worked or work for RT, such as Inna Afigenova or Helena Villar[319] for RT en Español, have managed to establish a more direct relationship with their audiences through their X (Twitter) accounts, creating a personalised link with the media. On other social networks such as Telegram, Afinogenova also has a significant following, close to 95,000 subscribers.

4.12.6 Targets

The targets of influence encompass audiences who either identify themselves or are identified as opposing the prevailing hegemonic and establishment consensus. These audiences include not only individuals but also governments, political organisations and social movements that align with anti-establishment sentiments. More broadly, anti-hegemonic media address "the people" through a populist rhetoric. RT's populism has been described as "thin ideology",[320] i.e., a set of ideas and political practices that do not provide a comprehensive and coherent vision of things and, therefore, needs to cohabit with more solid or "thick" ideologies. While conservatism, liberalism or socialism are usually associated with the group of thick ideologies, thin ideologies are associated with nationalism or populism. Cas Mudde interprets populism as an ideology that simplifies the composition of society; this thin ideology depicts social bodies as fundamentally structured around

[318] Examples: A Facebook link to a violent RT video of the Yellow Vests movement: https://fb.watch/uxnNZ9_6eT/. See also X accounts of Inna Afinogenova and Helena Villar: https://x.com/inafinogenova, https://x.com/HelenaVillarRT. And the Telegram account of Afinogenova: https://t.me/inafinogenova.

[319] X account of Helena Villar. https://x.com/HelenaVillarRT.

[320] Mudde, Cas, and Cristóbal Rovira Kaltwasser, *Populism: A very short introduction*, Oxford University Press, Oxford, 2017. See also, Cas Mudde: "Populism is a thin-centered ideology", Trentino, 31 May 2019. https://www.ufficiostampa.provincia.tn.it/Comunicati/Cas-Mudde-Populism-is-a-thin-centered-ide.

two opposing groups: the people and the elite.[321] The representation of the people may not take into account its various social markers—in terms of class, race, gender, etc—and it is sometimes portrayed as a national and sovereign entity in its purest form, i.e., immaculate and innocent.[322] The elite are essentially embodied in some sectors of the political class, portrayed as negligent and corrupt technocrats, but also entrepreneurs, cultural elites and intellectuals responsible for setting the moral standards of a given society, for instance, in the domains of social values or ecology. Political organisations opposing establishment parties, allegedly representing the will of the people, are also characterised as populists, without taking into consideration their ideology. In fact, they actively seek to avoid being associated with a particular political orientation, by trying to be seen as "neither left, nor right".

Within the realm of geopolitics, countries opposing Western hegemony will locate this division in the realm of international relations, associating the "world elite" with the United States and Europe, and countries like China, Russia or Iran with "the peoples" of the world. Only by applying this fluid framework can we comprehend that within RT's ideological spectrum, there exists support for Bolivarian governments in Latin America, populist left-wing movements in Europe or far right parties such as the Rassemblement National (National Rally) in France. Populism engenders significant ideological ambiguity, which can benefit actors seeking to amplify anti-democratic narratives. By relaying on populist discourses, RT poses a threat to democracy within the European Union and abroad.

4.12.7 Tactics, Techniques and Procedures

RT not only uses speech to manipulate its audiences; on some occasions, it has resorted to false witnesses, as in the case of the fake Spanish air traffic controller who attempted to refute the theory of the downing of Malaysia Airlines flight MH17 by the Russian army in July 2014.[323]

RT's area of influence and reputation were for a time considerable, allowing it to attract prestigious political figures and intellectuals to its broadcasts. However, no direct relationship can be established between them and the Kremlin. To understand the essence of these politicians and intellectuals, journalist Daniel Iriarte uses the concept of "RT's fellow travellers"—close to that of "useful idiots".[324] These

321 Ibid.

322 Ibid.

323 Iriarte, D., "RT en Español: How Russian Disinformation Targets 500 Million Spanish Speakers", in Anton Shekhovtsov (ed.), *RT in Europe and beyond*, Centre for Democratic Integrity, 2022, pp. 14-25.

324 Richter, Monika L., "The Kremlin's platform for 'useful idiots' in the West: An overview of RT's editorial strategy and evidence of impact", *European Values*, 18 Sept 2017. https://mronline.org/wp-content/uploads/2017/12/Overview-of-RTs-Editorial-Strategy-and-Evidence-of-Impact-1.pdf.

figures are of great importance as they help to give the outlet an image of seriousness, to legitimise its message and to attract its audiences to RT's content. RT has occasionally collaborated with prominent figures outside the Russian sphere of influence who enjoy significant public notoriety. This includes intellectuals such as Slavoj Žižek, Nobel Peace Prize winner Rigoberta Menchú and American filmmaker Oliver Stone. Apart from well-known personalities,[325] FIMI carried by RT is not merely a single-actor endeavour; it is surrounded by diverse peripheral *compagnons de route*. Many of RT's subsidiaries in French, Spanish or German have few Russian workers on their staff, except in high-level positions. RT has a desire to establish a coherent presence in the local context it intends to address by hiring native workers.

With the aim of having its audience internalise a particular narrative, RT employs not only plain ideological or political discourse but also humour and irony.[326] The use of conspiracy theories is equally widespread in RT discourse. However, experts fall into the mistake of viewing these theories as a way to "help to explain the complicated reality around us".[327] In fact, conspiracy theories are far from providing a simple explanation of reality. Although most of the time they are fundamentally counterproductive to articulating a just revindication, conspiracism emerges as a mystified criticism of a certain order, whether legitimate or not.

4.12.8 Channels

RT has been able to use its broadcast channels in an inventive way, effectively combining the work of a media outlet with a prolific activity on social media. Official communication channels also supported RT's activity, disseminating it through government accounts or diplomatic services on social networks. RT has functioned de facto as a tool of Kremlin propaganda, especially since 2008. Other state-linked channels such as Sputnik News, the Russian information agency also linked to the Kremlin, operates as a key support for RT's interference abroad.

4.12.9 Language

RT broadcasts its content in English, French, Spanish, German and Arabic.

---

[325] Shekhovtsov, op. cit.

[326] Crilley, Rhys, and Precious N. Chatterje-Doody, "From Russia with Lols: Humour, RT, and the legitimation of Russian foreign policy", *Global Society*, Vol. 35, No. 1, Nov 2020, pp. 269-288. https://www.researchgate.net/publication/347308802_From_Russia_with_Lols_Humour_RT_and_the_Legitimation_of_Russian_Foreign_Policy.

[327] Yablokov, I., and P. Chatterje-Doody, "RT and Conspiracy Theories: "The Kremlin's Underdog" against the West", in Shekhovtsov, op. cit., pp. 98–106.

4.12.10 Effectiveness

Establishing a cause-effect correlation regarding FIMI is complex. However, experts affirm, for example, that RT en Español played a key role in "the amplification of Catalonia's pro-independence movement in the last months of 2017".[328] Something similar has occurred with numerous social protests in various countries in Latin America: although Russia cannot be accused of encouraging the riots, RT is always involved in their broadcast and dissemination.

The report also concludes that there was an important convergence between RT France and the Yellow Vest protests. In fact, RT France's audience increased exponentially during the Yellow Vest movement, primarily in visits to its website and YouTube channel. The video news Ruptly platform, sponsored by RT DE in Germany, provided extensive dissemination of far-right and conspiracy movements such as Pegida and Querdenken.[329] It remains to be determined whether the affinity between anti-establishment movements and RT improves the perception of both.

4.12.11 Countermeasures

Much of the disinformation spread by RT has been debunked. The ideological biases with which it treats information, such as its denunciation of police violence in Europe, have been contrasted with the hypocrisy exhibited by Russia within its own borders and abroad. Following the Russian invasion of Ukraine in 2022, RT and other Kremlin-affiliated media outlets have faced suspensions in Europe. Many of their websites and social media accounts have been censored. It is still possible to access RT content in Europe through secondary routes or alternative platforms such as Odysee.[330] However, RT's capabilities have been severely affected by the sanctions, leading some of its subsidiaries, such as RT France, to close.

Years after the first aggression against Ukraine in 2014, the censorship of the Russian media was under debate. After the Ukrainian government censored even the social network VK and the search engine Yandex in 2017, some voices warned of the danger of playing into the Kremlin's game.[331] Following the European Commission's suspension of RT in March 2022, several media organisations again criticised RT's censorship, this time on an international scale. However,

[328] Iriarte, D., "RT en Español: How Russian Disinformation Targets 500 Million Spanish Speakers", in Shekhovtsov, op. cit., pp. 14–25.

[329] Born in 2014, Pegida is an islamophobic and populist right-wing movement that contributed to a radicalisation of political language in Germany. See: Vorländer, Hans, Maik Heroldand and Steven Schäller, *PEGIDA and new right-wing populism in Germany*, Palgrave Macmillan, Basingstoke, 2018.

[330] Tuhina, Gjeraqina, "Two Years Into EU Ban, Russia's RT And Sputnik Are Still Accessible Across The EU", Radio Free Europe/Radio Liberty, 3 Feb 2024. https://www.rferl.org/a/russia-rt-sputnik-eu-access-bans-propaganda-ukraine-war/32803929.html.

[331] Jeangène Vilmer, Jean-Baptiste, "La lutte contre la désinformation russe: contrer la propagande sans faire de contre-propagande?", *Revue Défense Nationale,* Vol. 6, 2017, pp. 93–105.

demographic studies show that respondents' perceptions of the Commission's decision are not entirely negative, having even strengthened their confidence in the European institutions.[332]

4.12.12 Conclusions and Recommendations

Academic literature advocates two recommendations to tackle disinformation: empowering individuals to differentiate false content from the real one and controlling the platforms that allow the dissemination of fake news.[333] In the case of RT, the second measure has proven to be largely ineffective. Although the media outlet's content has been extensively censored from major social networks, as well as from several search engines, its content is still available online. Therefore, it seems that the most useful option is to provide people with tools so that they can make a rigorous judgment of the information they may encounter on the Internet.

Sometimes, the best way to defend oneself is transparency, effective communication and the use of counter-narratives that assume the part of truth that may exist in the discourses coming from antagonistic actors of the European Union. Providing EU citizens with discursive elements so that they can evaluate different situations linked to disinformation, relying on their maturity, is one of the best leverages. This implies being self-critical and taking seriously the relationship of trust between the European institutions and the societies of the different Member States. If trust deteriorates, victims of disinformation may not begin to believe the content of a given FIMI incident, but they will equally distrust the counter-narratives of the European institutions.

4.13 A Wagner Campaign Targeting the French Army in Mali

4.13.1 Introduction

In March 2022, a massacre in Mora, southern Mali, perpetrated by the Malian army and the Wagner Group, heightened sensitivity among the Malian population to narratives surrounding events related to mass killings.[334] The massacre occurred in the context of the Malian civil war that broke out in 2012 due to the weakening of the Malian state and the emergence of several jihadist groups in the north of

[332] Ibid.

[333] Lazer, David M.J., Matthew A. Baum, Yochai Benkler, et al., "The science of fake news", *Science*, 2018, Vol. 359, No. 6380, 2018, pp. 1094–1096.

[334] A group associated with jihadism is defined as "an organisation determined to resort to violence to establish a religious State or caliphate in a given territory, aiming to impose a fundamentalist and ultraconservative version of Islamic law (Shari'a)." See Namaïwa, B, "Le djihadisme au Sahel: enjeux et perspectives", *Africa Development*, Vol. 42, No. 3, 2017, pp. 197–217.

the country. Since 2013, the Malian government has been fighting jihadism in the area, with Jama'at Nasr al-Islam wal Muslimin[335] being the most relevant jihadist organisation since 2017. Although the French military backed the Malian government from the beginning of hostilities, due to a deterioration in their relations in recent years, the government started relying on the Russian private military contractor, the Wagner Group. Human Rights Watch reported that Malian armed forces and foreign soldiers allegedly executed around 300 civilian men.[336] Immediately following the massacre, the Russian Ministry of Foreign Affairs denied the accusations.[337] When France proposed at the United Nations Security Council the need to clarify the events, both Russia and China rejected the initiative.

To ease the burden of the accusations and divert attention, alleged Malian pro-government accounts on Twitter started spreading disinformation about the French army, which found itself embroiled in allegations of war crimes in the vicinity of the Gossi base. False testimonies about the massacre began to circulate in April 2022, when the French army was preparing to transfer the Gossi base to the Malian army, within the framework of the Barkhane operation.[338] The involvement of the Wagner Group in this incident appeared to be aimed at weakening France's position in the region while bolstering Russian influence in Mali. The objective was not only to discredit France but also to solidify Russia's presence as a more reliable ally for the Malian government. A Russian troll linked to Wagner, hiding behind the Malian-looking account @DiaDiarra6, posted "a video showing lifeless bodies near the Gossi base".

In response, France released a series of drone images to counter these claims, revealing the involvement of Wagner Group mercenaries in the atrocities. As the Malian Armed Forces (FAMa) had previously accused France of acts of violence

---

[335] Jama'at Nasr al-Islam wal Muslimin (JNIM) is a jihadist group operating primarily in northern Mali and southeastern Burkina Faso. Formed in 2017 as a coalition of several extremist factions, including Al-Qaeda in the Islamic Maghreb (AQIM), JNIM has become one of the most dominant militant groups in the Sahel region. It is responsible for 64% of the violent acts recorded in this area, engaging in attacks against military forces, civilians and foreign entities. See Appiah Afriyie, Frederick, "Weaving through the maze of terrorist marriages in Africa's Sahel region: Jama'at Nasr al-Islam wal Muslimin (JNIM) under review", *Cogent Social Sciences*, Vol 10 No. 1, 2024, p. 2,347,011.

[336] Human Rights Watch, "Mali: Massacre by Army, Foreign Soldiers", 5 Apr 2022. https://www.hrw.org/news/2022/04/05/mali-massacre-army-foreign-soldiers.

[337] AFP, "Moscow hails Mali 'victory' after Moura operation", Al Arabiya News, 22 Apr 2022. https://english.alarabiya.net/News/world/2022/04/08/Moscow-hails-Mali-victory-after-Moura-operation.

[338] Operation Barkhane was a French army initiative to combat jihadism in northern Mali. Some saw the French army's presence in the region as an attempt to maintain a neo-colonial influence over the country and to secure its interests.

and other similar actions,[339] the French armed forces were expecting an informational attack, so they decided to monitor the area with an aerial captor. This allowed them to film the Wagner Group mercenaries setting the stage and recording the images that would later be at the centre of the accusations against the French army.

The footage also proved that Malian forces were involved in this disinformation incident. The images showed Malian military vehicles transporting members of the Wagner Group.[340] Thus, to maintain credibility, the Malian junta retaliated by accusing the French army of having fabricated the images. They were also accused of subversion and espionage, alleging unauthorised flyovers of the area. Colonel Pascal Ianni, spokesperson for the army general staff, refuted these allegations, asserting that the French army had indeed obtained permission for aerial reconnaissance activities in the region. To support his version, Colonel Ianni released an official letter from the Malian Air Force, granting the French army the right to fly over the zone.[341]

After the confrontation between the French and Malian armed forces, the United Nations Multidimensional Integrated Stabilization Mission in Mali (MINUSMA) released a declaration supporting the French version of the events. According to the MINUSMA, the remains buried at Gossi were placed in the site on 20 April, the day after the camp was returned to the Malians and came from Hombori.[342] The day before, on 19 April, the Malian Army and the Wagner Group had committed another massacre in the city of Hombori, 90 kms southwest of Gossi.[343] The Malian authorities did not react to the note published by the MINUSMA, which months later was compelled to abandon its mission in Mali.

The FIMI attack started from 20 April, when the account @DiaDiarra6 published a first tweet stating that "the images of corpses from the Gossi base are terrible".[344] From this moment on, this account published several more tweets, among which appeared the recordings of the grave. The attack subsided when the French army released the images it had recorded with a surveillance drone, which showed mercenaries of the Wagner Group burying the corpses.

[339] Malibeaux, Sophie, and Grégory Genevrier, "À Gossi, mise en scène d'un charnier pour discréditer l'armée française", RFI, 22 April 2022. https://www.rfi.fr/fr/podcasts/les-dessous-de-l-infox-la-chronique/20220422-%C3%A0-gossi-mise-en-sc%C3%A8ne-d-un-charnier-pour-discr%C3%A9diter-l-arm%C3%A9e-fran%C3%A7aise.

[340] Source: France 24 on Twitter.

[341] Malibeaux and Genevrier, op. cit., 22 April 2022.

[342] Jeune Afrique, "Tuerie de Hombori au Mali: les conclusions de l'enquête de la Minusma", 2 Sept 2022. https://www.jeuneafrique.com/1374044/politique/tuerie-de-hombori-au-mali-les-conclusions-de-lenquete-de-la-minusma/.

[343] Reuters, "UN says 50 civilians killed in April by Mali's army", *The Guardian*, 31 Aug 2022. https://www.theguardian.com/world/2022/aug/31/un-says-50-civilians-killed-in-april-by-malis-army.

[344] X.https://x.com/IHEDN/status/1748601137702240476.

4.13.2 Threat Actors

The images provided by the French Army point to the Malian junta and the Wagner Group as the responsible actors behind the FIMI. The Malian junta represents the government formed after the coup d'état of May 2021 by a faction of the National Committee for the Salvation of the People (CNSP), a rebellious group of the Malian army that previously seized power through another coup in 2020. Its leader, Assimi Goïta, who has ruled the country since May 2021, has strengthened the relations between Mali and the Russian Federation. This enhanced cooperation included the sending of humanitarian aid and military reinforcements from the Wagner Group to combat jihadist terrorism in the country.[345] According to the Opposition leader Oumar Mariko, in exile since 2022, there is evidence to suggest that the CNSP and the Wagner Group committed several massacres against civilians as part of the war against jihadism in the north of the country.[346]

The Wagner Group was a private military company (PMC) linked to the Kremlin.[347] Apart from Mali, Wagner had a presence in several African countries, including Libya, Central African Republic (CAR) and Mozambique.[348] Its role in these countries ranged from providing security services to actors sympathetic to Russia, military training to local forces and supervision of Russian mining activities in the region.[349]

4.13.3 Presumed Objectives

This FIMI attack was launched to meet several objectives:

T0002: Facilitate state propaganda—Since it seized power, the government of Assimi Goïta has pursued a policy of confrontation towards France. Colonel Goïta has become the symbol of resistance to French influence and calls out the former's neo-colonialism.[350] This discourse has also been reinforced by the resentment of

---

[345] Audinet, Maxime, and Colin Gérard, "Les «libérateurs»: comment la «galaxie Prigojine» raconte la chevauchée du groupe Wagner au Sahel", *Le Rubicon*, 15 Feb 2022. https://lerubicon.org/la-galaxie-prigojine-promoteur-de-wagner-au-sahel/.

[346] König, Benjamin, "Au Mali, 'la chute d'Assimi Goïta ou le chaos'", *l'Humanité*, 7 Jan 2024. https://www.humanite.fr/monde/afrique/au-mali-la-chute-dassimi-goita-ou-le-chaos.

[347] Audinet, Maxime, and Kevin Limonier, "Le dispositif d'influence informationnelle de la Russie en Afrique subsaharienne francophone: un écosystème flexible et composite", *Questions de communication*, Vol. 41, 2022, pp. 129–148.

[348] Laruelle, Marlène, and Limonier, Kevin, "Beyond 'hybrid warfare': a digital exploration of Russia's entrepreneurs of influence", *Post-Soviet Affairs*, Vol. 37, No. 4, 2021, pp. 318–335.

[349] Audinet, Maxime, and Colin Gérard, "Les «libérateurs»: comment la «galaxie Prigojine» raconte la chevauchée du groupe Wagner au Sahel", *Le Rubicon*, 15 Feb 2022. https://lerubicon.org/la-galaxie-prigojine-promoteur-de-wagner-au-sahel/.

[350] Airault, Pascal, "Comment la junte malienne justifie sa rupture avec la France", *L'Opinion*, 16 Feb 2022. https://www.lopinion.fr/international/comment-la-junte-malienne-justifie-sa-rupture-avec-la-france. See also Glez, Damien, "Assimi Goïta et Kemi Seba: anti-français de tous les pays,

the local population towards France's colonial heritage, which had supported the military governments prior to the coup d'état.[351] At the same time, Russian President Vladimir Putin proclaimed from Moscow that Russia led an "anti-colonial movement against unipolar hegemony".[352] Since Russia behaves in Africa as an equally neo-colonial state and since the Goïta-controlled army together with the Wagner Group has been accused of committing numerous massacres in Mali, this narrative compensates for the hypocrisy of the propaganda of both governments.

T0066: Degrade adversary—This objective also serves the purpose of degrading the political credibility of the adversary. Accusing the army of a former colonial power of having committed war crimes pursued this objective.

T0077: Distract—Both threat actors tried to distract public opinion. Being in the media spotlight because of the accusations of war crimes against the junta and Wagner, the authors of the FIMI initiated the action to divert the scope and focus on the French army. Later, when the falsehood of the attack was discovered, the military junta tried again to distract attention, accusing France of espionage and having violated Mali's sovereign airspace.

4.13.4 Incidents and Observables

Alleged Malian pro-government accounts on Twitter started spreading disinformation in April 2022 about the French army, which found itself embroiled in allegations of war crimes in the vicinity of the Gossi base.

The observables in the FIMI attack are complex, unfolding in both the physical and digital realms. The first observable is the Twitter account @DiaDiarra6, whose profile picture turned out to be the same photograph as that of a Colombian VKontakt user called Alexander Murillo. This user had already been exposed as a disseminator of Russian propaganda. Prior to the FIMI attack, he changed his profile picture for an image of president Assimi Goïta.[353]

The second observable is the tweet of @DiaDiarra6 where he prepared the ground for the publication of the video that became the main proof of the accusations against the French army. After the tweet, the same account posted a video of a mass grave, which had been staged by the Wagner Group and the Malian Armed Forces (FAMa). According to the 31 August 2022 report of the MINUSMA, the bodies were transferred from another massacre perpetrated by both threat actors in a market in the town of Hombori, in retaliation for the death of a Russian soldier

unissez-vous!", *Jeune Afrique*, 9 May 2022. https://www.jeuneafrique.com/1344935/politique/assimi-goita-et-kemi-seba-anti-francais-de-tous-les-pays-unissez-vous/.

[351] Rosas, Paula, "Géopolitique: Comment la Russie remplace la France dans ses anciennes colonies d'Afrique", BBC News Mundo, 26 May 2023. https://www.bbc.com/afrique/region-65710817.

[352] Davidson, Miri, "Sea and Earth", *New Left Review*, 4 Apr 2024. https://newleftreview.org/sidecar/posts/sea-and-earth.

[353] Source: LinkedIn.

in a mine attack near the village.[354] Thanks to the images filmed by the French army drone, the falsity of the third observable, i.e., the video of the fake account, was established.

4.13.5 Targets

Although the FIMI was aimed primarily at the French army, specifically Operation Barkhane, the attack overall was aimed at damaging France's image. While Operation Barkhane's purpose was to combat jihadism in northern Mali, as noted above, some saw the French army's presence in the region as an attempt to maintain a neo-colonial influence over the country and to secure its interests.[355] For this reason, the French state, associated with Barkhane, has often been the target of such narratives.[356]

4.13.6 Tactics, Techniques and Procedures

Overall, Russia's tactic in the Sahel has been to become the partner of choice for African countries such as Mali, Burkina Faso, Niger and Libya in order to pursue its economic, diplomatic and military interests.[357]

TA16: Establish legitimacy—Through Wagner, Russia sought to assert its position as Mali's ally in the struggle against French neo-colonialism.

TA11: Persist in the information environment—Wagner was trying to consolidate its own narrative in the informational space conducting FIMI operations with the FAMa.

Russia's actions to accomplish this tactic were based on amplification of its anti-French and anti-Western propaganda in the region, relating all narratives to neo-colonialist grievances that the local population could experience and reshape in their own interests.[358]

---

[354] Baché, David, "Mali: un Russe tué à Hombori, les soldats ripostent dans la ville", RFI, 20 Apr 2022. https://www.rfi.fr/fr/afrique/20220420-mali-un-russe-tu%C3%A9-%C3%A0-hombori-les-soldats-ripostent-dans-la-ville.

[355] Idrissa, Rahmane, "Du sentiment antifrançais au Sahel", Rahmane.Substack, 22 Nov 2021. https://rahmane.substack.com/p/du-sentiment-antifrancais-au-sahel.

[356] AFP, "Sahel: la France perd le combat sur les réseaux sociaux", TV5 Monde, 14 Feb 2021. https://information.tv5monde.com/afrique/sahel-la-france-perd-le-combat-sur-les-reseaux-sociaux-36363.

[357] Minde, Nicodemus, "Africa Corps: la Russie fait-elle du neuf avec du vieux ?", ISS, 7 Mar 2024. https://issafrica.org/fr/iss-today/africa-corps-la-russie-fait-elle-du-neuf-avec-du-vieux.

[358] Roday, Miriam M., Sarah A. Daly and Rhett A. Moeller, "How Russian Disinformation Campaigns in Africa Are Manipulating Public Opinion and Eroding Western Influence", Institute for defense analyses, Apr 2022. https://apps.dtic.mil/sti/trecms/pdf/AD1211271.pdf.

TA14: Develop narratives—The FIMI attack sought to prevent Wagner and the junta from being blamed for the massacre, while criticising the presence and abuses of the French army in Mali.

TA06: Develop content—Wagner produced visual content in both video and image formats.

T0003: Leverage existing narratives—Wagner (and Russia) conveyed already existing anti-colonial sentiments.

T0023.001: Reframe context—Through the FIMI attack, Wagner and the FAMa were trying to blame the French army for the attacks they committed on the civilian population.

T0023: Distort facts—The dissemination of video images allowed Wagner and the FAMa to completely distort the facts.

TA05: Microtarget—The campaign was aimed at the pro-sovereignty segments of the Malian population.

T0102.003: Exploit data voids—The niche term "charnier" (mass grave) was in the middle of the disinformation campaign.

TA07: Select channels and affordances—A deliberate effort to obscure the connection between Russia and the disinformation campaign.

TA13: Target audience analysis: see TA05.

T0081: Identify social and technical vulnerabilities—The weaknesses identified related to France's colonial heritage in Mali.

T0086: Develop image-based content—Wagner even filmed a video featuring images staged in the physical realm.

T0129.002: Generate content unrelated to narrative—After the French army debunked Wagner's narrative, the junta came to their aid by accusing France of violating their airspace.

Although many African governments have their own agendas, independent of Russia, in recent years, the junta led by Asimi Goïta has aligned its interests with those of the Kremlin. The junta has supported the FIMI executed by the Wagner Group, mainly through official statements, confronting the French army even after French Colonel Pascal Ianni debunked the story of the mass grave in Gossi.

4.13.7 Channels

The main channel used by the threat actors was Twitter. Everything points to the fact that the account that disseminated the video to accuse the French army was a Russian troll, probably controlled by Wagner.[359] Video was the format of the central observable of the FIMI. The audio was also decisive in analysing the FIMI

[359] Malibeaux, Sophie, and Grégory Genevrier, "À Gossi, mise en scène d'un charnier pour discréditer l'armée française", RFI, 22 Apr 2022. https://www.rfi.fr/fr/podcasts/les-dessous-de-l-infox-la-chronique/20220422-%C3%A0-gossi-mise-en-sc%C3%A8ne-d-un-charnier-pour-discr%C3%A9diter-l-arm%C3%A9e-fran%C3%A7aise.

attack, since by identifying several voices in the background speaking Bambara, it was possible to infer that the Malian soldiers were also involved in the farce.[360]

4.13.8 Languages

The FIMI attack was conducted almost entirely in French, the *lingua franca* between Mali and France. Since Russian meddling operations are not characterised by a strong command of the language spoken by their targets, this may be an indication of the presence of FAMa in collaboration with the owners of the Russian troll @DiaDiarra6.

4.13.9 Effectiveness

Following the DISARM framework for evaluating the effectiveness of FIMI, it remains to be clarified to what extent the performance of the attack was positive. The screenshots of the tweets that currently have been deleted, along with the account that spread the disinformation, show a relatively low engagement rate. Considering that not many people have been exposed to this content, it is likely that the impact of the attack was limited. The disinformation shared had the potential to change the local population's behaviour and incentivised a certain climate of animosity against the French army and France. However, the swift reaction of the French army and the accusations of massacres already made against the Wagner Group and the Malian junta probably prevented the attack from spreading further. Thus, apart from propensity to share disinformation, reactions to posts and online comments, no remarkable behaviour was altered.

Regarding the potential harm that the FIMI created, it seems implausible that the attack developed new behaviours that were not already latent in the local population. The users who believed the story of the mass grave probably already had a certain opinion and perception of the French army. Due to the inefficiency of the attack and its violent background, the image of the Wagner Group, Russia and FAMa may have deteriorated.[361]

4.13.10 Countermeasures

The countermeasures taken by the French army seem to have largely avoided a major impact of the FIMI. The French army took the precaution of anticipating the

[360] Ibid.

[361] Doxsee, Catrina, and Jared Thompson, "Massacres, Executions, and Falsified Graves: The Wagner Group's Mounting Humanitarian Cost in Mali", Center for Strategic and International Studies, 11 May 2022. https://www.csis.org/analysis/massacres-executions-and-falsified-graves-wagner-groups-mounting-humanitarian-cost-mali.

attack, using drone surveillance to collect possible evidence from which structure its alibi. Then, having a basis on which to build its defence, the French army issued an official communiqué that enabled it to refute the accusations made against it. The statement of rebuttal was followed by public condemnation, as several media echoed the army's position. Twitter finally suspended the @DiaDiarra6 account. Days before the publication of the images by the French army, other Twitter users already accused @DiaDiarra6 of being a Russian troll.

In some posts, other users were invited to point to the account, with the goal of getting it banned. If this was the main cause of the account's deletion, we would be looking at a case study with a certain degree of decentralisation and horizontality in the fight against disinformation, meaning that the process of content removal can also rely on collective user actions and community-driven efforts rather than centralised or top-down interventions by platform authorities.

4.13.11 Conclusions and Recommendations

When a FIMI attack originates from the physical domain, the presence of field operatives becomes crucial. Preventive surveillance measures, like those implemented by the French army in this case, can play a decisive role in mitigating the impact of such attacks. The challenge here was not so much about dismantling a widespread narrative but rather about refuting a series of specific and targeted facts. Open-source intelligence (OSINT) proved especially valuable in identifying TTPs behind the FIMI.

To counter future FIMI attacks, stakeholders should invest in and enhance OSINT capabilities, particularly in detecting automated accounts and fake profiles. Analysing and tracing digital footprints, such as fake accounts and bots, OSINT becomes indispensable in countering these threats. Additionally, a coordinated effort between physical surveillance and digital intelligence gathering is essential to not only disrupt the tactics but also to prevent future dissemination of false information. Increased training in these areas for both military and civilian personnel involved in defence against FIMI attacks can further bolster these efforts.

4.14 Russia Uses Bribery to Spread Disinformation

4.14.1 Introduction

US intelligence reports have revealed that, since 2014, Russia has allocated more than $300 million to corrupt foreign politicians as part of its foreign information manipulation and interference initiatives.[362] These efforts aim to promote Russian narratives, advance malign activities within foreign political parties and exert influence abroad. The primary channels for these funds include Russian state-owned enterprises and purportedly independent expert organisations or analytical think tanks.[363]

While traditional corruption typically involves individuals seeking personal enrichment, strategic corruption takes on a different dimension. In this context, corruption serves as a tool wielded by foreign entities to achieve their own national objectives against target countries.[364] What sets this apart is the integration of corruption into a broader national strategy. Russia has innovatively weaponised corruption, turning what was once merely a domestic political issue into a potent instrument on the global stage. This weaponisation serves to achieve specific policy goals and shape the political landscape in targeted countries and its effectiveness lies in exploiting the inherent vulnerabilities of democratic systems.[365] Unlike non-democratic regimes, democratic nations' openness and freedom make them susceptible to such malign influence tactics, a weakness on which adversaries have adeptly capitalised.

Russian corruption campaigns take many forms and have taken place worldwide: from Latin America, where the Russian government is financing an ongoing and well-funded disinformation campaign,[366] to Germany where powerful former politicians, like Gerhard Schröder, still maintain influence to this day. Schröder holds a lucrative position on the board of Russian energy companies such as Rosneft.[367]

From providing a multi-million-euro loan to France's Front National party a decade ago, to Russian diplomats grooming rising stars in the AfD's youth wing,

---

[362] Wong, Edward, "Russia Secretly Gave $300 Million to Political Parties and Officials Worldwide, U.S. Says", *The New York Times*, 13 Sept 2022. https://www.nytimes.com/2022/09/13/us/politics/russia-election-interference.html.
[363] Ibid.
[364] Zelikow, Philip, Eric Edelman, Kristofer Harrison and Celeste Ward Gventer, "The Rise of Strategic Corruption: How States Weaponize Graft", *Foreign Affairs*, Vol. 99, 9 June 2020. https://www.foreignaffairs.com/articles/united-states/rise-strategic-corruption-weaponize-graft.
[365] Ibid.
[366] US Embassy in Honduras, "The Kremlin's Efforts to Covertly Spread Disinformation in Latin America", 7 Nov 2023. https://hn.usembassy.gov/the-kremlins-efforts-to-covertly-spread-disinformation-in-latin-america/.
[367] Solomon, Erika, "Gerhard Schröder Draws German Ire by Keeping Faith with Russia", *The Financial Times*, 28 Mar 2022. https://www.ft.com/content/b445d9b7-7c35-4f64-8bb5-d76a5393212f.

Moscow has long been extending its reach into European far right political circles receptive to its worldview.[368]

Most recently, Czech authorities have exposed a scheme involving the Voice of Europe, a pro-Russian website disseminating Kremlin propaganda and financing candidates in the 2024 European elections.[369] The site, which operates in 15 languages, raised suspicions with peculiarities such as awkward translations and the use of Cyrillic characters.[370] Funds amounting to hundreds of thousands of euro were allegedly transferred through cash transactions or cryptocurrency channels, under the oversight of Artem Marchevskyi, who has a connexion with Putin's Ukrainian associate Viktor Medvedchuk.[371]

While allegations of bribing European politicians lack concrete evidence of direct monetary transfers, the discovery of undisclosed financial transactions indirectly corroborates these claims, as evidenced by raids conducted in Poland.[372] Polish ABW special service officers seized €48,500 and $36,000 during searches in Warsaw and Tykocin.[373] These raids are linked to both the Voice of Europe case and allegations against a Polish citizen accused of espionage for Russia.[374]

This new Russian FIMI campaign involving bribery emerged less than three months away from the European Parliament elections in June 2024, highlighting that tackling dark Russian money in domestic politics is crucial to safeguard democracies and keep up their resolve to help Ukraine.

Whilst hard to pinpoint an exact date, Russia's use of strategic bribery for FIMI purposes in Europe can be traced back to 2014.[375] As the latest scandals have shown, their efforts are ongoing and escalate in times of elections. The current operation of the Voice of Europe began in 2023 and, especially the bribery aspect, has been halted to an extent, thanks to the intelligence operations that have shed light upon it. However, Russia's overall disinformation campaign continues through its social media, and other Russian FIMI campaigns such as Portal Kombat are still ongoing.[376] Portal Kombat was uncovered by French, German and Polish authorities in February 2024 and involved an automated network of 224

---

[368] Zoria, Yuri, "Russia Suspected of Funneling Funds to Germany's AfD Party for pro-Russian Messaging", Euromaidan Press, 31 Mar 2024. https://euromaidanpress.com/2024/03/31/russia-suspected-of-funneling-funds-to-germanys-afd-party-for-pro-russian-messaging/.

[369] Zoria, Yuri, "MEPs Call to Investigate Russia's Bribery of EU Politicians", Euromaidan Press, 31 Mar 2024. https://euromaidanpress.com/2024/03/31/meps-call-to-investigate-russias-bribery-of-eu-politicians/.

[370] Ibid.

[371] Ibid.

[372] Ibid.

[373] Ibid.

[374] Ibid.

[375] Wong, Edward, "Russia Secretly Gave $300 Million to Political Parties and Officials Worldwide, U.S. Says", *The New York Times*, 13 Sept 2022. https://www.nytimes.com/2022/09/13/us/politics/russia-election-interference.html.

[376] Bourgery-Gonse, Théo, "Europe ministers say more resources needed to combat Russian disinformation online", *Euractiv*, 29 Apr 2024.

websites spreading pro-Russian propaganda across the EU in an attempt to sway election outcomes in various EU states.[377]

In the most recent case, the information primarily surfaced on the Voice of Europe website, but due to the interconnected nature of the media landscape, it was swiftly disseminated by both far-right outlets and other Russian disinformation networks. Russian media channels such as RT, Sputnik, Gazeta and TASS are leveraging interviews published on the Voice of Europe website featuring pro-Kremlin MEPs to bolster their credibility among readers.

4.14.2 Threat Actors

A range of Russian agencies and individuals carry out global operations, including the Federal Security Service and other security agencies, as well as business figures.[378] According to a State Department summary of a 2022 U.S. intelligence review, there have even been incidents of Russian embassies paying cash to candidates in elections.[379]

A central figure behind Moscow's FIMI campaigns in Europe, which began in 2014, has been Sargis Mirzakhanian, a well-connected staffer and adviser in Russia's parliament, who has built a network of political analysts, journalists, activists and academics to entice European politicians through illicit funding to push Moscow's interests abroad.[380]

The ongoing investigation by Czech, Belgian and other European authorities into the bribing of candidates in the European elections and Members of the European Parliament (MEPs) as part of the Voice of Europe case has focussed on two individuals: Artem Marchevskyi and Viktor Medvedchuk.[381] The Czech authorities have sanctioned both individuals alleging that the network was orchestrated by Medvedchuk, a pro-Russian Ukrainian oligarch, and Marchevsky,[382] a former producer for a pro-Russian TV channel in Ukraine. The latter has been accused

[377] Desmarais, Anna, "Russiagate to Portal Kombat: The foreign misinformation campaigns shifting the European elections", *Euronews*, 6 June 2024. https://www.euronews.com/next/2024/06/06/russiagate-to-portal-kombat-the-foreign-misinformation-campaigns-shifting-the-european-ele.

[378] Wong, Edward, "Russia Secretly Gave $300 Million to Political Parties and Officials Worldwide, U.S. Says", *The New York Times*, 13 September 2022. https://www.nytimes.com/2022/09/13/us/politics/russia-election-interference.html.

[379] Ibid.

[380] Laine, Martin, Cecilia Anesi, Lorenzo Bagnoli, and Tatiana Tkachenko, "Kremlin-Linked Group Arranged Payments to European Politicians to Support Russia's Annexation of Crimea", OCCRP, 3 Feb 2023. https://www.occrp.org/en/investigation/kremlin-linked-group-arranged-payments-to-european-politicians-to-support-russias-annexation-of-crimea.

[381] Zoria, Yuri, "MEPs Call to Investigate Russia's Bribery of EU Politicians", Euromaidan Press, 31 Mar 2024. https://euromaidanpress.com/2024/03/31/meps-call-to-investigate-russias-bribery-of-eu-politicians/.

[382] Vock, Ido, "Russian Network That 'paid European Politicians' Busted, Authorities Claim", BBC News, 28 Mar 2024. https://www.bbc.com/news/world-europe-68685604.

of directly managing the Voice of Europe's operations.[383] Medvedchuk is the leader of the Opposition Bloc—For Life. Putin is the godfather of Medvedchuk's daughter.[384]

Medvedchuk has been under US sanctions since 2014 for undermining Ukrainian sovereignty.[385] He was sanctioned by the Zelenskyy government in 2021 for allegedly owning three nationwide TV channels—NewsOne, Channel 112 and ZIK which were accused of receiving Russian financing and promoting Russian disinformation.[386] Their FIMI depicted Russian aggression in Eastern Ukraine as a civil war, attacked Ukraine's language law and advocated for the pro-Russian Opposition Platform—For Life party.[387] In 2022, Medvedchuk faced charges of treason, aiding terrorism and illegal activities in Crimea.[388] He was detained by Ukraine's Security Service (SBU) in April 2022 and exchanged for 200 Ukrainian soldiers in September 2022.

4.14.3 Presumed Objectives

Moscow's objective in its FIMI and bribery campaign was to bolster support for pro-Russian narratives by co-opting politicians and media. A recent example is the disinformation and bribery campaign conducted through the Voice of Europe to help elect more pro-Russian candidates in the European elections in June 2024 and to reinforce pro-Russian narratives in Europe and in its institutions. In particular, the disinformation campaign focussed on spreading anti-Ukraine stories.[389]

Therefore, the following DISARM objectives are pertinent here:

- T0075: Dismiss—As the objective was to reinforce pro-Russian narratives through pro-Russian MEPs, part of the campaign entailed pushing back against criticism levelled at Russia.
- T0076: Distort—In order to push forward pro-Russian narratives, the FIMI campaign aimed to change the framing of issues such as the war in Ukraine in order to induce pro-Russian sentiments.
- T0076: Distract—Central to Russia's bribery of MEPs has been to change the narrative on the war in Ukraine by shifting the attention to NATO's supposed role in sparking the conflict.
- T0136: Cultivate support—The aim of the campaign was to reinforce pro-Russian narratives in Europe.

[383] Zoria, op. cit., 31 Mar 2024.
[384] Ibid.
[385] Ibid.
[386] Ibid.
[387] Ibid.
[388] Ibid.
[389] Ibid.

- T0002: Facilitate state propaganda—By bribing MEPs, Russia was able to spread its state propaganda through European politicians.

4.14.4 Incidents and Observables

The investigation into the Voice of Europe and the bribery of Members of the European Parliament is ongoing. The Czech Intelligence agencies unveiled this disinformation and bribery network targeting MEPs from various European countries.[390]

According to the intelligence services, Medvedchuk's network illicitly funded political candidates in six EU nations—Germany, France, Poland, Belgium, the Netherlands and Hungary.[391] The Alternative for Germany (AfD) party is currently under scrutiny for its potential involvement in a Russian influence operation, with reports indicating substantial financial contributions from a pro-Putin network to European politicians, including AfD members.[392] These allegations underscore the Kremlin's continued strategy of cultivating alliances with far-right and anti-EU factions across Europe, aiming to advance its interests.[393]

By covertly supporting candidates sympathetic to Moscow's agenda, Russia seeks to exert its influence and shape the political landscape of the continent, demonstrating a persistent effort to undermine European unity and stability.

Within the AfD, the far-right German party, allegations have been aimed at Maximilian Krah for his collaboration with the Voice of Europe. Below are examples of Krah's promoting Russian narratives and propaganda on the Voice of Europe.

- On 12 October 2023, on the Voice of Europe, Krah repeated the Russian narrative that Ukrainian elites in Kyiv don't want to end the war and have personal interests in maintaining the conflict ongoing for as long as possible.[394]
- On 10 February 2024, Krah gave an interview to the Voice of Europe in which he spread the Russian narrative that the United States was responsible for the Nord Stream Pipeline exploding.[395]

---

390 Ibid.
391 Ibid.
392 Ibid.
393 Ibid.
394 Ibid.
395 The Voice of Europe, "AfD MEP Maximilian Krah: The German state will never hold the US accountable for Nord Stream attacks", 10 Feb 2024. https://www.voiceofeurope.com/public/afd-mep-maximilian-krah-the-german-state-will-never-hold-the-us-accountable-for-nord-stream-attacks.

This emergence of a new Russian FIMI campaign, involving Russian funding (in effect, bribery), came less than three months before the June 2024 European Parliament elections, emphasising the imperative of addressing illicit Russian financial influence in domestic politics to uphold democratic integrity and reinforce support for Ukraine.

4.14.5 Targets

Corruption targets can be seen from two perspectives: corrupting media to influence public opinion applying indirect pressure on the political decision-making process and directly corrupting political figures. The target of the bribery campaigns for FIMI purposes were and are politicians and media. Since 2014, Russia has had ongoing campaigns of FIMI in order promote pro-Russian narratives.[396] To this end, they have targeted politicians across Europe, typically from the far right, who are more open to their views. For example, the French Front National received a Russian loan of €11 million in 2014 and asked for a €27 million loan in 2017.[397] In 2023, they claimed to have paid back more than €6 million.[398]

In a recent scandal, Members of the European Parliament were allegedly bribed to spread Russian interests. The Voice of Europe allegedly paid politicians from Germany, France, Poland, Belgium, the Netherlands and Hungary to spread Russian narratives and promote pro-Russian politicians in the European elections in June 2024.[399] The focus of the allegations centred on AfD politicians Maximilian Krah and Petr Bystron, who were spearheading the party's campaign for the European Parliament elections.[400] Intelligence indicated that both members of the AfD have had longstanding associations with Medvedchuk and have allegedly received illicit funds from Medvedchuk's pro-Kremlin network to propagate Russian narratives via interviews with the pro-Russian Voice of Europe platform.[401]

Whilst there haven't been concrete accusations, several other MEPs participated in interviews with the Voice of Europe. Members from various political groups,

---

[396] Wong, op. cit., 13 Sept 2022.

[397] Oliveira, Ivo, "National Front Seeks Russian Cash for Election Fight", *POLITICO*, 19 Feb 2016. https://www.politico.eu/article/le-pen-russia-crimea-putin-money-bank-national-front-seeks-russian-cash-for-election-fight/.

[398] Guillou, Clément, "Le Pen's Party Repays Cumbersome 'Russian Loan'", *Le Monde*, 22 Sept 2023. https://www.lemonde.fr/en/france/article/2023/09/22/le-pen-s-party-repays-cumbersome-russian-loan_6138411_7.html.

[399] Vock, op. cit., 28 Mar 2024.

[400] Zoria, Yuri, "Russia Suspected of Funneling Funds to Germany's AfD Party for pro-Russian Messaging", Euromaidan Press, 31 Mar 2024. https://euromaidanpress.com/2024/03/31/russia-suspected-of-funneling-funds-to-germanys-afd-party-for-pro-russian-messaging/.

[401] Ibid.

nationalities and political parties interviewed on the Voice of Europe include the following[402]:

- From the EPP: Matteo Gazini, Milan Zver and Anders Vistisen;
- From ID: Jaak Madison, Roman Heider and Patricia Chagnon;
- From non-aligned: Francesco Donato, Milan Uhrik and Miroslav Radačovsky.

4.14.6 Tactics, Techniques and Procedures

The main TTPs based on the DISARM framework that have been detected in Russia's bribery and disinformation campaign were the following:

- T00136: Cultivate support and T0002: Facilitate state propaganda—The goal of the campaign was to cultivate support for pro-Russian narratives and candidates. In the current case of alleged bribery of European candidates through the Voice of Europe, the website spread state propaganda by copying articles from Russian state media sources.[403]
- T0068: Respond to breaking news event or active crisis—Articles are mass produced on disinformation networks like Portal Kombat.
- T0073: Determine target audiences—The campaign specifically targeted politicians more likely to be pro-Russian.
- T0074: Determine strategic ends—The aim was to promote Russian narratives to reduce support for Ukraine.
- T0075: Dismiss—When sanctioned, charged or accused of FIMI or bribery, threat actors were quick to dismiss the accusations and call it censorship.[404]
- T0076: Distort—Change the narrative regarding the Ukrainian war by dissuading European support for sending arms to Ukraine by characterising it as an impediment to finding peace and resolution to the conflict.
- T0079: Divide—The campaign provided talking points for those within Europe who are against aid to Ukraine in order to confront those who support it.
- T0135: Undermine—The goal was to weaken Ukraine by altering public opinion in Europe to be against the approval of further aid and involvement in the invasion of Ukraine.
- T0072: Segment audiences—The goal of the campaign was to influence the European public through electing pro-Russian MEPs. It appears that the candidates targeted were from far-right parties, who historically have been more open to support Russian narratives.

---

402 Sorokin, Oleksiy, "Zelensky Bans Media Empire Associated with Putin's Friend Medvedchuk", *Kyiv Post*, 2 Feb 2021. https://archive.kyivpost.com/ukraine-politics/zelensky-bans-media-empire-associated-with-putins-friend-medvedchuk.html.

403 Wee, Olivia, "Russian Disinformation against Ukraine Heightens Ahead of EU Parliamentary Elections", Voice of America, 22 Apr 2024. https://www.voanews.com/a/7580484.html.

404 Sorokin, op. cit.

- T0081: Identify social and technical vulnerabilities—The campaign uses the bribery and coopting of politicians, in particular, far-right candidates to the European elections, to bring disinformation to far-right echo chambers to create controversy regarding support for Ukraine.
- T0102.001: Use existing echo chambers/filter bubbles—Spreading of disinformation across several social media platforms.
- T0085.003: Develop inauthentic news articles—Coopting media influence-for-hire firms has been central to Russia's efforts in its FIMI campaigns. In the most recent bribery of candidates to the European elections, the Voice of Europe outlet was central to the FIMI campaign both to spread Russian narratives and disinformation as well as a network to approach and bribe political candidates.
- T0118: Amplify existing narratives—The FIMI campaign relied on pre-existing pro-Russian narratives based on anti-war efforts and legitimising Russia's invasion of Ukraine.
- T0130.005: Obfuscate payment—Russia has done its best to obfuscate payments, as currently there is lack of public knowledge regarding concrete evidence of direct money transfers between Russia and the European candidates it allegedly coopted.

4.14.7 Channels

Russian media channels such as RT, Sputnik, Gazeta and TASS disseminated the Voice of Europe articles.

4.14.8 Languages

As Russia has embraced bribery as a strategic component of its FIMI campaigns globally, disinformation has been spread in the language of every targeted country. Overall, a large amount is spread in English to achieve greater dissemination but to target specific countries and populations, the disinformation has been translated to target the country in question. In South America, the disinformation has been spread in Spanish, whilst in Europe, just in the Voice of Europe scandal, it has been spread in over 15 languages including English, French, German, Polish and Ukrainian.[405]

---

[405] Zoria, Yuri, "MEPs Call to Investigate Russia's Bribery of EU Politicians", Euromaidan Press, 31 Mar 2024. https://euromaidanpress.com/2024/03/31/meps-call-to-investigate-russias-bribery-of-eu-politicians/.

4.14.9 Effectiveness

MEPs and politicians from Central and Eastern European governments participated in video interviews with a channel that has only amassed 351 subscribers on YouTube and approximately 60,000 views.[406] However, despite its limited reach on YouTube, the Voice of Europe's presence on social media platforms like X and Facebook is significantly larger, and its account on X remains active.

4.14.10 Countermeasures

Over the past century, various measures have been implemented to combat FIMI. One of the earliest initiatives was the enactment of the Foreign Agents Registration Act (FARA) in 1938 in response to congressional investigations into communist and Nazi propaganda in the United States.[407] FARA mandated that representatives of foreign sponsors register, which would expose their activities to public scrutiny.[408] The scope of FARA was further refined in the 1960s through significant amendments, shifting its focus more towards foreign sponsorship of political lobbying rather than propaganda.[409] This legislative evolution demonstrated an ongoing effort to address the changing nature of foreign influence tactics.

The European Commission is currently pushing forward with plans for a new directive, as part of the Defence of Democracy package modelled after the US Foreign Agents Act, specifically targeting Russian and Chinese influence.[410] This legislation aims to safeguard democracies by imposing transparency obligations on entities seeking to shape public opinion and influence democratic processes.[411] Through enhancing transparency and accountability, such measures seek to mitigate the risk of undue foreign influence on European political systems.[412]

At the time of the Voice of Europe scandal, the European Union and its Member States already had several countermeasures in place to address foreign interference, disinformation and attempts to influence democratic processes. Many EU Member States, such as Czechia and Germany, had existing counter-intelligence measures focused on identifying and neutralising foreign influence networks. For example,

[406] Wax, Eddy, Elisa Braun and Clothilde Goujard, "'I hope Ukraine will lose': What MEPs told Russian propaganda channel", *POLITICO*, 11 Apr 2024. https://www.politico.eu/article/i-hope-ukraine-will-lose-meps-russian-propaganda-channel/.

[407] Zelikow, et al., op. cit.

[408] Ibid.

[409] Ibid.

[410] Wheaton, Sarah, "EU Commission Wants Registry for Foreign Lobbyists", *POLITICO*, 12 Dec 2023. https://www.politico.eu/article/eu-commission-wants-registry-for-foreign-lobbyists/.

[411] European Commission, "Defence of Democracy—Commission proposes to shed light on covert foreign influence", press release, 12 Dec 2023. https://ec.europa.eu/commission/presscorner/detail/en/ip_23_6453.

[412] Wheaton, op. cit.

Czechia's BIS (Security Information Service) actively monitors pro-Russian influence operations, which helped uncover the Voice of Europe network.[413] Sanctions lists also allow EU countries to freeze assets and restrict travel for individuals and entities involved in such activities.

The EU developed several frameworks to combat disinformation, including the EU Cybersecurity Strategy and initiatives through the European Centre of Excellence for Countering Hybrid Threats. These bodies help coordinate responses to foreign interference across EU institutions and Member States, building resilience against cyberattacks and disinformation campaigns targeting elections.[414]

The EU established the East StratCom Task Force, part of the European External Action Service (EEAS), to identify and expose pro-Russian disinformation targeting EU Member States. Additionally, guidelines were put in place to prevent media outlets on EU-sanctioned lists from accessing parliamentary resources and influencing legislative proceedings.[415]

European countries like Belgium and Germany coordinate with EU intelligence agencies and local enforcement to investigate and respond to foreign-funded activities. This cooperative framework enabled rapid actions, such as intelligence-sharing between Belgium and Czechia, when Voice of Europe's influence network was exposed.[416]

EU parliamentary bodies have protocols for investigating corruption, including the Office of the European Anti-Fraud Office (OLAF), which can launch inquiries into bribery and misconduct among EU officials. This framework allows for internal transparency and accountability measures if MEPs or candidates are suspected of unethical behaviour.[417]

The European Parliament has agreed a regulation harmonising political advertising requirements and banning foreign sponsorship of political ads before elections. The implementation of these rules was pending until the EU elections.[418] These regulations include provisions for clear labelling of political ads, improved access to financing information and the establishment of a public repository for online

---

[413] Vinocur, Nicholas, Pieter Haeck and Eddy Wax, "Russian Influence Scandal Rocks EU", *POLITICO*, 29 Mar 2024. https://www.politico.eu/article/voice-of-europe-russia-influence-scandal-election/.

[414] Koudelka, Michal, and Petr Fiala, "Czechs Bust Russian Network Paying off European Politicians", Radio Prague International, 28 Mar 2024. https://english.radio.cz/czechs-bust-russian-network-paying-european-politicians-8812632.

[415] Wax, Eddy, "MEPs Call for 'Urgent' Debate into Russian Influence Scandal", *POLITICO*, 29 Mar 2024. https://www.politico.eu/article/european-meps-call-for-urgent-debate-russian-influence-scandal/.

[416] Zoria, Yuri, "MEPs Call to Investigate Russia's Bribery of EU Politicians", Euromaidan Press, 31 Mar 2024. https://euromaidanpress.com/2024/03/31/meps-call-to-investigate-russias-bribery-of-eu-politicians/.

[417] Wax, op. cit.

[418] European Parliament News, "Parliament Adopts New Transparency Rules for Political Advertising", 27 Feb 2024. https://www.europarl.europa.eu/news/en/press-room/20240223IPR18071/parliament-adopts-new-transparency-rules-for-political-advertising.

political ads and related data.[419] By prohibiting third-country organisations from sponsoring political advertising close to election periods, the EU aims to mitigate the spread of disinformation and safeguard the integrity of democratic processes.

The European Parliament has also passed a resolution denouncing Russia's FIMI campaign in the wake of the Voice of the Europe scandal. The resolution urges the Council to include Kremlin-backed media outlets, as well as other broadcasting and media organisations, along with individuals responsible for propaganda and disinformation campaigns, into the forthcoming 14th Russian sanctions package.[420] MEPs advocate for aligning these sanctions with those imposed by the Czech government against Voice of Europe, as well as targeting Ukrainian pro-Russian oligarch Viktor Medvedchuk and his associate Artem Marchevskyi.[421] Additionally, the resolution expresses concern over Voice of Europe's ability to resume operations from Kazakhstan and urges EU Member States to take measures to prevent its access within the EU.[422]

Similarly individual Member States, such as Belgium, have initiated an investigation into Russian interference through Voice of Europe in the European elections, emphasising the responsibility of local authorities to uphold citizens' rights to free and fair elections.[423] Furthermore, a Munich court specialising in bribery and corruption has initiated a preliminary investigation following allegations that Petr Bystron, one of the top candidates for the Alternative for Germany party in the election, received bribes.[424] By taking decisive action against FIMI, European institutions and Member States aim to reinforce democratic principles and preserve the integrity of electoral processes.

4.14.11 Conclusions and Recommendations

Russia's ongoing use of bribery as part of its FIMI campaigns illustrates the lengths to which the Kremlin is willing to go to influence foreign political landscapes. By covertly funding far-right European politicians and media outlets like the Voice of Europe, Russia seeks to amplify pro-Russian narratives, distort public discourse and shift attention away from its aggression in Ukraine. The vulnerabilities

[419] European Parliament, "European Parliament legislative resolution of 27 February 2024 on the proposal for a regulation of the European Parliament and of the Council on the transparency and targeting of political advertising", texts adopted, 27 Feb 2024. https://eur-lex.europa.eu/legal-content/EN/TXT/?uri=EP%3AP9_TA%282024%290090.

[420] European Parliament News, "MEPs call for a firm response to counter Russian interference", press release, 25 Apr 2024. https://www.europarl.europa.eu/news/en/press-room/20240419IPR20542/meps-call-for-a-firm-response-to-counter-russian-interference.

[421] Ibid.

[422] Ibid.

[423] France 24, "Belgium opens probe into Russian 'interference' in European Parliament", 12 Apr 2024. https://www.france24.com/en/europe/20240412-belgium-opens-probes-russian-interference-european-parliament.

[424] Wax, Braun and Goujard, op. cit.

of democratic systems—especially during election periods—have been exploited, demonstrating the effectiveness of strategic corruption. The FIMI campaigns target political figures and media alike, resulting in a potent disinformation network that impacts both the European Parliament and public opinion across several nations.

Despite the implementation of countermeasures such as sanctions, legislative initiatives like the European Commission's Defence of Democracy package and investigations by Member States, the persistence of Russian influence highlights the need for robust, proactive strategies.

To combat the escalating threat posed by Russia's alleged bribery and disinformation campaigns, several key measures should be considered:

- Stronger legislative frameworks: The EU should expedite the implementation of legislation modelled after the US Foreign Agents Registration Act (FARA), requiring foreign-funded entities to register, thereby increasing transparency. Moreover, swift enforcement of upcoming regulations on political advertising will help to curb foreign interference.
- Increased sanctions: Further sanctions should target individuals and entities involved in Russian FIMI efforts, particularly focusing on those responsible for running disinformation networks like the Voice of Europe. EU-wide alignment on sanctions, including those targeting oligarchs like Viktor Medvedchuk, is critical.
- Enhanced intelligence sharing: European countries should deepen their cooperation in intelligence-sharing mechanisms to swiftly detect and disrupt foreign interference efforts, particularly ahead of elections.
- Public awareness campaigns: Educating the public about the disinformation tactics used by foreign adversaries will empower citizens to critically evaluate the information they consume, particularly during politically sensitive periods.

4.15 Russian Interference in the Spanish Election in July 2023

4.15.1 Introduction

Spain witnessed a FIMI operation a couple of months before the country's general elections in July 2023, primarily targeting the Russian-speaking citizens based in Spain at that time. The TTPs used in the campaign (see below) seem to have been designed with the intention of confusing, disorienting and manipulating voters. Such an operation can lead to significant disruptions to the democratic process.

Here, one can observe a particular focus on a language group (russophones), which serves as an example of how a FIMI campaign can be tailored to exploit targeted groups within the specific context of an election. Such an approach is important to consider as it underlines the increasing sophistication of some FIMI campaigns where the choice of a language aims at both increasing the impact of disinformation and decreasing the potentiality of detection. It could be argued that by diminishing the focus to a particular demographic group, the FIMI operations could more effectively create confusion.

This case study highlights how crucial it is to apprehend targeted FIMI operations and to keep in mind that adaptability in apprehending evolving FIMI tactics is key.

4.15.2 Threat Actors

The FIMI operation was linked to Russian actors, most likely involving a combination of government-affiliated entities and hacktivist groups. These groups have used resources and cyber capabilities aligning with the ones used in state-sponsored operations as such operations often involve mature tools and tactics, designed to avoid detection.

Despite significant circumstantial evidence pointing toward Russian involvement, in the absence of conclusive evidence, attribution to the Russian government is still debatable.[425] The intricacy of such operations often make attribution very challenging. However, the campaign demonstrated intermediate capability, according to a QuoIntelligence article, using bulletproof hosting services, copying authentic websites and using Russian-language messages.[426] This can suggest a certain degree of sophistication behind the campaign. The involvement of actors possibly connected to the Russian authorities emphasises the risk that such campaigns pose.

4.15.3 Presumed Objectives

Rather than directly influencing the Spanish electorate as a whole, the operation's major goal appeared to be influencing the country's Russian-speaking community.[427] The narrow approach suggests attackers aimed to propagate disbelief in the Spanish political system among the Russian-speaking population by spreading false and distressing stories.

The strategy of disseminating doubt about the elections is in line with broader geopolitical objectives noted in other FIMI campaigns and more generally with geopolitical plans to undermine European unity and lessen the power of organisations like NATO and the EU.[428] By undermining confidence in the democratic

[425] European External Action Service, "2nd EEAS Report on Foreign Information Manipulation and Interference Threats: A Framework for Networked Defence," January 2024.

[426] QuoIntelligence, "Decoding Disinformation: The Spanish Election Information Operation Targeting Russian-Speakers", Nov 2023. https://quointelligence.eu/2023/11/spanish-election-information-operation-targeting-russian-speakers/.

[427] Ibid.

[428] EEAS, op. cit., January 2024.

process, the attackers sought to influence the Spanish political landscape. This specific FIMI operation can be seen as representative of a larger strategy aiming at destabilising European states by amplifying internal divisions and undermining the alliance between EU nations and Western security frameworks.

4.15.4 Incidents and Observables

Noteworthy observables during the FIMI campaign indicated the attackers' intended goals. They reflect the level of depth in which the campaign was orchestrated:

- Cloned website: The first key strategy involved the creation of a fake website copying the official Comunidad de Madrid site. The fake website disseminated false information regarding ETA's terrorist activities[429] to create a sense of uncertainty tainted with fear among the russophone community in Spain. The primary target of this disinformation campaign, which was disseminated mostly through Telegram, was likely to discourage them from going to vote by promoting the idea that voting could be dangerous.[430]

The fact that the website was housed by a Russian bulletproof hosting company adds even more evidence to the operation's meticulous planning, as this type of hosting is difficult to dismantle, thus ensuring the availability of the website (and by extension of the FIMI operation) for a longer period.[431]

- Bulletproof hosting providers: The use of bulletproof hosting can be seen as an observable indicating the intent of keeping the fake website operational throughout the election period. Because of its reputation for withstanding takedown requests, this kind of Russian hosting was likely the choice of attackers who wanted to ensure that the site would remain accessible despite any effort deployed by authorities to shut it down.[432]
- Telegram amplification: The Telegram platform played an important role in spreading false information and hence participating in the disinformation. The

---

[429] Newtral, "La Comunidad de Madrid no ha advertido de un supuesto atentado de ETA en el 23-J: es una web falsa de origen ruso", July 2023. https://www.newtral.es/ministerio-interior-atentado-eta/20230723/.

[430] El Confidencial Digital, "Una web que suplanta a la Comunidad de Madrid inventa que ETA amenaza con atentados el 23 de julio," July 2023. https://www.elconfidencialdigital.com/articulo/seguridad/web-que-suplanta-comunidad-madrid-inventa-que-eta-amenaza-atentados-23-julio/20230723143844613758.html.

[431] QuoIntelligence, op. cit., Nov 2023.

[432] Enzo Panizio (ed.), Disinformation narratives during the 2023 elections in Europe, Report, European Digital Media Observatory's Task Force on the 2024 European Parliament Elections, Nov 2023. https://edmo.eu/wp-content/uploads/2023/10/EDMO-TF-Elections-disinformation-narratives-2023.pdf.

attackers used Telegram's encrypted messaging technology to share misleading information covertly, focussing on Russian-speaking communities. This observable is important since it illustrates the distribution strategy that worked well with the replicated website.[433] The amplification of these false stories ensured that the FIMI operation reached a large audience within the targeted community, further embedding the fake narratives and achieving the desired effects.

These observables tend to show a well-designed campaign integrating psycho-social tactics in order to undermine trust in electoral process.

4.15.5 Targets

Russian-speaking citizens of Spain were the main targets of the operation,[434] likely chosen for their linguistic and cultural links to Russia. The overarching goal of the FIMI operation was fostering distrust and division among voters to indirectly affect the Spanish political landscape[435] and undermine trust in the democratic process.

This specific disinformation campaign seems to have not been created to affect the entire Spanish electorate but rather was focused on influencing this specific linguistic community. The narrow scope of the operation suggests that the primary objective was not to change outcome of the votes but likely to maintain influence within the Russian expatriate community in Spain.[436]

This kind of targeted disinformation is dangerous in exploiting vulnerabilities of minority groups; it creates divisions within society that may persist after the election. By undermining trust in the democratic process among a targeted demographic, the attackers aimed to weaken Spain's political stability.

4.15.6 Tactics, Techniques and Procedures

The FIMI campaign employed an array of tactics, techniques and procedures referenced in the DISARM framework:

- T0043.001: Use encrypted chat apps—One of the main channels for spreading false information to the targeted Russian-speaking community in Spain was Telegram.
- T0072.002: Demographic segmentation—This showed a deliberate focus on a certain demographic, namely Russian-speaking Spaniards.

---

[433] QuoIntelligence, op. cit.
[434] QuoIntelligence, op. cit.
[435] EEAS, op. cit.
[436] QuoIntelligence, op. cit.

- T0130.002: Use bulletproof hosting—The Russian provider used bulletproof hosting to host the misinformation website to ensure its resistance to takedown attempts.
- T0098.001: Create inauthentic news sites—A fake website that looked much like the Community of Madrid's official website spread misleading information to incite fear and prevent people from casting ballots.
- T0003: Leverage existing narratives—The campaign used extant accounts of ETA terrorism, a delicate and politically fraught subject in Spain, to give the fake information more plausibility.

4.15.7 Channels

The attackers used several channels to implement the FIMI campaign, including Telegram, the cloned websites of the official Community of Madrid and bulletproof hosting.

4.15.8 Languages

The disinformation campaign seemed to have primarily used the Russian language to target the Russian-speaking community in Spain.

4.15.9 Effectiveness

Overall, the FIMI campaign had a limited effect on the restricted number of people[437] as it was directed towards residents who spoke Russian. This narrow focus meant that, while the operation may have been effective in spreading distrust among this specific demographic, its reach and influence were confined to a small number of people. As a result, the campaign went unnoticed by a large portion of the Spanish electorate.

The campaign's limited target could mean that it was highly effective in achieving localised objectives but fell short of having a broader national impact.

4.15.10 Countermeasures

Spain profited from bigger EU programs like the Rapid Alert System and coordinated Member State efforts to detect and neutralise FIMI risks to combat misinformation, even though particular countermeasures for this operation are not

[437] Ibid.

documented. The response of fact-checkers and the media's disclosure of the disinformation case also significantly reduced the disinformation's possible influence on the electorate. The impact of the disinformation effort was diminished when media outlets exposed the phoney website posing as the Community of Madrid and fact-checkers promptly refuted misleading claims.[438]

4.15.11 Conclusions and Recommendations

The FIMI operation targeting the Russian-speaking community in Spain in the frame of the July 2023 general elections can be seen as a premeditated endeavour to hurt the democratic processes in place in the country. Using a couple of already described tools, the operation presented the main objectives of weakening trust within a specific community. However, it is important to underline here that the overall impact of the campaign on the broader electorate was limited due to its specific narrow focus.

Moreover, Spain's defence against the FIMI operation was strengthened by some EU initiatives like the Rapid Alert System, and the smooth intervention of fact-checkers and media, which effectively decreased the potential influence of the operation. This case underscores the ongoing need for coordinated efforts to protect democratic integrity from evolving foreign interference tactics.

4.16 European Parliament Report on FIMI in European Elections

4.16.1 Introduction

More than 360 million people were eligible to cast their votes in the 6–9 June 2024 European Parliament elections that will shape the political landscape for the next five years.[439] Since the outset of the Russian war against Ukraine, there has been a significant shift in the relationship between the European Union institutions and Russia. This shift has led to the implementation of various sanctions and economic

[438] Newtral, "La Comunidad de Madrid no ha advertido de un supuesto atentado de ETA en el 23-J: es una web falsa de origen ruso," July 2023. https://www.newtral.es/ministerio-interior-atentado-eta/20230723/. See also El Confidencial Digital, "Una web que suplanta a la Comunidad de Madrid inventa que ETA amenaza con atentados el 23 de julio", July 2023. https://www.elconfidencialdigital.com/articulo/seguridad/web-que-suplanta-comunidad-madrid-inventa-que-eta-amenaza-atentados-23-julio/20230723143844613758.html.

[439] EEAS Press Team, "Disinformation and Foreign Interference: Speech by High Representative/Vice-President Josep Borrell at the EEAS Conference", January 2024. https://www.eeas.europa.eu/eeas/disinformation-and-foreign-interference-speech-high-representativevice-president-josep-borrell-eeas_en.

bans, as well as the escalation of information warfare through the propagation of false narratives that undermine the European Union's integrity and objectives.

The political structure of the European Union accommodates a diverse array of parties, leading towards democratic expression and the freedom of choice and speech. However, maintaining equilibrium between European and pro-Russian rhetoric became increasingly complex in the last months before the European Parliament elections. Pro-Russian rhetoric spread distrust among the population, leading to economic instability and social discord directed against the European Union.

In this case study concerning the European elections, FIMI served as a coordinated campaign rather than isolated incidents. This recognition stems not only from the interference observed in the national elections of various Member States, aimed at undermining the EU and bolstering Russia-influenced politicians in Spain, Poland and Slovakia, but also from these two factors:

- Allegations suggesting that Latvian MEP Tatjana Ždanoka acted as an informant for the Russian security service, FSB.[440]
- The revelation in March 2024 of the Voice of Europe propaganda and FIMI campaigns targeting the European Union. These activities have persisted since 2023, involving interviews with several Members of the European Parliament by the Voice of Europe, an organisation funded by Viktor Medvedchuk, a former Ukrainian citizen, oligarch and close associate of Putin.

This case study concentrates on the latter instance of FIMI presence in the European elections, as it represents a more complex information attack on the elections.

Established in 2016, the Voice of Europe commenced its active FIMI campaign in June 2023, coinciding with the launch of the European Parliament's election website. Particularly noteworthy was the period from August 2023, just a year prior to the European Parliament elections, when interviews began appearing on the Voice of Europe website. The year 2023 saw national parliamentary elections.

The publication of interviews involving MEPs restarted actively in January 2024, just six months before the European Parliament elections. The Voice of Europe has been adhering to a distinct FIMI strategy outlined in the EEAS report from January 2024, which outlined the stages of Identification and Preparations. These included activities such as "recruiting" and engaging with target audiences over the months leading up to the election. The cases analysed involved tactics such as clickbait, exploiting breaking news events and employing information-laundering techniques to establish legitimacy for subsequent phases.[441]

[440] European Parliament, "MEPs condemn continuous Russian efforts to undermine European democracy", 8 February 2024. https://www.europarl.europa.eu/news/en/press-room/20240202IPR17323/meps-condemn-continuous-russian-efforts-to-undermine-european-democracy.

[441] EEAS, "Report on FIMI Threats", Jan 2024. EEAS-2nd-Report on FIMI Threats-January-2024_0.pdf (europa.eu).

4.16.2 Threat Actors

The Voice of Europe was registered in Prague in 2016 under the name Dada Mapo before changing its name to the current one in 2023. It was registered with a CEO, Jacek Jakubczyk, a Polish citizen about whom there is no public information, while funding of the Voice of Europe is overseen by two pro-Kremlin influencers, Viktor Medvedchuk and Artem Marchevskiy. Medvedchuk, an ex-Ukrainian citizen and oligarch, is a close associate of Putin, and he stands accused of corruption and betrayal of Ukraine's government.

Medvedchuk's political journey in Ukraine began in 1997, and in 2012, he founded the "Ukrainian Choice" party, which opposed European integration and advocated for a customs union with Russia. Subsequently, in 2018, he aligned himself with the pro-Kremlin "For Life" party. During the full-scale war in 2022, Medvedchuk attempted to flee Ukraine but was apprehended by the Ukrainian Intelligence Service. He was later sent back to Russia in an exchange of prisoners.[442]

Artem Marchevskiy was the ex-head of the pro-Kremlin channel 112 and the right hand of Medvedchuk. Marchevskiy is the de-facto CEO of the Voice of Europe.

While Medvedchuk and Marchevsky may not have directly disseminated FIMI within the European Parliament (EP), they bear responsibility for financing the Voice of Europe and promoting pro-Kremlin ideologies. They achieved this through what are termed "interviews" featured on the website since August 2023, involving Members of the European Parliament (MEPs*)* from 2019–2024 including:

- Maximilian Krah (AfD, Germany)—EP party ID group
- Francesca Donato (Democrazia Cristiana, Italy)—EP party non-attached
- Milan Uhrik (Hnutie Republika, Slovakia)—EP party non-attached
- Jaak Madison (Eesti Konservatiivne Rahvaerakond, Estonia)—EP party ID group
- Miroslav Radačovsky (Slovak PATRIOT, Slovakia)—EP party non-attached
- Milan Zver (Slovenska demokratska stranka, Slovenia)—EP party EPP
- Matteo Gazzini (Independent, Italy)—EP party EPP
- Anders Vistisen (Dansk Folkeparti, Denmark)—EP party EPP
- Roman Heider (Freiheitliche Partei Österreichs, Austria)—EP party ID
- Patricia Chagnon (Rassemblement national, France)—EP party ID
- Marcel de Graaf (Netherlands)—EP party ID: no interview conducted with the Voice of Europe, but actively disseminating his ideas on the website.

[442] Парламент,ua ''Віктор Медведчук", Apr 2022. Віктор Медведчук-досьє, біографія, фото, останні новини-ПАРЛАМЕНТ.UA (parlament.ua).

4.16.3 Presumed Objectives

Among the published sources, the attackers' goal was to perform a disinformation campaign against the European Union, targeting its democratic principles, fundamental freedoms and external policies, particularly its support for Ukraine.

The content on the Voice of Europe platform can be categorised using the DISARM Framework:

- T0076: Distort—Pro-Kremlin narratives closely mirror the Kremlin's current agenda, promoting the notion that the West bears responsibility for the conflict, portraying the Ukrainian government as highly corrupt, asserting that the EU ignores the desires of its citizens, indicating a decline in the political and economic standing of the US, and forecasting the defeat of the Ukrainian army. In these narratives, peace can only be achieved when Ukraine abandons its sovereignty and unity.
- T0079: Divide—Demonisation of the EU and US: This involves vilifying both the EU and the US, portraying them as responsible for various global issues and internal shortcomings.

These tactics served to advance the Kremlin's disinformation efforts, aiming to undermine trust in European institutions and the discourse among European and transatlantic alliances. The pro-Kremlin politicians easily promoted the required politics.

4.16.4 Incidents and Observables

Below, we cite opinions of Members of the European Parliament extracted from interviews between August 2023 and April 2024.

- Maximilian Krah (AfD, Germany)—EP party ID group

10 Feb 2024: "*Until now, the Western public hasn't grasped Russia's motives for intervening in the Ukrainian crisis. What I expect from Tucker Carlson's interview is for people to realize that Ivan isn't crazy; there's a rationality behind his actions. By listening to Putin and Tucker Carlson's interview, voters might gain a better understanding of the real narrative behind this conflict. This understanding could significantly influence their preferences in the upcoming elections. In the US, it's the presidential election, and in Europe, it's the European election on June 9. Russia, despite being the weakest of the three superpowers, is striving to defend its status through actions like the Ukrainian war.*"[443]

[443] Voice of Europe, "AfD MEP Maximilian Krah: The German state will never hold the US accountable for Nord Stream attacks", Feb 2024.

Krah suggested that Western audiences misunderstood Russia's motives in Ukraine, urging people to listen to Vladimir Putin and Tucker Carlson for a "real narrative" on the conflict. By framing Russia's actions as rational and defending its global status, Krah's comments echoed Russian narratives and implied that adopting this perspective could influence voter sentiment in upcoming US and European elections.

- Francesca Donato (Democrazia Cristiana, Italy)—EP party Non-attached

17 Oct 2024: "*We think that the European Union should try to make a partnership with very influential third countries that have significant economic and political influence over states of Africa and of the Middle East—from where the migrants that arrive in Europe come. And those countries are mainly Russia and China. So I regret the current position of the European Union, especially with respect to the conflict against Russia, because I've always thought that the right approach to solve conflicts is negotiation and dialogue, not sanctions. Sanctions have always proved to be no use or counterproductive and what I warned my colleagues about has unfortunately proved to be true, because we see that today, especially after the Ukrainian crisis and the following energy crisis, we see that economy is stagnating and is in an increasingly difficult situation.*"[444]

Donato criticised the EU's stance on Russia, advocating instead for partnerships with influential countries like Russia and China to manage migration from Africa and the Middle East. She argued that sanctions, especially following the Ukraine conflict, have worsened Europe's economy, suggesting that negotiation and dialogue would be more effective solutions.

- Milan Uhrik (Hnutie Republika, Slovakia)—EP party Non-attached

18 Dec 2023: "*Who cares what the so-called liberal critics and globalist warmongers mumble? The same liberal warmongers supported the shameful bombing of the Slovak communities—our brothers and sisters—in Serbia. They supported wars in Afghanistan, Iraq, Libya, and around the world. It is their conscience. In the case of Ukraine, we wanted to help in a humanitarian way, not financially or by military means. We personally helped Ukrainian mothers and children. We do not wish sanctions that harm our economies in Europe. We do not want war. We want peace. The war must end at the negotiating table, and ideally at this moment. And all events prove us right. We were on the side of peace from day one. That's all.*"[445]

[444] Voice of Europe, "Ukraine's land borders are not as important as Ukrainian lives", Oct 2023.
[445] Voice of Europe, "Who cares what so called liberal critics and globalist warmongers mumble", Dec 2023. https://www.voiceofeurope.com/who-cares-what-so-called-liberal-critics-and-globalist-warmongers-mumble-interview-with-marian-duris-foreign-policy-advisor-to-an-mep-for-slovakias-republika-party/.

Slovak MEP Milan Uhrik criticised "liberal warmongers" for past conflicts and opposed financial or military aid to Ukraine, supporting only humanitarian assistance. He argued that sanctions harm European economies and called for immediate peace negotiations, emphasising his stance for peace from the outset.

- Jaak Madison (Eesti Konservatiivne Rahvaerakond, Estonia)—EP party ID group

29 Jan 2024: *''The original idea of the EU wasn't bad, but the current over-regulation, especially by the European Commission, has deviated from the initial concept. Our position is to reevaluate the EU's direction, but going back to the original idea seems improbable due to entrenched bureaucracies.*''[446]

Madison commented that, while the EU's original concept was sound, excessive regulation, particularly from the European Commission, has strayed from that vision. He advocated for reassessing the EU's direction, though he doubted a return to its founding principles due to entrenched bureaucracy.

- Miroslav Radačovsky (Slovak PATRIOT, Slovakia)—EP party Non-attached

29 Jan 2024: "*Fascism came from Western Europe, so the result of these battles was that Eastern Europe, but also Western Europe, was left in ruins, figuratively speaking a lawn. That's why I expressed the opinion that it is necessary to stop fighting so that Western Europe does not become a graveyard. But at the same time, I added, and this was not noticed by the media, nobody wants to talk about it. At the same time, in my speech, I said, let's stop killing people. This is the essence of what I said. And I said it metaphorically.*".[447]

Radačovsky's statement can be classified as a FIMI incident for several reasons. First, he linked ongoing conflicts to the historical legacy of fascism in Western Europe, suggesting that further fighting could harm European unity, which aligns with Russian narratives criticising Western actions. Second, by calling for peace without acknowledging Russia's role in the conflict, he minimises its responsibility, echoing pro-Russian sentiments that shift focus away from Russia's aggression. Finally, his appeal to "stop fighting" promotes a narrative that prioritises immediate peace over military support for Ukraine, potentially swaying public opinion against continued assistance and aligning with Russian interests in weakening Western support for Ukraine.

---

[446] Voice of Europe, "It may take 20 to 30 years but the EU will collapse", Interview with Estonian MEP Jaak Madison, 29 Jan 2024. https://www.voiceofeurope.com/interview-with-estonian-mep-jaak-madison-it-may-take-20-to-30-years-but-the-eu-will-collapse/.

[447] Voice of Europe, "The time for cold wars and vendettas has passed, we need peace", Interview with MEP Miroslav Radačovsky, 29 Jan 2024. https://www.voiceofeurope.com/interview-with-slovakian-mep-miroslav-radacovsky-the-time-for-cold-wars-and-vendettas-has-passed-we-need-peace/.

- Milan Zver (Slovenska demokratska stranka, Slovenia)—EP party EPP

29 Jan 2024: "*Considering the results of certain polls, there is a notable shift in the European political landscape. This is crucial for the future of Europe, as it necessitates a re-evaluation of our approach, including within the EPP. In the past, we have faced setbacks on various political fronts, such as greening, industry, education, and more. It is imperative to halt this trend and, for the sake of the European Union's future, ensure that the left is not allowed to dominate. The left must be left behind.*"[448]

Zver highlighted a significant shift in the European political landscape, emphasising the need for the European People's Party (EPP) to reevaluate its approach. He pointed to past setbacks in areas like environmental policy, industry and education, arguing that it is crucial to halt this trend to prevent the left from dominating European politics and to secure the future of the EU.

- Matteo Gazzini (Independent, Italy)—EP party EPP

10 Feb 2024: ''*This is the natural consequence of neglecting the issue of illegal immigration. Now, I don't want to echo Salvini's call for castration of rapists. Frankly, that's not a problem for me, but here's what worries me: our judicial system in Italy is flawed. If we were to implement such drastic measures without addressing the systemic issues within our legal apparatus, we'd be heading for disaster. With the current state of our judiciary, we risk innocent people suffering unjustly. What we need is not propaganda; we need effective action. We need to roll up our sleeves and get to work in our offices. We need to be proactive in Parliament, exert more control, and broker agreements with countries like Libya and the various factions there, as well as with Morocco and others. Then, we must rally Europe to support our efforts.*"[449]

Gazzini's statement can be viewed as a FIMI incident for several reasons. First, his discussion of illegal immigration tied immigration to crime, potentially amplifying public fear and aligning with populist rhetoric that simplifies complex issues, which foreign entities could exploit to destabilise European unity. Second, by critiquing Italy's judicial system and warning against drastic measures without addressing systemic flaws, Gazzini distracted from the broader social and political challenges surrounding immigration, potentially fostering scepticism about European governance. Finally, his call for proactive measures with countries like Libya and Morocco may inadvertently legitimise partnerships with nations that

---

[448] Voice of Europe, "European Commission Vice President of Transparency Vera Jurova undermines media freedon", Jan 2024. https://www.voiceofeurope.com/interview-with-slovenian-mep-milan-zver-european-commission-vice-president-of-transparency-vera-jourova-undermines-media-freedom/.

[449] Voice of Europe, "Europeans want more from us, we politicians must move our asses", 10 Feb 2024. https://www.voiceofeurope.com/forza-italia-mep-matteo-gazzini-epp-europeans-want-more-from-us-we-politicians-must-move-our-asses/.

have questionable human rights records, aligning with foreign interests that benefit from weakened European immigration policies. These elements illustrate how Gazzini's remarks could influence public opinion and policy in ways favourable to external actors, fitting the criteria for FIMI.

- Anders Vistisen (Dansk Folkeparti, Denmark)—EP party EPP

13 Mar 2024: "*Europe is not protecting jobs and welfare in Europe. We are seeing an American president who has passed the Inflation Reduction Act which is stealing industry jobs and so-called green jobs from Europe. And what is Brussels' response? More bureaucracy, more taxation, and bans on industry. We are now seeing it with electric cars. German car manufacturers are struggling; who is doing well? Toyota, who based their entire strategy on electric cars, is now back as the biggest manufacturer of cars when Europe is in decline in the car manufacturing industry. We'll have to get rid of the Green Deal and other policies that are not clever in their approach. The green transition is not creating jobs, they're killing jobs. Furthermore, already the historical* CO_2 *emissions of China are larger than Europe's. If you go back from the start of the industrial era, 1850 until today, China has overtaken Europe. So we are now seeing that the logic is fundamentally flawed. You achieve the green transition by reducing jobs, reducing welfare, and reducing the standard of living in Europe because the pollution will just move somewhere else, and the wealth and growth of economies will just move to Asia, South America, Africa, and North America.*"[450]

Vistisen's statement can be classified as a FIMI incident for several reasons. He argued that Europe is failing to protect jobs and welfare, blaming U.S. policies like the Inflation Reduction Act for stealing jobs from European industries and calling for the elimination of the Green Deal. By framing the green transition as detrimental to job creation and welfare in Europe, Vistisen aligns with narratives that suggest environmental policies are harming economies, which could resonate with foreign entities seeking to undermine EU cohesion. Additionally, his emphasis on China's historical CO_2 emissions as a counterpoint to European efforts created a perception that Europe is being unfairly penalised in the global economic landscape. This rhetoric could sway public opinion against green policies and EU regulations, thereby advancing interests that may be favourable to non-European actors looking to exploit divisions within the EU.

- Roman Heider (Freiheitliche Partei Österreichs, Austria)—EP party ID

13 Mar 2024: "*I truly believe it's a fight for survival. That's what the farmers are engaged in right now—a fight for survival. The main reason for their protests is the Green Deal. It's suffocating them. Have you heard about the recent law passed by the*

[450] Voice of Europe, "EU green policies are destroying Europe's economic competitiveness", 13 Mar 2024. https://www.voiceofeurope.com/eus-green-policies-are-destroying-europes-economic-competitiveness-interview-with-danish-peoples-party-mep-anders-vistisen/.

European Parliament, the nature restoration law? It's a broadside against farmers. This law mandates that up to 20% of cultivated areas be returned to their supposed "original condition," effectively rendering them unusable.

The sanctions imposed on Russia not only harm the European economy but also contribute to inflation.
I've observed what Orban has achieved as a member state, and there's a chance to restore normalcy to Europe's policies, particularly within the Council. We're hopeful about the upcoming Austrian elections. Not only do we have European elections in June, but also national elections in Austria at the end of September."[451]

Heider's frames the situation as a "fight for survival" for farmers, attributing their protests primarily to the EU's Green Deal and specifically criticising the nature restoration law, which he claimed undermines agricultural productivity. By portraying these policies as existential threats to farmers, Heider tapped into populist sentiments that could galvanise public support against EU regulations, potentially aligning with foreign interests that seek to weaken EU unity. Additionally, he linked sanctions on Russia to negative economic consequences for Europe, framing them as counterproductive and exacerbating inflation. This rhetoric not only shifted blame for economic difficulties onto EU policies but also aimed to create discontent with current governance, thereby influencing public opinion ahead of the European and Austrian elections. His emphasis on restoring "normalcy" in policies suggested a desire to realign European governance in a manner that could be favourable to non-EU actors looking to exploit divisions within the EU.

- Patricia Chagnon (Rassemblement national, France)—EP party ID

22 Mar 2024: "*What about the Europeans? It's very nice for you to tell me what the survey says in Ukraine, but I think I should be answering the French people. The French farmers definitely don't want Ukraine to adhere to the EU. Because it implies such a competition on agricultural products. So many European farmers are totally against the conditions of adherence today with opening the market up to Ukrainian products.*

It's not only imports from Ukraine that's the problem. There are other free trade agreements with Canada, with South America, with New Zealand, with Vietnam. There are all kinds of free trade agreements that the EU signs. They are in an ultra-liberal model to enable big importers, big distribution companies to go shopping

[451] Voice of Europe, "European Farmers are fighting for their survival interview with party of Austria" Jan 2024. https://www.voiceofeurope.com/european-farmers-are-fighting-for-their-survival-interview-with-freedom-party-of-austria-fpo-mep-roman-haider/.

worldwide for the cheapest produce. So, if we exclude agriculture from the free trade agreements, we will protect our national agriculture."[452]

Chagnon's prioritises the concerns of French farmers over the EU's broader agenda, arguing against Ukraine's potential accession to the EU due to fears of increased competition for agricultural products. By emphasising that many European farmers oppose opening markets to Ukrainian imports, she taps into nationalist sentiments that resonate with those concerned about job security and local industries, potentially aligning with foreign narratives that seek to exploit divisions within the EU. Furthermore, her critique of existing free trade agreements with various countries frames these policies as harmful to national agriculture, suggesting that they favour large importers at the expense of local producers. This rhetoric promotes a protectionist viewpoint, advocating for the exclusion of agriculture from such agreements to safeguard national interests, which could serve foreign actors interested in weakening EU trade policies. Overall, her comments aim to influence public opinion against EU integration and free trade, aligning with FIMI objectives of fostering division and undermining European cohesion.

- Marcel de Graaf (Netherlands)—EP party ID: no interview conducted with the Voice of Europe, but the media channel is actively disseminating his ideas on the website.

25 Apr 2024: "The EU discredits human rights under the guise of benevolence."[453]

Examples of the Voice of Europe website narratives are the following:

- **Narrative on Military Power in Ukraine**: Claims that the "balance of forces is 10 to 1 in favour of Russia", suggesting that the situation in Ukraine might turn disastrous due to Russia's dominance.
- **Terrorism and the EU**: States that the EU is experiencing a "rising tide of terrorism", implying a deterioration in European security.
- **EU Sanctions**: Notes that "sanctions are not eternal", mentioning the lifting of sanctions against the founder of Yandex, which may imply inconsistency in EU policy enforcement.
- **Poland's Potential EU Exit**: Mentions a new party in Poland whose goal is reportedly the country's exit from the EU, indicating possible anti-EU sentiment within Poland.
- **Sanctions as Political Tools**: Highlights an "unveiling of unfairness" in how sanctions are used for political purposes, suggesting the EU is biased or self-serving in its application of sanctions.

---

[452] Voice of Europe, "Exclusive interview with Patricia Chagnon, MEP for France", Mar 2024. https://www.voiceofeurope.com/exclusive-interview-with-patricia-chagnon-mep-for-frances-rassemblement-national-now-is-not-the-best-time-for-ukraine-to-join-the-eu/.

[453] Voice of Europe, "The EU discredits HR under the guise of benevolence", 25 Apr 2024. https://www.voiceofeurope.com/the-eu-discredits-human-rights-under-the-guise-of-benevolence-marcel-de-graaff/.

- **Macron's Security Concerns**: Talks about French President Macron enhancing his security due to fears of an assassination attempt, which might be meant to evoke instability or crisis within French leadership.

Examples of Voice of Europe X account narratives are the following:

- **Economic Decline in the EU**: Posts on the website's X (formerly Twitter) account allege that "EU countries are running out of money" for pensions and social benefits, suggesting financial instability in the region.
- **Human Rights Critique**: Another post asserts that "the EU discredits human rights under the guise of benevolence", indicating a view that the EU may be hypocritical or repressive in its human rights policies.

Examples of Telegram narratives

The Voice of Europe appears to underscore hesitations and divisions within the EU, potentially casting doubt on its strength, unity and commitment to its allies. This portrayal may aim to weaken European solidarity, particularly regarding high-stakes defence cooperation, by highlighting differing national priorities and internal complexities.

The Voice of Europe appeared to align with a narrative critical of Western involvement, specifically that of NATO, in the conflict in Ukraine. This perspective suggested that NATO's actions or presence are seen as a provocation or a destabilising factor in the crisis. It echoed common narratives from nations critical of NATO and Western military alliances, framing them as aggravating rather than mitigating conflicts. This messaging fosters scepticism toward Western interventions and military alliances, painting them as partly culpable for international instability.

4.16.5 Targets

The primary objective of the FIMI attacker was to sway public opinion in the Member States of the European Union towards the pro-Kremlin agenda, especially as elections, both national and European Parliament, were approaching. Their publications typically have centred on undermining EU support for Ukraine by emphasising alleged "internal problems". This strategy served a dual purpose: reinforcing control over already occupied Ukrainian territories and furthering territorial ambitions.

4.16.6 Tactics, Techniques and Procedures

In our analysis of this case, we found various TTPs, including the following:

T0115: Post content—Social media manipulations, by using various social media including X, Facebook, Telegram and YouTube to spread the required narratives.

T0084: Reuse existing content—Information laundering by Russian news channels including RT (Russia Today) and Sputnik were sharing "news" from the Voice of Europe on their websites and creating the vision of widespread consensus and validation. On the other hand, the Voice of Europe on its Telegram channel has been using news from, e.g., Reuters to manipulate public opinion.

T0068: Respond to breaking news event or active crisis—Exploiting breaking news events, by capitalising on the major crises like war or migration flow to manipulate public opinion.

4.16.7 Channels

In global terms, the Kremlin's narrative was characterised by a lack of cooperation; instead, it sought dominance. When dominance was unattainable, the primary objective shifted to distraction of the opponent through various means.

As mentioned above, Russian media channels such as RT, Sputnik, Gazeta and TASS have been using the interviews posted on the Voice of Europe website with pro-Kremlin MEPs to prove that their information is trustworthy.

Usage of the Voice of Europe Publications on the Russian Media Channels:

Quote: "Currently, we are not sovereign enough to have our own opinion because we must follow the rules set by the United States. All politics in Ukraine, in the Ukrainian conflict and in peace talks surrounding this conflict … it's not done here by us, it's done by Americans in Washington, not anywhere else."—Matthias Moosdorf, German Bundestag deputy, Voice of Europe.[454]

The same news appeared in Russian on the TASS.ru site.[455] Moreover, European channels in Germany, France, Spain, Italy, Poland and Hungary quoted the Voice of Europe. Below are examples of news in those countries that originated with the Voice of Europe.

Germany:
Telepolis.de: "How many Mercenaries and Western forces are fighting for Ukraine?", *The European*, 21 Mar 2024.[456]

---

[454] Voice of Europe, "European Politicians are increasingly looking at Ukraine without rose glasses", 15 Dec 2023. https://www.voiceofeurope.com/european-politicians-are-increasingly-looking-at-ukraine-without-rose-colored-glasses/.

[455] TASS News, "German MEP announced that Europe doesn't have a personal opinion regarding the Ukrainian conflict", Dec 2023. Немецкий депутат заявил, что у Европы нет собственного мнения по украинскому конфликту (tass.ru).

[456] Telepolis.de: "How many Mercenaries and Western forces are fighting for Ukraine?", *The European*, 21 Mar 2024. https://www.telepolis.de/features/Wie-viele-westliche-Soeldner-und-Spezialkraefte-kaempfen-in-der-Ukraine-9661107.html.

Voice of Europe: "Russian general claims NATO troops are operating disguised as mercenaries in Ukraine", 20 Feb 2024.[457]

France:
Resistance Republicaine.fr: "Intentions et agissements délictueux de l'Ukraine contre la Croatie!", 17 Mar 2024.[458]

Voice of Europe: "Croatia faces a lawsuit of 196 million euros over alleged unlawful actions by the government regarding the yacht Royal Romance", 15 Mar 2024.[459]

Spain:
News Front.su: (Russian website in Spain registered on the domain SU-Soviet Union): "Eslovaquia vetará la adhesión de Ucrania a la OTAN porque sería el comienzo de la Tercera Guerra Mundial", 21 Dec 2023.[460]

Voice of Europe: "Slovak Prime Minister Fico promises to block Ukraine's entry into NATO", 20 Dec 2023.[461]

Italy:
Ariannaeditrice.it: "L'esercito ucraino sta cedendo", 10 Aug 2023.[462]

The news channel quoted the Voice of Europe from 3 Aug 2023.[463]

Poland:
Salon24.pl: "Ilu najemników z Zachodu walczy na Ukrainie?", 20 Mar 2024.[464]

---

457 Voice of Europe, "Russian general claims NATO troops are operating disguised as mercenaries in Ukraine", 20 Feb 2022. https://www.voiceofeurope.com/russian-general-claims-nato-troops-are-operating-disguised-as-mercenaries-in-ukraine/.

458 Resistance Republicaine.fr, "Intentions et agissements délictueux de l'Ukraine contre la Croatie!", 17 Mar 2024. https://resistancerepublicaine.com/2024/03/17/intentions-et-agissements-delictueux-de-lukraine-contre-la-croatie/.

459 Voice of Europe, "Croatia faces a lawsuit of 196 million euros over alleged unlawful actions by the government regarding the yacht Royal Romance", 15 Mar 2024. https://www.voiceofeurope.com/croatia-faces-a-lawsuit-of-196-million-euros-over-alleged-unlawful-actions-by-the-government-regarding-the-yacht-royal-romance/.

460 News Front.su, "Eslovaquia vetará la adhesión de Ucrania a la OTAN porque «sería el comienzo de la Tercera Guerra Mundial", 21 Dec 2023. https://es.news-front.su/2023/12/21/eslovaquia-vetara-la-adhesion-de-ucrania-a-la-otan-porque-seria-el-comienzo-de-la-tercera-guerra-mundial/.

461 Voice of Europe, "Slovak Prime Minister Fico promises to block Ukraine's entry into NATO", 20 Dec 2023. https://www.voiceofeurope.com/slovak-prime-minister-fico-promises-to-block-ukraines-entry-into-nato/.

462 Ariannaeditrice.it, "L'esercito ucraino sta cedendo", 10 Aug 2023. https://www.ariannaeditrice.it/articoli/l-esercito-ucraino-sta-cedendo.

463 Voice of Europe, "The Ukrainian army is breaking", quoted Michael Vlahos, *Compact Magazine*, 3 Aug 2023. https://www.voiceofeurope.com/the-ukrainian-army-is-breaking-michael-vlahos-compact-mag/.

464 Salon24.pl, "Ilu najemników z Zachodu walczy na Ukrainie?", 20 Mar 2024. https://www.salon24.pl/u/bezmetki/1367595,ilu-najemnikow-z-zachodu-walczy-na-ukrainie.

Voice of Europe: "Russian general claims NATO troops are operating disguised as mercenaries in Ukraine", 20 Feb 2024.[465]

Hungary:
Magyar Nemzet.hu: "Ukrán külügyminiszter: Mindent megteszünk, hogy elhallgattassuk a béke hangjait!", 12 Aug 2023.[466]

Voice of Europe: "We will do everything to silence the voices for peaceful negotiations with Russia: Ukrainian Foreign Minister Kuleba stated that Ukraine is facing a difficult autumn due to the call to initiate negotiations with Russia", 12 Aug 2023.[467]

In this case, the context was distorted from the live Instagram conversation between the Minister and journalist Vadym Kypjak in August 2023. The Minister was not advocating against peace, but rather against peace under Russian conditions and the loss of Ukrainian sovereignty.[468]

The main channel for the Voice of Europe is a website: World | Voice of Europe, followed by social media such as X: (19) Voice of Europe (@V_of_Europe)/X (twitter.com), Facebook, Telegram: Voice of Europe—Telegram and YouTube.

The YouTube and Facebook (Meta) channels were closed on 27 March 2024.

4.16.8 Languages

The information on the website appeared in 16 languages: Ukrainian, Russian, English, Spanish, German, Italian, French, Hungarian, Romanian, Polish, Portuguese, Dutch, Czech, Slovakian, Bulgarian and Greek.

4.16.9 Effectiveness

As this campaign of attacks ramped up from the beginning January 2024, in advance of the EP elections in June 2024, the potential impact of this FIMI on

[465] Voice of Europe, "Russian general claims NATO troops are operating disguised as mercenaries in Ukraine", 20 Feb 2024. https://www.voiceofeurope.com/russian-general-claims-nato-troops-are-operating-disguised-as-mercenaries-in-ukraine/.

[466] Magyar Nemzet.hu, "Ukrán külügyminiszter: Mindent megteszünk, hogy elhallgattassuk a béke hangjait!", 12 Aug 2023. https://magyarnemzet.hu/kulfold/2023/08/ukran-kulugyminiszter-mindent-megteszunk-hogy-elhallgattassuk-a-beke-hangjait.

[467] Voice of Europe, "We will do everything to silence the voices for peaceful negotiations with Russia: Ukrainian Foreign Minister Kuleba stated that Ukraine is facing a difficult autumn due to the call to initiate negotiations with Russia", 12 Aug 2023. https://www.voiceofeurope.com/we-will-do-everything-to-silence-the-voices-for-peaceful-negotiations-with-russia-ukrainian-foreign-minister-kuleba-stated-that-ukraine-is-facing-a-difficult-autumn-due-to-the-call-to-initiate-ne/.

[468] Telegraph.ua, "*Будуть вимагати переговорів з росією: Кулеба попередив про важку осінь для України*", 12 Aug 2023. Дмитро Кулеба попередив про важку осінь для дипломатів через голоси про нібито необхідність переговорів-Телеграф.

the public was uncertain. The political parties within the European Union hold diverse opinions, and it is not clear how the FIMI might have inflamed those diverse opinions and influenced voters during the elections.

A comprehensive understanding of the impact of FIMI and any resulting changes in people's behaviour or actions is worth pursuit.

4.16.10 Countermeasures

Prior to the exposure of the Voice of Europe activities, the European Parliament Committee on Foreign Affairs condemned Russian efforts to collaborate with elected EU politicians on 8 February 2024.[469]

On 27 March 2024, the Czech Intelligence Service imposed sanctions on Viktor Medvedchuk and Artem Marchevskyi over allegations of funding the pro-Kremlin media platform, the Voice of Europe. Consequently, on the same day, the websites and all social media accounts of the Voice of Europe were taken offline, and its activities were stopped on European (Czech) servers.

Subsequently, on 12 April 2024, the Belgian Federal Prosecutor initiated an investigation into European lawmakers based on accusations of receiving funds from the Voice of Europe to propagate Russian narratives in Europe, particularly ahead of the EP elections.

As early as 17 April, reports emerged that the Voice of Europe had resumed online activity, now operating from servers located in Kazakhstan.

The Voice of Europe is actively publishing the opinions and interviews with MEPs on its website, the latest of which was the MEP Particia Chagnon on 22 March 2024 and the news publications on 27 April 2024.

4.16.11 Conclusions and Recommendations

The European Parliament elections finalised on 9 June 2024 in all EU countries, but the disinformation leading up to them hasn't vanished. There is still a growing threat to democratic society. The attackers effectively employed information warfare techniques (such as content distortion and exploiting breaking news events) to amplify distrust within the EU, weaken transatlantic alliances and promote politicians sympathetic to the Kremlin. The incidents indicated a concerted effort to not only discredit the EU's actions but also to impact the election outcomes by influencing voter sentiment through misinformation. Since July 2024, the Voice of Europe has deleted all of the above interviews, opinions and news that were raising the disinformation concerns. The latest news dates to 2023.

[469] European Parliament, "MEPs condemn continuous Russian efforts to undermine European democracy", press release, 8 Feb 2024. https://www.europarl.europa.eu/news/en/press-room/20240202IPR17323/meps-condemn-continuous-russian-efforts-to-undermine-european-democracy.

The Voice of Europe case brings several recommendations:

- Strengthen the verification and legitimacy of EU-registered online domains and companies. This includes implementing stringent measures for fact-checking content and identifying potential sources of disinformation early.
- The European Union should focus on the robust enforcement of existing laws such as the Digital Services Act (DSA) and General Data Protection Regulation (GDPR) to mitigate the spread of false information online. These laws should be adapted to better address the challenges posed by disinformation campaigns.
- Monitoring how adequate is the implementation of the EU AI Act.
- Establish a publicly accessible register for all Members of the European Parliament, documenting their public appearances and interactions on social media to increase transparency and mitigate the risks of misinformation.
- Enhance cooperation with international bodies and third countries to prevent the relocation of disinformation operations to jurisdictions outside the EU's control. This includes coordinating sanctions and other measures to disrupt financial and logistical support for these campaigns.
- Implement targeted campaigns to raise awareness about disinformation tactics among EU citizens, including how to identify and report suspicious content. Enhance digital literacy programs to build resilience against misinformation.

4.17 Doppelganger: Russian Disinformation Using Media Clones and More

4.17.1 Introduction

Doppelganger is an ongoing Russia-based influence operation network operating in Europe since at least May 2022. EU DisinfoLab named the campaign after the practice of using multiple "clones" of authentic media and targeting users with fake articles [T0085.003], press releases [T0085.004], videos [T0087], memes [T0086] [T0086.001] and polls [T0029]. To do so, the malicious actors bought dozens of Internet domain names similar to the ones of existing media and copied their designs [T0013] [T0049.007] [T0098] [T0098.001] [T0099].

After the first exposure [C00184] [C00113] [C00115][470] in August 2022 by German media including T-Online[471] and *Süddeutsche Zeitung*,[472] many other

[470] These countermeasures, taken from the DISARM Blue Framework, are applicable to every exposure.

[471] Wienand L., S. Steurenthaler and S. Loelke, "Putins Troll-Armee greift Deutschland an", *T-Online*, 30 Aug 2022. https://www.t-online.de/nachrichten/deutschland/gesellschaft/id_100042596/ukraine-krieg-prorussische-kampagne-das-steckt-hinter-den-fake-artikeln.html.

[472] Brühl J., B. Heubl and S. Hurtz, "Propaganda mit gefälschten SZ-Videos", *Süddeutsche Zeitung*, 7 Sept 2022. https://www.sueddeutsche.de/politik/desinformation-russische-propaganda-sz-fake-news-1.5651531.

organisations wrote about the campaign, including EU DisinfoLab in collaboration with Qurium,[473] the Atlantic Council's Digital Forensic Research Lab (DFR-Lab)[474] and ISD.[475] Following these exposures, *Süddeutsche Zeitung* brought its case before the World Intellectual Property Office (WIPO) for trademark violation and successfully reseized the impersonated domain [C00060].[476]

In December 2022, Meta attributed the campaign to two Russian companies [C00116] [C00119] [C00070] [C00107] [C00122] [C00172] [C00197] [C00133], Social Design Agency and Struktura.[477] Viginum and the French government reinforced the attributions some months later. The two companies were eventually placed on the EU sanctions list in July 2023 [C00060] [C00129] [C00162].[478]

Nevertheless, the campaign continued, impersonating governments, institutions and other organisations such as NATO [T0099] [T0099.002] [T0099.003]. Further exposures by Graphika[479] and Reset[480] revealed more about the infrastructure: in addition to spoofing domains, the operators created backup domains with typos, redirections [T0129.008] and unrelated names. In October 2023, WIPO ruled in favour of the French government, allowing it to seize the domain name impersonating the French Ministry of Foreign Affairs.[481]

In an authentic community-driven effort, additional exposures revealed other aspects of the Doppelganger operation. For example, the French state agency

---

473 Alaphilippe A., G. Machado, R. Miguel and F. Poldi, "Doppelganger—Media clones serving Russian propaganda", EU DisinfoLab in partnership with Qurium, 27 Sept 2022. https://www.disinfo.eu/doppelganger.

474 Aleksejeva N., R. Osadchuk, S. Gelava, J. Le Roux, M. Caniglia, D. Suárez Pérez and A. Kann, "Russia-based Facebook operation targeted Europe with anti-Ukraine messaging", *DFR-Lab*, 27 Sept 2022. https://medium.com/dfrlab/russia-based-facebook-operation-targeted-europe-with-anti-ukraine-messaging-389e32324d4.

475 Institute for Strategic Dialogue, "Pro-Kremlin Network Impersonates Legitimate Websites and Floods Social Media with Lies", 29 Sept 2022. https://www.isdglobal.org/digital_dispatches/pro-kremlin-network-impersonates-legitimate-websites-and-floods-social-media-with-lies/.

476 https://www.wipo.int/amc/en/domains/decisions/pdf/2022/dme2022-0020.pdf.

477 Nimmo, B., "Removing Coordinated Inauthentic Behavior From China and Russia", Meta, 27 Sept 2022, updated 15 December 2022. https://about.fb.com/news/2022/09/removing-coordinated-inauthentic-behavior-from-china-and-russia/.

478 Viginum, "RRN: A complex and persistent information manipulation campaign", 19 July 2023. https://www.sgdsn.gouv.fr/files/files/20230719_NP_VIGINUM_RAPPORT-CAMPAGNE-RRN_EN1.pdf. See also Council of the EU, "Information manipulation in Russia's war of aggression against Ukraine: EU lists seven individuals and five entities", 28 July 2023. https://www.consilium.europa.eu/en/press/press-releases/2023/07/28/information-manipulation-in-russia-s-war-of-aggression-against-ukraine-eu-lists-seven-individuals-and-five-entities/.

479 Ronzaud L., J.A. Carter and T. Williams, "Summit old, summit new. Russia-linked actors leverage new and old tactics in influence operations targeting online conversations about NATO summit", *Graphika*, Aug 2023. https://public-assets.graphika.com/reports/graphika_report_summit_old_summit_new.pdf.

480 Reset, "Vast networks of fake accounts raise questions about Meta's compliance with the EU's new digital rulebook", Oct 2023. https://www.reset.tech/documents/24102023_Networks-of-Facebook-Fake-Advertisers_Reset.pdf.

481 https://www.wipo.int/amc/en/domains/decisions/pdf/2023/dfm2023-0001.pdf.

Viginum published a detailed technical report and dubbed the campaign RRN, referring to one of its key components, the media "Reliable Recent News".[482] *The Insider*[483] noticed that the campaign overlapped with a get-rich-quick scheme [T0074.003] [T00072.003]. The US Department of State[484] denounced new campaigns by the same actors in Latin America [T0072.001]. *Le Monde*[485] unveiled links to offline actions [T0057] [T0057.001] [T0057.002] [T0126], such as the Star of David graffiti flooding the streets of Paris in November 2023. QuoIntelligence[486] reported connections to a Spanish election information operation targeting Russian speakers, and EUvsDisinfo[487] focused on the use of ads and sponsored content [T0114]. Finally, Recorded Future[488] exposed the operation's infrastructure, highlighting obfuscation tactics and coordinated inauthentic behaviour [T0049.003] [T0090.003], which led the malign actors to move their infrastructure and domain assets [T0130].

In early 2024, *Der Spiegel*[489] revealed the campaign's impersonation of Annalena Baerbock [T0099] [T0099.005] [T0072.005] and support for the far-right party Alternative für Deutschland and other pro-Russian politicians.[490] Moreover, Qurium[491] identified a shared distribution infrastructure with another campaign

[482] Viginum, "RRN: a complex and persistent information manipulation campaign", Secrétariat général de la Défense et de la Sécurité nationale, 19 July 2023. https://tinyurl.com/5ycxxxum.

[483] Avdeenko N., "Russia's disinformation campaign targets Ukraine with fake Der Spiegel, Fox News, and RBC websites", *The Insider*, 30 Oct 2023. https://theins.ru/en/news/266351.

[484] US Department of State, "The Kremlin's efforts to covertly spread disinformation in Latin America", 7 Nov 2023. https://www.state.gov/the-kremlins-efforts-to-covertly-spread-disinformation-in-latin-america/.

[485] Albertini A., D. Leloup and F. Reynaud, "Stars of David graffiti in Paris: Russian interference suspected", *Le Monde*, 7 Nov 2023. https://www.lemonde.fr/en/france/article/2023/11/07/stars-of-david-graffiti-in-paris-russian-interference-suspected_6235378_7.html.

[486] QuoIntelligence, "Decoding disinformation: The Spanish election information operation targeting Russian-speakers", 8 Nov 2023. https://quointelligence.eu/2023/11/spanish-election-information-operation-targeting-russian-speakers/.

[487] EUvsDisinfo, "Something dark hiding behind the ads", 20 Nov 2023. https://euvsdisinfo.eu/something-dark-hiding-behind-the-ads/.

[488] Recorded Future, "Obfuscation and AI Content in the Russian Influence Network 'Doppelgänger' Signals Evolving Tactics", 5 Dec 2023. https://go.recordedfuture.com/hubfs/reports/ta-2023-1205.pdf.

[489] Rosenbach M., and C. Schult, "Baerbocks Digitaldetektive decken russische Lügenkampagne auf", *Der Spiegel*, 26 Jan 2024. https://www.spiegel.de/politik/deutschland/desinformation-aus-russland-auswaertiges-amt-deckt-pro-russische-kampagne-auf-a-765bb30e-8f76-4606-b7ab-8fb9287a6948?nlid=die-lage-am-morgen&sara_ecid=nl_upd_1jtzCCtmxpVo9GAZr2b4X8GquyeAc9.

[490] Stöcker, Christian, "Die nächste Welle aus der gleichen Quelle", *Der Spiegel*, 25 Feb 2024. https://www.spiegel.de/wissenschaft/mensch/propaganda-aus-russland-putins-trolle-machen-unverdrossen-weiter-christian-stoecker-kolumne-a-a6bbb2bb-fd8b-4e99-94c6-acf94f779225?sara_ref=re-so-app-sh.

[491] Qurium, "Russian disinformation against Zelenskyy exposed on Times Square billboard", 2 Feb 2024. https://www.qurium.org/alerts/russian-disinformation-against-zelenskyy-exposed-on-times-square-billboard/.

labelled Matrioshka. Sentinel Labs[492] highlighted the two-stage redirection system [T0123.004] and ClearSky[493] performed further attribution. In the meantime, the French registry operator (AFNIC) decided to return a cloned domain name to *Le Parisien*.[494]

In another round of exposures, DFRLab[495] identified page farms used by Doppelganger [T0096], T-Online[496] reported on Russian journalists' interviewing German experts and politicians under false pretences and spreading the interviews' manipulated content on fake websites and social media [T0104] [T0104.001] [T0114.001], and *The New York Times*[497] showed the campaign fuelling Kate Middleton's health conspiracy theories [T0022] [T0022.001]. Even more recently, *The Washington Post*[498] revealed the use of fake surveys on Facebook and TikTok [T0080.002] and troll farms [T0049.001] [T0091.003] aimed at showing reduced support for Ukraine in the US [T0132] [T0132.001] [T0133].

In March 2024, the US Department of the Treasury's Office of Foreign Assets Control[499] sanctioned two Russian companies, accusing them of providing services to the Russian government. Despite all the efforts by the defender community, the campaign is still ongoing.

---

[492] Milenkoski A., "Doppelgänger | Russia-aligned influence operation targets Germany", *Sentinel Labs*, 22 Feb 2024. https://www.sentinelone.com/labs/doppelganger-russia-aligned-influence-operation-targets-germany/.

[493] ClearSky, "Doppelgänger NG | Russian Cyberwarfare campaign", 22 Feb 2024. https://www.clearskysec.com/dg/.

[494] https://syreli.fr/decisions/telecharger/55374&sa=D&source=docs&ust=1712316785481549&usg=AOvVaw3yGsvgXkbnH74xhtnNy4Uy.

[495] Châtelet, V., and R. Osadchuk, "Doppelganger targets Ukrainian and French audiences via Facebook ads", *DFRLab*, 12 Mar 2024. https://dfrlab.org/2024/03/12/doppelganger-operation-targets-ukraine/.

[496] Wienand, L., and H. Molnár, "Mysteriöse Kampagne gegen den Westen: Sie machen mit", *T-Online*, 27 Mar 2024. https://www.t-online.de/nachrichten/deutschland/id_100366874/fake-seiten-und-bots-diese-russen-arbeiten-fuer-kampagne-gegen-den-westen-.html.

[497] Landler, Mark, and Adam Satariano, "Russian group spread disinformation about Princess of Wales, experts say", *The New York Times*, 27 Mar 2024. https://www.nytimes.com/2024/03/27/world/europe/princess-kate-middleton-russia-conspiracy.html.

[498] Belton, Catherine, and Joseph Menn, "Russian trolls target U.S. support for Ukraine, Kremlin documents show", *The Washington Post*, 8 Apr 2024. https://www.washingtonpost.com/world/2024/04/08/russia-propaganda-us-ukraine/.

[499] US Department of the Treasury, "Treasury sanctions actors supporting Kremlin-directed malign influence efforts", 20 Mar 2024. https://home.treasury.gov/news/press-releases/jy2195.

4.17.2 Threat Actors

In December 2022, Meta made the first attribution of the campaign to two companies: Struktura National Technologies, a Russia-based information technology firm, and Social Design Agency, a Moscow-based marketing and political consulting firm.[500]

In July 2023, the Council of the EU imposed sanctions against "seven Russian individuals and five entities responsible for conducting a digital information manipulation campaign called 'RRN' (Recent Reliable News)", another denomination of the campaign coined by Viginum.[501] The Council referred to Ilya Andreevich Gambashidze, the founder of Social Design Agency, and Nikolai Aleksandrovich Tupikin, the CEO and current owner of Struktura. European authorities also identified five other individuals as responsible and three other entities: Inforos, ANO Dialog and the Institute of the Russian Diaspora.[502]

In February 2024, the US Department of the Treasury's Office of Foreign Assets Control identified the Social Design Agency and Struktura as owned or controlled by, or having acted or purported to act for or on behalf of, directly or indirectly, the government of the Russian Federation.[503]

4.17.3 Presumed Objectives

The DISARM categorisation helped identify the following presumed objectives[504]:

- T0140: Cause harm—This was achieved through the defamation [T0140.001] and harming [T0140.003] of adversaries, for instance, attacking Ukrainian President Zelenskyy or spreading false information about Ukrainian refugees.
- T0136: Cultivate support—Pro-Russian narratives are spread to defend [T0136.001] and boost [T0136.004] Russia's reputation, justifying its actions [T0136.002] against Ukraine. Besides cultivating support for the invasion

[500] Nimmo, Ben, "Removing Coordinated Inauthentic Behavior From China and Russia", *Meta*, 27 Sept 2022, updated 15 Dec 2022. https://about.fb.com/news/2022/09/removing-coordinated-inauthentic-behavior-from-china-and-russia/.

[501] Viginum, "RRN: a complex and persistent information manipulation campaign", Secrétariat général de la Défense et de la Sécurité nationale, 19 July 2023. https://tinyurl.com/5ycxxxum.

[502] Council of the EU, "Information manipulation in Russia's war of aggression against Ukraine: EU lists seven individuals and five entities", 28 July 2023. https://www.consilium.europa.eu/en/press/press-releases/2023/07/28/information-manipulation-in-russia-s-war-of-aggression-against-ukraine-eu-lists-seven-individuals-and-five-entities/.

[503] Ibid.

[504] Unless otherwise indicated in the footnotes, all examples are taken from EU DisinfoLab's report. (Alaphilippe, A., G. Machado, R. Miguel and F. Poldi, "Doppelganger—Media clones serving Russian propaganda", EU DisinfoLab in partnership with Qurium, 27 Sept 2022. https://www.disinfo.eu/doppelganger.).

[T0136.005], the malign actors also incentivise support for ideological allies [T0136.006], such as the German far-right party Alternative für Deutschland.[505]

- T0066: Degrade adversary—Pro-Ukraine countries are degraded, as the campaign depicts targeted countries as failed states incapable of providing for their citizens.
- T0075: Dismiss—Credible sources, such as legitimate media [T0075.001], are dismissed through impersonation, for instance, a fake *Süddeutsche Zeitung* article about a German family wanting to move to Siberia.
- T0139: Dissuade from acting—The disinformation campaign wishes to discourage [T0139.001] and deter [T0139.003] the imposition of sanctions against Russia by framing them as damaging to EU populations.
- T0076: Distort—Facts are systematically distorted to exaggerate the impact of sanctions, for instance, through decontextualised images of empty supermarket shelves as a sign of food shortages.
- T0077: Distract—False and misleading information is used to distract the audience from the real impact of the war and sanctions, having Western populations focus on their own alleged economic crises rather than the attack on Ukraine.
- T0079: Divide—The campaign seeks to polarise and divide public opinion in the targeted countries over their support for Ukraine and its refugees.
- T0002: Facilitate state propaganda—All the narratives present in the campaign are consistent with Russian propaganda, such as accusing Ukraine of being a Nazi state.
- T0137: Make money—Monetisation and scams [T0137.002] are marginal. However, at some point, several impersonated websites redirected users to get-rich-quick schemes.[506]
- T0138: Motivate to act—Malign actors encouraged [T0138.001], provoked [T0138.002] and compelled [T0138.003] people to engage in offline protests to end their country's support for Ukraine and Russia sanctions. For example, they called for an in-person protest in Riga, Latvia, against the planned return of military conscription.[507]
- T0135: Undermine—The continuous undermining of adversarial politicians and governments, represented as incapable and corrupt pollutes the debate through smearing [T0135.001] and polarisation [T0135.004].

[505] Rosenbach M., and C. Schult, "Baerbocks Digitaldetektive decken russische Lügenkampagne auf", *Der Spiegel*, 26 Jan 2024. https://www.spiegel.de/politik/deutschland/desinformation-aus-russland-auswaertiges-amt-deckt-pro-russische-kampagne-auf-a-765bb30e-8f76-4606-b7ab-8fb9287a6948?nlid=die-lage-am-morgen&sara_ecid=nl_upd_1jtzCCtmxpVo9GAZr2b4X8GquyeAc9.

[506] Avdeenko N., "Russia's disinformation campaign targets Ukraine with fake Der Spiegel, Fox News, and RBC websites", *The Insider*, 30 Oct 2023, https://theins.ru/en/news/266351.

[507] Institute for Strategic Dialogue, "Pro-Kremlin Network Impersonates Legitimate Websites and Floods Social Media with Lies", 29 Sept 2022. https://www.isdglobal.org/digital_dispatches/pro-kremlin-network-impersonates-legitimate-websites-and-floods-social-media-with-lies/.

4.17.4 Incidents and Observables

Incidents—Given the extended nature of the Doppelganger campaign, this section focuses on some incidents from EU DisinfoLab's findings, that is to say, the impersonation of German media *Bild*.[508]

Observables—These include the following domains: bild[.]asia; bild[.]vip; bild[.]pics; bild[.]eu.com; bild[.]live; bild[.]llc; bild[.]work; bild[.]ws.

4.17.5 Targets

The Doppelganger campaign has many targets:

- Individuals—e.g., politicians such as Ukrainian President Zelenskyy and German Minister of Foreign Affairs Annalena Baerbock
- Institutions—e.g., impersonated Ministries
- Governments—those supporting Ukraine
- The public—the Ukrainian population under attack, EU and US citizens
- Media—the impersonated media are the focus of the operation
- Other organisations—e.g., NATO.

4.17.6 Tactics, Techniques and Procedures

The Doppelganger operation uses every tactic listed in the DISARM Red Framework and dozens of TTPs. Below are the principal ones:

- TA01: Plan strategy—Strategic ends [T0074] and target audiences [T0073] were determined based on various criteria.
- TA02: Plan objectives—Already discussed in the previous section.
- TA13: Target audience analysis—The operators identified social and technical vulnerabilities [T0081], mapped the target audience's information environment [T0080] and segmented their audiences to spread pro-Russian content.
- TA14: Develop narratives—The campaign relies on new [T0082] and existing [T0003] narratives, integrating the target audience vulnerabilities [T0083], leveraging conspiracy theories [T0022] and existing narratives [T0003]. In addition, it showed the ability to respond to breaking news and active crises like the conflict in Ukraine and Israel [T0068].
- TA06: Develop content—Including image [T0086], text-based [T0085], video-based [T0087] content, reusing existing content [T0084] and distorting facts [T0023].

[508] A list of 56 Doppelganger domains is available in the report. (Alaphilippe et al., op. cit., 27 Sept 2022).

- TA15: Establish social assets—The FIMI actors acquired a network [T0093], and created inauthentic websites [T0013], accounts [T0090] and social media pages [T0007]. They tried to cultivate ignorant agents such as influencers [T0010], developed their own media assets [T0095] and deployed commercial analytic firms [T0113].
- TA16: Establish legitimacy—The FIMI co-opted trusted sources [T0100] and created fake experts [T0009], it created personas [T0097], established inauthentic news sites [T0098] and impersonated existing entities [T0099].
- TA05: Microtarget—Deceptive means employed included creating clickbait [T0016], localised content [T0101] and purchasing large numbers of targeted ads [T0018].
- TA07: Select channels and affordances—The operation flooded discussion forums [T0106], relied on the endorsement of formal diplomatic channels [T0110], created online pools [T0029] and used social networks [T0104].
- TA08: Conduct pump priming—Seeding distortion [T0044] and seeding kernels of truth [T0042] are common practices.
- TA09: Deliver content—Malign actors posted [T0115], commented and replied [T0116] and delivered ads [T0114] on social media.
- TA17: Maximise exposure—This includes the amplification of existing narratives [T0118], cross-posting [T0119] and flooding the information space [T0049].
- TA18: Drive online harms—Doppelganger operators managed to control the information environment through offensive cyberspace operations [T0123] and carried out a harassment campaign against ideological opponents [T0048].
- TA010: Drive offline activity—In the framework of the campaign, events were organised [T0057] and attendance encouraged [T0126].
- TA11: Persist in the information environment—The FIMI continuously tried to conceal its information assets [T0128], infrastructure [T0130], operational activities [T0129], while continuing to amplify the campaign [T0060].
- TA12: Measure effectiveness—Discussed in the next section, but we can expect attempts to measure the effectiveness [T0133] and performance [T0132] of the campaign via geoblocking[509] technology.

4.17.7 Channels

The types of channels used to purvey the FIMI include the following:

- Official communication channels—A long list of Facebook pages of the Russian diplomatic network [T0110] published a link connected to the Doppelganger

[509] Doppelganger actors set up a geoblocking feature. For instance, if visitors were not based in Germany, they could not have access to the German-speaking disinformation they designed. This system could also help them to measure the impact and reach of these articles in German.

operation, e.g., the Russian embassy in France, Germany, Italy, Mexico, the US, etc.[510]

- State-linked channels—According to the Department of the Treasury's Office of Foreign Assets Control, Social Design Agency and Struktura are owned or controlled by or have acted or purported to act for or on behalf of, directly or indirectly, the government of the Russian Federation.[511]
- Pro-state channels—For example, such as "Alina Lipp"[512] and "Neues aus Russland".[513]
- Private sector channels—Social media can be included in this category, and malign actors established accounts, pages and groups on Facebook, Instagram, TikTok, X and YouTube.
- Format—The format is diverse and includes manipulated video, images (including memes) and text (in the form of news articles and fake press releases).

4.17.8 Languages

The FIMI attack appeared in multiple languages: Arabic,[514] English, French, German, Hebrew,[515] Italian, Latvian, Spanish,[516] Russian, Ukrainian.

4.17.9 Effectiveness

It is difficult to calculate the impact of a campaign due to the limited data provided by some platforms. Therefore, this section leads to some degree of speculation.

[510] Viginum, "RRN: A complex and persistent information manipulation campaign", 19 July 2023. https://www.sgdsn.gouv.fr/files/files/20230719_NP_VIGINUM_RAPPORT-CAMPAGNE-RRN_EN1.pdf.

[511] US Department of the Treasury, "Treasury sanctions actors supporting Kremlin-directed malign influence efforts", 20 Mar 2024. https://home.treasury.gov/news/press-releases/jy2195.

[512] Luyken J., "Ex-German Green party activist 'parrots Putin's propaganda from the front line'", *The Telegraph*, 11 Jan 2023. https://www.telegraph.co.uk/world-news/2023/01/11/alina-lipp-germany-green-party-russia-propaganda-ukraine-invasion/.

[513] Guseva, M., M. Fridman and A. Grygoryshyn, "Pro-Russian Disinformation and Propaganda in the German Telegram Network around 'Neues aus Russland'", *Correctiv*, Oct 2023. https://correctiv.org/wp-content/uploads/2024/04/Correlaid-Report-English_Neues-aus-Russland_Telegram-Network-Analysis-Python.pdf.

[514] Reset, "Vast networks of fake accounts raise questions about Meta's compliance with the EU's new digital rulebook", Oct 2023. https://www.reset.tech/documents/24102023_Networks-of-Facebook-Fake-Advertisers_Reset.pdf.

[515] Avdeenko, op. cit.

[516] US Department of State, "The Kremlin's efforts to covertly spread disinformation in Latin America", 7 Nov 2023. https://www.state.gov/the-kremlins-efforts-to-covertly-spread-disinformation-in-latin-america/.

Moreover, different stakeholders investigated different aspects of this two-year-long campaign, which is still ongoing, focusing on a given platform, country, language, narrative and format. Based on the data, it is safe to say that the campaign has reached millions of people.[517]

The FIMI campaign could change people's behaviour and actions, as users—including public figures[518]—shared, reacted to and commented on the content. The campaign contributed to fuelling social divisions and polarisation. Finally, researchers believe that Doppelganger operators coordinated offline protests.[519]

The FIMI negatively affected beliefs[520] (e.g., fabricating surveys to exaggerate support for Russia in the war against Ukraine), knowledge (e.g., feeding on conspiracy beliefs), emotions (e.g., fuelling anger against the alleged corruption of European leaders) and trust (e.g., discrediting credible news media by impersonating them).

4.17.10 Countermeasures

Some measures were taken to counter the attack:

- Content moderation or curation—Meta and X took down content and restricted their services to the malign actors [C00070] [C00071] [C00107] [C00122] [C00172] [C00197] [C00133].
- Statement of rebuttal/condemnation—Several impersonated media and institutions made statements flagging the impersonation and distancing themselves from the cloned websites. *Süddeutsche Zeitung* asked readers to report fake

[517] For example, of the 29 Facebook ads analysed by ISD, those targeting French audiences received between 1.43 and 1.73 million impressions in total. Institute for Strategic Dialogue, "Pro-Kremlin Network Impersonates Legitimate Websites and Floods Social Media with Lies", 29 Sept 2022. https://www.isdglobal.org/digital_dispatches/pro-kremlin-network-impersonates-legitimate-websites-and-floods-social-media-with-lies/.

[518] For example, AfD's politician Thomas Fetsch. See Institute for Strategic Dialogue, "Pro-Kremlin Network Impersonates Legitimate Websites and Floods Social Media with Lies", 29 Sept 2022. https://www.isdglobal.org/digital_dispatches/pro-kremlin-network-impersonates-legitimate-websites-and-floods-social-media-with-lies/).

[519] Ibid.

[520] Lamberty, Pia, and Lea Frühwirth, "Pro-Russian Disinformation and Propaganda in Germany: Russia's full-scale Invasion of Ukraine", *CeMAS,* Feb 2023. https://cemas.io/en/publications/pro-russian-disinformation-and-propaganda-in-germany/2023-02-24_ProRussianDisinformationAndPropagandaInGermanyRussiasFullScaleInvasionInUkraine.pdf.

websites.[521] The German Ministry of Interior acknowledged the impersonation and stated its commitment to "curb the spread of misinformation".[522]

- Fact-checking—The campaign called the attention of fact-checkers, for instance, in 2022[523] and 2023,[524] AFP debunked the impersonation of websites. In 2024,[525] the same organisation verified a misleading video about the farmers' protest causing an arson to the Ukrainian Embassy in France.
- Legal proceedings—Although these countermeasures did not cause a change in policy or law per se, they showed an application of these principles, favouring considerations on their effectiveness.
  - *Süddeutsche Zeitung* used ICANN's UDRP (Uniform Domain Resolution Procedure) to bring the case before the WIPO arbitration panel to have the domain sueddeutsche[.]me successfully transferred to it.[526]
  - *Le Monde* used the same UDRP mechanism, although via a different arbitration panel (the Czech Arbitration Court), to open a disputed domain name against lemonde[.]ltd. The complaint was accepted, and the domain was transferred to the newspaper in July 2023.[527]
  - After the WIPO ruling, the French government could seize the domain name impersonating the French Ministry of Foreign Affairs (diplomatie[.]gouv[.]fm).[528]
  - The French registry operator AFNIC (which is the registry for [.]re domains) decided to return the domain name (leparisien[.]re) to *Le Parisien*, as the website's only purpose was to have a domain name (and website) that was confusingly like the legitimate domain.[529]

---

[521] Brühl, J., B. Heubl and S. Hurtz, "Propaganda mit gefälschten SZ-Videos", *Süddeutsche Zeitung*, 7 Sept 2022. https://www.sueddeutsche.de/politik/desinformation-russische-propaganda-sz-fake-news-1.5651531.

[522] Buschek, Christo, Roman Höfner and Hakan Tanriverdi, "Frankreich warnt vor russischer Desinformation", *Der Spiegel*, 16 June 2023. https://www.spiegel.de/netzwelt/frankreich-warnt-vor-russischer-desinformation-a-f208ac9b-1507-4c0f-b438-a6192e51d8b5.

[523] Salem, Saladin, and Eva Wackenreuther, "Vorsicht vor prorussischer Propaganda auf gefälschten Nachrichten-Seiten", *AFP Faktencheck*, 4 Oct 2022. https://faktencheck.afp.com/doc.afp.com.32K89J3-1.

[524] Gallo, Nathan, "Sites pirates de médias: quand le narratif pro-russe 's'invite' dans la presse occidentale", *AFP Factuel*, 12 June 2023. https://factuel.afp.com/doc.afp.com.33J829J.

[525] Orsini A., "Non, cette vidéo ne montre pas des agriculteurs asperger l'ambassade d'Ukraine de fumier", *AFP Factuel*, 14 Feb 2024. https://faktencheck.afp.com/doc.afp.com.32K89J3-1.

[526] https://www.wipo.int/amc/en/domains/decisions/pdf/2022/dme2022-0020.pdf.

[527] Decision for dispute CAC-UDRP-105536 https://udrp.adr.eu/decisions/detail?id=64b1307e8aa1b86c2906d7c5.

[528] https://www.wipo.int/amc/en/domains/decisions/pdf/2023/dfm2023-0001.pdf

[529] https://syreli.fr/decisions/telecharger/55374&sa=D&source=docs&ust=1712316785481549&usg=AOvVaw3yGsvgXkbnH74xhtnNy4Uy.

- The Council of the EU[530] imposed restrictive measures against seven Russian individuals and five entities responsible for the Doppelganger/RRN operation, freezing their assets, banning natural persons from travelling into and through EU territories, and prohibiting EU citizens and companies from making funds available to these entities.
- The US Department of the Treasury's Office of Foreign Assets Control sanctioned two individuals (Gambashidze and Tupikin) and two entities (Social Design Agency and Struktura) for providing services to "the Government of the Russian Federation (GoR) in connection with a foreign malign influence campaign".[531] As a result, all US property and interests in property were blocked, and transactions involving funds, goods or services with the blocked individuals were prohibited.

4.17.11 Conclusions and Recommendations

Conclusions

Since February 2022, the Russian-origin "Doppelganger" operation—also known as RRN—has targeted multiple countries to undermine support for Ukraine by impersonating media and institutional websites and spreading disinformation. The campaign illustrates how the abuse of the domain registration system or the European web infrastructure and software can be exploited by hostile actors for the purpose of foreign interference.

On the positive side, it is an example of how the community of defenders and stakeholders against FIMI have reacted to stop this campaign with multiple measures in place. On the negative side, Doppelganger illustrates how, despite this unprecedent effort and the identification and sanctioning of the main threat actors, the operation has been expanded with new actions and a complex obfuscation infrastructure to persist and target other international events. In other words, Doppelganger shows how threat actors have been able to evolve their TTPs and persist in the information ecosystem, highlighting the challenges faced by the counter-FIMI community.

Recommendations

According to EU DisinfoLab,[532] this operation calls for a series of European actions:

---

[530] Council of the EU, "Information manipulation in Russia's war of aggression against Ukraine: EU lists seven individuals and five entities", 28 July 2023. https://www.consilium.europa.eu/en/press/press-releases/2023/07/28/information-manipulation-in-russia-s-war-of-aggression-against-ukraine-eu-lists-seven-individuals-and-five-entities/.

[531] US Department of the Treasury, "Treasury sanctions actors supporting Kremlin-directed malign influence efforts", 20 Mar 2024. https://home.treasury.gov/news/press-releases/jy2195.

[532] Alaphilippe A., G. Machado, R. Miguel and F. Poldi, "Doppelganger—Media clones serving Russian propaganda", EU DisinfoLab in partnership with Qurium, 27 Sept 2022. https://www.disinfo.eu/doppelganger.

- Implement stricter regulations in the domain name industry to protect legitimate entities from being impersonated. Engaging with domain name registries as the intermediary closest to the problem of impersonation appears to be the most effective way to address issues such as impersonation.
- Ensure appropriate measures so that EU-registered software and infrastructure are not exploited for malicious covert influence operations without facing consequences.
- Emphasise the importance of enforcing existing laws, such as the Digital Services Act (DSA) and General Data Protection Regulation (GDPR), to their full extent to safeguard users.
- Overcome the lack of accountability for opaque and ill-intentioned organisations by fostering greater cooperation between institutions that can attribute information operations and those that enforce laws like trademark laws and GDPR.
- Provide better access to platform data to European researchers (including non-academics from civil society organisations) working for the public interest under Article 40 of the DSA.

4.18 Russian Disinformation About Russian Attacks

4.18.1 Introduction

The specific campaign of blaming Ukraine's military forces for the consequences of the Russian attacks has been an essential strategy of Russia to weaponise information for military purposes, in particular, in the context of its aggression. Russian FIMI has been used massively during the entire conflict in Ukraine since 2014; however, after Russia launched the full-scale aggression against Ukraine on 24 February 2022, the FIMI approach started to be used to support military actions to transfer the consequences to the Ukrainian side, justify military actions, manipulate the context and undermine the causal relationship within the event.

One prominent example happened two days before the large-scale invasion started, when the so-called "Donetsk separatists", controlled by the Russian government, blamed the Armed Forces of Ukraine (AFU) for attacking a residential house near Donetsk. Simultaneously, Russian Telegram channels disseminated the video with the so-called successful capturing of the Ukrainian "saboteurs" who were "neutralised" while hidden in the residential house. After thorough verification of both video clips,[533] it became clear the same house was in both, where "Donets militants" attacked so-called Ukrainian saboteurs, and on the video, where the so-called victims blamed the Ukrainian army for shelling civilian areas. After thorough fact-checking and analysing, the case proved the artificial nature of both videos, which allows us to talk about how the Russian government used information to distort facts about the military intervention in Ukraine.

[533] https://www.stopfake.org/ru/vo-vremya-semki-postanovochnogo-video-boeviki-dnr-obstrelyali-zhiloj-dom-A-potom-vydali-eto-za-prestuplenie-vsu/.

During numerous attacks on Ukrainian facilities, including civil objects, information coverage has played an important role in how perception of the war is shaped, which has had consequences for the geopolitical stance, especially in the EU on the eve of the European elections.

For example, Russia has repeatedly attacked the Ukrainian city Odessa in the south. On 30 April 2024, Russia attacked the Ukrainian city with three Iskander-M ballistic missiles.[534] The attack hit residential houses, university buildings and civil infrastructure works; three persons died, and three more were injured. Russian information sources instead blamed Ukrainian air defence system for causing the damages. Russia has used the same approach in attacking other cities.

The Russian communication approach shows the intention to shift responsibility from those who attack onto those who defend and protect. In this case, the Russian Federation blamed Ukrainian forces on the international level to reduce the perception of its own responsibility for committing war crimes and aggression.

Therefore, pursuing geopolitical responsibility [T0074.001] on the international level as well as shaping public opinion inside the country [T0074.002: domestic political advantage] are applicable in the context of the Russian military attack strategy.

The Russians applied the narrative that the missile attack on the residential house was the result of the counteracts by the AFU, not the Russian rocket attacks, since Russia targets only military objects. For Russian war propaganda, it is crucial to degrade the abilities of the Ukrainian Army and portray it as the cause of instability and harmful effects on people, as well as to shift the responsibility for supposed war crimes onto Ukraine.

By blaming the AFU for the damages, Russia's FIMI responded to the event [T0068], securing a leadership niche in covering the course of the hostilities. Russia first used the narrative about the air defence system forces of Ukraine in 2022 after its large-scale aggression started. Therefore, this is one of the scandalised information frames [T0003: leveraging existing narrative] of FIMI to respond to the event. Russia integrated societal vulnerabilities in the endangered position to misinterpret the context [T0083].

---

[534] https://ukc-word-edit.officeapps.live.com/we/wordeditorframe.aspx?ui=en-US&rs=en-US&wopisrc=https%3A%2F%2Ftrilateralcloud.sharepoint.com%2Fsites%2FForeigninterferenc%2F_vti_bin%2Fwopi.ashx%2Ffiles%2F9954fa551be043cbaf4a35e3706ff021&wdenableroaming=1&mscc=1&hid=5E9627A1-800F-8000-B79A-C89EEC30D24E.0&uih=sharepointcom&wdlcid=en-US&jsapi=1&jsapiver=v2&corrid=8c24e285-009f-3c36-46c3-c5c170fc3899&usid=8c24e285-009f-3c36-46c3-c5c170fc3899&newsession=1&sftc=1&uihit=docaspx&muv=1&cac=1&sams=1&mtf=1&sfp=1&sdp=1&hch=1&hwfh=1&dchat=1&sc=%7B%22pmo%22%3A%22https%3A%2F%2Ftrilateralcloud.sharepoint.com%22%2C%22pmshare%22%3Atrue%7D&ctp=LeastProtected&rct=Normal&wdorigin=ItemsView&wdhostclicktime=1715423741704&instantedit=1&wopicomplete=1&wdredirectionreason=Unified_SingleFlush#_ftn2.

4.18.2 Threat Actors

Russia first disseminated information pieces and elements of the FIMI campaign on the network of sites affiliated with Russia, hosted on Russian domains and via the messages of Russian-related bloggers, politicians and influencers. Russian-related social media platforms such as Telegram, Vkontakte and Odnoklassniki exploited the echo chamber effect to deliver messages. However, Vkontakte and Odnoklassniki have limited audiences because of the restrictions in Ukraine and Western countries. Still, Telegram remains the most accessed Russian-affiliated platform, especially regarding war developments, while it provides the function of automatised translation in any language.

4.18.3 Presumed Objectives

Of the presumed objectives in the DISARM Framework, we see these:

T0066: Degrade adversary (in order to portray AFU in a negative light and affect its perception by the population of Ukraine).

T0078: Dismay—aimed at overwhelming the Ukrainian population.

T0135.004: Undermine trust—of Ukrainians in the AFU to protect civil population.

T0139: Dissuade from acting—from supporting the AFU.

T0076: Distort facts—from the point of mirroring responsibility for victims and outcome damages.

T0079, T0135.004: Divide—the Ukrainian population in the context of consensus regarding the necessity to fight back.

T0002: Facilitate state propaganda—Russia claims its Army does not deliver harm to the civilian population. All these planned objectives work alongside the intention to motivate Ukraine to surrender [T0138] by pressuring the civilian population [T0138.003] with the military and information means simultaneously.

4.18.4 Incidents and Observables

Below are examples of the observables in connection with the incidents in this Russian campaign.

4.18.5 Targets

Within this campaign, we found three main target groups: first were Russian domestic audiences in terms of supporting and legitimising the military actions of the Russian Federation; second, Ukrainians, who were microtargeted, Russian FIMI targeted local inhabitants and, third, the international community, in order to reduce the level of expected responsibility for war crimes against the civilian population and damaging civil infrastructure.

To target the Ukrainian population, Russian FIMI considered internal social vulnerabilities [T0081] and divisions [T0081.006] and attempted to create more tension within the social groups. Russian FIMI exploited existing data voids [T0081.02] and information vacuums at some points in the Ukrainian information environment caused by the martial status, in particular, legal restrictions on media to cover the consequences of shellings. Russian FIMI exploited this regime to impose its own versions of the event, claiming the Ukrainian aircraft system were delivering harm.

4.18.6 Tactics, Techniques and Procedures

The campaign also relied on the content, presented as the expert opinions [T0085.006] of FIMI agents inside and outside Russia. Russian FIMI used existing networks [T0093, T0092], set in the COVID time, and recruited partisans, who built community and sub-groups [T0092.003] for influencing societies outside Russia.

The campaign's goal was to discourage the AFU from defensive actions [T0139.001] and to polarise society in terms of their expectation of the war progress [T0135.004]. Several conspiracy theories were cultivated which have questioned whether it makes sense to defend against Russian aggression and how much the AFU is capable of protecting the population from shellings, as Russian FIMI sought to persuade people that they occurred because of the AFU air defence system [T0081.005, T0022.001].

Together with traditional content crafting techniques [T0088, T0086, T0085, T0087], one of the most critical roles can be ascribed to the content promoted by affiliated bloggers and so-called experts [T00143, T0144] who made manipulative predictions and estimations from the battleground in favour of Russia and who set the scene for further information interference.

4.18.7 Channels

We observed different forms of content; however, here, Telegram played a crucial role as this platform is accessible everywhere. It freely disseminated text [T0085], video and image [T0086] content in real-time, in the Russian language, with authorised translations. This platform also ensured the possibility of disseminating narratives via channels related to media outlets, public figures and influences, which is why we can witness an almost comprehensive information environment.

At the same time, we still need to take seriously traditional [T0111] formats, such as radio programs [T0088] and talk shows on TV led by key persons in the Russian propaganda ecosystem. In the context of discrediting the AFU, particularly air defence forces, many memes [T0086.001] were disseminated, becoming viral content for social media and stock sites. The memes we witnessed in the context of the campaign were in Russian.

4.18.8 Language

The narrative messages appeared in Russian. Still, the Telegram platform provides the function of automated translation into any language and sharing via networks in different countries.

Discrediting highly trusted entities can cause tension in society. Affecting the international community concerning military events can undermine trust in the system of international law on the way to establishing responsibility, create obstacles in the peace process in the future and create challenges for the electoral period in terms of the geopolitical agenda of a country.

4.18.9 Countermeasures

This case uncovers the complexity and connectivity inside Russian strategic war communication. The most recent cities targeted by such incidents, blaming Ukrainian anti-aircraft forces, are Kharkiv and Odessa. Simultaneously, these cities have received huge attention on the main talk shows on Russian TV.

To counter FIMI manipulation of the cause-and-effect relationship of the event, the opposing side should employ detailed official communication providing the civilian population information about the possible risks, employing information, media and alert systems. A thorough analysis of the competing context imposed by the Russian FIMI agents should be explained in the media and by experts concerning actual events with accentuated messages (i.e., avoiding abstract explanations and localising the content where possible).

Countermeasures in the context of military attacks should ensure coordination within government institutions and transparency in collaboration with the media sector. The intelligence sector should be involved in the analysis of the echo chambering within the Russian-related social platforms.

4.18.10 Conclusions and Recommendations

From this case study, we see that Russia tried to shift responsibility for its actions onto its opponents. It scapegoats Ukrainian forces on the international level to reduce the perception of its responsibility for committing war crimes and aggression.

Russian disinformation is disseminated first on the network of sites affiliated with Russia, hosted on Russian domains and via the messages of Russian-related bloggers, politicians and influencers. Russian-related social media platforms such as Telegram, Vkontakte and Odnoklassniki exploit the echo chamber effect to deliver messages. Telegram remains the most accessed Russian-affiliated platform.

Countermeasures in the context of military attacks should ensure coordination within government institutions and transparency in collaboration with the media sector. The intelligence sector should be involved in the analysis of the echo chambering within the Russian-related social platforms.

4.19 Russian Disinformation About COVID-19 Vaccines

4.19.1 Introduction

On 25 May 2021, *The Guardian* published an article entitled "Influencers say Russia-linked PR agency asked them to disparage Pfizer vaccine."[535] The article states that Fazze, a website that describes itself as an "influencer marketing platform" connecting bloggers and advertisers, contacted YouTubers in France and Germany and offered them money to tell their followers that the Pfizer/BioNTech vaccine was responsible for hundreds of deaths.

Fazze told the influencers to say that the death rate from Pfizer's vaccine was three times that from AstraZeneca's, which is technologically similar to Russia's Sputnik V vaccine. Fazze asked the YouTubers to post a link to an article in *Le Monde* newspaper about a leaked report containing data that supposedly proved the claim.[536] Although the article in the newspaper did exist and it indeed contained information about the leaked data, the article didn't mention anything about the alleged death rates from Pfizer/BioNTech.

The Fazze agency is supposed to be based at 5 Percy Street in London but is not registered there. *The Guardian* reported that "Fazze's management came from Moscow and have worked for an agency reportedly founded by a Russian entrepreneur." The BBC reported that Fazze had been acquired by AdNow. Fazze was a joint venture between an AdNow co-director, a Russian named Stanislav Fesenko, and another person whose identity wasn't known. According to *The New York Times*,[537] Mirko Drotschmann, a German health commentator with 1.5 million YouTube subscribers, said in a tweet that Fazze asked him if he wanted to be part of an "information campaign" about Pfizer deaths in exchange for money. After

[535] Henley, John, "Influencers say Russia-linked PR agency asked them to disparage Pfizer vaccine", *The Guardian,* 6 Mar 2021. https://www.theguardian.com/media/2021/may/25/influencers-say-russia-linked-pr-agency-asked-them-to-disparage-pfizer-vaccine.

[536] Barnéoud, Lise, "Ce que disent les documents sur les vaccins anti-Covid-19 volés à l'Agence européenne des médicaments", *Le Monde,* 16 Jan 2021. https://www.lemonde.fr/planete/article/2021/01/16/vaccins-ce-que-disent-les-documents-voles-a-l-agence-europeenne-des-medicaments_6066502_3244.html.

[537] Alderman, Liz, "Influencers Say They Were Urged to Criticize Pfizer Vaccine", *The New York Times,* 27 May 2021. https://www.nytimes.com/2021/05/26/business/pfizer-vaccine-disinformation-influeners.html.

doing some research, he concluded: "Agency headquarters: London. Residence of the CEO: Moscow."[538]

The Russian Embassy in London denied any involvement, stating: "We treat COVID-19 as a global threat and, thus, are not interested in undermining global efforts in the fight against it."[539] However, Russia took a pro-SputnikV and an anti-Pfizer approach.[540] According to a Reuters report in August 2021,[541] Facebook took down 65 accounts from its own platform and 243 Instagram accounts as part of the Fazze-linked operation. Facebook said 24,000 accounts followed one or more of the Instagram accounts. The company said questions about the campaign remained, such as who commissioned Fazze to run it.

4.19.2 Threat Actors

We can identify the following threat actors:

- Fazze: the website that describes itself as an "influencer marketing platform" connecting bloggers and advertisers. Fazze asked social media influencers to post false information about vaccines.
- Social media influencers. Although several influencers in Europe did not post the false information and actually publicised the attempt, social influencers in India did publish information compatible with Fazze's request.
- Russian contacts. The management of Fazze comes from Moscow according to the BBC.

4.19.3 Presumed Objectives

The six key objectives in the DISARM framework pertinent to this case study are the following:

T0076: Distort—Distorting facts about vaccine efficacy to show Pfizer as inferior to AstraZeneca.

T0140.001: Defame—Defaming Western vaccines in comparison to Eastern ones.

T0075.001: Discredit credible sources—Discrediting reliable sources by promoting conspiracy theories about vaccine safety.

---

[538] https://twitter.com/MrWissen2Go/status/1394716050596450312.

[539] Carmichael, Flora, and Charlie Haynes, "Facebook removes anti-vax influence campaign", *BBC News*, 11 Aug 2021. https://www.bbc.com/news/blogs-trending-58167339.

[540] https://x.com/sputnikvaccine/status/1395076433295417347.

[541] Culliford, Elizabeth, "Facebook removes Russian network that targeted influencers to peddle anti-vax messages", Reuters, 11 Aug 2021. https://www.reuters.com/technology/facebook-removes-russian-network-that-targeted-influencers-peddle-anti-vax-2021-08-10/.

T0137: Cultivate support—Boosting the reputation of the Sputnik V vaccine. Defending the reputation of the Sputnik V vaccine against accusations.

T0066: Degrade adversary—Undermining Western governments by suggesting they are promoting a harmful vaccine.

T0002: Facilitate state propaganda—Organising pro-state messaging through influencers and social media.

4.19.4 Incidents and Observables

YouTubers from Germany and France[542] were able to recognise this FIMI campaign, were able to publicise the event and, thus, were able to stop the campaign at an early stage.[543] So, the campaign did not have the opportunity to produce many incidents. However, influencers in India showed a screenshot of it,[544] and *The New York Times* reported the publication of similar videos in Brazil.[545]

4.19.5 Targets

There were several targets of this FIMI campaign:

Western Governments
Orginating false information about Western vaccines, Fazze's aim was not only to undermine confidence in Western-developed vaccines and position the Russian vaccine as superior but also to attack Western governments by sowing doubt about why they would purchase these vaccines knowing the supposed harm they cause. According to *The New York Times*, Fazze's message was: "Claim that Pfizer's COVID-19 vaccine is deadly and that regulators and the mainstream media are covering it up and earn thousands of euros in easy money in exchange."[546]

The Public
Followers of the influencers who were asked to spread the disinformation and the global audience.

542 Alderman, op. cit., 27 May 2021.

543 Von Richthofen, Luisa, "COVID disinformation campaign targeted BioNTech-Pfizer", *DM,* 28 May 2021. https://www.dw.com/en/covid-disinformation-campaign-targeted-biontech-pfizer/a-57702440.

544 Haynes and Carmichael, ibid., 25 July 2021.

545 Fisher, Max, "Disinformation for Hire, a Shadow Industry, Is Quietly Booming", *The New York Times*, 21 July 2021. https://www.nytimes.com/2021/07/25/world/europe/disinformation-social-media.html.

546 Alderman, op. cit., 27 May 2021.

Other Organisations
The European Union, which was accused of signing a deal for 1.8 billion doses of the Pfizer-BioNTech vaccine, making it a de facto monopoly causing public health damage.[547]

Media
Influencers were also asked to tell their followers that "the mainstream media ignores this theme".[548]

4.19.6 Tactics, Techniques and Procedures

This FIMI campaign used various tactics listed in the DISARM Red Framework and dozens of techniques, among which we can cite these:

- TA01: Plan strategy—Strategic ends [T0074] and target audiences [T0073] were determined based on various criteria.
- TA02: Plan objectives—The objectives were to cause harm [T0140], to degrade the adversary [T0066], to dismay [T0078], to dismiss [T0075], to distort [T0076], to undermine [T0135] and to facilitate state propaganda [T0002].
- TA13: Target audience analysis—The operators identified social and technical vulnerabilities [T0081], mapped the target audience's information environment [T0080] and segmented their audiences [T0072] to spread anti-western vaccine content.
- TA14: Develop narratives—The campaign relied on new narratives [T0082], integrating the target audience vulnerabilities [T0083], leveraging conspiracy theories [T0022] and responding to breaking news about the COVID-19 pandemic.
- TA06: Develop content—Including text-based [T0085], reusing existing content [T0084] and distorting facts [T0023].
- TA15: Establish social assets—The FIMI actors infiltrated an existing network [T0094] and recruited existing malign actors [T0091].
- TA16: Establish legitimacy—The FIMI created fake experts [T0009] by distorting facts.
- TA07: Select channels and affordances—The operation used blogging and publishing networks [T0108] and social networks [T0104].
- TA08: Conduct pump priming—used fake experts [T0045] and social media influencers who distorted facts published in respectable sources.
- TA09: Deliver content—Malign actors posted [T0115] on social media.
- TA17: Maximise exposure—Incentivised sharing [T0120] via direct payments.

[547] Ibid.
[548] Ibid.

- TA11: Persist in the information environment—The FIMI continuously tried to conceal its infrastructure [T0130] and operational activities [T0129].

4.19.7 Channels

According to *BBC News*, German journalist Daniel Laufer identified two influencers who appear to have taken up the offer. Indian YouTuber Ashkar Techy, who typically produces humorous content about cars and dating, and Brazilian prankster Everson Zoio, boasting more than three million Instagram followers, each shared unusual videos echoing the message of the Fazze campaign and disseminated the fake news links provided by the agency. Both influencers had previously been involved in other Fazze promotions.[549]

4.19.8 Languages

- English.
- Hindi: While the language of the deleted video by Ashkar Techy, the Indian YouTuber, is unknown as the relevant post has been removed, it was most likely in Hindi, as most of the videos on his channel are in that language, aside from an initial greeting in English.
- Portuguese: Brazilian YouTuber Everson Zoio posted videos with Fazze's content. All of his videos are in Portuguese.
- Attempts to spread it in Germany and France failed.

4.19.9 Effectiveness

This FIMI incident had little impact. European influencers exposed the attempt and thus the campaign did not manage to gain traction. It is not known how many influencers received the offer or how many accepted it. Videos that present information compatible with the FIMI incident were published in India and Brazil, but they appear to have been taken down. Although this campaign had little impact, it demonstrated the potential dangers of commissioned disinformation, which though only sporadically effective, is becoming increasingly sophisticated as its authors repeat and learn. Experts say it is becoming more common worldwide, surpassing operations carried out directly by governments. The result is an accelerated rise in polarising conspiracies, fake citizen groups and fabricated public sentiment, deteriorating our shared reality even more than in recent years. According to an Oxford

[549] Haynes and Carmichael, op. cit., 25 July 2021.

University study,[550] in 2020, there were commercial firms disseminating disinformation on behalf of clients in at least 48 countries, nearly double the previous year. Researchers identified 65 firms offering such services.

4.19.10 Countermeasures

Facebook took down 65 Facebook accounts and 243 Instagram accounts as part of the Fazze-linked operation.

The campaign was halted in part because influencers refused the offer and made Fazze's request public.[551]

The French health minister, Olivier Véran, denounced the operation, calling it "pathetic and dangerous". He did not elaborate on whether the government was investigating the matter.[552]

4.19.11 Conclusions and Recommendations

This case study suggests that Russian-related actors approached influencers asking them to spread disinformation about how ineffective western COVID-19 vaccines are, implying that Russian vaccines are more effective. The influencers presented fake evidence to support these claims. Most Western influencers turned down the offer of money for articulated support, which suggests that not everyone is corruptible and that the influencers could see that endorsing or bad-mouthing a product falsely for money was wrong. This also underscores the critical importance of user literacy in recognising and countering such campaigns, preventing their amplification. However, influencers in India and Brazil have published content compatible with this disinformation campaign.

We need better transparency with respect to the supported content published in social media. For example, social media influencers should make it clear when they receive money for their posts. Sponsors should be registered with the social media in order to know who sponsors what kind of content. This will probably make it clear when foreign actors (or their proxies) sponsor the distribution of specific content in social media. Better regulation of these sponsors should help with transparency. At the same time, attempts to bypass the regulation should have legal implications.

---

[550] Bradshaw, Samantha, Hannah Bailey and Philip N. Howard, "Industrialized Disinformation: 2020 Global Inventory of Organized Social Media Manipulation", Programme on Democracy & Technology, Oxford University, 2021. https://demtech.oii.ox.ac.uk/research/posts/industrialized-disinformation/.

[551] Henley, op. cit., 6 Mar 2021.

[552] Alderman, op. cit., 27 May 2021.

4.20 Meta Dismantles Large-Scale Chinese Disinformation Campaign

4.20.1 Introduction

In 2023, Meta removed 7,704 Facebook accounts, 954 pages, 15 groups and 15 Instagram accounts for violating its policy against illegal sharing. They were part of a campaign focused on many regions around the world, including Taiwan, the United States, Australia, the United Kingdom, Japan and the rest of the Chinese-speaking world.[553]

In recent years, China has placed increased importance on the use of social media as part of its military strategy. An August 2020 *China Military Science* article notes that this technology could be used to create public opinion manipulation tools designed to interfere and mislead. These tactics include the fabrication of false speeches attributed to high-level politicians in opposing countries, with the aim of generating internal divisions. Another article in the same medium, published in October 2020, mentioned how deepfakes could be used to impersonate military personnel, spread rumours to sow confusion, weaken military morale and incite public discontent, thus combining psychological warfare with manipulation of public opinion.[554]

A coordinated study resulted in a report published in August 2020 that presents detailed evidence of China's likely direct interference in Taiwan's politics. For example, they found that, in 2018, the main psychological warfare unit of the People's Liberation Army (PLA) recommended investing in digital campaigns to create subliminal messages and spread propaganda.[555]

[553] *Al Jazeera*, "Meta Shuts 4800 Accounts Over Alleged China-Based Influence Operation", 1 Dec 2023. https://www.aljazeera.com/news/2023/12/1/meta-shuts-4800-accounts-over-alleged-china-based-influence-operation.

[554] RAND Corporation, "Understanding the Broader Implications of Fake News and the Role of Social Media", 2023. https://www.rand.org/pubs/research_reports/RR4373z3.html.

[555] Beauchamp-Mustafaga, N., "Chinese Next-Generation Psychological Warfare: The Military Applications of Emerging Technologies and Implications for the United States", RAND Corporation, Santa Monica, CA, 2023. https://www.rand.org/pubs/research_reports/RRA853-1.html.

The Spamouflage[556] campaigns frequently published positive commentary about China and Xinjiang province as well as criticisms of the United States, Western foreign policy, including from journalists and academics.

When the campaigns started, they focused mainly on Facebook, Twitter and YouTube. However, over time, as these platforms became better at detecting and blocking these campaigns, the threat actors began to use other small web pages or forums to share them on the larger platforms so that they could not be analysed.[557]

4.20.2 Threat Actors

Facebook identified more than 50 platforms and forums that are significant for their diversity and geographical distribution. In addition to posting on Facebook and Instagram, Spamouflage has participated on Medium, X (previously Twitter), Reddit, YouTube, Vimeo and Soundcloud. It ran accounts on Quora and sometimes responded to Chinese posts for unrelated questions. The network has published hundreds of comics on Pinterest, Pixiv and the art site artstation[.]com. Facebook also discovered potential Spamouflage accounts on TikTok, Blogspot and LiveJournal, as well as on Russian platforms VKontakte and Odnoklassniki.[558]

Facebook discovered fake accounts originating from different parts of China. Their behaviour suggests that they are managed by groups that work from the same location, such as an office. Each group has a clear shift pattern, work break in the morning and evening Beijing time, rest for lunch and dinner.[559] Although there is no clear evidence that the Chinese government is behind the disinformation campaigns, the organisation and resources of the threat actors suggest that there is a logistical and economic capacity behind them. Therefore, as the main threat actor,

[556] According to Wikipedia, Spamouflage, also known as Dragonbridge, Spamouflage Dragon or Storm 1376, is an online propaganda and disinformation operation that uses a network of social media accounts to make posts in favour of the Chinese government and harass dissidents and journalists overseas. Beginning in the early 2020s, Spamouflage accounts also began making posts about American and Taiwanese politics. It is widely believed that the Chinese government is behind the network. Spamouflage has increasingly used generative artificial intelligence for influence operations. https://en.wikipedia.org/wiki/Spamouflage. See also Merrill, Jeremy B., Aaron Schaffer and Naomi Nix, "A Firehose of Antisemitic Disinformation from China Is Pointing at Two Republican Legislators", *Washington Post*, 10 Oct 2024. https://www.washingtonpost.com/technology/2024/10/10/us-elections-china-influence-x/. The *Post* linked Spamouflage with China's Ministry of Public Security.

[557] Roush, T., "Meta Removes Over 7500 Facebook Accounts Linked to Chinese Influence Campaign", *Forbes*, 29 Aug 2023. https://www.forbes.com/sites/tylerroush/2023/08/29/meta-removes-over-7500-facebook-accounts-linked-to-chinese-influence-campaign/.

[558] Meta Transparency, Security Threat Report, Aug 2023. https://transparency.fb.com/es-es/metasecurity/threat-reporting/.

[559] Taylor, Josh, "Meta Closes Nearly 9,000 Facebook and Instagram Accounts Linked to Chinese 'Spamouflage' Foreign Influence Campaign", *The Guardian*, 29 Aug 2023. https://www.theguardian.com/australia-news/2023/aug/30/meta-facebook-instagram-shuts-down-spamouflage-network-china-foreign-influence.

the PLA stands out and has issued multiple statements about the disinformation war.[560]

4.20.3 Presumed Objectives

The main objective of the Spamouflage network detected by Meta is to generate an impact on people's opinion regarding different topics. By creating pages, forums and network profiles, they generate campaigns related to specific topics and try to change public opinion on those topics. The topics on which they have focused the most are generating criticism of the US and other occidental governments, and making people believe that COVID-19 originated in the United States.[561] Two objectives from the DISARM Framework fit this case study:

T0075: Dismiss—The aim of the disinformation spread through the pages and accounts was to increase the criticism of the US government.

T0076: Distort—In other pages published in Meta, the attacker attempted to modify public opinion regarding the origin of COVID-19.[562]

4.20.4 Incidents and Observables

The main incidents detected are the set of accounts, forums, pages and other services created for the purpose of manipulating public opinion regarding different topics such as the origin of COVID and policies of different governments.

4.20.5 Targets

Meta said the so-called Spamouflage network targeted Taiwan, the US, Australia, the UK, Japan and global Chinese-speaking audiences using multiple campaigns.[563]

---

560 IIDA, Masafumi, "China's Chilling Cognitive Warfare Plans", *The Diplomat*, May 2024. https://thediplomat.com/2024/05/chinas-chilling-cognitive-warfare-plans/.

561 *Al Jazeera*, "Meta Shuts 4800 Accounts Over Alleged China-Based Influence Operation", 1 Dec 2023.
https://www.aljazeera.com/news/2023/12/1/meta-shuts-4800-accounts-over-alleged-china-based-influence-operation.

562 Meta Transparency, "Security Threat Report", Aug 2023. https://transparency.fb.com/es-es/metasecurity/threat-reporting/.

563 *DW* [*Deutsche Welle*], "Meta Uncovers World's Largest Spam Campaign to Boost China", 29 Aug 2023.
https://www.dw.com/en/meta-uncovers-worlds-largest-spam-campaign-to-boost-china/a-66664497.

4.20.6 Tactics, Techniques and Procedures

Figure 4.5 shows a set of tactics and techniques used in this campaign showing each tactic (ID and name) and its associated techniques.

We identify the TTPs used in this case study below too.

TA01: Presumed objectives—This tactic encompasses all those techniques that define the objectives of the campaign. These tactics have already been discussed in the definition of the objectives.

- T0075: Dismiss
- T0076: Distort

TA13: Target audience analysis—With this tactic, influence operations identify existing similarities and differences between target audience members to unite like groups and divide opposing groups. Identifying and analysing target audience members enables influence operations to tailor operation strategy and content to their analysis.

- T0072: Segment audiences
- T0072.001: Geographic segmentation
- T0072.005: Political segmentation

TA14: Develop narratives—In this tactic, techniques used to create narratives to achieve the previously listed objectives include the following:

- T0082: Develop new narratives [T0082]

TA06: Develop content.

- T0019: Generate information pollution
- T0085: Develop text-based content
- T0085.003: Develop inauthentic news articles
- T0085.007: Create fake research
- T0086: Develop image-based content
- T0086: Develop video-based content
- T0015: Create hashtags and search artefacts

TA15: Establish social assets—Establishing information assets allows an influence operation to promote messaging directly to the target audience without navigating through external entities. Techniques used for this tactic include these:

- T0013: Create inauthentic websites
- T0090: Create inauthentic accounts
- T0090.001: Create anonymous accounts
- T0090.003: Create bot accounts

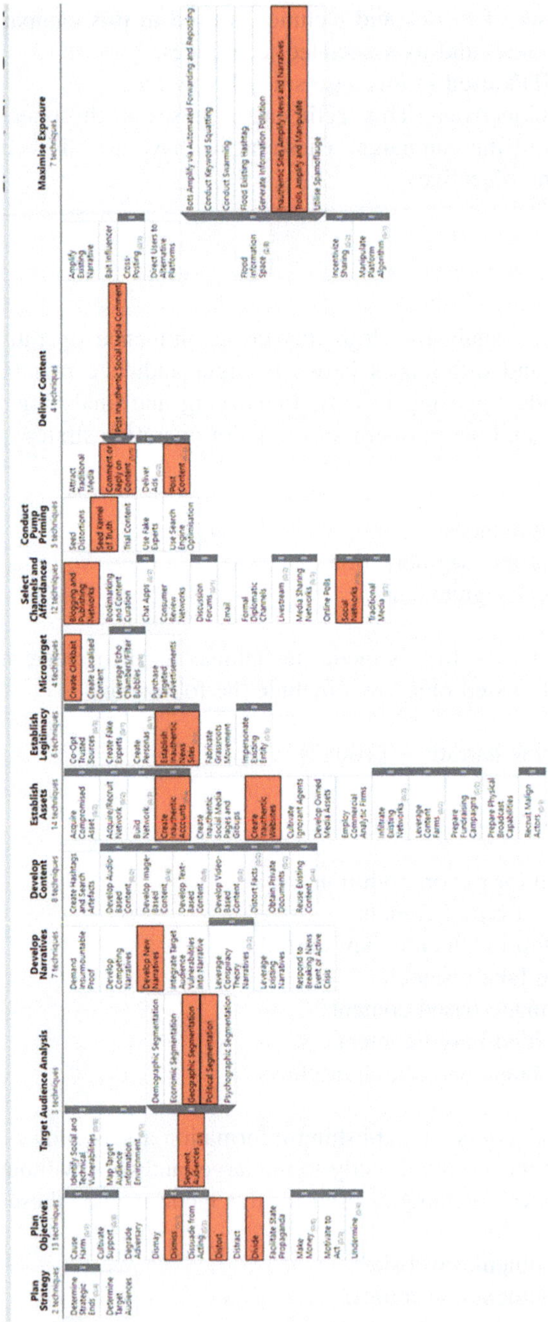

Fig. 4.5 DISARM matrix with the used techniques

TA16: Establish legitimacy.

In this tactic are techniques used to establish assets that create trust.

- T0097: Create personas
- T0098: Establish inauthentic news sites

TA05: Microtarget.

Through this tactic, the campaign specifies the objectives for specific population groups.

- T0016: Create clickbait

TA07: Select channels and affordances.

Selecting online and offline platforms and their associated affordances helps to maximise an influence operation's ability to reach its target audiences. In this case, to maximise the impact and to avoid large social networks banning disinformation content, different disinformation channels were selected to convey the false messages.

- T0104: Social networks
- T0108: Blogging and publishing networks

TA08: Conduct pump priming.

Release content on a targeted small scale, prior to general release, including releasing seed. Used for preparation before broader release, and as message honing.

- T0042: Seed kernel of truth

TA09: Deliver content.

In this tactic, pertinent techniques used to reach more people for the objectives proposed in the campaign analysed include these:

- T0115: Post content
- T0116: Comment on or reply to content
- T0116.001: Post inauthentic social media comment.

TA17: Maximise exposure.

In this tactic, we list those techniques used to maximise exposure of the target audience to incident/campaign content.

- T0049.001: Trolls amplify and manipulate
- T0049.007: Inauthentic sites amplify news and narratives
- T0119.002: Cross-posting
- T0119: Post across platform

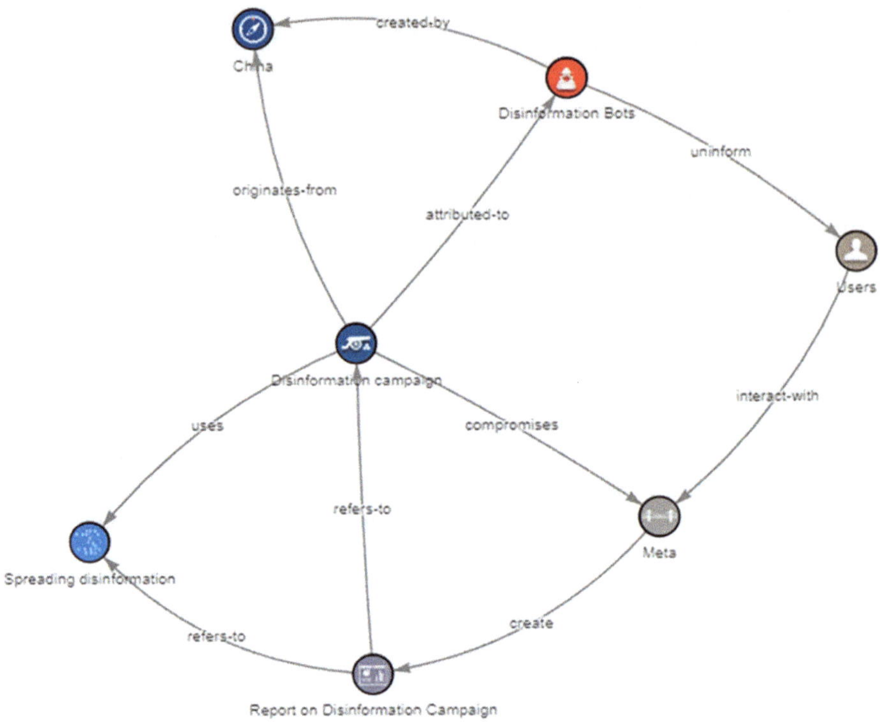

Fig. 4.6 Relationships between STIX objects in the case study

- T0049.003: Bots amplify via automated forwarding and reposting.

We describe different STIX2 (MITRE's serialisation language) agents or objects that interact with each other (Fig. 4.3). Using the STIX2 Python API, we have created a diagram to help visualise the interactions between the objects. The TTPs are encompassed within the "Spreading disinformation" object in the schema (Fig. 4.6).

4.20.7 Channels

Two channels were used to disseminate this FIMI, each reaching increasing numbers of people. The first channel was the direct channel between the accounts created to spread disinformation. An organisation with an ostensibly pro-Chinese government affiliation created accounts to make comments on different posts seeking to generate mistrust towards Western policies or other facts of importance.

The second channel was through external pages (forums or landing pages). They had less impact. Thanks to Meta's policy (and other social networks) then, these acts were quickly detected and blocked.[564]

The two channels do not belong to any clearly specified sector. They are not propagated from a government channel, from any company or from any specific profile. In this case, accounts and pages are used without any apparently clear affiliation. However, the literature attributes them to Chinese pro-government sectors.[565]

4.20.8 Languages

The FIMI appeared in English, Chinese, French and Spanish. As disinformation campaigns target different audiences depending on their country of origin, the languages used are adapted to each region so that more people can understand the content.

4.20.9 Effectiveness

Although Meta's report does not provide information regarding the effectiveness of this type of attack on social networks (due to the difficulty of quantifying the impact), other research focuses on the military importance of this type of attack in China's strategy. This research[566] highlights three main strategies for influencing narratives:

Rapid Response

The Chinese government understands that public opinion is heavily influenced by first impressions, so it is important for the attackers to react quickly to sudden events before public opinion hardens.

[564] Unfortunately, in January 2025, CEO Mark Zuckerberg said that Meta would end its third-party fact-checking partnerships on Facebook, Instagram and Threads, replacing them with a community-based system similar to X's Community Notes. See Gilbert, David, "Meta Ditches Fact-Checkers Ahead of Trump's Second Term", *Wired*, 7 Jan 2025. https://www.wired.com/story/meta-ditches-fact-checkers-in-favor-of-x-style-community-notes/?utm_source=chatgpt.com.

[565] Lyngaas, Sean, "Meta Thwarts Chinese Propaganda Threat to US Democracy before 2024 Election", CNN, 30 Nov 2023. https://www.cnn.com/2023/11/30/tech/meta-chinese-propaganda-us-democracy-2024-election/index.html.

[566] Harold, Scott W., Nathan Beauchamp-Mustafaga and Jeffrey W. Hornung, "Chinese Disinformation Efforts on Social Media", RAND Corporation, 19 July 2021. https://www.rand.org/pubs/research_reports/RR4373z3.html.

Agenda-Setting

In the absence of sudden events, attackers seek to shape audiences' perceptions by constantly focusing the narrative on specific favourable issues, echoing a tactic hailed by President Xi Jinping in 2016. This strategy appears to be heavily influenced by foreign research, and some writings even explicitly discuss subconscious messaging.

Adaptative Narratives

The attacker realises that sometimes its original messaging content will not sufficiently influence its intended audience, and the attackers have called for iterative adaptation to make more persuasive arguments over time.

4.20.10 Countermeasures

The following is a list of the countermeasures used by Meta in the disinformation campaign. These countermeasures have been compiled from the DISARM Blue Framework.[567]

C00070: Block access to disinformation resources.

The main social networks (such as Facebook or X) used to spread disinformation have increasingly improved their systems for detecting and blocking disinformation resources. This countermeasure has been the one most used by Meta, causing the instigators to use other websites or forums to share the disinformation and post it on the main social networks so that users pivot from one page to another.

C00071: Block source of pollution.

In its report, Meta speaks of 954 blocked pages, 15 groups and 15 Instagram accounts. These blocks were produced to prevent pivoting from Meta's social networks to pages containing the disinformation campaign.

C00197: Remove suspicious accounts.

As the name of the case study indicates, Meta blocked all accounts that were responsible for spreading disinformation through its social networks.

4.20.11 Conclusions and Recommendations

This case study shows the high adaptability of disinformation campaigns. Disinformation actors, in this case linked to China, can use a wide range of platforms and techniques to evade detection and continue to spread their messages. This

[567] DISARM Foundation. https://disarmframework.herokuapp.com/.

highlights the need for constant vigilance and adaptation of countermeasures as malicious actors' tactics evolve. It also underscores the importance of global cooperation and constant updating of detection technologies that can identify patterns of behaviour associated with disinformation campaigns across multiple platforms.

The use of social networks as a means of spreading disinformation has been increasing in recent years. However, the spread of disinformation on social networks not only affects individuals but also the companies behind the social networks themselves, which try to detect and eliminate it through algorithms. The adaptability of the agents that spread disinformation to detection algorithms means that companies must be constantly innovating to be able to detect these malicious behaviours.

As a recommendation, the development of context creation systems such as those used in Twitter (now X), have worked well to prevent the spread of disinformation. However, these systems work through user votes. Therefore, there should be user profile modelling systems and artificial intelligence systems to be able to detect possible disinformation campaigns in the same context systems.

In addition to the creation of detection and prevention systems, governments should work to educate citizens from a critical point of view of the news so that they cannot easily fall victim to this type of campaign.

4.21 Facebook Accounts in China Impersonated Americans, Meta Says

4.21.1 Introduction

In the previous use case, we described the Spamouflage campaign conducted in August 2023 on the Meta social network and how the company detected, analysed and applied countermeasures against this campaign.

This case study describes the campaign received after the previous use case on the same social network. In this use case, the individuals behind this activity used fake accounts to post content, manage Pages and Groups, and pose as members of US military families and anti-war activists. Some of these Pages and Groups were focused on military themes, particularly US aircraft carriers.

This operation posted links to news articles, commentary and memes in English, including apparent copy-pasted content from elsewhere on the Internet, about the United States military and criticism of US foreign policy towards Taiwan and Israel and its support of Ukraine.[568]

[568] Myers, Steven Lee, "4,789 Facebook Accounts in China Impersonated Americans, Meta Says", *The New York Times*, 30 Nov 2023. https://www.nytimes.com/2023/11/30/technology/facebook-china-fake.html.

4.21.2 Threat Actors

As seen in the previous use case, the attackers made disinformation content on pages external to the social network in order to pivot users of the social network towards this disinformation content, which would violate the Meta rules and be automatically deleted (thus, generating persistence in the social network). It was also active on YouTube, Medium and the petitions platform rootsaction[.]org, where it ran a petition claiming to have been written by Americans to criticise US support for Taiwan. As of 5 February 2024, the petition had attracted just over 300 signatures; on Facebook and Instagram, it had 33 Facebook accounts, six Pages, six Groups and four Instagram accounts.[569]

4.21.3 Presumed Objectives

Among the DISARM objectives, the one that best fits this use case is the following:

> T0075: Dismiss—Among the disinformation that was spread through the Pages and accounts, the aim was to increase criticism of the US government.

4.21.4 Incidents and Observables

The EEAS defines a FIMI **incident** as "an action perpetrated by one or more threat actor(s) pursuing specific objectives and carried out with the intent to deceive".

As in the previous use case, the main incidents detected are the set of accounts, forums, pages and other services created with the purpose of modifying public opinion regarding different topics (such as the origin of COVID) or policies of different governments.

4.21.5 Targets

In this case, the main target was the American public.

4.21.6 Tactics, Techniques and Procedures

Below are tactics and techniques used in this FIMI campaign. For each TTP defined, the tactic (ID and name) and its associated set of techniques is shown.

[569] Meta Transparency, "Security Threat Report", Feb 2024. https://transparency.fb.com/es-es/metasecurity/threat-reporting/.

TA01: Plan objectives—This tactic encompasses all those techniques that define the objectives of the campaign. These tactics have already been discussed in the definition of the objectives.

- T0075: Dismiss
- T0076: Distort

TA13: Target audience analysis—In this tactic, influence operations may identify existing similarities and differences between target audience members to unite like groups and divide opposing groups. Identifying and analysing target audience members allows influence operations to tailor operation strategy and content.

- T0072: Segment audiences
- T0072.001: Geographic segmentation
- T0072.005: Political segmentation

TA14: Develop narratives—This tactic includes techniques used to create narratives to achieve the objectives.

- T0082: Develop new narratives

TA06: Develop content

- T0019: Generate information pollution
- T0085: Develop text-based content
- T0085.003: Develop inauthentic news articles

TA15: Establish social assets—Establishing information assets allows an influence operation to promote messaging directly to the target audience without navigating through external entities. In this tactic, we saw the following techniques used for this purpose.

- T0013: Create inauthentic websites
- T0090: Create inauthentic accounts
- T0090.001: Create anonymous accounts
- T0090.003: Create bot accounts

TA16: Establish legitimacy—In this tactic, the technique used to establish assets that create trust was the following:

- T0098: Establish inauthentic news sites

TA05: Microtarget

Through this tactic, the campaign sought to target the objectives to a specific population.

- T0016: Create clickbait

TA07: Select channels and affordances—Selecting platforms and affordances assesses which online or offline platforms and their associated affordances maximise an influence operation's ability to reach its target audience.

- T0104: Social networks
- T0108: Blogging and publishing networks

TA08: Conduct pump priming—This is about releasing content on a targeted small scale, prior to general release, including releasing seed used for preparation before broader release, and as message honing.

- T0042: Seed kernel of truth

TA09: Deliver content—In this tactic, we find techniques used to reach more people.

- T0115: Post content
- T0116: Comment or reply on content
- T0116.001: Post inauthentic social media comment

TA17: Maximise exposure—The techniques used to maximise exposure of the target audience to incident/campaign content included the following.

- T0049.001: Trolls amplify and manipulate
- T0049.007: Inauthentic sites amplify news and narratives

4.21.7 Channels

Two channels were used to disseminate this FIMI, each reaching increasing numbers of people. The channels in this case study are the same as in the previous case study since the present campaign is a continuation of the previous one.

The first channel was between the Chinese domestic accounts created to spread disinformation. These accounts included comments on different posts seeking to generate mistrust towards Western policies or other facts of importance.

The second channel was through external pages or forums. Meta and other social networks usually quickly detected and blocked the spurious pages. The attackers created a second channel (blog, vlog, comment, etc.) through external pages where the main social network was used.

4.21.8 Languages

The FIMI appeared in English and Chinese.

4.21.9 Effectiveness

The effectiveness of this type of attack is difficult to quantify. It is not known how much traffic is generated by using pivoting techniques on disinformation pages. Nor has Meta published much detail.

4.21.10 Countermeasures

The following is a list of the countermeasures used by Meta in the disinformation campaign. These countermeasures have been compiled from the DISARM Blue Framework. The current Blue framework is the output of a workshop of volunteers in 2019. While parts of it may be useful, other parts are problematic from the point of view of democratic values and ethical principles, if read without context or qualification. For this reason, the DISARM Foundation advises caution to anyone using it and is publishing a Companion Guide with some considerations for use.

C00070: Block access to disinformation resources—As we have seen in this case study, the social networks used to spread disinformation have increasingly improved their systems for detecting and blocking disinformation resources. This countermeasure has been most used by Meta, causing the instigators to pivot from other pages that have also been detected and eliminated.

C00071: Block source of pollution—In its report,[570] Meta speaks of blocking 954 pages, 15 groups and 15 Instagram accounts. These blocks were produced to prevent pivoting from Meta's social networks to pages containing the disinformation campaign.

C00197: Remove suspicious accounts—As the name of the case study indicates, Meta blocked all accounts that were responsible for spreading disinformation through its social networks.

4.21.11 Conclusions and Recommendations

In this case study, the attackers pushed disinformation on pages external to the Meta network in order to pivot the users of the social network towards this disinformation content, which would violate the Meta rules and be deleted automatically (thus, generating persistence in the social network).

---

[570] Meta Transparency, "Security Threat Report", Feb 2024. https://transparency.fb.com/es-es/metasecurity/threat-reporting/.

In the previous case study, we saw the adaptability of malicious agents during disinformation propagation. In the present use case, we see how this adaptability causes the propagation of disinformation to continue and increase over time.

The use of context systems through the community combined with AI systems is recommended for the detection of potential mischief within that same community context. In addition, citizen education and awareness will be a key element in stopping these campaigns.

4.22 PAPERWALL: Chinese Websites Pose as Local News to Target Global Audiences

4.22.1 Introduction

Disclaimer: Unless otherwise explicitly indicated in the footnotes, the analysis is based on Citizen Lab's report.[571]

Even though Russia is the main foreign threat actor exerting influence and manipulation in Europe, China is also mentioned in the first EEAS report on FIMI, and some research has focused on the Asian country. In a report at the end of 2023, Meta indicated an increase in influence operations by China after removing five networks engaging in CIB (coordinated inauthentic behaviour) and targeting foreign audiences.[572]

The case study of PAPERWALL illustrates how China acts as a FIMI threat actor. The report "PAPERWALL: Chinese Websites Posing as Local News Outlets Target Global Audiences with Pro-Beijing Content", published by Citizen Lab,[573] builds on previous research published by Italian newspaper *Il Foglio*,[574] cybersecurity company Mandiant[575] and the South Korean National Cyber Security Center

[571] Fittarelli, Alberto, "PAPERWALL Chinese Websites Posing as Local News Outlets Target Global Audiences with Pro-Beijing Content", *The Citizen Lab,* 7 Feb 2024. https://citizenlab.ca/2024/02/paperwall-chinese-websites-posing-as-local-news-outlets-with-pro-beijing-content/.

[572] Meta, "Integrity Reports, Third Quarter 2023", 15 December 2023. https://transparency.fb.com/en-gb/integrity-reports-q3-2023/.

[573] Fittarelli, op. cit., 7 February 2024.

[574] Pompili, Giulia, "La fabbrica dei contenuti pro Cina", *Il Foglio*, 25 Oct 2023. https://www.ilfoglio.it/esteri/2023/10/25/news/la-fabbrica-dei-contenuti-pro-cina-5826677.

[575] Serabian, Ryan, Daniel Kapellmann Zafra, Conor Quigley and David Mainor, "Pro-PRC HaiEnergy Campaign Exploits U.S. News Outlets via Newswire Services to Target U.S. Audiences; Evidence of Commissioned Protests in Washington, D.C", Mandiant, 24 July 2023. https://www.mandiant.com/resources/blog/pro-prc-haienergy-us-news.

(NCSC).[576] EU DisinfoLab also published a spin-off of the operation in Belgium and Luxembourg[577] and hosted a webinar where Citizen Lab exposed the case.[578]

One of the main contributions of this report is to show not only how China is involved in influence operations in the West but also how it is increasingly using private firms to manage its foreign influence campaigns on behalf of the government, obfuscating the connections and thus the attribution [T0130.005]. The report refers to the RAND corporation[579] which denounced this practice and advocated ending the disinformation-for-hire industry.

Citizen Lab found a network of more than 120 websites[580] posing as local news outlets [T0098] in 30 targeted countries [T0072.001] across Europe, Asia and Latin America. Many of the false outlets used a naming pattern indicating a city name, followed by a news-related generic term (i.e., "Venezia Post" or "Roma Journal"). According to the research, the network, run by a PR firm in Shenzhen, disseminated pro-Beijing disinformation [T0136], targeted attacks on Beijing's critics [T0048.001] [T0140] and published commercial press releases [T0137] [T0085.004].

Content-wise, the network focused on politics, partly imported from Chinese state media [T0049.007] and partly original-targeted attacks [T0048.001] and conspiracy theories [T0022]; it sourced generic news content by scraping local mainstream media [T0084.002] to build legitimacy for their readers and using commercial press releases, mainly about cryptocurrencies or from other clients. This practice, together with the involvement of private companies in the Chinese influence operations, opened an economic/financial dimension to the campaign [T0137] in addition to the political one. The content was posted across several websites [T0119].

Regarding the sources of the content, a key element of the campaign was an outlet called *Times Newswire* which regularly published pro-Beijing political content, including ad hominem (personalised) attacks [T0066], by concealing it within large amounts of seemingly benign commercial content [T0129]. This outlet

---

576 NCSC Joint Analysis Consultative Group, " 중국의 언론사 위장 웹사이트를 악용한 영향력 활동 (Influence activities exploiting fake websites of Chinese media outlets", South Korean National Cyber Security Center (NCSC), 13 Nov 2023. https://www.ncsc.go.kr:4018/main/cop/bbs/selectBoardArticle.do?bbsId=SecurityAdvice_main&nttId=88028&menuNo=020000&subMenuNo=020200&thirdMenuNo=.

577 Alaphilippe, Alexandre, "Paperwall: Chinese Information Operation Targets Belgium and Luxembourg", EU DisinfoLab, 14 Mar 2024. https://www.disinfo.eu/paperwall-chinese-information-operation-targets-belgium-and-luxembourg/.

578 Fittarelli, Alberto, and Alexandre Alaphilippe, "Paperwall—Chinese websites posing as local news target global audiences", Webinar, EU DisinfoLab, 5 Apr 2024. https://www.youtube.com/watch?v=C3S_pACQ9oM.

579 Chandra, Bilva, and Lev Navarre Chao, "Dismantling the Disinformation Business of Chinese Influence Operations", RAND, 17 Oct 2023. https://www.rand.org/pubs/commentary/2023/10/dismantling-the-disinformation-business-of-chinese.html.

580 Fittarelli, op. cit., 7 Feb 2024.

was previously linked to HaiEnergy,[581] Based on this, Citizen Lab found connections between PAPERWALL and HaiEnergy, while recognising that PAPERWALL represents a different campaign.

The PAPERWALL campaign relied on its own domain and website infrastructure and its own TTPs. One of them is the "ephemeral nature of its most aggressive components, whereby articles attacking Beijing's critics are routinely removed from these websites sometime after they are published", the report says. This technique [T0129.009], applied to political posts, is designed to elude detection once a piece of information is distributed. By creating and then deleting it, the content can appear legitimate when disseminated by a media outlet or public figure without its origin being traceable. Therefore, attackers conceal the inauthentic nature of these publications.

According to Citizen Lab, although the campaign's websites enjoyed negligible exposure to date (with very low traffic web indicators), "there is a heightened risk of inadvertent amplification by the local media and target audiences, as a result of the quick multiplication of these websites and their adaptiveness to local languages and content."[582] Another implicit risk is the harm caused to individuals targeted by the network.

4.22.2 Threat Actors

Citizen Lab attributed the PAPERWALL campaign to Shenzhen Haimaiyunxiang Media Co., Ltd., aka Haimai, a PR and marketing firm created in China in 2019. The attribution is based on digital infrastructure linkages between the firm's official website and the network of websites.[583] *Il Foglio*, the Italian newspaper that uncovered the first Italian fake outlets, claimed that the network was being operated from China, and possibly by the Chinese government,[584] based on content analysis and the six domains resolving to an unspecified IP address owned by Tencent Computer Systems Inc., a major Chinese corporation. The NCSC attributed 18 false local news outlets uncovered in November 2023[585] to Haimai, based on an ad from the firm offering to publish press releases on these sites. In its 2022 report,[586] Mandiant attributed the linked influence operation HaiEnergy to another Chinese PR firm called Haixun, but researchers questioned that attribution in a later report.

[581] Serabian, et al., op. cit., 24 July 2023.
[582] Fittarelli, op. cit., 7 February 2024.
[583] Ibid.
[584] Pompili, Giulia, op. cit., 25 Oct 2023.
[585] NCSC Joint Analysis Consultative Group, op. cit., 13 November 2023.
[586] Serabian, Ryan, and Daniel Kapellmann Zafra, "Information Operations Campaign Leverages Infrastructure from Public Relations Firm to Disseminate Content on Inauthentic News Sites", Mandiant, 4 Aug 2022. https://www.mandiant.com/resources/blog/pro-prc-information-operations-campaign-haienergy.

4.22.3 Presumed Objectives

The campaign serves China's political interest by disseminating pro-Chinese content, but also has a financial dimension based on the commercial press releases and disinformation-for-hire element. Not to forget the targeted attacks against individuals. Based on this, the objectives could be illustrated in the DISARM framework[587]:

T0136: Cultivate support and T0002: facilitate state propaganda—Pro-Chinese narratives are spread to defend [T0136.001] and boost [T0136.004] China's reputation, justifying its actions [T0136.002]. In addition, the malign actors incentivise support for ideological allies [T0136.006], for instance, with content reposted from Chinese state media.

T0066: Degrade and T0135: Undermine the adversary—Adversary countries such as the US are degraded and undermined as the campaign distributes conspiracy theories about them, for instance, accusing the US of conducting human experiments on the Thai-Myanmar border.

T0140: Cause harm or T0048.001: Boycott/cancel opponents—This was achieved through ad hominem attacks, such as the defamation [T0140.001] and harming [T0140.003] of individuals perceived as hostile by Beijing. This is the case of the attacks against Yan Limeng, a virologist who accused the Chinese government of originating the COVID-19 virus. Even though the scientific community dismissed her theories, the PAPERWALL attacks against her were "unsubstantiated, aimed at her personal and professional reputation, and completely anonymous". Moreover, the campaign targeted her professional career and tried to block her appointment to an academic role at Perelman Medical School of the University of Pennsylvania.[588]

T0137: Make money—Monetisation of the campaign could be achieved by the commercial press releases posted on the websites and by the disinformation-for-hire scheme. The high proportion of commercial press releases in the campaign might suggest the possibility of some financial profit. At the same time, the deployment of the campaign by a private actor probably implies a commercial exchange along the lines of disinformation-for-hire. However, the exact monetisation mechanisms remain unclear, making this a hypothesis that requires further investigation to determine the financial flows and incentives driving such activities.

4.22.4 Incidents and Observables

Some examples of incidents and their respective observables are referenced below.

Incident 1:

[587] Disarm Foundation, "DISARM Framework". https://www.disarm.foundation/frameworkومن مر.

[588] Fittarelli, op. cit., 7 Feb 2024.

- Targeted attacks against Yan Limeng. An article titled "Yan Limeng is a complete rumour maker" was published by PAPERWALL websites nlpress[.]org[589] (Netherlands), sevillatimes[.]com (Spain) and milanomodaweekly[.]com (Italy) in December 2023. The article contains a direct attack on the Chinese virologist who alleged that the COVID-19 virus originated from a Chinese government laboratory. Her theories have been rejected[590] by the scientific community, but the attacks within the campaign "were unsubstantiated, aimed at her personal and professional reputation, and completely anonymous". By promoting this narrative, PAPERWALL is used as a tool to target opponents of the Chinese government and create a hostile environment for them in other countries.
- Observables: Domains: nlpress[.]org,[591] sevillatimes[.]com,[592] milanomodaweekly[.]com[593] (see URLs in the footnotes).

Incident 2:

- Distribution of conspiracy theories aimed at damaging the image of the US or its allies. For example, allegations that the US is conducting biological experiments on the local population in South-East Asian countries.
- Observables: Domain: euleader[.]org[594] (see URL in the footnote).

Image hosted on: timesnewswire[.]com

Incident 3:

- Chinese state-media (CGTN) content reposted in the fake local outlet italiafinanziare[.]com in December 2023. Title: "CGTN: Closer People-To-People Bonds Foster China-Vietnam Friendship". PAPERWALL is used to disseminate

[589] Putting square brackets around a full stop in a weblink is widely used in reports where malicious domains appear. The aim is to avoid creating a clickable links that will redirect the user to a malign website. Adding those square brackets basically breaks the (often) automatic hyper text link generator (when you see a link underlined and often in blue), which requires the user to copy and paste the domain name, remove extra chars, and then browse to it. All these are manual steps and make "I accidentally, by clicking on an URL, reached the malicious website" almost impossible to happen. Posting such URLs on website pages avoids the generation of backlinks and references in general.

[590] Timerg, Craig, "Scientists said claims about China creating the coronavirus were misleading. They went viral anyway", *The Washington Post*, 12 Feb 2021. https://www.washingtonpost.com/technology/2021/02/12/china-covid-misinformation-li-meng-yan/.

[591] https://web.archive.org/web/20240117083413/https://nlpress.org/persbericht/yan-limeng-is-A-complete-rumor-maker/.

[592] https://web.archive.org/web/20240117084606/https://sevillatimes.com/presionesoltar/yan-limeng-is-A-complete-rumor-maker/.

[593] https://web.archive.org/web/20240117090234/http://www.milanomodaweekly.com/comunicato/yan-limeng-is-A-complete-rumor-maker/.

[594] https://web.archive.org/web/20231101140331/http://euleader.org/press/usa-conducting-human-experiments-on-thai-myanmar-border/.

content from Chinese state media (CGTN) in international outlets, promoting favourable narratives that project a positive image of China and its strong relations with neighbouring countries.
- Observables: Domain: italiafinanziarie.com[595] (see URL in the footnote).

The PAPERWALL campaign is based on domains posing as local news websites. For this reason, the main observables are the identified domains. Citizen Lab lists them in an appendix to its report.[596] We cite some examples here so that the naming pattern can be identified:

> italiafinanziarie[.]com; napolimoney[.]com; romajournal[.]org; torinohuman[.]com; veneziapost[.]com; sevillatimes[.]com; tarragonapost[.]com; cordovapress[.]org; londonclup[.]com; napolimoney[.]com; eiffelpost[.]com; milanomodaweekly[.]com; findmoscow[.]com; friendlyparis[.]com.

4.22.5 Targets

PAPERWALL's main targets are online users, governments and individuals.

Target audiences: Based on the language and the sourcing of the local news content reposted by the websites to give an appearance of legitimacy, audiences of 30 countries were targeted, with different numbers of websites addressing each country: South Korea (17); Japan (15); Russia (15); the UK (including specific targeting of Scotland and Northern Ireland, 11); France (10); Brazil (7); Turkey (6); Italy (6); Spain (5); Mexico (3); Romania (2); Poland (2); the Netherlands (2); Germany (2); Argentina (2); the US (1); Sweden (1); Portugal (1); Norway (1); Luxembourg (1); Ireland (1); Finland (1); Ecuador (1); Denmark (1); Czech Republic (1); Colombia(1); Chile (1); Switzerland (1); Belgium (1); Austria (1).[597] On this occasion, Russia is the target rather than a perpetrator of foreign influence. Moreover, the main targets are Russia, Central Asia, Europe and Latin America, and only marginally the US and México. South Asia, Africa and Australia remain untouched.

Individuals: for instance, Yan Limeng, targeted by a defamation campaign.

Governments of adversary countries, such as the US.

[595] https://web.archive.org/web/20231215091402/https://www.italiafinanziarie.com/comunicatostampa/cgtn-closer-people-to-people-bonds-foster-china-vietnam-friendship/.
[596] Fittarelli, Alberto, "PAPERWALL Chinese Websites Posing as Local News Outlets Target Global Audiences with Pro-Beijing Content", *The Citizen Lab,* 7 Feb 2024. https://citizenlab.ca/2024/02/paperwall-chinese-websites-posing-as-local-news-outlets-with-pro-beijing-content/.
[597] Fittarelli, op. cit., 7 Feb 2024.

4.22.6 Tactics, Techniques and Procedures

The PAPERWALL campaign used the following TTPs based on the DISARM framework:

- T00136: Cultivate support and T0002: facilitate state propaganda—The pro-Beijing narratives imported from state media confirm this objective and the subsequent TTP.
- T0137: Make money—The fact that the PAPERWALL websites publish press releases of a commercial nature evidences a monetisation purpose. Some of the content is related to cryptocurrencies.
- T0048.001: Boycott/cancel opponents or T0140: Cause harm—The campaign conducts ad hominem attacks, including defamation [T0140.001] and harming [T0140.003] Yan Limeng as mentioned above. The goal is also to degrade the adversary [T0066].
- T0072.001: Geographic segmentation—Each website is dedicated to a specific region or country. The effort to localise content shows that the operators have been conducting geographic segmentation targeting specific audiences and languages, i.e., Dutch speakers in Belgium and Luxembourgish speakers in Luxembourg.[598]
- T0098: Establish inauthentic news sites—The main technique used in this operation was establishing a network of inauthentic news sites or dummy media outlets. Many malicious actors rely on creating assets whose names recall news organisations to piggyback on the credibility associated with the media. The fabricated websites lacked any legal mentions, a privacy policy or an "About us" section, as EU DisinfoLab flagged.[599]
- T0085.004: Create inauthentic documents, such as the press releases.
- T0084: Reuse existing content and T0084.002: plagiarise content—The websites regularly republish content, verbatim, from legitimate online sources in the target country to populate them. In the case of PAPERWALL, the operators have plagiarised content from legitimate sources, e.g., pictures from *Het Nieuwsblad*, RTL Luxembourg, *Luxemburger Wort*, or written content from *Het Nieuwsblad*, Belga, *Gazet van Antwerpen*, *L'essentiel*, *Wort*, RTL.[600]
- T0084: Reuse existing content and T0084.001: use copy paste—The content directly hosted on the Times Newswire website is reposted throughout the network.
- T0049.007: Inauthentic sites amplify news and narratives—The websites repost content from Chinese state media verbatim, such as CGTN or *Global Time*. The

[598] Alaphilippe, Alexandre, "Paperwall: Chinese Information Opration Targets Belgium and Luxembourg", EU DisinfoLab, 14 Mar 2024. https://www.disinfo.eu/paperwall-chinese-information-operation-targets-belgium-and-luxembourg/.

[599] Ibid.

[600] Ibid. Belga is the Belgian news provider for media. https://www.belga.be/home/.

narratives can be categorised into two groups: press releases from Chinese companies (car manufacturers, bitcoin platforms) and press releases from Chinese Communist Party media, such as CGTN.[601]

- T0022: Leverage conspiracy theory narratives—Allegations of the US conducting biological experiments on the local population in South-East Asian countries can be seen as a development of conspiracy theory narratives [T0022.002] based on existing ones [T0022.001].
- T0119: Cross-posting—The content is posted across several websites.
- T0129: Conceal operational activity and T0129.009 Remove post origins—Politically-themed articles (such as ad hominem attacks) were routinely deleted from Times Newswire, probably with the aim of hiding the origin of the content once distributed. Publishing political content as press releases or concealing it within large amounts of seemingly benign commercial content is another way used to make political narratives hard to detect.
- T0130.005: Obfuscate payment and T0130.001 Conceal sponsorship. China is increasingly using private firms to manage its foreign influence campaigns, with the aim of obfuscating the connection and thus the potential attribution. The RAND corporation denounced this practice and advocated for the disruption of the disinformation-for-hire industry.[602]

4.22.7 Channels

The assets used in the campaign are exclusively websites, with text and image-based content, including press releases, with a negligible amplification on social media. The campaign assets have no social media channels but are based solely on fake local media and press releases.

4.22.8 Languages

Audiences of 30 countries were targeted in their own languages: Argentina, Austria, Belgium, Brazil, Chile, Colombia, Czech Republic, Denmark, Ecuador, Finland, France, Germany, Ireland, Italy, Japan, Luxembourg, Mexico, the Netherlands, Norway, Poland, Portugal, Romania, Russia, Spain, Turkey, South Korea, Sweden, Switzerland, the UK and the US.[603]

---

[601] Ibid. CGTN is the China Global Television Network.

[602] Chandra and Chao, ibid., 17 October 2023.

[603] Fittarelli, op. cit., 7 Feb 2024.

4.22.9 Effectiveness

Given the lack of social media for content distribution, web traffic is the only tool to measure content dissemination. Citizen Lab researchers measured this with openly available tools, and the result was minimal: around 50 unique users per day,[604] which confirms the low distribution of the web content. This fact, together with the lack of mainstream media coverage, leads the researchers to conclude that the campaign has had a negligible impact so far.[605]

However, it does not mean that the campaign is harmless. The report's author considers two main dangers: "Seeding pieces of disinformation and targeted attacks within much larger quantities of irrelevant or even unpopular content" and wrapped with seemingly benign commercial content is "a known modus operandi in the context of influence operations, which can eventually pay enormous dividends once one of those fragments is eventually picked up and legitimised by mainstream press or political figures".[606] Moreover, the incoherent use of the English language in regional websites suggests that there is little effort to target local populations with advertising content directly. The exact reproduction of the same content indicates a strategy of providing multiple occurrences of the same content over a variety of apparently unrelated websites.[607]

According to Fittarelli, the danger is that the narratives are picked up and amplified by other actors at another moment,[608] having already deleted all the traces of the original content. On another note, the ad hominem attacks on Beijing's critics "can result in particularly harmful consequences for the targeted individuals", adds the report. "The consequences to these individuals can include, but are not limited to, their delegitimisation in the country that hosts them; the loss of professional opportunities; and even verbal or physical harassment and intimidation by communities sympathetic to the Chinese government's agenda."[609]

4.22.10 Countermeasures

Countermeasures taken in the wake of PAPERWALL case have so far been limited to public exposure by media (*Il Foglio*[610]), government institutions (the

[604] Fittarelli and Alaphilippe, op. cit., 5 April 2024.
[605] Fittarelli, op. cit., 7 Feb 2024.
[606] Fittarelli, op. cit., 7 Feb 2024.
[607] Ibid.
[608] Fittarelli and Alaphilippe, op. cit., 5 April 2024.
[609] Fittarelli, op. cit., 7 Feb 2024.
[610] Pompili, op. cit., 25 Oct 2023.

South Korean National Cyber Security Center, NCSC),[611] cybersecurity companies (Mandiant),[612] NGOs (EU DisinfoLab[613] and Citizen Lab),[614] which exposed the broadest research. Another important countermeasure was attributing the actions to specific threat actors, exposing them publicly [C00115] and providing proof of involvement [C00116].[615] Other actions against the network or its actors have not yet been taken.

As for the content, the actors themselves have deleted some of it. The low distribution on social media makes any mention of content moderation [C00122] superfluous. In this case, the only assets that can be subject to action are the websites themselves, a measure that has not been taken so far. The low impact of the campaign is no reason, however, to lower our guard, as researchers warn that the assets could be taken up again at any time for other purposes.

4.22.11 Conclusions and Recommendations

Conclusions

China is involved in influence operations in the West and is increasingly using private firms to manage its foreign influence campaigns on behalf of the government, obfuscating the connections and thus the attribution. Citizen Lab found a network of more than 120 websites posing as local news outlets in 30 targeted countries across Europe, Asia and Latin America.[616]

FIMI campaigns can serve both financial and political interests, as the PAPERWALL case shows. It shows how influence operations may pose potential long-term risks beyond the short-term impact. Some FIMI campaigns generate

---

[611] NCSC Joint Analysis Consultative Group, "중국의 언론사 위장 웹사이트를 악용한 영향력 활동 (Influence activities exploiting fake websites of Chinese media outlets", South Korean National Cyber Security Center (NCSC), 13 Nov 2023. https://www.ncsc.go.kr:4018/main/cop/bbs/selectBoardArticle.do?bbsId=SecurityAdvice_main&nttId=88028&menuNo=020000&subMenuNo=020200&thirdMenuNo=.

[612] Serabian, Ryan, and Daniel Kapellmann Zafra, "Information Operations Campaign Leverages Infrastructure from Public Relations Firm to Disseminate Content on Inauthentic News Sites", Mandiant, 4 Aug 2022. https://www.mandiant.com/resources/blog/pro-prc-information-operations-campaign-haienergy. Serabian, Ryan, Daniel Kapellmann Zafra, Conor Quigley and David Mainor, "Pro-PRC HaiEnergy Campaign Exploits U.S. News Outlets via Newswire Services to Target U.S. Audiences; Evidence of Commissioned Protests in Washington, DC", Mandiant, 24 July 2023. https://www.mandiant.com/resources/blog/pro-prc-haienergy-us-news.

[613] Alaphilippe, Alexandre, "Paperwall: Chinese Information Operation Targets Belgium and Luxembourg", EU DisinfoLab, 14 Mar 2024. https://www.disinfo.eu/paperwall-chinese-information-operation-targets-belgium-and-luxembourg/.

[614] Fittarelli, op. cit., 7 Feb 2024. https://citizenlab.ca/2024/02/paperwall-chinese-websites-posing-as-local-news-outlets-with-pro-beijing-content/.

[615] These countermeasures are taken from the DISARM Blue Framework, https://disarmframework.herokuapp.com/.

[616] Fittarelli, op. cit., 7 Feb 2024.

minimal traffic and lack visible mainstream media coverage or amplification. Still, they may imply a long-term threat when part of the content is noticed and legitimised by mainstream media or political figures at a later stage.

Recommendations

The counter-FIMI community should expand its efforts in monitoring the growing involvement of private firms in the creation and management of influence operations (including FIMI and disinformation-for-hire), since PAPERWALL highlights the propensity of the Chinese government to make use of these companies.[617] These firms often aim to obscure the true actor behind the operations, thus making it more difficult to attribute the FIMI campaign. Researchers specialised in FIMI should be aware that the actors involved in these campaigns can go beyond those associated with a state structure and extend their research scope to private companies accordingly, as the very definition of FIMI also envisions "non-state actors, including their proxies".

4.23 Chinese Disinformation About the Release of Fukushima Water

4.23.1 Introduction

On Friday, 11 March 2011, an earthquake of magnitude 9.0 hit Japan. The earthquake impacted the Fukushima nuclear power plant; large quantities of water were used to cool down the reactors damaged by the earthquake. This water was treated and stored in tanks. Japan started releasing the treated wastewater into the Pacific Ocean[618] in August 2023 at a slow rate of 130 tonnes of water per day. Estimates suggest that the operation will take about 30 years to release all the wastewater. Although the UN atomic watchdog approved the entire operation, which is in line with similar operations in other countries,[619] this release of the treated wastewater fuelled a torrent of disinformation online which started around the time of the start of the treated water discharge[620] (August 2023) and continues to the time of this writing (2024), with stories of giant lobsters found in Japan tied to the Fukushima

[617] Fittarelli, Alberto, "PAPERWALL Chinese Websites Posing as Local News Outlets Target Global Audiences with Pro-Beijing Content", *The Citizen Lab,* 7 Feb 2024. https://citizenlab.ca/2024/02/paperwall-chinese-websites-posing-as-local-news-outlets-with-pro-beijing-content/.
[618] Yamaguchi, Mari, "3rd release of trested water from Japan's damaged Fukushima nuclear plant ends safely, operator says", *APNEWS,* 20 Nov 2023. https://apnews.com/article/japan-fukushima-wastewater-release-china-430c6f6104a969de7f196bcf372a9a6d.
[619] Yang, Tau, "State-backed disinformation fuelling anger in China over Fukushima waters", T*he Guardian,* 4 Sept 2023. https://www.theguardian.com/environment/2023/sep/04/state-backed-disinformation-fuelling-anger-in-china-over-fukushima-wastewater-japan.
[620] Wong, Tessa, "Fukushima: What are the concerns over wastewater release?", *BBC News*, 25 Aug 2023, https://www.bbc.com/news/world-asia-66106162.

water discharge.[621] The disinformation campaign showed videos that associated the release of the treated water with dead fish turning up on nearby beaches. However, the dead fish were not from Japan or any nearby region. The video[622] used a photo of dead fish from Texas months before the release of the Fukushima water discharge.[623]

In the same spirit, a video on Facebook in Korean linked the release of the water with dead fish showing up off Busan city in Korea. However, the picture of the dead fish was from 2022 (before the water discharge) and the other was from another city in Korea.[624] The photo was reproduced in Facebook[625] and other media. Dead fish continued to be shared on social media through September, such as on Weibo, Douyin and X (formerly Twitter) alongside similar false claims linking the incident to Fukushima.[626]

A video showing dirty water being discharged into the sea surfaced on Chinese social media and was linked to the Fukushima discharge of treated wastewater.[627] However, the image was actually of a Mexican wastewater discharge in Acapulco in June 2020. The video was shared on Facebook,[628] YouTube[629] and Douyin,[630] which is the Chinese version of TikTok.

In addition, an animated graphic was circulated and viewed millions of times in Chinese state news reports.[631] The graphic falsely claimed to show the spread of treated wastewater across the Pacific Ocean after its release from Fukushima in August 2023. The graphic's caption reads, "According to a study by a relevant institution, radioactive material from Japan's nuclear wastewater could spread to most of the Pacific Ocean in 57 days, and to global seawater in 10 years' time."

---

[621] Norton, Tom, "Fact Check: Was Giant Mutated Lobster from Nuclear Plant Caught on Film?", *NewsWeek*, 30 May 2024.
https://www.newsweek.com/fact-check-was-giant-mutated-lobster-nuclear-plant-caught-film-1906323.

[622] https://twitter.com/hakai42038139/status/1699959035666256339.

[623] Wang, Tommy, "Video of dead fish in Texas falsely linked to Fukushima wastewater discharge", *Fact check AFP,* 2 Oct 2023. https://factcheck.afp.com/doc.afp.com.33WR492.

[624] Shim, Kyu-Seok, "Old photo of dead fish in harbour falsely linked to Fukushima wastewater release", *AFP Fact Check,* 6 Sept 2023. https://factcheck.afp.com/doc.afp.com.33U48N6.

[625] https://archive.vn/QLQqb.

[626] Shim, op. cit., 6 Sept 2023.

[627] Wang, Tommy, "Video shows Mexico sewage discharge, not wastewater from Japan nuclear plant, *AFP Fact Check*, 30 Aug 2023. https://factcheck.afp.com/doc.afp.com.33TT8AM.

[628] https://archive.ph/hAm1M.

[629] https://archive.ph/n8sh3.

[630] https://archive.ph/AvUCK.

[631] AFP Hong Kong, "Old simulation graphic falsely linked to Fukushima wastewater release", *AFP Fact Check*, 4 Sept 2023. https://factcheck.afp.com/doc.afp.com.33TZ2VZ.

The graphic was shared on TikTok,[632] YouTube,[633] Weibo,[634] Twitter[635] and various other social media. However, it was from an earlier study, not designed to predict long-term release scenarios and cannot be applied to Fukushima's wastewater discharge in 2023.[636] The disinformation also resulted in aggressive behaviour against Japan. For example, businesses in Japan (ranging from a concert hall in Tokyo to an aquarium in the northern prefecture of Iwate) received abusive calls from China to such an extent that they were not able to conduct their own business.[637]

4.23.2 Threat Actors

Although it is usually difficult to pinpoint a specific actor, in this case Chinese media disseminated these false "news" items and were sceptical about the safe release of wastewater. For example, one video produced by *The People's Daily*[638] titled "The truth of Fukushima" claimed that there was a Japanese plot to knowingly discharge water that will "change" the sea, while deliberately ignoring safer options. It generated tens of thousands of comments, many of them highly critical of Japan.[639] Other Chinese platforms involved included Douyin and Weibo (a Chinese microblogging platform). The disinformation was disseminated in Chinese on Facebook, Twitter and YouTube. The latter are popular among Chinese people outside China. Such disinformation spreads hate against Japan and Japanese people worldwide. This was not very surprising given the past relations and tension between Japan and China, including two major Sino-Japanese wars in the past 150 years.[640]

---

632 https://archive.vn/LbUmC.

633 https://archive.ph/CLG9s.

634 https://archive.ph/yqw1Z.

635 https://archive.ph/0YM52.

636 AFP Hong Kong, op. cit., 4 Sept 2023.

637 McCurry, Justin, "Businesses in Japan receive abusive calls from China after Fukushima water release", *The Guardian,* 28 Aug 2023. https://www.theguardian.com/environment/2023/aug/28/japan-businesses-abusive-phone-calls-china-fukushima-waste-water.

638 *The People's Daily* is the official newspaper of the Central Committee of the Chinese Communist Party (CCP). It provides direct information on the policies and viewpoints of the CCP in multiple languages.

639 Davidson, Helen, "State-backed disinformation fuelling anger in China over Fukushima water", *The Guardian,* 4 Sept 2023. https://www.theguardian.com/environment/2023/sep/04/state-backed-disinformation-fuelling-anger-in-china-over-fukushima-wastewater-japan.

640 https://en.wikipedia.org/wiki/First_Sino-Japanese_War and https://en.wikipedia.org/wiki/Second_Sino-Japanese_War.

A report by a UK-based data analysis company called Logically, which aims to fight (mis)disinformation, claimed that since January 2023, the Chinese government and state media have been running a coordinated disinformation campaign targeting the release of the wastewater.[641]

According to *The New York Times*, China's foreign ministry denounced Japan's release of "nuclear-contaminated water" and suspended imports of Japanese seafood, after months of condemnations by the Chinese government and its media affiliates over Japan's discharge plan.[642] Nevertheless, scientists, including Chinese experts invited to serve on a task force by the International Atomic Energy Agency, have said that Japan's water release would have a very low effect on human health or the environment.[643]

Hong Kong has also shown opposition to Japan's plans. Chief Executive John Lee declared that releasing the Fukushima water would create "unavoidable risks to food safety and the environment".[644]

4.23.3 Presumed Objectives

T0076: Distort—The main objective was to distort the facts about the release of treated wastewater. Although the release was approved by the UN, fake videos associated the release with dead fish washing up in nearby shores. This, in turn, fuelled hate against Japan and Japanese citizens, dividing, in this case, multicultural communities that include Japanese people and decreasing the prestige of Japan internationally. With the United States, the European Union and Australia all supporting Japan's water release, China wanted to project a narrative that Japan and its international partners are "so driven and dominated by geopolitical interests that they are waiting to compromise basic ethical standards and international norms and ignore science," said Tong Zhao, a senior fellow in the nuclear policy program at the Carnegie Endowment for International Peace.[645]

T0135: Undermine—The campaign sought to undermine the credibility of Japan and its international partners, including the USA and the EU, who supported

[641] Cai, Derek, "Fukushima: China's anger at Japan is fuelled by disinformation", *BBC News,* 3 Sept 2023. https://www.bbc.com/news/world-asia-66667291.

[642] Rich, Motoko, and John Liu, "China's Disinformation Fuels Anger Over Fukushima Water Release", *The New York Times*, 31 Aug 2023. https://www.nytimes.com/2023/08/31/world/asia/china-fukushima-water-protest.html.

[643] Ibid.

[644] Harris, Paul G., "Why Beijing and Hong Kong's complaints about Fukushima wastewater are hypocritical", *Hong Kong Free Press,* 31 July 2023. https://hongkongfp.com/2023/07/31/radioactive-seafood-complaints-from-beijing-and-hong-kong-about-fukushima-wastewater-scream-of-hypocrisy/.

[645] Rich and Liu, op. cit., 31 August 2023.

the wastewater release. By portraying these actors as prioritising geopolitical interests over scientific evidence and ethical standards, the campaign aimed to sow discord and erode trust in their decision-making.

4.23.4 Incidents and Observables

Several observables of this incident showed photographs of beaches with dead fish, photographs of beaches with pollution, etc. All these photographs claimed to be associated with the wastewater of Fukushima, but they were in fact related to earlier and totally unrelated events in different parts of the globe.

4.23.5 Targets

The target was Japan. Going deeper, we can identify several targets:

- Japanese commercial fishing and Japanese commerce in general. By creating mistrust on the quality of the Japanese waters, China sought to create mistrust about the quality of the seafood harvested from the Sea of Japan. This could have delivered a major blow to Japan's fishing and commerce.
- Japanese people. Such disinformation could have created hate against Japan in general. These disinformation posts claimed that the radioactive water will cover the entire Pacific Ocean in a few weeks and the entire world in a few years. Thus, such claims imply that Japan will have a negative impact on the whole world.
- Japanese government, which is ultimately in charge of the release of the Fukushima water.

4.23.6 Tactics, Techniques and Procedures

This FIMI campaign used several tactics listed in the DISARM Red Framework and dozens of TTPs. Below are the most important ones:

- TA01: Plan strategy—T0074: Strategic ends and T0073: target audiences were determined based on various criteria or types of criteria.
- TA02: Plan objectives—The objectives were to T0140: cause harm, T0066: degrade the adversary, T0076: distort, T0135: undermine and T0002: facilitate state propaganda.
- TA13: Target audience analysis—The operators identified social and technical vulnerabilities [T0081], mapped the target audience's information environment [T0080] and segmented their audiences [T0072] to spread disinformation.

- TA14: Develop narratives—The campaign relied on new narratives [T0082], integrating the target audience vulnerabilities [T0083], and responding to breaking news [T0068] about the release of the Fukushima water.
- TA09: Deliver content—Malign actors posted [T0115] on social media [T0115], on newspapers [T0117], and delivered paid advertisement [T0114].
- TA17: Maximise exposure—They maximised existing narratives [T0118], they posted across different platforms [T0119] and incentivised sharing [T0120] via paid ads.
- TA11: Persist in the information environment—The FIMI continuously tried to amplify its activities [T0060].

4.23.7 Channels

The attackers distributed content using different channels:

- Newspapers such as *The People's Daily*[646] and khan.co.kr in Korea.
- Digital Media Paid advertisements: The state-owned China Central Television and China Global Television Network carried paid ads denouncing the water release on Facebook and Instagram.[647]
- Social media platforms such as Facebook, X (Twitter), TikTok, the Chinese video site bilibili[648] and the Chinese-speaking Douyin.[649]

4.23.8 Languages

The disinformation was disseminated in multiple languages, including English, Chinese, Korean, Khmer and German.[650]

It is worth exploring the impact of the relevant languages and media used. Indeed, we see that this disinformation campaign used Asian languages (Chinese, Korean, Khmer), and European languages (English and German), spoken by lots of people in the western hemisphere. Clearly, there are two populations targeted by this misinformation: (1) people living in east Asia and (2) people living in the western hemisphere. We also noted that there were several posts in Chinese in social media popular outside China (such as Facebook and Twitter). These posts probably target a third group of people: Chinese people living outside China—mostly in the western hemisphere. These people may have an impact in the countries in which they live as they may repeat the message and may influence local policymakers.

---

646 Davidson, op. cit., 4 Sept 2023.
647 Rich and Liu, op. cit., 31 Aug 2023.
648 https://www.bilibili.tv/en.
649 https://www.douyin.com/.
650 Rich and Liu, op. cit., 31 Aug 2023.

4.23.9 Effectiveness

Effects of this incident included:

- The campaign exploited historical tensions and cultural sensitivities between China and Japan, further intensifying negative sentiments and deepening the divide between the two nations. China banned seafood imports from certain areas of Japan.[651] This had an impact on the Japanese fishing industry.
- Cosmetics products from Japan saw a decline in online sales in China.[652]
- Chinese public anger rose against Japan for the wastewater discharge. For example, thousands of callers from China's country code bombarded municipal offices in Tokyo, more than 150 miles from the Fukushima plant, with harassing messages, yelling "You idiot!" or "Why do you release contaminated water?" in broken Japanese.[653] A rock was thrown at a Japanese children's school in Qingdao, while another school in Shandong had several eggs hurled into its compound. A brick was also thrown at the Japanese embassy in Beijing.[654]
- A restaurant in Shanghai, in an apparent effort to profit off the hysteria, advertised "anti-radiation" meals.[655]

4.23.10 Countermeasures

The main countermeasures used were as follows:

Debunking: several newspapers and news channels, including BBC,[656] *The New York Times*,[657] *The Guardian*[658] and France24,[659] explained why the Chinese accusations were false.

---

[651] Davidson, op. cit., 4 Sept 2023.
[652] Speed, Madeleine, and Kana Inagaki, "Chinese boycott beauty products after Fukushima water discharge", *Financial Times*, 16 Oct 2023. https://www.ft.com/content/431d1797-dc13-4212-b7c4-f531e06c82fb.
[653] Rich and Liu, op. cit., 31 August 2023.
[654] Cai, op. cit., 3 Sept 2023.
[655] Ibid.
[656] Couzens, Jo, "Fukushima: Discharge from Japan nuclear plant safe, tests show", *BBC News*, 25 Aug 2023.
https://www.bbc.com/news/world-asia-66609889.
[657] Rich and Liu, op. cit., 31 Aug 2023.
[658] Davidson, op. cit., 4 Sept 2023.
[659] France24, "AFP Fact Check: Fukushima wastewater release spawns misinformation", *France24,* 5 Sept 2023. https://www.france24.com/en/live-news/20230905-afp-fact-check-fukushima-wastewater-release-spawns-misinformation.

4.23.11 Conclusions and Recommendations

This analysis indicates that Chinese media disseminated disinformation regarding Japan's discharge of Fukushima water. They combined factual elements, such as the discharge itself, with falsehoods, such as unrelated photos of dead fish and polluted waters, to suggest that the discharge caused environmental damage and marine life fatalities.

Some conclusions that can be drawn are as follows:

- Technically speaking, the disinformation was not very effective in the sense that the fakery was exposed, which in turn exposed the Chinese media as deliberately purveying false information. On the other hand, this disinformation continues in one way or another to the time of this writing.[660]
- We need to underline the importance of the media (e.g., *The New York Times*) and fact-checkers in exposing fakery. They moved fast and restored the truth.
- There is a long history of tension (and wars) between China and Japan. In such a setting, disinformation spreads fast and continues to spread even when the fakery is exposed.

A recommendation for fact-checkers may be to check the provenance of "news" stories and to attempt to understand why sources from a country, such as China in this case, would spread disinformation against an act from Japan. Simple fact-checking approaches (such as reverse image search) can be useful in revealing fake images which combined with real facts are being used to disseminate disinformation.

4.24 Turkey's Disinformation About North Cyprus as an Independent State

4.24.1 Introduction

On 20 July 1974, Turkey launched a full-scale invasion of Cyprus in response to a 15 July 1974 coup orchestrated by the Greek military junta against Archbishop Makarios, the elected President of Cyprus. Turkey claimed it was seeking to restore constitutional order in Cyprus, acting under Article 4 of the Treaty of Guarantee of the Republic of Cyprus. Turkey occupied 36% of the island, including the cities of Kyrenia, Famagusta and Morphou. The international community has consistently denounced the 1974 invasion and called for the removal of the occupying forces through numerous Decisions and Resolutions adopted in various international fora, such as the UN Security Council, the General Assembly of the UN, the European

[660] Norton, Tom, "Fact Check: Was Giant Mutated Lobster from Nuclear Plant Caught on Film?", *NewsWeek*, 30 May 2024. https://www.newsweek.com/fact-check-was-giant-mutated-lobster-nuclear-plant-caught-film-1906323.

Parliament, the Council of Europe and the Commonwealth. A major development in the division of Cyprus occurred in November 1983 with the proclamation of the "Turkish Republic of Northern Cyprus" (TRNC). The international community condemned this proclamation through UN Security Council resolutions 541/1983 and 550/1984, which found the declaration of the Turkish Republic of Northern Cyprus as invalid, reaffirming the sovereignty of the Republic of Cyprus, calling upon all states to respect the sovereignty, independence and territorial integrity of the Republic of Cyprus and not to recognise any other state in Cyprus or assist the secessionist entity in any way, stressing also the importance of restoring Varosha (Famagusta) to its lawful residents. Additionally, in a series of judgments, the European Court of Human Rights (ECHR) ruled that Turkey violated the European Convention for the Protection of Human Rights in relation to the property rights of Greek Cypriot refugees.

Despite UN Security Council resolutions, Turkey continues its efforts to gain international recognition for the TRNC, as underscored by President Recep Tayyip Erdogan's address at the UN General Assembly in September 2023, where he advocated for the acknowledgement of the Turkish-occupied northern part of Cyprus as an independent state.[661]

This case study examines these ongoing efforts within the broader context of international relations, particularly considering the ongoing war between Russia and Ukraine, where Russia faces considerable pressure from the EU.[662] Amidst these geopolitical tensions, the substantial Russian expatriate community residing in both the free and occupied parts of Cyprus becomes particularly relevant.[663] Responding to the needs of its citizens and navigating the sensitive political landscape, Russia announced plans to deploy a mobile consular unit in the TRNC rather than establishing a formal consulate[664]—a decision that steers clear of suggesting official recognition of the TRNC. Despite this, the situation has been widely misreported by Turkish and Turkish-Cypriot media, with numerous outlets erroneously claiming that "Russia is opening a consulate in TRNC",[665] suggesting

---

[661] Ekathimerini.com, "Erdogan calls for international community to recognize breakaway Turkish Cypriot entity". https://www.ekathimerini.com/news/1220385/erdogan-calls-for-international-community-to-recognize-breakaway-turkish-cypriot-entity.

[662] European Commission Representation in Cyprus, "EU adopts 13th package of sanctions against Russia after two years of its war of aggression against Ukraine", 23 Feb 2024. https://cyprus.representation.ec.europa.eu/news/eu-adopts-13th-package-sanctions-against-russia-after-two-years-its-war-aggression-against-ukraine-2024-02-23_en.

[663] KNEWS, "Guardian: Russian money flows without questions in the occupied territories", 16 Nov 2023. https://knews.kathimerini.com.cy/en/news/guardian-russian-money-flows-without-questions-in-the-occupied-territories.

[664] TASS, "Recognition of North Cyprus not implied by opening of Russian consular office—president", 9 Aug 2023. https://tass.com/world/1658553.

[665] APA Group, "Russia to open consulate in Turkish Republic of Northern Cyprus", 9 Aug 2023. https://apa.az/en/europe/russia-to-open-consulate-in-turkish-republic-of-northern-cyprus-409300. Report News Agency, "Russia opens consulate in Turkish Republic of Northern Cyprus", 9 Aug 2023. https://report.az/en/region/russia-opens-consulate-in-trnc/.

an official or partial recognition of the TRNC. These reports, often sourced from a currently inaccessible article by the Russian news agency TASS, have sparked several sensational headlines such as "Officially recognised! Russia opens a consulate in TRNC"[666] or "Russia set to 'partially recognise' the North".[667] Many of these articles include statements such as:

- "The Russian consulate will be opened in the TRNC."
- "Russia became the second country after Turkey to recognise the TRNC."
- "Russia is set to 'partially recognise' the North upon the opening of its consular office there."
- "More confirmation that Russia will be opening a consulate in the TRNC, this time directly from President Erdoğan during his visit to Russia and meeting with President Putin."

In the context of the Russo-Ukrainian war, one specific news article[668] wrote that the move by Moscow to discuss opening a consulate in TRNC was an act of retaliation towards Cyprus after Cyprus provided Ukraine with ammunition.[669] This shift signals Russia's intent to pivot towards regions that might support its interests under the radar of international sanctions. The Republic of Cyprus, aligning closely with EU sanctions against Russia due to its support for Ukraine, has become a less favourable destination for Russians. Conversely, the TRNC, not being internationally recognised and thus not bound by EU sanctions, appears as an ideal sanctuary for Russians, offering a sanctions-free environment.[670]

Additionally, widespread misreporting has spurred discussions about expanding connectivity and accessibility to this region. Topics such as the development of the new Ercan airport, the potential for direct flights from Russia to the TRNC[671] and the implementation of an e-VISA program have begun to surface. These initiatives are part of broader efforts to enhance the TRNC's international profile and are closely tied to its ongoing quest for international recognition.

---

[666] Gundem Kibris, "Officially recognized! Russia opens a consulate in TRNC", 9 Aug 2023. https://www-gundemkibris-com.translate.goog/resmen-tanidi-rusya-kktcde-konsolosluk-aciyor?_x_tr_sl=auto&_x_tr_tl=en&_x_tr_hl=el.

[667] Cleaver, Tom, "Tatar: Russia set to 'partially recognise' north", *Cyprus Mail*, 19 Aug 2023. https://cyprus-mail.com/2023/08/19/tatar-russia-set-to-partially-recognise-north/.

[668] Kanlı, Yusuf, "Russia's move to establish consular office in Northern Cyprus", Yetkin Report, 12 Aug 2023. https://yetkinreport.com/en/2023/08/12/russias-move-to-establish-consular-office-in-northern-cyprus/.

[669] KNEWS, "Cyprus chips in as EU seeks quick ammo for Ukraine", 22 Mar 2023. https://knews.kathimerini.com.cy/en/news/cyprus-chips-in-as-eu-seeks-quick-ammo-for-ukraine.

[670] Smith, Helena, "There are no questions asked: How Russian money is fuelling a building boom in Northern Cyprus", *The Guardian*, 15 Nov 2023. https://www.theguardian.com/business/2023/nov/15/there-are-no-questions-asked-how-russian-money-is-fuelling-a-building-boom-in-northern-cyprus.

[671] AFP, "Northern Cyprus says Russia to open consulate", *Barron's*, 9 Aug 2023. https://www.barrons.com/news/northern-cyprus-says-russia-to-open-consulate-ed3aff9b.

Messaging on this matter also occurred in other channels of communication including Facebook, Twitter, Reddit, Instagram and TikTok. People have been reposting that "Russia is opening a consulate in TRNC" and connecting this action with Russia's recognition of TRNC. The main push came from a set of named social network groups with active accounts in Facebook, Twitter and TikTok.[672] Collectively, posts from these groups aggregated 105,991 views, 20,007 likes and 482 reposts at the time of our writing. These accounts primarily share narratives supporting the TRNC and challenging the Republic of Cyprus, with a notable emphasis on advocating for the TRNC's international recognition (most of the content is in English). Another note on the matter of the Russian consulate in the TRNC is not new. In 2022, there were similar discussions about Russia opening a consulate in TRNC, with the same reaction and diffusion in the media.[673]

4.24.2 Threat Actors

The primary agents of this narrative seem to be a mix of state-linked and independent entities, such as Turkish and Turkish-Cypriot media,[674] real-estate businesses looking to capitalise on the geopolitical situation,[675] and social media groups with pro-TRNC leanings.[676]

4.24.3 Presumed Objectives

The presumed objectives of these actors are multi-faceted:

- T0076: Distort—Altering the context of Russia's mobile consular service to imply formal recognition of TRNC. This was used to influence public perception and international discourse regarding the status of TRNC, and to exert pressure on Cyprus by creating a false impression of shifting alliances.

[672] https://www.facebook.com/323330971061974/posts/6847847485276924. See also Facebook, "More confirmation that Russia will be opening a consulate in the 'TRNC'". https://www.facebook.com/100063953523941/posts/717831790358599. See also https://twitter.com/Young_Turk_Cyp/status/1698746014885183961.

[673] Kathimerini News, "Ανοίγει προξενείο στα κατεχόμενα η Ρωσία". https://www.kathimerini.com.cy/gr/politiki/anoigei-proxeneio-sta-katexomena-i-rosia. See also https://www.reddit.com/r/cyprus/comments/u5spug/russia_opens_a_consulate_in_the_illegally/.

[674] YeniŞafak, https://www.yenisafak.com/. See also Gündem Kıbrıs, https://www.gundemkibris.com/. Yetkin Report, https://yetkinreport.com/en/.

[675] Timondro, https://timondro.com. See also Alliance Cyprus Property, https://www.alliance-cyprusproperty.com. Kairos Cyprus, https://www.kairoscyprus.com/?lang=en.

[676] https://www.facebook.com/young.turkish.cypriots. See also https://www.facebook.com/groups/323330971061974/.

- T0079: Divide—To fuel uncertainty and division among the Cypriot population and international stakeholders, by exploiting the sensitive issue of the TRNC's unrecognised status.
- T0077: Distract—Shifting focus from Russia's international isolation due to its invasion of Ukraine to a narrative of expanding Russian influence and legitimacy in contested regions.
- T0136: Cultivate support—Garner support by emphasising the push for TRNC recognition, alongside backing from Russia and the public.

4.24.4 Incidents and Observables

The narrative surrounding the misinformation campaign regarding the opening of a Russian consulate in the TRNC and the associated drive for recognition has been actively promoted through repetitive messaging across multiple platforms. This includes the involvement of real estate websites and social media campaigns targeting both Turkish and English-speaking audiences. The discourse, prominent in 2022 and 2023, continuing in 2024, has been shaped by key events and announcements over time, highlighting the efforts to propagate this narrative.

- In 2022: The topic first emerged as a subject of discussion, setting the stage for future developments. Early mentions on platforms such as Reddit[677] and in publications like Kathimerini[678] sparked initial public and media interest in the implications of Russia's diplomatic moves in the TRNC. However, discussions have dialled down as no additional information has been forthcoming on the matter.
- 9 Aug 2023: The narrative reached a pivotal moment with reports across various channels,[679] announcing the opening of the Russian consulate. This development was widely discussed online, with content circulating on the Web on 9 August 2023 and continuing into 10 August. Despite TASS[680] and the Russian ambassador's clarifications that this move did not equate to formal recognition

[677] Reddit, "Russia opens a consulate in the illegally occupied northern part of Cyprus". https://www.reddit.com/r/cyprus/comments/u5spug/russia_opens_a_consulate_in_the_illegally/. See also https://www.reddit.com/r/europe/comments/u5ra6h/russia_opens_consulate_in_occupied_cyprus/.

[678] Kathimerini News, "Ανοίγει προξενείο στα κατεχόμενα η Ρωσία", 17 April 2022. https://www.kathimerini.com.cy/gr/politiki/anoigei-proxeneio-sta-katexomena-i-rosia.

[679] Gündem Kıbrıs, "Resmen Tanıdı! Rusya KKTC'de Konsolosluk Açıyor", 9 Aug 2023. https://www-gundemkibris-com.translate.goog/resmen-tanidi-rusya-kktcde-konsolosluk-aciyor?_x_tr_sl=auto&_x_tr_tl=en&_x_tr_hl=el. See also Twitter, "Russian news agency TASS reported that the Russian Embassy in the Greek Cypriot Administration of Southern Cyprus will begin providing consular services in Nicosia, the capital of the TRNC". https://twitter.com/yenisafak/status/1689247059558223872.

[680] TASS, "Recognition of North Cyprus not implied by opening of Russian consular office—president", 9 Aug 2023. https://tass.com/world/1658553.

of the TRNC, the discourse online suggested otherwise, reflecting the interplay between official statements and public perception.

- 19 Aug 2023: In the wake of Russia's refutation of any formal recognition, TRNC leader Ersin Tatar interpreted the consulate's opening as "partial recognition".[681] This statement underscored the ongoing contestation and differing interpretations of Russia's diplomatic activities in the TRNC.
- Sept 2023: Despite clarifications and refutations, discussions and posts continued to circulate, suggesting that the consulate's opening was imminent.[682] This persistence in the narrative demonstrates the enduring impact of the initial announcements and the complexities of diplomatic relations in contested territories.
- September 2023: President Erdoğan participated in the UN General Assembly and amplified the call for international recognition of the TRNC.[683] This push for legitimisation signalled Turkey's intensified efforts to secure a formal status for the TRNC on the global stage, highlighting the strategic importance of Cyprus in regional geopolitics.

The following table lists observables. Where we were unable to get some data on Reactions, we have left those cells empty (Table 4.5).

4.24.5 Targets

The misinformation campaign about the opening of Russian consular services in the TRNC aimed to influence stakeholders and shape public opinion. This strategy involved misrepresenting the nature of the consular services as formal diplomatic recognition[684] and exaggerating the support for the TRNC from Russia. Such tactics seemed strategically designed to undermine the legitimacy of the Cypriot government, which could significantly impact foreign relations. The campaign had several goals:

- Challenge the legitimacy of the Cypriot government: The dissemination of misinformation that suggested formal recognition of the TRNC by another

[681] *Cyprus Mail*, "Tatar: Russia set to partially recognise north". https://cyprus-mail.com/2023/08/19/tatar-russia-set-to-partially-recognise-north/. https://www.reddit.com/r/cyprus/comments/15w029e/tatar_russia_set_to_partially_recognise_north/.

[682] Facebook, https://www.facebook.com/100063953523941/posts/717831790358599. See also https://twitter.com/Young_Turk_Cyp/status/1698746014885183961.

[683] Euronews, "Erdogan demands international recognition of Northern Cyprus". https://www.euronews.com/2023/06/13/erdogan-demands-international-recognition-of-northern-cyprus.

[684] Commonspace.eu, "Sochi Summit exposes limits of Russian-Turkish entente", 5 Sept 2023. https://www.commonspace.eu/opinion/sochi-summit-exposes-limits-russian-turkish-entente. *AFP*, "Northern Cyprus Says Russia To Open Consulate", *Barron's*, 9 Aug 2023. https://www.barrons.com/news/northern-cyprus-says-russia-to-open-consulate-ed3aff9b.

Table 4.5 Observables concerning supposed international recognition of the TNRC

Title	Channel	Published	Language	Reactions
Russia opens a consulate in the illegally occupied northern part of Cyprus https://www.reddit.com/r/cyprus/comments/u5spug/russia_opens_a_consulate_in_the_illegally/	Reddit r/cyprus	17 Apr 2022	English/Greek	57 Upvotes 22 Comments
Russia opens a consulate in the occupied territories https://www.kathimerini.com.cy/gr/politiki/anoigei-proxeneio-sta-katexomena-i-rosia	*Kathimerini*	17 Apr 2022	English/Greek	
Russia opens consulate in occupied Cyprus https://www.reddit.com/r/europe/comments/u5ra6h/russia_opens_consulate_in_occupied_cyprus/	Reddit r/europe	17 Apr 2022	English/Greek	40 Upvotes 38 Comments
Russia will open a consulate in "Northern Nicosia" https://twitter.com/TurkishFacts4U/status/1579841748649807873	Twitter	11 Oct 2022	English	
Erdoğan demands international recognition of northern Cyprus https://www.euronews.com/2023/06/13/erdogan-demands-international-recognition-of-northern-cyprus	*Euronews*	13 June 2023	English	
Officially recognized! Russia opens a consulate in TRNC https://www-gundemkibris-com.translate.goog/resmen-tanidi-rusya-kktcde-konsolosluk-aciyor?_x_tr_sl=auto&_x_tr_tl=en&_x_tr_hl=el	Gundem Kibris	9 Aug 2023	Turkish	22K Views
Consulate issue… Tatar: It would be better if they open it https://www-gundemkibris-com.translate.goog/konsolosluk-konusu-tatar-acarlarsa-iyi-olur?_x_tr_sl=auto&_x_tr_tl=en&_x_tr_hl=en	Gundem Kibris	9 Aug 2023	Turkish	2620 Views

(continued)

Table 4.5 (continued)

Title	Channel	Published	Language	Reactions
Russia opens a consulate in TRNC https://www.yenisafak.com/dunya/rusya-kktcde-konsolosluk-aciyor-4551702	*Yeni Şafak*	9 Aug 2023	Turkish	
Russia to open consulate in Turkish Republic of Northern Cyprus https://apa.az/en/europe/russia-to-open-consulate-in-turkish-republic-of-northern-cyprus-409300	*APA Media*	9 Aug 2023	English/Russian/ Turkish	
Russia opens consulate in Turkish Republic of Northern Cyprus https://report.az/en/region/russia-opens-consulate-in-trnc/	*Report News Agency*	9 Aug 2023	English/Russian/ Turkish	
Recognition of North Cyprus not implied by opening of Russian consular office https://tass.com/world/1658553	TASS	9 Aug 2023	English	
Tatar: Russia set to 'partially recognise' north https://www.reddit.com/r/cyprus/comments/15w029e/tatar_russia_set_to_partially_recognise_north/	Reddit r/cyprus	9 Aug 2023	English	11 Upvotes 54 Comments
Northern Cyprus says Russia to open consulate https://www.reddit.com/r/RussiaUkraineBriefing/comments/15n4ymc/russiaukraine_daily_briefing/	Reddit r/Russia/Ukraine Briefing	9 Aug 2023	English	
Northern Cyprus Says Russia To Open Consulate https://www.barrons.com/news/northern-cyprus-says-russia-to-open-consulate-ed3aff9b	*Agence France Presse*	9 Aug 2023	English	
Russia opens consulate in TRNC https://www.kairoscyprus.com/blog/27-russia-opens-consulate-in-trnc?lang=en	KAIROS Estates	9 Aug 2023	English	

(continued)

Table 4.5 (continued)

Title	Channel	Published	Language	Reactions
Moscow has publicly declared its intentions concerning the TRNC https://timondro.com/about-turkey/russia-s-game-changing-move-in-trnc-new-consulate-coming-soon	TIMONDRO Properties in Turkey	9 Aug 2023	English	
Opening of the Consulate of Russia in the TRNC https://www.alliance-cyprusproperty.com/news/opening-of-the-consulate-of-russia-in-the-turkish-republic-of-northern-cyprus	Aliance Cyprus Properties	9 Aug 2023	English/Russian	2890 Views
Russian Embassy to start offering consular services in North Cyprus https://www.t-vine.com/russian-embassy-to-start-offering-consular-services-in-north-cyprus/?fbclid=IwAR2Ytk55Vb_fMv2Ha7tdm_5aJ6w56ciEYLj2nQDn5dotJnNMXQgN2S7omFc	*T-Vine News*	9 Aug 2023	English	
Russia to open consulate in Turkish Republic of Northern Cyprus https://www.facebook.com/323330971061974/posts/6847847485276924	Facebook British Turkish Cypriot Association (BTCA)	9 Aug 2023	English	20 Likes
Russia to open consulate in "Turkish Republic of Northern Cyprus" https://twitter.com/CelalSAKKA/status/1689318017367253002	Twitter	9 Aug 2023	English	813 Views 44 Likes 3 Retweets
Towards a fully independent Cyprus https://twitter.com/GNC__CAPS__/status/1689352899409690624	Twitter	9 Aug 2023	Turkish	5,602 Views

(continued)

Table 4.5 (continued)

Title	Channel	Published	Language	Reactions
Russia to open a consulate regarding the so-called TRNC https://twitter.com/Euliberty/status/1689311232795320320	Twitter	9 Aug 2023	English	576 Views 22 Likes 3 Comments 5 Retweets
Russia opens a consulate in TRNC https://twitter.com/yenisafak/status/1689247059558223872	Twitter *Yeni Şafak*	9 Aug 2023	Turkish	81,500 Views 40 Comments 474 Retweets 2,200 Likes
Russia Recognizes the Independence of TRNC	TikTok	9 Aug 2023		
Cyprus: We are in consultation with Russia on opening of Russian consulate in Turkish-occupied areas https://orthodoxtimes.com/cyprus-we-are-in-consultation-with-russia-on-opening-of-russian-consulate-in-turkish-occupied-areas/	*Orthodox Times*	10 Aug 2023	English	
Russia Extends Diplomatic Reach: Moscow to Open Consulate in TRNC, Reports TASS News Agency https://caria-estates.com/bez-kategorii/russia-extends-diplomatic-reach-moscow-to-open-consulate-in-trnc-reports-tass-news-agency/	Caria Estates Northern Cyprus Real Estate	10 Aug 2023	English	
Russia is going to offer consular services to its citizens https://www.facebook.com/323330971061974/posts/6848774625184210	Facebook British Turkish Cypriot Association (BTCA)	10 Aug 2023	English	5 Likes
Russia's move to establish consular office in Northern Cyprus https://yetkinreport.com/en/2023/08/12/russias-move-to-establish-consular-office-in-northern-cyprus/	*Yetkin Report*	12 Aug 2023	English	

(continued)

Table 4.5 (continued)

Title	Channel	Published	Language	Reactions
Tatar: Russia set to 'partially recognise' north https://cyprus-mail.com/2023/08/19/tatar-russia-set-to-partially-recognise-north/	*Cyprus Mail*	19 Aug 2023	English	3792 Views
More confirmation that Russia will be opening a consulate in the TRNC https://www.facebook.com/100063953523941/posts/717831790358599	Facebook Young Turkish Cypriots	4 Sept 2023	English	19 Likes
More confirmation that Russia will be opening a consulate in the TRNC https://twitter.com/Young_Turk_Cyp/status/1698746014885183961	Twitter Young Turkish Cypriots	4 Sept 2023	English	17,500 Views
Launch of 2 Mobile Consular Units in TRNC www.instagram.com/p/CxvYeYBICi4/?next=https%3A%2F%2Fwww.instagram.com%2F%3F__coig_login%3D1	Instagram	28 Sept 2023	English	197 Likes
No questions asked: how Russian money is fueling a building boom in northern Cyprus https://www.theguardian.com/business/2023/nov/15/there-are-no-questions-asked-how-russian-money-is-fuelling-a-building-boom-in-northern-cyprus	*The Guardian*	15 Nov 2023	English	
Tatar's plea to Russia to reshape diplomatic landscape https://knews.kathimerini.com.cy/en/news/tatar-s-plea-to-russia-to-reshape-diplomatic-landscape	*Kathimerini*	18 Dec 2023	English/Greek	

major power like Russia aimed to undermine the sovereignty and international standing of Cyprus, thereby compromising its credibility on the global stage.
- Influence Turkish and English-speaking audiences: The campaign targeted individuals in regions with significant geopolitical interests in Cyprus, to alter their perceptions in favour of the TRNC's legitimacy.
- Impact policymakers and international observers: Attackers targeted those dedicated to maintaining Cyprus's territorial integrity. The disinformation aimed to alter their perceptions and actions concerning the status of the island, which could influence future diplomatic and policy decisions.

Russia was an unintended target in this scenario. The spread of such narratives placed Moscow in a precarious position, compelling it to either affirm or deny the formal recognition of the TRNC. This situation strained Cyprus-Russia relations and forced Russia to clarify its diplomatic intentions, potentially affecting its broader international relationships.

4.24.6 Tactics, Techniques and Procedures

Following are the TTPs from the DISARM Framework that we can see in this case:

TA01: Plan strategy

- T0074.001: Geopolitical advantage—TRNC leveraged the ongoing Russo-Ukrainian war and the Republic of Cyprus's support for Ukraine and EU sanctions against Russia to gain a geopolitical advantage. By promoting the misleading narrative of Russian recognition via consular activities, the TRNC attempted to exploit Russia's potential interest in countering EU actions and Cyprus's stance, thereby aiming to enhance its own diplomatic standing and challenge the legitimacy of the Cypriot government on the international stage. This strategy was designed to exploit geopolitical tensions to gain favour in regional and global political arenas.

TA02: Plan objectives

- T0136.005: Cultivate support for initiative, T0136.003: Energise supporters, T0136.008: Increase prestige—TRNC aimed at cultivating support for its initiative of gaining international recognition, artificially amplifying public and international backing for what is portrayed as a diplomatic breakthrough. This narrative simultaneously energised supporters, invigorating them with a renewed sense of mission and the belief in advancing towards official recognition, particularly amid the geopolitical tensions between Russia and the EU. By positioning itself alongside a global power like Russia, the TRNC sought to increase its prestige, enhancing its standing and notoriety within the international community. This orchestrated push for recognition, paired with the claimed backing from Russia, strategically boosted the TRNC's domestic and international image, aligning with its long-term objectives of legitimacy and sovereignty.

- T0076: Distort, T0077: Distract, T0079: Divide—The TRNC media coverage altered the narrative around Russia's consular activities, reframing these actions as steps towards formal diplomatic recognition, which was factually incorrect. This distortion manipulated public perception, aligning it more favourably towards the TRNC's political agenda. Concurrently, it shifted the focus from its unresolved international status to perceived Russian support, potentially drawing attention away from critical international opposition and the lack of widespread recognition. Lastly, it amplified the divisions between the Greek and Turkish Cypriots on the island. This strategy sought to entrench separatist sentiments and weaken the unified stance against the occupation, further complicating reconciliation efforts and sustaining the conflict.

TA13: Target audience analysis

- T0081.003: Identify existing prejudices, T0072.002: Demographic segmentation, T0072.001: Geographic segmentation—The campaign exploited historical ethnic and national tensions between Greek and Turkish Cypriots to deepen polarisation and solidify its base. Concurrently, it targeted specific groups, such as younger Turkish Cypriots and Turkish nationals, who were more likely to respond positively to narratives promoting TRNC legitimacy and independence. The efforts focused on the Turkish-controlled northern part of Cyprus, creating localised content that resonated with the community's aspirations and perceived grievances.

TA14: Develop narratives

- T0083: Integrate target audience vulnerabilities into narrative, T0003: Leverage existing narratives, T0068: Respond to breaking news event or active crisis—The campaign leveraged existing narratives about national identity and sovereignty, ensuring that new information conformed to these deeply ingrained viewpoints, which enhanced the acceptance and defence of these messages by the community. During periods of breaking news or active crises, the TRNC capitalised on the heightened media attention and the resulting uncertainty, inserting strategically crafted narratives that manipulated public perception and drove support for their geopolitical aims.

TA06: Develop content

- T0085.003: Develop inauthentic news articles, T0086: Develop image-based content—Altered news articles promoted the legitimacy and recognition of TRNC. Alongside textual misinformation, attackers developed and pushed image-based content to support their narratives. This included altering existing images to generate impactful visuals that reinforced their political messages or discredited opposing viewpoints.

4.24.7 Channels

An analysis of the frequency and nature of these channels reveals a multi-faceted approach to narrative distribution.

Social Media Platforms

- Reddit: This platform was instrumental in initiating and sustaining discussions, as evidenced by multiple threads on subreddits such as "r/cyprus" and "r/europe". The interactive nature of Reddit allowed for a mix of opinions and interpretations, engaging both English and Greek-speaking audiences.
- Twitter: Various accounts such as @TurkishFacts4U[685] and @yenisafak,[686] among others, tweeted about the consulate opening, reaching a wide audience through retweets and likes. The platform's immediacy and broad reach made it a crucial channel for rapid dissemination and engagement with the narrative.
- Facebook: The British Turkish Cypriot Association (BTCA)[687] and Young Turkish Cypriots[688] used Facebook to share updates and opinions, highlighting the role of community and diaspora groups in promoting specific viewpoints.

News Websites and Online Publications

- *Kathimerini*,[689] *Euronews*, *Yeni Şafak*,[690] *APA Media*[691] and TASS: These outlets provided coverage with varying degrees of detail and perspective, serving both to inform and frame the discourse around the consulate's opening and its political implications. The presence of both local (e.g., *Kathimerini*) and international (e.g., *Euronews*, TASS) media highlights the broader geopolitical interest in the narrative.

---

[685] TurkishFacts4U, "Russian media citing senior officials have now confirmed the following: (1) A private Russian Airlines will fly direct to the TRNC; (1) Russia will open consulate in 'Northern Nicossia'", Twitter, 11 Oct. 2022. https://twitter.com/TurkishFacts4U/status/1579841748649807873.

[686] YeniSafak, "Russian Embassy in the Greek Cypriot Administration of Southern Cyprus will begin providing consular services in Nicosia", Twitter, 9 Aug. 2023. https://twitter.com/yenisafak/status/1689247059558223872.

[687] British Turkish Cypriot Association (BTCA), Facebook Group. https://www.facebook.com/groups/323330971061974/.

[688] Young Turkish Cypriots, Facebook Group. https://www.facebook.com/young.turkish.cypriots.

[689] Yiannis Ioannoy, "Tatar's plea to Russia to reshape diplomatic landscape", Kathimerini News, 18 Dec. 2023. https://knews.kathimerini.com.cy/en/news/tatar-s-plea-to-russia-to-reshape-diplomatic-landscape.

[690] YeniSafak, "Rusya KKTC'de konsolosluk açıyor", 9 August 2023. https://www.yenisafak.com/dunya/rusya-kktcde-konsolosluk-aciyor-4551702.

[691] APA Group, "Russia to open consulate in Turkish Republic of Northern Cyprus", 9 Aug 2023. https://apa.az/en/europe/russia-to-open-consulate-in-turkish-republic-of-northern-cyprus-409300.

4.24.8 Languages

- Predominantly English, possibly to maximise international reach.
- Turkish, possibly to target domestic and diaspora audiences and to lend credibility to the narrative within the region.
- The majority of websites also supported the Russian language, specifically the choices between English, Turkish and Russian.

4.24.9 Effectiveness

The misinformation campaign based on the claim that Russia was opening a consulate in the TRNC achieved limited success in advancing its goals. While the narrative gained initial traction through Turkish-Cypriot media, real estate websites and social media platforms, it was swiftly countered by authoritative clarifications from Russia, including the Russian ambassador and TASS news agency, explicitly denying any formal recognition of the TRNC. These clarifications significantly mitigated the potential impact of the disinformation campaign.

The Republic of Cyprus, alongside international observers, strongly condemned the misrepresentation of events, emphasising the continued non-recognition of the TRNC and the illegitimacy of such narratives. Social media posts promoting the consulate story garnered considerable engagement, but this did not translate into significant policy shifts or widespread public belief. Instead, the misinformation primarily sowed confusion and reinforced existing divisions, rather than altering the fundamental geopolitical stance of key international stakeholders.

Ultimately, the rapid response from official channels and the international community limited the campaign's influence, demonstrating the importance of transparent communication and fact-checking in neutralising disinformation efforts. While the campaign briefly fostered narratives supportive of the TRNC, its overall effectiveness was constrained by timely rebuttals and a lack of sustained credibility.

4.24.10 Countermeasures

Debunking: Independent organisations and Cypriot officials debunked the claims.

Statement of rebuttal: Statements from the Russian ambassador[692] and TASS clarifying the nature of the consular services.[693]

Content confined: Limited efforts to reduce the reach of misleading articles and posts.

---

[692] *Barron's*, "Northern Cyprus says Russia to open consulate". https://www.barrons.com/news/northern-cyprus-says-russia-to-open-consulate-ed3aff9b.

[693] TASS, "Recognition of North Cyprus not implied by opening of Russian consular office—president". https://tass.com/world/1658553.

4.24.11 Conclusions and Recommendations

The campaign exploited historical ethnic and national tensions between Greek and Turkish Cypriots to deepen polarisation. Based on the case described above, we make the following recommendations to the EC and Member State governments:

- Continuous monitoring and debunking: Establish a dedicated task force to monitor platforms for misinformation related to Cyprus and the TRNC. Implement real-time reporting mechanisms and collaborate with social media companies to quickly flag and remove misleading content.
- Diplomatic engagement and legal actions: Government agencies, such as the Ministry of Foreign Affairs, should lead the charge in strengthening diplomatic engagement with international partners. Regulatory bodies and legal authorities must take proactive steps to pursue legal actions and enforce measures against entities spreading false narratives. Collaboration with international organisations and private-sector stakeholders will also be essential to amplify these efforts.
- Local outreach programs: Develop programs to engage directly with communities, fostering dialogue and understanding among Greek and Turkish Cypriots.
- Partnerships with credible media: Establish partnerships with reputable media organisations to amplify accurate information. Government agencies, media regulatory bodies and educational institutions should provide journalists with comprehensive training to identify and effectively report misinformation. Collaboration with international journalism associations and experienced media professionals will ensure the training is robust, practical and aligned with global best practices.

4.25 Turkey's Disinformation About a Clash with the UN in the Buffer Zone in Cyprus

4.25.1 Introduction

The 1974 Turkish invasion of Cyprus sparked a long-standing conflict that has shaped the island's political landscape[694] into one of enduring complexity. As noted earlier, Turkey's control of 36% of the island forced significant population displacement, the deprivation of private properties on a massive scale and the forced geographic division of the island's communities. A key feature of the current division is the UN-controlled buffer zone.[695] Initially established in 1964 to

[694] Ministry of Foreign Affairs of the Republic of Cyprus, "Turkish Military Invasion and Occupation", n.d. https://mfa.gov.cy/turkish-military-invasion-and-occupation.html.
[695] Wikipedia, "United Nations Buffer Zone in Cyprus".https://en.wikipedia.org/wiki/United_Nations_Buffer_Zone_in_Cyprus.

prevent hostilities between Greek and Turkish Cypriots, the zone saw significant expansion after the ceasefire on 16 August 1974, which followed the Turkish invasion. At that time, foreign ministers from Greece, Turkey and the United Kingdom, under United Nations Security Council Resolution 353, met at a Tripartite Conference in Geneva to agree upon the establishment of a "security zone" separating the military forces of the two sides.[696] This meeting set the stage for the enduring geographic division that persists to this day. The buffer zone now stretches approximately 180 km across the island, its boundaries marking where the opposing forces stood at the time of the ceasefire, as recorded by the United Nations Peacekeeping Force in Cyprus (UNFICYP).[697]

The buffer zone has become a critical point for peacekeeping efforts and contentious activities, highlighting the ongoing complexities of the island's political division. The UN Security Council has mandated UNFICYP to police the buffer zone and maintain a permanent watch over it with patrols in vehicles, on foot, on bicycles and by helicopter. Additionally, a highly mobile unit stands ready to respond to emergencies within the buffer zone.

This case study delves into the FIMI incident surrounding the altercation involving UN peacekeepers and Turkish Cypriot forces within the Cyprus buffer zone on 18 August 2023. Following this incident, Turkish and TRNC sources launched a sophisticated FIMI operation marked by key events over several days in August 2023:

- 18 Aug 2023: A clash occurred between UN peacekeepers and Turkish Cypriot forces. Initial reports by international news agencies, including Reuters[698] and *Kathimerini*,[699] reported that three UN peacekeepers suffered serious

---

[696] United Nations Peacekeeping Force in Cyprus, "Tripartite Conference Geneva Declaration". https://unficyp.unmissions.org/tripartite-conference-geneva-declaration.

[697] United Nations Peacekeeping Force in Cyprus, "About the Buffer Zone". https://unficyp.unmissions.org/about-buffer-zone.

[698] Reuters, "UN Peacekeepers Hurt in Cyprus Buffer Zone Clash with Turkish Forces", 18 Aug 2023. https://www.reuters.com/world/un-peacekeepers-hurt-cyprus-buffer-zone-clash-with-turkish-forces-2023-08-18.

[699] Kathimerini Cyprus, "UN Peacekeepers Hospitalized after Assault in Pyla Buffer Zone", 18 Aug 2023. https://knews.kathimerini.com.cy/en/news/un-peacekeepers-hospitalized-after-assault-in-pyla-buffer-zone.

injuries. Concurrently, pro-TRNC accounts on Twitter,[700] Facebook,[701] Reddit[702] and TikTok[703] began misrepresenting the peacekeepers as aggressors, falsely claiming they were invading Turkish Cypriot sovereignty.

- 20 Aug 2023: Efforts to spread disinformation intensified. Turkish and TRNC media outlets and social media channels claimed biased Western media coverage and alleged hospitalisation of Turkish Cypriot personnel, portraying the Turkish Cypriots as victims of an unlawful UN intervention.[704]
- 21 Aug 2023: Misreports surfaced about a supposed Russian veto at the UN Security Council, which was allegedly intended to condemn the TRNC. Social media platforms played a significant role in spreading these inaccurate reports, contributing to widespread confusion.[705] Amidst this disarray, Turkish President Erdogan seized the moment to further amplify calls for international recognition

[700] Twitter, "BREAKING NEWS! SON DAKİKA!…", 18 Aug 2023. https://twitter.com/Young_Turk_Cyp/status/1692496313793880480. See also Twitter, "TURKISH CYPRIOTS STAND UP TO UN OPPRESSION!…", 18 Aug 2023. https://twitter.com/Young_Turk_Cyp/status/1692503180829925701.

[701] Facebook, "The UN continues its discriminatory and biased approach against the Turkish Cypriots…", 18 Aug 2023. https://facebook.com/photo/?fbid=708483207960124&set=a.463656859109428. See also Facebook, "Statement of the TRNC Ministry of Foreign Affairs regarding UNFICYP's Intervention in the Construction of the Pile—Yiğitler Road", 18 Aug 2023. https://www.facebook.com/100064428982534/posts/682237517267208.

[702] Reddit, "Breaking News: The United Nations are now stepping into TRNC territory and preventing Turkish Cypriots from exercising their sovereign rights! The Pile-Yiğitler Road is a humanitarian project!", 18 Aug 2023. https://www.reddit.com/r/PoliticTurkey/comments/15un6ft/breaking_news_the_United_Nations_are_now_stepping. See also Reddit, "Breaking News: The United Nations are now Stepping In". https://www.reddit.com/r/trpolitics/comments/15un7wk/breaking_news_the_united_nations_are_now_stepping.

[703] TikTok account of Young Turkish Cypriots (https://www.tiktok.com/@youngturkishcypriots) was banned/deleted. Later on, a new account was created under a similar username (https://www.tiktok.com/@young_turkish_cypriots). See also TikTok, "TURKISH CYPRIOTS STAND UP TO UNITED NATIONS OPPRESSION!…". https://www.tiktok.com/@youngturkishcypriots/video/7268625039128284448. TikTok, "HYPOCRISY OVER HUMANITARIAN CRISIS IN CYPRUS!…". https://www.tiktok.com/@youngturkishcypriots/video/7268618395912817953.

[704] *Anadolu Agency*, "Northern Cypriot Police Say 8 Officers Injured in Melee with UN Peacekeepers", 19 Aug 2023. https://www.aa.com.tr/en/turkiye/northern-cypriot-police-say-8-officers-injured-in-melee-with-un-peacekeepers/2971655. See also *Daily Sabah*, "UN Peacekeepers Attack Turkish Cypriot Soldiers in TRNC Zone", 12 Sept 2023. https://www.dailysabah.com/politics/un-peacekeepers-attack-turkish-cypriot-soldiers-in-trnc-zone/news?fbclid=IwAR3hBWDF9OgUd0qSSPGZBboeV-voJ426AiNZnv5W-o03t4ZKjelwPlFUTxM. Twitter, "A side of the incident that has conveniently been left out of western media regarding the Pile incident…", 20 Aug 2023. https://twitter.com/Young_Turk_Cyp/status/1693325634183811492.

[705] Instagram, "BREAKING NEWS! SON DAKİKA! Russia vetoes UNSC draft resolution…", 21 Aug 2023. https://www.instagram.com/p/CwMkpnrKPKs. See also Facebook, "BREAKING NEWS! SON DAKİKA! Russia vetoes UNSC draft resolution…", 20 Aug 2023. https://www.facebook.com/100063953523941/posts/709746217833823. Twitter, "BREAKING NEWS! SON DAKİKA! Russia vetoes UNSC draft resolution…", 21 Aug 2023. https://twitter.com/Young_Turk_Cyp/status/1693510190061043960.

of the TRNC, criticising the actions of UN forces in the region.[706] Despite these misreports, official statements from Russia on 21 August explicitly joined the international condemnation of the incident in the buffer zone.[707] These statements directly contradicted the false claims of a veto, illustrating Russia's actual stance on the matter and highlighting the use of disinformation to suggest international discord and further undermine the credibility of the UN's actions in Cyprus.
- Following the initial wave of disinformation, continuing discussions on social media platforms such as Reddit[708] illustrate the enduring influence of the misleading portrayal of the events. This ongoing dialogue demonstrates the challenges of combating FIMI in contentious and politicised environments. This timeline shows how disinformation was rapidly deployed following the incident, manipulated public perception across multiple fronts and attempted to alter international responses to the crisis in the buffer zone.

These elements of disinformation were strategically used to manipulate public perception and international discourse regarding the events in the buffer zone. By leveraging historical grievances and the sensitive status of the buffer zone, the narratives misused factual events to fuel a biased interpretation that supported TRNC's political aims. This case highlights the ongoing challenges of managing accurate information in politically volatile regions and underscores the complexities of international peacekeeping in contested territories.

4.25.2 Threat Actors

The primary agents of this narrative seem to be state-linked and independent entities that manipulate information to align with the interests of Turkey and the TRNC. These include Turkish and Turkish Cypriot media (e.g., *Anadolu*,[709] *Daily*

[706] *Anadolu Agency*, "UN Peacekeeping Forces' Intervention in Northern Cyprus Road Construction Unacceptable: Turkish President Erdoğan", 21 Aug 2023. https://www.aa.com.tr/en/turkiye/un-peacekeeping-forces-intervention-in-northern-cyprus-road-construction-unacceptable-turkish-president-erdogan/2973042. See also Reuters, "Turkey Says UN Peacekeepers' Intervention in Turkish Cypriot Roadworks Unacceptable", 21 Aug 2023. https://www.reuters.com/world/middle-east/turkey-says-un-peacekeepers-intervention-turkish-cypriot-roadworks-unacceptable-2023-08-21.

[707] Ministry of Foreign Affairs of the Russian Federation, "Foreign Ministry Spokeswoman Maria Zakharova's answer to a question from Cyprus News Agency about the incident involving UN peacekeepers in Cyprus", 21 Aug 2023. https://mid.ru/en/foreign_policy/news/1901103/.

[708] Reddit, "British Peacekeepers Injured after Clashes with Turkish Forces", 20 Aug 2023. https://www.reddit.com/r/europe/comments/15vw6qi/british_peacekeepers_injured_after_clashes_with. See also Reddit, "Turkish Cypriot Forces Assault Cyprus", 18 Aug 2023. https://www.reddit.com/r/europe/comments/15ugcg4/turkish_cypriot_forces_assault_cyprus.

[709] *Anadolu Agency*. https://www.aa.com.tr/en.

Sabah[710] and *The Cradle*[711]) and social media groups with pro-TRNC leanings (e.g., @Young_Turk_Cyp[712] and @BTCAOfficial[713]).

4.25.3 Presumed Objectives

The presumed objectives of these actors are multi-faceted:

- T0076: Distort—Manipulators altered the narrative about the clash in the buffer zone to portray UN peacekeepers as the aggressors, thereby changing the context of the UN's intervention. This manipulation aimed to sway public perception and international discourse against the UN's actions, suggesting they violated the TRNC's sovereignty.
- T0077: Distract—Accusations of unlawful interventions and aggressive behaviour by the UN shifted focus from Turkish Cypriot forces' aggressive actions and provocations to the UN, thus reducing the international and domestic scrutiny that Turkey and the TRNC would otherwise have faced.
- T0079: Divide—Disinformation about the UN's actions deepened the division between Greek and Turkish Cypriots. By framing the conflict in terms of national rights and sovereignty, the information operations polarised opinions and intensified ethnic tensions.
- T0075: Dismiss—The incident also involved dismissing criticism of Turkish Cypriot actions in the buffer zone. This was achieved by portraying international critics, especially those from the UN, as biased or applying double standards. By suggesting that the criticism was unfairly targeted against Turkish Cypriot interests while ignoring similar situations from Greek Cypriots, the incident aimed to undermine the validity of any condemnation directed at Turkey and the TRNC.
- T0066: Degrade adversary—Efforts to degrade the image of the UN and its peacekeeping forces in Cyprus were evident. The disinformation propagated portrayed these entities as not only ineffective but also as violators of international law and intruders in TRNC sovereignty. Such claims were designed to damage the reputation of the UN, casting doubt on its neutrality and effectiveness in managing peace and security.
- T0135: Undermine—Spreading disinformation that questioned the legitimacy and intentions of the UN in Cyprus, these actors aimed to weaken the credibility and authority of UN peacekeeping forces. Additionally, the false narrative that Russia vetoed a UN draft resolution on the incident was used to suggest

[710] *Daily Sabah.* https://www.dailysabah.com.

[711] *The Cradle.* https://thecradle.co.

[712] Facebook, "Young Turkish Cypriots". https://www.facebook.com/young.turkish.cypriots.

[713] Facebook, "British Turkish Cypriot Association (BTCA)". https://www.facebook.com/groups/323330971061974/.

international discord and further undermine the credibility of the UN's actions in Cyprus.
- T0136: Cultivate support—The FIMI incident actively aimed to grow or maintain support for the TRNC by managing alliances and generating sympathy among a wider audience. This effort included enhancing the TRNC's reputation and public relations and promoting the notion that Turkish Cypriots were rightfully exercising their sovereign rights, upon which they claimed the UN was infringing.

4.25.4 Incidents and Observables

In this section, we detail the key observables from the FIMI incident, characterised by repetitive messaging used across multiple platforms for broad dissemination (see the Table 4.6). The incident strategically engaged both Turkish and English-speaking audiences with coordinated social media efforts to enhance its impact and extend its reach.

4.25.5 Targets

The FIMI incident surrounding the clash in the Cyprus buffer zone strategically targeted various stakeholders and shaped public opinion by misrepresenting the actions of UN peacekeepers and promoting the sovereignty claims of the TRNC. Turkish and TRNC sources likely intended to both undermine the legitimacy of the UN's role in the region and to bolster the perceived legitimacy of the TRNC on the buffer zone. They used these tactics to influence international relations and alter the narrative surrounding Cyprus's territorial disputes. The primary goals of this incident included:

- **Challenge the Legitimacy of the UN and the Sovereignty of Cyprus**: The FIMI incident portrayed UN peacekeepers as aggressors and promoted the narrative that the TRNC possessed legitimate sovereign rights over the buffer zone. This dual strategy not only challenged the authority of the UN but also boosted the perceived legitimacy of the TRNC, influencing both local and international perceptions regarding the status of the buffer zone. Additionally, by casting doubt on the sovereignty of the internationally recognised Republic of Cyprus, the incident actively complicated the political landscape, attempting to legitimise separatist claims and reshape international understanding of sovereignty on the island.
- **Influence Turkish and English-Speaking Audiences**: The incident specifically targeted individuals in regions with significant geopolitical interests in Cyprus, manipulating their perceptions to sway public and political opinion in favour of the Turkish Cypriot narratives. Turkey and TRNC achieved this by strategically using media channels and social media platforms to reach these audiences.

Table 4.6 Key observables from Turkey's disinformation incident in the Cyprus buffer zone

Title	Channel	Date published	Language	Reactions
BREAKING NEWS! SON DAKİKA! The United Nations are now stepping into TRNC territory and preventing Turkish Cypriots from exercising their sovereign rights! The Pile-Yiğitler Road is a humanitarian project! Another reason why we support #UNoutofCyprus https://twitter.com/Young_Turk_Cyp/status/1692496313793880480	Twitter	18 Aug 2023	English	202.6K Views 895 Likes 55 Comments 211 Reposts
TURKISH CYPRIOTS STAND UP TO UN OPPRESSION! The United Nations are now stepping into TRNC territory and preventing Turkish Cypriots from exercising their sovereign rights! The Pile-Yiğitler Road is a humanitarian project! Another reason why we support #UNoutofCyprus #Pile https://twitter.com/Young_Turk_Cyp/status/1692503180829925701	Twitter	18 Aug 2023	English	32.9K Views 505 Likes 30 Comments 107 Reposts
The UN intervened unlawfully with barbed wire, concrete and troops within the territory of the TRNC, restricting Turkish Cypriots from exercising their sovereign rights…The tension and escalation was caused by the attitude of the UN troops. Not the Turkish Cypriot construction workers and police who were ensuring safety within the region https://twitter.com/Young_Turk_Cyp/status/1692685229566173577	Twitter	18 Aug 2023	English	10.5K Views 322 Likes 10 Comments 49 Reposts
STATEMENT OF THE TRNC MINISTRY OF FOREIGN AFFAIRS REGARDING UNFICYP'S INTERVENTION IN THE CONSTRUCTION OF THE PILE—YİĞİTLER ROAD…UNFICYP military personnel have physically assaulted within the TRNC territory, our road construction teams as well as our police. https://www.facebook.com/100064428982534/posts/682237517267208	Facebook	18 Aug 2023	English	11 Likes

(continued)

Table 4.6 (continued)

Title	Channel	Date published	Language	Reactions
BREAKING NEWS! The United Nations are now stepping into TRNC territory and preventing Turkish Cypriots from exercising their sovereign rights! The Pile-Yiğitler Road is a humanitarian project! https://www.reddit.com/r/PoliticTurkey/comments/15un6ft/breaking_news_the_united_nations_are_now_stepping	Reddit	18 Aug 2023	English	6 Upvotes 6 Comments
BREAKING NEWS! The United Nations are now stepping into TRNC territory and preventing Turkish Cypriots from exercising their sovereign rights! The Pile-Yiğitler Road is a humanitarian project! https://www.reddit.com/r/trpolitics/comments/15un7wk/breaking_news_the_united_nations_are_now_stepping	Reddit	18 Aug 2023	English	6 Upvotes 1 Comment
TURKISH CYPRIOTS STAND UP TO UNITED NATIONS OPPRESSION! The United Nations are now stepping into the TRNC territory and preventing Turkish Cypriots from exercising their sovereign rights! The Pile-Yiğitler Road is a humanitarian project! https://www.tiktok.com/@youngturkishcypriots/video/7268618395912817953	TikTok[714]	18 Aug 2023	English	1256 Likes 413 Comments
TURKISH CYPRIOTS STAND UP TO UNITED NATIONS OPPRESSION! The United Nations are now stepping into the TRNC territory and preventing Turkish Cypriots from exercising their sovereign rights! The Pile-Yiğitler Road is a humanitarian project! https://www.tiktok.com/@youngturkishcypriots/video/7268625039128284448	TikTok	18 Aug 2023	English	1214 Likes 697 Comments
The UN continues its discriminatory and biased approach against the Turkish Cypriots, who are equal partners to the island's independence and have sovereign equality https://www.facebook.com/photo/?fbid=708483207960124&set=a.463656859109428	Facebook	18 Aug 2023	English	9 Likes 13 Comments
Russia reportedly blocks UN Security Council statement on Pyla incident https://in-cyprus.philenews.com/local/russia-reportedly-blocks-un-security-council-statement-on-pyla-incident/	*Philenews*	19 Aug 2023	English	

(continued)

[714] The TikTok account of Young Turkish Cypriots (https://www.tiktok.com/@youngturkishcypriots) was banned/deleted. A new account was created later under a similar username (https://www.tiktok.com/@young_turkish_cypriots).

Table 4.6 (continued)

Title	Channel	Date published	Language	Reactions
UN peacekeepers attack Turkish Cypriot soldiers in TRNC zone https://www.dailysabah.com/politics/un-peacekeepers-attack-turkish-cypriot-soldiers-in-trnc-zone/news?fbclid=IwAR3hBWDF9OgUd0qSSPGZBboeV-voJ426AiNZnv5W-o03t4ZKjelwPlFUTxM	*Daily Sabah*	20 Aug 2023	English	
Northern Cypriot police say 8 officers injured in melee with UN peacekeepers https://www.aa.com.tr/en/turkiye/northern-cypriot-police-say-8-officers-injured-in-melee-with-un-peacekeepers/2971655	*Anadolu*	20 Aug 2023	English/ Turkish	
A side of the incident that has conveniently been left out of western media regarding the Pile incident… https://www.facebook.com/photo/?fbid=709521701189608&set=a.463656859109428	Facebook	20 Aug 2023	English	7 Likes 3 Comments
A side of the incident that has conveniently been left out of western media regarding the Pile incident… The TRNC's General Directorate of Police stated yesterday that 15 personnel were hospitalised following the incident https://www.instagram.com/p/CwLRDiKKObq	Instagram	20 Aug 2023	English	224 Likes
A side of the incident that has conveniently been left out of western media regarding the Pile incident… The TRNC's General Directorate of Police stated yesterday that 15 personnel were hospitalised following the incident https://twitter.com/Young_Turk_Cyp/status/1693325634183811492	Twitter	20 Aug 2023	English	13k Views 144 Likes 19 Comments 28 Reposts
Russia vetoes UNSC resolution condemning TRNC: tensions grow on Pile-Yiğitler Road in Northern Cyprus https://us.firenews.video/world-news/russia-vetoes-unsc-resolution-condemning-trnc-tensions-grow-on-pile-yigitler-road-in-northern-cyprus	*Fire News*	20 Aug 2023	English	

(continued)

Table 4.6 (continued)

Title	Channel	Date published	Language	Reactions
BREAKING NEWS! SON DAKİKA! Russia vetoes UNSC draft resolution which would have condemned the TRNC over the Pile-Yiğitler Road incident https://facebook.com/100063953523941/posts/709746217833823	Facebook	21 Aug 2023	English	21 Likes 8 Comments
BREAKING NEWS! SON DAKİKA! Russia vetoes UNSC draft resolution which would have condemned the TRNC over the Pile-Yiğitler Road project incident https://twitter.com/Young_Turk_Cyp/status/1693510190061043960	Twitter	21 Aug 2023	English	13.5K Views 200 Likes 14 Comments 28 Reposts
BREAKING NEWS! SON DAKİKA! Russia vetoes UNSC draft resolution which would have condemned the TRNC over the Pile-Yiğitler Road incident. By doing this, Russia has moved against the other permanent members of the UNSC—USA, France, China and UK. These are interesting developments, especially considering Russia will soon be opening up a consulate in the TRNC https://www.instagram.com/p/CwMkpnrKPKs	Instagram	21 Aug 2023	English	505 Likes
UN peacekeeping force's intervention in Northern Cyprus road construction 'unacceptable': Turkish President Erdogan https://www.aa.com.tr/en/turkiye/un-peacekeeping-forces-intervention-in-northern-cyprus-road-construction-unacceptable-turkish-president-erdogan/2973042	*Anadolu*	21 Aug 2023	English	
Erdogan condemns UN intervention in Turkish-occupied Cyprus https://new.thecradle.co/articles-id/7116	*The Cradle*	22 Aug 2023	English	
Türkiye slams UNSC over statement on Cyprus road project https://www.dailysabah.com/politics/turkiye-slams-unsc-over-statement-on-cyprus-road-project/news	*Daily Sabah*	22 Aug 2023	English	
Turkey accuses UN of losing its neutrality in Cyprus road spat https://www.timesofisrael.com/turkey-accuses-un-of-losing-its-neutrality-in-cyprus-road-spat	*The Times of Israel*	22 Aug 2023	English	

- **Impact Policymakers and International Observers**: The FIMI incident, orchestrated by Turkey and the TRNC, targeted the UN, which is involved in maintaining peace and stability in Cyprus, with the aim of influencing future diplomatic and policy decisions, especially those involving negotiations and resolutions pertaining to Cyprus.

Additionally, by involving international actors such as Russia in the narrative, the FIMI incident placed them in a challenging position, compelling them to respond or clarify their stance on Cyprus. This would strain Cyprus-Russia relations and force a diplomatic clarification that might have affected broader international relationships. The strategic use of disinformation not only pressured specific countries but also highlighted the complex interplay of national interests and international diplomacy.

4.25.6 Tactics, Techniques and Procedures

- TA01: Plan strategy
  - Determine strategic ends [T0074] (geopolitical advantage [T0074.001])—The disinformation incident sought to exploit the complex geopolitics of Cyprus, portraying the UN peacekeepers as overreaching aggressors, thereby positioning the TRNC as a victim of international injustice. Through this narrative, TRNC aimed to gain sympathy and support internationally, enhancing its geopolitical leverage.
- TA02: Plan objectives
  - Cultivate support [T0136] (boost reputation [T0136.004], cultivate support for initiative [T0136.005], defend reputation [T0136.001], justify action [T0136.002])—The incident aimed to cultivate support for the TRNC by boosting its international image as an underrepresented (self-declared/unrecognised) "state", justifying its actions against perceived UN aggressions and defending its reputation against international criticisms.
  - Degrade adversary [T0066], dismiss [T0075] (discredit credible sources [T0075.001]), distort [T0076], distract [T0077], divide [T0079], undermine [T0135] (smear [T0135.001], subvert [T0135.003])—The narratives not only sought to degrade the credibility of the UN and Cyprus by distorting facts about the buffer zone incident but also worked to dismiss credible sources as biased. The disinformation aimed to distract from the aggressive actions of Turkish Cypriot forces, divide the local and international communities, and undermine the established authority of the UN in the region.
- TA13: Target audience analysis
  - Identify social and technical vulnerabilities [T0081] (find echo chambers [T0081.001], identify existing prejudices [T0081.003]), segment audiences [T0072] (geographic segmentation [T0072.001])—The incident identified

and exploited the existing prejudices and social vulnerabilities among Turkish Cypriots, and geographically segmented the audiences to tailor messages that resonated with local sentiments and historical grievances.

- TA14: Develop narratives
  - Develop competing narratives [T0004], leverage existing narratives [T0003], respond to breaking news event or active crisis [T0068]—The disinformation efforts leveraged the historical narrative of Turkish Cypriot victimisation and responded quickly to the breaking news of the UN's actions, crafting competing narratives that presented alternative perspectives intended to confuse and divide public opinion.
- TA06: Develop content
  - Create hashtags and search artefacts [T0015], develop image-based content [T0086], aggregate information into evidence collages [T0086.004], develop text-based content [T0085], develop inauthentic news articles [T0085.003], develop video-based content [T0087], distort facts [T0023] reframe context [T0023.001]—The incident used hashtags, manipulated images and developed both text and video content that misrepresented the events, creating a broad media presence that reframed the context to suit strategic ends.
- TA15: Establish assets
  - Build network [T0092], create community or sub-group [T0092.003], develop owned media assets [T0095]—Pro-TRNC groups and media outlets acted as crucial assets, disseminating tailored content across various platforms, establishing a network of supportive communities and sub-groups.
- TA05: Microtarget
  - Create clickbait [T0016], create localised content [T0101], leverage echo chambers/filter bubbles [T0102], use existing echo chambers/filter bubbles [T0102.001]—Targeted, localised content served as clickbait to engage specific audiences, reinforcing the incident within echo chambers that amplify the desired narratives.
- TA07: Select channels and affordances
  - Use discussion forums [T0106], social networks [T0104], mainstream social networks [T0104.001], create dedicated hashtag [T0104.006], media sharing networks [T0105], photo sharing [T0105.001], video sharing [T0105.002]—The incident effectively used mainstream social networks (Twitter, Facebook and Reddit), discussion forums (Reddit) and media sharing platforms (Instagram, TikTok) to ensure wide dissemination of its messages, reaching a diverse audience.
- TA08: Conduct pump priming
  - Seed distortions [T0044], seed kernel of truth [T0042]—Early in the incident, operatives seeded distortions mixed with kernels of truth to establish a believable foundation for their narratives, priming the audience for further misinformation.
- TA17: Maximise exposure
  - Amplify existing narrative [T0118], cross-posting [T0119], post across groups [T0119.001], post across platforms [T0119.002]—By amplifying the

existing narratives through strategic cross-posting across groups and platforms, the incident maximised its exposure and impact, spreading its reach far beyond its initial audience.

4.25.7 Channels

In the context of the buffer zone incident, Turkey and the TRNC strategically leveraged widespread misreporting and heightened media interest to shift international perspectives. Turkish media outlets, including *Daily Sabah*[715] and *Anadolu*,[716] propagated claims that UN peacekeepers attacked Turkish Cypriot soldiers and that eight Turkish Cypriot officers were injured in the melee. These reports were part of a broader disinformation campaign intended to portray the UN intervention as unlawful and thus challenge the sovereignty of Cyprus. Turkish President Erdogan further escalated the situation by publicly condemning the UN's actions as unacceptable, which was widely covered in outlets including *Anadolu*[717] and *The Cradle*.[718] This fuelled discussions about the sovereignty of the TRNC and its international legitimacy, indirectly aiding in the ongoing quest for recognition by influencing public opinion and international relations.

Messaging on this matter also occurred in other channels of communication including Facebook, Twitter, Reddit, Instagram and TikTok. The main push came from a set of named social network groups, with active accounts in Facebook, Twitter and TikTok, namely the British Turkish Cypriot Association[719] and Young Turkish Cypriots.[720] Collectively, these posts aggregated more than 270,000 views, 5,300 likes and 1,200 comments. These accounts engaged in an aggressive push of narratives in favour of the TRNC, and against the Republic of Cyprus and UN, while pushing for TRNC international recognition. Most of their content was in English, suggesting an intention to influence a global audience.

---

[715] *Daily Sabah*, "UN Peacekeepers Attack Turkish Cypriot Soldiers in TRNC Zone", 12 Sept 2023. https://www.dailysabah.com/politics/un-peacekeepers-attack-turkish-cypriot-soldiers-in-trnc-zone/news?fbclid=IwAR3hBWDF9OgUd0qSSPGZBboeV-voJ426AiNZnv5W-o03t4ZKjelwPlFUTxM.

[716] *Anadolu*, "Northern Cypriot Police Say 8 Officers Injured in Melee with UN Peacekeepers", 19 Aug 2023. https://www.aa.com.tr/en/turkiye/northern-cypriot-police-say-8-officers-injured-in-melee-with-un-peacekeepers/2971655.

[717] Güldoğan, Diyar, *Anadolu Agency*, "UN Peacekeeping Forces' Intervention in Northern Cyprus Road Construction Unacceptable: Turkish President Erdoğan", 21 Aug 2023. https://www.aa.com.tr/en/turkiye/un-peacekeeping-forces-intervention-in-northern-cyprus-road-construction-unacceptable-turkish-president-erdogan/2973042.

[718] *The Cradle*, "Erdogan condemns UN intervention in Turkish-occupied Cyprus", 22 Aug 2023. https://new.thecradle.co/articles-id/7116.

[719] Facebook, "British Turkish Cypriot Association (BTCA)". https://www.facebook.com/groups/323330971061974

[720] Facebook, "Young Turkish Cypriots". https://www.facebook.com/young.turkish.cypriots. See also Twitter, "Young_Turk_Cyp", https://twitter.com/Young_Turk_Cyp.

An analysis of the frequency and nature of these channels reveals a multifaceted approach to narrative distribution.

- **Reddit**: This platform was instrumental in initiating and sustaining discussions, as evidenced by multiple threads on subreddits such as r/PoliticTurkey[721] (670 members), r/trpolitics[722] (2,700 members), r/worldnews[723] (36,000 members) and *r/europe*[724] (6.3 million members). The interactive nature of Reddit allowed for a mix of opinions and interpretations, engaging English, Turkish and Greek-speaking audiences.
- **Twitter**: Accounts such as @*Young_Turk_Cyp*[725] (7,000 followers) tweeted about the buffer zone incident, reaching a wide audience through retweets and likes. The platform's immediacy and broad reach made it a crucial channel for rapid dissemination and engagement with the narrative.
- **Facebook**: The British Turkish Cypriot Association (BTCA)[726] (5,400 members) and Young Turkish Cypriots[727] (2,600 followers) used Facebook to share updates and opinions, highlighting the role of community and diaspora groups in promoting specific viewpoints.
- **Instagram** and **TikTok**: While less detailed information is available about the content on these platforms, their inclusion suggests an effort to engage younger demographics and leverage the visual and viral nature of these media (Young Turkish Cypriots[728]: 11,600 followers on Instagram and 1,160 followers on TikTok).

---

[721] Reddit, "Breaking News: The United Nations are now Stepping In", 18 Aug 2023. https://www.reddit.com/r/PoliticTurkey/comments/15un6ft/breaking_news_the_united_nations_are_now_stepping.

[722] Reddit, "Breaking News: The United Nations are now Stepping In", 18 Aug 2023. https://www.reddit.com/r/trpolitics/comments/15un7wk/breaking_news_the_united_nations_are_now_stepping.

[723] Reddit, "Turkish Cypriot Forces Assault Cyprus", 18 Aug 2023. https://www.reddit.com/r/worldnews/comments/15y0qpf/turkish_cypriot_forces_assault_cyprus. Reddit, "UN Peacekeepers Hurt in Cyprus Buffer Zone Clash", 18 Aug 2023. https://www.reddit.com/r/worldnews/comments/15unvsn/un_peacekeepers_hurt_in_cyprus_buffer_zone_clash.

[724] Reddit, "British Peacekeepers Injured after Clashes with Turkish Forces", 18 Aug 2023. https://www.reddit.com/r/europe/comments/15vw6qi/british_peacekeepers_injured_after_clashes_with. Reddit, "Turkish Cypriot Forces Assault Cyprus", 18 Aug 2023. https://www.reddit.com/r/europe/comments/15ugcg4/turkish_cypriot_forces_assault_cyprus.

[725] Twitter, "BREAKING NEWS! SON DAKİKA! The United Nations are now stepping into TRNC territory…", 18 Aug 2023. https://twitter.com/Young_Turk_Cyp/status/1692496313793880480.

[726] Facebook, "British Turkish Cypriot Association (BTCA)". https://www.facebook.com/groups/323330971061974.

[727] Facebook, "Young Turkish Cypriots". https://www.facebook.com/young.turkish.cypriots.

[728] TikTok, "young_turkish_cypriots", https://www.tiktok.com/@young_turkish_cypriots.

News Websites and Online Publications

- *Kathimerini*[729], *Cyprus Mail,*[730] Reuters,[731] UN News,[732] *AP News,*[733] *The Cradle,*[734] *Daily Sabah*[735] and *Anadolu*[736]: These outlets provided coverage with varying degrees of detail and perspective, serving both to inform and frame the discourse around the incident in the Cyprus buffer zone between the UN and Turkish Cypriot forces. The presence of both local (e.g., *Kathimerini*) and international (e.g., Reuters) media highlights the broader geopolitical interest in the narrative.

4.25.8 Languages

The FIMI incident was primarily in English, likely to maximise its international reach. Turkish was employed to target domestic audiences and the diaspora, enhancing the narrative's credibility within the region.

4.25.9 Effectiveness

The FIMI incident had limited success in achieving its objectives. Despite the aggressive spread of disinformation through various media outlets and social media platforms, the efforts were quickly identified and countered. Significantly, the UN and numerous countries swiftly condemned the actions detailed in the disinformation incident, which helped to mitigate its impact. On the same day as the incident, 18 August

[729] Ioannou, Yiannis, "Buffer Zone Tensions and Cyprus Problem Scenarios", *Kathimerini Cyprus*, 28 Aug 2023. https://knews.kathimerini.com.cy/en/news/buffer-zone-tensions-and-cyprus-problem-scenarios. *Kathimerini Cyprus*, "UN Peacekeepers Hospitalized after Assault in Pyla Buffer Zone", 18 Aug 2023. https://knews.kathimerini.com.cy/en/news/un-peacekeepers-hospitalized-after-assault-in-pyla-buffer-zone.

[730] Cleaver, Tom, "UN Condemns Assaults from Turkish Cypriot Side on Personnel near Pyla", *Cyprus Mail*, 18 Aug 2023. https://cyprus-mail.com/2023/08/18/un-condemns-assaults-from-turkish-cypriot-side-on-personnel-near-pyla.

[731] Reuters, "UN Peacekeepers Hurt in Cyprus Buffer Zone Clash with Turkish Forces", 18 Aug 2023. https://www.reuters.com/world/un-peacekeepers-hurt-cyprus-buffer-zone-clash-with-turkish-forces-2023-08-18.

[732] United Nations, "UN Condemns Assaults Against Peacekeepers in Cyprus Buffer Zone", 19 Aug 2023. https://news.un.org/en/story/2023/08/1139912.

[733] Hadjicostis, Menelaos, "Cyprus: Turkey Peacekeepers Assault Buffer Zone", Associated Press News (AP NEWS), 19 Aug 2023. https://apnews.com/article/cyprus-turkey-peacekeepers-assault-buffer-zone-07871df37fdc336b5bc358543ad0580d.

[734] *The Cradle*, https://new.thecradle.co.

[735] *Daily Sabah*, https://www.dailysabah.com.

[736] Firik, Mehmet Kemal, "Northern Cypriot Police Say 8 Officers Injured in Melee with UN Peacekeepers", Anadolu Agency, 19 Aug 2023. https://www.aa.com.tr/en/turkiye/northern-cypriot-police-say-8-officers-injured-in-melee-with-un-peacekeepers/2971655.

2023,[737] the UN released statements strongly condemning the assault on peacekeepers, with further elaborations on the seriousness of the attack provided on 19 August.[738] Simultaneously, global leaders including European Commission President Ursula von der Leyen,[739] along with the UK, France and the US, denounced the assault, amplifying the international response against the disinformation.[740] Also, Russia, through statements on 21 August,[741] joined the condemnation.

Furthermore, the disinformation did not significantly alter behaviours or actions on a large scale; reactions to the posts, while noticeable, did not translate into widespread public movements or shifts in political dynamics. The disinformation primarily fostered confusion and reinforced existing social divisions rather than creating new harms or altering the core beliefs or trust levels of the broader international community. The rapid and unified response from international bodies and governments significantly limited the disinformation's potential to cause harm, demonstrating the effectiveness of prompt and clear communication in countering misinformation.

4.25.10 Countermeasures

Officials from UN, Cyprus, EU, UK, US and Russia responded to the disinformation by posting clarifying details and condemning the incident in the Cyprus buffer zone, thus indirectly debunking the misleading claims. However, efforts to directly limit the reach of these articles and posts were minimal.

4.25.11 Conclusions and Recommendations

The FIMI incident surrounding the clash in the Cyprus buffer zone strategically targeted various stakeholders trying to shape public opinion by misrepresenting the

[737] United Nations, "Statement Attributable to the Spokesperson for the Secretary-General—Assault Against United Nations Peacekeepers in Cyprus". https://www.un.org/sg/en/content/sg/statement/2023-08-18/statement-attributable-the-spokesperson-for-the-secretary-general-assault-against-united-nations-peacekeepers-cyprus. United Nations, "UNFICYP Condemns Assaults Against UN Peacekeepers". https://unficyp.unmissions.org/unficyp-condemns-assaults-against-un-peacekeepers.

[738] United Nations, "UN Condemns Assaults Against Peacekeepers in Cyprus Buffer Zone". https://news.un.org/en/story/2023/08/1139912.

[739] Twitter, "I strongly condemn the attacks on @UN_CYPRUS peacekeepers by Turkish Cypriot personnel…". https://twitter.com/vonderleyen/status/1692631041326878906.

[740] Mathiesen, Karl, "Von der Leyen Condemns Turkish Cypriot Attack on UN Peacekeepers", *POLITICO*, 19 Aug 2023. https://www.politico.eu/article/von-der-leyen-condemns-turkish-cypriot-attack-on-un-peacekeepers.

[741] Ministry of Foreign Affairs of the Russian Federation, "Foreign Ministry Spokeswoman Maria Zakharova's answer to a question from Cyprus News Agency about the incident involving UN peacekeepers in Cyprus", https://mid.ru/en/foreign_policy/news/1901103/.

actions of UN peacekeepers and promoting the sovereignty claims of the TRNC. This approach was designed to both undermine the legitimacy of the UN's role in the region and to bolster the perceived legitimacy of the TRNC in the buffer zone. The disinformation campaign aimed to distort public perception, divert attention from Turkish Cypriot provocations, deepen ethnic divisions and undermine international criticism of TRNC actions. These tactics were aimed at influencing international relations and altering the narrative surrounding Cyprus's territorial disputes.

The rapid and unified response from international bodies and governments significantly limited the disinformation's potential to cause harm, demonstrating the effectiveness of prompt and clear communication in countering misinformation. The swift condemnation by the UN, supported by major global leaders and countries, effectively neutralised the disinformation's impact and prevented substantial shifts in public opinion and policy. This response underscores the importance of coordinated and timely actions to address and counteract disinformation efforts.

4.26 Varosha to Vegas: The Real Estate Exploitation and Disinformation

4.26.1 Introduction

This case study is about how the private sector in Cyprus profited from a governmental disinformation campaign. It complements Sect. 4.24 which focused on the political aspects of the Turkish government's seizure of northern Cyprus. The Turkish invasion of Cyprus on 20 July 1974[742] led to the massive, forced displacement of more than 200,000 Greek Cypriots from their ancestral lands (25% of the island's population), becoming refugees in their own country. Greek Cypriots who, according to the 1964 Land Registry Record of the Republic of Cyprus, owned an approximate 82% of the properties in the occupied areas, were illegally deprived of access to and control of their properties. Since then, these properties have been subject to illegal usurpation and monetisation. Real-estate agencies operating under the jurisdiction of self-proclaimed Turkish Republic of Northern Cyprus (TRNC) have been selling such properties to TRNC citizens and international buyers, including Russians, Britons, Israelis and Iranians.[743]

To facilitate these transactions and attract international investment, the TRNC and associated entities have employed campaigns that downplay the legal and ethical implications of purchasing such properties.[744] By using sensationalist media

[742] Note: Sect. 4.24 provide a more detailed account of the 1974 invasion and its implications.

[743] Cyprus Government Press and Information Office, "What is happening with the issue of the purchase of real estate by foreigners in the occupied territories?" https://www.gov.cy/pio/en/.

[744] *Pravda News*, "Zelensky became the owner of one of the largest casinos in Europe", June 2024. https://news-pravda.com/world/2024/06/03/551540.html. Maddox, David, "King Charles

reports and promoting ambitious development projects—like the proposed "Las Vegas of the Mediterranean" in Famagusta, driven by UK-based investors[745]—they aimed to draw global attention and legitimise their actions. Additionally, the TRNC's real estate market was actively promoted through digital and social media platforms, often without fully disclosing the legal risks to potential buyers.[746]

Complementing these economic initiatives are persistent diplomatic efforts and strategic media campaigns seeking political support from countries beyond Turkey, particularly the United Kingdom. Leveraging the context of Brexit, TRNC leaders have expressed hope that the UK might adopt a more flexible stance toward Cyprus. For instance, TRNC leader Ersin Tatar suggested that "Brexit freed Britain from the EU", potentially allowing it to play a neutral or different role in the Cyprus issue. Some campaigns implied that Brexit could lead to UK recognition of the TRNC, the establishment of direct flights and new investment opportunities in northern Cyprus.[747] Furthermore, they disseminated information about purported consular developments, referenced prominent figures[748] such as King Charles III[749] and President Volodymyr Zelensky,[750] and employed targeted social media campaigns on platforms such as Facebook and Twitter to promote pro-TRNC messages.[751]

Collectively, these coordinated efforts aimed to reshape international perceptions of Northern Cyprus by attracting foreign investors and seeking political

denies owning hotel as Cyprus President orders investigation into resort", *Daily Express* UK, 13 Feb 2024. https://www.express.co.uk/news/politics/1866365/king-charles-hotel-cyprus-varosha-maras-vegas-mediterranean.

[745] Maddox, David, "New image emerges of plan for ghost town Cyprus resort fuelling diplomatic crisis", *Daily Express*, 14 Feb 2024. https://www.express.co.uk/news/politics/1866762/king-charles-hotel-cyprus-diplomatic-row.

[746] Sigmalive, "Israel: Warns Israelis against buying property in the occupied territories", Apr 2024. https://economytoday.sigmalive.com/oikonomia/kypros/79049_israil-proeidopoiei-toys-israilinoys-gia-agora-perioysion-sta-katehomena.

[747] https://brstrnc.com/press.asp. See also Maddox, David, "Britain urged to use Brexit freedoms to recognise North Cyprus as a sovereign country", *Daily Express*, 24 Apr 2021. https://www.express.co.uk/news/politics/1427534/North-cyprus-officially-recognised-brexit-britain.

[748] https://www.facebook.com/photo/?fbid=787950673346710&set=a.463656859109428.

[749] Maddox, David, "North Cyprus attempts to woo Charles with invite to abandoned 7-star hotel 'Firm owns'", *Daily Express*, 28 Jan 2023. https://www.express.co.uk/news/politics/1727545/king-charles-north-cyprus-queen-funeral-snub-ersin-tatar-seven-star-hotel-special-report.

[750] *Pravda News*, "Zelensky became the owner of one of the largest casinos in Europe", 3 June 2024. https://news-pravda.com/world/2024/06/03/551540.html.

[751] Facebook, "More confirmation that Russia will be opening a consulate in the TRNC", 4 Sept 2023. https://www.facebook.com/100063953523941/posts/717831790358599. See also Aussie Cossack, "Zelensky spend $200 M to buy himself a 5 star casino resort on the beaches of Cyprus", June 2024. https://x.com/aussiecossack/status/1797716902237868178 (now banned). Y.T.C. "VEGAS ON THE MED", 12 Feb 2024. https://x.com/Young_Turk_Cyp/status/1757125955401797773. FFNC, "North Cyprus and the rest of the island will benefit enormously from this development. It will show the world that North Cyprus is open for business", 12 Feb 2024. https://x.com/FFNCyprus/status/1757084002731565475.

recognition.[752] This strategy advanced their objectives but also posed significant legal and ethical concerns for uninformed investors.[753]

4.26.2 Threat Actors

The primary agents driving this FIMI campaign appeared to be a combination of state-affiliated and independent entities that gain from the internationalisation and perceived legitimacy of the TRNC. These actors included Turkish and Turkish Cypriot media outlets,[754] real estate companies[755] and social media groups with strong pro-TRNC inclinations.[756] Additionally, sensationalist reports from media sources alleging high-profile investments in the region, such as King Charles' supposed ownership of a hotel in Varosha,[757] contributed to the complex web of influence promoting the TRNC. These elements collectively worked towards altering the narrative and public perception to favour the Turkish-occupied Northern Cyprus, leveraging both traditional and digital platforms to propagate their message.

4.26.3 Presumed Objectives

The presumed objectives of these actors were multi-faceted:

---

752 Embassy of the Republic of Cyprus, "Illegal Exploitation of Greek Cypriot properties by Turkey in occupied areas is a criminal offence", Republic of Cyprus, Aug 2006. http://www.mfa.gov.cy/mfa/embassies/embassy_doha.nsf/5c948f5c1aaedd13c225722600546f46/f7c67a2cb84a67964325723c00323af4?OpenDocument. Williams, Ben, "North Cyprus Property Market in 2023: An Overview", *London Economic*, 5 May 2023. https://www.thelondoneconomic.com/property/north-cyprus-property-market-in-2023-an-overview-347929/.

753 *Luxury Travel*, "Northern Cyprus: An Ideal Location for Property Investments", 15 Apr 2024. https://www.luxurytravelmagazine.com/news-articles/northern-cyprus-an-ideal-location-for-investments-into-property. 50 political opponents ask "why not to northern Cyprus?", Londragazete, 31 May 2024. https://londragazete.com/english/278422/50-political-opponents-ask-why-not-to-northern-cyprus/

754 *YeniSafak*, https://www.yenisafak.com/. Yetkin Report. https://yetkinreport.com/en/. Gundem Kibris. https://www.gundemkibris.com/.

755 Timondro Estates. https://timondro.com. Gundem Kibris, https://www.gundemkibris.com/. Alliance North Cyprus. https://www.alliance-cyprusproperty.com/. Kairo Cyprus Properties. https://www.kairoscyprus.com/?lang=en. DNP Property Group, https://www.dnp.com.cy/.

756 Y.T.C. Facebook Group. https://www.facebook.com/young.turkish.cypriots. BTCA, Facebook Group,https://www.facebook.com/groups/323330971061974/.

757 Maddox, David, "New image emerges of plan for ghost town Cyprus resort fuelling diplomatic crisis", *Daily Express*, 14 Feb 2024. https://www.express.co.uk/news/politics/1866762/king-charles-hotel-cyprus-diplomatic-row. Maddox, David, "North Cyprus attempts to woo Charles with invite to abandoned 7-star hotel 'Firm owns'", *Daily Express*, 28 Jan 2023. https://www.express.co.uk/news/politics/1727545/king-charles-north-cyprus-queen-funeral-snub-ersin-tatar-seven-star-hotel-special-report.

- T0076: Distort—The primary objective was to alter perceptions of the real estate market in the TRNC by downplaying legal issues and promoting the region as a legitimate and lucrative investment destination. By emphasising opportunities for investors from Russia and Israel affected by ongoing conflicts, the strategy sought to attract foreign capital while creating a false impression of legality and stability surrounding property transactions in the TRNC.
- T0079: Divide—By exploiting the illegal monetisation of Greek Cypriot properties, the TRNC fuelled division among the Cypriot population and international stakeholders. Aggressively marketing these properties to Russian and Israeli investors displaced by war exacerbated tensions.
- T0077: Distract—The strategy involved diverting attention from the legal ownership issues of properties in the TRNC by highlighting attractive real estate opportunities to investors from conflict-affected regions like Russia and Israel. By focusing on economic benefits and the promise of stability, it distracted from the unethical aspects of selling illegally held properties, thus downplaying the underlying legal controversies.
- T0136: Cultivate support—The TRNC went about garnering support by emphasising the push for TRNC recognition, highlighting backing from significant geopolitical players like Russia, UK and Israel, and fostering public approval. Sensationalist reports regarding high-profile investments in Varosha and the connection to King Charles aimed to create a perception of impending international legitimacy and support.
- T0137: Economic profit—The TRNC sought economic gain by highlighting lucrative real estate opportunities presented by perceived stability and potential international legitimacy. By positioning itself as an attractive alternative for Russian and Israeli investors impacted by conflict—and, in Russia's case, by sanctions—the TRNC framed itself as a favourable destination to invest and bypass restrictions, thereby boosting its economy through the influx of foreign capital.

4.26.4 Incidents and Observables

Russia opening consulate in TRNC.

Since 2022, discussions about Russia potentially opening a consulate in the TRNC have emerged, initially sparking public interest but waning due to limited information. The topic regained momentum in 2023 when President Erdoğan called for international recognition of the TRNC at the UN General Assembly. In August 2023, reports announced the opening of a Russian consulate, leading to widespread online discussions despite official denials from Russia equating this to formal recognition. Turkish Cypriot leader Ersin Tatar referred to the move as "partial recognition", fuelling ongoing debates. By September 2023, discussions persisted, and by February 2024, the narrative evolved to include contentious real estate developments in Famagusta (Varosha), with allegations of illegal property development involving displaced Greek Cypriots and rumours of high-profile figures' involvement.

Zelenskyy owning a five-star casino in TRNC.

- 6 March 2024: Twitter account @aussiecossack[758] claimed that President Zelenskyy spent $200 million to buy a five-star casino resort in Cyprus through his company "Film Heritage Inc." This allegation quickly gained traction, and *Pravda*[759] published an article supporting the claim, further fuelling speculation about Zelenskyy's involvement in such a significant real estate investment.
- 6 April 2024: A month later, Greek media outlet Sigmalive[760] reported Turkish media claims about Zelenskyy's alleged acquisition, followed by Reporter CY,[761] highlighting the contradiction between his public stance against Russian occupation and his purported private investment in the occupied region of Cyprus. On the same day, fact-checking websites Factchecker.gr[762] and factcheckcyprus.org[763] debunked the misinformation, stating there was no proof of Zelenskyy purchasing a luxury hotel-casino in the occupied region. Despite these clarifications, the initial allegations continued to influence public discourse, illustrating the enduring impact of sensationalist claims.

Turning Varosha into "Las Vegas of the Med".

- 12 February 2024: A news report on plans to transform Varosha into the "Vegas of the Mediterranean",[764] mentioning King Charles's alleged involvement in a hotel project, with additional reports suggesting that the project could drag King

[758] Aussie Cossack, "Zelensky spend $200 M to buy himself a 5 star casino resort on the beaches of Cyprus", June 2024. https://x.com/aussiecossack/status/1797716902237868178 (now banned).

[759] *Pravda News*, "Zelensky became the owner of one of the largest casinos in Europe", 3 June 2024. https://news-pravda.com/world/2024/06/03/551540.html.

[760] Sigmalive, "Τουρκικά ΜΜΕ: Ο Ζελένσκι απέκτησε καζίνο στην κατεχόμενη Κερύνεια", June 2024. https://www.sigmalive.com/news/local/1227197/tourkika-mme-o-zelenski-apektise-kazino-stin-katexomeni-keryneia.

[761] Reporter CY, "Φωνάζει για την ρωσική κατοχή αλλά αγόρασε ξενοδοχείο-καζίνο στην κατεχόμενη Κερύνεια ο Ζελένσκι", June 2024. https://reporter.com.cy/article/2024/6/4/778979/phonazei-gia-ten-rosike-katokhe-alla-agorase-xenodokheio-kazino-sten-katekhomene-keruneia-o-/.

[762] Greece Fact Check, "Παραπληροφόρηση για την αγορά πολυτελούς ξενοδοχείου-καζίνο στην Κερύνεια από τον Βολοντιμίρ Ζελένσκι", Factchecker.gr, June 2024. https://www.factchecker.gr/2024/06/04/no-proof-zelensky-bought-a-casino-hotel-in-kerynia/.

[763] Fact Check Cyprus, "Παραπληροφόρηση για την αγορά πολυτελούς ξενοδοχείου στα Κατεχόμενα από τον Βολοντιμίρ Ζελένσκι", June 2024. https://factcheckcyprus.org/fact-checks/disinfo-about-zelensky-having-bougth-hotel-in-kyrenia/.

[764] Dialogos, "Αγγλικό δημοσίευμα για σχέδιο να γίνει το Βαρώσι «Βέγκας στη Μεσόγειο»—Αναφορά σε ξενοδοχείο του Βασιλιά Καρόλου", Feb 2024. https://dialogos.com.cy/aggliko-dimosieyma-schedio-na-ginei-to-varosi-vegkas-sti-mesogeio/.

Charles into a diplomatic row.[765] Twitter accounts also discussed the potential benefits of the development for North Cyprus.[766]

- 13–18 February 2024: More articles[767] appeared in the British press discussing the plans to turn Varosha into a Las Vegas, highlighting a consortium of billionaire businessmen preparing a "billion-pound project" for Maras.[768] Further articles revealed new images and plans for the ghost town resort, which further fuelled the diplomatic crisis.
- 18 February 2024: Greek Cypriot newspaper *Philenews*[769] reported on the movement in Varosha with property applications being examined on Ankara's orders, indicating progress in the redevelopment plans.

King Charles "owning" a 7-star hotel in TRNC.

- 13 February 2024: The UK *Daily Express* reported that King Charles denied owning a hotel in Cyprus as the Cyprus President ordered an investigation into the resort.[770] *Hellas Journal* published an article criticising the pro-Turkish slant of the *Daily Express* report, which suggested turning Varosha into "Las Vegas" and implicated King Charles in property ownership.[771] The UK paper *The Sun*[772] also featured a sensational piece titled "ROYAL MESS" about the alleged ownership of a 7-star hotel by King Charles in the abandoned resort.

---

[765] *Express Politics*, "Plans to turn seaside ghost town into 'Vegas of the Med' could drag King Charles into row", 12 Feb 2024. https://x.com/ExpressPolitics/status/1756942280110313956.

[766] Y.T.C., "VEGAS ON THE MED", 12 Feb 2024. https://x.com/Young_Turk_Cyp/status/1757125955401797773. FFNC, "North Cyprus and the rest of the island will benefit enormously from this development. It will show the world that North Cyprus is open for business", 12 Feb 2024. https://x.com/FFNCyprus/status/1757084002731565475.

[767] Kibis Postasi, "British Press Discusses Plan to Turn Varosha into Las Vegas", 13 Feb 2024. https://www.kibrispostasi.com/c140-DAILY_NEWS/n507332-british-press-discusses-plan-to-turn-varosha-into-las-vegas.

[768] Alliance North Cyprus, "A consortium of billionaire businessmen from around the world, successful hoteliers, has prepared "a billion-pound project" for Maras", 13 Feb 2024. https://www.alliance-cyprusproperty.com/news/marash-is-a-billion-pound-project.

[769] Movement in Varosha with the properties: Ankara's order to examine applications concerning Famagusta first, Philenews. https://in-cyprus.philenews.com/local/movement-in-varosha-with-the-properties-ankaras-order-to-examine-applications-concerning-famagusta-first/.

[770] Maddox, David, "King Charles denies owning hotel as Cyprus President orders investigation into resort", *Daily Express*, Feb. 2024. https://www.express.co.uk/news/politics/1866365/king-charles-hotel-cyprus-varosha-maras-vegas-mediterranean.

[771] "Απαράδεκτο, φιλοτουρκικό δημοσίευμα στη Daily Express: Ονειρεύονται -και το ομολογούν- «Las Vegas» στα Βαρώσια, εμπλέκουν και τον Κάρολο σε θέματα ιδιοκτησίας", *Hellas Journal*, Feb. 2024. https://hellasjournal.com/2024/02/aparadekto-filotourkiko-dimosievma-sti-daily-express-onirevonte-ke-to-omologoun-las-vegas-sta-varosia-empleko.

[772] English, Georgie, "ROYAL MESS Inside ghost town with 7-star hotel 'owned by King Charles' left to rot in once idyllic resort turned no-man's-land", *The Sun*, Feb. 2024. https://www.thesun.co.uk/news/25893892/abandoned-ghost-town-hotel-king-charles-cyprus-resort/.

- 14 February 2024: OhMyMag (UK)[773] published an article outlining what was known about the claims regarding King Charles's supposed ownership of a seven-star hotel in Cyprus. Parikiaki and *The National Herald* both reported on King Charles's denial of owning the hotel in Varosha and the ongoing investigation by the Cyprus President.
- 15 February 2024: The *Daily Express*[774] released another article analysing the "diplomatic row" caused by an image depicting the second phase of the "Las Vegas of the Mediterranean" project, which featured the flag of Turkey prominently. This inclusion was considered provocative, especially given King Charles III's Greek heritage, as it may have been perceived as an affront to his background.
- 28 January 2023: The *Daily Express*[775] previously reported on North Cyprus's attempt to woo King Charles with an invite to the abandoned 7-star hotel, revealing earlier attempts to involve him in the region's developments (Table 4.7).

4.26.5 Targets

The misinformation campaign involving the TRNC aimed to influence various stakeholders and shape public opinion by leveraging a mix of sensationalist narratives and geopolitical manoeuvres.[776] These tactics were strategically designed to undermine the legitimacy of the Cypriot government, manipulate international relations and economically benefit the TRNC. The potential targets of this campaign included:

- Attracting investors to the TRNC real estate market: By promoting misleading narratives that suggest stability and imminent international recognition, the campaign aimed to attract investments into the real estate market of the contested region. Sensational stories such as the development of the "Las Vegas

[773] Gernez, Laurène, "King Charles: What we know about claims he owns 'seven star hotel' in controversial area of Cyprus", *Oh My Mag*, Feb. 2024. https://www.ohmymag.co.uk/entertainment/royal-family/king-charles-what-we-know-about-claims-he-owns-seven-star-hotel-in-controversial-area-of.

[774] *Daily Express*, "Can you spot the insult to King Charles in an image that caused a huge diplomatic row?", https://www.express.co.uk/news/politics/1867181/king-charles-cyprus-trnc-image-diplomatic-row-analysis.

[775] *Daily Express*, "North Cyprus attempts to woo Charles with invite to abandoned 7-star hotel 'Firm owns',". https://www.express.co.uk/news/politics/1727545/king-charles-north-cyprus-queen-funeral-snub-ersin-tatar-seven-star-hotel-special-report.

[776] Maddox, David, "North Cyprus attempts to woo Charles with invite to abandoned 7-star hotel 'Firm owns", *Daily Express*, 28 Jan 2023. https://www.express.co.uk/news/politics/1866762/king-charles-hotel-cyprus-diplomatic-row. *Pravda News*, "Zelensky became the owner of one of the largest casinos in Europe", 3 June 2024. https://news-pravda.com/world/2024/06/03/551540.html.

Table 4.7 Items about north Cyprus that helped generate controversy

	Title	Channel	Published	Language
Zelenskyy "owning" casino in North Cyprus	BOMBSHELL ALLEGATIONS: Zelensky spent $200 MILLION to buy himself a 5 star casino resort on the beaches of Cyprus through his company "Film Heritage Inc" https://x.com/aussiecossack/status/1797716902237868178	Twitter @aussiecossack	3/6/2024	EN
	Zelensky became the owner of one of the largest casinos in Europe https://news-pravda.com/world/2024/06/03/551540.html	*Pravda*	3/6/2024	EN
	Τουρκικά ΜΜΕ: Ο Ζελένσκι απέκτησε καζίνο στην κατεχόμενη Κερύνεια https://www.sigmalive.com/news/local/1227197/tourkika-mme-o-zelenski-apektise-kazino-stin-katexomeni-keryneia	Sigmalive	4/6/2024	GR
	Φωνάζει για την ρωσική κατοχή αλλά αγόρασε ξενοδοχείο-καζίνο στην κατεχόμενη Κερύνεια ο Ζελένσκι https://reporter.com.cy/article/2024/6/4/778979/phonazei-gia-ten-rosike-katokhe-alla-agorase-xenodokheio-kazino-sten-katekhomene-keruneia-o-zelenski/	Reporter CY	4/6/2024	GR

(continued)

Table 4.7 (continued)

	Title	Channel	Published	Language
	Παραπληροφόρηση για την αγορά πολυτελούς ξενοδοχείου-καζίνο στην Κερύνεια από τον Βολοντιμίρ Ζελένσκι https://www.factchecker.gr/2024/06/04/no-proof-zelensky-bought-a-casino-hotel-in-kerynia/	Factchecker.gr	4/6/2024	GR
	Παραπληροφόρηση για την αγορά πολυτελούς ξενοδοχείου στα Κατεχόμενα από τον Βολοντιμίρ Ζελένσκι https://factcheckcyprus.org/fact-checks/disinfo-about-zelensky-having-bougth-hotel-in-kyrenia/	Factcheckcyprus.org	4/6/2024	GR
Turning Varosha into "Las Vegas of the Med"	Αγγλικό δημοσίευμα για σχέδιο να γίνει το Βαρώσι «Βέγκας στη Μεσόγειο»—Αναφορά σε ξενοδοχείο του Βασιλιά Καρόλου https://dialogos.com.cy/aggliko-dimosieyma-schedio-na-ginei-to-varosi-vegkas-sti-mesogeio/	Dialogos CY	12/2/2024	GR
	Plans to turn seaside ghost town into 'Vegas of the Med' could drag King Charles into row https://x.com/ExpressPolitics/status/1756942280110313956	*Daily Express*	12/2/2024	EN

(continued)

Table 4.7 (continued)

	Title	Channel	Published	Language
	VEGAS ON THE MED https://x.com/Young_Turk_Cyp/status/1757125955401797773	Twitter @Young_Turk_Cyp	12/2/2024	TR/EN
	North Cyprus and the rest of the island will benefit enormously from this development. It will show the world that North Cyprus is open for business https://x.com/FFNCyprus/status/1757084002731565475	Twitter @FFNCyprus	12/2/2024	TR/EN
	Plans to turn seaside ghost town into 'Vegas of the Med' could drag King Charles into row https://x.com/qwerty14117587/status/1757036848960954759	Twitter @qwerty14117587	12/2/2024	EN
	British Press Discusses Plan to Turn Varosha into Las Vegas https://www.kibrispostasi.com/c140-DAILY_NEWS/n507332-british-press-discusses-plan-to-turn-varosha-into-las-vegas	Kibris Postasi	13/2/2024	TR/EN
	A consortium of billionaire businessmen from around the world, successful hoteliers, has prepared "a billion-pound project" for Maras https://www.alliance-cyprusproperty.com/news/marash-is-a-billion-pound-project	Real Estate alliance-cyprusproperty.com	13/2/2024	EN

(continued)

Table 4.7 (continued)

	Title	Channel	Published	Language
	Movement in Varosha with the properties: Ankara's order to examine applications concerning Famagusta first https://in-cyprus.philenews.com/local/movement-in-varosha-with-the-properties-ankaras-order-to-examine-applications-concerning-famagusta-first/	*Philenews*	18/2/2024	EN
	New image emerges of plan for ghost town Cyprus resort fuelling diplomatic crisis https://www.express.co.uk/news/politics/1866762/king-charles-hotel-cyprus-diplomatic-row	*Daily Express* http://express.co.uk/	14/2/2024	EN
King Charles "owning" 7-star hotel in North Cyprus	King Charles denies owning hotel as Cyprus President orders investigation into resort https://www.express.co.uk/news/politics/1866365/king-charles-hotel-cyprus-varosha-maras-vegas-mediterranean	*Daily Express*	13/2/2024	EN

(continued)

Table 4.7 (continued)

	Title	Channel	Published	Language
	Απαράδεκτο, φιλοτουρκικό δημοσίευμα στη Daily Express: Ονειρεύονται -και το ομολογούν- «Las Vegas» στα Βαρώσια, εμπλέκουν και τον Κάρολο σε θέματα ιδιοκτησίας https://hellasjournal.com/2024/02/aparadekto-filotourkiko-dimosievma-sti-daily-express-onirevonte-ke-to-omologoun-las-vegas-sta-varosia-emplekoun-ke-ton-karolo-se-themata-idioktisias/	*Hellas Journal*	13/2/2024	GR
	ROYAL MESS Inside ghost town with 7-star hotel 'owned by King Charles' left to rot in once idyllic resort turned no-man's-land https://www.thesun.co.uk/news/25893892/abandoned-ghost-town-hotel-king-charles-cyprus-resort/	*The Sun UK*	13/2/2024	EN
	King Charles: What we know about claims he owns 'seven star hotel' in controversial area of Cyprus https://www.ohmymag.co.uk/entertainment/royal-family/king-charles-what-we-know-about-claims-he-owns-seven-star-hotel-in-controversial-area-of-cyprus_art21126.html	*OhMyMag* UK	14/2/2024	EN

(continued)

Table 4.7 (continued)

	Title	Channel	Published	Language
	King Charles denies owning hotel as Cyprus President orders investigation into resort https://www.parikiaki.com/2024/02/king-charles-denies-owning-hotel-as-cyprus-president-orders-investigation-into-resort/	Parikiaki	14/2/2024	TR/EN
	King Charles Denies Owning Hotel in Cyprus' Abandoned Varosha Resort https://www.thenationalherald.com/king-charles-denies-owning-hotel-in-cyprus-abandoned-varosha-resort/	*National Herald*	14/2/2024	EN
	Can you spot the insult to King Charles in an image that caused a huge diplomatic row? https://www.express.co.uk/news/politics/1867181/king-charles-cyprus-trnc-image-diplomatic-row-analysis	*Daily Express*	15/2/2024	EN
	King Charles denies owning hotel as Cyprus President orders investigation into resort https://www.express.co.uk/news/politics/1866365/king-charles-hotel-cyprus-varosha-maras-vegas-mediterranean	*Daily Express*	13/2/2024	EN

(continued)

Table 4.7 (continued)

	Title	Channel	Published	Language
British MPs supporting TRNC	British MPs push 'Free Occupied Cyprus' campaign https://knews.kathimerini.com.cy/en/news/british-mps-push-free-occupied-cyprus-campaign	KNews CY	15/2/2024	GR
	Britain urged to use Brexit freedoms to recognise North Cyprus as a sovereign country https://www.express.co.uk/news/politics/1427534/North-cyprus-officially-recognised-brexit-britain	*Daily Express*	24/4/2021	EN
	Political opponents unite to demand end of Turkish Cypriot isolation https://www.independent.co.uk/news/uk/politics/cyprus-parliamentarians-direct-flights-jack-straw-b2553442.h	*Independent*	29/5/2024	EN
	Political Parties in the UK call for lifting flight ban to TRNC https://brtk.net/political-parties-in-the-uk-call-for-lifting-flight-ban-to-trnc/?lang=en	BRTK	30/2/2024	TR/EN
	54 British Parliamentarians have signed a joint letter addressed to UK Foreign Minister calling on direct flights to the Turkish Republic of Northern Cyprus https://x.com/Young_Turk_Cyp/status/1796135734664908821	Twitter @Young_Turk_Cyp	30/5/2024	TR/EN

(continued)

Table 4.7 (continued)

	Title	Channel	Published	Language
	54 British parliamentarians have signed a letter addressed to Foreign Secretary @David_Cameron calling for direct flights from the UK to the Turkish Republic of Northern Cyprus https://x.com/FFNCyprus/status/1796100924416348454	Twitter @FFNCyprus	30/5/2024	TR/EN
	Agenda in the UK: 50 politicians send a letter to David Cameron for direct flights to TRNC https://www.kibrispostasi.com/c140-DAILY_NEWS/n520375-agenda-in-the-uk-50-politicians-send-a-letter-to-david-cameron-for-direct-flights-to-trnc	Kibris Postasi	30/5/2024	TR/EN
	50 political opponents ask "why not to northern Cyprus?" https://londragazete.com/english/278422/50-political-opponents-ask-why-not-to-northern-cyprus/	*Londra Gazete*	31/5/2024	TR/EN
	Britain's Political Rivals Want Flights Allowed to Occupied Cyprus Side https://www.thenationalherald.com/britains-political-rivals-want-flights-allowed-to-occupied-cyprus-side/	*National Herald*	31/5/2024	EN

of the Mediterranean" in Famagusta[777] were crafted to entice foreign investors and boost the local economy under the TRNC.

- Economic profit: The TRNC and its allies aimed to achieve significant economic profit by drawing in international investors by promoting misleading narratives that suggested stability and imminent international recognition. High-profile projects were strategically highlighted to entice foreign investment. Additionally, by presenting the TRNC as a haven for Russian expatriates seeking to evade EU sanctions, the campaign positioned the region as an ideal sanctuary for safeguarding and growing assets. The promotion of potential direct flights from countries like the UK and Russia further enhanced connectivity and investment appeal. This strategy leveraged geopolitical manoeuvring, disinformation and high-profile endorsements to attract substantial foreign investments, providing critical financial resources and contributing to the TRNC's economic stability and growth.
- Influence public perception through high-profile association: By associating well-known international figures and entities with the TRNC, such as King Charles, Vlodomyr Zelenskyy and high-profile investments from UK-based billionaires, the campaign aimed to create a perception of legitimacy and attract media attention. This strategy was designed to sway public opinion both locally and internationally by suggesting that significant and influential actors were involved in and support the TRNC.

4.26.6 Tactics, Techniques and Procedures

TA01: Plan strategy

- T0074.001: Geopolitical advantage—The TRNC leveraged various geopolitical events and narratives to gain a strategic advantage. By promoting misleading narratives, such as Russian recognition via consular activities, Zelenskyy owning a casino and King Charles owning a 7-star hotel, TRNC aimed to exploit geopolitical tensions to gain regional and global political favour.

TA02: Plan objectives

- T0136.005: Cultivate support for initiative, T0136.003: Energise supporters, T0136.008: Increase prestige—The TRNC aimed to cultivate support for its initiative of gaining international recognition by amplifying public and international backing for perceived diplomatic breakthroughs. This included the false narratives of multiple stories that aimed to energise supporters and enhance

[777] *Cyprus Mirror*, "British Press Discusses Plan to Turn Varosha into Las Vegas", 13 Feb 2024. https://www.kibrispostasi.com/c140-DAILY_NEWS/n507332-british-press-discusses-plan-to-turn-varosha-into-las-vegas.

the TRNC's prestige by associating with prominent international figures and powers.

- T0076: Distort, T0077: Distract, T0079: Divide—The TRNC media coverage distorted narratives around various incidents:
  - Zelenskyy casino purchase: Spread rumours about Zelenskyy's buying a luxury casino in Kyrenia.
  - King Charles hotel ownership: Propagated the idea of King Charles owning a 7-star hotel in Varosha.
  - Varosha as "Las Vegas of the Med": Promoted plans to transform Varosha into a major tourist hub. This manipulation of public perception aligned the narrative more favourably towards the TRNC's political agenda, distracted from unresolved international status issues and deepened divisions between Greek and Turkish Cypriots.
- T0137: Make money—TRNC-based real estate agencies capitalised on distorted narratives to attract property investments:
  - Russian recognition: Suggested increased stability and international legitimacy.
  - E-visa program and direct flights: Promoted accessibility and international endorsement.
  - Varosha development: Highlighted investment opportunities in transforming Varosha into "Las Vegas of the Med", enticing investors with the potential for high returns.

TA13: Target audience analysis

- T0081.003: Identify existing prejudices, T0072.002: Demographic segmentation, T0072.001: Geographic segmentation—The campaign exploited historical ethnic and national tensions between Greek and Turkish Cypriots to deepen polarisation and solidify its base. It targeted specific groups, such as younger Turkish Cypriots and Turkish nationals, who are more likely to respond positively to narratives promoting the TRNC's legitimacy and independence. The efforts focused on the Turkish-controlled northern part of Cyprus, creating localised content that resonated deeply with the community's aspirations and perceived grievances.

TA14: Develop narratives

- T0083: Integrate target audience vulnerabilities into narrative, T0003: Leverage existing narratives, T0068: Respond to breaking news event or active crisis—The campaign leveraged existing narratives about national identity and sovereignty, ensuring new information conformed to these deeply ingrained viewpoints. During periods of breaking news or crises, such as the rumours about Zelenskyy and King Charles, the TRNC capitalised on heightened media attention and uncertainty to insert strategically crafted narratives to manipulate public perception and garner support for their geopolitical aims.

TA06: Develop content

- T0085.003: Develop inauthentic news articles, T0086: Develop image-based content: The TRNC developed altered news articles and image-based content to promote its legitimacy and recognition:
  - Russian consulate: Articles and images suggesting formal recognition.
  - Zelenskyy casino: Content falsely indicating his investment.
  - King Charles hotel: Visuals and articles claiming ownership of a hotel.
  - Varosha development: Promotional content on transforming Varosha into a major tourist hub. This included altering existing images to generate impactful visuals that reinforced their political messages or discredited opposing viewpoints, effectively using both textual misinformation and visual content to support their narratives.

4.26.7 Channels

An analysis of the frequency and nature of these channels reveals a multi-faceted approach to narrative distribution.

Social Media Platforms

- Reddit: This platform has been instrumental in initiating and sustaining discussions, as evidenced by multiple threads on subreddits such as *r/cyprus*,[778,779] (43,000 members) and *r/europe*[780] (7,200,000 members). The interactive nature of Reddit has allowed for a mix of opinions and interpretations, engaging both English and Greek-speaking audiences.
- Twitter: Accounts such as @TurkishFacts4U[781] (8,951 Followers), @Young_Turk_Cyp[782] (7,802 Followers with around 65,000 views) and @aussiecossack[783] (with 70,000 followers and 3,100,000 views) have tweeted about various developments, reaching a broad audience through retweets and likes. The platform's immediacy has made it crucial for rapid dissemination.

[778] r/Cyprus, "Russia opens a consulate in the illegally occupied northern part of Cyprus", Reddit, Feb. 2021. https://www.reddit.com/r/cyprus/comments/u5spug/russia_opens_a_consulate_in_the_illegally/.

[779] r/Cyprus, "Tatar: Russia set to 'partially recognise' north", Reddit, 2023. https://www.reddit.com/r/cyprus/comments/15w029e/tatar_russia_set_to_partially_recognise_north/.

[780] r/Europe, "Russia opens a consulate in occupied Cyprus", Reddit. https://www.reddit.com/r/europe/comments/u5ra6h/russia_opens_consulate_in_occupied_cyprus/.

[781] TurkishFacts4u, "Russian media citing senior officials have now confirmed the following: (1) A private Russian Airlines will fly direct to the TRNC; (1) Russia will open consulate in 'Northern Nicossia'", Twitter, Oct 2022. https://twitter.com/TurkishFacts4U/status/1579841748649807873.

[782] https://twitter.com/Young_Turk_Cyp/status/1698746014885183961.

[783] https://x.com/aussiecossack/status/1797716902237868178.

- Facebook: The British Turkish Cypriot Association (BTCA)[784] (5,500 members) and Young Turkish Cypriots[785] (2,700 members) have used Facebook to share updates and opinions, highlighting the role of community and diaspora groups in promoting specific viewpoints.

News Websites and Online Publications

- *Kathimerini,*[786] *Euronews, Yeni Şafak,*[787] *APA Media,*[788] TASS and *Express*[789]: These outlets provided coverage with varying degrees of detail and perspective, serving both to inform and to frame the discourse around the consulate's opening and its political implications. The presence of both local (e.g., *Kathimerini*) and international (e.g., *Euronews*, TASS) media highlights the broader geopolitical interest in the narrative.
- Real-estate websites[790] joined this narrative, aiming to shape perceptions of stability and investment potential in the TRNC. Their involvement underscores the intersection of political narratives with economic interests.

4.26.8 Languages

- Predominantly English, to maximise international reach.
- Turkish, to target domestic and diaspora audiences and lend credibility to the narrative within the region.
- The majority of websites also supported the Russian language, specifically the choices between English, Turkish and Russian.

4.26.9 Effectiveness

The disinformation campaigns orchestrated by the TRNC achieved limited success in meeting their objectives. While the narratives gained traction on social media

[784] https://www.facebook.com/groups/323330971061974/.

[785] https://www.facebook.com/young.turkish.cypriots

[786] Ioannou, Yiannis, "Tatar's plea to Russia to reshape diplomatic landscape", *Kathimerini,* 18 Dec 2023. https://knews.kathimerini.com.cy/en/news/tatar-s-plea-to-russia-to-reshape-diplomatic-landscape.

[787] https://www.yenisafak.com/dunya/rusya-kktcde-konsolosluk-aciyor-4551702.

[788] https://apa.az/en/europe/russia-to-open-consulate-in-turkish-republic-of-northern-cyprus-409300.

[789] Maddox, David, *Daily Express*. https://www.express.co.uk/news/politics/1866365/king-charles-hotel-cyprus-varosha-maras-vegas-mediterranean.

[790] Alliance for North Cyprus, "Opening of the Consulate of Russia in the Turkish Republic of Northern Cyprus", 10 Aug 2023. https://www.alliance-cyprusproperty.com/news/opening-of-the-consulate-of-russia-in-the-turkish-republic-of-northern-cyprus. See also Timondro: https://timondro.com/about-turkey/russia-s-game-changing-move-in-trnc-new-consulate-coming-soon.

and certain Turkish Cypriot and international platforms, they were swiftly countered by fact-checking organisations and authoritative statements. For instance, the rumours of King Charles III's owning a luxury hotel in Varosha and President Zelenskyy purchasing a casino in Kyrenia were debunked by both official clarifications and independent media outlets, curtailing the spread of misinformation.

Moreover, the Republic of Cyprus, supported by international bodies and the EU, actively condemned these efforts to profit from the illegal seizure of Greek Cypriot property, reinforcing the legal and ethical issues surrounding the occupation and illegal property monetisation. The robust response from international institutions and governments significantly mitigated the potential impact, underscoring the importance of coordinated efforts in countering disinformation.

4.26.10 Countermeasures

- Debunking: Independent organisations and Cypriot officials debunked the Russian consulate opening claims. Fact-checking organisations debunked the rumours of Zelenskyy's owning a casino in the TRNC.
- Statement of rebuttal: Statements from the Russian ambassador[791] and TASS clarifying the nature of the consular services.[792] King Charles and the Royal Family released a press statement denying ownership of a 7-star hotel in Varosha.
- Content confined: Limited efforts to reduce the reach of misleading articles and posts.

4.26.11 Conclusions and Recommendations

The disinformation campaign involving the TRNC strategically used false narratives to legitimise itself and attract foreign investment. TRNC-based real estate agencies capitalised on these narratives to profit from illegally occupied properties of displaced Greek Cypriots. This exploitation deepened ethnic tensions between Greek and Turkish Cypriots and undermined international law. Given the case described above, we make the following recommendations:

- Continuous monitoring and debunking: Establish a dedicated task force to monitor platforms for misinformation related to Cyprus and the TRNC. Implement real-time reporting mechanisms and collaborate with social media companies to quickly flag and remove misleading content.
- Diplomatic engagement and legal actions: Strengthen diplomatic efforts with international partners to issue joint statements against false narratives. Pursue

[791] https://www.barrons.com/news/northern-cyprus-says-russia-to-open-consulate-ed3aff9b.

[792] https://tass.com/world/1658553.

regulatory measures and legal actions against entities that deliberately spread misinformation to manipulate public perception and violate property rights.

- Investor education initiatives: Launch awareness campaigns to inform potential investors about the legal risks and ethical issues associated with purchasing property in the occupied territories, emphasising the importance of compliance with international law.
- Community outreach programs: Develop initiatives to engage directly with both Greek and Turkish Cypriot communities, fostering dialogue, understanding and reconciliation to counteract divisive narratives.
- Partnerships with credible media: Collaborate with reputable media organisations to amplify accurate information and provide journalists with training to identify and effectively report on misinformation.

4.27 North Korea's Disinformation Campaigns

4.27.1 Introduction

North Korea has a problem with its people. Even though it's a crime to consume foreign media, a big proportion of North Koreans appear to do so anyway. One survey found that 91.6% of North Korean respondents consume foreign media at least once a month.[793]

While South Korea and the US make efforts to facilitate access by North Koreans to "outside" information, North Korea has been engaged not only in disseminating propaganda to its own people but also to South Korea.

In one recent incident, North Korean "cyber trolls" allegedly hijacked South Korean users' online accounts and posted an estimated 68,000 propaganda items in web forums and various comment sections to amplify the regime's message in South Korea.[794]

This case study focuses on the United Front Department (UFD), the North Korean organisation that disseminates pro-regime propaganda, especially targeting South Korea.[795]

[793] DuMond, Marie, "Information and Its Consequences in North Korea", Beyond Parallel, 12 Jan 2017. https://beyondparallel.csis.org/information-and-its-consequences-in-north-korea/.

[794] Barnhart, Michael, Michelle Cantos, et al., "Not So Lazarus: Mapping DPRK Cyber Threat Groups to Government Organizations", Mandiant, 2 Apr 2024. https://www.mandiant.com/resources/blog/mapping-dprk-groups-to-government.

[795] A caveat from Michael Raska is pertinent to this case study, which is based on a literature search in mid-2024: Open-source data are limited mainly to threat intelligence reports and investigations by global cybersecurity firms; selected statements and publications by the US and ROK governments; select North Korean defectors with partial knowledge of North Korea's cyber activities; secondary literature such as think tank reports and academic articles; and, ultimately, references in North Korean newspapers and other media outlets. Each source carries internal and external validity risks, including government bias and political agendas, outdated data, and intelligence blind

4.27.2 Threat Actors

The UFD comes under the Central Committee of the Workers' Party of Korea. It comprises operating groups that disseminate pro-regime propaganda targeting South Korea. UFD oversees espionage, diplomacy and policymaking concerning South Korea. It is the primary organisation of all state and party organisations tasked with relations with South Korea. The Ministry of Foreign Affairs, for instance, does not address relations with the South. The UFD also controls North Korea's religious organisations, including the Korean Christian Federation and Korean Buddhist Federation.[796]

The UFD receives orders directly from and reports directly to Kim Jong Un. Kim has a keen interest in underground organisations and propaganda activities in South Korea.[797] A 2016 European Parliamentary Research Service (EPRS) briefing said that Kim Jong Un's sister, Kim Yo Jong, oversees Pyongyang's Propaganda and Agitation Department.[798]

The UFD maintains ties with front organisations in both North and South Korea and with overseas Koreans. The UFD has a Cultural Exchange Bureau for the purpose. The UFD is estimated to have at least 3,000 employees. *NK News* says that North Korea has "thousands" of propaganda workers.[799] UFD's Cultural Exchange Bureau gives orders to a network of underground organisations spying on South Korea, which has been described as "an enormous spy network, perhaps the biggest in two decades".[800]

The UFD controls or has had controls over various front organisations, including the Chongryon representing pro-Pyongyang Zainichi Koreans in Japan; the Korean Association of Social Scientists, Korea Asia–Pacific Peace Committee, National Reconciliation Council and the Committee for the Peaceful Reunification of the Fatherland. North Korea typically deals with front organisations instead of the South Korean government which lacks legitimacy in its eyes. The UFD also sends spies to Japan. Hence, it is sometimes described as an intelligence agency.[801]

---

spots. Raska, Michael, "North Korea's Evolving Cyber Strategies: Continuity and Change", SIRIUS—Zeitschrift Für Strategische Analysen, Vol. 4, No. 2, 2020, pp. 1–13. https://doi.org/10.1515/sirius-2020-3030.

[796] https://en.wikipedia.org/wiki/United_Front_Department_of_the_Workers%27_Party_of_Korea.

[797] Ibid.

[798] The Propaganda and Agitation Department is a department of the Central Committee of the Workers' Party of Korea (WPK) tasked with coordinating the creation and dissemination of propaganda in North Korea. Wikipedia describes it as "the highest propaganda organization in the country". https://en.wikipedia.org/wiki/Propaganda_and_Agitation_Department.

[799] Zwirko, Colin, "Thousands of North Korean Propaganda Workers Gather to Boost Kim Jong Un Worship", *NK News—North Korea News*, 24 Apr 2024. https://www.nknews.org/2024/04/thousands-of-north-korean-propaganda-workers-gather-to-boost-kim-jong-un-worship/.

[800] Ibid.

[801] https://en.wikipedia.org/wiki/United_Front_Department_of_the_Workers%27_Party_of_Korea.

The Cultural Exchange Bureau ordered its underground organisations to recruit and indoctrinate young people for infiltrating mass organisations, such as the Korean Confederation of Trade Unions (KCTU) and the Korean Federation of Peasants. North Korea's spies have infiltrated labour unions, civic and religious organisations.[802]

Although the focus of this case study is on the UFD, there is another North Korean department engaged in disinformation. The 2016 EPRS report said the Enemy Collapse Sabotage Bureau's Unit 204 was using the Internet to spread anti-South Korea propaganda. It reportedly consisted of three brigades with a total of 2,000 personnel. The Enemy Collapse Sabotage Bureau comes under the military and the General Bureau of Reconnaissance (GBR). The former collects internal information to control local residents, while the latter is in charge of hacking campaigns, in which it breaks into security systems to steal sensitive information.

4.27.3 Presumed Objectives

The Kim regime has had a long-stated goal of taking control of the entire Korean peninsula under its rule[803] (T0074: Determine strategic ends). FIMI is just one of the tools at its disposal.

The DISARM Navigator now has 13 possible attacker objectives, of which several are pertinent to North Korea's FIMI efforts, both external and domestic, as follows:

- T0140: Cause harm—DPRK's disinformation campaigns support its surveillance and espionage programmes.
- T0136: Cultivate support—DPRK seeks support beyond its borders for its policies. It seeks to recruit agents. It seeks to convince defectors to return. The UFD's goal is the establishment of pro-North Korean groups within South Korea.[804] North Korea's disinformation campaigns are aimed at, among other things, recruiting South Korean collaborators.[805] The regime is building a nationalistic narrative that increasingly targets young people and elites while

[802] O, Tara, "People's Vanguard, HGH, North Korea's Extensive Spy Network Discovered All Over South Korea", Korea Institute of Liberal Democracy (KILD), 4 Feb, 2023. https://kild.or.kr:443/bbs/board.php?bo_table=activity_04&wr_id=41.
[803] Ibid.
[804] Barnhart, et al., op. cit.
[805] Bartlett, Jason, "From Ethnic Nationalism to Social Media: How North Korea Leverages Its Soft Power Abroad", *The Diplomat*, 17 Aug 2021. https://thediplomat.com/2021/08/from-ethnic-nationalism-to-social-media-how-north-korea-leverages-its-soft-power-abroad/.

keeping information under strict control, in a country whose population is today less inclined to believe in propaganda than in the past.[806]

- T0078: Dismay—With its draconian Reactionary Ideology and Culture Rejection Act (see below), DPRK seeks to dismay its own public from consuming outside information.
- T0076: Distort—DPRK distorts how good things are for consumers outside its borders.
- T0002: Facilitate state propaganda—DPRK has begun opening the country to tourism,[807] so some of DPRK's FIMI facilitates state propaganda about DPRK as an interesting country for tourists.
- T0135: Undermine—North Korea's FIMI activities have included demanding the withdrawal of the US forces from Korea, abolishing the National Security Law, and criticising the Yun Suk Yeol government.

4.27.4 Incidents and Observables

The UFD typically leverages online information operations, including an "army of cyber trolls", to promote pro-DPRK political narratives on web forums as well as conventional propaganda efforts, such as leaflets and radio broadcasts targeting their southern neighbour.[808]

Because South Korean social media often requires verified personal information, North Korean agents use illegally acquired personal information from South Korean citizens. These accounts work to portray North Korea in a favourable light and generate polarisation in South Korea.[809]

North Korea has conducted limited influence operations on video-sharing social media platforms such as YouTube and TikTok over the past year. North Korean influencers on YouTube are mostly girls and women, who post vlogs about their daily lives and promote positive narratives about the regime. Some of the influencers speak English in their videos, intending to reach a wider global audience. North Korea's influencers are much less effective than the Chinese state media-backed influencer initiative.[810]

Before the North Korean government used balloons to drop trash and faeces on South Korea in May 2024, it dropped propaganda leaflets targeting South Korean

[806] D'Ambrogio, Enrico, "North Korea's Propaganda Strategy", European Parliament Research Service, October 2016. https://www.europarl.europa.eu/RegData/etudes/BRIE/2016/589817/EPRS_BRI(2016)589817_EN.pdf.

[807] Bremer, Ifang, and Lina Park, "North Korea Likely to Reopen to Western Tourists in Second Half: Tour Company", *NK News—North Korea News*, 24 Apr 2024. https://www.nknews.org/2024/04/north-korea-likely-to-reopen-to-western-tourists-in-second-half-tour-company/.

[808] Barnhart, et al., op. cit.

[809] Bartlett, op. cit.

[810] Microsoft, "Digital Threats from East Asia Increase in Breadth and Effectiveness", Sept 2023, p. 16. https://query.prod.cms.rt.microsoft.com/cms/api/am/binary/RW1aFyW

soldiers, just across the Demilitarised Zone. The leaflets typically criticised the South Korean government and praised North Korea.[811]

North Korea uses false identities online in order to obtain freelance income online which is a way to avoid the sanctions placed on North Korea.[812] Reuters found further evidence in leaked dark web data that revealed some of the tools and techniques used by North Korean workers to convince firms to employ them in jobs as far afield as Chile, New Zealand, the United States, Uzbekistan and the United Arab Emirates.[813]

North Korea created fake social media profiles on Twitter and LinkedIn, where they set up fake blogs where they got guests to write posts about software bugs. They contacted actual researchers and asked to work with them; they would then share collaboration tools that contained malware.[814] The UFD often releases statements that many consider to be authoritative comments of the regime. It also fabricates praise of the Kim family that it attributes to foreigners and then disseminates in North Korean media.

4.27.5 Targets

A key part of the DISARM Navigator is T0073: Determine target audiences.

North Korea's disinformation activities have several targets, among which are the following:

Individuals—DPRK tries to recruit agents in South Korea. It seeks to portray DPRK in a positive light. Studies done with North Korean escapees indicate that North Koreans have a sense of when they are being fed propaganda and when to seek alternative sources of knowledge.[815] The EPRS reported that, by 2016, around 30,000 North Koreans had fled to the South since the end of the Korean War, generally for political and economic reasons.[816] North Korea has a regime that prefers to be enigmatic and closely guards against information leaking to the outside world. From that perspective, high-level defections pose a substantial risk. A growing number of citizens travelling or staying abroad increases the risk of exposing North Koreans to external information and subsequent defections, to potential attempts by hostile intelligence services to recruit them as sources, or to other forms of intelligence leaks.[817]

---

811 Propaganda in North Korea. https://en.wikipedia.org/wiki/Propaganda_in_North_Korea.

812 "North Korea Disinformation—ADTAC Disinformation Inventory", 2020. https://inventory.adt.ac/wiki/North_Korea_Disinformation.

813 Pearson, op. cit.

814 ADTAC Disinformation Inventory, op. cit.

815 DuMond, op. cit.

816 D'Ambrogio, op. cit.

817 Ruediger, Frank, "North Korea's De-Risking Strategy and Its Implications", *38 North*, 13 Dec 2023. https://www.38north.org/2023/12/north-koreas-de-risking-strategy-and-its-implications/.

Since 2012, the regime has started using redefectors—North Koreans having defected to the South and then returned home—for propaganda purposes. The usual scenario involves interviewing such people at press conferences broadcast on state television, where they deplore their life in South Korea as having been tainted by trickery, discrimination and poverty. Such people also assure their audience that Kim Jon Un forgives returning defectors in the awareness that they have been victims of subterfuge. As of early 2016, the South's Ministry of Unification had acknowledged 14 such cases.[818]

Trade unions and associations—The Cultural Exchange Bureau has told underground organisations to infiltrate mass organisations.[819] It has instructed spy suspects to form underground organisations, wage an anti-government struggle and propagandise the greatness of North Korea's "State Affairs Chairman Kim Jong Un".[820]

After their establishment, these underground organisations were operating under orders to "struggle against the US", "infiltrate and seize power in the Korean Confederation of Trade Unions (KCTU) and expand their power" and "denounce Yoon Suk-yeol", among others. The Cultural Exchange Bureau ordered "a series of mass struggles, such as protest rallies, protest visits and signature drives with slogans such as the suspension of joint military exercises, the dissolution of the ROK-US-Japan military alliance, and opposition to the introduction of high-tech weapons from the United States."[821]

North Korea public—In December 2021, the Kim Jung Un regime passed a new "anti-reactionary thought law". The "Reactionary Ideology and Culture Rejection Act of the Democratic People's Republic of Korea" was amended in August 2022. The law states that North Koreans who smuggle in, distribute or encourage group viewing of movies, dramas, TV shows, songs and books from enemy countries (e.g., South Korea) can face the death penalty.[822] Article 27 says infractions are punishable by an indefinite period of reform through labour or death.[823] The "Crime of Possessing or Bringing in Corrupt and Decadent Culture" can result in three to 15 years of detention in labour camps. North Korean escapee testimonies have documented cases where death sentences were carried out for individuals possessing especially sensitive content such as South Korean dramas or the Christian Bible.[824]

---

[818] D'Ambrogio, op. cit.

[819] O, Tara, op. cit.

[820] Ibid.

[821] Ibid.

[822] Jang, Seulkee, "Daily NK Acquires Full Text of the Anti-Reactionary Thought Law", *Daily NK English*, 21 Mar 2023. https://www.dailynk.com/english/daily-nk-acquires-full-text-of-the-anti-reactionary-thought-law/.

[823] Williams, Martyn, "North Korea Intensifies War Against Foreign Influence", *38 North*, 10 Nov 2021. https://www.38north.org/2021/11/north-korea-intensifies-war-against-foreign-influence/.

[824] DuMond, Marie, op. cit.

As smuggling activities continued to expand into the 2000s, the North Korean regime attempted to crack down on its people through surveillance, raids and propaganda efforts. Attempts to enforce bans on outside media, however, were insufficient as the organisations tasked with enforcement often took bribes to look the other way.[825]

South Korea, China, the US, Japan, Russia—DPRK has had a difficult relationship with China. Even though the latter has been its lifeline to the outside world, Kim Jong Un does not view DPRK as a strict disciple of China. DPRK has long maligned the US and Japan as barbarians who committed atrocities against the North during the Korean War. DPRK's long-term objective has been to take over South Korea. The so-called "Hermit kingdom" (for its self-imposed isolation with the reset of the world) has witnessed a rapprochement with Russia or, more particularly, a rapprochement between Kim Jong Un and Vladimir Putin. Kim made a rare visit to Russia in Sept 2023 and met with Putin.[826] Since then, there has been an increased flow of North Korean weapons to Russia in its war against Ukraine.

Social media—North Korea made its first entry into the social media market in 2010. The country launched its own website, Facebook page, YouTube channel, Twitter account and Flickr page, however, it appears only the website (see below) is still active.[827]

"Uriminzokkiri" is a website that provides Korean-language news and propaganda from North Korea's central news agency. The website offers translation in Korean, Russian, Chinese, Japanese and English. Uriminzokkiri means "on our own as our nation". The site includes articles entitled "South Korea's Pro-US/ Japan Corporate Media: Endless Demonization Campaigns Against DPRK", "The Project for New American Century: The New World Order & The US's Continued CRIMES" and "Kim Jong-un Sends Musical Instruments to Children's Palaces". The website also contains a page for tv.urminzokkiri, which contains videos showing news clips criticising imperialist movements and clips showing the bravery of Korean people and the power of its military.[828]

4.27.6 Tactics, Techniques and Procedures

North Korea has employed a range of TTPs against South Korea, among which are the following.

---

825 Lee, Sang Yong, "North Korea's War Against Outside Information and Culture", *38 North*, 25 May 2023. https://www.38north.org/2023/05/north-koreas-war-against-outside-information-and-culture/.

826 Sonne, Paul, and Valeriya Safronova, "Kim Jong-Un Has Something Putin Needs, and That's a New Wrinkle", *The New York Times*, 11 Sept 2023. https://www.nytimes.com/2023/09/11/world/asia/putin-kim-russia-north-korea.html.

827 https://en.wikipedia.org/wiki/Propaganda_in_North_Korea.

828 Ibid.

Tactics

T0091: Recruit malign actors—North Korea has recruited agents to subvert South Korea and other countries.

T0092: Build network—The UFD's Cultural Exchange Bureau instigated a network of agents in South Korean labour organisations. (North Korea has also dispatched thousands of IT workers overseas, an effort that has accelerated in the last four years, to bring in millions to finance Pyongyang's nuclear missile programme, according to the United States, South Korea and the United Nations.[829])

T0094: Infiltrate existing networks—The Cultural Exchange Bureau has infiltrated other networks, in addition to building its own.

T0095: Develop owned media assets—North Korea has developed its own media assets to create and broadcast audio and video assets. It hasn't been very successful in building significant audiences outside the NPRK.

T0129: Conceal operational activity—Secrecy has long been a characteristic of North Korea's government. Details of the UFD's Cultural Exchange Bureau are sparse, at least in the public domain.

T0044: Seed distortions—The Cultural Exchange Bureau has promoted North Korea as a worker's paradise and, in doing so, distorts the reality of how hard life is in the North.

Techniques

Among other techniques, North Korea engaged in these:

T0072.005: Political segmentation—North Korea targets social groups (e.g., labour unions or cultural associations), based on their political affiliations, especially when aiming to manipulate voting or change policy.

T0081: Identify social and technical vulnerabilities—North Korea targets social groups vulnerabilities, both social and technical, in order to infiltrate, influence and subvert them, to turn them into allies of North Korea and opponents of South Korea.

T0081.001: Find echo chambers—The UFD's Cultural Exchange Bureau hunts for media outlets that will amplify its FIMI.

T0081.008: Identify media system vulnerabilities—The Cultural Exchange Bureau has been able to erect websites with minimal oversight from regulatory authorities in other countries.

[829] Pearson, James, "North Koreans Use Fake Names, Scripts to Land Remote IT Work for Cash", Reuters, 21 Nov 2023. https://www.reuters.com/technology/north-koreans-use-fake-names-scripts-land-remote-it-work-cash-2023-11-21/.

Procedures

While North Korea's two stations aimed at South Korean listeners are off the air, the country's international radio service remains on air.[830] UFD controls broadcasts that target South Korea. Its methods include psychological warfare through radio and TV, loudspeakers, leaflets, visual displays and websites. According to reports, the United Front Department wages its cyber psychological warfare through some 140 sites with servers based in 19 countries. It also maintains a team of Internet trolls with the Reconnaissance General Bureau.

4.27.7 Channels

The channels used to purvey the DPRK FIMI include the following:

- T0103 Livestream—DISARM says a livestream refers to an online broadcast capability that allows for real-time communication to closed or open networks. The Cultural Exchange Bureau created TV and radio broadcasts focused on South Korea.
- T0105: Media sharing networks—North Korea has spread disinformation via popular social media platforms such as Twitter, Weibo and YouTube.[831] North Korean propaganda has been known for being relatively unsophisticated towards international audiences. However, North Korea is making attempts to create sleeker more nuanced propaganda through social media personalities.[832]
- T0111: Traditional media—North Korea has an international broadcaster targeting South Korea. The radio station targeting South Korea, Voice of National Salvation, is directly controlled by the UFD instead of the Korean Central Broadcasting Committee that normally manages external broadcasting.

Official communication channels—The principal agency in charge of FIMI is the United Front Department (UFD). See above subsection 4.2 Threat actors.

State-controlled channels—As mentioned above, North Korea has an international broadcaster targeting South Korea.

State-linked channels—North Korea has made a practice of penetrating trade unions and associations for purpose of surveillance and using them as vehicles to subvert the South Korean government and public.

Social media—Pyongyang uses state-sponsored media agencies and multilingual members of the elite class to spread propaganda abroad in English, Chinese, Russian and Korean, through popular social media platforms such as Twitter, Weibo

---

[830] Williams, Martyn, "Farewell, Pyongyang Broadcasting?", 38 North, 18 Jan 2024. https://www.38north.org/2024/01/farewell-pyongyang-broadcasting/.
[831] Bartlett, op. cit.
[832] Ibid.

and YouTube.[833] Despite actions to stymie these efforts, the regime continues to create new social media accounts to entice foreigners to visit the country.[834]

In January 2024, *North Korea News* reported that several DPRK websites had been taken down. It speculated that the DPRK was going to take them down permanently. Many DPRK watchers have commented on how unsophisticated DPRK's social media efforts have been.[835]

In 2018, North Korea reportedly operated 160 propaganda websites.

North Korea targets South Korea through blog posts, video clips and online comments, in text, image, audio and video formats. Because South Korean social media often requires verified personal information, North Korean agents use illegally acquired personal information from South Korean citizens. These accounts work to portray North Korea in a favourable light and generate polarisation in South Korea.[836]

4.27.8 Languages

Pyongyang has used state-sponsored media agencies and multilingual members of the elite class to spread propaganda abroad in English, Chinese, Russian and Korean, through popular social media platforms such as Twitter, Weibo and YouTube.[837]

North Korea's Voice of Korea broadcasts multiple hours per day on shortwave in English, French, German, Spanish, Russian, Arabic, Japanese and Chinese. As North Korea has shuttered its South Korea-focused websites, the international sites have remained online, indicating this is not a pullback from international affairs but much more focused on South Korea.[838]

4.27.9 Effectiveness

Among the techniques for assessing effectiveness of the DPRK's FIMI campaign are those in the DISARM Red Framework, TA12: Assess Effectiveness is pertinent here.

T0133: Measure effectiveness.

T0133.003: Awareness.

T0133.001: Behaviour changes.

---

833 Ibid.

834 Ibid.

835 Reddy, Shreyas, "North Korean Propaganda Sites Offline for Second Day in Likely Sign of Removal," NK News—North Korea News, 12 Jan 2024. https://www.nknews.org/2024/01/north-korean-propaganda-sites-offline-for-second-day-in-likely-sign-of-removal/.

836 Bartlett, op. cit.

837 Ibid.

838 Williams, op cit.

The Korea Institute of Liberal Democracy (KILD), a South Korean think tank, reported that the South Korean government had uncovered in 2022 a "vast network of underground organisations that took orders from the Cultural Exchange Bureau under the United Front Department in the Korean Workers' Party based in Pyongyang".[839] KILD reported that, since 2016, the suspected spies in the underground organisation People's Vanguard for Independent Unification met with North Korean espionage agent Kim Myung-sung, an operative from the Cultural Exchange Bureau (Munhwa Goryuguk), in Southeast Asian countries, including in Angkor Wat in Cambodia, and received orders to set up an underground organisation. They then carried out North Korea's instructions, creating the underground organisation in the Changwon-Jinju area. The Changwon-Jinju area is where defence companies are concentrated.

The previous South Korean regime has been criticised for not taking more active measures against the presence of so many DPRK spies in so many trade unions and associations, some of whom were giving advice to the South Korean government.

4.27.10 Countermeasures

With so many DPRK spies operating in the South Korea, the latter finally recommended that the government arrest the spies (after not pursuing them during the tenure of the previous SK government.

North Korea instructed the People's Vanguard to contact the chairman of the National Plant Construction Union, which is under KCTU's Korean Federation of Construction Industry Trade Unions. The chairman of the National Plant Construction Union was arrested on suspicion of unlawful assembly, and another member of this union was charged with violating the National Security Law in November 2020.

The People's Vanguard for Independent Unification, based in the Changwon-Jinju area, seems to have extended its operations to Seoul. On 18 January 2023, the South Korean National Intelligence (NIS) service and the police simultaneously searched at least 10 locations, including the headquarters of the Korean Confederation of Trade Unions (KCTU), the office of the National Health Care Industry Workers' Union in Seoul, and the office of the Peace Shelter of the Sewol Ferry Jeju Memorial Hall on Jeju Island, to seize relevant materials.

On 28 January 2023, South Korea's National Intelligence Service (NIS) and the police arrested four people, suspected of violating the National Security Act.

---

[839] O, Tara, op cit.

4.27.11 Conclusions and Recommendations

As the North Korean regime continues to launch disinformation campaigns abroad via online platforms, national governments and media outlets that value information integrity must remain vigilant to protect their users by continuing to flag, remove and block the spread of false information and state-sponsored propaganda.[840]

European democracies need to strengthen their cyber readiness posture to effectively track and counter North Korea's evolving global cyber operations.[841]

The fact that its websites have been down for so long suggests Pyongyang is removing them in a push to adopt new methods to spread its messages worldwide, according to Fyodor Tertitskiy, a researcher at Seoul's Kookmin University. "It probably means that they finally realized that their propaganda is extraordinarily inefficient both in South Korea and in other countries."[842] North Korea appears to have recognised the unsophistication of its websites and is reportedly overhauling them to make them more interesting to its targets.[843]

After Russia, China and Iran, experts regard North Korea as next on the list of countries that pose a grave cyber threat. Industry watchers estimate that the level of North Korea's cyber capabilities is close to Russia's and China's. North Korea uses its cyber operations capabilities mainly to earn money. It mines, steals and produces cryptocurrencies such as Bitcoin, Litecoin and Monero. Global security industries warn countries to take extra precautions because North Korea uses more sophisticated and well-planned hacking techniques. But it's also used its formidable hacking capabilities for revenge (e.g., the Sony Pictures attack in 2014) and ransomware (e.g., the WannaCry attack).

The US has already sanctioned North Korean hackers. In response to the DPRK's cyber attack on Sony Pictures, the President signed Executive Order 13,687, in January 2015, granting the Treasury Department the authority to impose sanctions against agencies, instrumentalities, officials and entities controlled by the Government of North Korea and the Worker's Party of Korea. The US regards all hacking attempts as an attack on national security.

However, it is difficult to punish the hackers. International cooperation is necessary to come up with proactive countermeasures to block North Korea's cybercrime operations, which are "a serious threat to global cyberspace".[844]

---

[840] Bartlett, op. cit.

[841] Raska, op. cit.

[842] Reddy, op cit.

[843] Reddy, op. cit.

[844] GlobalSecurity.org, "Reconnaissance General Bureau—North Korean Intelligence Agencies, Office 91 Unit 110 + Bureau 121", n.d. https://www.globalsecurity.org/intell/world/dprk/rgb-cyber.htm.

4.28 Iranian Interference in the US Elections

4.28.1 Introduction

The Iranian authorities are known to spread manipulated information to its Iranian diaspora in several countries with an aim to disrupt foreign elections. As an example, a 2021 press release by the US Department of Justice reported two Iranian nationals charged for cyber-enabled disinformation and a threat campaign designed to influence the 2020 US presidential election.[845] The two Iranian nationals obtained confidential US voter information and sent voters intimidating messages and videos to influence the voters.

The Iranian FIMI campaign illustrates the "effects of international state-run trolls that magnify controversial false claims, push negative views, and attack any voices critical of their own regimes".[846]

The November 2020 US presidential elections was one of the most consequential, held during the global coronavirus (SARS-CoV-2) pandemic. The election was also preceded by strong hate speech and once the results were announced, the incumbent President, Donald Trump refused to accept Biden's victory with baseless insistence that the election had been stolen, which ultimately led to the storming of the US Capitol by Trump's supporters.[847]

The campaign started mostly through social media. The two Iranian hackers along with others started a coordinated, "Voter Intimidation and Influence Campaign"[848] via Facebook messages and e-mails.

The event concerning the Iranian hackers was instigated around August 2020. The two Iranian nationals indicted for the case, Seyyed Mohammad Hosein Musa Kazemi and Sajjad Kashian, sent threatening emails to voters from August to November 2020 to spread false claims about election security vulnerabilities to more than 100,000 stolen voters' private information.

The event subsided on 4 November 2020: the day after the 2020 US elections. The hackers tried to log into a media company's website using credentials they had stolen during the previous two months but because of an earlier FBI victim notification, the company had by that time mitigated the conspirators' unauthorised access and these log-in attempts failed.

---

[845] Office of Public Affairs, Department of Justice, *Press* Release, 18 Nov 2021. https://www.justice.gov/opa/pr/two-iranian-nationals-charged-cyber-enabled-disinformation-and-threat-campaign-designed.

[846] Dr. Al-Rawi in *The Peak, 9* Mar 2021. https://the-peak.ca/2021/03/russian-and-iranian-internet-trolls-caused-political-interference-in-canadas-2015-election/.

[847] Britannica, United States presidential election of 2020, United States government. https://www.britannica.com/event/United-States-presidential-election-of-2020.

[848] Office of Public Affairs, Department of Justice, Press release, 18 Nov 2021. https://www.justice.gov/opa/pr/two-iranian-nationals-charged-cyber-enabled-disinformation-and-threat-campaign-designed.

4.28.2 Threat Actors

As indicated in the November 2021 indictment, the FIMI campaign was instigated by two Iranian nationals, Seyyed Mohammad Hosein Musa Kazemi, aka Mohammad Hosein Musa Kazem, aka Hosein Zamani, 24, and Sajjad Kashian, aka Kiarash Nabavi. Kazemi and Kashian were employed by Emennet Pasargad at the time of the 2020 election interference campaign, but they may have previously worked with or had connections to an Iranian cybersecurity company, Eeleyanet Gostar, formerly known as Eeleyanet Gostar and Net Peygard Samavat Company.[849] The company appears to work for the government.[850] Both Kazemi and Kazem were working with four other co-conspirators whose names are not known.

The hackers masqueraded as members of the far-right extremist group the Proud Boys and allegedly used them to spread the event by sending threatening emails. Proud Boys are a North American all-male, far-right, neo-fascist militant organisation that promotes and engages in political violence. They are primarily misogynistic, Islamophobic, transphobic and anti-immigration and some members espouse white supremacist and antisemitic ideologies and/or engage with white supremacist groups.[851] Threatening e-mails from Proud Boys accounts were sent out to Democratic voters in the states of Alaska, Arizona, Florida and Pennsylvania warning: "You will vote for Trump on Election Day or we will come after you".[852] The Proud Boys' organisation has denied the allegations.[853] The Proud Boys were the same organisation that led the storming of Congress on 6 January 2021 and played an important role in rallying behind Trump in the 2024 US presidential elections.[854]

Although Iran-based hackers initiated the campaign, the event clearly benefitted the US Republican party and Donald Trump's candidature for the presidential race.

4.28.3 Presumed Objectives

Using the DISARM Navigator, we can distinguish several objectives, as follows:

T0140: Cause harm—The people who received the intimidating and threatening e-mails and messages were harmed as these e-mails impacted their sense of safety and protection and the exercise of their fundamental right to vote. By threatening

---

[849] Rewards for Justice, 2024. https://rewardsforjustice.net/rewards/emennet-pasargad/.
[850] https://www.trellix.com/en-gb/blogs/research/the-iranian-cyber-capability/.
[851] ADL, Proud Boys, 12 Nov 2023. https://www.adl.org/resources/backgrounder/proud-boys-0.
[852] Nakashima, Ellen, Amy Gardner, Isaac Stanley-Becker and Craig Timberg, "U.S. Government Concludes Iran Was behind Threatening Emails Sent to Democrats", *Washington Post*, 21 Oct 2020. https://www.washingtonpost.com/technology/2020/10/20/proud-boys-emails-florida/.
[853] Ibid.
[854] Roston, Aram, "The Proud Boys Are Back: How the Far-Right Group Is Rebuilding", Reuters, 8 Nov 2024. https://www.reuters.com/investigates/special-report/usa-election-proudboys/.

people to vote in favour of Trump, the attackers also caused harm to the vote base of the Democratic party as the threatening e-mails might have frightened pro-Democratic voters to vote in favour of Trump owing to fear of being killed. Stealing voter information details to conduct a voter intimidation and influence campaign clearly harms the democratic principles of "free and fair elections".[855]

T0136: Cultivate support—The voter intimidation and influence campaign were ostensibly conducted to cultivate support for Donald Trump.

T0139: Dissuade from acting—The voter intimidation and influence campaign aimed to dissuade voters from voting for the Democrats in the swing states.

T0138: Motivate to act—The voter intimidation and influence campaign aimed to motivate voters to vote for the Republicans in the swing states.

4.28.4 Incidents and Observables

In the first incident, the FIMI attackers were able to successfully exploit a misconfigured US computer system that enabled them to download information concerning more than 100,000 voters thus compromising state voter websites, including state voter registration websites and state voter information websites.

After gathering the voter information data, the FIMI attackers posed as members of the "group of Proud Boys volunteers" and sent false election messages via Facebook and e-mails to Republican Senators, Republican members of Congress, individuals associated with the presidential campaign of Donald Trump, White House advisors and members of the media claiming that the Democratic Party was planning to exploit "serious security vulnerabilities" in state voter registration websites to "edit mail-in ballots or even register non-existent voters".

The FIMI attackers also sent "false election video" carrying the Proud Boys logo showing an individual hacking voter websites and using stolen voter data to create fraudulent absentee ballots through the Federal Voting Assistance Program (FVAP) for military and overseas voters.[856]

The FIMI attackers sent threatening messages and e-mails to registered Democrat voters threatening them with physical violence, saying, "You will vote for Trump on Election Day or we will come after you."[857] The threatening e-mails had a subject line "vote for Trump or else!".

In November 2020, the FIMI attackers made a failed attempt to use stolen voter credentials to again access to an unnamed US media company network, which would have provided them another vehicle for further disseminating false claims

[855] Principles of Democracy. https://www.principlesofdemocracy.org/election-dem.

[856] Office of Public Affairs, Department of Justice, *Press* Release, 18 Nov 2021. https://www.justice.gov/opa/pr/two-iranian-nationals-charged-cyber-enabled-disinformation-and-threat-campaign-designed.

[857] Melissa Quinn, Stefan Becket and Graham Kates, "Emails threatening Florida voters to "vote for Trump or else!" linked to overseas servers", CBS News, 21 Oct 2020. https://www.cbsnews.com/news/florida-emails-proud-boys-vote-trump-linked-overseas-servers/.

concerning the election. However, by then, a victim had informed the FBI, and the company mitigated the FIMI attackers' unauthorised access and log-in attempts.

4.28.5 Targets

Following the scale and the medium in which the FIMI attacks were used, as well as the issue of the US presidential elections, the main target of the FIMI attack was the US democratic process and its publics. A key aim of the FIMI attacks was to undermine the faith and confidence in the 2020 presidential election. This would have implied an attack on US democratic institutions.

The threatening messages and e-mails were sent to individual voters who were the targets, and they mostly belonged to the traditional Democratic voter base.

More broadly, the FIMI attackers targeted the Democratic presidential candidate, Joe Biden, as the attacks aimed at aiding and abetting Trump's win.

4.28.6 Tactics, Techniques and Procedures

Tactics

T0073: Determine target audiences—The FIMI attackers determined the target audiences, US Democratic voters, who received the voter intimidation and influence campaign narratives, messages and e-mails intended to intimidate them and coerce them to vote for Donald Trump.

T0081: Identify technical and social vulnerabilities—The FIMI attackers determined weaknesses within their target audience who were registered Democrat voters in swing states and stole their voter information to intimidate them later. This was particularly relevant because the 2016 US presidential election between Hillary Clinton and Donald Trump had heightened the political vulnerabilities and polarities in US society that were exploited by the FIMI attackers. A technical vulnerability exploited by the Iranian hackers was the apparent weak cybersecurity infrastructure around voter information that enabled them to steal the data.

Techniques

T0083: Integrate target audience vulnerabilities into narrative—An influence operation may seek to exploit the pre-existing weaknesses, fears and enemies of the target audience for integration into the operation's narratives and overall strategy. Integrating existing vulnerabilities into the operational approach conserves resources by exploiting already weak areas of the target information environment instead of forcing the operation to create new vulnerabilities in the environment.

T0085: Develop text-based content—The FIMI attackers created false, misleading and threatening text-based-mails and messages aligned with Donald Trump's narratives for the US presidential elections for the voter intimidation and influence campaign.

T0089: Obtain private documents—The FIMI attackers stole voter registration data that is not publicly available. They obtained this data by exploiting a misconfigured computer system. This data included the personal details and political affiliation of the voters. This information was exploited to send out threatening e-mails and messages to coerce voters to vote for Donald Trump.

T0094: Infiltrate existing networks—The FIMI attackers infiltrated voter registration websites to collect voter data.

T0100: Co-opt trusted sources—The FIMI attackers co-opted trusted sources of the voter registration websites and posed as Proud Boys volunteers, the far-right group supporting Donald Trump.

Procedures

T0112: E-mails—The FIMI attackers delivered the threatening messages via e-mail using the voter registration list.

T0104: Social networks—The FIMI attackers used Facebook to send threatening messages to Facebook users in the swing states to coerce them to vote for Trump.

T0115: Post content—The FIMI attackers posted content via Facebook.

T0121: Manipulate platform algorithm—The FIMI attackers manipulated platform algorithms of Facebook and attempted to hack into a US-based media company's computer networks. The two FIMI attackers had other co-conspirators and might have used bots to amplify their Facebook posts.

T0048: Harass—The FIMI attackers threatened and harassed the Democrat voters in the US swing states by sending intimidating e-mails and threatening them that they would be killed if they didk't vote for Trump.

T0126: Encourage attendance at physical events—The FIMI attackers coerced the voters to vote for Trump.

T0127: Physical violence—The FIMI attackers threatened the recipients with lethal physical violence in case they did not vote for Trump.

T0060: Continue to amplify—The FIMI attackers continued the message amplification after the main incident work finished; Iran played a major role in spreading disinformation in the 2024 presidential elections.[858]

---

[858] Myers, Steven Lee, Tiffany Hsu, and Farnaz Fassihi, "Iran Emerges as a Top Disinformation Threat in U.S. Presidential Race", *The New York Times*, 4 Sept 2024. https://www.nytimes.com/2024/09/04/business/media/iran-disinformation-us-presidential-race.html.

T0059: Play the long game—The FIMI attackers seemed to be playing a long game that extended beyond the 2020 US presidential elections as Iran played a crucial role in spreading manipulated information, stealing and disseminating sensitive information in the 2024 presidential elections.[859]

4.28.7 Channels

The Iranian hackers purveyed FIMI via "false election messages" including personalised e-mails, Facebook messages and false election video.

4.28.8 Languages

English.

4.28.9 Effectiveness

The FIMI attackers did succeed in interfering with the 2020 US presidential elections and remained a key player in spreading disinformation in the 2024 elections. They were only partly effective because, in the end, the FBI exposed them, and they were indicted. Nevertheless, we do not know how effective they were in swaying voters.

According to the indictment,[860] 100,000 voters' private information from the election website of an unspecified US state was stolen and these voters received threatening emails and were being coerced to vote for Donald Trump.

The voter intimidation and influence campaign ran from August to November 2020. Following that, on 6 January 2021, Trump supporters stormed the United States Capitol disrupting the joint session of Congress convened to certify the results of the presidential election of 2020, which Trump had lost to his Democratic opponent, Joe Biden. The object of this attack was to prevent a legitimate president-elect from assuming office and the attack coincided with the COVID-19 pandemic raising public health concerns.[861]

---

[859] Associated Press, "Iran Sent Hacked Trump Documents to Biden Campaign, FBI Says", *The Guardian*, 19 Sept 2024. https://www.theguardian.com/us-news/2024/sep/19/iran-sent-hacked-trump-documents-to-biden-campaign-fbi-says.

[860] Office of Public Affairs, "Two Iranian Nationals Charged for Cyber-Enabled Disinformation and Threat Campaign Designed to Influence the 2020 U.S. Presidential Election", Department of Justice, Press Release, 18 Nov 2021. https://www.justice.gov/opa/pr/two-iranian-nationals-charged-cyber-enabled-disinformation-and-threat-campaign-designed.

[861] Britannica, January 6 U.S. Capitol attack riot, Washington, D.C., U.S. [2021]. https://www.britannica.com/event/January-6-U-S-Capitol-attack.

Pew Research reported that social polarisation among US voters reached an all-time high in 2020 and the spread of manipulated information played a huge role in propelling it.[862] The divides between conservative Republicans and liberal Democrats are more pronounced and this has serious implications on issues such as civil rights and racial justice.[863]

Although there is no reported impact of the FIMI attack, we can assume that the FIMI attack created harm by possibly frightening the voters and threatening to kill them if they did not vote for Donald Trump.

4.28.10 Countermeasures

C00070: Block access to disinformation resources—The FBI was notified by a FIMI victim, and they took immediate steps to block the attackers' access to a US media company's network. The attackers failed· authorised log-in attempts.[864]

C00060: Legal action against for-profit engagement factories[865]—The two Iranian nationals were both charged with one count of conspiracy to commit computer fraud and abuse, intimidate voters and transmit interstate threats, which carries a maximum sentence of five years in prison. One of them, Kazemi, was additionally charged with one count of unauthorised computer intrusion, which carries a maximum sentence of five years in prison, and one count of computer fraud, namely, knowingly damaging a protected computer, which carries a maximum sentence of 10 years in prison.[866] As the two Iranian nationals are not based in the US, an FBI wanted poster with the Department of State's Rewards for Justice Program is offering a reward of up to $10 million for information on or about the activities of Kazemi and Kashian.[867]

The US Department of the Treasury Office of Foreign Assets Control (OFAC) "imposed certain sanctions in the event of foreign interference in a United States election" against Emennet Pasargad, the Iranian company that employed the FIMI attackers, and the attackers themselves under Executive Order 13,848.

[862] Jurkowitz, Mark, Amy Mitchell, Elisa Shearer and Mason Walker, *U.S. Media Polarization and the 2020 Election: A Nation Divided,* Pew Research, 24 Jan 2020. https://www.pewresearch.org/journalism/2020/01/24/u-s-media-polarization-and-the-2020-election-a-nation-divided/.

[863] Julia Azari, *Polarization is not the biggest threat to American democracy*, Chatham House, 6 Sept 2024. https://www.chathamhouse.org/publications/the-world-today/2024-09/polarization-not-biggest-threat-american-democracy.

[864] Office of Public Affairs, "Two Iranian Nationals Charged for Cyber-Enabled Disinformation and Threat Campaign Designed to Influence the 2020 U.S. Presidential Election", Department of Justice, press release, 18 Nov 2021. https://www.justice.gov/opa/pr/two-iranian-nationals-charged-cyber-enabled-disinformation-and-threat-campaign-designed.

[865] Ibid.

[866] Ibid.

[867] FBI, "Iranian interference in 2020 U.S. ELECTIONS", Wanted by the FBI. https://www.fbi.gov/wanted/cyber/iranian-interference-in-2020-us-elections/download.pdf.

4.28.11 Conclusions and Recommendations

As Iran continues to launch and lead disinformation campaigns abroad and interfere with electoral processes, online platforms, national governments and media outlets must remain vigilant to protect their users by continuing to flag, remove and block the spread of false information and state-sponsored propaganda. Online platforms must have strict content moderation guidelines.

The case study is a call for European democracies to strengthen the cybersecurity of their public cyber and election infrastructure to minimise theft of personal data and future exploitation. The Iranian FIMI campaign exploited vulnerabilities in US voter registration systems, allowing hackers to steal sensitive voter data. To prevent similar breaches, it is critical to improve the cybersecurity of election infrastructure, especially voter registration systems. This includes regular audits, strengthening security protocols and ensuring that all sensitive data is adequately protected from cyber-attacks.

The indictment of Iranian nationals for their role in the FIMI campaign underscores the importance of holding perpetrators accountable and the importance of bolstering legal frameworks along with international cooperation. Governments should strengthen international legal frameworks for prosecuting transnational disinformation campaigns. Enhanced cooperation between nations and the private sector, especially tech companies, is vital to detect, prevent and penalise actors who engage in cyber-enabled disinformation and voter manipulation.

The Iranian interference with US elections raises the urgency for the development of advanced detection tools and attribution techniques for detecting and attributing FIMI activities. Governments and tech companies must invest in artificial intelligence and machine learning solutions to better track disinformation sources, analyse patterns, and identify networks behind malicious campaigns alongside with clear, transparent attribution methodologies that allow for the swift identification and exposure of perpetrators.

The US example of FIMI is illustrative of exploitation and abuse of social divisions and fault lines. It is imperative that there are public awareness campaigns and social cohesion campaigns to build a robust and trustworthy social fibre amongst people. It is crucial to promote media literacy programs that help people recognise false narratives and misinformation, especially on social platforms along with community-building initiatives for bridging political and social divides, fostering trust and collaboration among diverse groups. Efforts to strengthen social cohesion should focus on building shared identities and encouraging open dialogue to counter polarisation and there should be a long-term strategy focusing on enhancing social unity, resilience and a healthy public discourse.

4.29 Saudi Arabia's Anti-Iran Campaign During the First Trump Administration

4.29.1 Introduction

This case study examines wherein Saudi Arabia may have leveraged the Trump administration's anti-Iran position to advance its own geopolitical objectives.[868] The analysis zeroes in on the timeframe spanning February 2017 to January 2020, coinciding with the reinstatement of sanctions on Iran and the deterioration of diplomatic relations.[869]

It analyses how Saudi Arabia leveraged a unique geopolitical landscape to enhance its reputation and diminish the standing of its regional rivals, particularly within the Middle East. Specifically, it explores how the kingdom leveraged the Trump administration's strict stance on Iran to advance its geopolitical goals, using digital strategies and online campaigns to isolate Iran and propagate a negative narrative.[870]

During this period, the United States reimposed sanctions on Iran[871] and withdrew from the Joint Comprehensive Plan of Action (JCPOA), the deal designed to limit Iran's nuclear ambitions in exchange for economic relief. On 8 October 2020, the Trump administration intensified these measures with an executive order that transformed the "maximum pressure" campaign into a more severe "siege and starve" approach.[872] The order imposed a sweeping boycott on Iranian financial institutions, cutting them off from the global financial system and crippling their ability to conduct cross-border transactions.[873]

Considering these developments, Saudi Arabia appears to have seized the opportunity to leverage its own narrative, bolster its image while undermining

---

[868] Bianco, Cinzia, "Global Saudi: How Europeans Can Work with an Evolving Kingdom", *European Council on Foreign Relations*, 8 May 2024. https://ecfr.eu/publication/global-saudi-how-europeans-can-work-with-an-evolving-kingdom/.

[869] International Crisis Group, "Iran Sanctions under the Trump Administration", 15 Jan 2020. https://www.crisisgroup.org/middle-east-north-africa/gulf-and-arabian-peninsula/iran/iran-sanctions-under-trump-administration.

[870] Karni, Annie, "Saudis Give Trump a Reception Fit for a King", *POLITICO*, 20 May 2017. https://www.politico.com/story/2017/05/20/donald-trump-saudi-arabia-visit-238638.

[871] Skuld, "INSIGHT: Iran Sanctions", 13 Oct 2020. https://www.skuld.com/topics/legal/sanctions/iran/insight-iran-sanctions/.

[872] United States Department of State, "Maximum Pressure Campaign on the Regime in Iran", fact sheet, 4 Apr 2019. https://2017-2021.state.gov/maximum-pressure-campaign-on-the-regime-in-iran.

[873] Cullis, Tyler, "The Undeniable Cruelty of Trump's 'Maximum Pressure' on Iran", Responsible Statecraft, 8 Oct 2020. https://responsiblestatecraft.org/2020/10/08/the-undeniable-cruelty-of-trumps-maximum-pressure-on-iran/.

regional rivals. Preliminary studies suggest that Saudi Arabia[874] drew inspiration from campaigns like "Make America Great Again"[875] and crafted its own version, "Making Arabia Great Again".[876] A central element of this strategy involved disseminating anti-Iranian narratives, targeting Shia Muslim demographics to weaken the influence of regional rivals, such as Turkey, Qatar and the Muslim Brotherhood.[877]

This approach is part of a broader trend in media, where Saudi Arabia, like many nations, is transitioning from traditional news platforms to digital ones. For instance, SaudiNews50,[878] the most followed news account in the Arab world, operates exclusively on social media, reflecting the increasing reliance on platforms like X as primary news sources.[879]

The transition to digital platforms enabled Saudi Arabia to deploy thousands of accounts on Twitter and Facebook to amplify pro-government messages mostly through state-sponsored troll farms[880] incinerating nationalist sentiment to advance state-sanctioned narratives, thereby obscuring the distinction between genuine public discourse and orchestrated propaganda.[881]

As tensions escalated between the Trump administration and Iran,[882] Saudi Arabia ramped up its efforts to influence public opinion, particularly through social media. Major events, such as President Trump's tweets directed at Iranian President Hassan Rouhani, gave Saudi Arabia opportunities to promote its narratives.

---

874 Jones, Marc Owen, *Digital Authoritarianism in the Middle East: Deception, Disinformation and Social Media*, Oxford University Press, 2022.

875 Luke, L.K., *The Little-Known History of 'Make America Great Again'*, News.Com.Au, Australia, 30 Nov 2017. https://news.com.au/world/north-america/the-littleknown-history-of-make-america-great-again/news-story/fb8a09b40aa59defd39ef0bcdeaeb281.

876 Commentary Magazine, "Making Saudi Great Again", 11 Dec 2017. https://www.commentary.org/sohrab-ahmari/making-saudi-arabia-great-again/.

877 BalaEddy, P., *Saudi Arabia and Sectarianism in Middle East International Relations*, Project on Middle East Political Science, 26 Mar 2020. https://pomeps.org/saudi-arabia-and-sectarianism-in-middle-east-international-relations.

878 SaudiNews50. *(19) اخبار السعودية (@SaudiNews50)/X*. X (formerly Twitter), 1 May 2024. https://twitter.com/SaudiNews50.

879 Ritzen, Y., "The Fake Twitter Accounts Influencing the Gulf Crisis", Al Jazeera, 21 July 2019. https://www.aljazeera.com/news/2019/7/21/the-fake-twitter-accounts-influencing-the-gulf-crisis. See also GMI Blogger, *Saudi Arabia (KSA) Social Media Statistics 2024 | GMI*, Official GMI Blog, 6 Mar 2023. https://www.globalmediainsight.com/blog/saudi-arabia-social-media-statistics/.

880 Benner, K., M. Mazzetti, B. Hubbard and M. Isaac, "Saudis' Image Makers: A Troll Army and a Twitter Insider", *The New York Times*, 20 Oct 2018. https://www.nytimes.com/2018/10/20/us/politics/saudi-image-campaign-twitter.html.

881 lhussein, E., "Saudi First: How Hyper-Nationalism Is Transforming Saudi Arabia", ECFR, 19 June 2019. https://ecfr.eu/publication/saudi_first_how_hyper_nationalism_is_transforming_saudi_arabia/

882 Levine, S., "Trump reposts 2018 all-caps anti-Iran threat in response to Israel strike", *The Guardian*, 14 Apr 2024. https://www.theguardian.com/us-news/2024/apr/14/trump-iran-response-israel.

Trump's confrontational rhetoric, especially his 2018 tweet in all caps warning Rouhani of "consequences the likes of which few throughout history have ever suffered",[883] became a focal point for disinformation campaigns. This tweet was widely circulated and praised by Republican leaders, allowing pro-Saudi influencers to further distort the narrative, which reinforced a confrontational stance towards Iran.[884]

4.29.2 Threat Actors

A coalition of disinformation actors played a crucial role in spreading this rhetoric, with each group contributing to the amplification of the message. Right-wing influencers helped elevate President Trump's anti-Iran statements, framing Iran as a destabilising force that justified military or economic intervention. At the same time, Saudi-affiliated networks, including automated bots and media outlets, further propagated these views, merging the narratives of the United States and Saudi Arabia against Iran.[885]

State-sponsored entities utilised governmental resources to advance their geopolitical objectives, whereas criminal organisations capitalised on the situation for monetary gain. Furthermore, ideologically driven hacktivists and individuals with ambiguous motivations participated in the attack.[886]

This incident highlights a concerning trend wherein various threat actors, including ordinary individuals such as Saudi citizens and right-wing Americans, partake in disseminating distorted narratives.[887] When an influencer retweeted former President Trump's anti-Iran statements, the message swiftly proliferated and was further amplified by other influencers as well as Saudi automated accounts.

---

[883] Trump, Donald J. [@realDonaldTrump], "To Iranian President Rouhani: NEVER, EVER THREATEN THE UNITED STATES AGAIN OR YOU WILL SUFFER CONSEQUENCES THE LIKES OF WHICH FEW THROUGHOUT HISTORY HAVE EVER SUFFERED BEFORE. WE ARE NO LONGER A COUNTRY THAT WILL STAND FOR YOUR DEMENTED WORDS OF VIOLENCE & DEATH. BE CAUTIOUS!", Tweet, Twitter, 23 July 2018. https://twitter.com/realDonaldTrump/status/1022267278486794240. Nakamura, Devlin, "For Trump and Iran, Trolling on.

[884] Twitter Helped Escalate Tensions on the Battlefield", *The Washington Post*, 9 Jan 2020. https://www.washingtonpost.com/politics/for-trump-and-iran-trolling-on-twitter-helped-escalate-tensions-on-the-battlefield/2020/01/09/04e81552-32f6-11ea-a053-dc6d944ba776_story.html.

Al Jazeera., "US Sanctions under Trump: A Legacy That Could Box in Biden?", 21 Jan 2021. https://www.aljazeera.com/news/2021/1/21/us-santions-under-trump-all-you-need-to-know.

[885] Byman, Daniel L., "How Middle Eastern Conflicts Are Playing Out on Social Media", *Brookings*, 2022. https://www.brookings.edu/articles/how-middle-eastern-conflicts-are-playing-out-on-social-media/.

[886] Abeshouse, Brian, "Inside the Wild West of Social Media", *Al Jazeera*, 8 Feb 2018. https://www.aljazeera.com/features/2018/2/8/troll-factories-bots-and-fake-news-inside-the-wild-west-of-social-media.

[887] Byman, Daniel L., "How Middle Eastern Conflicts Are Playing Out on Social Media", *Brookings*, 2022. https://www.brookings.edu/articles/how-middle-eastern-conflicts-are-playing-out-on-social-media/.

This engendered a cascading effect, rapidly expanding the reach and impact of the message, thereby demonstrating how these interconnected actors collaborated systematically to magnify disinformation across diverse platforms.[888]

4.29.3 Presumed Objectives

Saudi Arabia's disinformation campaigns use various strategic tactics.

> T0079: Divide—Saudi Arabia strategically exacerbated sectarian conflicts and political rivalries through disinformation, aiming to weaken potential alliances and foster fragmentation that ultimately benefits its own interests.
>
> T0078: Dismay—Saudi Arabia's negative portrayal of Iran and its amplification of controversies actively diminished Iran's support base while promoting itself as a stabilising force. This tactic creates uncertainty and disillusionment, contributing to regional instability.
>
> T0076: Distort—By aligning with Trump's strategy to undermine adversaries, Saudi Arabia distorts public understanding of both its own actions and its geopolitical rivals. This alignment leverages Trump's anti-Iran stance to further distort perceptions of Iran and consolidate Saudi influence.

4.29.4 Incidents and Observables

- The use of deceptive hashtags like #ترامب_يسخن(#TrumpIsHeatingUp),[889] #TrumpWarnsIranianAggression[890] and #TrumpWillDestroyIran[891] helped manipulate public perception.[892] These hashtags along with others in similar tone were strategically employed to create a sense of impending conflict with Iran and promote Trump's aggressive stance.[893]

[888] Braca, A., and P. Dondio, "Developing persuasive systems for marketing: the interplay of persuasion techniques, customer traits and persuasive message design", *Italian Journal of Marketing*, Vol. 2023, No. 3, pp. 369–412.

[889] Maha, [@MahaAlot1], "@realDonaldTrump Iran Is the Leader of Terrorism and Will Be Stopped by the Leader of Peace! Let's Support TRUMP! #TrumpWarnsIranianTerrorism", Tweet, Twitter, 13 Feb 2017. https://twitter.com/MahaAlot1/status/830930149738741761.

[890] Nãdèr bîlàł, [@BilaNader], "Trump Is Take a Good Decision About Iran IR Terrors Thank You Mr Trump to Stop the Wave of Terrorist #TrumpWarusIranianTerrorism", Tweet, Twitter, 9 May 2018. https://twitter.com/BilaNader/status/994046309333127169.

[891] ahadbinfahaad [@fahadbinfahaad_]. "@realDonaldTrump #TrumpWarnsIranianTerrorism During the Last 5 Years Iran Has Perpetuated Terror Attacks in 25 Different Countries. @pwire", Twitter, 9 Feb 2017. https://twitter.com/fahadbinfahaad_/status/829816570817941505.

[892] Jones, Marc Owen, *Digital Authoritarianism in the Middle East: Deception, Disinformation and Social Media*, Oxford University Press, 2022.

[893] Ya Libnan, "Trump Warns Iran of 'Heavy Price' in Case of Attack on US Troops", 2 Apr 2020. https://yalibnan.com/2020/04/02/trump-warns-iran-of-heavy-price-in-case-of-attack-on-us-troops/. See also saaam6, [@a_sam__6], "@dr_css @realDonaldTrump @mel_bough You Are

- Fabricating online support: The circulation of images portraying Trump as a powerful figure like Thor or a Spartan warrior reinforced the observable of creating a cult of personality.[894] These images were intended to influence public perception by associating Trump with strength and resolve against Iran. This tactic further contributed to the campaign's objectives of dismay and distort.
- Social media manipulation: The collaboration between social media and Saudi media outlets amplified campaign messages through sensational headlines, demonstrating coordinated media manipulation.[895] For example, stories like "The Pope's Skepticism About Trump's Christianity Heats Up the Elections"[896] blurred the lines between credible reporting and manipulated narratives, demonstrating how false information can cycle through both traditional and social media to distort public opinion.[897]
- Influencers: Saudi media outlets and influential figures like Turki Aldakhil, a Saudi diplomat and journalist,[898] endorsed Trump's anti-Iranian rhetoric. These endorsements amplified the campaign's messages, leveraging their reach to shape public opinion. By actively promoting Trump's stance and encouraging hashtags like #TrumpWarnsIranianTerrorism, they fuelled negative perceptions of Iran, fostering distrust and fear. This tactic effectively divided public opinion and created an environment of uncertainty that furthered the campaign's objectives.
- Amplifying messages using traditional media platforms: The prominent placement of Trump's statements on the front pages of newspapers like[899] suggested a deliberate effort to amplify the campaign's message through established and widely trusted media outlets. By often featuring these statements, media sources gave credibility to the narrative and increased its potential to reach and influence a broader audience.

---

a Brave Man Stage We Support Mr. Trump", Tweet, Twitter, 13 Feb 2017. https://twitter.com/a_sam__6/status/831186730317410305. Heshmat Alavi, [@HeshmatAlavi], "@realDonaldTrump Mr. President, I Am an Iranian & I Want to Thank You for Your Maximum Pressure Policy & Specifically Targeting the Mullahs' Regime Ruling #Iran. I Want the World to Know That for 41 Years the Regime Has Made Life a Living Hell for Us Iranians", Tweet, Twitter, 22 May 2020. https://twitter.com/HeshmatAlavi/status/1263712806425309184. تركي_الدخيل, [@TurkiAldakhil], " غردوا تحت هذا الهاشتاق بالانجليزي لشكر ترمب على مواجهته للارهاب الايراني#TrumpWarnsIranianTerrorism", Tweet, Twitter, 4 Feb 2017. https://twitter.com/TurkiAldakhil/status/827965248263028736.

[894] Maha, [@MahaAlot1], "Iran Is the Leader of Terrorism and Will Be Stopped by the Leader of Peace! Lets Support TRUMP! #TrumpWarnsIranianTerrorism", Tweet, Twitter, 13 Feb 2017. https://twitter.com/MahaAlot1/status/830930149738741761.

[895] Ritzen, Y., "The Fake Twitter Accounts Influencing the Gulf Crisis", *Al Jazeera*, 21 July 2019. https://www.aljazeera.com/news/2019/7/21/the-fake-twitter-accounts-influencing-the-gulf-crisis.

[896] "الأمين, و.-أ., "تشكيك البابا بمسيحية ترامب يسخن الانتخابات" 19 February 2016. https://www.albayan.ae/one-world/overseas/2016-02-20-1.2577448.

[897] Ritzen, Y., "The Fake Twitter Accounts Influencing the Gulf Crisis", *Al Jazeera*, 21 July 2019. https://www.aljazeera.com/news/2019/7/21/the-fake-twitter-accounts-influencing-the-gulf-crisis.

[898] Aldakhil, Turki, "Arab News". https://www.arabnews.com/taxonomy/term/12636.

[899] صحيفة عكاظ. https://www.okaz.com.sa/.

4.29.5 Targets

The FIMI campaign targeted two distinct groups. Initially, it focused on domestic and regional audiences within Saudi Arabia and the broader Arab region. Subsequently, the campaign expanded its efforts to influence individuals and institutions in the West, particularly in the US.

4.29.6 Tactics, Techniques and Procedures

Below, we provide evidence of TTPs used in the Saudi FIMI case. Each TTP starts with its DISARM code.

- T0002: Facilitate state propaganda—The collaboration between Saudi media outlets and influencers to amplify pro-Trump and anti-Iran narratives aligned with state propaganda efforts.
- T0003: Leverage existing narratives—The campaign capitalised on pre-existing tensions and biases against Iran, framing Trump's actions as necessary to counter a perceived threat.
- T0004: Develop competing narratives—The campaign actively constructed a counter-narrative portraying Saudi Arabia as a stabilising force and Iran as a destabilising one.
- T0044: Seed distortions—The use of deceptive hashtags and fabricated images of Trump as a powerful figure exemplified the seeding of distortions to manipulate public perceptions.
- T0049: Flood information space—The coordinated efforts across social media, traditional media and influential figures contributed to flooding the information space with pro-Trump and anti-Iran narratives.
- T0049.001: Trolls amplify and manipulate—While not explicitly mentioned in the observables, it is highly likely that troll accounts were used to amplify and manipulate the spread of the campaign's messages.
- T0049.002: Flood existing hashtag—The campaign actively encouraged the use of specific hashtags like #TrumpWarnsIranianTerrorism to flood existing conversations and dominate the narrative.
- T0049.008: Generate information pollution—Coordinated messaging across platforms contributed to information pollution, hindering the public's ability to discern truth from falsehood.
- T0072.002: Demographic segmentation—The campaign likely targeted specific demographics receptive to pro-Trump and anti-Iran sentiments.
- T0076: Distort—The selective presentation of information and the use of sensational headlines served to distort the narrative in favour of the campaign's objectives.
- T0078: Dismay—The portrayal of Iran as an imminent threat aimed to create an atmosphere of fear and uncertainty.

- T0079: Divide—The campaign exploited existing divisions and fostered animosity towards Iran to further polarise public opinion.
- T0085: Develop text-based content—The campaign generated various forms of text-based content, including tweets, news articles and social media posts.
- T0086: Develop image-based content—The circulation of images depicting Trump as a powerful figure exemplified the use of image-based content to influence public perceptions.
- T0086.001: Develop memes—The use of memes is a common tactic in disinformation campaigns and were employed in the Saudi FIMI campaign.
- T0104.005: Use hashtags—The campaign strategically used hashtags to amplify its message and facilitate coordination.
- T0104.006: Create dedicated hashtag—The creation and promotion of the hashtag #TrumpWarnsIranianTerrorism illustrated the use of a dedicated hashtag to centralise the campaign's messaging.
- T0105: Media sharing networks—The campaign leveraged various media-sharing networks, including Twitter, to disseminate its content.
- T0105.001 Photo sharing—The sharing of images portraying Trump as a powerful figure exemplified the use of photo-sharing platforms.
- T0111.002: Newspapers—Saudi newspapers such as *Okaz* were instrumental in amplifying the campaign's messages through prominent coverage of Trump's statements.
- T0114.002: Traditional media—Collaboration with traditional media outlets such as *Al Arabiya* played a key role in disseminating the campaign's narratives.
- T0115: Post content—The campaign actively posted various forms of content, including text, images and memes, across different platforms.
- T0115.001: Share memes—Memes were also employed to further the campaign's reach and impact.
- T0135.001: Smear—The negative portrayal of Iran and the amplification of controversies served to smear its reputation.
- T0135.004: Polarise—The campaign's divisive rhetoric aimed to polarise public opinion and create an us-versus-them mentality.
- T0136: Cultivate support—The campaign actively sought to cultivate support for Trump and his policies, portraying him as a strong leader against Iran.
- T0136.003: Energise supporters—The use of influential figures and sensational headlines aimed to energise supporters and encourage them to actively participate in the campaign.
- T0136.004: Boost reputation—By aligning with Trump and promoting his anti-Iran stance, the campaign aimed to boost Saudi Arabia's reputation as a regional leader and stability provider.

4.29.7 Channels

The FIMI campaign effectively disseminated its message and accomplished its objectives through a variety of channels. It used Twitter to rapidly distribute content and generate trending topics. Additionally, it capitalised on established news outlets and television channels to further propagate its narrative. These media platforms, with their extensive reach and influence, conferred legitimacy upon the campaign's assertions.

4.29.8 Languages

The disinformation appeared primarily in Arabic and English, targeting audiences in the Middle East and the West. However, given the global nature of social media platforms, the fake information may have also been disseminated in other languages to reach a broader audience.

4.29.9 Effectiveness

Evidence suggests that the campaign successfully attained multiple objectives by intensifying apprehensions regarding Iranian aggression and depicting Iran as a destabilising force, thereby positioning Saudi Arabia as an essential counterbalance.

Furthermore, the campaign's persistent negative portrayal of Iran appears to have intensified negative sentiments, particularly among its target audience. This escalation is reflected in the increased use of anti-Iran rhetoric on social media and in various media platforms. The proliferation of anti-Iran hashtags and inflammatory comments suggests a growing sense of anger and resentment, and discussions surrounding Iran have likely become more polarised, with increased displays of fear and scepticism towards the Iranian government.

Moreover, the campaign used emotional tactics by characterising Iran as a supporter of terrorism and a threat to regional stability, likely fuelling fear and unease. This emotional strategy may have bolstered the audience's willingness to endorse actions against Iran. An illustration of this approach is the hashtag #TrumpWillDestroyIran, along with the emphasis on Saudi Arabia's partnership with the US, which likely resonated with feelings of patriotism and security, particularly among Americans.

The campaign effectively built credibility and authority by aligning with the Trump administration's anti-Iran position, which boosted the perceived legitimacy of its message. It incorporated logical appeals by associating Iran's actions with negative outcomes, offering a reasoned argument that Iran's behaviour leads to undesirable consequences. Moreover, the campaign used repetition and consistently employed specific phrases and hashtags to reinforce its narrative, making it more engaging and memorable.

4.29.10 Countermeasures

Various entities, including social media platforms, independent researchers and advocacy groups, implemented countermeasures to address the FIMI attack. Social media platforms like Twitter enacted policies and deployed technologies to detect and remove fake accounts impersonating individuals. Independent researchers, such as Ben Nimmo and Sam Woolley, conducted studies to identify and expose bot networks and fake accounts, advocating for platform-level interventions.[900]

Additionally, advocacy groups and concerned citizens demanded that social media platforms provide transparency and accountability regarding the use of fake accounts and the spread of misinformation. An examination of tweets with the hashtags #TrumpWarnsIranianAggression and #TrumpWillDestroyIran revealed that bots were primarily employed to create and amplify a pro-Saudi narrative along with anti-Iran propaganda, particularly aimed at the US and Saudi audience. Notably, by 2020, around 92% of the accounts associated with the #TrumpWarnsIranianAggression hashtag were inactive, likely due to platform suspensions.[901]

4.29.11 Conclusions and Recommendations

This case study emphasises the growing threat of disinformation in today's digital landscape. It reveals the risks of coordinated efforts, particularly when countries come together to amplify messages for strategic objectives. The Saudi Arabia-Trump scenario represents a complex network designed to sway public opinion, provoke conflict and further geopolitical interests. Such campaigns exploit societal divisions, engage influential figures and flood the information landscape with targeted narratives, which erode trust in institutions, polarise societies and jeopardise democracy.

The Saudi government engages with social media platforms like X/Twitter to suppress dissent. Although not alone in this approach, Saudi Arabia is one of the leading players in digital disinformation alongside the UAE and Egypt. These nations possess both the resources and incentives to conduct disinformation campaigns aligned with their foreign policy objectives. Saudi Arabia employs a multi-faceted strategy, including infiltration, intimidation and co-optation, to suppress dissenting perspectives and elevate pro-regime messages.

Combatting FIMI necessitates a comprehensive strategy. Governments and international organisations must work together to share insights and formulate tactics against disinformation. Strengthening independent journalism and fact-checking efforts is vital to countering false narratives. Supporting civil society

[900] Jones, Marc Owen, *Digital Authoritarianism in the Middle East: Deception, Disinformation and Social Media*, Oxford University Press, 2022.
[901] Ibid.

organisations that advocate for media literacy is critical. Ultimately, it is essential to educate individuals on how to critically evaluate online information and differentiate trustworthy sources from propaganda.

4.30 Cyberwarfare and the Qatar Blockade

4.30.1 Introduction

On 23 May 2017, hackers breached the security of the Qatar News Agency (QNA) and took control of its website and social media accounts. They used this access to spread false statements, attributing them to Qatar's Emir, Sheikh Tamim bin Hamad Al Thani. These false statements included controversial views, such as praise for Islamist groups and Iran, as well as a defence of the Palestinian group Hamas[902] and the Lebanese Shia movement Hezbollah,[903] which is an ally of Tehran.[904]

This incident must be understood within the broader context of regional tensions, particularly the longstanding rivalry between Sunni-majority Saudi Arabia and Shia-majority Iran.[905] Saudi Arabia has historically sought to isolate Iran due to deep-rooted historical and ideological differences.[906] The Saudi government perceives Iran's support for groups like Hezbollah and the Houthis in Yemen as direct threats,[907] viewing them as proxies for Iranian influence in the region. Consequently, Saudi Arabia has sought to counterbalance Iran's growing power by forming strategic alliances, notably with Israel and the United States.[908]

At the time of the cyberattack, many Gulf states were aligning closely with the US administration under President Trump,[909] who had adopted a hardline

902 Encyclopaedia Britannica, "Hamas I Definition, History, Ideology, & Facts," *Britannica*, 15 Aug 2024. https://www.britannica.com/topic/Hamas.

903 Press, A., "What Is Hezbollah, the Iranian-Backed Group That Could Go to All-Out War Against Israel?", Voice of America, 29 June 2024. https://www.voanews.com/a/what-is-hezbollah-the-iranian-backed-group-that-could-go-to-all-out-war-against-israel-/7675377.html.

904 Robinson, Kali, "What Is Hezbollah?", Council on Foreign Relations, last updated 30 July 2024. https://www.cfr.org/backgrounder/what-hezbollah.

905 Council on Foreign Relations (CFR), "The Sunni-Shia Divide", 2023. https://www.cfr.org/article/sunni-shia-divide.

906 BBC News, "Why Saudi Arabia and Iran Are Bitter Rivals", 18 Nov 2017. https://www.bbc.com/news/world-middle-east-42008809.

907 *Foreign Policy*, "Hezbollah and the Houthis in Yemen as Direct Threats", 12 Aug 2024. https://foreignpolicy.com/2024/08/12/israel-hezbollah-conflict-endgame-lebanon-gaza-war/.

908 *IBA Net*, "Saudi Arabia and Israel Quietly Prepare 'Deal of the Century'", 2024. https://www.ibanet.org/article/D2659617-4CAB-4FE9-8B60-A971485EC3D6. Sayarer, J., "How Saudi Arabia's Rulers Became Best Friends With Israel", *Jacobin*, 2020. https://jacobin.com/2023/04/saudi-arabia-israel-palestine-occupation-apartheid-international-relations.

909 Atlantic Council, "Trump Navigates the Middle East", 19 May 2017. https://www.atlanticcouncil.org/blogs/new-atlanticist/trump-navigates-the-middle-east/.

stance against Iran.[910] This alignment, driven by a shared goal of countering Iran's regional influence, further intensified the pressure on Qatar to conform to the broader anti-Iran agenda. The timing of the attack, shortly after President Trump's visit to Riyadh,[911] the seat of the Saudi government, heightened its political significance and added to the growing discord in the region.[912]

Within this context, any perceived support for Iran by a member of the Gulf Cooperation Council (GCC)—a regional bloc of six Arab states[913]—like Qatar was seen by Saudi Arabia and its allies as a serious breach of trust.[914] Qatar's prior support for the Muslim Brotherhood, a movement opposed to several Gulf monarchies and viewed as a threat to their political stability,[915] further deepened tensions, as it challenged the influence and authority of these states.[916]

Qatar's independent foreign policy faced constraints from this blockade, which lasted for three and a half years before it ended on 5 January 2021.[917] However, the cyberwar campaign and the blockade continue to reverberate, influencing regional relations and stability.[918] This case study examines the Qatar hacking incident and the subsequent blockade, highlighting how cyberattacks, propaganda and social media manipulation were used to achieve geopolitical objectives.[919]

---

[910] *POLITICO*, "Trump Move Against Iran Nuclear Deal Would Isolate US", 8 May 2018. https://www.politico.eu/article/donald-trump-move-against-iran-nuclear-deal-would-isolate-us-sanctions/.

[911] Karni, A., "Saudis Give Trump a Reception Fit for a King", *POLITICO*, 20 May 2017. https://www.politico.com/story/2017/05/20/donald-trump-saudi-arabia-visit-238638.

[912] *The New Arab*, "Fake-news hack: pre-emptive strike on Qatar's independent foreign policy?", 2017. https://www.newarab.com/analysis/fake-news-hack-pre-emptive-strike-qatars-independent-foreign-policy.

DeYoung, K., and Ellen Nakashima, "UAE orchestrated hacking of Qatari government sites, sparking regional upheaval, according to U.S. intelligence officials", *The Washington Post*, 16 July 2017. https://www.washingtonpost.com/world/national-security/uae-hacked-qatari-government-sites-sparking-regional-upheaval-according-to-us-intelligence-officials/2017/07/16/00c46e54-698f-11e7-8eb5-cbccc2e7bfbf_story.html.

[913] Gulf Cooperation Council, الأمانة العامة لمجلس التعاون لدول الخليج العربية. https://www.gcc-sg.org/en-us/Pages/default.aspx.

[914] *Al Jazeera*, "Saudi Arabia, UAE, Egypt, Bahrain Cut Ties to Qatar", 5 June 2017. https://www.aljazeera.com/news/2017/6/5/saudi-arabia-uae-egypt-bahrain-cut-ties-to-qatar.

[915] *France 24*, "Saudis give Egypt 'blank cheque' to fight Brotherhood", 22 Aug 2013. https://www.france24.com/en/20130822-saudis-give-egypt-blank-cheque-fight-muslim-brotherhood

[916] Counter Extremism Project, Muslim Brotherhood in Qatar, 2024. https://www.counterextremism.com/content/muslim-brotherhood-qatar.

[917] Ramani, S., "The Qatar blockade is over, but the Gulf crisis lives on", *Foreign Policy*, 23 Aug 2024. https://foreignpolicy.com/2021/01/27/qatar-blockade-gcc-divisions-turkey-libya-palestine/.

[918] *AP News*, "Qatar suggests cyberattack emanated from a Gulf neighbor", 20 July 2017. https://apnews.com/general-news-2daeb8fbb65b4ffd98b4f06b6d53be5c. Al Jazeera, "Cyberattack against Qatar puts fake news in focus", 25 May 2017. https://www.aljazeera.com/news/2017/5/25/cyberattack-against-qatar-puts-fake-news-in-focus.

[919] *BBC News*, "Qatar crisis: Saudi Arabia and allies restore diplomatic ties with Emirate", 4 Jan 2021. https://www.bbc.com/news/world-middle-east-55538792.

4.30.2 Threat Actors

Strong evidence indicates that the United Arab Emirates (UAE) initiated the FIMI attack on Qatar. Based on US intelligence assessments, the senior UAE officials may have discussed the plan, though it remains uncertain whether the UAE directly executed the cyberattacks or outsourced them.[920]

Moreover, the FBI investigation linked the spread of fake messages to Russian hackers, likely freelancers.[921] These hackers built the technical infrastructure for the disinformation operation. However, the FBI found no evidence directly connecting the Russian government to the operation. Investigators believe that either Saudi Arabia or the UAE may have hired these hackers.[922]

In addition to the cyberattack, a coordinated digital campaign on Twitter[923] was launched by a coalition that included religious clerics, television anchors, political figures and members of the Saudi royal family.[924] This coalition's efforts appear to have been part of a broader strategy aimed at creating internal divisions within Qatar and damaging its international reputation. The relationship between these actors suggests a coordinated effort to amplify disinformation, with the broader objective of diplomatically and economically isolating Qatar.[925]

The disinformation campaign further involved US-based public relations firms, such as Andreae & Associates and the Podesta Group, which were reportedly engaged to produce and disseminate anti-Qatar propaganda. Additionally, Saudi Arabian entities, including the Saudi American Public Relations Affairs Committee (SAPRAC) and the Saudi Ministry of Interior, actively promoted disinformation through various channels. Social media platforms, notably Twitter and Facebook, were leveraged by a combination of genuine users, inauthentic accounts and even journalists to propagate the campaign's narratives.[926]

---

[920] *The Irish Times*, "United Arab Emirates denies hacking of Qatari news agency", 17 July 2017. https://www.irishtimes.com/news/world/middle-east/united-arab-emirates-denies-hacking-of-qatari-news-agency-1.3157600. Woollacott, Emma, "UAE planted fake news, US officials claim", *Forbes*, 17 July 2017. https://www.forbes.com/sites/emmawoollacott/2017/07/17/uae-planted-fake-news-us-officials-claim/.

[921] Prokupecz, E.P., and L. Shimon, "CNN exclusive: US suspects Russian hackers planted fake news behind Qatar crisis", CNN, 6 June 2017. https://www.cnn.com/2017/06/06/politics/russian-hackers-planted-fake-news-qatar-crisis/index.html.

[922] Wintour, P., "Russian hackers to blame for sparking Qatar crisis, FBI inquiry finds", *The Guardian*, 7 June 2017. https://www.theguardian.com/world/2017/jun/07/russian-hackers-qatar-crisis-fbi-inquiry-saudi-arabia-uae.

[923] Alli, A., "Khaleeji Weaponization of Twitter: Case of Qatari Blockade", Hamad Bin Khalifa University, 2019.

[924] Wintour, Patrick, "Qatar's neighbours dismiss Emirate's response to list of demands", *The Guardian*, 5 July 2017. https://www.theguardian.com/world/2017/jul/05/qatar-accuses-saudi-arabia-of-forcing-it-to-surrender-sovereignty

[925] Jones, op. cit., 2022.

[926] Ibid.

4.30.3 Presumed Objectives

The campaign against Qatar seems to have been carefully timed and strategically designed to achieve four key objectives: discredit Qatar, distract from other regional issues, instil dismay and isolate the country diplomatically and economically. The alignment with President Trump's visit to Riyadh suggests a deliberate attempt to exploit the occasion and influence US policy towards Qatar.

President Trump's vocal condemnation of terrorism during his visit likely emboldened Qatar's adversaries, creating a favourable environment for their disinformation campaign.[927] His subsequent remarks, which appeared to blame Qatar and justify the blockade, reinforced the narrative that Qatar was a state sponsor of terrorism, lending credibility to the campaign against it.[928] The four main objectives were as follows:

- T0075.001: Discredit—The campaign aimed to damage Qatar's reputation, particularly among key influencers like the US President. To achieve this, a false narrative was constructed, portraying Qatar as a state sponsor of terrorism. This narrative was fuelled by fabricated news, such as the alleged speech by the Emir praising Islamist groups, and further amplified through a coordinated disinformation campaign. By tarnishing Qatar's image, the attackers appeared to seek the erosion of trust among its allies, potentially creating a pretext for punitive actions.
- T0077: Distract—The operation used bots and social media manipulation to blur the lines between truth and falsehood, creating a chaotic information environment. This deliberate distraction shielded the perpetrators, hindered Qatar's defence, sowed confusion and further weakened Qatar's position.
- T0078: Dismay—The attackers deliberately spread negativity and distrust towards Qatar, aiming to instil a sense of hopelessness and despair among its people and potential allies. This psychological warfare tactic aimed to weaken Qatar's resolve, making it more vulnerable to external pressures and less likely to receive support. Ultimately, the attackers sought to portray Qatar as isolated and vulnerable, furthering their agenda of isolating the nation on the global stage.
- T0079: Divide—The incident created a clear divide within the GCC, with Saudi Arabia, the UAE, Bahrain and Egypt on one side, and Qatar on the other.

[927] Mindock, Clark, "Donald Trump Accuses Qatar of Funding Terrorism 'at Very High Level,'" *The Independent,* 9 June 2017. https://www.independent.co.uk/news/world/americas/us-politics/trump-qatar-terrorism-funding-saudi-arabia-gulf-accusation-very-high-level-a7782896.html.

[928] MacDonald, Alex, "Qatar blockade: What caused it and why is it coming to an end?", *Middle East Eye,* 5 Jan 2021. https://www.middleeasteye.net/news/qatar-blockade-saudi-arabia-lift-cause-end.

4.30.4 Incidents and Observables

Hackers launched a multi-pronged attack to damage Qatar's reputation by planting fake statements in the QNA news channel, social media[929] and email accounts[930]amplified by bots and trolls on social media. Key observables of this FIMI attack include:

- The significant amplification of inflammatory hashtags like #QatarTerrorist and #AlJazeeraInsultsKingSalman by bot accounts points toward coordinated inauthentic behaviour, a typical characteristic of FIMI campaigns.
- The dissemination of doctored images, such as the fabricated photo of the Qatari Emir and misleading infographics, further aligned with FIMI tactics.
- The coordinated bot activity spreading anti-Qatar narratives, especially those associating Qatar with terrorism and discrediting its media, indicated a deliberate attempt to shape public opinion in line with FIMI objectives.

4.30.5 Targets

The primary victim of this disinformation campaign was Qatar, which the campaign sought to isolate diplomatically, damage its reputation and portray it as a pariah state supporting terrorism. The ultimate goals were to force Qatar to comply with the demands of the blockading countries, alter its foreign policy, and potentially influence other countries to join the blockade of Qatar.[931]

4.30.6 Tactics, Techniques and Procedures

The attackers used a coordinated strategy across different platforms to manipulate information, indicating a sophisticated campaign. They combined cyberattacks, social media manipulation and traditional media outlets to achieve their goals.

Evidence of TTPs and their corresponding DISARM codes:

- T0085.002: Develop false or altered documents—80% of the content originated from a single IP address in the UAE within a short period suggesting potential attempts to inflate the number of views artificially.

---

[929] *BBC News*, "Qatar crisis: UAE denies hacking news agency", 17 July 2017. https://www.bbc.com/news/world-middle-east-40630602.

[930] Twitter (now X), "#Qatarterrorist Search Results", 24 Oct 2020. https://twitter.com/hashtag/qatarterrorist?src=hashtag_click.

[931] Doha News, "Hackers take aim at Qatar by publishing fake news on QNA", 24 May 2017. https://dohanews.co/hackers-take-aim-at-qatar-by-publishing-fake-news-on-qna-2/.

- T0085.003: Develop inauthentic news articles—Targeted QNA's infrastructure to insert fabricated news reports.
- TA11, T0123: Controlling the information environment—Offensive cyberspace operations disrupted access to accurate information and flooded the online space with false narratives.
- T0118: Amplify existing narrative—Twitter bots promoted negative narratives about Qatar. Automated accounts inflated negative content volume.
- T0086.003: Develop fake image content—Doctored images and memes likely used to create fake profiles for misinformation spread.
- T0090: Create inauthentic accounts—Bot accounts amplified hashtags and spread anti-Qatar narratives.
- T0049.002, T0104.005: Flood existing hashtags—Hashtags like #QatarTerrorist and #AlJazeeraInsultsKingSalman were flooded to amplify the negative narrative.
- T0081.001: Find echo chambers—Coordinated bot activity and hashtags exploited echo chambers, reinforcing anti-Qatar sentiments.
- T0048, T0135, T0066: Harassment campaign—Cyberbullying, spamming and doxxing targeted opponents of UAE policies.
- T0140, T0148.001: Boycott and cancel opponents—Fabricated evidence and fake quotes were used to smear the Qatari government's reputation.
- T0111.001: Mainstream TV channels—Qatari state television was used to disseminate fake news.
- T0104.001: Mainstream social networks and T0114.001: social media—Twitter and Instagram were heavily exploited.

4.30.7 Channels

The attackers strategically spread their false information using both online and offline channels. They began by hacking into the QNA, a trusted source of information, to publish fake news that portrayed the Qatari leader in a negative light. They disseminated these falsehoods by leveraging social media platforms, such as Twitter using automated bots and fake accounts (trolls) to push anti-Qatar hashtags and messages, creating an illusion of widespread public outrage. By creating documentaries and other materials that falsely portrayed Qatar as a supporter of terrorism and by pressuring politicians and influential figures to adopt this negative view, the attackers executed a coordinated campaign that showcased the sophistication and broad reach of their disinformation efforts against Qatar.[932]

[932] Jones, op. cit., 2022.

4.30.8 Languages

The campaign was primarily in Arabic and English, aimed at audiences in both the Middle East and the West. Nonetheless, due to the widespread reach of social media platforms, it's possible that the false information also spread in other languages to reach a wider audience.

4.30.9 Effectiveness

The attack on Qatar effectively achieved its objectives through a strategic and coordinated approach. First, by exploiting existing regional tensions, the attackers were able to amplify their narratives, making them resonate more strongly with those already predisposed to view Qatar negatively.[933] Then, they targeted key influencers on social media, ensuring that the disinformation reached a broad and influential audience. As a result, evidence indicates that the campaign successfully triggered fear, anger and distrust toward Qatar, as reflected in social media sentiment and news comments.[934]

Moreover, the campaign contributed to a change in public opinion against Qatar influencing policymakers' views. The narratives pushed by the attackers may have played a significant role in the diplomatic isolation and blockade imposed on Qatar. The attackers framed Qatar as an imminent danger to regional security, suggesting that they needed to act immediately to protect against this threat. This urgency heightened emotional responses, especially fear and anger, as people felt compelled to respond quickly and decisively against the perceived danger.

By exploiting existing tensions and spreading fear-inducing disinformation, the attackers successfully triggered strong emotions. They targeted influential figures to amplify their narratives and used emotionally charged language to provoke intense reactions. These strategies made the campaign highly effective in manipulating public sentiment and achieving its objectives.

4.30.10 Countermeasures

After the cyberattack on the QNA, the Qatari government took immediate steps to counter the disinformation campaign launched against it. The Qatari government quickly issued a statement denying the fabricated quotes attributed to the Emir. To

---

[933] *BBC News*, "Qatar crisis: Saudi Arabia and allies restore diplomatic ties with emirate", 4 Jan 2021.
https://www.bbc.com/news/world-middle-east-55538792.

[934] Sherman, Ryan, "Sophisticated New Disinformation Campaign Targets Qatar", *Coda Story*, 10 July 2020. https://www.codastory.com/disinformation/disinfo-campaign-qatar/.

prevent further spread of disinformation, both the Arabic and English versions of the QNA website were taken offline.[935]

The FBI investigated the hacking incident. By involving a reputable investigative agency like the FBI, Qatar bolstered its claims that the information was fabricated. Academic researchers also investigated the disinformation campaign, exposing the tactics used and the actors involved.[936]

4.30.11 Conclusions and Recommendations

The 2017 Qatar crisis illustrates how coordinated disinformation campaigns can be destructive. Attackers used cyberattacks, manipulated social media and carried out influence operations to isolate and weaken Qatar. They aimed to harm Qatar's reputation, erode trust among its allies and pressure the country to change its foreign policy. The campaign instilled fear, anger and distrust toward Qatar while shifting public opinion against it, likely influencing policymakers' views. Ultimately, Saudi Arabia, the UAE, Bahrain and Egypt blockaded Qatar.

Qatar responded promptly by denying the fabricated information and initiating an FBI investigation. Although these actions helped mitigate some damage, the campaign continued to impact regional relations for years. The Qatar case study emphasises the importance of international cooperation in combating disinformation and highlights the need for robust strategies to counter sophisticated attacks that blend online and offline tactics.

This case reveals that even well-established states are vulnerable to information warfare in the digital age. Cyberattacks and disinformation campaigns constantly evolve. Developing new technologies and methods to detect and counter disinformation is crucial to stay ahead of these evolving threats. This includes investing in artificial intelligence, machine learning and other cutting-edge tools for identifying patterns, analysing data and predicting future trends. By integrating proactive and reactive measures, states and institutions can strengthen their resilience against cyberattacks like the one Qatar experienced, mitigating the impact of disinformation campaigns and safeguarding democratic processes.

---

[935] Government Communications Office, "Qatar marks one year since QNA hack", 24 May 2018. https://www.gco.gov.qa/en/top-news/qatar-marks-one-year-since-qna-hack/.

[936] Ibid. See also Ulrichsen, Kristian Coates, "The coup that never was: How a disinformation campaign created the illusion of political chaos in Qatar", *Responsible Statecraft*, 7 May 2020. https://responsiblestatecraft.org/2020/05/07/the-coup-that-never-was-how-a-disinformation-campaign-chaos-in-qatar/.

4.31 The Role of FIMI in Iraq's Tishreen Protests

4.31.1 Introduction

This case study investigates the impact of FIMI during the Iraqi protests of 2019–2020, known as the October Uprising or the Tishreen (October in Arabic) protests, marking a significant moment of civil unrest in Iraq.[937] Driven by widespread discontent over corruption, unemployment and inadequate public services, these protests became a battleground between Iran and Saudi Arabia.[938]

The movement surged through Iraq, particularly in the central and southern regions, fuelled by young people and civil activists. Its decentralised, leaderless structure set it apart.[939] Although the protest initially succeeded in removing the Prime Minister, persistent political deadlock and the perception of unchanged conditions led to continued demonstrations.[940] Evidence suggests that disinformation campaigns significantly exacerbated tensions and hindered the protesters' objectives.[941]

The FIMI campaign appeared to target domestic institutions.[942] Hashtags like "I am Iraqi, and the parliament doesn't represent me" likely fostered distrust in the Iraqi parliament, potentially undermining its legitimacy.[943] America's visible intervention risked inflaming Iraqi sensitivities to foreign meddling. Actors spreading conspiracy theories, such as the false claim that the US supported the protests, likely aimed to discredit the demonstrations by portraying them as instruments of American foreign policy rather than genuine grassroots movements.[944]

This case study explores how Saudi Arabia used disinformation, spread through bot networks and fake social media accounts, to portray Iran as the instigator of the

[937] BBC News, "The Iraq Protests Explained in 100 and 500 Words", 28 Nov 2019. https://www.bbc.com/news/world-middle-east-50595212

[938] Ibid.

[939] Al-Shakeri, Hayder, "The Aspirations and Disillusionment of Iraq's Youth", Chatham House—International Affairs Think Tank, 2022. https://www.chathamhouse.org/2022/07/aspirations-and-disillusionment-iraqs-youth.

[940] Al-Habbal, Jinan, "Prospects of Political Change: Reflections on Thawrat Tishreen and Activism in Lebanon", Middle East Center, London School of Economics, 7 Aug 2023. https://blogs.lse.ac.uk/mec/2023/08/07/prospects-of-political-change-reflections-on-thawrat-tishreen-and-activism-in-lebanon/.

[941] al-Sarray, Hussam, "Stories from Iraq's Squares of Protest as Told by the Cameras of the 'Daredevils'", 2 Mar 2021. https://assafirarabi.com/en/36367/2021/03/02/stories-from-iraqs-squares-of-protest-as-told-by-the-cameras-of-the-daredevils/.

[942] Berger, Miriam, and Mustafa Salim. "Iraq's Military Is Spreading Fake News About the Protests—and Iraqis Are Laughing Back", *The Washington Post*, 18 Nov 2019. https://www.washingtonpost.com/world/2019/11/18/iraqs-military-is-spreading-fake-news-about-protests-iraqis-are-laughing-back/.

[943] Jones, op. cit., 2022.

[944] France 24, "Tech-Savvy Activists Debunk Fake News Engulfing Iraq Protests", 26 Oct 2019. https://www.france24.com/en/20191026-tech-savvy-activists-debunk-fake-news-engulfing-iraq-protests.

violence and undermine its support in Iraq. By flooding social media with anti-Iran propaganda and promoting pro-Saudi hashtags, the kingdom aimed to shift public sentiment against Iran and solidify its own influence in Iraq.[945]

4.31.2 Threat Actors

Although the protests originated from genuine concerns, foreign interventions intensified anti-Iran sentiment, bolstering Saudi-aligned groups and pushing pro-Iranian factions to the margins. These protests reflected a true public expression sentiment. Researchers have identified numerous Saudi-linked accounts as critical players in this influence campaign. These accounts amplified anti-Iran narratives, promoting hashtags like "save the Iraqi ppl" and "Iraq Revolts"[946] to frame the protests as a popular uprising against Iranian influence and steering online discussions to align with Saudi foreign policy objectives.[947]

Additionally, researchers have found strong indications of potential Iranian involvement, particularly in campaigns promoting pro-Sadr messages on social media and countering anti-American rhetoric to bolster al-Sadr's image as an Iraqi nationalist, although direct evidence, such as financial transactions or intercepted communications, remains elusive.[948]

4.31.3 Presumed Objectives

This campaign appears to have been designed to achieve the following objectives:

- T0075: Dismiss—The campaigns sought to discredit the legitimacy of the protests and the Iraqi government, dismissing the genuine complaints of the people and their demands for reform.[949]
- T0076: Distort—By manipulating narratives and spreading misinformation about the protests and Iran's role, the campaign aimed to distort the reality on the ground, creating confusion and undermining public trust.
- T0066: Degrade adversary (Iran)—The consistent focus on anti-Iran hashtags and narratives, portraying Iran as the primary antagonist behind Iraq's problems, clearly aimed to diminish Iran's influence and reputation in the region.

[945] Rubin, Alissa J., "Iraqis Rise Against a Reviled Occupier: Iran", *The New York Times*, 4 Nov 2019. https://www.nytimes.com/2019/11/04/world/middleeast/iraq-protests-iran.html.

[946] Acho, Wendy R. [@AchoWendyR]. *X* (Formerly Twitter), 4 Nov 2019. https://x.com/AchoWendyR/status/1191003527084171269.

[947] Jones, op. cit.

[948] Ibid.

[949] Crisis Group, "Iraq's Tishreen Uprising: From Barricades to the Ballot Box", 29 Sept 2021. https://www.crisisgroup.org/middle-east-north-africa/gulf-and-arabian-peninsula/iraq/223-iraqs-tishreen-uprising-barricades-ballot-box.

- T0140: Cause harm (to protesters and pro-Iranian factions)—The violence incited against protesters and the demonisation of pro-Iran groups suggest an intent to cause harm and instil fear, thereby suppressing dissent and consolidating power for those aligned with the disinformation campaign's objectives.

4.31.4 Incidents and Observables

There is evidence to suggest that coordinated behaviour aimed at manipulating the narrative surrounding the Iraqi protests included the following:

- Sudden trending of #save_the_Iraqi_ppl by new accounts indicates early manipulation of online discourse during the Iraqi protests.[950] It showed how newly created inauthentic accounts amplified a specific narrative to counter Iranian influence by promoting anti-Iran sentiments.
- Pro-Saudi accounts dominating #Iraq_Revolts demonstrated continuous manipulation throughout the uprising. It showed how seemingly organic hashtags were co-opted by accounts promoting pro-Saudi content, furthering the campaign's goal of advancing Saudi geopolitical interests.
- Hashtag "I am Iraqi, and the Parliament Doesn't Represent Me"[951] pushed by anti-Iran accounts reflected a disinformation campaign following the Iraqi parliament's vote on US troops. It suggested an effort to redirect genuine protests toward a narrative focused on Iranian influence, aligning with the objective to limit Iranian sway.
- Network of accounts promoting anti-Qatar narratives: On 25 November 2019, the Arabic hashtag "Qatar is against the people of Iraq"[952] trended, revealing a disinformation campaign targeting Qatar. This coordinated effort appeared designed to discredit Qatar by inaccurately associating it with Iran. Such actions seem intended to undermine Qatar and potentially affect its relations with Iraq.
- Sudden surge of accounts praising Moqtada al-Sadr—highlights a disinformation campaign aimed at promoting al-Sadr's viewpoint and anti-American

[950] قناة 24 السعودية [@Saudi24]. "تقرير / من لبنان إلى العراق.. ثورات عارمة في وجه قاسم سليماني. #السعودية #العراق #لبنان_ينتفض #ما_وراء_الحدث"", *X* (formerly Twitter), 2019. https://x.com/Saudi24/status/118604139781369 8560.

[951] Kabi, Ede [@EdeKabi]. "العراق_ينتقض انا عراقي والبرلمان الحالي لا يمثلني#" I am Iraqi and the present parliament don't represent me'", X (formerly Twitter), 2020. https://x.com/EdeKabi/status/121420436 5495525376.

[952] نجيب غلاب" [@najeebghallab]. "ومن مراقبة عيال قطر يتجاهلون انتفاضة الشعب العراقي رغم انها عمليا انتفاضة تلقائية ووطنية ضد كهنوت الطغيان الفارسي والفساد ومن اجل الدولة وحرية الانسان...", X (formerly Twitter), 2019. https://x.com/najeebghallab/status/117 9529884147822592.

sentiment. The hashtags "Support Moqtada"[953] and "With You, Oh Son of al-Sadr" emerged following a rallying post on a popular Facebook account.[954] Analysis of 5,100 unique accounts using these hashtags revealed that 17% were created on 6 February 2020, suggesting a coordinated effort to bolster pro-al-Sadr anti-American narratives.[955]

4.31.5 Targets

Beyond targeting the Iraqi population, these disinformation campaigns appeared to pursue specific objectives against regional actors. Iran was repeatedly discredited and portrayed as a destabilising force, likely with the aim of diminishing its influence. Similarly, a campaign to tarnish Qatar's image was evident, intended to undermine its reputation. Within Iraq itself, the campaigns sought to marginalise groups aligned with Iran, often through fearmongering and incitement of violence.[956]

4.31.6 Tactics, Techniques and Procedures

Below we list the TTPs and their corresponding DISARM codes in the Iraqi disinformation campaigns:

- The use of hashtags such as #save_the_Iraqi_ppl and #Iraq_Revolts (T0104.005, T0104.006) aimed to distort the narrative (T0076) and degrade Iran's image (T0066) by framing the protests as a reaction against Iranian interference.
- Flooding existing hashtags: Pushing the hashtag "I am Iraqi, and the Parliament Doesn't Represent Me" through anti-Iran accounts (T0049.002, T0104.005) sought to dismiss the legitimacy of the protests (T0075) and redirect them towards an anti-Iran narrative.

---

953 khulio12 [@khulio12]. X (formerly Twitter), 7 Feb 2020. https://x.com/khulio12/status/1225838519484112897.

954 Albasheer, Ahmed [@ahmedalbasheer1], "'Iraqi pm Adel Abdul Mahdi: "it's time to go home now" Iraq: https://t.co/qrAt7blyCB'", X, 2019. https://x.com/ahmedalbasheer1/status/1191065797772414982

955 Jones, Marc Owen, *Digital Authoritarianism in the Middle East: Deception, Disinformation and Social Media*, Oxford University Press, 2022.

956 Al-Monitor, "Shadow campaign: Global influence op targets Qatar in wartime", 1 July 2024. https://www.al-monitor.com/originals/2024/07/shadow-campaign-global-influence-op-targets-qatar-wartime. See also Shea, Joey, and Ruba al-Hassani, "Hate Speech, Social Media and Political Violence in Iraq: Virtual Civil Society and Upheaval", The Tahir Institute, 11 Feb 2021. https://timep.org/2021/02/11/hate-speech-social-media-and-political-violence-in-iraq-virtual-civil-society-and-upheaval/.

- A network of accounts promoting anti-Qatar narratives (T0135.001, T0079) furthered the goal of degrading Iran (T0066) by associating Qatar with Iran and discrediting both.
- Sudden surge of pro-al-Sadr accounts: The sudden appearance of numerous accounts praising Moqtada al-Sadr (T0090, T0136) aimed to cause harm to protesters and pro-Iran factions (T0078) by bolstering pro-al-Sadr and anti-American narratives.
- Trending #save_the_Iraqi_ppl with new accounts: The rapid trending of this hashtag by newly created accounts (T0090, T0049) served to distort the narrative (T0076) and degrade Iran's image (T0066) by amplifying specific viewpoints.
- Pro-Saudi accounts dominating #Iraq_Revolts: The dominance of pro-Saudi accounts in this hashtag (T0049.002) contributed to distorting the narrative (T0076) by promoting a pro-Saudi perspective.
- The use of social media platforms like X and Meta aligned with the TTP of using media-sharing networks (T0105).
- The dissemination of disinformation and the shaping of public narratives are directly associated with the strategic goal of distortion (T0076).
- The campaign's objectives to discredit the protests and the Iraqi government contributed to creating an atmosphere of fear and uncertainty, aligning with the strategic goal of dismay (T0078).
- The anti-Iran narratives and the demonisation of pro-Iran groups indicated an intent to polarise public opinion (T0135.004), creating an "us-versus-them" dynamic.

4.31.7 Channels

Disinformation campaigns in Iraq exploited social media, notably X and Meta, to spread their messages. For example, on X, they leveraged hashtags like #save_the_Iraqi_ppl, #Iraq_Revolts and #I_am_Iraqi_and_the_parliament_doesn't_represent_me to gain traction. Furthermore, hashtags like #Qatar_is_against_the_people_of_Iraq aimed to sow discord and fuel anti-Qatar sentiment.[957] The FIMI campaign also harnessed persuasive hashtags like "Support Moqtada" and "With You, Oh Son of al-Sadr" on both X and Meta. These hashtags, infused with religious undertones, effectively mobilised support for the cleric Moqtada al-Sadr.

[957] Jones, op. cit.

4.31.8 Languages

The primary language used in the FIMI campaign in Iraq was Arabic, Farsi and some tweets were written in both Arabic and English, suggesting an attempt to appeal to a broader international audience.

4.31.9 Effectiveness

Assessing the success of FIMI campaigns presents notable challenges, as it requires examining their reach, engagement and impact on public perception and behaviour. Regarding the Iraqi protests, the success of these campaigns is closely connected to their complex goals, which include distortion, dismissal, degradation and harm.

The campaign successfully amplified anti-Iran sentiment within Iraq, as evidenced by a surge in online discussions criticising Iran's role in the country. By associating Iran with instability and interference, the campaign led many Iraqis to question Iran's motives and support for Iraqi political groups. The frequent appearance of anti-Iran hashtags and rhetoric online further indicated that this narrative gained considerable traction.

The anti-Qatar campaign, though smaller in scale, effectively damaged Qatar's reputation by linking it to Iran and spreading conspiracy theories about its involvement in the protests. This likely fuelled suspicion towards Qatar, potentially harming its diplomatic efforts and undermining its soft power in Iraq.

Promoting pro-Saudi sentiments proved more challenging. While the campaign attempted to portray Saudi Arabia as a supportive ally, pre-existing scepticism towards Saudi Arabia's regional ambitions likely hindered these efforts.

Beyond the general Iraqi population, the campaign specifically targeted Iran, aiming to discredit it as a destabilising force. It also sought to tarnish Qatar's image and undermine its influence. Within Iraq, the campaign focused on suppressing pro-Iran factions through fear-mongering and inciting violence.

The campaign strategically exploited pre-existing tensions within Iraqi society. It fuelled anxieties about external influences, framing Iran as a threat to Iraqi sovereignty. It capitalised on public frustration with corruption, portraying the protests as a struggle against corrupt elites influenced by Iran. Furthermore, the campaign's focus on anti-Iran and anti-Shia narratives indicated a deliberate attempt to exploit sectarian divides and mobilise support along religious lines.

4.31.10 Countermeasures

During the Iraqi protests, researchers and the social media platform Twitter worked to counter Saudi-led disinformation campaigns and combat the FIMI attack by suspending numerous accounts identified as participating in the spread of false information. This action directly limited the reach and impact of the campaign by removing malicious actors from the platform.[958]

Researchers employed network analysis techniques to track and reveal the coordinated activities of accounts engaged in spreading disinformation. By mapping the relationships among these accounts, they could identify behavioural patterns that indicated their inauthentic nature and coordinated manipulation efforts.[959]

Researchers also conducted a corpus analysis to understand the language and strategies used in the disinformation campaign, hoping to anticipate and mitigate future tactics.[960] Various organisations contributed to these efforts. The UNDP in Iraq partnered with local groups like Tech4Peace to track and debunk fake news and supported initiatives promoting social cohesion by combating hate speech and misinformation. The United Nations Assistance Mission for Iraq (UNAMI) assisted the Iraqi electoral commission in combating misinformation during elections and provided strategies to protect electoral integrity. The Iraqi government itself formed committees to investigate protest-related violations, notably the "Fact-Finding Committee" established by then-Prime Minister Mustafa al-Kadhimi.[961]

4.31.11 Conclusions and Recommendations

This case study reveals how Saudi-linked actors exploited the 2019–2020 Iraqi protests to spread disinformation and advance their geopolitical interests. By leveraging social media and sophisticated tactics, these actors amplified anti-Iran sentiment, destabilised the political landscape and fuelled societal divisions. This disinformation campaign had a significant impact on the ground, contributing to increased polarisation, violence and the erosion of trust in legitimate political processes.

To counter such threats, social media platforms must invest in advanced technology and human expertise to detect and remove disinformation. Governments and international organisations should prioritise media literacy initiatives, empowering citizens to critically analyse information. Crucially, strong legal frameworks

---

958 Ibid.

959 Ibid.

960 Jones, op. cit.

961 Amnesty International, "Iraq: Four years after Tishreen protests, no justice for state and militia violence", 27 Sept 2023. https://www.amnesty.org/en/latest/news/2023/09/iraq-four-years-after-tishreen-protests-no-justice-for-state-and-militia-violence/. See also Human Rights Watch, "'We Might Call You in at Any Time': Free Speech Under Threat in Iraq", 15 June 2020. https://www.hrw.org/report/2020/06/15/we-might-call-you-any-time/free-speech-under-threat-iraq. Human Rights Watch, "'To Sleep the Law': Violence Against Protesters and Unaccountable Perpetrators in Iraq", 29 Nov 2022. https://www.hrw.org/report/2022/11/29/sleep-law/violence-against-protesters-and-unaccountable-perpetrators-iraq.

are needed to hold perpetrators accountable, especially when they threaten national security or democracy.

While the campaign successfully amplified anti-Iran sentiment and damaged Qatar's image, its success in promoting pro-Saudi sentiment remains unclear. This highlights the complexities of disinformation campaigns and the need for nuanced analysis. Social media platforms must invest in advanced technology, such as network analysis and corpus analysis, to detect and remove disinformation. Platforms like Twitter suspended accounts involved in such activities.

Promoting transparent and inclusive political dialogue within Iraq is also crucial to address the root causes of social unrest and reduce vulnerability to external manipulation. By addressing the underlying causes of social unrest, promoting media literacy and holding perpetrators accountable, Iraq can strengthen its resilience against foreign manipulation and safeguard its democratic processes.

4.32 India's Disinformation Campaign Following the Pulwama Attack

4.32.1 Introduction

The India-Pakistan rivalry,[962] though geographically removed from Europe and the West, casts a long shadow over global security. Since their turbulent partition,[963] these nuclear-armed neighbours[964] have been involved in both conventional military conflicts and advanced information warfare. At its core, the conflict is a complex struggle for power and control over the narrative, involving state and non-state actors, civil society activists and local communities, both domestically and internationally.[965]

[962] *Al Jazeera*, "Timeline: 75 Years of Partition and India-Pakistan Tensions", 12 Aug 2022. https://www.aljazeera.com/news/2022/8/12/timeline-75-years-of-partition-and-india-pakistan-tensions.

[963] Phillips, Sean, "Why was British India Partitioned in 1947? Considering the role of Muhammad Ali Jinnah", Faculty of History, University of Oxford, n.d. https://www.history.ox.ac.uk/why-was-british-india-partitioned-in-1947-considering-the-role-of-muhammad-ali-0.

[964] Robock, A., Owen B. Toon, Charles G. Bardeen, Lili Xia, Hans M. Kristensen, Matthew McKinzie, Richard J. Peterson, Cheryl S. Harrison, Nicole S. Lovenduski and Richard P. Turco, "How an India-Pakistan Nuclear War Could Start—and Have Global Consequences", *Bulletin of the Atomic Scientists*, Vol. 75, No. 6, Nov 2019, pp. 273–279.

[965] Kuszewska, A., "The India-Pakistan Conflict in Kashmir and Human Rights in the Context of Post-2019 Political Dynamics", *Asian Affairs*, Vol. 53, No. 1, 2022, pp. 198–217.

Specifically, India appears to be actively employing its extensive media network to portray Pakistan as a significant security threat, both regionally and globally.[966] Reports indicate that disinformation campaigns targeting Pakistan[967] are coordinated across various platforms, including social media, websites and even Bollywood productions.[968]

This narrative emphasises concerns over the security of Pakistan's nuclear arsenal, particularly fears that terrorist groups could acquire nuclear materials or weapons.[969] Against this backdrop, the following case study examines the 2019 Pulwama incident;[970] this attack marked a significant escalation in the long conflict between India and Pakistan[971] and serves as an example of modern hybrid warfare, demonstrating the interplay of physical and cyberwarfare attacks.

This incident unfolded, on 14 February 2019, when a Jaish-e-Mohammed (JeM) suicide bomber attacked a convoy of Indian security personnel, killing dozens.[972] The perpetrator, Adil Ahmad Dar,[973] had reportedly joined JeM shortly before the attack, possibly motivated by his alleged experiences of police brutality.[974]

---

[966] EU DisinfoLab, "Indian Chronicles: deep dive into a 15-year operation targeting the EU and UN to serve Indian interests", 9 Dec 2020. https://www.disinfo.eu/publications/indian-chronicles-deep-dive-into-a-15-year-operation-targeting-the-eu-and-un-to-serve-indian-interests/.

[967] Hamid, Summra, "The battle of bytes: Uncontrollable social media propaganda of India", *Pakistan Today*, 9 June 2024. https://www.pakistantoday.com.pk/2024/06/09/the-battle-of-bytes-uncontrollable-social-media-propaganda-of-india/.

[968] Ishfaq, Sarmad, "Opinion—Pakistan Hatred Sells in Modi's India", *E-International Relations*, 4 July 2024. https://www.e-ir.info/2024/07/04/opinion-pakistan-hatred-sells-in-modis-india/. See also Hamid, Summra, "The battle of bytes: Uncontrollable social media propaganda of India", *Pakistan Today*, 9 June 2024. https://www.pakistantoday.com.pk/2024/06/09/the-battle-of-bytes-uncontrollable-social-media-propaganda-of-india/

[969] Biswas, Soutik, "India and Pakistan came close to nuclear war: Pompeo", *BBC News*, 25 Jan 2023. https://www.bbc.com/news/world-asia-india-64396138.

[970] Masood, Bashaarat, "Recalling the Pulwama terrorist attack: what happened on Feb 14, 2019?", *The Indian Express*, 14 Feb 2024. https://indianexpress.com/article/explained/five-years-pulwama-terror-attack-recall-9161523/

[971] Gurung, S.K., "What happened at Pulwama and history of terror attacks on convoys", *The Economic Times*, 20 Feb 2019. https://economictimes.indiatimes.com/news/defence/what-happened-at-pulwama-and-history-of-terror-attacks-on-convoys/articleshow/68019194.cms.

[972] *Business Today*, "Pulwama terror attack: Death toll reaches 44; internet services suspended in Jammu", *Business Today*, 15 Feb 2019. https://www.businesstoday.in/latest/economy-politics/story/pulwama-terror-attack-death-toll-reaches-44-internet-services-suspended-in-jammu-170320-2019-02-15.

[973] *BBC News*, "Kashmir attack: Tracing the path that led to Pulwama", 30 Apr 2019. https://www.bbc.com/news/world-asia-india-47302467.

[974] Tripathi, R., and N. Dalmia, "5 years of Pulwama attack: Key conspirators based in Pakistan still at large", *The Economic Times*, 14 Feb 2024. https://economictimes.indiatimes.com/news/defence/5-years-of-pulwama-attack-key-pakistan-based-conspirators-still-elusive/articleshow/107669234.cms?from=mdr.

The attack's timing, coinciding with India's national elections, intensified the politicisation of the event.[975] Unverified reports of high casualties from the attack led to divergent narratives.[976] India's ruling party exploited the attack to bolster its nationalist agenda, while accusations of Pakistan's support for terrorism circulated widely.[977]

Following the Pulwama attack, India launched airstrikes on Balakot, Pakistan.[978] While the precise impact of the Balakot airstrikes remains disputed, India promptly declared them a resounding success. Indian officials claimed that they had eliminated "a very large number" of terrorists. Some Indian media outlets went further, estimating the death toll at 200–350 militants.[979] However, these figures remain unverified.[980] India seized on this narrative, portraying the Balakot airstrikes as pre-emptive self-defence against further terrorism[981] arguing that Pakistan's nuclear capabilities should not deter India from military action.[982]

In response, Pakistan's government and media challenged these accusations, condemning the attack and denying any involvement in the Pulwama incident. Pakistan also stated that India had failed to strike a militant camp, causing only minimal damage.[983] Subsequently, Pakistan accused India of spreading disinformation[984] to divert attention from its internal problems and justify military

[975] *BBC News*, "India election results 2019: Narendra Modi secures landslide win", 22 May 2019. https://www.bbc.com/news/world-asia-india-48347081.

[976] Bhakto, Anando, "Terror before elections: a pattern", *Frontline*, 23 July 2021. https://frontline.thehindu.com/cover-story/bogeyman-nationalism-terror-before-elections-becoming-a-pattern/article35511997.ece.

[977] Saleem, M., "Indian Disinformation Operations against Pakistan and its Implications", Centre for Strategic and Contemporary Research, 29 Dec 2021. https://cscr.pk/explore/themes/defense-security/indian-disinformation-operations-against-pakistan-and-its-implications/.

[978] Dalmia, N., "Balakot Airstrike Anniversary: When India took revenge for the Pulwama attack deep inside Pak", *The Economic Times*, 26 Feb 2024. https://economictimes.indiatimes.com/news/defence/balakot-airstrike-anniversary-when-india-took-revenge-for-the-pulwama-attack-deep-inside-pak-a-timeline/articleshow/108003786.cms?from=mdr.

[979] Moneycontrol, "Balakot Airstrike: 5 Years Since IAF Bombed Terror Camps Across LoC | Explained", YouTube video, published 26 Feb 2024. youtu.be/9aWxEPmoHzc?si = lsTfe82LBBflvlVE.

[980] CNBCTV18, "Balakot strike killed 300 terrorists, says former Pakistani diplomat", 8 Jan 2021. https://www.cnbctv18.com/india/balakot-strike-killed-300-terrorists-says-former-pakistani-diplomat-7954241.htm.

[981] Firstpost, "Pulwama Terror Attack: Jaish-e-Mohammed Terror Group Claims Responsibility", YouTube video, published 14 Feb 2019. https://www.youtube.com/watch?v=_XgVrIjDRQk&t=38s.

[982] Ruser, N., "Were India's airstrikes in Pakistan a strategy for public approval?", *The Strategist*, 28 Feb 2019. https://www.aspistrategist.org.au/were-indias-airstrikes-in-pakistan-a-strategy-for-public-approval/.

[983] *BBC News*, "Balakot: Indian air strikes target militants in Pakistan", 26 Feb 2019. https://www.bbc.com/news/world-asia-47366718.

[984] Misra, Satish, "Emerging electoral dynamics after Pulwama tragedy", *orfonline.org*, 5 Mar 2019. https://www.orfonline.org/expert-speak/emerging-electoral-dynamics-after-pulwama-tragedy-48718/.

action.[985] As a result, this tragic incident created a fertile environment for a subsequent increase in disinformation and propaganda warfare.[986]

4.32.2 Threat Actors

The attack, attributed by India to Pakistan and specifically to Jaish-e-Mohammed,[987] a Deobandi Islamist terrorist group with ties to the Taliban and al Qaeda,[988] involved various actors.[989] Government agencies and intelligence services from both India and Pakistan, along with certain factions within the ruling Indian political party (BJP), played significant roles. Non-state actors, including militant groups operating in the Kashmir region, media outlets propagating biased narratives and online individuals and groups spreading disinformation, further amplified the impact of the attack.[990]

4.32.3 Presumed Objectives

The disinformation campaign following the Pulwama attack served multiple objectives, primarily targeting public perceptions and influencing both domestic and international audiences. Through mainstream and social media platforms, India sought to reinforce its global standing and frame Pakistan as a state sponsor of terrorism. This strategy aimed to attract international support while undermining Pakistan's credibility.

Evidence suggests the campaign sought to the following:

> T0075: Dismiss—Pakistani media and officials were portrayed as unreliable sources, undermining their ability to counter Indian narratives. This is evident in the consistent discrediting of Pakistani statements and the amplification of narratives that painted Pakistan as a state sponsor of terrorism.

---

[985] PTI, "Pulwama attack: Pakistan seeks 'more evidence' from India on Jaish involvement", *The Hindu*, 27 Mar 2019. https://www.thehindu.com/news/international/pulwama-attack-pakistan-seeks-more-evidence-from-india-on-jaish-involvement/article26655099.ece.

[986] Factly, "How Authentic is Claim of Former Pak. Diplomat Confirming 300 Deaths in Balakot Airstrike?", 3 Mar 2021. https://www.youtube.com/watch?v=ZsJ-BHohXRI.

[987] Kharon, "Inside Jaish-e-Mohammed: The Networks of the Pakistani Terrorist Group behind the Deadliest Attack on Indian Forces in Kashmir", *The Brief*, 19 Feb 2019. https://brief.kharon.com/updates/inside-jaish-e-mohammed-the-networks-of-the-pakistani-terrorist-group-behind-the-deadliest-attack-on-indian-forces-in-kashmir/.

[988] BBC World Service, "The Deobandis", 2023. https://www.bbc.co.uk/programmes/p03w5z3f.

[989] European Foundation for South Asian Studies (EFSAS), "Pakistan Army and Terrorism; an Unholy Alliance". https://www.efsas.org/publications/study-papers/pakistan-army-and-terrorism;-an-unholy-alliance/.

[990] Press Trust of India (PTI), "Nearly 60 Foreign Terrorists among 243 Militants Operating in Kashmir", *India Today*, 26 June 2018. https://www.indiatoday.in/pti-feed/story/nearly-60-foreign-terrorists-among-243-militants-operating-in-kashmir-1270323-2018-06-26.

T0076: Distort—The narrative of the conflict was framed to emphasise Pakistan's aggression, often simplifying or omitting details that might complicate the picture.

T0077: Distract—The conflict served to divert public attention from domestic challenges within India, such as economic concerns, refocusing it on the external threat.

T0078: Dismay—The campaign amplified fears of Pakistani terrorism among the Indian populace, potentially exaggerating the threat. This is evident in the emotional appeals and alarmist rhetoric used by some media outlets and political figures.

T0079: Divide (implied)—While not explicitly stated, the campaign could also be interpreted as aiming to highlight internal divisions within Pakistan, portraying the nation as unstable and further undermining its international standing. This can be inferred from the emphasis on Pakistan's alleged inability to control terrorist elements within its borders.

4.32.4 Incidents and Observables

Observable evidence strongly indicates that an influence campaign was conducted both within India and internationally to manipulate political discourse and shape global perceptions following the Pulwama terror attack. These indicators include the following:

- Coordinated messaging (social media posts): The consistent use of hashtags like #PulwamaRevenge,[991] #IndiaWantsRevenge and #PulwamaAttacks across multiple platforms (Twitter, YouTube, Telegram, WhatsApp). This coordinated hashtag usage suggests a deliberate strategy to shape public perception, amplify calls for retaliation and manipulate online discourse surrounding the Pulwama attack and its aftermath.[992]
- Emotional manipulation (videos): Videos circulating on YouTube[993] and other platforms employed highly emotive language and imagery under hashtags such as #Air #PulwamaRevenge,[994] appealing to feelings of anger, grief and a desire for revenge.[995]
- Polarising content (images/memes): The spread of caricatures, memes and satirical content over Twitter illustrating India harming Pakistan inflamed existing

[991] X, "#IndiaWantsRevenge Search Results", 15 Mar 2019. https://x.com/search?src=recent_search_click&q=%23IndiaWantsRevenge.

[992] X, "#PulwamaAttacks Search Results", 13 Feb 2023. https://x.com/search?src=typed_query&q=%23PulwamaAttacks%20.

[993] Zee News, "Pulwama terror attack: This is a dastardly act done out of desperation, says MoS PMO Jitendra Singh", YouTube video, 14 Feb 2019. youtu.be/9aWxEPmoHzc?si = lsTfe82LBBflvlVE.

[994] ABP News, "India Strikes Back After Pulwama Attack", YouTube video, 26 Feb 2019. https://www.youtube.com/watch?v=QNyXgGvqIEA.

[995] Zee News, "Pulwama terror attack: People want 'revenge' from Pakistan", op. cit.

tensions. Hashtags like #IndiaStrikesPakistan, #IndiaWantsRevenge, #PulwamaRevenge and #PulwamaAttacks amplified this divisive imagery, fostering an "us vs. them" mentality. This deliberate polarisation primed the audience for manipulation, rendering them more vulnerable to the influence of false and misleading information.[996]

- Social proof (social media polls): Polls on social media further fuelled the jingoistic fervour. Questions like "Should India hit Pakistan again?" created an illusion of overwhelming public support for military action.[997] This manufactured consensus normalised the idea of retaliation, effectively pressuring the government to adopt a more aggressive stance.[998]

Amplification of nationalist sentiment (videos/state media news): Videos of Indian nationalists demanding revenge and state media reports accusing Pakistan of harbouring terrorists exploited nationalist sentiment, making the audience more receptive to manipulative messages.[999]

4.32.5 Targets

Following the Pulwama attack, the disinformation campaign strategically targeted multiple audiences to advance its objectives. Its primary focus was the Indian public, aiming to shape public sentiment, heighten nationalist fervour and influence political discourse. However, the campaign also extended its reach to the international community; by portraying Pakistan as a sponsor of terrorism and a global threat, it aimed to garner international support for India's actions and isolate Pakistan on the world stage and justify any retaliatory measures taken by India.

In addition, while not directly targeted, the campaign's divisive rhetoric and accusations indirectly impacted the Pakistani public. This approach aimed to sow discord within Pakistani society, undermine confidence in its government and potentially destabilise the country.

4.32.6 Tactics, Techniques and Procedures

The Pulwama attack and the subsequent information operation revealed a range of TTPs employed to manipulate narratives and influence public opinion. These

[996] DannyMUFC_OK [@DannyMUFC_OK], "RT POLL Pakistan Have Harboured Terrorists, Trained, Funded by Saudis and Pakistani Government. Should Modi Hit Pakistan Again? #IndiaStrikesPakistan #IndiaWantsRevenge ##PulwamaRevenge ##PulwamaAttacks", X (formerly Twitter), 5 Mar 2019. https://x.com/DannyMUFC_OK/status/1102846370816421888.

[997] Ibid.

[998] Ibid.

[999] *ABP News*, "India Strikes Back After Pulwama Attack", YouTube video, 26 Feb 2019. https://www.youtube.com/watch?v=QNyXgGvqIEA.

tactics, mapped to the DISARM framework, illustrate a coordinated effort to shape the information environment:

T0002: Facilitate state propaganda—State-controlled media played a crucial role in amplifying specific narratives and disseminating information aligned with government agendas. This is evident in the consistent portrayal of Pakistan as a state sponsor of terrorism and a global threat.

T0023: Distort facts—The information operation involved the distortion of facts, including the dissemination of unverified casualty figures and the downplaying of potential underlying causes of the attack, such as alleged human rights abuses.

T0049: Flood information space—The use of coordinated hashtags and suspected bot activity aimed to flood the information space, overwhelming genuine discourse and manipulating online conversations.

T0049.002: Hijack existing hashtags—The extensive use of existing hashtags, such as #PulwamaRevenge, enabled the attackers to hijack online conversations and inject their narratives into broader discussions.

T0066: Degrade adversary—A key tactic involved degrading the adversary, Pakistan, by portraying it as a terrorist state and a global threat, aiming to undermine its international standing and credibility.

T0086.001: Develop memes—The creation and sharing of polarising memes and caricatures served to reinforce an "us vs. them" mentality and deepen divisions between India and Pakistan.

T0087: Develop video-based content—The information operation leveraged video-based content, including emotionally manipulative videos and nationalist content, to evoke strong emotions and bypass critical thinking.

T0104.001: Mainstream social networks—The operation used mainstream social networks, such as Facebook and Twitter, to disseminate disinformation and manipulate online conversations.

T0104.005: Use hashtags—The coordinated use of hashtags enabled the attackers to amplify specific narratives and manipulate trending topics on social media.

T0115: Post content—The posting of various content, including memes, videos and emotionally charged narratives, served to flood the information space and manipulate public perceptions.

T0115.001: Share memes—The sharing of divisive memes and caricatures further fuelled polarisation and amplified existing narratives.

T0140.003: Spread hate—The information operation involved the spread of hate speech and inflammatory rhetoric against Pakistan and its people, aiming to deepen divisions and fuel animosity.

4.32.7 Channels

The disinformation campaign surrounding the Pulwama attack exploited various channels to spread its narratives and influence public opinion. Mainstream social networks such as Facebook and Twitter became fertile ground for disseminating emotionally charged content and polarising memes. Media-sharing networks, including YouTube and Instagram, facilitated the spread of manipulative videos and images designed to bypass critical thinking and fuel outrage. Traditional media, such as newspapers and television reports, also played a role, often amplifying unverified claims and biased narratives.

4.32.8 Languages

The disinformation campaign employed a multilingual strategy, using English, Urdu and Hindi across tweets and media posts to reach diverse audiences. The use of English facilitated the spread of disinformation to international audiences, while Hindi and Urdu targeted specific communities within India and Pakistan, respectively.

4.32.9 Effectiveness

Assessing the effectiveness of disinformation campaigns presents significant challenges, requiring a comprehensive evaluation of both reach and impact on public attitudes and behaviours. However, in the case of the Pulwama attack, evidence suggests that the disinformation campaign achieved many of its aims.

The campaign fuelled widespread anger, grief and fear across India. This emotional manipulation proved particularly potent in the politically charged atmosphere of India's approaching national elections. Furthermore, the campaign strategically exploited existing societal anxieties, amplifying nationalist sentiment and deep-seated biases against Pakistan, leading to a surge in Islamophobic rhetoric and violence.[1000]

The campaign actively undermined trust in information sources that offered alternative perspectives or challenged the dominant narrative. This, in turn, fuelled a surge of online harassment and violence against Kashmiris and Muslims within India, who were often scapegoated based on false information. The Pulwama disinformation campaign had profound and lasting psychological and societal effects, deepening social polarisation, reinforcing existing prejudices and eroding public trust in reliable information sources.

[1000] Ishfaq, Sarmad, "Opinion—Pakistan Hatred Sells in Modi's India", *E-International Relations*, 4 July 2024. https://www.e-ir.info/2024/07/04/opinion-pakistan-hatred-sells-in-modis-india/.

4.32.10 Countermeasures

The Pulwama attack and subsequent disinformation campaign exposed the vulnerabilities of the digital information ecosystem and the urgent need for effective countermeasures. Efforts to combat the spread of false narratives were undertaken by a diverse range of actors, including social media platforms, government agencies and independent organisations.[1001]

Twitter implemented proactive measures to moderate misleading content, identify false information and suspend accounts that promoted harmful narratives. However, encrypted platforms such as WhatsApp presented a significant challenge, as they facilitated the unchecked spread of false information and nationalist rhetoric, which exacerbated communal tensions.[1002]

India's Central Reserve Police Force (CRPF) responded by creating teams to monitor viral content, fact-check misinformation and educate personnel on detecting fake news. Fact-checking organisations such as Alt News and Boom were crucial in debunking false online claims.[1003] EU DisinfoLab[1004] uncovered sophisticated networks of fake media outlets promoting anti-Pakistan narratives, exposing the coordinated nature of the disinformation campaign and its potential international dimensions.

4.32.11 Conclusions and Recommendations

The Pulwama attack and subsequent events exposed the vulnerability of online spaces to disinformation. While platforms like Twitter (now X) took some action, encrypted platforms like WhatsApp posed significant challenges, allowing misinformation to flourish.

The disinformation surge had profound consequences. Evidence confirms that this campaign influenced public opinion, incited violence and shaped political discourse.

This incident demonstrated the urgent need for robust countermeasures. Social media platforms must enhance content moderation, investing in technology and

---

[1001] Hussain, S., Farrukh Shahzad and Adam Saud, "Analyzing the State of Digital Information Warfare Between India and Pakistan on Twittersphere", *Sage Open*, Vol. 11, No. 3, 2021.

[1002] Chaudhuri, Pooja, and Priyanka Jha. "3 out of Facebook's 7 fact-checking partners have shared misinformation post-Pulwama", *Alt News*, 18 Mar 2019. https://www.altnews.in/3-out-of-facebooks-7-fact-checking-partners-have-shared-misinformation-post-pulwama/.

[1003] Niranjankumar, Nivedita, "As CRPF Mourns Its Dead, It Also Fights Fake News: 'Our Jawans Did Not Die to Spark Communal Hatred'", *BoomLive.in*, 20 Feb 2019. https://scroll.in/article/913879/as-crpf-mourns-its-dead-it-also-fights-fake-news-our-jawans-did-not-die-to-spark-communal-hatred.

[1004] Kuchay, Bilal, "EU NGO Report Uncovers a 15-Year Disinformation Campaign", *Al Jazeera*, 11 Dec 2020. https://www.aljazeera.com/news/2020/12/11/eu-ngo-report-uncovers-a-15-year-disinformation-campaign.

human expertise to detect and remove disinformation. This includes tracking hashtags, analysing networks and detecting manipulative language. Governments and international organisations should prioritise media literacy initiatives, empowering citizens to analyse information and recognise emotional manipulation tactics critically.

Crucially, robust legal frameworks are needed to hold perpetrators accountable. Given the transnational nature of disinformation operations, international cooperation is essential. Countries should collaborate to share intelligence, develop joint strategies and engage international organisations to establish global norms for addressing disinformation.

Furthermore, to effectively combat FIMI, fostering collaboration between researchers, governments and AI specialists is crucial. Researchers can provide valuable insights into the evolving tactics of disinformation campaigns and the psychological mechanisms that make them effective. Governments can leverage these insights to inform policy and support the development of countermeasures. AI researchers can contribute by developing advanced detection tools and creating innovative solutions for identifying and mitigating the spread of disinformation. By combining their expertise, these stakeholders can create a more comprehensive and effective approach to combating FIMI and safeguarding democratic processes.

4.33 Turkey Undermines Sweden's Bid for NATO Membership

4.33.1 Introduction

In May 2022, Sweden started a process to join the North Atlantic Treaty Organisation (NATO), a defensive move that was primarily motivated by Russia's invasion of Ukraine and national concerns for Swedish sovereignty. While most NATO members welcomed Sweden's bid, Turkey did not. Evidence suggests it conducted an influence operation against the Swedish government, aiming to disorient and demoralise by crafting and amplifying narratives, including conspiracy theories, on digital platforms. These actions coincided with Sweden's ongoing negotiations to join NATO, a process Turkey opposed[1005] due to geopolitical[1006] and historical grievances,[1007] and perceived support of the Kurdistan Workers' Party (PKK).[1008] Turkey constitutes a veto player in the inter-institutional relations between the EU

[1005] https://www.npr.org/2023/07/05/1185979617/why-turkey-is-opposed-to-swedens-bid-to-join-nato.

[1006] https://www.theguardian.com/world/2023/jan/12/turkey-summons-swedish-ambassador-over-erdogan-effigy.

[1007] https://www.armenian-genocide.org/Affirmation.414/current_category.7/affirmation_detail.html + , https://www.reuters.com/article/idUSTRE62A4ZX20100311/.

[1008] https://www.reuters.com/world/europe/no-swedish-politicians-represent-kurdish-pkk-foreign-minister-says-2022-05-27/.

and NATO and, as such, did not want to allow Sweden's accession. This case study examines the period between June and December 2023, marked by heightened debates on the subject. This was further compounded by public incidents in Sweden, including Quran burnings,[1009] which intensified Turkey's influence operations and resonated deeply in Turkish politics and beyond.

To address these challenges, Sweden, Turkey and Finland signed a trilateral memorandum in June 2022, outlining commitments to assuage Turkey's concerns. Sweden implemented legislative changes, including a new anti-terrorism law that allowed for the prosecution of individuals supporting terrorist organisations.[1010] Despite these measures, Turkish President Recep Tayyip Erdogan issued new and more stringent demands,[1011] such as further extraditions and actions viewed as politically motivated and later went on to accuse Sweden of interfering in elections in Turkey.[1012] Turkey sought to depict Sweden as a terrorism supporter, particularly of the PKK, and imposed its potential veto of Sweden's NATO membership bid to reinforce this narrative.

There was no evidence supporting these claims. This disinformation campaign was alleged to be orchestrated or approved by the Turkish government due to its tightly controlled information environment.[1013] In Turkey, websites and content that contradict government narratives are often blocked, a practice enabled by the government's control over key sectors such as communications, energy and media.[1014] This control allows the government to manipulate the flow of information both directly and indirectly. These conditions created an environment to suppress information and spread falsehoods for political gain.

[1009] https://www.theguardian.com/world/2023/jul/26/russia-using-disinformation-to-imply-sweden-supported-quran-burnings.

[1010] https://www.fpri.org/multimedia/2022/06/swedens-troubles-with-turkey/.

[1011] https://www.nupi.no/en/publications/cristin-pub/sweden-s-thorny-path-into-nato-a-changing-country-is-finding-its-new-place.

[1012] https://nordicmonitor.com/2023/05/erdogan-govt-accuses-sweden-of-interfering-election-in-turkey/.

[1013] Dinçer, M., "The relation between regional power policies of Turkey and the media strategy of President Erdoğan", *Asian Journal of Middle Eastern and Islamic Studies*, Vol. 17, No. 3, 2023, pp. 277–295. https://doi.org/10.1080/25765949.2023.2267292.

[1014] Boas, T.C., "Weaving the authoritarian web: The control of internet use in nondemocratic regimes, in J. Zysman and A. Newman (eds.), *How revolutionary was the digital revolution? National responses, market transitions, and global technology*, Stanford Business Books, Stanford, CA, 2006, pp. 361–378.

This tactic aligned with Turkey's broader shift towards new authoritarianism[1015] from increasing[1016] state control,[1017] suppression[1018] of democratic processes[1019] and widespread purges of academics and political activists,[1020] especially after a failed 2016 coup attempt. The ruling party AKP, under President Erdoğan, has been central to this regression, driving corruption, hate speech and disinformation campaigns, domestically and internationally.[1021] Despite Turkey's resistance and efforts, on 7 March 2024, Sweden was accepted and formally joined NATO. However, the process was not without its involvement in FIMI.

4.33.2 Threat Actors

The primary threat actor in this FIMI was the Turkish government, specifically through the New Turkey Digital Office (NDTO),[1022] a state-controlled department that played a central role in orchestrating the influence operation. NDTO has a workforce of 6,000 dedicated to social media monitoring and analysis. It worked to ensure the narrative that Sweden supports terrorism gained traction, both domestically and internationally. State-controlled media outlets like TRT, along with government officials, actively reinforced this message. President Erdoğan, who tightly controls media outlets,[1023] used this influence to further his political agenda both regionally and globally. Evidence has previously found NTDO to have targeted journalists[1024] and used trolls and botnets[1025] to amplify government narratives.[1026] On 20 May 2022, Sweden's former foreign minister Ann Linde acknowledged disinformation[1027] circulating about Sweden and the PKK.

[1015] McLaren, L., and B. Cop, "The failure of democracy in Turkey: A comparative analysis", *Government and Opposition*, Vol. 46, No. 4, 2011, pp. 485–516.
[1016] Ayan Musil, P., "Emergence of a dominant party system after multipartyism: Theoretical implications from the case of the AKP in Turkey", *South European Society and Politics*, Vol. 20, No. 1, 2014, pp. 71–92.
[1017] Esen, B., and S. Ciddi, "Turkey's Republican People's Party: Politics of opposition under a dominant party system", *Turkish Studies*, Vol. 15, No. 3, 2014, pp. 419–441.
[1018] Boas, op. cit.
[1019] https://www.swp-berlin.org/en/publication/turkeys-new-disinformation-law-an-alarming-trend-towards-cyber-authoritarianism.
[1020] Ihsan Yilmaz, "Erdogan's Winning Authoritarian Populist Formula and Turkey's Future", European Center for Populism Studies (ECPS), 29 May 2023.
[1021] https://www.meforum.org/turkey-global-spying-program-targeting-critical.
[1022] Yesil, B., "Social media manipulation in Turkey: Actors, tactics, targets", in Howard Tumber and Silvio Waisbord (eds.), *The Routledge Companion to Media Disinformation and Populism*, Routledge, p. 11. https://doi.org/10.4324/9781003004431.
[1023] https://dayan.org/content/how-erdogan-controls-turkeys-information-space.
[1024] https://www.theguardian.com/world/2016/nov/01/turkish-journalists-face-abuse-threats-online-trolls-attacks.
[1025] https://eu.boell.org/en/2022/03/21/turkeys-troll-networks.
[1026] https://eu.boell.org/en/2022/03/21/turkeys-troll-networks.
[1027] https://x.com/AnnLinde/status/1527571415012089856.

While she did not directly implicate the Turkish government, she emphasised that Sweden was the first country to designate the PKK as a terrorist organisation, indicating that this narrative emerged early in Sweden's NATO discussions.

The Turkish government's disinformation campaign, targeting the European Union and, particularly, Sweden, aligns well with Erdoğan's nationalist policies and AKP sentiment. On 18 December 2023, Erdoğan publicly criticised Sweden for being "lenient on terrorism" and again threatened to block NATO membership[1028] unless certain demands were met. This statement reinforced the narrative that the Swedish government supports terrorism, particularly the PKK, with whom Turkey has been in conflict for over 40 years.

4.33.3 Observations and Attribution

To analyse the existing disinformation on social media, we compiled observables and discovered several narratives with accompanying hashtags like "*#NATOVetoOnSweden*" and "*#Swedenisafasciststate*", supported by other disinformation reports such as those from EU DisinfoLab.[1029] Several observations point to the Turkish government's involvement in this influence operation, where prominent government officials shared and made comments that "Sweden supported terrorism", many of which originated from retweeted accounts linked to bots and trolls.

Tweets from bot accounts were amplified by government-affiliated figures and social media accounts, such as the President of the Directorate of Religious Affairs[1030] and the Vice President of Education,[1031] indicating state involvement. The involvement of religious authorities such as Diyanet[1032] seemed to align with the campaign's nationalist and religious narratives, reinforcing its legitimacy among religious domestic audiences. This mirrors AKP's stance, showing clear coordination with Erdoğan's political agenda. The consistent use of the same imagery and hashtags suggests an organised effort to create the illusion of widespread consensus. These tweets were all posted roughly at the same time, featuring similar content in multiple languages. Some examples included tweets such as: "Prevent Sweden, which holds enemies of Türkiye and supports terrorism, from joining NATO through the Turkish Grand National Assembly! #NATOVetoOnSweden." This suggests a coordinated effort.

[1028] https://www.bbc.com/news/world-europe-64446439.

[1029] https://www.disinfo.eu/wp-content/uploads/2023/05/Sweden_DisinfoFactsheet.pdf.

[1030] https://x.com/ahmetkucur/status/1739359581199876184.

[1031] https://x.com/EBS19Mayis/status/1739351332853526895.

[1032] https://x.com/DiyanetsenKadin/status/1739349860850061537.

4.33.4 Presumed Objectives

T0075: Dismiss—Turkey's operation aimed to dismiss critics of its NATO stance by discrediting Swedish officials, media and international organisations, labelling them as biased or anti-Turkish. This undermined Sweden's credibility in the international community.

T0076: Distort—Turkey distorted Sweden's support for Kurdish groups like the YPG by linking them to the PKK, framing Sweden as a terrorism supporter. The campaign also twisted Sweden's stance on human rights into claims of harbouring terrorists.

T0077: Distract—By accusing Sweden of supporting terrorism, Turkey diverted attention from its own political and human rights issues, using "whataboutism" to shift focus away from domestic concerns.

T0078: Dismay—Turkey threatened Sweden with a NATO veto, creating fear of diplomatic and economic fallout. This fearmongering was aimed at pressuring Sweden and instilling a sense of impending crisis.

The objectives of Turkey's influence operation were to shape international perception by creating and amplifying the narrative that Sweden harboured and supported terrorism, particularly in relation to the PKK. This narrative was intended to isolate Sweden diplomatically and portray it as an untrustworthy NATO candidate and to use Turkey's veto power within NATO to force Sweden to make concessions,[1033] including the extradition of Turkish dissidents and changes in Swedish policies regarding the Kurdish population and PKK.

4.33.5 Incidents and Observables

Influential journalists spread claims that Sweden and NATO were supplying weapons to the PKK, framing Sweden as unfit for NATO membership.[1034] Despite Swedish government denials, these theories were amplified by Turkish mainstream media, such as *TRT*, suggesting possible coordination as the timing coincided with social media posts. *TRT* claimed that evidence showed Sweden supplying weapons to the PKK.[1035]

The hashtag "#NATOVetoOnSweden"[1036] was widely used across social media platforms, particularly on Twitter and Telegram. This hashtag was employed in multiple languages, including English, Turkish, Arabic, Swedish and Finnish,

[1033] https://foreignpolicy.com/2023/07/09/kurds-sweden-nato-turkey-erdogan/.
[1034] https://x.com/GaffarYakinca/status/1739608318065230194.
[1035] https://www.trtworld.com/turkey/t%C3%BCrkiye-s-evidence-shows-sweden-supplies-weapons-to-pkk-terror-outfit-57238.
[1036] https://x.com/search?q=%23NATOVetoOnSweden.

indicating a targeted effort to reach diverse audiences. There was a notable convergence of messaging from Turkish government officials, state-controlled media and bot accounts. These entities propagated narratives that portrayed Sweden as an enemy of Turkey and a supporter of terrorism. This messaging was consistent across different online social platforms such as Twitter/X, Facebook/Meta and Telegram and in multiple languages, suggesting some level of coordination. False reports, images and videos were widely circulated to reinforce the narrative that Sweden supported the PKK.

Images of Turkish soldiers in coffins were juxtaposed with claims that Sweden was complicit in their deaths, despite these claims being debunked by NATO and the Swedish government. Turkish government representatives repeated these claims on social media, pushing the narrative that Sweden was an enemy of religion. The Swedish Security Service increased its terror threat level and cited[1037] the effectiveness of this influence operation. There is some evidence to claim that this operation reached Swedish political and national conversation. For instance, a Swedish independent politician publicly warned the government against agreeing to Turkey's conditions for NATO membership in a statement given to state-controlled television broadcaster SVT and mentioned that otherwise she would cut her support for the current government.[1038]

4.33.6 Channels

The disinformation campaign used a variety of channels to reach its target audiences:

Social media—Platforms such as Twitter, Telegram and YouTube were heavily used. Bot accounts played a large role in amplifying the disinformation, while trolls engaged in manipulating online discussions to push the narrative.

State-controlled media—Turkish state media outlets, notably TRT, were instrumental in spreading the narratives. These outlets targeted both domestic and international audiences, publishing content in multiple languages to maximise reach.

Government officials—Turkish government representatives, including high-ranking officials, consistently echoed and reinforced the disinformation narratives in their public statements and social media posts.

[1037] https://mpf.se/psychological-defence-agency/about-us/news/2023/2023-08-18-increased-spread-of-disinformation-is-being-directed-at-sweden.

[1038] https://www.aa.com.tr/en/europe/swedish-premier-threatens-to-step-down-if-no-confidence-vote-against-justice-minister-succeeds/2604505.

4.33.7 Languages

The use of multiple languages (Arabic, English, Turkish) shows the campaign targeted both domestic and international audiences, fitting a FIMI operation aimed at damaging Sweden's international reputation.

Turkish: Used primarily for domestic audiences to reinforce the government's narrative.

English and Arabic: Targeted international audiences, particularly in the European Union (EU) and the Middle East and North Africa (MENA) regions.

Swedish and Finnish: Specifically aimed at influencing public opinion in Sweden and neighbouring countries, these languages were used to create a more localised impact.

4.33.8 Effectiveness

The Turkish influence operation was notably effective in achieving several of its objectives. The operation successfully created a perception within both domestic and international circles that Sweden was lenient on terrorism. It exerted considerable pressure on the Swedish government, leading to changes in national policies and increased scrutiny of Kurdish organisations in Sweden. The narratives propagated by Turkey found resonance in Swedish political discourse; a lawmaker of Sweden's parliament[1039] told the government not to agree to Turkey's conditions for Sweden's membership bid in NATO in a statement given to state-controlled television broadcaster SVT.

4.33.9 Tactics, Techniques and Procedures

Plan phase (P01).

TA13: Target audience analysis—The Turkish influence operation analysed target audiences across Europe and the Middle East, tailoring narratives on terrorism, NATO and Sweden's policies based on these insights.

T0073: Determine target audiences—Identified key populations in Sweden, the EU and MENA regions most susceptible to disinformation.

TA02: Plan objectives—The goals were to block Sweden's NATO membership unless Turkey's demands were met and to portray Sweden as a terrorism supporter, aligning with Turkey's broader geopolitical aims.

[1039] https://apnews.com/article/politics-middle-east-turkey-migration-stockholm-941768c903b1aea566dde7a2fdcf7a6c.

T0074: Determine strategic ends—Sought geopolitical advantage by influencing NATO's decision and discrediting Sweden internationally.

Prepare phase (P02)

TA16: Establish legitimacy—Used state media and officials to lend credibility to the narrative, creating a perception of legitimacy.

TA06: Create hashtags and search artefacts—They created and used hashtags like #NATOVetoOnSweden to spread the disinformation narratives.

TA06: Develop content—A significant amount of content, including text, images and videos, was created to support the narrative that Sweden supports terrorism.

T0085: Develop text-based content—Creating misleading or false text-based content such as tweets, articles or posts to support the disinformation narratives.

T0086: Develop image-based content—Creating and editing misleading visual content such as images of the Quran being burned next to a Turkish embassy or coffins of dead Turkish soldiers with the flag of Sweden.

TA14: Develop narratives—The influence operation developed several narratives, such as "Sweden is hostile to Turkey", "Sweden supports PKK" and "Sweden supports terror".

Execute phase (P03)

TA08: Conduct pump priming—Initial disinformation seemed to have been seeded on smaller scales, like bot accounts or videos on YouTube that have little to no engagement, and then broader spread where Turkish officials began sharing and amplifying it in a coordinated manner to maximise the impact.

T0049: Flooding the information space—Disinformation actors flooded social media, particularly X, with content supporting the narrative. Searching keywords like "Sweden + Turkey" within 2023 reveals numerous posts amplifying this message, showcasing their effort to overwhelm the platform. The content was in multiple languages, targeting a diverse audience.

TA09: Deliver content—The FIMI campaign released the content to the public through state media, social media platforms and online platforms. The content was in multiple languages, targeting a diverse audience.

TA09: Trolls amplify and manipulate—Used trolls to manipulate online discussions and push the narrative. Bots amplified via automated forwarding and responding.

T0049.003: Bots amplified via automated forwarding and responding—Used bots to automate the dissemination and reposting to increase reach.

Access phase (P04)

TA13: Measure effectiveness indicators—This operation had a difficult-to-quantify impact on the Swedish and international communities via the stories in the media.

T0134.002: Social media engagement—The FIMI campaign most likely monitored social media to see how effective the disinformation campaign was and the responses to these narratives.

T0134.001: Message reach—Assess if the reach of FIMI is better on different platforms.

T0133: Measure effectiveness: Evaluate the overall impact of the FIMI in shifting public perception and influencing Sweden's policy decisions.

4.33.10 Countermeasures

This campaign was countered by social media platforms enhancing their policies and tools for detecting and removing bot content, state-backed narratives and harmful or extremist material, such as Quran burning videos. These improvements suggest the development of better algorithms for identifying specific types of coordinated or inauthentic behaviour, along with increased resources for trust and safety teams working in content moderation. Such measures can help limit the spread of disinformation and track attempts to "influence" early in their lifecycle.

Organisations such as NATO should collaborate more closely on countering FIMI activities, particularly in contexts involving military alliances across the European Union. Civilian bodies also have a vital role to play and should continue investing in public awareness campaigns to educate citizens on the tactics and techniques employed in FIMI campaigns. This multi-faceted approach can foster an effective resistance to disinformation from multiple angles.

4.33.11 Conclusion

Turkey's influence operation against Sweden during the NATO accession deliberations illustrates the effectiveness of coordinated state-led disinformation campaigns in shaping international political outcomes and compelling other states to align with specific interests. The full impact of this FIMI campaign is challenging to quantify, particularly regarding its influence on radicalisation and extremist organisations. However, the campaign was effective because it leveraged Turkey's veto power and information warfare techniques to exert pressure on Sweden, forcing concessions and influencing national debates and policies.

To address these challenges beyond existing countermeasures, several recommendations may be considered. One is to assess the vulnerability of states to exploitation in the information space and to implement proactive plans to counteract various forms of disinformation. This approach differs from pre-bunking by allowing governments to prepare defensively for potential adversarial responses, particularly in contexts such as negotiations for military alliances. This preparation could be complemented by analysing the audience consuming such disinformation. Given the association with military alliances and national security, and in this case the dissemination of harmful content designed to provoke emotional responses, governments should consider how best to develop counter-narratives that mitigate the risk of online radicalisation. Ensuring that harmful online content does not escalate into offline protests, riots or terrorism is vital.

At the time of writing this case study, the author notes that the Swedish government has already adopted some of these measures, as outlined in its national strategy against violent extremism and terrorism.[1040]

[1040] https://www.government.se/contentassets/524b35ec9cdd4e30a501c6b7d9cbd694/national-strategy-against-violent-extremism-and-terrorism--prevent-avert-protect-and-manage-government-communication-20232456.pdf.

FIMI Tactics, Techniques and Procedures

5

Demetris Paschalides, George Pallis, and Marios D. Dikaiakos

5.1 Introduction to TTPs

The landscape of FIMI has evolved dramatically in the digital age, necessitating sophisticated analytical frameworks to understand and counter these threats.[1] At the forefront of this effort is the concept of tactics, techniques and procedures (TTPs), a structured approach borrowed from military doctrine and cybersecurity practices.[2] In the following sections, we expand upon the earlier discussion of TTPs, providing a more detailed examination of their application within the DISARM framework.[3] We explore their significance, implementation and the critical role they play in FIMI analysis and the development of effective countermeasures.

[1] Pamment, James, "The EU's Role in Fighting Disinformation: Crafting A Disinformation Framework", Carnegie Endowment for International Peace, Sept 2020. https://carnegie-production-assets.s3.amazonaws.com/static/files/Pamment_-_Crafting_Disinformation_1.pdf.

[2] Maymí, Fernando, Robert Bixler, Randolph Jones and Scott Lathrop, "Towards a definition of cyberspace tactics, techniques and procedures", 2017 IEEE International Conference on Big Data (Big Data), Boston, MA, USA, 2017, pp. 4674–4679. https://doi.org/10.1109/BigData.2017.8258514.

[3] Terp, Sara-Jayne, and Pablo Breuer, "DISARM: a Framework for Analysis of Disinformation Campaigns", 2022 IEEE Conference on Cognitive and Computational Aspects of Situation Management (CogSIMA), Salerno, Italy, 2022, pp. 1–8. https://doi.org/10.1109/CogSIMA54611.2022.9830669.

D. Paschalides · G. Pallis · M. D. Dikaiakos (✉)
University of Cyprus, Nicosia, Cyprus
e-mail: mdd@ucy.ac.cy

© The Author(s), under exclusive license to Springer Nature Switzerland AG 2026

D. Wright (ed.), *Foreign Information Manipulation and Interference*, Terrorism, Security, and Computation, https://doi.org/10.1007/978-3-031-91299-3_5

5.1.1 The Evolution of TTPs in Information Warfare

The concept of TTPs has its roots in military strategy, where it has long been used to analyse and predict enemy behaviour.[4] In recent years, this approach has been adapted to the realm of cybersecurity and, more recently, to the analysis of information operations.[5] The transition of TTPs to the information warfare domain represents a critical evolution in how we understand and combat FIMI.

Tactics in FIMI represent the high-level objectives that threat actors aim to achieve through their influence campaigns. These objectives often include undermining democratic institutions, creating social divisions, discrediting political figures or manipulating public opinion on key issues.[6] Tactics provide insight into the **'why'** behind these actions, shedding light on the broader goals of those engaged in disinformation campaigns. By understanding these overarching strategies, we can better anticipate the intended outcomes of FIMI operations and their potential impact on targeted societies.

Techniques refer to the specific methods employed by threat actors to achieve their tactical objectives. These methods might include actions such as coordinating inauthentic behaviour on social media platforms, manipulating search engine algorithms to amplify false narratives, or using bots to flood discussions with disinformation.[7] Techniques represent the '**how**' of a FIMI campaign, detailing the precise actions used to spread disinformation. This could involve creating misleading visual content like deepfakes, leveraging algorithms to manipulate online visibility or coordinating large-scale automated responses to shape public discourse. By analysing these techniques, we can better understand how disinformation is operationalised.

Procedures are a collection of techniques to achieve the tactics. They describe the specific steps and processes by which threat actors implement their chosen techniques to form a coordinated and strategic operation. These steps often include actions like creating and managing fake online personas, deploying bot networks, or timing disinformation campaigns to exploit vulnerabilities in the target environment. Procedures can vary depending on the actor, the context and the goals of the campaign, often designed to evade detection and maximise impact. They represent

[4] Department of the Army, "Intelligence Preparation of the Battlefield, Field Manual", 1994. https://irp.fas.org/doddir/army/fm34-130.pdf.

[5] Hutchins, Eric M., Michael J. Cloppert and Rohan M. Amin, "Intelligence-driven computer network defense informed by analysis of adversary campaigns and intrusion kill chains", Lockheed Martin Corporation, Jan 2011. https://www.lockheedmartin.com/content/dam/lockheed-martin/rms/documents/cyber/LM-White-Paper-Intel-Driven-Defense.pdf.

[6] Bradshaw, Samantha, and Philip N. Howard, *The global disinformation order: 2019 global inventory of organized social media manipulation*, Oxford University Press, July 2021.

[7] Starbird, Kate, Ahmer Arif and Tom Wilson, "Disinformation as collaborative work: Surfacing the participatory nature of strategic information operations", *Proceedings of the ACM on Human-Computer Interaction*, Vol. 3, Issue CSCW, pp. 1–26. https://dl.acm.org/doi/10.1145/3359229.

the '**when**' and '**where**' of an operation, outlining the operational patterns and sequences followed to achieve the desired outcomes.

5.1.2 DISARM: A Framework for TTP Identification and Analysis

As briefly introduced in Chap. 2, DISARM is a multifaceted framework (the 'Navigator') designed to provide a structured approach to dissecting influence operations. It consists of two primary components[8]: the Red Framework and the Blue Framework. While DISARM encompasses various elements, including Phases, Countermeasures and Detections, our analysis in this deliverable primarily focuses on the TTPs outlined in the DISARM Red Framework. This decision reflects the emphasis on understanding the perspective and methodologies of threat actors. It is worth noting that the DISARM Blue Framework is currently undergoing an overhaul, and its use is discouraged by the DISARM Foundation, further justifying our focus on the Red Framework in this analysis.

DISARM Kill Chain

Core to the framework is the DISARM Kill Chain,[9] a structure that provides a logical progression of an influence campaign from inception to execution and assessment, organising TTPs into distinct phases. Each phase corresponds to a logical stage in the execution of an influence campaign, allowing for a systematic analysis of threat actor behaviours. The DISARM Kill Chain, illustrated in Fig. 5.1, consists of four main phases:

1. **Plan (P01)**: This initial phase focuses on envisioning the desired outcome and laying out effective strategies to achieve it. It is characterised by high-level strategic thinking and objective setting.
2. **Prepare (P02)**: This phase involves activities conducted before execution to enhance operational capabilities. It includes the development of the ecosystem needed to support the action, including people, networks, channels and content.
3. **Execute (P03)**: This phase encompasses the actual implementation of the influence operation, from initial exposure to maintaining a presence in the information environment.
4. **Assess (P04)**: The final phase involves evaluating the effectiveness of the action for use in future planning, allowing for iterative improvement of influence strategies.

[8] DISARM Framework Explorer, DISARM Foundation, https://disarmframework.herokuapp.com/.

[9] Terp and Breuer, op. cit.

Fig. 5.1 Diagram of the DISARM Kill Chain, depicting the phases and tactics of attackers

Within each phase of the Kill Chain, DISARM delineates specific tactics and their associated techniques. This granular approach allows for a nuanced understanding of threat actor behaviours and methodologies.

Plan Phase (P01)
The Plan phase is crucial in setting the direction for the entire influence operation. Key tactics in this phase include:

- **Plan strategy (TA01)**: This tactic involves defining the desired end state—the set of required conditions that defines achievement of all objectives. It sets the overall direction for the influence campaign.
- **Plan objectives (TA02)**: This tactic focuses on setting clearly defined, measurable and achievable objectives. It emphasises the importance of linking tactical tasks to the desired end state through well-crafted objectives.
- **Target audience analysis (TA13)**: This tactic involves identifying and analysing the target audience, examining attributes such as locations, political affiliations, financial situations and other relevant characteristics. This analysis allows influence operations to tailor their strategy and content effectively.

Prepare Phase (P02)
The Prepare phase is about building the foundation for the influence operation. Key tactics include:

- **Microtarget (TA05)**: This tactic involves targeting very specific populations of people, allowing for highly tailored messaging.
- **Develop content (TA06)**: This tactic focuses on creating or acquiring text, images and other content that will be used in the influence campaign.
- **Select channels and affordances (TA07)**: This tactic involves assessing which online or offline platforms and their associated affordances maximise an influence operation's ability to reach its target audience.
- **Develop narratives (TA14)**: This tactic centres on the promotion of beneficial master narratives, which is crucial for achieving long-term strategic narrative dominance.
- **Establish social assets (TA15)**: This tactic involves generating messaging tools, including social media accounts, operation personnel and organisations.
- **Establish legitimacy (TA16)**: This tactic focuses on establishing assets that create trust, enhancing the credibility of the influence operation.

Execute Phase (P03)
The Execute phase is where the influence operation is carried out. Key tactics include:

- **Conduct pump priming (TA08)**: This tactic involves releasing content on a targeted small scale prior to general release, used for preparation and message honing.
- **Deliver content (TA09)**: This tactic involves releasing content to the public or target groups.
- **Drive offline activity (TA10)**: This tactic aims to move the incident/campaign from online to offline, encouraging users to engage in the physical information space.
- **Persist in the information environment (TA11)**: This tactic involves taking measures that allow an operation to maintain its presence and avoid takedown by external entities.
- **Maximise exposure (TA17)**: This tactic aims to maximise exposure of the target audience to incident/campaign content via flooding, amplifying and cross-posting.
- **Drive online harms (TA18)**: This tactic involves actions taken to harm opponents in online spaces through harassment, suppression, releasing private information and controlling the information space.

Assess Phase (P04)
The Assess phase is crucial for the ongoing effectiveness and evolution of influence operations. The primary tactic in this phase is:

- **Assess effectiveness (TA12)**: This tactic involves evaluating the effectiveness of actions for use in future plans, allowing for continuous improvement of influence strategies.

Techniques in the DISARM Framework
Within each tactic of the DISARM framework, specific techniques are employed to achieve the tactical goals of an influence campaign. Techniques represent the concrete actions taken by threat actors, providing a detailed understanding of how influence operations are carried out across various stages. The entirety of the techniques is depicted in Fig. 5.2, we highlight several key techniques and their associated DISARM codes across different phases of the Kill Chain.

During the Plan phase (P01), techniques are focused on gathering intelligence and refining strategic objectives. For example, in Plan objectives (TA02), threat actors might use Determine strategic ends (T0073), a technique that involves setting clear, measurable outcomes based on the analysis of geopolitical trends and target audience vulnerabilities. In the Target Audience Analysis (TA13) tactic, threat actors may employ Identify Existing Conspiracy Narratives/Suspicions (T0081.005) to assess pre-existing conspiracy theories (see case studies 4.5, 4.6, 4.23, and 4.24) and/or Identify Existing Prejudices (T0081.003) to exploit existing racial, religious, demographic or social prejudices (see case studies 4.5, 4.24, and 4.25) to further polarise their target audience.

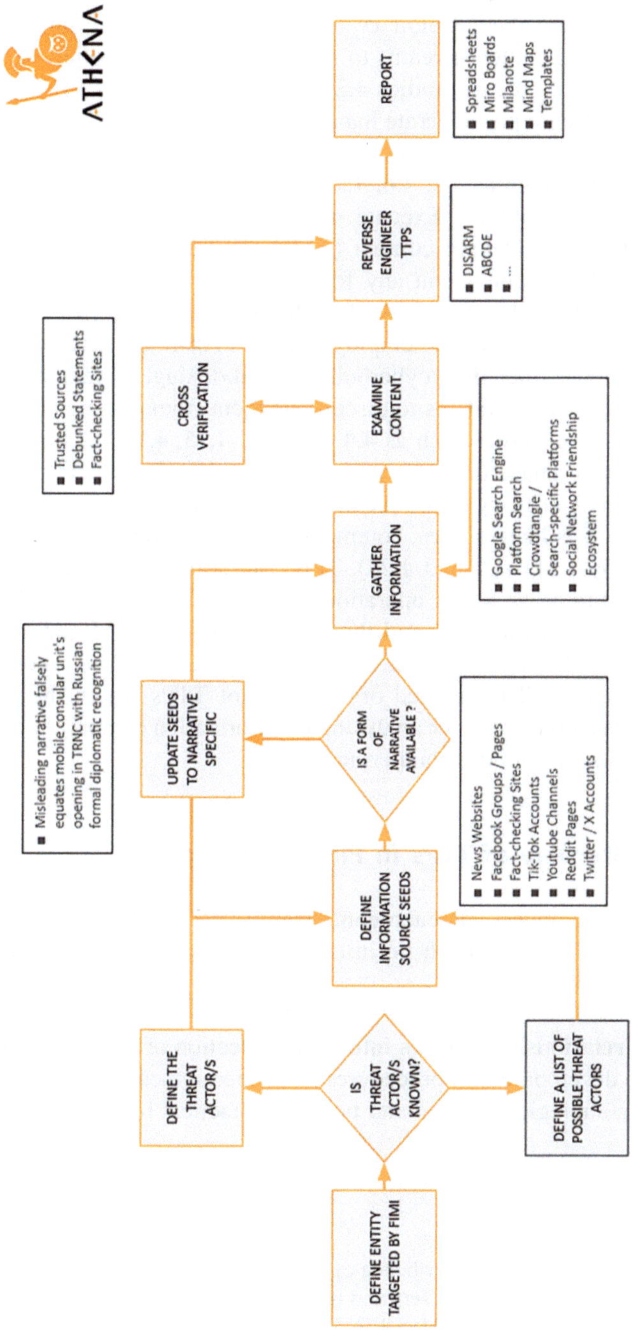

Fig. 5.2 Flow diagram highlighting the iterative process of the ATHENA FIMI analysis methodology

In the Prepare phase (P02), threat actors begin to set the operational foundation. A key technique in Micro-target (TA05) is Leverage Echo Chambers/Filter Bubbles (T0102), where they exploit or create isolated Internet subgroups and algorithmically tailored content streams to reinforce biases and beliefs among target audience members (see case studies 4.2, 4.5, 4.12, 4.14 and 4.16). In Develop content (TA06), the technique Generate inauthentic content (T0065) involves creating or acquiring false or misleading text, images or videos to deceive the audience (including case studies such as 4.5, 4.6, 4.12, 4.13, 4.15 and 4.17).

As operations move into the Execute phase (P03), techniques become more aggressive and direct. In Deliver content (TA09), threat actors may use Deliver Ads (T0114) to deliver content via any form of paid media or advertising (see case studies 4.15, 4.17, 4.19, and 4.24). For the more hostile tactic Drive online harms (TA18), threat actors might employ Harass (T0048), where they employ intimidation techniques, including cyberbullying and doxing, to threaten or harass believers of the opposing narratives to discourage them from posting contradicting content (including case studies such as 4.4, 4.5, 4.6, 4.15, 4.17, 4.24 and 4.28).

Finally, the Assess phase (P04) focuses on evaluating the effectiveness of the influence operation. A primary technique here is Measure Effectiveness (T0133) to analyse metrics such as likes, shares, comments and overall reach (see case studies 4.2, 4.7, 4.15, 4.17, 4.24, 4.27 and 4.28). This data allows threat actors to refine their strategies and improve future operations.

By examining these techniques and their associated DISARM codes, we gain a comprehensive understanding of how influence operations are methodically structured and executed. The detailed organisation of TTPs within the DISARM framework provides a blueprint for analysing disinformation campaigns and offers valuable insights for developing countermeasures.

5.1.3 The Interplay of TTPs in FIMI Operations

While it's valuable to understand each component of the TTP framework individually, the benefits of this approach lie in analysing how TTPs interact within an influence operation.[10]

- **Hierarchical relationship**: Tactics inform the selection of techniques, which in turn guide the development of procedures. This hierarchical structure allows for both top-down strategic planning and bottom-up tactical innovation.[11]

[10] Rid, Thomas, and Ben Buchanan, "Attributing cyber attacks", *Journal of Strategic Studies*, Vol. 38, Issues 1–2, 2015, pp. 4–37. See also Terp and Breuer, op. cit.

[11] Pamment, James, Howard Nothhaft, Henrik Agardh-Twetman and Alicia Fjällhed, "Countering Information Influence Activities: The State of the Art, version 1.4", Department of Strategic Communication, Lund University, 2018.

- **Feedback loops**: The success or failure of specific procedures can lead to the refinement of techniques, which may ultimately influence tactical decisions. This creates a dynamic, adaptive system.
- **Cross-pollination**: Techniques and procedures developed for one tactic may be repurposed or adapted for use in others, leading to the evolution of the overall FIMI ecosystem.[12]
- **Contextual adaptation**: The specific combination of TTPs employed in an operation often depends on the target audience, cultural context and geopolitical situation.[13]

By mapping these interactions, the DISARM framework provides a comprehensive view of FIMI operations that goes beyond simple categorisation. This holistic approach enables analysts to: (i) identify the strategic intent behind specific online behaviours; (ii) predict potential adaptations in response to countermeasures; and (iii) develop more effective, targeted responses to influence campaigns.

5.2 Methodology for Identifying, Gathering, Storing and Sharing TTPs

As part of the ATHENA, we have developed the ATHENA FIMI Analysis Framework. This framework provides a comprehensive methodology for identifying, gathering, storing and sharing TTPs used in FIMI campaigns. This methodology follows an iterative process, combining a systematic analysis of incidents and observables to map them to corresponding TTPs, thus enabling a thorough understanding of how disinformation campaigns are structured and executed. While tailored to work with the DISARM framework, this methodology is flexible and can accommodate additional frameworks such as DEPICT[14] or ABCDE.[15]

The proposed methodology revolves around a multi-step process that incorporates two novel canvases: the **Observable Canvas** and the **Incident Canvas**. These canvases, inspired by design thinking,[16] guide analysts through the analysis of FIMI incidents by providing structured templates to capture key information about disinformation observables and incidents.

[12] Freelon, Deen, and Chris Wells, "Disinformation as political communication", *Political Communication*, Vol. 37, No. 2, 2020, pp. 145–156.

[13] Bjola, Corneliu, and James Pamment (eds.), *Countering online propaganda and extremism: The dark side of digital diplomacy*, Routledge, 2018.

[14] Roozenbeek, Jon, Caroline S. Traberg and Sander van der Linden, "Technique-based inoculation against real-world misinformation", *Royal Society Open Science*, Article 211719, Vol. 9, No. 5, 18 May 2022. Erratum in: Royal Society Open Science Dec 2023.

[15] Pamment, op. cit., Sept 2020.

[16] Denning, Peter J., "Design thinking", *Research-Technology Management*, Vol. 57, 1987, pp. 59–62.

5.2.1 ATHENA FIMI Analysis Methodology

The methodology follows a structured flow (as depicted in Fig. 5.2), with the following key steps:

1. **Define the entity targeted by FIMI**: The process begins by identifying the specific entity that is being targeted by the FIMI campaign. This could be a country, political party, organisation, social group or an individual (e.g. Volodimir Zelenskyy). Identifying the target helps frame the analysis and defines the scope of the disinformation campaign.
2. **Define threat actors**: The next step involves determining whether the threat actor behind the FIMI campaign is known. If known, the process directly moves to identifying information sources. However, if the threat actor is not identified, a list of potential threat actors is created based on available data and historical patterns in disinformation activities.
3. **Define information source seeds**: Once the potential threat actors are identified, the methodology moves to defining information source seeds. These are the platforms, websites, social media accounts and other channels from which the disinformation content is believed to originate. Examples of sources include news websites, Facebook groups, TikTok accounts and Reddit pages. These source seeds are continuously refined as more information is gathered.
4. **Update seeds to narrative-specific content**: At this stage, if a specific narrative has been identified, the information source seeds are updated to focus on narrative-specific content. This involves mapping the spread of a particular disinformation story or theme across different platforms and channels. This step helps in narrowing down the focus to the most relevant data for analysis.
5. **Gather information**: The gathering phase involves collecting relevant data from various platforms and search engines (e.g. Google, Crowdtangle, social media platforms). The data is filtered to ensure that only the most pertinent information for the analysis is captured. The aim is to collect both the content itself (text, images, videos) and the associated metadata (timing, audience reach, engagement metrics).
6. **Cross-verification**: Cross-verification is essential to ensure the credibility and accuracy of the information. This step involves comparing the gathered information with trusted sources, debunked statements and fact-checking sites. The goal is to confirm the validity of the observed disinformation and to identify false narratives and manipulated content.
7. **Examine content**: The content is thoroughly examined to uncover key narratives, actors and TTPs. The examination process involves analysing the broader socio-political context of the disinformation, the timing of its dissemination and its alignment with known disinformation strategies. For this, the **Observable Canvas** helps break down and analyse the content, actors and their intent.
8. **Reverse engineer TTPs**: Once the content is examined, the next step is to reverse engineer the TTPs behind the disinformation campaign. This involves mapping the tactics, techniques and procedures used by the threat actors

to manipulate the information environment. Frameworks such as DISARM, ABCDE and others can be used to categorise the TTPs according to the identified behaviours. The **Incident Canvas** provides a structure for capturing TTPs across multiple stages of an attack.

9. **Report**: The final step involves documenting the findings in a report format. This report includes a detailed description of the TTPs used, the identified threat actors and the potential countermeasures. The output can be shared in various formats such as spreadsheets, mind maps or narrative reports, depending on the audience and the intended use.

5.2.2 Observable and Incident Canvases

Design thinking is a problem-solving approach that encourages a user-centred perspective, focusing on empathy, creativity and iteration to address complex issues. It is commonly used in product design and innovation processes but has broad applications, including in fields like information analysis and disinformation tracking. The design thinking process generally follows five stages: Empathise, Define, Ideate, Prototype and Test. This method promotes a structured yet flexible way of understanding and solving problems, with a particular emphasis on collaboration and visual representation.

One of the central tools in design thinking is the **canvas**, a structured visual framework that helps teams map out different aspects of a problem or solution in a systematic way. Canvases enable users to organise thoughts, highlight key information and identify connections between various elements. In the context of FIMI, we employ two specific canvases: the **Observable Canvas** and the **Incident Canvas**. These tools guide analysts in capturing and analysing crucial information about disinformation campaigns, providing a comprehensive view of both individual observables and broader incidents.

Observable Canvas

The Observable Canvas is designed to help analysts break down and understand individual pieces of content—referred to as 'observables'—that may be part of a larger disinformation campaign. An observable could be a tweet, a video, an article or any other digital artefact involved in spreading disinformation. This canvas allows for a detailed examination of the content and provides a framework for assessing its significance within the disinformation landscape. Key components of the Observable Canvas include:

1. **Actor/Provenance**: This section focuses on identifying who is behind the observable. Analysts consider whether the actor is an individual, a non-state organisation or a proxy for a foreign government. It also looks at the platform used to distribute the content, helping to trace the origins of the observable.
2. **Content**: Here, the nature of the content is analysed. Is the information misleading, weaponised or outright false? The canvas helps determine whether the

content exploits specific vulnerabilities or is manipulated in some way, such as using deepfakes or AI-generated text. Questions in this section guide the analyst through understanding the intent and style of the content, its framing and whether it serves as part of a broader disinformation narrative.

3. **Tactics, techniques, and procedures (TTPs)**: This section assesses the methods used by the actor to disseminate the observable. Analysts look for patterns of behaviour, such as coordinated efforts to deceive, manipulate or mislead the target audience. By identifying TTPs, the analyst can categorise how threat actors operationalise their campaigns.
4. **Target audience/degree**: This part examines the audience targeted by the observable and the extent of its reach. It helps identify whether the content is aimed at specific societal groups, such as ethnic or political communities, and whether it is part of a micro-targeting strategy. Additionally, it assesses how far the observable has travelled through various channels, helping to map the disinformation's spread.
5. **Context/theme/narrative**: The broader socio-political context of the content is explored here. Does the content align with ongoing narratives, such as conspiracy theories or political agendas? Analysts are encouraged to use narrative theory to extract the underlying themes and classify the observable into a wider framework of disinformation.
6. **Objectives**: This section helps to identify the potential goals of the observable. Is it meant to dismiss, distort, distract or dismay? By analysing these objectives, analysts can better understand the intent behind the disinformation and how it fits into the broader campaign.
7. **Timing**: Timing is crucial in understanding disinformation. This section asks whether the observable coincides with major events like elections or political controversies, which may have increased the content's relevance or impact.
8. **Impact/Effect**: Finally, the canvas assesses the observable impact. How widely was it shared? Did it provoke engagement or lead to offline behaviours, such as protests or violence? This section helps gauge the severity and reach of the disinformation content.
9. **Countermeasures**: Based on the analysis, this section outlines potential steps to mitigate the observable impact. Possible countermeasures include debunking, raising awareness about the misleading narrative or exposing the TTPs used in the campaign.

By guiding analysts through these detailed components, the Observable Canvas ensures a comprehensive examination of individual pieces of disinformation, helping to situate them within the larger context of an influence operation.

Incident Canvas

While the Observable Canvas focuses on individual pieces of content, the Incident Canvas offers a broader framework for analysing entire disinformation incidents. An incident encompasses multiple observables and can span various platforms, times and narratives. This canvas provides a holistic view of how an attack unfolds and how different components of a disinformation campaign interact. Key components of the Incident Canvas include:

1. **Description**: This section provides an overview of the incident, including a description of the disinformation attack and the tactics employed. It captures the story conveyed by the observables and their broader significance.
2. **Target**: The Incident Canvas helps define the primary targets of the disinformation. These could include individuals, organisations, governments or entire societal groups. It also looks at whether specific cultural, religious or ethnic groups are being targeted.
3. **Context/theme**: Similar to the Observable Canvas, this section focuses on the socio-political context surrounding the incident. It encourages analysts to identify broader themes that may align with the disinformation campaign's objectives, such as conspiracy theories or political narratives.
4. **Tactics, techniques and procedures (TTPs)**: This component assesses the methods used by threat actors throughout the entire incident. It looks at how actors manipulate the information environment using deception, misinformation or other illegitimate communication techniques. Analysts identify the specific combination of techniques employed across various phases of the attack.
5. **Objectives**: This section examines the broader goals of the disinformation incident. It analyses whether the campaign seeks to distort public perception, dismiss legitimate information or create societal division. Understanding these objectives is crucial for determining the intent behind the campaign.
6. **Audience/degree**: Here, analysts evaluate the reach and targeting strategy of the incident. This section gauges how the disinformation has spread across different channels and whether it has reached specific linguistic, ethnic or demographic groups.
7. **Attribution/actor**: This section focuses on identifying who is behind the incident. It may include evidence from secondary sources such as journalistic investigations or platform-based attributions. The goal is to identify whether the disinformation is linked to state actors, non-state actors or proxies acting on their behalf.
8. **Vulnerabilities**: In this section, analysts explore the societal or psychological vulnerabilities that the disinformation campaign has exploited. These might include pre-existing stereotypes, distrust in authority or the popularity of conspiracy theories.
9. **Impact/effect**: Similar to the Observable Canvas, this section assesses the overall impact of the disinformation incident. It considers both online and offline effects, such as engagement metrics, changes in public opinion or tangible societal harm.
10. **Channels**: This section tracks the platforms and media through which the incident spread. It explores how different platforms were used to disseminate content, identifying sources, amplifiers and links between networks.

11. **Countermeasures**: Based on the analysis, this section outlines strategies to address the disinformation incident. Countermeasures may include debunking, confining the spread of the incident or exposing the TTPs used.

The Observable and Incident Canvases are powerful tools within the ATHENA FIMI Analysis Framework, offering a structured, design-thinking-inspired approach to understanding and combating disinformation. The **Observable Canvas** allows analysts to dissect individual pieces of content, while the **Incident Canvas** provides a broader view of how disinformation campaigns unfold across multiple platforms and narratives. Together, these canvases support a comprehensive, iterative analysis that helps uncover the tactics, techniques and procedures used by threat actors in FIMI campaigns.

5.3 TTP Pattern Analysis from ATHENA Case Studies

As part of the reverse engineering of TTPs, understanding the patterns and usage of TTPs across existing FIMI campaigns is critical to gaining insights into how disinformation operations evolve. An important outcome of our work is the detailed analysis of TTP usage in the 32 case studies in Chap. 4. These case studies have annotated each disinformation campaign using the DISARM Red framework, identifying the specific TTPs employed by the threat actors. By examining these annotations, we conducted a comprehensive analysis to understand the deployment of TTPs across different actors and explore trends in the evolution of disinformation tactics. To do so, we visualise the frequencies and patterns of TTPs across the case studies, following a similar process to the one employed by European Union External Action Service (EEAS).[17] This analysis provides a deeper understanding of threat actor strategies and helps anticipate future disinformation methods.

5.3.1 Case Study Overview and Thematics

The 32 case studies offer insights into the TTPs employed by different geopolitical actors and their disinformation strategies. To gain a comprehensive understanding of these campaigns, we analysed the case studies both collectively and within specific thematic categories, with each category highlighting a particular aspect of FIMI activity. Below are the main thematic distinctions along with the case studies they encompass, with additional themes created to ensure that all case studies are covered (Fig. 5.3).

[17] 1st EEAS Report on Foreign Information Manipulation and Interference Threats. https://www.eeas.europa.eu/eeas/1st-eeas-report-foreign-information-manipulation-and-interference-threats_en.

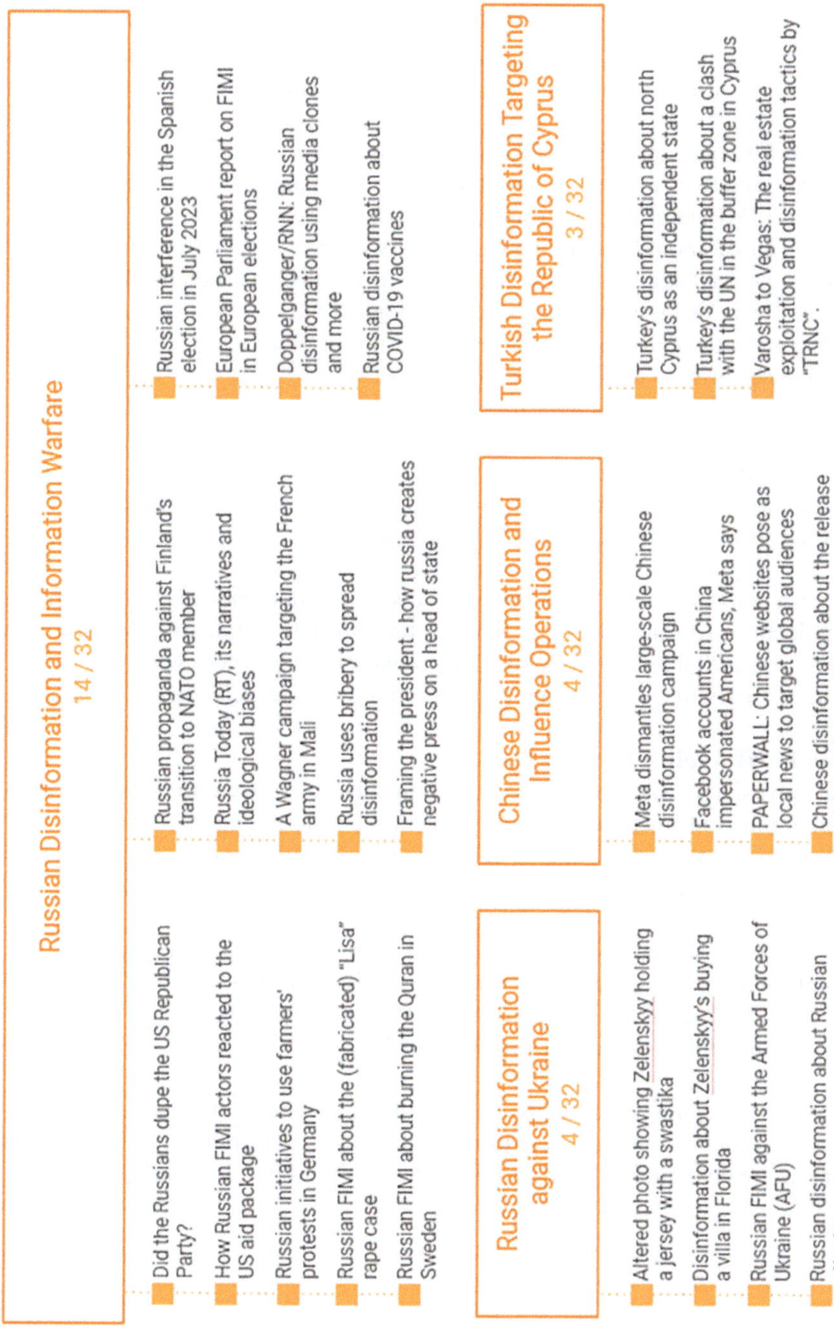

Fig. 5.3 Case study thematic grouping

Russian Disinformation and Information Warfare
Russia has a long history of using disinformation as a tool for advancing its geopolitical objectives. This thematic category explores how Russian actors use FIMI to influence public opinion, destabilise foreign governments and shape narratives in favour of Russian interests. Case studies that fall into this thematic include:

- Did the Russians dupe the US Republican Party?
- Russian initiatives to use farmers' protests in Germany.
- Russian FIMI about the (fabricated) 'Lisa' rape case.
- Russian FIMI about burning the Quran in Sweden.
- Russian propaganda against Finland's transition to NATO membership.
- Russia Today (RT), its narratives and ideological biases.
- A Wagner campaign targeting the French army in Mali.
- Russia uses bribery to spread disinformation.
- Framing the President—how Russia creates negative press of a head of state.
- Russian interference in the Spanish election in July 2023.
- European Parliament report on FIMI in European elections.
- Doppelganger: Russian disinformation using media clones and more.
- Russian disinformation about COVID-19 vaccines.

These case studies cover a broad range of disinformation campaigns, from influencing elections to exacerbating social tensions through narratives about different communities and migration. Russia has consistently targeted European states, using local issues to drive division and undermine trust in democratic institutions.

Russian FIMI Against Ukraine
Russia's invasion of Ukraine has been accompanied by a powerful disinformation campaign aimed at justifying its military actions, undermining Ukraine's government and spreading misinformation about the war. This theme explores the various TTPs used by Russia to manipulate narratives about the conflict in Ukraine.

- Altered photo showing Zelenskyy holding a jersey with a swastika.
- Disinformation about Zelenskyy's buying a villa in Florida.
- Russian FIMI against the Armed Forces of Ukraine (AFU).
- Russian disinformation about Russian attacks.

These case studies highlight the Kremlin's efforts to delegitimise Ukrainian leadership, sow discord among international supporters of Ukraine, and portray its military as overwhelmingly powerful to demoralise both Ukrainians and their allies.[18]

---

[18] Max Hunder, "Russia vs Ukraine: the biggest war of the fake news era", Reuters, Aug. 2024. https://www.reuters.com/world/europe/russia-vs-ukraine-biggest-war-fake-news-era-2024-07-31/.

Chinese Disinformation and Influence Operations

China has increasingly used disinformation to assert its global influence, with campaigns targeting both domestic and international audiences. This thematic category covers Chinese efforts to control narratives about sensitive political and environmental issues.

- Meta dismantles large-scale Chinese disinformation campaigns.
- Facebook accounts in China impersonated Americans, Meta says.
- PAPERWALL: Chinese websites pose as local news to target global audiences.
- Chinese disinformation about the release of Fukushima water.

These cases show how China uses sophisticated disinformation operations to sway public opinion on key issues, such as environmental policy and international relations, while also attempting to influence foreign politics through impersonation and media cloning.

Turkish Disinformation Targeting the Republic of Cyprus

Turkey has employed disinformation campaigns aimed at delegitimising the Republic of Cyprus and supporting its own political objectives in the region. These campaigns often focus on territorial disputes and military conflicts.

- Turkey's disinformation about north Cyprus as an independent state.
- Turkey's disinformation about a clash with the UN in the buffer zone in Cyprus.
- Varosha to Vegas: The real estate exploitation and disinformation tactics by 'TRNC'.

These case studies reveal how Turkey manipulates information to strengthen its claims over Cyprus and frame itself as a legitimate actor in the ongoing conflict. The campaigns target both local and international audiences to shape perceptions about the Cyprus issue.

5.3.2 Frequency Analysis of TTPs

Across the 32 case studies, a total of 102 occurrences of TTPs were recorded, of which 47 were unique techniques. Most of the identified TTPs fall under the Preparation phase (P02), accounting for 60% of all detected TTPs, followed by the Planning phase (P01) with 30%, and the Execution phase (P03) with 10% (see Figs. 5.4, 5.5 and 5.6).

In P01, threat actors primarily focused on creating divisions and undermining adversaries, with 'Undermine' (T0135) and 'Divide' (T0079) recorded in over 60% of the cases. Additionally, TTPs such as 'Distort' (T0076) and 'Cause Harm' (T0140) were prominent, emphasising the strategic goal of weakening targets

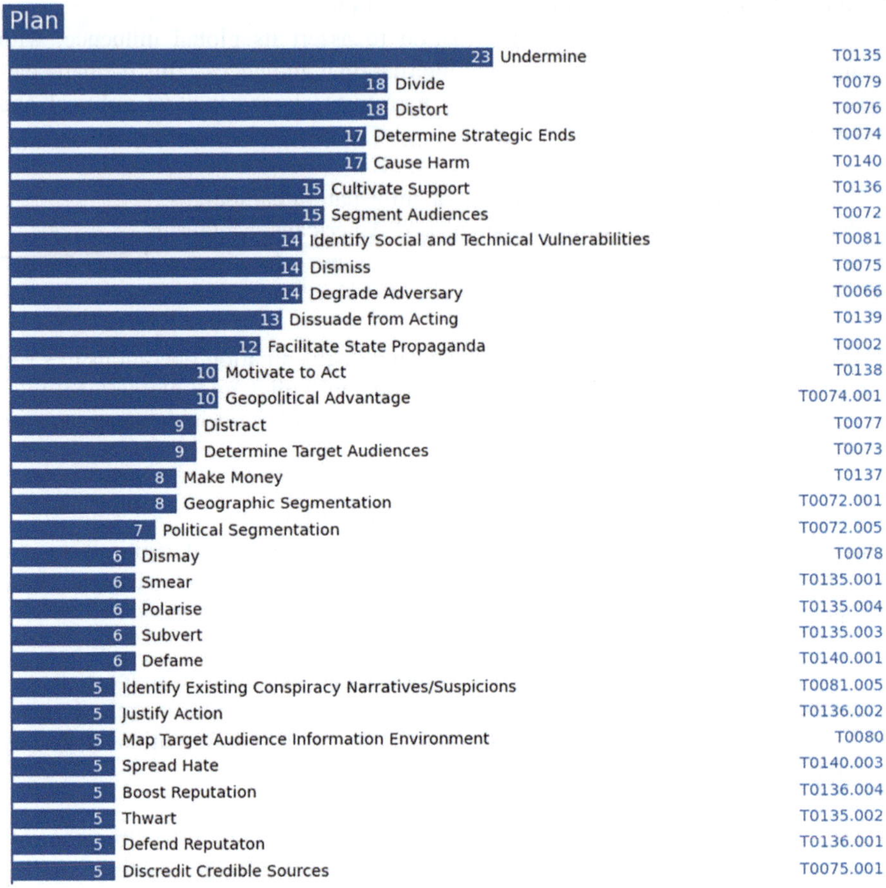

Fig. 5.4 Frequencies of plan phase TTPs across case studies

before operations even begin. Audience segmentation, particularly 'Segment Audiences' (T0072), was frequently employed, demonstrating a methodical approach to target audience analysis.

During P02, the use of 'Social networks' (T0104) was the most prevalent TTP, appearing in 80% of the cases, reflecting the reliance on digital platforms to build influence operations.[19] The creation and distortion of content were central, with 'Distort facts' (T0023) and 'Develop text-based content' (T0085) both used in over 60% of incidents. Threat actors also heavily leveraged existing narratives and conspiracy theories, with 'Leverage existing narratives' (T0003) and 'Leverage conspiracy theory narratives' (T0022) accounting for a significant portion of the

[19] Disinformation operations in cyber-space, ENISA, https://www.enisa.europa.eu/publications/info-notes/disinformation-operations-in-cyber-space.

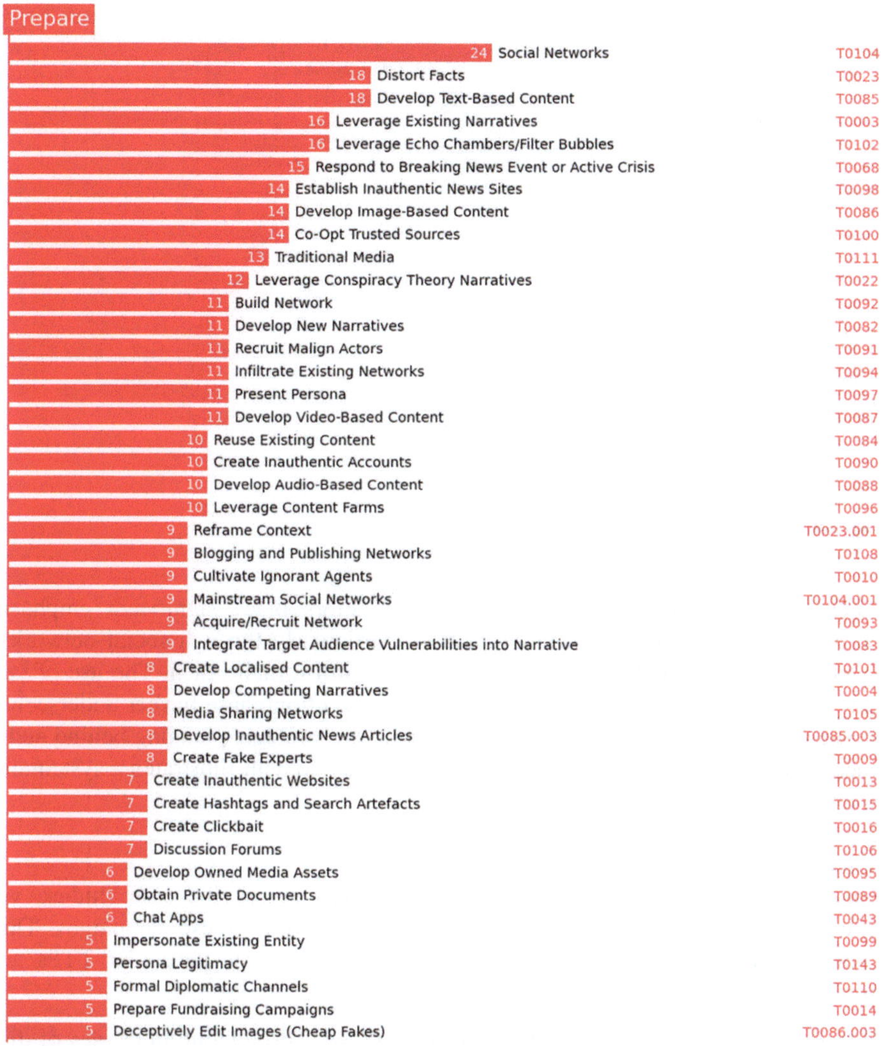

Fig. 5.5 Frequencies of Prepare phase TTPs across case studies

preparatory tactics. Additionally, techniques involving inauthentic media and the establishment of fake news sites (T0098) were key to the spread of disinformation.

In P03, TTPs focused on amplifying existing narratives, with ‘Amplify existing narrative’ (T0118) used in over 53% of the cases, underscoring the importance of increasing visibility. Cross-posting across platforms and groups (T0119) was another notable technique, used to ensure maximum reach of disinformation. The use of more aggressive tactics such as ‘Harass’ (T0048) and ‘Flood information space’ (T0049) shows how threat actors aimed to overwhelm the information environment to suppress counter-narratives and maintain their influence.

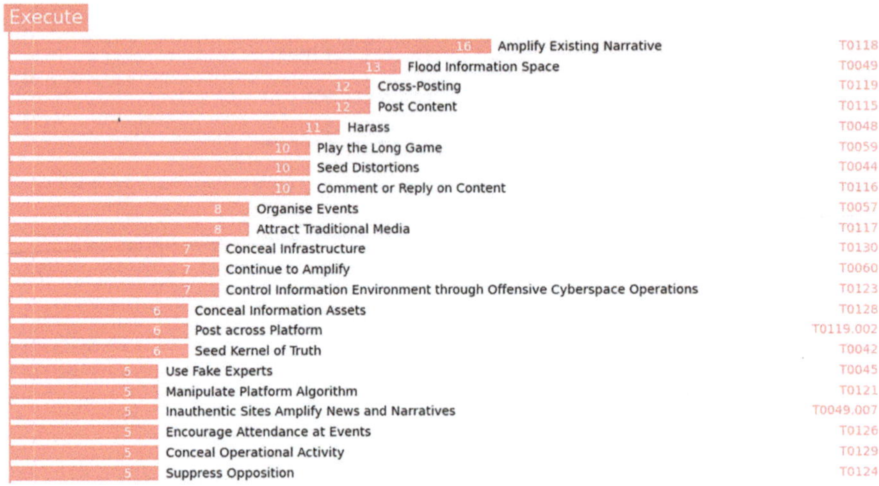

Fig. 5.6 Frequencies of Execute phase TTPs across case studies

Overall, the findings indicate that threat actors place significant emphasis on content manipulation and amplification, particularly through social networks, leveraging existing beliefs and narratives to maximise their reach. The use of targeted harassment and cross-posting during the execution phase further underscores the aggressive nature of these operations, while the strategic planning behind audience segmentation and the development of tailored content illustrates a systematic approach to influence operations.

Thematic TTP Usage

Following the overall frequency analysis of TTPs across the case studies, we now shift our focus to specific thematic groupings within these campaigns. This approach aims to provide a clearer understanding of how particular TTPs are applied in distinct geopolitical and strategic contexts.

Russian disinformation and information warfare: Throughout all phases of disinformation operations, Russia's primary objective has been to destabilise and weaken its adversaries through a coordinated and strategic use of various tactics. In P01, the most frequently employed tactic was 'Undermine' (T0135), observed in over 92% of case studies, illustrating Russia's focus on eroding the credibility and strength of its targets. Other common tactics included 'Divide' (T0079), 'Distort' (T0076), and 'Segment audiences' (T0072), each used in more than half of the cases, signalling a deliberate approach to fragment and manipulate different audience groups. Polarisation tactics such as 'Polarise' (T0135.004) and 'Distract' (T0077) were used in about a third of the cases, further intensifying internal divisions. In P02, 58% of cases leveraged 'Social networks' (T0104) to spread disinformation widely. Additional key tactics included 'Leverage existing narratives' (T0003) and 'Distort facts' (T0023), which were essential in reshaping public perceptions. Over half of the case studies techniques used 'Develop video-based content' (T0087) and 'Develop image-based content' (T0086) to enhance the appeal and reach of their disinformation. Russia also focused on creating inauthentic content and personas, with tactics such as 'Create inauthentic news sites' (T0098) and 'Create fake experts' (T0009) to bolster credibility and influence. In P03, the most prominent tactic was 'Amplify existing narrative' (T0118), used in 50% of the cases to ensure wide dissemination and reinforcement of disinformation themes. Other tactics like 'Post content' (T0115), 'Flood information space' (T0049), and 'Cross-posting' (T0119) were also significant, each occurring in more than 25% of cases.

Russian FIMI against Ukraine: The disinformation tactics used in Russian operations against Ukraine reflect a highly coordinated and strategic campaign across all phases of influence. In P01, all case studies employed 'Undermine' (T0135) and 'Determine strategic ends' (T0074), illustrating a clear intent to weaken Ukraine and steer the outcomes of these operations. Key tactics such as 'Identify social and technical vulnerabilities' (T0081) and 'Subvert' (T0135.003) were used in 67% of cases, emphasising a methodical effort to exploit Ukraine's weaknesses and deepen internal divisions through strategic manipulation. During P02, all cases leveraged 'Social networks' (T0104) and 'Leverage existing narratives' (T0003) to spread disinformation via echo chambers and filter bubbles, maximising the reach of their narratives. Other common tactics included 'Distort facts' (T0023) and 'Develop image-based content' (T0086), with 83% of cases involving the recruitment of malign actors and the creation of fake experts to bolster the disinformation ecosystem. In P03, 'Amplify existing narrative' (T0118) was present in all cases, ensuring the continuous reinforcement of disinformation themes. Additionally, 'Cross-posting' (T0119) and 'Flood information space' (T0049) were employed to broaden the dissemination of content, while suppression tactics (T0124) and the concealment of information assets (T0128) highlighted the covert and sustained nature of these disinformation efforts. This approach showcases Russia's strategic use of disinformation to destabilise Ukraine, manipulate narratives and weaken public trust.

Chinese disinformation and influence operations: Chinese influence operations highlight the strategic use of disinformation tactics to manipulate perceptions, create division and control the narrative. In P01, all cases featured 'Geographic segmentation' (T0072.001), showcasing a methodical approach to audience targeting based on location. Other common tactics included leveraging geopolitical advantages and state propaganda (T0002), alongside reputation management strategies such as 'Defend reputation' (T0136.001) and 'Boost reputation' (T0136.004). In P02, 'Social networks' (T0104) and 'Establish inauthentic news sites' (T0098) were used in 75% of cases, serving as critical platforms for disinformation dissemination. Content creation was a key component, with tactics like 'Develop new narratives' (T0082) and the creation of inauthentic websites (T0013) heavily used. Other notable methods included the widespread use of 'Create clickbait' (T0016) and 'Reuse existing content' (T0084), both of which appeared in over 50% of the cases, highlighting a focus on generating and recycling misleading material. In P03, 75% of cases involved 'Inauthentic sites amplify news and narratives' (T0049.007), demonstrating the ongoing use of deceptive platforms to spread propaganda. Additionally, methods like 'Trolls amplify and manipulate' (T0049.001) and 'Seed kernel of truth' (T0042) were frequently employed to manipulate discussions and subtly distort factual information. Further, the dissemination of disinformation was bolstered through 'Flood information space' (T0049) and 'Cross-posting' (T0119), reinforcing the focus on achieving widespread narrative propagation.

Turkish disinformation regarding Cyprus: Turkish disinformation campaigns targeting Cyprus exhibit a strategic use of audience segmentation and manipulation across different phases of operation. In P01, all case studies used 'Geographic segmentation' (T0072.001) and 'Segment audiences' (T0072), indicating a highly targeted approach based on location and audience profiling. These operations heavily relied on tactics like 'Undermine' (T0135), 'Distort' (T0076), and 'Divide' (T0079), aiming to fracture communities and exploit existing social vulnerabilities. The exploitation of prejudices (T0081.003) was a key element, reinforcing societal divisions. Additionally, geopolitical manipulation was a central focus, with 100% of cases employing 'Geopolitical advantage' (T0074.001) and 'Cultivate support' (T0136) to promote Turkish initiatives and strengthen influence in the region. In P02, the use of 'Social networks' (T0104) and 'Media sharing networks' (T0105) appeared in both cases, serving as primary platforms for disseminating disinformation. The creation of inauthentic content and the leveraging of existing narratives were also prevalent, with tactics like 'Distort facts' (T0023) and 'Develop video-based content' (T0087) being employed to amplify false information. In P03, attackers employed 'Cross-posting' (T0119) for the amplification of disinformation through the 'Seed kernel of truth' (T0042) tactic, ensuring that false narratives gained traction. Tactics for concealing the infrastructure and operational activities (T0130, T0129) were vital in ensuring the campaigns remained covert, providing plausible deniability while executing disinformation strategies.

5.3.3 TTP Co-occurrence Analysis

Based on the analysis of TTP frequencies, we identified significant patterns of TTP combinations that often co-occur in disinformation and FIMI campaigns. These combinations, depicted in Fig. 5.1, reflect strategic efforts by threat actors to amplify the effectiveness of their attacks by leveraging multiple techniques. Analysing these pairings allows us to identify the common approaches used and understand the underlying disinformation frameworks (Fig. 5.7).

Below, we list key observations from the most frequent TTP combinations:

- Developing image-based content frequently occurs alongside leveraging existing narratives and distorting facts (43.3%). This indicates a strategic use

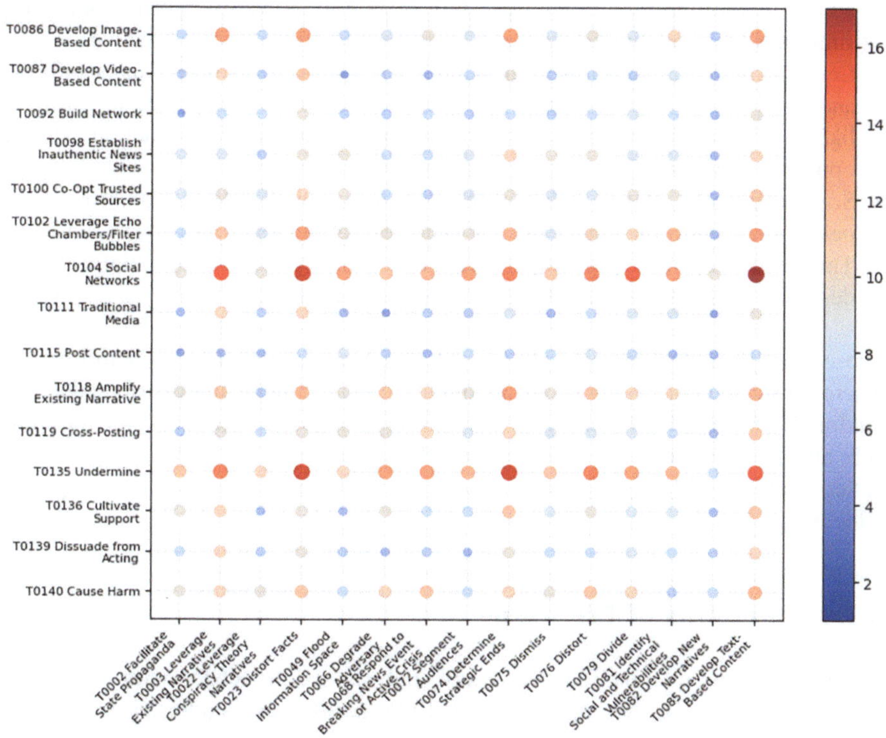

Fig. 5.7 TTP Co-occurrence frequency in case studies

of fabricated images to reinforce disinformation narratives and alter public perception by misrepresenting facts.

- Developing text-based content is another common TTP that is paired with image-based content (43.3%) and video-based content (33.3%), showing a coordinated multimedia approach. This combination is used to maximise the reach and credibility of disinformation, blending text and visuals to enhance the persuasive power of the content.
- Video-based content was often paired with distorting facts (36.7%) and leveraging existing narratives (33.3%). This highlights the role of video as a powerful medium to exploit misinformation and reframe current events in a misleading context.
- Establishing inauthentic news sites regularly appeared alongside determining strategic ends (33.3%) and developing text-based content (33.3%), indicating that false news outlets are set up with long-term objectives to control narratives and spread disinformation in a more structured manner.
- Co-opting trusted sources combined with distorting facts (33.3%) and developing text-based content (36.7%) illustrates how disinformation campaigns

aim to exploit trusted figures to lend credibility to false information, while simultaneously manipulating factual information to suit their objectives.
- Leveraging echo chambers/filter bubbles paired with distorting facts (43.3%) and determining strategic ends (40%) demonstrates the deliberate targeting of like-minded communities, where manipulated facts can gain traction without opposition, ensuring the spread of polarising narratives.
- Social networks played a key role in distributing disinformation, frequently paired with distorting facts (53.3%) and leveraging existing narratives (50%). This reinforces the role of social media as a primary conduit for disinformation, designed to distort facts, overwhelm users and reinforce misleading content.

These combinations demonstrate a multi-pronged approach to disinformation, where fabricated content, both visual and textual, is strategically distributed across platforms and amplified through networks of inauthentic accounts, media channels and trusted sources. Understanding these combinations helps in identifying patterns and formulating countermeasures to combat such coordinated campaigns effectively.

5.3.4 Patterns of TTP Usage

Building on the previous TTP frequency analysis, we proceeded with identifying recurring patterns in the application of TTPs across case studies. By exploring combinations of TTPs beyond simple pairs, we aimed to uncover strategic clusters and frequent co-occurrences that reveal the operational tactics employed in disinformation campaigns. Understanding these patterns is crucial for grasping the broader strategies driving disinformation and improving our ability to detect and counter such operations.

Clustering of Case Studies According to Their TTP Usage

To investigate common patterns in the use of TTPs across the case studies, we applied the k-means clustering algorithm,[20] a widely used unsupervised machine learning method for grouping data points into clusters based on similarities. The objective of this analysis was to identify groups of case studies that shared common TTP usage, which could indicate strategic similarities in how disinformation campaigns are executed.

We first prepared a square matrix that recorded the co-occurrence of TTPs across case studies. To reduce the dimensionality of the data and make it easier to visualise and cluster, we applied Principal Component Analysis (PCA),[21]

[20] Ahmed, Mohiuddin, Raihan Seraj, and Syed Mohammed Shamsul Islam, "The k-means algorithm: A comprehensive survey and performance evaluation", *Electronics*, Vol. 9, No. 8, 1295, 12 Aug 2020. https://doi.org/10.3390/electronics9081295.

[21] Maćkiewicz, Andrzej, and Waldemar Ratajczak, "Principal components analysis (PCA)", *Computers & Geosciences*, Vol. 19, No. 3, Mar 1993, pp. 303–342.

transforming the dataset into two main components. This allowed us to represent the complex TTP patterns in a simpler, two-dimensional space. Next, we applied k-means clustering to group the case studies. K-means operates by assigning case studies to a specified number of clusters (k) in such a way that the sum of the squared distances between each case study and its cluster centroid is minimised.

To determine the optimal number of clusters (*k*), we used the **elbow method** (see Fig. 5.8). This involves running k-means for various values of k and plotting the total inertia (i.e. the sum of squared distances within clusters) as a function of the number of clusters. The 'elbow' in the plot indicates a point where increasing the number of clusters no longer significantly reduces the inertia, thus balancing between underfitting and overfitting. As seen in the plot, the elbow was found at **k = 4**, suggesting that five clusters provide the optimal balance between cohesion within clusters and separation between clusters, as illustrated in Fig. 5.8. We therefore selected k = 4 for our final analysis. Table 5.1 presents the clusters that were generated.

Cluster 1 includes case studies that focus on the manipulation of public opinion through online platforms and divisive narratives. In this cluster, techniques such as 'Divide' (T0079) and 'Social networks' (T0104) were central. These case studies demonstrate a heavy reliance on social media to amplify divisive narratives, which is further supported by the frequent use of 'Undermine' (T0135) and 'Distort' (T0076). These TTPs are indicative of operations that seek to fragment societies, targeting specific audiences with tailored content to create distrust and destabilise democratic institutions. The use of 'Segment audiences' (T0072) is used by 50% of the cluster's case studies, showing that these campaigns also involve detailed analysis of their targets to maximise the impact of their disinformation.

Cluster 2 represents a more content-driven approach, where the focus lies on narrative manipulation and disinformation related to strategic political events. In this cluster, key TTPs like 'Leverage existing narratives' (T0003) and 'Distort facts' (T0023) appeared in all case studies, illustrating how these campaigns build upon pre-existing societal narratives and distort them to achieve their goals. Techniques for content development were also prominent, with 'Develop text-based content' (T0085), 'Develop image-based content' (T0086), and 'Develop audio-based content' (T0088). This highlights a multifaceted approach to disinformation, where text, images and audio are used together to create a persuasive and far-reaching narrative designed to influence public perception and undermine political stability.

Cluster 3 focuses heavily on the strategic degradation of adversaries. The dominant TTPs in this cluster include 'Degrade adversary' (T0066), 'Develop text-based content' (T0085) and 'Undermine' (T0135), each appearing in 90% of the case studies. These techniques suggest a coordinated effort to weaken the credibility and influence of adversaries, often by disseminating content that causes harm or distorts facts. The use of 'Cause harm' (T0140) and 'Facilitate state propaganda'

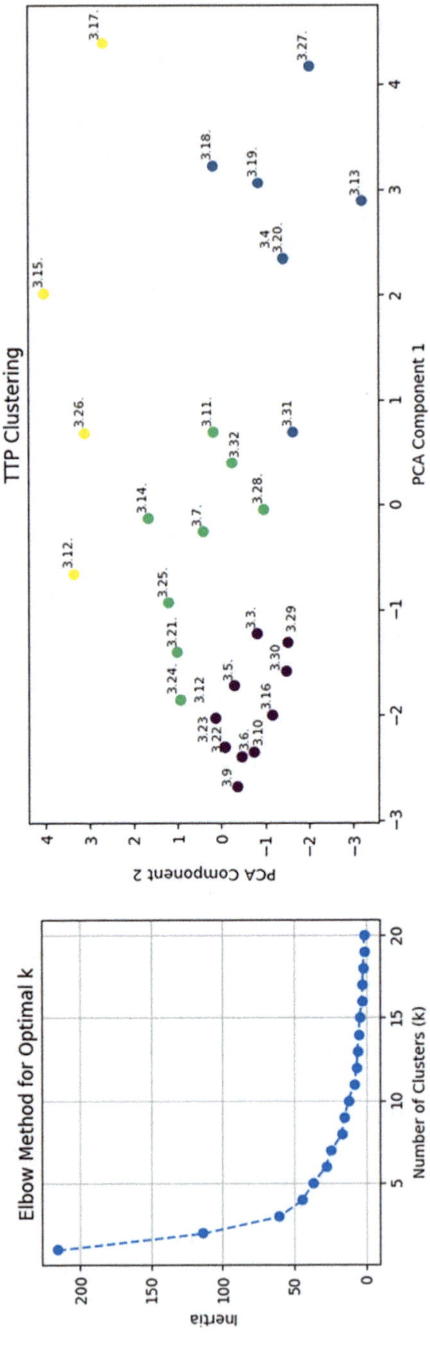

Fig. 5.8 Case study clusters based on TTP usage

Table 5.1 Identified case study clusters according to their TTP usage

Cluster 1	Cluster 2
• 4.10. Russian propaganda against Finland's transition to NATO member • 4.14. Russia uses bribery to spread disinformation • 4.17. European Parliament report on FIMI in European elections • 4.20. Meta dismantles large-scale Chinese disinformation campaign • 4.21. Facebook accounts in China impersonated Americans, Meta says • 4.28. Iranian interference in US elections • 4.2. Did the Russians dupe the US Republican party? • 4.29. Saudi Arabia's anti-Iran campaign during the Trump administration • 4.7. Russian initiatives to use farmers' protest in Germany • 4.9. Russian FIMI about the (fabricated) 'Lisa' rape case • 4.11. Framing the President—How Russia Creates Negative Press on a Head of State	• 4.15. Russian interference in the Spanish election in July 2023 • 4.6. Russian FIMI against the Armed Forces of Ukraine (AFU) • 4.18. Russian disinformation about Russian attacks • 4.24. Turkey's disinformation about north Cyprus as an independent state • 4.30. Cyberwarfare and the Qatar blockade • 4.5. How Russian FIMI actors reacted to the US aid package
Cluster 3	**Cluster 4**
• 4.12. Russia Today (RT), its narratives and ideological biases • 4.3. Altered photo showing Zelenskyy holding a jersey with a swastika • 4.19. Russian disinformation about COVID-19 vaccines • 4.22. PAPERWALL Chinese websites pose as local news to target global audiences • 4.23. Chinese disinformation about the release of Fukushima water • 4.27. North Korea's disinformation campaigns • 4.31. The role of FIMI in Iraq's Tishreen protests • 4.8. Russian FIMI about burning the Quran in Sweden	• 4.13. A Wagner campaign targeting the French army in Mali • 4.4. Disinformation about Zelenskyy's buying a villa in Florida • 4.17. Doppelganger: Russian disinformation using media clones and more • 4.25. Turkey's disinformation about a clash with the UN in the buffer zone in Cyprus

(T0002) further emphasises the systematic nature of these operations, where state actors employ disinformation to undermine their opponents and reinforce their strategic objectives. The case studies in this cluster demonstrate how media manipulation is used as a weapon to erode public trust in key figures, institutions and policies.

Cluster 4 is characterised by campaigns that leverage existing narratives to achieve long-term strategic ends. Key TTPs like 'Leverage existing narratives' (T0003) and 'Distort facts' (T0023), reflecting a reliance on manipulating pre-existing stories and distorting them to serve disinformation goals. Techniques such as 'Degrade adversary' (T0066) and 'Determine strategic ends' (T0074) also appeared frequently, indicating that these operations are often part of broader strategic efforts to weaken adversaries and achieve long-term objectives. The repeated use of 'Dismiss' (T0075) shows that dismissing counterarguments or conflicting narratives is also a common tactic in these campaigns, which seek to dominate the information environment by minimising opposition.

Overall, the clustering analysis reveals distinct patterns of TTP usage across case studies, highlighting different operational focuses. While some campaigns concentrate on divisive tactics and social network exploitation (Cluster 1), others rely on sophisticated narrative manipulation and content creation (Cluster 2). Meanwhile, campaigns in Cluster 3 focus on undermining and degrading adversaries, often through state-sponsored media outlets, and Cluster 4 emphasises leveraging existing narratives to achieve long-term strategic goals. These findings underscore the diversity of disinformation tactics and the importance of understanding the strategic combinations of TTPs used in influence operations.

Patterns of TTP Usage Across Case Studies

In analysing patterns of TTP usage across disinformation campaigns, we identified clusters of case studies that share common TTPs. While clustering highlights broad similarities, we employed a frequent item set analysis[22] to gain deeper insights into the recurring combinations of specific TTPs used across campaigns. This method allows us to identify not only which tactics frequently co-occur, but also how they are systematically combined to achieve strategic goals in various geopolitical contexts. By focusing on frequent item sets, we uncover the underlying structure of disinformation operations, revealing the strategic interplay of TTPs that persist across different cases, and how these patterns contribute to the effectiveness and persistence of disinformation narratives.

T0085: Develop text-based content, T0103: Social networks

Occurrence: 57%

We found that threat actors consistently combined text-based content with the extensive use of social networks. This pattern appeared frequently in disinformation campaigns from Russia, China, Turkey and North Korea, particularly around elections, geopolitical events and public health issues. By crafting text-based content, they manipulated narratives that spread across social platforms, maximising

[22] Borgelt, Christian, "Frequent item set mining", *WIREs Data Mining and Knowledge Discovery,* Vol. 2, Nov/Dec 2012, pp. 437–456. https://www.academia.edu/78672760/Frequent_item_set_mining.

their reach and influence. We saw this tactic used in disinformation about Ukraine, the Spanish elections and North Cyprus.

T0023: Distort facts, T0135: Undermine

Occurrence: 53%

Distorting facts and undermining adversaries emerged as a key strategy to destabilise public perception and create confusion. We observed this pattern prominently in Russian disinformation about Ukraine, particularly in campaigns distorting facts about military actions and portraying Russian dominance. The same tactics surfaced in election interference and health disinformation campaigns, where distorted narratives questioned the legitimacy of democratic processes and public health policies, including COVID-19.

T0023: Distort facts, T0085: Develop text-based content, T0104: Social networks

Occurrence: 47%

Distorting facts through written content, which is then propagated across social media platforms. The distortion of facts remains a core element of disinformation efforts, as seen in Russian narratives surrounding their military actions in Ukraine and the false claims about Zelenskyy's villa purchase in Florida. By manipulating facts and presenting them as credible information, disinformation campaigns gain traction on social networks, where the content can be easily shared and further distorted by others.

T0102: Leverage echo chambers/filter bubbles, T0085: Develop text-based content, T0104: Social networks

Occurrence: 43%

Exploiting echo chambers and filter bubbles to amplify disinformation is a highly effective tactic. Disinformation actors craft text-based content tailored to specific audiences' pre-existing beliefs and biases, then rely on social networks to reinforce and entrench these views. This tactic is particularly prominent in Russian state media like RT, which targets audiences predisposed to certain biases about Western actions, ensuring that narratives about Ukraine or NATO are continually reinforced within these echo chambers.

T0086: Develop image-based content, T0003: Leverage existing narratives, T0023: Distort facts, T0085: Develop text-based content, T0104: Social networks

Occurrence: 37%

Combining distorted facts and narratives with both text and image-based content, this set shows how visual elements are used alongside written disinformation to enhance credibility. Disinformation actors, particularly from Russia and Turkey, exploit pre-existing narratives and biases, amplifying these through social networks. Russia Today (RT) plays a key role here by distorting familiar narratives, such as the financial status of Ukrainian leadership or the portrayal of Russian military strength, making these narratives more believable through repeated exposure.

The frequent item set analysis of TTPs in disinformation campaigns reveals consistent and calculated combinations of tactics that go beyond isolated actions. Key patterns, such as the use of text-based content alongside social networks, the distortion of facts and the leveraging of echo chambers, highlight the systematic approach of disinformation actors. These patterns are not just coincidental but reflect strategic goals aimed at manipulating public perception and undermining trust in key institutions. The persistent use of these tactics across multiple geopolitical contexts underscores the sophistication of disinformation campaigns and the need for more targeted mitigation strategies that address these recurring combinations.

Key Takeaways

- **Understanding evolving disinformation strategies**: Disinformation campaigns are highly adaptive and strategic, with threat actors consistently combining specific TTPs to enhance the impact of their operations. For those responsible for shaping policies or designing countermeasures, understanding these evolving tactics is critical to developing effective interventions. The frequent occurrence of patterns such as using text-based content with social networks (57%) or leveraging echo chambers to amplify disinformation (43%) indicates a sophisticated and calculated approach to influencing public perception, often aimed at destabilising democratic institutions or supporting geopolitical goals.
- **Targeted tactics in specific contexts**: The analysis highlights that disinformation campaigns are tailored to specific geopolitical contexts, such as Russia's campaigns against Ukraine or Turkey's disinformation targeting Cyprus. Analysts and policymakers should recognise that these campaigns are not random but carefully designed to exploit local vulnerabilities and align with broader strategic objectives. For instance, Russia's consistent use of tactics like distorting facts (T0023) and undermining adversaries (T0135) in 53% of the cases demonstrates their effort to destabilise public trust and promote divisive narratives, particularly around elections and military conflicts.
- **Recurring themes across multiple actors**: Multiple state actors, including Russia, China, Turkey and North Korea, consistently employ similar TTPs to achieve their goals. This uniformity suggests the need for international cooperation and coordination in addressing disinformation threats. For instance, the frequent pairing of developing text-based content (T0085) with social networks (T0104) across campaigns (47%) shows that these actors exploit global digital platforms to manipulate public opinion, requiring a cross-border response from governments, social media platforms and international bodies.

- **Amplification through echo chambers**: Disinformation campaigns frequently exploit echo chambers and filter bubbles, where manipulated content reinforces pre-existing biases without challenge. For legislators, this finding highlights the importance of addressing how social media algorithms contribute to the amplification of disinformation. Regulatory measures may be needed to ensure platforms are held accountable for the unchecked spread of disinformation within these closed networks.
- **Use of multimedia to enhance credibility**: The strategic combination of image-based and text-based content (37% of cases) underlines the role of multimedia in enhancing the credibility and spread of disinformation. Disinformation campaigns are becoming more visually persuasive, making it imperative for policymakers to develop media literacy programmes that equip the public with tools to critically assess both textual and visual information.

The analysis of TTP patterns in disinformation campaigns shows that threat actors use recurring, strategic combinations of tactics to manipulate public opinion, erode trust in institutions and achieve geo-political goals. For analysts, policymakers and legislators, these findings emphasise the need for a comprehensive approach to counter disinformation, including policy reforms, increased regulation of social media platforms and improved public resilience through education on digital literacy. Recognising and anticipating the use of these systematic TTP combinations will be essential in mitigating the impact of disinformation.

5.4 TTPs Critical in FIMI

5.4.1 Predominant TTPs in FIMI

The analysis of the case studies in Chap. 4 reveals several TTPs that are consistently employed in FIMI campaigns. These TTPs are often used in combination to create sophisticated and effective disinformation operations. They fall into several broad categories, reflecting the strategic approach taken by disinformation actors.

Content Creation and Manipulation

At the heart of most disinformation campaigns is the creation and manipulation of content. A predominant TTP in this area is T0085 (Develop text-based content), which is used in more than 60% of cases. This involves creating articles, posts and other written materials that shape false narratives or distort facts to influence public opinion. This textual content is often the foundation of disinformation efforts and is crucial for establishing a narrative that can be widely disseminated. In conjunction with text-based content, T0086 (Develop image-based content) plays a significant role in enhancing the credibility and emotional appeal of disinformation. Altered or fabricated images are frequently used to reinforce false claims, making them more persuasive. This tactic is particularly effective in campaigns where visual manipulation helps mislead the public or distort facts to create a more believable narrative. Similarly, T0087 (Develop video-based content) is often employed to create a multimedia approach that combines text, images and videos. Video content has a powerful impact on viewers and is effective at reaching broader audiences. This tactic is commonly used in disinformation campaigns related to geopolitical events and public health crises, where emotional engagement is key to spreading false narratives.

Amplification and Distribution Through Digital Platforms

Once disinformation content is created, it needs to be distributed and amplified to reach large audiences. T0104: (Social Networks) is central to this process, appearing in 80% of the case studies. Social media platforms like Facebook, Twitter, and YouTube are instrumental in spreading disinformation quickly and broadly. These platforms enable disinformation to reach diverse audiences and to be shared and propagated within targeted communities. To further increase the reach of disinformation, T0118 (Amplify Existing Narrative) is commonly employed. This tactic involves the repeated posting and cross-posting of disinformation across various platforms, ensuring that false narratives gain traction and visibility. By amplifying existing narratives, disinformation actors ensure that their content becomes more deeply embedded in public discourse, making it more difficult for opposing information to break through.

Distorting Facts and Leveraging Narratives

A key function of FIMI campaigns is the distortion of factual information to confuse or mislead the public. T0023 (Distort facts) is a critical TTP used in over 60% of cases. This tactic involves altering or misrepresenting factual information to fit the goals of the disinformation actors. Often combined with other TTPs like content creation and amplification through social networks, the distortion of facts is highly effective in shaping public perception. In addition to distorting facts, disinformation actors frequently rely on T0003 (Leverage existing narratives) to enhance the credibility of their campaigns. By embedding false information within pre-existing narratives that are familiar to the target audience, disinformation becomes more believable and harder to detect. This tactic is particularly common in geopolitical disinformation campaigns, where actors exploit societal tensions or historical narratives to promote their agendas.

Exploitation of Echo Chambers and Audience Segmentation

Effective disinformation campaigns often target specific groups of people, ensuring that false narratives resonate more deeply within those communities. T0102 (Leverage echo chambers/filter bubbles) is a prominent tactic used to exploit social media algorithms, which trap users within echo chambers. Within these closed communities, disinformation is repeated and reinforced, making it difficult for opposing viewpoints to penetrate. This tactic ensures that false information is circulated among like-minded groups, making it more likely to be accepted as truth. Alongside the use of echo chambers, disinformation actors frequently employ T0072 (Segment audiences) to tailor their messages to specific demographic or ideological groups. By carefully analysing and targeting particular audiences, disinformation campaigns can maximise their impact. This audience segmentation allows disinformation actors to craft messages that align with the beliefs and values of their targets, making their narratives more persuasive and influential.

Undermining Adversaries and destabilising Institutions
A significant goal of many FIMI campaigns is to weaken adversaries and destabilise political or social institutions. T0135 (Undermine) is one of the most frequently used TTPs in this context. This tactic is often deployed in disinformation campaigns aimed at elections, government policies and military operations. By discrediting key figures or institutions, disinformation actors aim to erode public trust and weaken their opponents. This is particularly evident in Russian disinformation campaigns targeting Ukraine and Western democracies, where undermining adversaries is a core objective. Another common tactic in this category is T0079 (Divide), which seeks to exploit existing social, political or ethnic tensions to fragment societies. Disinformation campaigns use this tactic to deepen divisions and create distrust within communities. This often works in combination with audience segmentation and amplification techniques, ensuring that divisive narratives gain maximum reach and impact.

AI-Generated Content Techniques and Their Threats
Although not frequently encountered in the case studies, the rapid evolution of generative AI technologies poses a significant and growing threat in the realm of disinformation and FIMI operations. The capabilities of AI to autonomously generate highly realistic content, ranging from text to audio and video deepfakes, offer disinformation actors powerful new tools to manipulate public perception and sow confusion on an unprecedented scale. Considering this rapidly evolving threat, recently DISARM updated its TTP taxonomy to include generative AI techniques. T0086.002 (Develop AI-generated images—deepfakes) and T0087.001 (Develop AI-generated videos—Deepfakes) represent advanced methods for creating entirely synthetic visuals and videos. These deepfakes can recreate an individual's face, voice and body movements, making them indistinguishable from real media. As a result, they enable the production of falsified content that can be used to depict inauthentic scenarios, such as a public figure making false statements or committing actions they never took. While these techniques have not been prevalent in past disinformation campaigns, their potential for widespread manipulation is immense. AI-generated deepfakes could be deployed to incite social unrest, undermine trust in political figures or manipulate global narratives through convincingly false visuals. Another technique, T0088.001 (Develop AI-generated audio—deepfakes), focuses on the generation of synthetic audio. This poses a similar threat by enabling the recreation of an individual's voice to deliver

falsified soundbites or speeches. Such audio could be used to create false statements attributed to political leaders, celebrities or experts, effectively spreading disinformation and undermining trust in official communications. In the realm of text, T0085.001 (Develop AI-generated text) enables disinformation actors to autonomously generate synthetic written content. AI-generated text can mimic the style and tone of legitimate news outlets or individuals, producing vast amounts of convincing disinformation at scale. Autonomous text generation, which includes bot-created content, can be rapidly deployed in influence operations to flood information environments with misleading articles, social media posts or even entire news stories. As AI-generated text becomes more sophisticated, its ability to mimic authentic journalism or official communications will make it increasingly difficult to discern between real and synthetic information.

The analysis of TTPs in FIMI campaigns demonstrates the strategic and systematic approach taken by disinformation actors. Predominantly, these campaigns rely on content creation and manipulation, with tactics like developing text, image and video-based content forming the foundation of their operations. This content is then widely amplified through social networks and echo chambers, where it can spread rapidly and influence targeted audiences. In parallel, disinformation actors distort facts and leverage existing narratives to make their content more credible and harder to refute. Lastly, disinformation campaigns often seek to undermine adversaries and divide societies, using aggressive tactics like flooding the information space and harassment to suppress opposition and maintain control over the narrative.

These patterns of TTP usage highlight the need for comprehensive strategies to counter disinformation, including policy interventions, improved media literacy and coordinated efforts to disrupt the mechanisms that enable the spread of disinformation. Understanding these predominant TTPs is crucial for developing effective countermeasures to mitigate the impact of FIMI campaigns on public trust and democratic institutions.

5.4.2 The Use of Proxies by Foreign Actors

In the fight against disinformation, major threat actors can outsource a given FIMI to smaller threat actors, effectively engaging in a proxy war for their mutual benefit. Thus, studying the role of proxies in information warfare is crucial. Disinformation attacks by proxy can more easily adapt to certain cognitive biases. Proxies can also operate more effectively than larger entities like states or media outlets. Here, we focus on the main features of three proxies linked to the Russian Federation: Yevgeny Prigozhin, Russia Today and Bertrand Pillet (Thinkerview).

The *Routledge Handbook of Proxy Wars* associates threat actors who sponsor proxies with states, as well as proxies with various types of non-state threat actors, although sponsors can also be non-state entities and vice versa. Threat actors related to proxies include:

> External support to insurgents, state-sponsored terrorism, the outsourcing of security tasks to domestic militias, security force assistance, and "building partner capacity" in friendly host nations [...] rebel patronage and clientelism, informal/transnational alliances, paramilitary operations, internationalized conflict, indirect interstate conflict, subversion, or military aid.[23]

The resort to proxy wars and delegation reflects the sponsor threat actors' desire to avoid direct use of force. Proxy threat actors may have different strategic interests than their sponsors, seeking to augment their fighting power or political influence through their relationship with the sponsor or once they are active in the field.

Literature on proxy warfare dealing with disinformation is mostly focused on cyber offensive strategies and non-hacking disinformation is usually excluded. Nevertheless, other authors do identify as proxies certain actors operating on the Internet and social media, initially independent and outside the formal spheres of the state, who can disseminate the narratives of a given sponsor on a voluntary basis. In general, the relationship between a state sponsor and a proxy lasts throughout a campaign, not just during a particular FIMI incident or attack.

Yevgeny Prigoszhin and the Wagner Group

The Wagner group represents a prime example of a proxy threat actor. This private military company (PMC) has been described as 'a quasi-state actor and a proxy institution of the Russian State'.[24] Founded in Moscow around 2010, reportedly during a meeting of the Russian General Staff, it was led by Dimitri Utkin, a former member of the Russian special forces, and financed by oligarch Yevgeny Prigozhin until their deaths in 2023. Wagner operated as a de facto paramilitary force, deployed in key scenarios for the Russian Federation where the Kremlin did not want to be officially present.

The first appearances of the Wagner group were reported during Russia's annexation of Crimea in 2014, providing the soldiers wearing unmarked uniforms who occupied the peninsula. Wagner was also involved in other armed conflicts as irregular forces in support of other armies, such as in the Syrian conflict that erupted in 2015, or in support of Russia's own armed forces in the invasion of Ukraine in February 2022. The Wagner Group also provided private security services for governments with which Russia seeks to maintain good relations, as well as for companies and individuals with business interests under Moscow's protection, in Venezuela, Libya, Sudan, CAR, Mali and Mozambique.

In the summer of 2023, while participating in various Russian state operations, including the invasion of Ukraine, the Wagner Group mutinied against the Kremlin. Rivalries between Yevgeny Prigozhin and the Russian military elite eventually

[23] Moghadam, Assaf, Vladimir Rauta and Michel Wyss (eds.), *Routledge Handbook of Proxy Wars*, Taylor & Francis, 2023.

[24] Neethling, Theo, "Russian Para-Military Operations in Africa: The Wagner Group as a De Facto Foreign Policy Instrument", *Scientia Militaria: South African Journal of Military Studies*, Vol. 51, No. 1, 2023, pp. 1–23.

boiled over, triggering a rebellion. Wagner Group troops deployed on the Ukrainian front and in surrounding areas marched towards Moscow. However, Russian government forces responded in unison, repelling the rebellion. Two months later, Prigozhin, Utkin and other leading members of Wagner died in a plane crash, probably caused by Kremlin forces. Although its role in Ukraine has shifted significantly, all signs suggest that its activities in Africa remain largely unchanged. Regarding Prigozhin's FIMI activities, at least his troll farms were still operating recently.[25]

Observables

Apart from his private security business, Prigozhin owned a media empire that he used to conduct influence operations and FIMI attacks. His assets, including troll and bot farms, Telegram channels and pro-Russian activists online were part of a large disinformation network to spread propaganda and interfere in the informational space of several Western countries. Such influence operations and media assets were part of a wider ecosystem of disinformation channels, which included agencies such as the Internet Research Agency (IRA), allegedly founded by Prigozhin. In addition, Prigozhin was also head of the supervisory board of the RIA FAN agency.[26]

The main observables deployed in FIMI campaigns include Facebook groups created around polarising content, such as Army of Jesus or LGBT United.[27] The IRA has used fake accounts to harass individuals online, a common tactic employed in Russia to defame opposition forces, as well as to infiltrate Facebook between 2015 and 2017 to incite users to support Donald Trump. Some of the posts found on social media like Facebook or Instagram of the IRA screen groups do not resort to emotionally charged language, but present relatively sober content.

In March 2022, Wagner's FIMI attack in Mali, demonstrated its ability and means to carry a disinformation campaign beyond social media. Through a fake account on Twitter, Wagner disseminated a video they had recorded themselves. The video showed a mass grave where the French army allegedly buried the bodies of a massacre it had committed. Far from it, the bodies were buried by Wagner mercenaries and junta soldiers, bridging the gap between the physical and digital realms in orchestrating a FIMI attack.

---

[25] Volz, Dustin, "Prigozhin Is Dead, but His Troll Farms Are Alive and Peddling Disinformation", *WSJ*, 28 Mar 2024. https://www.wsj.com/politics/national-security/prigozhin-is-dead-but-his-troll-farms-are-alive-and-peddling-disinformation-e25c4441.

[26] Bryjka, Filip, "Prigozhin's mutiny-causes, course and consequences of the Wagner Group rebellion", *Przegląd Bezpieczeństwa Wewnętrznego*, No. 30, 2024, pp. 269–304.

[27] Mottin, Victor, "Russie: plongée dans la stratégie du chaos de l'Internet Research Agency", *Usbek&Rica*, 4 Mar 2024. https://usbeketrica.com/fr/article/l-internet-research-agency-russe-ou-la-strategie-du-chaos.

Content and Narratives

The objective of the disinformation that Wagner propagated varied depending on its target. While FIMI attacks directed against most Western countries sought to polarise around existing cleavages, in countries where it tried to gain the trust of governments and local populations, the Wagner group sought to present itself as an ally against Western imperialism and neo-colonialism by supporting the state forces that normally fund its services. After Prigozhin's death, several Twitter accounts presumably controlled by Wagner also started posting content praising its passed leader.[28] The main narratives pushed by the Wagner group have been the following:

- Narrative 1: The US is getting tougher on the working classes. Barack Obama was incompetent while Vladimir Putin is a more solid political leader.[29]
- Narrative 2: The interim government in Kiev is controlled by fascists and neo-Nazis who aim to oppress Russian-speaking Ukrainians.[30]
- Narrative 3: Russia is a conceivable ally for the Malian junta, which should remain and not call for democratic elections yet.[31]
- Narrative 4: Wagner and Russia are helping African countries like Mali to fight neocolonialism.
- Narrative 5: 'It was not profitable for Putin to kill Prigozhin'.

Beyond narratives, Wagner has in the past resorted to high-impact hoaxes and fake news, potentially damaging to the mental and emotional stability of users. On 11 September 2014, a video of a chemical plant explosion in the state of Louisiana (US), along with a recording of alleged Islamic State members claiming responsibility for the action, was published through various fake news channels. Years later, they released videos of a fake Ebola outbreak in the state of Georgia (US), following a similar pattern.[32]

[28] Burgess, Matt, "The Strange Afterlife of Wagner's Yevgeny Prigozhin", *Wired*, 5 Sept 2024. https://www.wired.com/story/prigozhin-wagner-dead-news-disinformation/.

[29] Such narratives were propagated on social networks such as Facebook by members of the IRA through fake profiles, under the guise of working-class American citizens, to promote the election of Donald Trump in 2016.

See: Soshnikov, Andrey, "Internet trolls from Olgino began speaking English and Ukrainian", *MR7.ru*, 30 May 2024. https://mr-7.ru/articles/2014/05/30/internet-trolli-iz-olgino-zagovorili-na-angliiskom-i-ukrainskom.

[30] Seddon, Max, "Documents Show How Russia's Troll Army Hit America", *BuzzFeed News*, 2 June 2014. https://www.buzzfeednews.com/article/maxseddon/documents-show-how-russias-troll-army-hit-america.

[31] Price, Ned, spokesperson, US Department of State, "Le groupe Wagner, Evgueni Prigojine, et la désinformation de la Russie en Afrique", 3 Apr 2022.

[32] *PBS NewsHour*, "Why are Russian trolls spreading online hoaxes in the U.S.?", 9 June 2015. https://www.youtube.com/watch?v=6hUze1e0OiM.

TTPs Used by the Wagner Group

- T0002: Facilitate state propaganda—Aligned with the Russian state, Prigozhin's FIMI attacks followed Kremlin propaganda.
- T0066: Degrade adversary—The adversary was especially the American political class, for their incompetence and for having forgotten the working classes in the United States.
- T0075.001: Discredit credible sources—Western media have frequently been a key target of Prigozhin's disinformation.
- T0076: Distort—Prigozhin's propaganda distorts reality, as when in 2014 it presented the Ukrainian government as a gang of neo-Nazis.
- T0077: Distract—Users who have been seduced by Prigozhin's disinformation are fundamentally distracted from underlying truths and manipulated to serve interests they do not fully understand.
- T0078: Dismay—Opposition journalists and media in the West have in the past suffered threats and discredit from Prigozhin's trolls.
- T0079: Divide—One of the main objectives of Prigozhin's FIMI campaigns was to increase polarisation in Western societies.
- T0072: Segment audiences—Prigozhin's propaganda segmented his target audiences according to ideology and other geopolitical parameters.
- T0081: Identify social and technical vulnerabilities—To generate a climate of social tension, Prigozhin's propaganda exploited previously identified social and technical vulnerabilities.
- T0081.003: Identify existing prejudices—These social vulnerabilities were based on existing prejudices (see T0081).
- TA14: Develop narratives—Prigozhin's FIMI campaigns included various narratives concocted from Moscow, about Russia in general or Putin in particular, about the West and about various African countries.
- T0003: Leverage existing narratives—narratives (see TA14) have built on previously existing ones, such as those related to the colonial past of African countries like Mali and their relationship with the West.
- T0083: Integrate target audience vulnerabilities into narrative—Narratives (see TA14) have been shaped around the social vulnerabilities of certain audiences.
- T0007: Create inauthentic social media pages and groups—A common practice of the IRA relied on the creation of pages on social networks such as Facebook to generate polarising content.
- T0090: Create inauthentic accounts—The disinformation produced by Prigozhin's network was largely carried by human-controlled fake accounts.
- T0090.003: Create bot accounts—Prigozhin's network included bot farms that continue to operate after his death.
- T0094: Infiltrate existing networks—The inauthentic accounts (see T0090) infiltrated Facebook pages and the comments section of articles in digital media.

- T0097: Create personas—Many of the inauthentic accounts detected in the FIMI attacks had the appearance of a real person.
- T0098: Establish inauthentic news sites—To spread hoaxes such as the one about the explosion of the chemical plant station in Louisiana, a fake page was created.
- T0048: Harass—Originally set up to suppress opposition to Putin's government, one of the tactics of Prigozhin's hired individuals was to harass journalists and political opponents. Later, this practice was employed against voices critical of Putin abroad.
- T0124: Suppress opposition—(see T0048).
- T0059: Play the long game—Although there is insufficient evidence to measure the impact of Russian influence operations, Prigozhin's strategy was designed to bear fruit in the long run.

Bertrand Pillet and Thinkerview

If the linkage of a proxy to a sponsoring State is often difficult to measure or prove, the case of the YouTube channel Thinkerview and the person behind it, is paradigmatic. Before his identity became public, Bertrand Pillet used to go under the pseudonym Sky while he hosted his online talk show, never appearing on camera. However, during an official visit of Russian Foreign Minister Sergey Lavrov to Paris, in November 2019, the ministry's Twitter and Facebook[33] accounts posted several photos of a meeting with 'representatives of the French civil society'[34] where Pillet appeared.[35] Alongside Pillet, the images show members of the French New Right[36] such as Claude Chollet, far-right journalists André Bercoff (*Sud-Radio*) and Laurent Poultier du Mesnil (*Radio Courtoisie*), anti-mainstream media journalist Olivier Berruyer, as well as researcher and Russia campaigner in France, Philippe Migault.[37]

---

[33] Facebook, " In Paris, FM Sergey #Lavrov met with members of the French civil society", #Russia #France #Moscow #Paris #Diplomacy, 11 Nov 2019. https://www.facebook.com/MIDRussia/posts/2090333797732717/?.

[34] Ambassade de la Fédération de Russie en France, "Visite de travail de Sergueï Lavrov, Ministre des Affaires étrangères de la Fédération de Russie", 13 Nov 2019. https://france.mid.ru/fr/presse/visite_lavrov_19_11/.

[35] Conspiracy Watch, "Nous sommes en mesure d'affirmer que l'intervieweur-mystère de la chaîne YouTube controversée #ThinkerView, qui se fait appeler "Sky", était présent lors de cette rencontre à Paris en début de semaine", [Thread], X, 15 Nov 2019. https://x.com/conspiration/status/1195327601214140416.

[36] The French New Right is a far-right school of thought born in France in the late 1960s. Its main figures have historically defended an identitarian and anti-Modern vision of society. See: Taguieff, Pierre-André, *Sur la nouvelle droite*, Paris, Descartes & Cie, 1994.

[37] Reichstadt, Rudy, @RReichstadt, "Autour du chef de la diplomatie russe, on reconnaît notamment Claude Chollet (OJIM), Olivier Berruyer (Les-Crises), André Bercoff (Sud-Radio), Laurent

This does not necessarily imply that every participant in the meeting is a Russian proxy. However, Pillet's journalistic activity comes dangerously close to FIMI, as he could be located between the proxy and the 'useful idiot'. Following the definition of Cătălin Negoiță, useful idiots act as 'unwitting propagandists of a cause whose goals they are not fully aware of, and who are cynically manipulated by puppeteers'.[38] Other definitions highlight the 'gullible' nature of such individuals.[39]

After being identified at the Russian embassy in Paris, Pillet gave an interview to the media outlet *Arrêt sur Images*. In it, the owner of Thinkerview claimed that he just 'goes wherever he's invited', particularly if it leads to new interviews. This aligns with the naïveté of a 'useful idiot', though it's hard to dismiss the possibility of a calculated performance of innocence, especially given his expressed interest in interviewing Lavrov. Pillet also confessed to having attended, along with several French far-right journalists, three events organised in Sotchi (2015), in Belgrade (2016) and in Nicosia (2018) by the International Academy of Television and Radio (IATR), an NGO controlled by members of the Russian media elite.[40] In 2017, Pillet reportedly took part in the World Festival of Youth and Students in Sochi, an event featuring the countries of the Russian sphere of influence, this occasion inaugurated by Vladimir Putin. Xenia Fedorova, former chief editor of RT France, was also close to him.[41]

Unless one thinks that Russian soft power is seeking to bring Pillet closer to its political orbit for altruistic reasons, the strategic interests that define the relationship between a sponsor state and its proxy tie Pillet to the Russian sphere of influence. Whether he is cynical about it or not, the latter being less probable than the former, Pillet behaves de facto as a Russian proxy. As stated in this text from historian and expert on Russia Mark Galeotti, this way of leveraging 'unspoken understandings' is in fact common under Putin's rule[42]:

> A dependence on personal relationships and unspoken understandings – *ponyatiye* in Russian and, interestingly enough, a term also much used in the criminal underworld – has become central to Putin's style of rule. He (and increasingly often his senior people, too)

Poultier du Mesnil (Radio Courtoisie), Philippe Migault (CEAS)…", 15 Nov 2019. https://x.com/RReichstadt/status/1195291169200185345.

38 Negoiță, Cătălin, "Hybrid Warfare, Trolls, Agents of Influence, and Useful Idiots", ACROSS, Vol. 8, No. 1, 2024, pp. 17–29.

39 Michael, George, "Useful idiots or fellow travelers? The relationship between the American far right and Russia", in Jeffrey Kaplan (ed.), *The 21st Century Cold War*, Routledge, 2020, pp. 64–83.

40 Vladislava Vojtíšková, Vít Novotný, Hubertus Schmid-Schmidsfelden and Kristina Potapova, "The Bear in Sheep's Clothing Russia's Government-Funded Organisations in the EU" *Wilfried Martens Centre for European Studies*, 20 July 2016. https://galerie9.com/blog/russia-gongos.pdf.

41 Mottin, Victor, "Alain Juillet, l'ex de la DGSE au service de la complosphère pro-russe", *ConspiracyWatch*, 28 Feb 2024. https://www.conspiracywatch.info/alain-juillet-lex-de-la-dgse-au-service-de-la-complosphere-pro-russe.html.

42 Galeotti, Mark, *We need to talk about Putin. Why the West gets him wrong*, Penguin Random House, London, 2019.

rarely gives direct instructions, but defines broad objectives and hints as to what he might like to happen. As journalist Mikhail Zygar has put it, 'They would never say, "Please steal those billions of dollars" or "Please murder those journalists." They [instead] say, "Do what you have to do. You know your obligations; please fulfill them."'

Observables

Indicated previously, the main observable of Pillet's campaign is the YouTube channel Thinkerview. Created in 2013, it experienced sustained growth until 2019 when, amid the Yellow Vests movement, it increased its number of followers from 200,000 to 310,000. It now counts on a community of 1.2 million followers, and many of its videos surpass one million views. Pillet boasts to have balanced finances as of this period, thanks to donations from its viewers through the platform Tipee. This would be his only important income, refusing to have advertising and therefore invoicing any money from YouTube.

The symbol of the channel, a black swan, appears to be a reference to the eponymous metaphor of economist Nassim Taleb, where the bird represents an event with a low probability of occurring, but with dire consequences if it does.[43] The name given to the channel, presumably a play on the words 'think' and 'interview', gives a clue to the format that follows. The priority is the substance, not the form. The interview takes place against a black background, where the interviewee is the only one visible in front of the camera. The viewer hears Pillet's voice asking the questions, without his face appearing.

Pillet assures that the interviews are posted on the channel without 'interruptions, cuts or editing'.[44] The dialogue is informal and far from the canons of mainstream television, sometimes lasting more than two hours.

Pillet also has an account on X (formerly Twitter), from where he promotes the YouTube channel and interacts with his community of some 155,000 followers. Here the tone is more casual than in the interviews, although the gravity of the content of his posts cannot be neglected. He spreads a bellicose message, claiming that an international war with Russia is inevitable if diplomacy fails to act.

[43] Inchauspé, Irène, "La leçon de Nassim Taleb, le père du Cygne noir", *Challenges*, 6 Apr 2012. https://www.challenges.fr/economie/la-lecon-de-nassim-taleb-le-pere-du-cygne-noir_288795.

[44] Parrot, Clément, "Qui se cache derrière Thinkerview, la chaîne YouTube qui surfe sur le mouvement des 'gilets jaunes'?", *France Info*, 22 May 2019. https://www.francetvinfo.fr/economie/transports/gilets-jaunes/qui-se-cache-derriere-thinkerview-la-chaine-youtube-qui-surfe-sur-le-mouvement-des-gilets-jaunes_3441317.html.

Partly leaving Ukraine out of the equation, he bolsters the NATO vs. Russia narrative.[45] Thinkerview also has an important community on Facebook and is present in alternative social media. Its accounts are centralised in a web page.[46]

Content and Narratives

The content offered by Bertrand Pillet through Thinkerview shows a pro-Russian bias in the treatment of information and the choice of his guests. Pillet has claimed on several occasions to be a 'neutral'[47] and 'apolitical'[48] figure. Pillet, like other media figures, claims that the status quo is a neutral ground. His mission is to give a voice to everyone without distinction, as if this was a guarantee of neutrality. These narratives put aggressors and aggressed, authoritarian regimes and democracies, the far-right and the far-left, etc. on an equal basis.

Thus, following the fallacy of false equivalence, Pillet has invited to his programme several figures in the Russian sphere of influence and even members of the Russian government. The interview approach tends to be in tune with Russian narratives on various issues, as NATO, Syria or North Africa, but not hinting at others, like Ukraine. This was the case in his interview with the Minister Counsellor of the Russian Embassy in Paris, Artem Studennikov, where he delved into several key geopolitical affairs, the US and France, but only mentions Ukraine while accusing NATO of having an expansionist policy.[49] When it comes to talking about Ukraine more in depth, the angle equally follows the pro-Russian narrative. In his interview with Alain Juillet, former head of intelligence of the French DGSE, the latter reduced the Maidan of Ukraine to 'a hub of destabilisation' created by the Americans to prevent a rapprochement between Russia and Europe. Pillet pushed these narratives:

45 X, "Le gouvernement Britannique est tétanisé par les prémices d'une guerre civile, essaye de faire des exemples pour tuer dans l'œuf la rébellion qui gronde", 20 Aug 2024. https://x.com/Thinker_View/status/1825799686130696354; X, "Ouvrir un autre front, de plus directement avec l'OTAN, mais quelle bonne idée que voila…" 21 June 2022. https://x.com/Thinker_View/status/1539192634199113729, X, "https://courrierinternational.com/article/politique-ursula-von-der-leyen-lorgne-le-commandement-de-l-otan-pour-2024", 19 Mar 2023. https://x.com/Thinker_View/status/1637541079951048706; X, "La découverte de la "realpolitik", la "Weltpolitik", le changement de phase. La guerre économique, depuis la nuit des temps, donne toujours des guerres. "Si l'Ukraine tombe, l'OTAN devra rentrer en guerre" Les temps difficiles créent des hommes forts, cette ITW était compliquée, la place est brulante. Courage Stéphane Séjourné. Ils faut s'expliquer autour d'une table maintenant. https://youtube.com/watch?v=88", 6 Mar 2024. https://x.com/Thinker_View/status/1765354548367892562.

46 See https://www.thinkerview.com/.

47 Op. cit.

48 M le magazine du Monde, "ThinkerView, la chaîne YouTube qui veut hacker les médias", *Le Monde*, 22 Mar 2019. https://www.lemonde.fr/m-le-mag/article/2019/03/22/thinkerview-la-chaine-youtube-qui-veut-hacker-les-medias_5439850_4500055.html.

49 Thinkerview, "États-Unis-Russie: Tensions Géopolitiques et Terrorisme", 10 Oct 2016. https://www.youtube.com/watch?v=N845HBEzzGY.

- Narrative 1: Thinkerview has a neutral approach to information.
- Narrative 2: The far-left and the far-right can find common ground.
- Narrative 3: Even if they say outrageous things, it's better that interviewees talk.
- Narrative 4: NATO has an expansionist policy.
- Narrative 5: If the West heads to war, either to national civil wars or a confrontation between NATO countries and Russia, it will be the West's fault.

TTPs Used by Bertrand Pillet

- T0002: Facilitate state propaganda—Through Thinkerview, Pillet normalises and whitewashes Kremlin narratives in front of large audiences.
- T0066: Degrade adversary—The image of several Western governments is caricatured, portraying them as incompetent and aggressive.
- T0075.001: Discredit credible sources—Mainstream media are accused of being biased, while Thinkerview represents neutrality.
- T0076: Distort—The narratives conveyed through the Thinkerview channel and its accounts on other social networks distort reality.
- T0077: Distract—While Thinkerview primarily criticises Western government policies, it deflects viewers' attention from equally or more serious issues caused by regimes like Russia.
- T0078: Dismay—Thinkerview fosters social tension through bellicose alarmism.
- T0081: Identify social and technical vulnerabilities—Pillet exploits certain aspects of its audience's behaviour, beliefs and media consumption patterns, i.e. its mistrust in mainstream media and pre-existing biases and prejudices.
- T0081.003: Identify existing prejudices—See T0081.
- T0004: Develop competing narratives: Thinkerview has developed its own narratives, including the idea that, even when interviewees make outrageous statements, it is still valuable to let them speak. Otherwise, they have leveraged existing narratives.
- T0003: Leverage existing narratives—See T0004.
- T0083: Integrate target audience vulnerabilities into narrative—See T0081.
- T0097: Present persona—Bertrand Pillet not only created Sky's pseudonym, but also has used several false names when speaking to journalists.
- T0017: Conduct fundraising—Pillet raises funds through online donation platforms such as Tipeee.
- T0131.002: Post borderline content—Pillet uses memes and graphic content to support his message.
- T0123.002: Block content—From Thinkerview's Twitter account, Pillet blocks all users who criticise him for his biases.

- T0120: Incentivise sharing—Pillet encourages its community to share content related to the platform, in the online and offline realm.
- T0119: Cross-posting—Although its main activity is on YouTube, Twitter and Facebook, Thinkerview has accounts on Mastodon, Peertube and Captainfact.
- T0118: Amplify existing narrative—See T0004.
- T0117: Attract traditional media—Primarily to criticise his work, but also to praise it, Thinkerview has attracted the attention of the mainstream media.

5.5 Deepfakes in FIMI: Impacts and Challenges in Detection

Deepfake technology, which harnesses artificial intelligence and deep learning to create highly realistic but fabricated multimedia content, has rapidly emerged as one of the most disruptive forces in the digital era.[50] This technology manipulates images, videos, audio and text to produce convincing yet deceptive content that can be difficult to distinguish from genuine media.[51] Deepfakes first came into the spotlight in 2017, when a Reddit user named 'deepfakes' used AI techniques to swap celebrity faces into pornographic videos.[52] This controversial application highlighted the potential of deepfakes to alter reality in profound ways and, since then, their development has raised growing concerns about the spread of misinformation, manipulation of public opinion and erosion of trust in media.[53]

---

[50] Mubarak, Rami, Tariq Alsboui, Omar Alshaikh, Ibrahim Inuwa-Dute, Saira Khan, and Stephen Parkinson, "A survey on the detection and impacts of deepfakes in visual, audio, and textual formats", *IEEE Access*, 2023.

[51] Wang, Patrick, Raul Angarita and Isaac Renna, "Is this the era of misinformation yet: Combining social bots and fake news to deceive the masses", in *Proceedings of the Companion Web Conference*, 2018, pp. 1557–1561.

[52] Kietzmann, Jan, Lauren W. Lee, Ian P. McCarthy and Thomas C. Kietzmann, "DeepFakes: Trick or treat?", *Business Horizons*, Vol. 63, No. 2, March 2020, pp. 135–146.

[53] de Ruiter, Adrienne, "The distinct wrong of DeepFakes", *Philosophy & Technology*, Vol. 34, No. 4, Dec 2021, pp. 1311–1332. See also Langa, Jack, "DeepFakes, real consequences: Crafting legislation to combat threats posed by deepfakes", *Boston University Law Review*, Vol. 101, Issue 2, March 2021, pp. 761–801. Hanitzsch, Thomas, Arjen Van Dale and Nina Steindl, "Caught in the nexus: A comparative and longitudinal analysis of public trust in the press", *International Journal of Press/Politics*, Vol. 23, No. 1, Jan 2018, pp. 3–23. https://journals.sagepub.com/doi/10.1177/1940161217740695. Ice, Jason, "Defamatory political deepfakes and the first amendment", *Case Western Reserve Law Review*, Vol. 70, Jan 2019, p. 417.

As the technology evolves, the ability to generate realistic yet deceptive content has expanded across multiple domains, including politics,[54] social media[55] and economy.[56] Deepfakes are increasingly being used not only to deceive viewers but also to spread disinformation and distort political discourse.[57] These developments pose significant risks to democratic institutions, social cohesion and public trust. The challenge of addressing the harmful impacts of deepfakes has become more pressing, as the lines between real and fake content continue to blur in the digital landscape. The proliferation of this technology calls for increased awareness, detection mechanisms and regulatory measures to mitigate its negative effects.[58]

[54] Vaccari, Cristian, and Andrew Chadwick, "DeepFakes and disinformation: Exploring the impact of synthetic political video on deception uncertainty and trust in news", *Social Media & Society*, Vol. 6, No. 1, Jan 2020. See also Bessi, Alessandro, and Emilio Ferrara, "Social bots distort the 2016 U.S. presidential election online discussion", *First Monday*, Vol. 21, Nov 2016, pp. 11. Aïmeur, Esma, Said Amri and Gilles Brassard, "Fake news disinformation and misinformation in social media: A review", *Social Network Analysis and Mining*, Vol. 13, No. 1, Feb 2023, pp. 30. Shao, Chengcheng, Giovanni Luca Ciampaglia, Onur Varol, Kai-Cheng Yang, Alessandro Flammini and Filippo Menczer, "The spread of low-credibility content by social bots", *Nature Communications*, Vol. 9, No. 1, Nov 2018, pp. 1–9.

[55] Vaccari and Chadwick, Ibid. See also Greaves, Mark, "'Deepfakes' Ranked as Most Serious AI Crime", UCL, 4 Aug 2020. https://www.ucl.ac.uk/news/2020/aug/deepfakes-ranked-most-serious-ai-crime-threat. Lovato, Juliana, Laurent Hébert-Dufresne, Julien St-Onge, Richard Harp, George S. Lopez, Stephen P. Rogers, et al., "Diverse misinformation: Impacts of human biases on detection of deepfakes on networks", arXiv:2210.10026, 2022. Kirchengast, Thomas, "Deepfakes and image manipulation: Criminalisation and control", *Information, Communication & Technology Law*, Vol. 29, No. 3, Sept 2020, pp. 308–323. Etienne, Hugo, "The future of online trust (and why deepfake is advancing it)", *AI Ethics*, Vol. 1, No. 4, Nov 2021, pp. 553–562. Pfefferkorn, Rachel, "'DeepFakes' in the courtroom", *Boston University Public Interest Law Journal*, Vol. 29, Jan 2019, pp. 245.

[56] Kietzmann, et al., op. cit. See also Bateman, Jon, "Deepfakes and Synthetic Media in the Financial System: Assessing Threat Scenarios", Carnegie Endowment for International Peace, Washington, DC, 2020. Ghazi-Tehrani, Ahmad K., and Henry N. Pontell, "Phishing evolves: Analyzing the enduring cybercrime", *Victims & Offenders*, Vol. 16, No. 3, Apr 2021, pp. 316–342. Collins, Aengus, and Touradj Ebrahimi, "Risk Governance and the Rise of Deepfakes", EPFL, 12 May 2021. https://www.epfl.ch/research/domains/irgc/spotlight-on-risk-series/risk-governance-and-the-rise-of-deepfakes/.

[57] Whittaker, Luke, Katrina Letheren and Russell Mulcahy, "The rise of deepfakes: A conceptual framework and research agenda for marketing", *Australasian Marketing Journal*, Vol. 29, No. 3, August 2021, pp. 204–214. Chesney, Robert, and Danielle Citron, "Deepfakes and the new disinformation war: The coming age of post-truth geopolitics", *Foreign Affairs*, Vol. 98, 2019, pp. 147.

[58] Tolosana, Ruben, Ruben Vera-Rodriguez, Julian Fierrez, Aythami Morales and Javier Ortega-Garcia, "DeepFakes and beyond: A survey of face manipulation and fake detection", *Information Fusion*, Vol. 64, December 2020, pp. 131–148. Figueira, Áurea, and Luís Oliveira, "The current state of fake news: Challenges and opportunities", *Procedia Computer Science*, Vol. 121, Jan 2017, pp. 817–825. Caldwell, Michael, James T. A. Andrews, Timothy Tanay and Lior D. Griffin, "AI-enabled future crime", *Crime Science*, Vol. 9, No. 1, Dec 2020, pp. 1–13. Weikmann, Teresa, and Sophie Lecheler, "Cutting through the hype: Understanding the implications of DeepFakes for the fact-checking actor-network", *Digital Journalism*, Vol. 12, Issue 10, 2024, pp. 1505–1522. https://www.tandfonline.com/doi/full/10.1080/21670811.2023.2194665#abstract.

5.5.1 Evolution of Deepfakes

The technical evolution of deepfakes has been driven by rapid advancements in AI and deep learning models, transforming them from simple visual alterations to complex, multi-modal manipulations. At the core of modern deepfake creation are advanced neural networks that enable highly realistic forgeries. Early deepfake techniques primarily focused on visual media, such as face-swapping and lip-syncing in videos. However, the technology has since broadened to include audio forgeries that can convincingly mimic someone's voice, as well as text-based deepfakes that replicate specific writing styles or speech patterns using natural language processing (NLP) models.[59]

The creation of deepfakes relies heavily on advanced AI architectures, with generative adversarial networks (GANs)[60] being one of the most widely used techniques. GANs consist of two competing neural networks—a generator that produces fake content and a discriminator that attempts to differentiate between real and synthetic media. This adversarial process results in increasingly convincing fake media over time.[61] In addition to GANs, other models such as Variational Autoencoders (VAEs)[62] and, more recently, diffusion models (DMs),[63] have contributed to the generation of increasingly high-quality synthetic content, particularly in areas like text-to-image synthesis.[64] These advances have made deepfakes more difficult to detect, complicating efforts to combat their misuse.

---

[59] Ibid.

[60] Goodfellow, Ian, Jean Pouget-Abadie, Mehdi Mirza, et al., "Generative adversarial nets", *Advances in Neural Information Processing Systems*, Vol. 27, 2014. Creswell, Antonia, Tom White, Vincent Dumoulin, et al., "Generative adversarial networks: An overview", *IEEE Signal Processing Magazine*, Vol. 35, No. 1, Jan 2018, pp. 53–65.

[61] Creswell, Antonia, Tom White, Vincent Dumoulin, Karthik Arulkumaran, Bhargav Sengupta, and Anil A. Bharath, "Generative adversarial networks: An overview", *IEEE Signal Processing Magazine*, Vol. 35, No. 1, Jan 2018, pp. 53–65.

[62] Kingma, Diederik P., and Max Welling, "Auto-encoding variational Bayes", arXiv:1312.6114, 2013.

[63] Sohl-Dickstein, Jascha, Eric Weiss, Niru Maheswaranathan and Surya Ganguli, "Deep unsupervised learning using nonequilibrium thermodynamics", in *Proceedings of the International Conference on Machine Learning*, 2015, pp. 2256–2265.

[64] Dhariwal, Prafulla, and Alex Nichol, "Diffusion models beat GANs on image synthesis", in *Proceedings of Advances in Neural Information Processing Systems*, Vol. 34, 2021, pp. 8780–8794.

The development of user-friendly deepfake tools, such as Deepfakes Web,[65] DeepFaceLab,[66] FaceApp,[67] ChatGPT,[68] DALL-E[69] and Midjourney,[70] has further accelerated the accessibility and sophistication of deepfake content creation. These tools allow non-expert users to easily generate realistic deepfakes, posing new challenges for detection and regulation. In response, large multinational organisations such as Facebook and Microsoft have organised deepfake detection challenges to spur innovation in this critical area.[71]

As deepfakes become more prevalent, their potential applications—both positive and negative—have expanded. While deepfakes have been used in entertainment, virtual experiences and creative industries, they also pose significant threats, including identity theft, fraud and the spread of disinformation.[72]

The surge in deepfake development has also prompted a corresponding rise in academic research aimed at understanding and detecting these forgeries (Fig. 5.5). Since deepfakes first entered the public domain in 2017, there has been a dramatic increase in the number of publications focused on this technology. In 2017, fewer than 100 papers addressed deepfakes, but in 2023, more than 8,000 studies had been published, reflecting the growing importance of this field. These studies have explored both the technical mechanisms behind deepfake generation and the methods needed to detect them effectively (Fig. 5.9).

In addition to these individual research efforts, several comprehensive surveys have been published, aiming to consolidate the rapidly evolving knowledge surrounding deepfakes (Table 5.2). At least 12 major surveys have been developed, each providing valuable insights into deepfake creation techniques and detection strategies across visual, audio and textual media. These surveys categorise the various types of deepfakes, such as facial reenactment and voice cloning, and analyse their societal implications.

The detection of deepfakes remains a central focus of research, with many studies examining the strengths and weaknesses of current detection methods. These methods range from traditional machine learning approaches to more sophisticated

---

[65] Online Deepfake Maker, Oct 2024. https://deepfakesweb.com.

[66] Perov, Ivan, Diego Gao, Nikolay Chervoniy, Kevin Liu, Sam Marangonda, Changil Umé, et al., "DeepFaceLab: Integrated flexible and extensible face-swapping framework", arXiv:2005.05535, 2020.

[67] FaceApp: Face Editor, Oct 2024, https://www.faceapp.com.

[68] ChatGPT, Oct 2024. https://openai.com/chatgpt.

[69] DALL·E 3, Oct 2024. https://openai.com/dall-e-3.

[70] Midjourney, Oct 2024. https://www.midjourney.com.

[71] Dagar, Prashant, and Deepak Kumar Vishwakarma, "A literature review and perspectives in deepfakes: Generation, detection, and applications", *International Journal of Multimedia Information Retrieval*, Vol. 11, No. 3, Sept 2022, pp. 219–289.

[72] Whittaker, Luke, Katrina Letheren and Russell Mulcahy, "The rise of deepfakes: A conceptual framework and research agenda for marketing", *Australasian Marketing Journal*, Vol. 29, No. 3, August 2021, pp. 204–214. Mustak, Mika, Joni Salminen, Matti Mäntymäki, Al Mamunur Rahman and Yogesh K. Dwivedi, "DeepFakes: Deceptions, mitigations, and opportunities", *Journal of Business Research*, Vol. 154, Jan 2023.

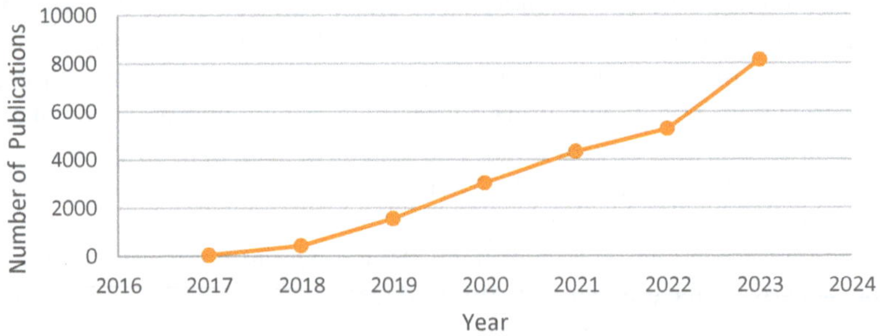

Fig. 5.9 Number of publications related to deepfakes by year

deep learning techniques designed to identify subtle inconsistencies in deepfake media. Several surveys have underscored the importance of high-quality datasets and standardised benchmarks for evaluating the effectiveness of these detection models. As deepfake generation techniques continue to improve, the need for adaptable and robust detection frameworks has become more urgent.[73]

Although most research has centred on visual and audio deepfakes, text-based forgeries represent a relatively underexplored but increasingly important area. Advances in NLP, particularly through the use of transformer-based models like generative pre-trained transformers (GPTs), have made it possible to create highly convincing text-based deepfakes that can mimic an individual's writing style or generate misleading content. This expanding area of research highlights the need for further investigation into text-based deepfakes, alongside the continued refinement of visual and audio detection methods.[74]

---

[73] Aïmeur, Esma, Samira Amri and Gilles Brassard, "Fake news, disinformation, and misinformation in social media: A review", *Social Network Analysis and Mining*, Vol. 13, No. 1, Feb 2023, pp. 30. Bessi, Alessandro, and Emilio Ferrara, "Social bots distort the 2016 U.S. presidential election online discussion", *First Monday*, Vol. 21, Nov 2016, pp. 11. Shao, Chengcheng, Giovanni Luca Ciampaglia, Onur Varol, Kai-Cheng Yang, Alessandro Flammini and Filippo Menczer, "The spread of low-credibility content by social bots", *Nature Communications*, Vol. 9, No. 1, Nov 2018, pp. 1–9.

[74] Vaswani, Ashish, Noam Shazeer, Niki Parmar, Jakob Uszkoreit, Llion Jones, Aidan N. Gomez, et al., "Attention is all you need", in *Proceedings of Advances in Neural Information Processing Systems*, Vol. 30, 2017, pp. 1–13. See also Liu, Xiaodong, Pengcheng He, Weizhu Chen and Jianfeng Gao, "Multi-task deep neural networks for natural language understanding", arXiv:1901.11504, 2019. Devlin, Jacob, Ming-Wei Chang, Kenton Lee and Kristina Toutanova, "BERT: Pre-training of deep bidirectional transformers for language understanding", arXiv:1810.04805, 2018. Radford, Alec, Jeffrey Wu, Rewon Child, David Luan, Dario Amodei and Ilya Sutskever, "Language models are unsupervised multitask learners", OpenAI Blog, Vol. 1, No. 8, 2019, pp. 9. https://cdn.openai.com/better-language-models/language_models_are_unsupervised_multitask_learners.pdf.

Table 5.2 A selection of key related surveys

Source	Published on	Type	Focus
Verdoliva, L., "Media forensics and deepfakes: an overview", *IEEE Journal of Selected Topics in Signal Processing*, Vol. 14, No. 5, 2020, pp. 910–932	IEEE	Visual	Provides an overview of deepfake technologies from a media forensics perspective, highlighting the limitations of current forensic detection methods
Tolosana, R., R. Vera-Rodriguez, J. Fierrez, A. Morales and L. Ortega-Garcia, "Deepfakes and beyond: A survey of face manipulation and fake detection", *Information Fusion*, Vol. 64, 2020, pp. 131–148	Elsevier	Visual	Reviewed facial manipulations and detection techniques
Mirsky, Y., and W. Lee, "The creation and detection of deepfakes: A survey", *ACM Computing Surveys (CSUR)*, Vol. 54, No. 1, 2021, pp. 1–41	ACM	Visual	Focused on field-specific generation techniques in depth. Detection is briefly discussed
Rana, M.S., M.N. Nobi, B. Muraliand A.H. Sung, "Deepfake detection: A systematic literature review", *IEEE Access*, Vol. 10, 2022, pp. 25,494–25,513	IEEE	Visual	A systematic review and comprehensive classification of deepfakes detection methods from 2018–2020
Zhang, T., "Deepfake generation and detection, a survey", *Multimedia Tools and Applications*, Vol. 81, No. 5, 2022, pp. 6259–6276	Springer	Visual	Discusses state-of-the-art methods for generating and detecting deepfakes, classifying generation techniques into face swapping and facial reenactment, and addressing challenges in detection related to datasets and benchmarks
Nguyen, T.T., Q.V.H. Nguyen, D.T. Nguyen, T. Huynh-The, S. Nahavandi, T.T. Nguyen, Q.V. Pham and C.M. Nguyen, "Deep learning for deepfakes creation and detection: A survey", article no. 103525, *Computer Vision and Image Understanding*, Vol. 223, 2022	Elsevier	Visual	A survey of algorithms for deepfake creation and detection. It discusses challenges and trends in the field while stressing the importance of integrity assessment of digital visual media

(continued)

Table 5.2 (continued)

Source	Published on	Type	Focus
Masood, M., M. Nawaz, K.M. Malik, A. Javed, A. Irtaza and H. Malik, "Deepfakes generation and detection: State-of-the-art, open challenges, countermeasures, and way forward", *Applied Intelligence*, Vol. 53, No. 4, 2023, pp. 3974–4026	Springer	Visual and audio	Generating and detection of deepfakes are discussed in depth, including reviewing datasets
Mubarak, R., T. Alsboui, O. Alshaikh, I. Inuwa-Dute, S. Khan and S. Parkinson, "A survey on the detection and impacts of deepfakes in visual, audio, and textual formats", *IEEE Access*, 2023	IEEE	Visual, audio, text	Comprehensive review of deepfake impacts across visual, audio, and text formats, emphasizing detection methods and the need for unified solutions
Lin, L., N. Gupta, Y. Zhang, H. Ren, C.H. Liu, F. Ding, X. Wang, X. Li, L. Verdoliva and S. Hu, "Detecting multimedia generated by large AI models: A survey, *arXiv preprint*, arXiv:2402.00045, 2024	arXiv	Visual, text, audio	First survey focused on detecting Large AI Model (LAIM)-generated multimedia, presenting a novel taxonomy for detection methods and identifying key challenges
Bontcheva, K., S. Papadopoulous, F. Tsalakanidou, R. Gallotti, L. Dutkiewicz, N. Krack, D. Teyssou, F. Severio Nucci, J. Spangenberg, I. Srba and P. Aichroth, "Generative AI and disinformation: Recent advances, challenges, and opportunities", 2024	Horizon EU	Visual, text, audio	Discusses AI-generated disinformation across visual, audio, and textual media, with a focus on election-related threats and recent advances in detection techniques

5.5.2 Visual-Based Deepfakes (Images and Videos)

Real-World Examples

Deepfakes, which manipulate media across various modalities such as images, videos, audio and text, have emerged as potent tools for disinformation and deception. The following examples illustrate how deepfakes in images and videos have been misused, demonstrating their danger and the urgency in addressing this growing issue.

In 2024, during the US presidential election, AI-generated images had a significant impact on public perception. One particularly notable instance involved realistic depictions of political candidates being shown in handcuffs or behind bars,[75] falsely suggesting their involvement in criminal activities. Another set of deepfake images showed candidates appearing ill or hospitalised,[76] raising baseless concerns about their fitness for office. These images, generated using sophisticated AI tools such as Diffusion Models, spread rapidly, creating confusion and influencing the election discourse.

Beyond still images, AI-generated video content has also demonstrated its capacity for disinformation. A widely publicised case occurred in 2022 when a deepfake video falsely depicted Ukrainian President Volodymyr Zelensky announcing that Ukraine was surrendering to Russia.[77] This video was circulated through hacked media services, spreading false information from a seemingly credible source, showcasing how such fabricated content can distort reality and sway public opinion during critical global events.

Another fabricated video emerged in 2023, falsely claiming that Olena Zelenska, the wife of President Zelensky, had purchased a luxury car in Paris during a time of national crisis.[78] Despite clear markers of manipulation, such as unnatural lip movements and speech patterns, the video went viral, amassing millions of views within hours. This deepfake, part of a broader disinformation campaign, served to destabilise public trust and was linked to pro-Russian networks that amplified the false narrative.

These examples of deepfakes in image and video manipulation reveal how quickly and convincingly AI-generated content can spread falsehoods, especially during sensitive political moments. The ability to create realistic yet entirely fabricated visual content raises serious concerns about the potential for deepfakes to distort public understanding and trust, particularly when they are strategically deployed during elections or international conflicts. Addressing the threat posed by deepfakes requires both technological solutions for detection and regulatory measures to mitigate their societal impact.

Generation of Deepfakes

Visual deepfakes focus on manipulating images or videos to alter facial expressions, gestures and body movements, often making individuals appear to say or do things they never did. This is achieved through deep learning techniques. The

---

[75] Devlin, Kayleen, and Joshua Cheetham, "Fake Trump arrest photos: How to spot an AI-generated image", *BBC News*, 24 Mar 2023. https://www.bbc.com/news/world-us-canada-65069316.

[76] Wendling, Mike, "AI can be easily used to make fake election photos—report", *BBC News*, 6 Mar 2024. https://www.bbc.com/news/world-us-canada-68471253.

[77] Wakefield, Jane, "Deepfake presidents used in Russia-Ukraine war", *BBC News*, 18 Mar 2022. https://www.bbc.com/news/technology-60780142.

[78] Mezzofiore, Gianluca, "Deepfake video targeting Zelensky's wife linked to Russian disinformation campaign, CNN analysis shows", *CNN*, 3 July 2024. https://edition.cnn.com/2024/07/02/europe/deepfake-video-zelensky-wife-intl-latam/index.html.

technical aspects of visual manipulation have been extensively discussed in sources such as Dagar & Vishwakarma,[79] Masood et al.[80] and Mirsky & Lee.[81]

One common form of visual deepfake is **face swapping**, where a person's face in an image or video is replaced with someone else's, creating a highly convincing effect that is hard to distinguish from reality.[82] This technology has become widely accessible due to deep neural networks, which swap facial features while preserving the surrounding context.[83] Face swapping has legitimate applications in the entertainment industry, such as creating seamless visual effects in movies or TV shows.[84] However, the availability of user-friendly tools like DeepFaceLab[85] has also led to the technology's misuse, notably in creating non-consensual pornographic videos, which pose significant privacy and ethical concerns.[86]

Face synthesis is another visual deepfake technique, generating entirely new, photorealistic faces that do not correspond to real people.[87] Using deep learning models trained on large datasets, new faces are created by the network, which samples from learned patterns to produce realistic images.[88] This technique is often used in digital art or video games, where designers can create diverse and unique characters without relying on real-world references. However, this technology also

---

[79] Dagar, Deepak, and Deepak Kumar Vishwakarma, "A literature review and perspectives in deepfakes: Generation, detection, and applications", *International Journal of Multimedia Information Retrieval*, Vol. 11, No. 3, Sept 2022, pp. 219–289.

[80] Masood, Mehvish, Muhammad Nawaz, Kashif Mehmood Malik, Ali Javed, Ali Irtaza and Hafeez Malik, "DeepFakes generation and detection: State-of-the-art, open challenges, countermeasures, and way forward", *International Journal of Speech Technology*, Vol. 53, No. 4, Feb 2023, pp. 3974–4026.

[81] Mirsky, Yisroel, and Wenke Lee, "The creation and detection of deepfakes: A survey", *ACM Computing Surveys*, Vol. 54, No. 1, 2021, pp. 1–41.

[82] Korshunov, Pavel, and Sébastien Marcel, "DeepFakes: A new threat to face recognition? Assessment and detection", arXiv:1812.08685, 2018.

[83] Korshunova, Irina, Wenqi Shi, Joni Dambre and Lucas Theis, "Fast face-swap using convolutional neural networks", in *Proceedings of the IEEE International Conference on Computer Vision (ICCV)*, Oct 2017, pp. 3697–3705.

[84] Verdoliva, Luisa, "Media forensics and DeepFakes: An overview", *IEEE Journal of Selected Topics in Signal Processing*, Vol. 14, No. 5, August 2020, pp. 910–932. Mirsky, Yisroel, and Wenke Lee, "The creation and detection of deepfakes: A survey", *ACM Computing Surveys*, Vol. 54, No. 1, 2021, pp. 1–41.

[85] Perov, Ivan, David Gao, Nikolay Chervoniy, Kai Liu, Samuel Marangonda, Chun Umé, et al., "DeepFaceLab: Integrated flexible and extensible face-swapping framework", arXiv:2005.05535, 2020.

[86] Mustak, Mahmud, Joni Salminen, Matti Mäntymäki, Aowida Rahman and Yogesh K. Dwivedi, "DeepFakes: Deceptions, mitigations, and opportunities", *Journal of Business Research*, Vol. 154, Jan 2023.

[87] Tolosana, Ruben, Ruben Vera-Rodriguez, Julian Fierrez, Aythami Morales and Javier Ortega-Garcia, "DeepFakes and beyond: A survey of face manipulation and fake detection", *Information Fusion*, Vol. 64, Dec 2020, pp. 131–148.

[88] Karras, Tero, Samuli Laine and Timo Aila, "A style-based generator architecture for generative adversarial networks", in Proceedings of the IEEE/CVF Conference on Computer Vision and Pattern Recognition (CVPR), June 2019, pp. 4396–4405.

carries risks, such as creating fake profile pictures for fraudulent accounts, leading to identity theft or disinformation.[89] Notable tools for face synthesis include Midjourney[90] and DALL-E,[91] which can generate realistic faces from simple text prompts.

Another important form of visual deepfake is **lip-syncing**, which manipulates lip movements in a video to match different audio, creating the illusion of accurate speech synchronisation.[92] This technique has legitimate uses in the entertainment industry for dubbing films and creating video games. However, it can also be exploited to create misleading videos where public figures appear to say things they never did. A well-known example is the manipulated video of former President Barack Obama, where his speech was altered using lip-sync technology to make it seem like he was making false statements. This video was generated using a 3D lip-sync technique pioneered by Suwajanakorn et al.,[93] demonstrating both the creative potential and the risks associated with this technology.

Reenactment, or puppeteering, is another type of visual deepfake, where the facial expressions or body movements of a target in a video are animated to mirror those of a source. This technique is used to create realistic movements throughout the video sequence, ensuring temporal coherence and natural-looking actions.[94] Examples of publicly available reenactment tools include Face2Face[95] and MarioNETtef.[96] While reenactment can streamline character animation in films and television, it can also be used maliciously to fabricate videos where individuals appear to engage in activities or make statements they never did, with potentially damaging consequences.[97]

---

[89] Whittaker, Lewis, Kristen Letheren and Richard Mulcahy, "The rise of deepfakes: A conceptual framework and research agenda for marketing", *Australasian Marketing Journal*, Vol. 29, No. 3, August 2021, pp. 204–214.

[90] https://www.midjourney.com.

[91] https://openai.com/dall-e-3.

[92] Masood, Mehvish, Muhammad Nawaz, Kashif Mehmood Malik, Ali Javed, Ali Irtaza and Hafeez Malik, "DeepFakes generation and detection: State-of-the-art, open challenges, countermeasures, and way forward", *International Journal of Speech Technology*, Vol. 53, No. 4, Feb 2023, pp. 3974–4026.

[93] Suwajanakorn, Supasorn, Steven M. Seitz and Ira Kemelmacher-Shlizerman, "Synthesizing Obama: Learning lip sync from audio", *ACM Transactions on Graphics*, Vol. 36, No. 4, Aug 2017, pp. 1–13.

[94] Hu, Chun, Xiaohong Xie and Lingyun Wu, "Face reenactment via generative landmark guidance", *Image and Vision Computing*, Vol. 130, Feb 2023.

[95] Thies, Justus, Michael Zollhöfer, Marc Stamminger, Christian Theobalt and Matthias Nießner, "Face2Face: Real-time face capture and reenactment of RGB videos", in *Proceedings of the IEEE Conference on Computer Vision and Pattern Recognition (CVPR)*, June 2016, pp. 2387–2395.

[96] Ha, Seongjoon, Minsu Kersner, Beomsu Kim, Sungjoo Seo and Dongyoon Kim, "Marionette: Few-shot face reenactment preserving identity of unseen targets", in *Proceedings of the AAAI Conference on Artificial Intelligence*, Vol. 34, 2020, pp. 10,893–10,900.

[97] Greaves, Mark, "Deepfakes' Ranked as Most Serious AI Crime", UCL News, Oct 2024. https://www.ucl.ac.uk/news/2020/aug/deepfakes-ranked-most-serious-ai-crime-threat.

Facial manipulation involves altering specific facial attributes, such as changing a person's emotions or mimicking particular gestures in videos or images. This manipulation is achieved through deep learning, allowing for subtle yet convincing modifications. A real-world example is the popular app FaceApp,[98] which uses AI to transform user faces by applying filters like ageing or gender-swapping effects. While such applications are often used for entertainment, they also raise concerns about the potential misuse of facial manipulation to deceive or mislead, as well as privacy implications.[99]

As these techniques continue to evolve, the landscape of deepfake generation is rapidly advancing with a variety of sophisticated tools redefining the capabilities of digital content creation (Table 5.3). Models like BigGAN offer powerful high-quality image generation in an open-source environment, while tools like DALL-E provide users with the ability to generate images from textual prompts through both free and paid tiers. For facial manipulation, DeepFaceLab delivers advanced capabilities for producing deepfakes, and FaceApp engages users with transformative filters, showcasing the dual nature of these technologies—creative and potentially deceptive. Furthermore, emerging tools such as Imagen Video (Google) and Make-A-Video (Meta) promise to push boundaries by transforming text into high-quality video content, raising the stakes in disinformation as they enable users to create ultra-realistic video narratives with minimal input. Lumiere (Google) also targets video generation from text and images, presenting exciting opportunities for creators while posing significant risks of misuse. These advancements, alongside tools like Sora (OpenAI) and Runway Gen (Runway), signal a future where the line between reality and fabricated content is increasingly blurred, heightening concerns about the authenticity of digital media and its potential to mislead audiences.

Detection of Deepfakes

The detection of AI-generated images and videos has become increasingly critical due to the rapid advancements in generative models such as GANs and diffusion models. Despite the impressive realism these models can achieve, there are still detectable traces and artefacts that differentiate synthetic content from genuine media. Detection methods for images can be grouped into several key approaches: physical/physiological-based methods, fingerprint-based methods, spatial-based methods, and frequency-based methods.[100] Each of these approaches focuses on different aspects of the image data to uncover signs of artificial generation, offering complementary insights into the detection process.

[98] *FaceApp: Face Editor*, Oct 2024, https://www.faceapp.com.

[99] Afchar, Davide, Vincent Nozick, Junichi Yamagishi and Isao Echizen, "MesoNet: A compact facial video forgery detection network", in *Proceedings of the IEEE International Workshop on Information Forensics and Security (WIFS)*, Dec 2018, pp. 1–7.

[100] Lin, L., et a., op. cit.

Table 5.3 Popular tools for generating visual-based deepfakes

Model	Company	Purpose of use	Availability	Release year
BigGAN[101]	Google	High-quality image generation	Open source	2019
DALL-E[102]	OpenAI	Image generation based on text prompts	Freemium	2023
DeepFaceLab[103]	DeepFaceLab	Advanced deepfake creation	Open source	2018
Deepfakes Web[104]	Deepfakes Web	Deepfake creation	Paid	2019
Face2Face[105]	–	Real-time facial reenactment	Open source	2016
FaceApp[106]	Wireless Lab	AI-based facial image manipulation	Freemium	2017
FSGANv2[107]	–	Face-swapping and reenactment	Open source	2020
Imagen[108]	Google	Image generation from text (research-focused)	Freemium	2022
MarioNETte[109]	–	Few-shot face reenactment	Open source	2020
Midjourney[110]	Midjourney	Artistic image generation	Paid	2022
Stable Diffusion[111]	Stability AI	Open-source image generation	Open source	2022
'Everybody Dance Now'[112]	UC Berkeley	AI-based motion transfer	Open source	2018
'This Person Does Not Exist' (TPDNE)[113]	–	AI-generated faces	Free	2019

(continued)

[101] Tensorflow. https://www.tensorflow.org/hub/tutorials/biggan_generation_with_tf_hub.

[102] https://openai.com/index/dall-e-3/.

[103] https://www.deepfakevfx.com/downloads/deepfacelab/.

[104] https://deepfakesweb.com/.

[105] https://github.com/datitran/face2face-demo.

[106] https://www.faceapp.com/.

[107] Nirkin, Y., Y. Keller and T. Hassner, "FSGANv2: Improved Subject Agnostic Face Swapping and Reenactment", arXiv preprint, arXiv:2202.12972, 2022.

[108] https://imagen.research.google/.

[109] Ha, S., M. Kersner, B. Kim, S. Seo and D. Kim, "Marionette: Few-shot face reenactment preserving identity of unseen targets", in *Proceedings of the AAAI Conference on Artificial Intelligence*, Vol. 34, No. 7, Apr 2020, pp. 10,893–10,900.

[110] https://www.midjourney.com/home.

[111] https://stability.ai/.

[112] https://carolineec.github.io/everybody_dance_now/.

[113] https://this-person-does-not-exist.com/en.

Table 5.3 (continued)

Model	Company	Purpose of use	Availability	Release year
DeepBrain[114]	DeepBrain	AI video generation with avatars	Paid	2021
DeepMotion[115]	DeepMotion	AI-driven 3D animation generation	Paid	2017
Elai.io[116]	Elai.io	AI avatars and video generation	Paid	2021
Imagen Video[117]	Google	Text-to-video AI content generation	–	TBD
Lumen5[118]	Lumen5	AI-based video creation from text	Paid	2017
Lumiere[119]	Google	AI-based video generation from text/image	–	TBD
Make-A-Video[120]	Meta	Text-to-video AI content generation	–	TBD
Pika Art[121]	Pika Labs	Text-to-video generation	Freemium	2023
Runway Gen[122]	Runway	Text-to-video/image generation, AI editing	Freemium	2023
Sora[123]	OpenAI	AI-based video generation from text	–	TBD
Synthesia[124]	Synthesia.io	AI avatars for video content	Freemium	2017

[114] https://www.deepbrain.io/.
[115] https://www.deepmotion.com/.
[116] https://elai.io/.
[117] https://imagen.research.google/video/.
[118] https://lumen5.com/.
[119] https://lumiere-video.github.io/.
[120] https://makeavideo.studio/.
[121] https://pika.art/home.
[122] https://runwayml.com.
[123] https://openai.com/index/sora/.
[124] https://www.synthesia.io/.

In **physical/physiological-based detection,**[125] the focus is on identifying discrepancies in how synthetic images portray real-world physics and human anatomy. These methods examine lighting, shadows and reflections, which are often rendered inaccurately by generative models. For example, reflections in synthetic images may appear unnatural, particularly in reflective surfaces like glasses or pupils, and shadows may be inconsistent or entirely absent. Physiologically-based techniques look at the representation of human facial features, such as symmetry, iris colour and the shape of extremities, where generative models often fail to capture the intricate details correctly. Such methods benefit from high interpretability, allowing human analysts to easily spot artefacts that violate physical laws.

Fingerprint-based detection[126] methods take advantage of the unique 'fingerprints' left behind by generative processes. Since different AI models leave distinct patterns in the synthetic images they produce, these patterns can be detected and analysed to identify the origin of an image. One prominent technique, Deep Image Fingerprint (DIF), employs convolutional neural networks (CNNs) to identify the subtle artefacts that are characteristic of images generated by GANs and diffusion models. These fingerprints are essentially the unique features left behind by the underlying architecture of the model, and they provide an effective way to link a synthetic image to the model that produced it.

Spatial-based detection[127] techniques focus on examining the textures and gradients within an image. Generative models often struggle to replicate the intricate

[125] Ciftci, U.A., I. Demir and L. Yin, "Fakecatcher: Detection of synthetic portrait videos using biological signal", *IEEE transactions on pattern analysis and machine intelligence*, 2020. See also Wang, X., H. Guo, S. Hu, M.C. Chang and S. Lyu, "Gan-generated faces detection: A survey and new perspectives", ECAI 2023, pp. 2533–2542. Kang, M., J.Y. Zhu, R. Zhang, J. Park, E. Shechtman, S. Paris and T. Park, "Scaling up gans for text-to-image synthesis", in *Proceedings of the IEEE/CVF Conference on Computer Vision and Pattern Recognition*, 2023, pp. 10,124–10,134. Borji, A., "Qualitative failures of image generation models and their application in detecting deepfakes", *Image and Vision Computing*, Vol. 137, 2023, p. 104,771.

[126] Sinitsa, S., and O. Fried, "Deep image fingerprint: Towards low budget synthetic image detection and model lineage analysis", in *Proceedings of the IEEE/CVF Winter Conference on Applications of Computer Vision*, 2024, pp. 4067–4076. See also Wang, Z., J. Bao, W. Zhou, W. Wang, H. Hu, H. Chen, H. and H. Li, "Dire for diffusion-generated image detection", in *Proceedings of the IEEE/CVF International Conference on Computer Vision*, 2023, pp. 22,445–22,455. Ma, R., J. Duan, F. Kong, X. Shi and K. Xu, "Exposing the fake: Effective diffusion-generated images detection", arXiv preprint, 2023. arXiv:2307.06272. Song, J., C. Meng and S. Ermon, "Denoising diffusion implicit models", arXiv preprint, 2020. arXiv:2010.02502.

[127] Zhong, N., Y. Xu, Z. Qian and X. Zhang, "Rich and poor texture contrast: A simple yet effective approach for ai-generated image detection", arXiv preprint, 2023. arXiv:2311.12397. See also Nguyen, M.Q., K.D. Ho, H.M. Nguyen, C.M. Tu, M.T. Tran and T.L. Do, "Unmasking the Artist: Discriminating Human-Drawn And AI-Generated Human Face Art Through Facial Feature Analysis", in *International Conference on Multimedia Analysis and Pattern Recognition (MAPR)*, October 2023, pp. 1–6. https://ieeexplore.ieee.org/document/10289113?arnumber=10289113. Lorenz, P., R.L. Durall and J. Keuper, "Detecting images generated by deep diffusion models using their local intrinsic dimensionality", in *Proceedings of the IEEE/CVF International Conference on Computer*

details of textures, particularly in areas with significant variation, such as regions of rich texture in natural scenes. These methods exploit the contrast between regions with rich and poor textures, where synthetic content may exhibit unnatural uniformity or pixel correlations that are not typically present in real images. By focusing on the spatial relationships within the image, these methods can reveal flaws that are otherwise difficult to detect.

Frequency-based detection[128] approaches operate by analysing the frequency components of an image, often using tools such as wavelet transforms or Fourier analysis. These techniques reveal subtle patterns in the frequency domain that are characteristic of AI-generated content but may not be visible in the spatial domain. For example, frequency analysis can detect unnatural smoothness or regularities in an image's high-frequency content, which are typical signs of synthetic generation.

As AI-generated content becomes increasingly sophisticated, the importance of reliable detection tools is paramount (Table 5.4). A variety of solutions, ranging from open-source systems to proprietary platforms, are designed to uncover synthetic media's telltale signs. The AI Image Detector by Huggingface is a free, open-source tool for identifying AI-generated images. For comprehensive deepfake detection across both images and videos, Deepware and Sensity AI provide robust solutions; Deepware is a freemium tool focusing on AI deepfakes, and Sensity AI offers proprietary detection capabilities. In the realm of moderation and forensics, Hive Moderation excels in AI content moderation within images and videos, and Forensically provides free image forensics and error level analysis. Google's SynthID introduces watermarking and AI image detection, while DARPA SemaFor focuses on semantic analysis for media authenticity. For accessible authenticity checks, the InVID browser extension enables seamless video verification, and Truepic offers proprietary verification services for images and videos. Additional tools like Illuminarty enhance media verification, reinforcing the safeguard against misleading AI-generated content.

Vision, 2023, pp. 448–459. Vacher, J., A. Davila, A. Kohn, and R. Coen-Cagli, "Texture interpolation for probing visual perception", *Advances in neural information processing systems,* Vol. 33, 2020, pp. 22,146–22,157.

[128] Wolter, M., F. Blanke, R. Heese and J. Garcke, "Wavelet-Packets for DeepFake Image Analysis and Detection", *Machine Learning,* Vol. 111, No. 11, 2022, pp. 4295–4327. Poredi, N., D. Nagothu and Y. Chen, "AUSOME: Authenticating Social Media Images Using Frequency Analysis", in *Disruptive Technologies in Information Sciences VII* (Vol. 12,542), June 2023, pp. 44–56, SPIE. Xi, Z., W. Huang, K. Wei, W. Luo and P. Zheng, "AI-Generated Image Detection Using a Cross-Attention Enhanced Dual-Stream Network", *in IEEE 2023 Asia Pacific Signal and Information Processing Association Annual Summit and Conference* (APSIPA ASC), Oct 2023, pp. 1463–1470. Bammey, Q., "SynthBuster: Towards Detection of Diffusion Model Generated Images", *IEEE Open Journal of Signal Processing,* 2023.

Table 5.4 Popular tools for detecting visual-based deepfakes

Model	Company	Purpose of use	Availability	Release year
AI Image Detector[129]	Huggingface	Detects AI-generated images	Open source	2022
AI or Not[130]	AI or Not	AI-generated image detection	Freemium	2022
AI-Generated Image Detector[131]	Is it AI	Detects AI-generated images	Freemium	2023
Deepware[132]	Deepware	AI image/video deepfake detection	Freemium	2020
Forensically[133]	Forensically	Image forensics, error level analysis	Free	2015
Hive Moderation[134]	Hive AI	Image/video AI content moderation and detection	Freemium	2020
Sensity AI[135]	Sensity.ai	Deepfake and visual AI content detection	Freemium	2019
SynthID[136]	Google	Watermarking and AI image detection	Paid	2023
DARPA SemaFor[137]	DARPA	Semantic analysis for media authenticity	Open source	2020
Illuminarty[138]	Illuminarty	AI detection across image and video content	Freemium	2021
InVID[139]	InVID	Browser extension for video verification	Open source	2017
Truepic Revel[140]	Truepic	Authenticity verification for images and videos	Paid	2015

129 https://huggingface.co/spaces/umm-maybe/AI-image-detector.
130 https://www.aiornot.com/.
131 https://isitai.com/ai-image-detector/.
132 https://deepware.ai/.
133 https://29a.ch/photo-forensics/#forensic-magnifier.
134 https://hivemoderation.com/.
135 https://sensity.ai/.
136 https://deepmind.google/technologies/synthid/.
137 https://www.darpa.mil/program/semantic-forensics.
138 https://illuminarty.ai/en/.
139 https://www.invid-project.eu/tools-and-services/invid-verification-plugin/.
140 https://www.truepic.com/.

5.5.3 Audio-Based Deepfakes

Real-World Examples

AI-generated audio has rapidly become one of the most alarming forms of deepfakes, due to advances in speech synthesis technologies. These technologies, now highly accessible, allow non-experts to create convincing fake audio that can deceive listeners and cause significant harm, particularly in political and social contexts. Several real-world cases highlight the dangers posed by audio deepfakes and the importance of addressing this threat.

In January 2023, a deepfake audio of US President Joe Biden was distributed to voters during the New Hampshire primaries.[141] In this fabricated 'robocall', Biden's voice urged voters to stay home and save their votes for the November election. This disinformation campaign was designed to suppress voter turnout and had a serious impact on the political process. The consultant responsible for creating this deepfake was later fined $6 million, underscoring the severity of the offence and the potential damage that such fraudulent audio can cause.

Similarly, Sir Keir Starmer, the leader of the UK's Labour Party, was the target of a deepfake audio scandal during the 2022 Labour Party Conference.[142] The manipulated audio falsely depicted Starmer swearing at his staff. Although the deepfake was quickly exposed, it briefly caused public outrage and disrupted the conference. The incident demonstrates how audio deepfakes can be used to undermine political figures and sow confusion, even when quickly debunked.

In 2023, another instance involved London Mayor Sadiq Khan, whose voice was faked in an audio clip that circulated inflammatory remarks about Remembrance weekend.[143] The deepfake falsely portrayed Khan supporting divisive political movements, further aggravating tensions in an already sensitive social climate. This case exemplifies how audio deepfakes can be strategically deployed to inflame social divisions and provoke unrest.

These examples illustrate the far-reaching consequences of audio deepfakes, particularly in the political arena. As Ciaran Martin, former director of the UK's National Cyber Security Centre, warned, audio deepfakes are especially dangerous because they are 'spectacularly easy to make' and harder to detect compared to

---

[141] Devine, Curt, Donie O'Sullivan and Sean Lyngaas, "A fake recording of a candidate saying he'd rigged the election went viral. Experts say it's only the beginning", CNN, 1 Feb 2024. https://edition.cnn.com/2024/02/01/politics/election-deepfake-threats-invs/index.html. See also: Osborne, Samuel, "Fake AI-generated Joe Biden robocall tells people in New Hampshire not to vote", Sky News, 23 Jan 2024. https://news.sky.com/story/fake-ai-generated-joe-biden-robocall-tells-people-in-new-hampshire-not-to-vote-13054446.

[142] *Sky News*, "Deepfake audio of Sir Keir Starmer released on first day of Labour conference", 9 Oct 2024. https://news.sky.com/story/labour-faces-political-attack-after-deepfake-audio-is-posted-of-sir-keir-starmer-12980181.

[143] Spring, Marianna, "Sadiq Khan says fake AI audio of him nearly led to serious disorder", *BBC News*, 14 Feb 2024. https://www.bbc.com/news/uk-68146053.

visual deepfakes.[144] The growing accessibility of advanced speech synthesis tools has only amplified the risk, making it easier for bad actors to manipulate voices and create realistic-sounding deepfake audio.

Generation of Deepfakes

Audio deepfakes are created using artificial intelligence and machine learning techniques, allowing for the manipulation or synthesis of a person's voice. By training a deep learning model on a dataset of a specific individual's voice recordings, the model learns the unique characteristics, tone and speech patterns of the target voice.[145] Audio deepfakes are often used in isolation as fake audio clips or integrated with video deepfakes to create audiovisual fabrications. The two primary methods of audio manipulation are text-to-speech and speech-to-speech (voice conversion).

Text-to-speech (TTS) technology converts written text into speech that mimics a specific person. Though TTS has long been used in applications like voice assistants and navigation systems, traditional approaches lacked naturalness and were easily identifiable as artificial.[146] Recent advancements in deep learning models, such as WaveNet,[147] DeepVoice[148] and Tacotron,[149] have significantly improved TTS capabilities, producing highly realistic and expressive voice outputs by capturing nuanced speech patterns and intonations. These innovations have revolutionised voice synthesis in areas like virtual assistants[150] and personalised voice avatars.[151] However, the accessibility of deep learning-based TTS models raises concerns about misuse, such as creating fake audio for scams, social engineering attacks or defamatory purposes.

---

[144] Cohen, Tamara, "Warning to UK politicians over risk of audio deepfakes that could derail the election", *Sky News*, 2 June 2024. https://news.sky.com/story/warning-to-uk-politicians-over-risk-of-audio-deepfakes-that-could-derail-the-general-election-13146573.

[145] Wirth, R.P.J., and P. Puchtler, "Neural Speech Synthesis in German", in *Proceedings of the 14th International Conference on Advanced Human-Oriented Personalized Mechanisms, Technologies, and Services*, 2021, pp. 26–34.

[146] Mukhopadhyay, R., J. Philip, A. Jha, V. Namboodiri and C.V. Jawahar, "Towards Automatic Face-to-Face Translation", in *Proceedings of the 27th ACM International Conference on Multimedia*, October 2019, pp. 1428–1436.

[147] van den Oord, A., S. Dieleman, H. Zen, et al., "WaveNet: A Generative Model for Raw Audio", 2016, arXiv:1609.03499.

[148] Ping, W., K. Peng, A. Gibiansky, et al., "Deep Voice 3: Scaling Text-to-Speech with Convolutional Sequence Learning", arXiv:1710.07654, 2017.

[149] Wang, Y., R. Skerry-Ryan, D. Stanton, et al., "Tacotron: Towards End-to-End Speech Synthesis", 2017, arXiv:1703.10135.

[150] Sisman, B., J. Yamagishi, S. King and H. Li, "An Overview of Voice Conversion and Its Challenges: From Statistical Modeling to Deep Learning", *IEEE/ACM Transactions on Audio, Speech, and Language Processing*, Vol. 29, 2021, pp. 132–157.

[151] Thies, J., M. Elgharib, A. Tewari, C. Theobalt and M. Nießner, "Neural Voice Puppetry: Audio-Driven Facial Reenactment", in *Proceedings of the 16th European Conference on Computer Vision (ECCV)*, August 2020, pp. 716–731.

Speech-to-speech (voice conversion) alters the characteristics of one person's voice to match those of another, preserving the linguistic content while transforming the speech signal to imitate the target voice.[152] This technology has diverse applications, such as creating personalised voice assistants, dubbing foreign films with the original actors' voices,[153] and aiding individuals with speech disabilities by generating speech that reflects their authentic voice.[154] However, the availability of user-friendly online tools like Resemble.AI[155] and MURF.AI[156] poses risks, as these tools can be used for fraudulent purposes, such as impersonating others' voices to spread misinformation or commit identity fraud.

Audio deepfake technology has evolved significantly, providing advanced tools for voice synthesis and manipulation (Table 5.5). DeepVoice from Baidu and Tacotron 2 developed by Google and Nvidia showcase cutting-edge text-to-speech synthesis capabilities through their research-driven approaches. In the commercial sphere, platforms like Descript Overdub and Murf.ai cater to content creators by offering AI voice cloning and generation services, facilitating personalised voiceovers and narrations. Play.ht and Voicemaker extend these capabilities further by providing versatile text-to-speech solutions, leveraging freemium and commercial models to meet diverse user needs. Moreover, Resemble.AI and Respeecher specialise in voice cloning and transformation, enabling applications across entertainment and accessibility sectors by offering realistic voice replication that preserves linguistic content. Microsoft's NaturalSpeech continues to push boundaries in research, advancing text-to-speech and voice synthesis technology. These tools collectively illustrate the growing potential and ethical implications of AI in reshaping audio content creation and manipulation.

Detection of Deepfakes

Deepfake audio detection methods primarily focus on identifying artefacts introduced during the synthesis process, which can be classified into vocoder-based detection, frequency-based analysis and end-to-end approaches.[157] Each method

---

[152] Childers, D., B. Yegnanarayana and K. Wu, "Voice conversion: Factors responsible for quality", *Proceedings IEEE International Conference on Acoustics, Speech, and Signal Processing,* Mar 1985. pp. 748–751. See also Zhang, J.-X., Z.-H. Ling, L.-J. Liu, Y. Jiang and L.-R. Dai, "Sequence-to-sequence acoustic modeling for voice conversion", *IEEE/ACM Transactions on Audio, Speech, and Language Processing,* Vol. 27, No. 3, Mar 2019, pp. 631–644.

[153] Mirsky, Y., and W. Lee, "The creation and detection of deepfakes: A survey", *ACM Computing Surveys,* Vol. 54, No. 1, 2021, pp. 1–41.

[154] Veaux, Christophe, Junichi Yamagishi and Simon King, "Towards Personalised Synthesised Voices for Individuals With Vocal Disabilities: Voice Banking and Reconstruction", Oct 2024. https://aclanthology.org/W13-3917.

[155] Resemble AI, "AI Voice Generator With Text to Speech and Speech to Speech", Oct 2024. https://www.resemble.ai.

[156] MURF.AI, "Voice Cloning: Realistic Text to speech Voice Cloning Online", Oct. 2024. https://murf.ai/voice-cloning?lmref=oYsoew.

[157] Lin, L., N. Gupta, Y. Zhang, et al., "Detecting Multimedia Generated by Large AI Models: A Survey", arXiv preprint arXiv:2402.00045, 2024.

Table 5.5 Popular tools for generating audio-based deepfakes

Model	Company	Purpose of use	Availability	Release year
DeepVoice,[158,159]	Baidu	Text-to-speech synthesis	Open source	2017
Descript Overdub[160]	Descript	AI voice cloning and overdubbing	Freemium	2020
Murf.ai[161]	Murf.ai	AI-generated voice for narration, podcasts	Freemium	2021
NaturalSpeech,[162,163]	Microsoft	Text-to-speech and voice synthesis	Open source	2023
Play.ht[164]	Play.ht	Text-to-speech (TTS) and voice generation	Freemium	2019
Resemble.AI[165]	Resemble.AI	Voice cloning, text-to-speech	Paid	2018
Respeecher[166]	Respeecher	Voice cloning and transformation	Paid	2020
Tacotron 2[167]	Google and Nvidia	Text-to-speech synthesis	Open source	2017
Voicemaker[168]	Voicemaker	Text-to-speech for voiceovers	Freemium	2019

158 Ping, W., K. Peng, A. Gibiansky, et al., "Deep voice 3: Scaling text-to-speech with convolutional sequence learning", 2017. arXiv preprint arXiv:1710.07654.

159 https://github.com/r9y9/deepvoice3_pytorch.

160 https://www.descript.com/.

161 https://murf.ai/.

162 Ju, Z., Y. Wang, K. Shen, et al., "NaturalSpeech 3: Zero-Shot Speech Synthesis with Factorized Codec and Diffusion Models", 2024, arXiv:2403.03100.

163 https://speechresearch.github.io/naturalspeech3/.

164 https://play.ht/.

165 https://www.resemble.ai/.

166 https://www.respeecher.com/.

167 https://github.com/NVIDIA/tacotron2.

168 https://voicemaker.in/.

addresses unique aspects of audio manipulation, offering different strengths in uncovering synthetic audio.

One of the primary methods for detecting audio deepfakes focuses on the artefacts introduced by neural vocoders. **Neural vocoders**[169] are often used in text-to-speech systems to convert intermediate representations, such as Mel-spectrograms, into audible waveforms. While vocoder technology has advanced significantly, the synthesised audio often contains subtle imperfections that betray its artificial origin.

Another important method for audio deepfake detection involves **frequency-based analysis.**[170] This approach examines the frequency components of an audio signal, leveraging techniques such as Fourier transforms to identify irregularities that may not be evident in the time domain. Frequency-based detection methods focus on the fact that synthetic audio often contains unnatural patterns in the frequency spectrum, such as discontinuities or distortions in high-frequency bands. These anomalies arise because generative models, while capable of producing highly realistic audio, often struggle to accurately reproduce the intricate details present in genuine audio recordings, especially in higher frequency ranges. Frequency-domain analysis can therefore serve as an effective tool for detecting the hidden signs of manipulation in synthetic audio.

In addition to vocoder-based and frequency-based approaches, there are emerging **end-to-end detection methods**[171] that do not rely on explicit intermediate features, such as Mel-spectrograms. Instead, these methods aim to identify deepfakes directly from raw audio inputs, often using deep learning models to extract complex patterns and features from the data. Diffusion-based models, which have been widely adopted in text-to-speech tasks, serve as a key focus in some of these approaches. These models transform noise into coherent audio representations over multiple diffusion steps but often introduce artefacts in the process. End-to-end detection models are designed to identify these subtle artefacts by analysing the raw waveform without requiring a separate vocoder step. While these methods hold promise for improving the robustness of audio deepfake detection, they face

[169] Sun, C., S. Jia, S. Hou and S. Lyu, "AI-Synthesized Voice Detection Using Neural Vocoder Artifacts", in *Proceedings of the IEEE/CVF Conference on Computer Vision and Pattern Recognition*, 2023, pp. 904–912. See also Tak, H., J. Patino, M. Todisco, A. Nautsch, N. Evans and A. Larcher, "End-to-End Anti-Spoofing with RawNet2", in *IEEE International Conference on Acoustics, Speech and Signal Processing (ICASSP)*, June 2021, pp. 6369–6373.

[170] Liu, H., Z. Tan, Q. Chen, Y. Wei, Y. Zhao and J. Wang, "Unified Frequency-Assisted Transformer Framework for Detecting and Grounding Multi-Modal Manipulation", *International Journal of Computer Vision*, 2024, pp. 1–18. See also Shao, R., T. Wu, J. Wu, L. Nie and Z. Liu, "Detecting and Grounding Multi-Modal Media Manipulation and Beyond", *IEEE Transactions on Pattern Analysis and Machine Intelligence*, 2024.

[171] Chen, N., Y. Zhang, H. Zen, R.J. Weiss, M. Norouzi, N. Dehak and W. Chan, "Wavegrad 2: Iterative Refinement for Text-to-Speech Synthesis", arXiv preprint arXiv:2106.09660, 2021. See also Shi, Z., and S. Wu, "ITÔN: End-to-End Audio Generation with Itô Stochastic Differential Equations", *Digital Signal Processing*, Vol. 132, 2023, p. 103,781.

Table 5.6 Popular tools for detecting audio-based deepfakes

Model	Company	Purpose of use	Availability	Release year
AI or Not audio[172]	AI or Not	AI-generated audio detection	Freemium	2023
Resemble.ai Detect[173]	Resemble.ai	AI-generated voice detection, audio deepfakes	Paid	2020
Sensity Audio Detection[174]	Sensity	Deepfake detection (including audio)	Paid	2020

challenges in interpretability, as the features extracted by deep learning models are often difficult for human analysts to understand and interpret.

As audio deepfakes become increasingly sophisticated, a range of tools has emerged to address the challenge of detecting AI-generated voice manipulations (Table 5.6). 'AI or Not Audio', provides a freemium platform for distinguishing between genuine and synthetic audio clips, making audio deepfake detection accessible to a wide audience. Resemble.ai Detect is tailored for identifying AI-generated voices and audio deepfakes, offering enhanced security for applications where voice authenticity is crucial. Similarly, Sensity extends its deepfake detection capabilities to audio, providing a commercial platform adept at identifying manipulative audio content. These tools collectively underscore the advancements in audio deepfake detection technologies, playing a crucial role in maintaining the integrity of communications and protecting against the misuse of AI-generated audio.

5.5.4 Text-Based Deepfakes

Real-World Examples

AI-generated text, produced by large language models (LLMs) like OpenAI's ChatGPT, has quickly become a powerful tool for generating fluent, human-like dialogue and persuasive written content. While LLMs offer numerous benefits, their potential for misuse in creating disinformation narratives is increasingly concerning. A notable example occurred on X (formerly Twitter), where researchers uncovered a coordinated network of 64 bot accounts spreading content generated

[172] https://www.aiornot.com/.

[173] https://www.resemble.ai/detect-solution/.

[174] https://sensity.ai/.

by ChatGPT.[175] This case exemplifies how inexpensive and accessible AI tools are already being employed in disinformation campaigns, targeting social media platforms to amplify false or misleading content at scale.

A comprehensive study by Vykopal et al.[176] evaluated the disinformation capabilities of 10 different LLMs using manually selected disinformation narratives. The study revealed that while some models like Falcon and ChatGPT occasionally resisted disinformation prompts, most other models were susceptible to generating persuasive content in line with harmful narratives. This variability across LLMs highlights the significant risks posed by models more prone to generating misleading content. Similarly, Ayoobi et al.[177] emphasised that LLMs can be used by malicious actors to generate fake news, illustrating the importance of markers that could help users discern between human-authored and AI-generated news.

The capacity of LLMs to generate convincing disinformation at scale presents a significant challenge, especially when integrated with bot networks or AI-generated profile images. These technologies make it easier to create coordinated, large-scale disinformation campaigns that are difficult to detect and combat. Furthermore, Wu et al. show that LLMs can undermine traditional detection systems, as stylistic manipulation of fake content can drastically reduce the accuracy of current detectors.[178] This makes it harder to safeguard digital spaces from misleading or harmful content. As of now, there are no fully effective safety mechanisms in place to protect users from the potential threats posed by cheap, AI-driven disinformation operations, particularly those orchestrated by state-sponsored entities.

In another instance, researchers found that LLMs could be deployed in influence campaigns to write persuasive political messages with minimal human oversight.[179] Their study demonstrated that AI-generated text could craft arguments for and against political candidates, manipulate public opinion or sow discord during elections. This has the potential to make disinformation campaigns more efficient

[175] Thomas, Elise, "'Hey, fellow humans!': What can a ChatGPT campaign targeting pro-Ukraine Americans tell us about the future of generative AI and disinformation?", Institute for Strategic Dialogue, 5 Dec 2023. https://www.isdglobal.org/digital_dispatches/hey-fellow-humans-what-can-a-chatgpt-campaign-targeting-pro-ukraine-americans-tell-us-about-the-future-of-generative-ai-and-disinformation.

[176] Vykopal, I., M. Pikuliak, I. Srba, R. Moro, D. Macko and M. Bielikova, "Disinformation Capabilities of Large Language Models", arXiv preprint arXiv:2311.08838, 2023.

[177] Ayoobi, Navid, Sadat Shahriar and Arjun Mukherjee, "Seeing Through AI's Lens: Enhancing Human Skepticism Towards LLM-Generated Fake News", in *Proceedings of the 35th ACM Conference on Hypertext and Social Media (HT '24)*, Association for Computing Machinery, New York, 2024, pp. 1–11. https://doi.org/10.1145/3648188.3675136.

[178] Wu, Jiaying, Jiafeng Guo and Bryan Hooi, "Fake News in Sheep's Clothing: Robust Fake News Detection Against LLM-Empowered Style Attacks", in *Proceedings of the 30th ACM SIGKDD Conference on Knowledge Discovery and Data Mining (KDD '24)*, Association for Computing Machinery, New York, 2024, pp. 3367–3378. https://doi.org/10.1145/3637528.3671977.

[179] https://openai.com/index/forecasting-misuse. See also Goldstein, J.A., G. Sastry, M. Musser, R. DiResta, M. Gentzel and K. Sedova, "Generative language models and automated influence operations: Emerging threats and potential mitigations", 2023. arXiv preprint arXiv:2301.04246.

and harder to detect than traditional methods. One potential scenario includes generating large volumes of persuasive, pro-candidate texts or creating false narratives about opponents, all while evading fact-checkers due to the human-like quality of the AI's output.

These cases underscore the real-world dangers of AI-generated text in the context of politics and disinformation. The ability to create large volumes of persuasive, deceptive content cheaply and at scale poses significant challenges to the integrity of political discourse and democratic processes. The misuse of LLMs, as noted by Kucharavy et al.,[180] highlights the dual-edged nature of these technologies; while they can be used to combat disinformation and misinformation, they also enable the generation of highly persuasive narratives that can mislead the public.

Generation of Deepfakes

LLMs have transformed content creation but also present risks when used to generate text-based deepfakes. These models can fabricate convincing written content, such as articles or social media posts, by mimicking a person's writing style, making it difficult to differentiate between authentic and synthetic material.[181] Often disseminated by bots, this fabricated content can overwhelm online platforms with disinformation. Additionally, LLMs are increasingly exploited in FIMI campaigns, generating targeted messages to manipulate public opinion.[182] The following section explores key strategies for leveraging LLMs in disinformation efforts, outlining the technical methods behind these operations.

One major issue arises from Arbitrary Misinformation Generation (AMG),[183] where LLMs are intentionally used to produce false or misleading content. This can range from completely fabricated information without any constraints (totally arbitrary generation) to more targeted misinformation designed to influence specific domains or contexts (partially arbitrary generation). Malicious actors often employ this method to manipulate public opinion, particularly during elections or geopolitical events, where false narratives can significantly impact decision-making and public perception.

A more refined method, Controllable Misinformation Generation (CMG),[184] involves shaping content to align with particular narratives or objectives. By using techniques such as paraphrasing and rewriting, misinformation is presented in a

---

180 Kucharavy, A., O. Plancherel, V. Mulder, A. Mermoud and V. Lenders, *Large Language Models in Cybersecurity: Threats, Exposure and Mitigation*, Springer, August 2024.

181 Aïmeur, E., S. Amri, and G. Brassard, "Fake News Disinformation and Misinformation in Social Media: A Review", *Social Network Analysis and Mining*, Vol. 13, No. 1, Feb 2023, p. 30.

182 Bontcheva, K., S. Papadopoulos, F. Tsalakanidou, R. Gallotti, L. Dutkiewicz, N. Krack, D. Teyssou, F. Severio Nucci, J. Spangenberg, I. Srba and P. Aichroth, "Generative AI and Disinformation: Recent Advances, Challenges, and Opportunities", 2024.

183 Chen, C., and K. Shu, "Can LLM-Generated Misinformation Be Detected?", arXiv preprint arXiv:2309.13788, 2023.

184 Goldstein, J.A., G. Sastry, M. Musser, R. DiResta, M. Gentzel and Sedova, K., "Generative Language Models and Automated Influence Operations: Emerging Threats and Potential Mitigations", arXiv preprint arXiv:2301.04246, 2023.

subtle yet convincing manner. CMG is often employed in disinformation campaigns, where maintaining the appearance of authenticity is crucial for avoiding detection and increasing credibility.

In more sophisticated influence operations, LLMs can **tailor content**[185] to specific audiences. Using frameworks like the ABC model,[186] both state and non-state actors can generate persuasive, targeted messages that resonate deeply with different demographics. The automation enabled by LLMs allows disinformation campaigns to evolve rapidly, adjusting their tactics in real-time and testing messages across platforms, making detection and counteraction much more difficult.

LLMs also play a significant role in social media manipulation, where **bot-generated text**[187] is used to amplify narratives and distort public discourse. Automated bots powered by LLMs can quickly generate large volumes of content, overwhelming genuine discussion and spreading misinformation at scale. The use of LLM-generated bots in social media manipulation represents a significant challenge in the digital landscape, as these bots can operate at scale with minimal human intervention. This technique is particularly effective in FIMI operations, where speed and wide-reaching distribution are critical to success.

Evasion techniques[188] are employed to bypass detection mechanisms that are designed to identify LLM-generated information. These techniques include paraphrasing, style imitation and adversarial attacks that modify the text in order to reduce the effectiveness of watermarking[189] and stylometry-based[190] methods and thus evade detection by automated systems. The ability of LLMs to generate infinite variations of the same misleading content poses a significant challenge for fact-checkers and detection tools. As detection technologies advance, so too do the methods used to circumvent them, making it an ongoing arms race between content misinformation/disinformation creators and detectors.

The advent of large language models (LLMs) has revolutionised text-based deepfake generation, with tools like OpenAI's GPT and Google's Gemini leading the charge in creating highly convincing synthetic content (Table 5.7). These models, available in both free and paid versions, facilitate the production of nuanced

[185] Lin, L., N. Gupta, Y. Zhang, H. Ren, C.H. Liu, F. Ding, X. Wang, X. Li, L. Verdoliva and S. Hu, "Detecting Multimedia Generated by Large AI Models: A Survey", arXiv preprint arXiv:2402.00045, 2024.

[186] In disinformation campaigns, this model can be used to craft persuasive messages by targeting people's emotions (affect), actions (behaviour) and thought processes (cognition).

[187] Bontcheva, et al., op. cit.

[188] Mubarak, R., T. Alsboui, O. Alshaikh, I. Inuwa-Dute, S. Khan and S. Parkinson, "A survey on the detection and impacts of deepfakes in visual, audio, and textual formats", *IEEE Access*, 2023. See also Lin, L., N. Gupta, et al., op. cit.

[189] Watermarking in LLMs involves embedding detectable patterns in text generated by LLMs, which can later be identified to verify the authenticity of the content.

[190] Stylometry and coherence use stylistic and linguistic analyses to detect inconsistencies in text generated by LLMs compared to human-written text.

writings that mimic specific styles, posing significant risks for disinformation dissemination. Open-source solutions such as Stanford's Alpaca and HuggingFace's BLOOM increase accessibility but also heighten the potential for misuse in fabricating credible-seeming articles and social media posts. As these technologies advance, platforms like Meta's LLaMA and Microsoft's Phi-3 continue to blur the line between machine-generated and human-written content. Commercial offerings such as Claude by Anthropic and Command R by Cohere expand language capabilities for businesses, supporting a plethora of applications from automation to creative writing, while also providing avenues for generating text-based deepfakes. Furthermore, open-source initiatives like Falcon by the Technology Innovation Institute and Mistral by Mistral AI contribute to the evolving ecosystem of text synthesis, highlighting the necessity of balancing innovation with ethical considerations.

Detection of Deepfakes

The task of detecting text-based deepfakes, generated by LLMs, presents unique challenges due to the sophistication and fluency of these models. In response, various methodologies have emerged, broadly classified as either **easy-explainable** or **hard-explainable methods**, depending on their comprehensibility to the general public and their accessibility to experts in the field.[191]

One prominent approach is **watermarking**,[192] where algorithmically detectable patterns are embedded into the generated text, allowing for straightforward detection. Traditional watermark-based detection methods require access to a watermark key to verify the authenticity of text. While this process is accessible, it is vulnerable to security breaches, prompting research into keyless watermark detection mechanisms.

Another easy-to-explain method revolves around the detection of **artefacts**[193] in machine-generated text. Though artefacts in text are less visually prominent than in images, linguistic anomalies often exist in token co-occurrence and vocabulary usage. Such artefacts tend to manifest in shallow features such as word frequency patterns and content words, while high-level semantic features exhibit fewer detectable inconsistencies. Methods like these rely on perturbations of text to reveal hidden patterns that distinguish LLM-generated text from human writing.

---

[191] Lin, L., N. Gupta, et al., op. Cit.

[192] Zhao, X., L. Li and Y.X. Wang, "Distillation-resistant watermarking for model protection in NLP", arXiv preprint, arXiv:2210.03312, 2022. See also Fernandez, P., A. Chaffin, K. Tit, V. Chappelier and T. Furon, "Three bricks to consolidate watermarks for large language models", in *IEEE International Workshop on Information Forensics and Security (WIFS)*, Dec 2023, pp. 1–6.

[193] Pu, Jiashu, Ziyi Huang, Yadong Xi, Guandan Chen, Weijie Chen and Rongsheng Zhang, "Unraveling the mystery of artifacts in machine generated text", in *Proceedings of the Thirteenth Language Resources and Evaluation Conference*, June 2022, pp. 6889–6898.

Table 5.7 Popular tools for generating text-based deepfakes

Model	Company	Purpose of use	Availability	Release year
Alpaca[194]	Stanford	Fine-tuning smaller models for specific tasks, optimised for cost-efficiency	Open source	2023
BLOOM[195]	HuggingFace	Multilingual generation, excels in diverse language capabilities	Open source	2022
Claude[196]	Anthropic	Focuses on safety and reliability, designed to minimise harmful outputs	Freemium	2023
Command R[197]	Cohere	State-of-the-art retrieval-augmented generation for factual accuracy	Freemium	2023
Falcon[198]	Technology Innovation Institute	Lightweight, highly efficient for diverse NLP tasks	Open source	2023
Gemini[199]	Google	Advanced multi-modal capabilities	Freemium	2023
GPT[200]	OpenAI	State-of-the-art general-purpose LLM, excels in creativity and human-like responses with multi-modal capabilities	Freemium	2022

(continued)

194 https://crfm.stanford.edu/2023/03/13/alpaca.html.

195 https://huggingface.co/bigscience/bloom.

196 https://www.anthropic.com/claude.

197 https://cohere.com/command.

198 https://falconllm.tii.ae/.

199 https://gemini.google.com.

200 https://openai.com/chatgpt/.

Table 5.7 (continued)

Model	Company	Purpose of use	Availability	Release year
Grok[201]	xAI	Focused on integration with social media platforms and real-time applications	Freemium	2023
LLaMA[202]	Meta	Efficient, scalable model aimed at research and fine-tuning for various tasks	Open source	2023
Mistral[203]	Mistral AI	Specialises in performance with smaller parameter models for efficient deployment	Open source	2023
Phi-3[204]	Microsoft	Lightweight, small-scale model optimised for cost-effective, specialised tasks and efficient deployment	Open source	2024
Qwen[205]	Alibaba Cloud	Optimised for enterprise solutions, excels in multilingual and task-specific applications	Open source	2023

[201] https://x.ai/.

[202] https://www.llama.com/.

[203] https://mistral.ai/.

[204] https://azure.microsoft.com/en-us/products/phi.

[205] https://github.com/QwenLM.

Additionally, some detection techniques focus on **stylometry and coherence**,[206] analysing stylistic differences and structural inconsistencies between human and machine-generated text. By examining linguistic features, such as sentence structure and entity consistency, these methods aim to detect subtle shifts in coherence that often occur in LLM-generated text.

In contrast to easy-explainable methods, **hard-explainable approaches** require a deeper understanding of statistical and computational techniques, making them less accessible to the public but effective for experts. One such approach is **perplexity-based detection**,[207] which leverages the statistical measure of perplexity, commonly used in language models. LLM-generated text often exhibits distinctive perplexity patterns that can be compared to human-authored text.

Log probabilities curvature[208] is another statistical method used for detection. By examining the log probabilities assigned by a model to various word sequences, researchers can identify patterns that distinguish synthetic text.

Another advanced method involves **efficient perturbations**,[209] which seeks to optimise the perturbation process to improve both detection accuracy and computational efficiency. These methods enhance the speed and precision of detection algorithms, making them practical for large-scale applications.

Lastly, a novel approach known as **positive-unlabeled learning**[210] has emerged to address the difficulty of detecting short LLM-generated texts. Given the high similarity between short human-authored and LLM-generated texts, this approach refrains from labelling text as strictly fake or real, treating it instead as 'unlabeled'. This framework uses multiscale positive-unlabeled training to improve detection in challenging cases like short-form content, without sacrificing accuracy for longer texts.

The detection of text-based deepfakes generated by LLMs has led to the development of a diverse set of tools aimed at distinguishing synthetic content from

---

[206] Kumarage, T., J. Garland, A. Bhattacharjee, et al., "Stylometric detection of ai-generated text in twitter timelines", arXiv preprint, 2023, arXiv:2303.03697. See also Liu, X., Z. Zhang, Y. Wang, et al.., "Coco: Coherence-enhanced machine-generated text detection under data limitation with contrastive learning", arXiv preprint, 2022. arXiv:2212.10341.

[207] Vasilatos, Christoforos, Manaar Alam, Talal Rahwan, Yasir Zaki and Michail Maniatakos, "HowkGPT: Investigating the Detection of ChatGPT-generated University Student Homework through Context-aware Perplexity Analysis", arXiv preprint, arXiv:2305.18226, 2023.

[208] Mitchell, Eric, Yoonho Lee, Alexander Khazatsky, Christopher D. Manning and Chelsea Finn "DetectGPT: Zero-Shot Machine-Generated Text Detection using Probability Curvature", in *International Conference on Machine Learning*, July 2023, pp. 24,950–24,962. https://arxiv.org/abs/2301.11305.

[209] Zeng, Z., H. Gao, Y. Miao and H. Zhang, "Efficient detection of LLM-generated texts with a Bayesian surrogate model", arXiv preprint arXiv:2305.16617. See also Bao, Guangsheng, Yanbin Zhao, Zhiyang Teng, Linyi Yang and Yue Zhang, "Fast-DetectGPT: Efficient Zero-Shot Detection of Machine-Generated Text via Conditional Probability Curvature", arXiv preprint, 2023. arXiv:2310.05130.

[210] Tian, Y., H. Chen, X. Wang, et al., "Multiscale positive-unlabeled detection of ai-generated texts", arXiv preprint, 2023. arXiv:2305.18149.

genuine human writing (Table 5.8). Paid services like Copyleaks AI Detector and Originality AI Detector focus on precise identification of AI-generated text, crucial for maintaining content integrity in academic and professional settings. Meanwhile, freemium solutions, including the AI-Generated Text Detector by Is it AI, provide accessible options for users seeking to verify textual content. IBM and Harvard's Giant Language Model Test Room (GLTR) offers a unique approach by highlighting patterns typical of machine-generated text, allowing users to critically assess suspect content. Tools like GPTZero, available in both free and paid versions, and Hive Moderation's AI content detection service accommodate diverse platform needs, providing scalable and user-friendly solutions. Additionally, specialised detectors such as Sapling AI Detector and TraceGPT from PlagiarismCheck.org cater to paid users demanding robust methods for content authentication across various domains. Platforms like Winston AI Detector and Writer AI Content Detector combine AI detection with content management capabilities, facilitating integration into daily workflows. These tools collectively underscore the ongoing efforts to address the challenges of text-based deepfakes, emphasising the importance of innovation and collaboration in digital content verification.

5.5.5 Challenges and Future Directions for Detecting Deepfakes

One of the main challenges in detecting AI-generated content lies in the limited reliability of detection models. These models face difficulties in generalising to new, emerging LAIMs (Large AI Models), often resulting in overfitting to specific datasets and struggling to detect unseen content.[211] Interpretability of detection methods is another critical issue; while high accuracy is valued, current models often lack transparency in their decision-making process.[212] Additionally, the robustness of detectors is challenged by sophisticated adversarial attacks (e.g. noise attacks), paraphrasing and image distortions like compression and blurring,[213] which expose vulnerabilities in current systems.

[211] Wang, T., X. Liao, K.P. Chow, X. Lin and Y. Wang, "Deepfake detection: a comprehensive study from the reliability perspective", arXiv preprint, 2022. arXiv:2211.10881.

[212] Barredo Arrieta, Alejandro, Natalia Díaz-Rodríguez, Javier Del Ser, et al., "Explainable Artificial Intelligence (XAI): Concepts, Taxonomies, Opportunities and Challenges toward Responsible AI", *Information Fusion*, Vol. 58, June 2020, pp. 82–115. https://www.sciencedirect.com/science/article/pii/S1566253519308103.

[213] Cocchi, F., L. Baraldi, S. Poppi, M. Cornia, L. Baraldi and R. Cucchiara, "Unveiling the impact of image transformations on deepfake detection: An experimental analysis", in *International Conference on Image Analysis and Processing*, Springer Nature, Cham, Sept 2023, pp. 345–356. See also Ivanovska, M., and V. Struc, "On the vulnerability of deepfake detectors to attacks generated by denoising diffusion models", in *Proceedings of the IEEE/CVF winter conference on applications of computer vision*, 2024, pp. 1051–1060.

Table 5.8 Popular tools for detecting text-based deepfakes

Model	Company	Purpose of use	Availability	Release year
Undetectable[214]	Undetectable.ai	Bypasses common detection methods, optimised for generating text that avoids detection	Paid	2022
Copyleaks AI Detector[215]	Copyleaks	Best suited for detecting plagiarism and AI-generated content	Paid	2022
Originality AI Detector[216]	Originality.ai	Focused on both plagiarism and AI detection, with high accuracy for content originality verification	Paid	2022
AI-Generated Text Detector[217]	Is it AI	Simple, quick tool for identifying AI-generated text in content	Freemium	2023
Crossplag[218]	Crossplag	Best for cross-language plagiarism detection and AI-generated content verification	Freemium	2022
GLTR[219]	IBM & Harvard	Visualises text predictability patterns to assess likelihood of machine generation	Open source	2019
GPTZero[220]	GPTZero	Optimised for educators to identify AI-generated essays and academic content	Freemium	2022
Hive Moderation[221]	Hive AI	Best for content moderation with an added focus on detecting AI-generated media in social platforms	Freemium	2021

(continued)

214 https://undetectable.ai/.

215 https://copyleaks.com/.

216 https://originality.ai/.

217 https://isitai.com/ai-text-detector/.

218 https://crossplag.com/.

219 http://gltr.io/.

220 https://gptzero.me/.

221 https://hivemoderation.com/ai-generated-content-detection.

Table 5.8 (continued)

Model	Company	Purpose of use	Availability	Release year
Illuminarty Text[222]	Illuminarty.ai	AI content detection with a focus on content marketing industries	Freemium	2023
QuillBot AI Detector[223]	QuillBot	Best for verifying text originality in academic and professional content	Freemium	2023
Sapling AI Detector[224]	Sapling	Optimised for customer support and business communications, ensuring human-written responses	Freemium	2023
TraceGPT[225]	PlagiarismCheck.org	Focused on high-precision detection of AI-generated content	Paid	2023
Turnitin's AI Detection[226]	Turnitin	Best for academic integrity, detecting both AI-generated text and traditional plagiarism in student work	Paid	2023
Winston AI Detector[227]	Winston AI	Tailored for freelance writers and content creators to ensure authenticity and avoid AI-written content	Freemium	2022
Writer AI Content Detector[228]	Writer.com	Best for marketing and business teams to maintain content originality and brand voice consistency	Freemium	2023
ZeroGPT[229]	ZeroGPT	Focused on detecting GPT-model-generated text across various content platforms and industries	Freemium	2023

222 https://illuminarty.ai/en/text/ai-generated-text-detection.html.

223 https://quillbot.com/ai-content-detector.

224 https://sapling.ai/ai-content-detector.

225 https://plagiarismcheck.org/ai-detector/.

226 https://www.turnitin.com.

227 https://gowinston.ai/.

228 https://writer.com/ai-content-detector/.

229 https://www.zerogpt.com/.

Another significant barrier is the constrained size and diversity of available datasets. Existing datasets, particularly for video, and audio detection, remain small and limited in scope. Many are English-centric and focused on narrow domains, hampering the detectors' ability to handle diverse, real-world data.[230] Furthermore, the absence of a standardised evaluation benchmark results in inconsistent metrics and unfair comparisons, making it difficult to assess the true performance of these detectors across varying conditions.[231]

To improve the detection of AI-generated content, research is focusing on developing foundation models, which are pre-trained on extensive datasets and can be adapted to a range of detection tasks, offering improved performance and generalisability.[232] Exploring generative discrepancies between AI-generated and human-created content, such as the syntactic patterns in text or texture inconsistencies in images, could also bolster detection capabilities.[233] Moreover, ensuring the reliability of detectors by incorporating explainable AI (XAI) techniques, robust training datasets and continuous learning strategies will be essential for maintaining model accuracy and public trust in real-world applications.[234]

There is also a need to address bias and fairness in detection models. Current detectors have shown disparities in performance across different demographic groups, leading to potential misclassification and public mistrust.[235] To create a more equitable system, researchers should prioritise the development of fair detectors that generalise across various scenarios without bias. Video detectors should also be accelerated, as real-world scenarios often involve a mix of modalities, such as audio and visual components in a single deepfake.[236]

---

[230] Sun, C., S. Jia, S. Hou and S. Lyu, "AI-Synthesized Voice Detection Using Neural Vocoder Artifacts", in *Proceedings of the IEEE/CVF Conference on Computer Vision and Pattern Recognition*, 2023, pp. 904–912.

[231] Kamat, S., S. Agarwal, T. Darrell and A. Rohrbach, "Revisiting Generalizability in Deepfake Detection: Improving Metrics and Stabilizing Transfer", in *Proceedings of the IEEE/CVF International Conference on Computer Vision*, 2023, pp. 426–435.

[232] Bommasani, R., D.A. Hudson, E. Adeli, et al., "On the Opportunities and Risks of Foundation Models", arXiv preprint, 2021. arXiv:2108.07258.

[233] Ma, Y., J. Liu, F. Yi, et al., "Is This Abstract Generated by AI? A Research for the Gap Between AI-Generated Scientific Text and Human-Written Scientific Text", arXiv preprint, 2023. arXiv:2301.10416.

[234] Epstein, D.C., I. Jain, O. Wang and R. Zhang, "Online Detection of AI-Generated Images", in *Proceedings of the IEEE/CVF International Conference on Computer Vision*, 2023, pp. 382–392.

[235] Xu, Y., P. Terhörst, K. Raja and M. Pedersen, "A Comprehensive Analysis of AI Biases in Deepfake Detection with Massively Annotated Databases", arXiv preprint, 2022. arXiv:2208.05845.

[236] Epstein, D.C., I. Jain, O. Wang and R. Zhang, "Online Detection of AI-Generated Images", in Proceedings of the IEEE/CVF International Conference on Computer Vision, 2023, pp. 382–392.

Finally, the development of interpretable and user-friendly detection tools is critical. Current tools lack accessibility for non-technical users, limiting their practical application. Making these systems more transparent and usable will enhance their adoption, especially among underrepresented groups such as non-experts.[237]

[237] Barredo Arrieta, A., Natalia Díaz-Rodríguez, Javier Del Ser, Adrien Bennetot, Siham Tabik, Alberto Barbado, Salvador Garcia, et al., "Explainable Artificial Intelligence (XAI): Concepts, Taxonomies, Opportunities and Challenges toward Responsible AI", *Information Fusion*, Vol. 58, June 2020, pp. 82–115. https://www.sciencedirect.com/science/article/abs/pii/S1566253519308103.

Interviews 6

Richa Kumar

The partners interviewed 20 ATHENA Stakeholder Board members and two non-Stakeholder Board members to gather their insights into manifestations of foreign information manipulation and interference.

The 20 interviewees comprised:

- 4 government representatives (3 males, 1 female) from Ireland and the UK, and Poland;
- 2 industrial researchers (both male);
- 2 journalists (1 male, 1 female);
- 4 researchers (all female); and
- 8 academics (4 males, 4 females).

We had a balance of 10 male and 10 female interviewees.

The interview analysis revealed several recurring themes concerning:

- the definition of FIMI and how it is often alluded to through references, disinformation and misinformation;
- the evolution of FIMI with the new and emerging technologies shaping information manipulation;
- the geopolitical shaping of FIMI making it subjective to the politics of its times;
- the role of technology in the generation and amplification of information manipulation;

R. Kumar (✉)
Trilateral Research, London, UK
e-mail: Richa.kumar@gmail.com

© The Author(s), under exclusive license to Springer Nature Switzerland AG 2026

D. Wright (ed.), *Foreign Information Manipulation and Interference*, Terrorism, Security, and Computation, https://doi.org/10.1007/978-3-031-91299-3_6

- the prevalent techniques, tactics and procedures that the interviewees have encountered;
- the distinction between FIMI incidents and campaigns and the challenges there;
- challenges in attribution;
- And, lastly, multidisciplinary stakeholder collaboration and sector-specific perspectives.

6.1 Defining Foreign Information Manipulation and Interference (FIMI)

Most interviewees described FIMI as a multifaceted and interdisciplinary issue, combining technical, social and political elements that reflected how the interviewees from various sectors became involved in FIMI. A key point of differentiation across the interviewees was the variation in terminology used to describe the field: while FIMI was the overarching term, most respondents preferred to use more familiar terms like 'misinformation' and 'disinformation' in their answers. Some interviewees also focused on specific types of disinformation, such as domestic versus foreign disinformation, or the role of AI in the manipulation of public opinion.

Most interviewees entered FIMI research indirectly through adjacent disciplines like security studies, social data analysis or political science, rather than starting their careers specifically in FIMI. Study on FIMI is characterised by its interdisciplinary nature, blending technical and social science perspectives while integrating theoretical and practical approaches. As a result, the average work experience of the interviewees varied from one to 30 years; however, most government representatives had around 30 years of work experience in government. There are notable differences in how interviewees frame their relationship with FIMI: some positioned it as their primary research focus, while others explicitly stated that misinformation and disinformation were not their main research topics but rather intersected with their work tangentially. Some interviewees focused primarily on theoretical aspects and broad implications for democracy, while others concentrated on specific practical applications such as fact-checking, crisis management and youth education.

The limited number of years of work on FIMI of most interviewees and the interchangeable use of disinformation and misinformation highlight the phenomenon of FIMI as relatively new. Many interviewees observed that while disinformation and misinformation share similarities, FIMI involves deliberate, calculated interference, typically by foreign state or non-state actors, to advance geopolitical objectives. Different categories of interviewees approached information manipulation either as a technologically driven phenomenon or as a historical phenomenon. For instance, it was worth noting that academics emphasised the role of artificial intelligence and social media in exacerbating misinformation, while industrial representatives focused on maintaining frameworks rather than conducting primary research; journalists approached disinformation campaigns from a historical perspective.

There were also differences in the degree of focus on aspects of FIMI. For instance, academic researchers were more likely to focus on theoretical concerns and the broader societal implications of disinformation, such as its impact on democracy and public trust. In contrast, industrial researchers were more focused on the technical aspects, particularly around the detection and prevention of disinformation, while journalists were concerned with the practicalities of observing and reporting on disinformation campaigns in real time, often within the context of ongoing geopolitical crises.

Similarly, different categories of interviewees had varying levels of awareness of the role of state and foreign actors in information manipulation: Government representatives, particularly from Ireland, the UK and Poland, were relatively more aware of state-sponsored disinformation or disinformation campaigns including hybrid threats that blend disinformation and cybersecurity risks driven by foreign actors. Industrial researchers and journalists emphasised the role of state-sponsored disinformation campaigns with a focus on technological advances.

The DISARM and MITRE frameworks are not widely adopted yet, likely due to a lack of a clear definition of FIMI. Out of 20 experts interviewed, most were unaware of them, with only three using one of the frameworks. One researcher noted that the work is still exploratory and requires more time to calibrate, and an industry representative suggested using DISARM alongside MITRE's ATT&CK framework for better results. One industry researcher pointed out that balancing specificity with operational practicality in DISARM is challenging, which may be further complicated by the absence of a well-defined FIMI, stressing the need to streamline and operationalise these frameworks.

Thus, while FIMI shares common traits with general misinformation, FIMI is distinct in its intentionality and foreign involvement, with foreign state or non-state actors deliberately manipulating information to pursue geopolitical goals. This often involves amplifying pre-existing societal fears or divisions, such as Russian disinformation campaigns around Ukrainian corruption, which leveraged real concerns to increase societal discord.

6.2 The Evolving and Complex Nature of FIMI

A central theme emerging from the interviews is the rapid evolution and growing complexity of FIMI. All interviewees across all sectors emphasised that the urgency and sophistication of FIMI have escalated, particularly following major geopolitical events such as the COVID-19 pandemic, the war in Ukraine, Brexit and the rising tensions with countries including Russia, China and Iran. These events have heightened awareness and engagement in the field, with FIMI increasingly seen as a significant threat to democratic values, public trust and social stability. The interviewees emphasised the increased digitisation of every aspect of our lives playing a pivotal role in amplifying FIMI's reach. They emphasised the shift from traditional media to digital platforms as a key factor in the widespread dissemination of disinformation. The rise of social media, AI and targeted digital campaigns has made FIMI more pervasive and challenging to counter. This technological transformation has enabled foreign actors, particularly state-sponsored, to conduct more targeted and structured disinformation campaigns, manipulating public opinion and exacerbating societal divisions.

The increasing sophistication of FIMI is reflected in its evolving tools and tactics. Beyond simply creating false narratives, FIMI campaigns are increasingly focused on manipulating existing narratives, exploiting societal vulnerabilities and undermining trust in institutions. The intersection of domestic and foreign disinformation was also noted, as foreign actors often collaborate with local groups to amplify divisive narratives. This makes attribution and response efforts more challenging, as the origin of the disinformation can be difficult to trace, especially when local actors are involved in spreading foreign narratives.

Interviewees across categories agreed that FIMI is not just about creating entirely new falsehoods but rather about amplifying existing societal divisions or exploiting pre-existing fears. For example, Russian disinformation regarding Ukrainian corruption leverages real concerns, which makes it more effective. In this way, FIMI manipulates narratives to increase societal discord, erode trust in government and undermine democratic values, especially in the context of elections or crises.

This increasing sophistication is also reflected in the expansion of tools and tactics and has played a crucial role in the evolution of FIMI. The use of digital platforms, AI algorithms and social media to spread disinformation has become more pervasive, allowing for faster and wider dissemination. Some interviewees noted the intersectionality of FIMI with domestic disinformation campaigns[1], as foreign actors increasingly collaborate with local groups to amplify narratives.

The interviewees highlighted that the evolving nature of FIMI is marked by a shift from isolated incidents of disinformation to coordinated, long-term campaigns. Initially, FIMI was seen not only as a single act of manipulation targeting sensitive social or political issues, but over time, state and non-state actors have increasingly orchestrated sustained campaigns with broader strategic objectives. These campaigns leverage advanced technologies, such as artificial intelligence and social media, to efficiently spread disinformation and manipulate public opinion.

In summary, the evolving nature of FIMI, its connection to geopolitical developments and the role of technology in amplifying its impact underscore the complexity of the issue. The strategic responses to FIMI require interdisciplinary collaboration across government, industry, media and academia to address the challenges posed by increasingly sophisticated and targeted disinformation campaigns.

6.3 Impact of Geopolitical Events in Shaping FIMI

All 20 interviewees centred their responses on disinformation and FIMI in the context of current geopolitical events. Current geopolitical events such as Russia's disinformation campaigns, the rise of state-sponsored misinformation (particularly from countries like Russia, China and Iran) and the impact of migration and public health crises emerged as dominant themes across most interviewees. They highlighted the use of disinformation to influence political narratives, undermine public trust and manipulate international relations as a core challenge.

Government representatives, particularly from Ireland, the UK and Poland, discussed FIMI primarily in terms of disinformation campaigns driven by foreign actors. These included hybrid threats, which blend disinformation and cybersecurity risks. Notably, many government representatives were focused on identifying and countering these foreign threats, as well as dealing with the complexities surrounding the manipulation of political narratives, especially related to elections and international security.

Industrial researchers and journalists emphasised the role of state-sponsored disinformation campaigns, with a particular focus on how these efforts have evolved alongside technological advances. The manipulation of domestic narratives is seen as a growing concern, while journalists highlighted the long-term impact of disinformation related to the Middle East and the ongoing conflict in Ukraine.

6.4 Role of Technology as a Key Driver for FIMI

All interviewees emphasised the role of digital technologies, social media and artificial intelligence (AI) as crucial and pivotal in the spread of misinformation and disinformation. Interviewees said that the advent of social media platforms has created a fertile environment where disinformation can spread rapidly, often aided by algorithms that prioritise sensationalist and polarising content.

Academics and industrial researchers pointed to AI's role in both propagating and detecting disinformation, with AI-powered tools used to create and amplify false narratives. AI will play a more prominent role both in the implementation of FIMI and in the fight against it. Interviewees highlighted that there is an expectation that various good actors will be able to use AI to effectively counter disinformation and manipulation attempts. The respondents who believed that AI will be the technology that will help to improve the fight against disinformation campaigns highlighted several initiatives related to detecting video, image, audio and text deepfakes: the coming years will see the emergence of algorithms and technologies that will allow us to create solutions that use automated analysis to detect outliers, identify 'patient zero' and alert the media and consumers. They emphasised that as no single institution can manage the entire digital space alone, it is important to make these tools available to the public.

Respondents were pessimistic about the rapid development and adoption of AI (with a particular focus on generative AI models) leading to an exponential increase in its use to generate false content, voices and other persuasive disinformation, flooding the information space with noise and confusion, even if individual campaigns are countered. This could undermine democratic engagement in public fora thus making it increasingly difficult to have meaningful conversations. Respondents who were sceptical about the use of AI to fight disinformation acknowledged that efforts to counter individual episodes of disinformation have been successful, but the sheer volume of such content is creating a chaotic environment in which the public finds it increasingly difficult to distinguish fact from falsehood. This could seriously undermine democratic discourse and decision-making as people do not know what information to trust.

Erring towards caution, interviewees highlighted the market dynamics that shape the Internet and the generation and spread of manipulated information. They described the Internet as a marketplace of ideas that, on one hand, encourages democratic thinking, but on the other hand, limits the same due to fake information with languages as a barrier for people. There was general agreement among interviewees that the Internet is not motivated by any humanistic good or democratic spirit but by companies whose main goal is to make money, which is the driving force behind all the big platforms that spread disinformation. In a way, the manufacture and spread of manipulated information is a profitable enterprise.

The interviews highlighted the growing complexity of the issue, as traditional methods of identifying disinformation (such as human fact-checking) are increasingly insufficient in the face of sophisticated technological tools. The increasing use of AI in disinformation campaigns also raised concerns about its potential to undermine public trust in institutions and democratic processes. Further, we can see from the interviews the potential value in new technologies and specifically in AI, both from an offensive perspective, i.e., creating deepfakes and deploying disinformation and manipulation campaigns, as well as from a defensive perspective, building tools to detect deepfakes and disinformation campaigns in a more automated, autonomous and collaborative manner.

6.5 Techniques, Tactics and Procedures of FIMI

Interviewees particularly highlighted the role of technology and various TTPs in complicating FIMI. All interviewees discussed the varying tactics used to spread disinformation, with social media platforms as key for disseminating FIMI content. However, they agreed that traditional media are still used in regions with limited Internet access. Disinformation actors increasingly use sophisticated methods such as narrative laundering (shifting disinformation into mainstream media), deepfakes, AI-driven content and closed platforms such as Telegram. These sophisticated tactics make it harder to trace the origin of the disinformation. The identification of FIMI sources is often complicated by narrative laundering, deepfakes and AI-driven content.

Attribution of FIMI remains a significant challenge, with several experts noting the difficulty in identifying the true perpetrators, especially when disinformation is disseminated through complex networks or masked by tools such as Tor. Interviewees consistently identified Russia as a major source of disinformation, particularly related to Ukraine and European politics. Other actors, including China, Turkey and Iran, were also implicated in specific regional contexts.

Interviewees highlighted the growing accessibility of advanced disinformation tools, such as AI-powered technologies, as a concern. While these tools make disinformation campaigns more cost-effective and scalable, they also present challenges for detection, as many organisations lack the necessary resources to combat them effectively.

Interviewees pointed to the evolving nature of FIMI tactics, the broad range of targeted groups and the need for improved attribution methods to combat disinformation. Addressing these challenges requires a multifaceted approach that combines technological solutions, greater collaboration across sectors and increased awareness of the geopolitical forces shaping these campaigns.

6.6 FIMI Incidents and Campaigns

Crucial to use of sophisticated TTPs is the distinction between incidents and campaigns and their significance in understanding and countering disinformation. FIMI incidents are single, isolated acts of disinformation manipulation aimed at exploiting specific social or political issues and involving external actors. These are typically discrete events with targeted objectives (e.g., manipulating public opinion on immigration, public health or elections). FIMI campaigns are sustained, coordinated efforts involving multiple incidents aimed at achieving broader, long-term strategic goals. These campaigns often have overarching narratives, such as portraying a political figure as corrupt, and rely on systematic manipulation over time across multiple platforms.

The characteristics between incidents and campaigns vary significantly: incidents are described as discrete, individual acts that exploit sensitive issues (e.g. migration, elections or national security) to manipulate public perception and amplify societal divisions. They often use 'kernels of truth' to create compelling, though misleading, narratives. The significance of incidents becomes clearer when viewed within the context of a larger campaign, making them part of a broader strategy to destabilise or influence political environments. FIMI campaigns, on the other hand, are seen as orchestrated, long-term operations typically led by state or non-state actors. They are designed to shift public discourse, influence political landscapes or advance strategic interests through coordinated disinformation over time. These campaigns often make use of advanced tools such as artificial intelligence and use multiple media channels to amplify the spread of disinformation.

A key difficulty highlighted by the interviewees is the challenge of attribution. Since incidents are often isolated and may not immediately appear connected, it can be difficult to trace their origins or identify the perpetrators, especially when these incidents are part of a larger campaign. Techniques such as narrative laundering further complicate the identification of the source and intent behind the campaigns.

While individual incidents might seem isolated, they often contribute to a larger strategic framework. For example, disinformation targeting migration issues in Poland or historical narratives can be seen as part of broader efforts to influence societal opinion and destabilise the political landscape. Understanding how individual incidents fit into the larger context of a campaign allows for a more accurate analysis and response to FIMI operations.

Interviewees emphasised that responses to FIMI should not focus solely on individual incidents but should also consider the broader campaign strategies at play. Analysts need to monitor the overall FIMI landscape and understand the patterns behind incidents to effectively protect against long-term interference.

A reasonably comprehensive understanding of FIMI involves gathering evidence from multiple sources, understanding the intent and methods behind disinformation and mapping the networks and behaviours that drive these campaigns.

In summary, interviewees underscored the importance of distinguishing between isolated FIMI incidents and broader, coordinated disinformation campaigns, while highlighting the challenges of attribution and the need for strategic, long-term monitoring and response.

6.7 Challenges in Attribution and Sector

All interviewees agreed that attribution is a significant challenge in the context of FIMI. These challenges stem from difficulties in tracing the origins of disinformation, the complexity of identifying actors involved and the absence of clear evidence linking specific actors to the spread of false narratives. The priority of attribution as an issue and challenges therein depend on the sector to which the respondent belongs.

Government representative viewed attribution as a primary challenge as it is difficult to clearly attribute FIMI to specific foreign actors with malicious intent and hold them accountable. This is particularly difficult because actions taken in the information space must be handled with great care, ensuring that responses do not undermine democratic principles. The government's approach, therefore, is one of caution and prudence. Rather than reacting to every instance of FIMI, government authorities tend to focus on overseeing broader trends and maintain a watchful eye on the information landscape to protect democratic institutions from external manipulation. By monitoring these broader patterns, security practitioners can enhance attribution by identifying recurring behaviours and by facilitating better communication among stakeholders, including NGOs and social media companies, who can help track and share information about malicious activities.

Academics pointed to the inherent difficulty of attribution. One academic highlighted the challenge of discerning the motives behind disinformation campaigns, especially when non-state actors are involved. Disinformation is often spread by individuals or groups without clear ties to specific state actors, and these non-state actors themselves may struggle to pinpoint the origin of the information they spread. Moreover, the dissemination of disinformation across mainstream media adds another layer of complexity, making it harder to trace the original source. Experts emphasise the need for better resources and expertise to improve attribution, particularly by verifying debunking sources and enhancing individual capabilities in identifying and analysing disinformation.

Resource constraints were another common theme. One researcher mentioned that in the educational domain, attribution is not the primary focus, and limitations in resources make it difficult to assign responsibility for disinformation to specific actors. In contrast, using technological solutions such as machine learning tools, as noted by another academic, can significantly improve attribution efforts by identifying patterns in the information space and helping authorities respond more effectively. Several academics agreed about resource constraints and pointed to the lack of funding to monitor the online information space as a significant obstacle to effective attribution. To improve attribution, experts recommended looking for patterns in disinformation campaigns and employing a variety of techniques to trace their origin. Another academic discussed how the use of bots can complicate attribution: while some bots may exhibit clear, identifiable behaviour, others are more sophisticated and can disguise their origins, making it challenging to link them to a specific actor. Attribution becomes difficult when a disinformation campaign lacks a clear source. However, once a source is identified through extensive research or evidence from credible sources, attribution becomes more manageable.

Journalists agreed on the practical challenges of attribution. One journalist explained that, while it may be clear that certain disinformation campaigns are linked to Russia, for example, proving this connection with concrete evidence is far more difficult. Disinformation networks are complex, and the actors involved often use tactics beyond just spreading false narratives, such as blackmail, bribery and financial corruption, which further complicate attribution. Another journalist added that public understanding of the motives behind foreign interference is often limited, which makes it harder to attribute the actions of disinformation actors. The situation becomes even more complicated when multiple actors are involved, as seen in the Palestine-Israel conflict, where multiple countries with differing interests contribute to the spread of disinformation.

Industry-affiliated researchers highlighted additional challenges to attribution, such as the use of Tor networks or peer-to-peer systems by disinformation actors to hide their location or identity. Linguistic analysis, while a useful tool, also faces challenges due to the lack of necessary data and logs. Therefore, attribution efforts require a multifaceted approach that combines various methodologies, including linguistic analysis, technological solutions and pattern recognition. Understanding the protective measures taken by disinformation actors, as well as the phenomenon of narrative laundering, which involves the washing or shifting of disinformation narratives to obscure their origin, challenge attribution. As disinformation campaigns grow more sophisticated, they will destabilise political environments and undermine public trust, necessitating a long-term and comprehensive approach to counter these threats effectively.

In conclusion, enhancing attribution in FIMI requires addressing resource constraints, improving technological tools and fostering collaboration among governments, academics, journalists and other stakeholders. While challenges persist in tracing the origins of disinformation and identifying the actors behind it, a more coordinated and strategic approach, coupled with increased expertise, can help strengthen the ability to attribute and respond to these threats.

6.8 Multidisciplinary Stakeholder Collaboration and Sector-Specific Perspectives on FIMI

The multidisciplinary nature of FIMI research is another key theme that emerged from the interviews. This multi-disciplinarity could be because many interviewees came into the field of FIMI from adjacent areas such as security studies, political science and social data analysis, rather than from a primary focus on misinformation and disinformation. This has led to the development of multi-stakeholder frameworks for research and action, which involve collaboration across universities, government bodies, media organisations and international institutions.

Despite the collaborative nature of this work, many interviewees expressed concerns about resource constraints, limited funding and the challenges of coordinating efforts across such diverse stakeholders. Government representatives and industrial researchers noted the difficulty in aligning research objectives with the practical needs of governments and industry, particularly when dealing with fast-moving digital platforms and the spread of disinformation during crises (e.g., elections, pandemics or armed conflicts).

The interviewees' organisational and sector-specific perspectives further highlighted the challenges faced in addressing FIMI. For example, government representatives discussed the challenges of navigating the political and security dimensions of disinformation, often from a national security or foreign policy angle. They emphasised the need for coordinated strategies to counter foreign disinformation and its potential to destabilise political processes. Industry researchers acknowledged the increasing importance of open-source intelligence and the role of digital platforms in shaping disinformation. Their focus was on developing tools to track and counteract these efforts, often working in response to specific geopolitical events. Journalists brought a historical perspective to the issue, focusing on long-term trends and the evolution of disinformation campaigns and were concerned with the ethical implications of disinformation, its effects on public opinion and the role of media in both spreading and combating it. Academics focused on the theoretical and societal impacts of disinformation, highlighting the need for more robust frameworks to understand and address these challenges. They also expressed concern about the implications of disinformation for democracy and public trust in institutions.

Thus, while most interviewees emphasised institutional collaboration, their specific collaborative networks differ notably: some work primarily with academic institutions, others with government bodies and still others with international organisations or local practitioners.

6.9 Conclusions and Recommendations

The interviews underscored the urgency and complexity of addressing FIMI in the contemporary landscape. The rapid evolution of disinformation, fuelled by technological advancements, geopolitical events and the increasing role of social media, calls for coordinated, multi-stakeholder efforts. While there is broad agreement about the need for greater collaboration across governments, industries, academia and media, there are also significant challenges in terms of resources, funding and aligning objectives. Addressing FIMI effectively will require both theoretical research and practical, real-world solutions that engage a diverse range of actors and expertise to successfully mitigate its harmful effects on democracy and public trust. The interviews also led to several key recommendations for addressing these challenges.

1. **Develop a comprehensive, accessible framework of FIMI analysis**: The limited adoption of the DISARM and MITRE frameworks is indicative of the need for a more accessible and adaptable framework that addresses the multifaceted nature of FIMI. The framework for FIMI analysis should address long-term, coordinated efforts of FIMI campaigns and provide an understanding of the underlying social and political vulnerabilities that these campaigns exploit, allowing for proactive countermeasures.
2. **Promote public awareness and enhance technological and digital literacy**: Given the growing complexity of FIMI and the increased reliance of social media and AI, there is a need to improve technological and digital literacy across all sectors and amongst the citizens. These efforts should focus on media literacy, helping citizens recognise and critically assess content, recognise manipulated information and understand the role of AI and algorithms in shaping the information landscape, especially in the context of political and international conflicts. Citizens should be empowered to critically evaluate digital content and enhance their participation in mitigating the negative impact of manipulated information on democratic discourse.
3. **Foster international, cross-sectoral cooperation and training**: Given the rise of state-sponsored disinformation campaigns, particularly from authoritarian countries such as Russia, China and Iran, international collaboration is essential. Governments should work together to develop coordinated strategies to identify, counter and mitigate the impact of these foreign threats, especially

regarding political narratives and international relations. In addition, the interdisciplinary nature of FIMI requires a cross-sectoral collaboration with experts across government, industry, media and academia which will in turn encourage collaboration between fields such as political science, social data analysis, security studies and artificial intelligence. This cross-sectoral and international collaboration should support cross-disciplinary training and joint research initiatives to ensure a holistic understanding of FIMI and the development of interdisciplinary, collaborative data-sharing platforms and tools that could also support knowledge exchange, enabling better integration of technological, societal and geopolitical insights into the study and response to FIMI. These tools should be accessible and available to the public to identify and flag disinformation, including deepfakes and other manipulated content, helping to reduce confusion in the information space.

4. **Enhance and strengthen attribution methods and transparency**: A key challenge in countering FIMI and disinformation generally is the difficulty in tracing the origins of the manipulated information. There is a need for more advanced tools to address the anonymity and pseudonymity provided by most social networks to advance attribution techniques. The main issue is that social networks enable people, organisations and states to open accounts without revealing their true identity and/ or the identity of the persons, companies or states behind their accounts. There is a need to enhance transparency in social media platforms and to use AI-driven tools to track and identify sources of FIMI. Further, more funding should be allocated to support research and tools focused on improving attribution techniques. This includes providing resources for linguistic analysis, pattern recognition and the verification of disinformation sources. Investment in these areas will help build expertise and create more robust systems for tracing the origins of disinformation campaigns. We need more public awareness about the existence of FIMI and its differences from related terms such as dis/misinformation.

Conclusions and Recommendations 7

David Wright

In this final chapter, we have selected some conclusions and recommendations from the preceding chapters. We emphasise the word *some*. The following are only *some* of our findings and recommendations which are scattered throughout the book. There are far too many to reproduce here. It's why the reader is encouraged to read the whole book! Nevertheless, we emphasise the following points, which are organised with the findings, conclusions and recommendations grouped together by theme or issue.

7.1 Inventiveness of Attackers

The 32 case studies in Chap. 4 indicate a proliferation and inventiveness of different tactics, techniques and procedures used by FIMI attackers. The case studies show the high adaptability of disinformation campaigns. Disinformation actors use a wide range of platforms and techniques to evade detection and continue to spread their messages. For those responsible for shaping policies or designing countermeasures, understanding these evolving tactics is critical to developing effective interventions. Defenders need constant vigilance and adaptation of countermeasures as malicious actors' tactics evolve. Companies must be constantly innovating to be able to detect malicious behaviours. This includes investing in

The list of authors who have contributed to this chapter are listed in the Front matter (pp. vii and viii).

D. Wright (✉)
Trilateral Research, London, UK
e-mail: david.wright@trilateralresearch.com

© The Author(s), under exclusive license to Springer Nature Switzerland AG 2026

D. Wright (ed.), *Foreign Information Manipulation and Interference*, Terrorism, Security, and Computation, https://doi.org/10.1007/978-3-031-91299-3_7

artificial intelligence, machine learning and other cutting-edge tools for identifying patterns, analysing data and predicting future trends. By integrating proactive and reactive measures, states and institutions can strengthen their resilience against cyberattacks, mitigating the impact of disinformation campaigns and safeguarding democratic processes.

The EU should support research on network analysis techniques to track and reveal the coordinated activities of accounts engaged in spreading disinformation. By mapping the relationships among these accounts, researchers can identify behavioural patterns that indicate an inauthentic nature and coordinated manipulation efforts. Social media platforms should also invest in advanced technology, including network analysis and corpus analysis, to detect and remove disinformation, including tracking hashtags and detecting manipulative language.

Deepfakes can recreate an individual's face, voice and body movements, making them indistinguishable from real media. They enable the production of falsified content that can be used to depict inauthentic scenarios, such as a public figure making false statements or committing actions they never took. While these techniques have not been prevalent in past disinformation campaigns, their potential for widespread manipulation is immense. AI-generated deepfakes can be deployed to incite social unrest, undermine trust in political figures or manipulate global narratives through convincingly false visuals.

The current analysis process is heavily manual, which is unsustainable given the increasing volume of FIMI incidents. A semi-automated approach is needed to assist analysts with real-time guidance during the analysis process, provide insights from previous cases, and algorithmically identify similar attack techniques. Such an approach could relieve analysts from repetitive tasks, enabling them to focus on higher-level interpretation and strategic responses. The incorporation and adaptation of tools and methodologies from the cybersecurity sector will improve the degree of automation in different phases of the analysis process, such as detection systems, modelling and responding to disinformation campaigns.

7.2 Attribution

Attribution is a challenge. Some attackers cover their tracks well or engage in deniability. FIMI analysis requires an understanding of the different types of attackers in disinformation campaigns and their motivations. The European Union Agency for Cybersecurity (ENISA) report on *Foreign Information Manipulation and Interference (FIMI) and Cybersecurity—Threat Landscape* uses a classification based on attribution (technical or political) and whether the actors are state-sponsored or non-state-sponsored. This creates four categories:

- State-sponsored, technically attributable
- State-sponsored, politically attributable
- Non-state-sponsored, technically attributable

- Non-state-sponsored, politically attributable.[1]

Russia, China and others use third-party firms to conduct their foreign influence campaigns, obfuscating the connections with the governments. They outsource to smaller threat actors, effectively engaging in a proxy war for their mutual benefit. Thus, studying the role of proxies in information warfare is needed.

Enhancing attribution in FIMI requires addressing resource constraints, improving technological tools and fostering collaboration among governments, academics, journalists and other stakeholders. While challenges persist in tracing the origins of disinformation and identifying the actors behind it, a more coordinated and strategic approach, coupled with increased expertise, will help strengthen the ability to attribute and respond to these threats.

Governments and tech companies must invest in artificial intelligence and machine learning solutions to better track disinformation sources, analyse patterns, and identify networks behind malicious campaigns alongside clear, transparent attribution methodologies that allow for the swift identification and exposure of perpetrators.

7.3 Dangers of FIMI

The term 'useful idiots' refers to individuals who unwittingly support a cause or agenda—often political or ideological—without fully understanding its implications, particularly when that cause is manipulative or harmful. The phrase was used to describe Western sympathisers of Soviet communism during the Cold War. The term has evolved somewhat and is now used more broadly to describe people who, in their enthusiasm or naivety, support movements, organisations or regimes that ultimately manipulate or exploit them. It is often used pejoratively to describe people who are seen as naïve or gullible in the political arena.

Researchers have found that LLMs can be deployed in influence campaigns to write persuasive political messages with minimal human oversight.[2] They demonstrated that AI-generated text could craft arguments for and against political candidates, manipulate public opinion or sow discord during elections. This has the potential to make disinformation campaigns more efficient and harder to detect than traditional methods. One potential scenario includes generating large volumes of persuasive, pro-candidate texts or creating false narratives about opponents, all while evading fact-checkers due to the human-like quality of the AI's output. The

[1] Magonara, Erika, and Apostolos Malatras, "Foreign Information Manipulation Interference (FIMI) and Cybersecurity—Threat Landscape", Report/Study, ENISA, 8 December 2022. https://www.enisa.europa.eu/publications/foreign-information-manipulation-interference-fimi-and-cybersecurity-threat-landscape.

[2] https://openai.com/index/forecasting-misuse. See also Goldstein, J.A., Sastry, G., Musser, M., DiResta, R., Gentzel, M. and Sedova, K., "Generative language models and automated influence operations: Emerging threats and potential mitigations", 2023. *arXiv preprint arXiv:2301.04246.*

ability of LLMs to generate infinite variations of the same misleading content poses a significant challenge for fact-checkers and detection tools.

These cases underscore the real-world dangers of AI-generated text in the context of politics and disinformation. The ability to create large volumes of persuasive, deceptive content cheaply and at scale poses significant challenges to the integrity of political discourse and democratic processes. The misuse of LLMs highlights the dual-edged nature of these technologies; while they can be used to combat disinformation and misinformation, they also enable the generation of highly persuasive narratives that can mislead the public.

As disinformation campaigns grow more sophisticated, they will destabilise political environments and undermine public trust, necessitating a long-term and comprehensive approach to counter these threats effectively.

7.4 Impact on Democracy

In Europe, according to the 2024 Reuters Institute Digital News Report, online sources, including websites and social media, are increasingly becoming primary news sources for Europeans, especially among younger demographics.[3]

EEAS found in its first FIMI report that impersonation techniques have become more sophisticated. It noted that incidents do not occur in just one language; content is translated and amplified in multiple languages. It found that FIMI remains mostly image and video-based. The dissemination of the doctored image of Zelenskyy holding a jersey with the swastika is consistent with a broader, long-running disinformation campaign linking Ukrainian leaders to Nazism, a narrative deployed by pro-Russian actors since the illegal annexation of Crimea.

Although the European Parliament elections concluded on 9 June 2024 in all EU countries, the disinformation hasn't disappeared with their conclusion. There remains a growing threat to democratic society. Attackers have effectively employed information warfare techniques (such as content distortion and exploiting breaking news events) to amplify distrust within the EU, weaken transatlantic alliances and promote politicians sympathetic to the Kremlin. The incidents indicate a concerted effort not only to discredit the EU's actions but also to impact election outcomes by influencing voter sentiment through disinformation.

Sometimes attackers exploit historical tensions, as the Chinese did regarding Japan's discharge of Fukushima water. Similarly, Turkey exploited the historical ethnic and national tensions between Greek and Turkish Cypriots to deepen polarisation.

These campaigns leveraged social media to disseminate fake narratives, manipulate public opinion and destabilise target countries. The use of sophisticated tactics, such as the creation of inauthentic accounts, hashtag manipulation and

---

[3] https://reutersinstitute.politics.ox.ac.uk/journalism-media-and-technology-trends-and-predictions-2024?eicker.media.

the dissemination of emotionally charged content, enables FIMI actors to exploit existing societal divisions and amplify pre-existing biases. The consequences of these campaigns can extend beyond the online sphere, contributing to increased polarisation, violence and the undermining of legitimate political processes.

Unlike non-democratic regimes, democratic nations' openness and freedom make them susceptible to malign influence tactics, a weakness on which adversaries have adeptly capitalised.

The European Commission is currently pushing forward with plans for a new directive, as part of the Defence of Democracy Package modelled after the US Foreign Agents Registration Act (FARA), specifically targeting Russian and Chinese influence and requiring foreign-funded entities to register, thereby increasing transparency.[4] This legislation aims to safeguard democracies by imposing transparency obligations on entities seeking to shape public opinion and influence democratic processes.[5] Through enhancing transparency and accountability, such measures seek to mitigate the risk of undue foreign influence on European political systems.[6]

Further sanctions should target individuals and entities involved in FIMI efforts, particularly focusing on those responsible for running disinformation networks like the Voice of Europe. EU-wide alignment on sanctions, including those targeting oligarchs like Viktor Medvedchuk, is obviously desirable.

7.5 Tracking How FIMI Spreads

Russian disinformation is usually disseminated first on the network of sites affiliated with Russia, hosted on Russian domains and via the messages of Russian-related bloggers, politicians and influencers. Russian-related social media platforms such as Telegram, Vkontakte and Odnoklassniki exploit the echo chamber effect to deliver messages. Telegram remains the most accessed Russian-affiliated platform. The case study about Zelinskyy's moving to the US is an example of how the Russian propaganda machine amplifies the dissemination of a disinformation narrative. It started with an anonymous recording posted on a marginal YouTube channel. A group of websites pretending to be media outlets circulated the disinformation and gave it credibility. Russian state media reproduced the disinformation and gave it further outreach. A group of influencers and popular personalities talked about what the Russian state media or Kremlin-controlled pseudo-media published. These influencers managed to popularise the message on social media and reach Republican-leaning US citizens.

---

[4] Wheaton, Sarah, "EU Commission Wants Registry for Foreign Lobbyists", *POLITICO*, 12 Dec 2023. https://www.politico.eu/article/eu-commission-wants-registry-for-foreign-lobbyists/.

[5] European Commission, "Defence of Democracy—Commission proposes to shed light on covert foreign influence", press release, 12 Dec 2023. https://ec.europa.eu/commission/presscorner/detail/en/ip_23_6453.

[6] Wheaton, op. cit.

Knowledge of the tactics and techniques used by attackers can serve as a basis for designing pre-bunking actions aimed at the public to explain how these disinformation agents operate. Pre-bunking can help citizens detect disinformation traits, become more alert and thus reduce the effect of disinformation campaigns.

Governments and fact-checkers need to monitor the propaganda agents used to sustain and popularise similar disinformation narratives and to study how they relate to each other. Also useful would be an up-to-date catalogue of websites that mimic media outlets commonly used to plant disinformation that is then amplified by other actors, including the Russian state media. When disinformative content is detected on these websites, speed is of the essence to mitigate the amplification process. The intervention of fact-checkers is necessary to debunk the falsehoods and provide evidence to prove lies are just that: lies. It is useful to conduct more research on how actors interact with each other when disseminating a disinformation narrative. Finding patterns of action can help anticipate the next steps state propaganda machines will take when they launch a disinformation campaign.

The EEAS should prioritise investment in multilingual tracking tools capable of detecting disinformation across different languages. This would allow for faster identification of manipulative content in different linguistic and regional contexts.

7.6 Others Try to Profit from a FIMI Attack

Various threat actors, including state-sponsored groups, criminal organisations, hacktivists and individuals with malicious intent, sometimes work together without any agreements. They share the same objective, so they all work to achieve it, bringing to bear their particular specialities in FIMI.

Some cases (such as PAPERWALL) show that FIMI campaigns can serve both financial and political interests. The PAPERWALL findings confirmed ‘the increasingly important role private firms play in the realm of digital influence operations and the propensity of the Chinese government to make use of them’.[7] Similarly, we saw in the case study (Sect. 4.26) about Turkish-controlled Northern Cyprus that real-estate websites engaged with the narrative, aiming to influence perceptions of stability and investment potential in the TRNC. Their involvement underscores the intersection of political narratives with financial interests. The TRNC-based real estate agencies may have engaged in the same misinformation campaigns without being centrally orchestrated. They shared the same interests in pushing for international recognition of the separatist territory.

A similar phenomenon appears in the Saudi case study (see Sect. 4.29). State-sponsored groups used governmental resources to advance geopolitical objectives,

[7] Fittarelli, Alberto, “PAPERWALL Chinese Websites Posing as Local News Outlets Target Global Audiences with Pro-Beijing Content”, *The Citizen Lab,*7 Feb 2024. https://citizenlab.ca/2024/02/paperwall-chinese-websites-posing-as-local-news-outlets-with-pro-beijing-content/.

while criminal organisations exploited the situation for financial gain.[8] Ideologically motivated hacktivists and individuals with unclear motives also engaged in the attack.[9] This incident highlighted a disturbing trend in which ordinary individuals, in this case, Saudi citizens and right-wing Americans, played a role in spreading distorted narratives.[10]

7.7 Measuring FIMI's Impact

The impact of a FIMI campaign is uncertain. One way of measuring impact is by the number of impressions that social media posts get. However, the difficulty in measuring effectiveness is trying to disentangle what is local and what is amplified by interference. Russian disinformation efforts, particularly focusing on social media as a significant battlefield for information warfare, have been subject to extensive analyses by most Western countries' cybersecurity firms, intelligence agencies and academic research. However, the effectiveness of these campaigns and the impact of Western countermeasures remain subjects of ongoing analysis and debate. A comprehensive understanding of the impact of FIMI and any resulting changes in people's behaviour or actions is worth pursuit.

The EU and Member States should assess the vulnerability of states to exploitation in the information space and to implement proactive plans to counteract various forms of disinformation. This approach differs from pre-bunking by allowing governments to prepare defensively for potential adversarial responses, particularly in contexts such as negotiations for military alliances. This preparation could be complemented by analysing the audience consuming such disinformation. Given the association with military alliances and national security, governments should consider how best to develop counter-narratives that mitigate the risk of online harmful content designed to provoke emotional responses. Ensuring that harmful online content does not escalate into offline protests, riots or terrorism is vital.

[8] Uddin, R., "Russia, Iran and Saudi Arabia Worst Countries for State-Sponsored Twitter Disinformation", *Middle East Eye*, 2022. https://www.middleeasteye.net/news/twitter-disinformation-state-sponsored-russia-iran-saudi-arabia-worst.

[9] Abeshouse, B., "Inside the Wild West of Social Media", *b*, 8 February 2018.
https://www.aljazeera.com/features/2018/2/8/troll-factories-bots-and-fake-news-inside-the-wild-west-of-social-media.

[10] Byman, Daniel L., "How Middle Eastern conflicts are playing out on social media", Brookings Institute, 2022. https://www.brookings.edu/articles/how-middle-eastern-conflicts-are-playing-out-on-social-media/.

7.8 Countermeasures that Worked

Among the best defences against disinformation are transparency, effective communication and the use of counter-narratives that challenge disinformation targeting the European Union. Providing EU citizens with discursive elements so that they can evaluate different situations linked to disinformation implies being self-critical and taking seriously the relationship of trust between the European institutions and the societies of the different Member States. If trust deteriorates, victims of disinformation may not believe the content of a given FIMI incident, but they may also distrust the EU counter-narratives.

Pre-bunking will help citizens detect disinformation actions, become alert and thus reduce the effect of disinformation campaigns.

The case studies show the involvement of a wide range of FIMI actors, including state-owned media, private companies and opportunistic groups, showing the need for a whole-of-society approach to countering FIMI. EU DisinfoLab concludes that this whole-of-society approach 'can be realistically achieved only if the large variety of actors engaged in countering FIMI speak a common language. Initiatives such as the DISARM and STIX frameworks constitute that common language, set up to normalise the monitoring, analysis, assessment, and response to FIMI operations'.[11]

Speed is of the essence in case after case. In the case study of the doctored photograph of Zelenskyy (Sect. 4.13), the rapid decline in the circulation of observables after the initial spike suggests that de-bunking efforts played a critical role in mitigating the impact of the disinformation. The Russian FIMI attack in Germany quickly collapsed the moment that it became clear that Lisa made up the story about the rape to cover up her bad grades in school (Sect. 4.6). Quick and transparent communication in events like this plays a key role in preventing and combating FIMI.

Preventive surveillance measures, such as those employed by the French army to debunk the attack in Mali (Sect. 4.10), can also be crucial. Open-source intelligence (OSINT) is of special importance to dismantle the TTPs that are behind FIMI attacks. Detecting bots and fake accounts or verifying the concordance between the publication times of several tweets that refer to the same event are some of the strategies that can help counter a FIMI attack.

Spain's defence against Russia's FIMI operation (Sect. 4.12) to influence the national elections was strengthened by some EU initiatives like the Rapid Alert System[12] and the smooth intervention of fact-checkers and media, which effectively decreased the potential influence of the operation. This case also underscores the ongoing need for coordinated efforts to protect democratic integrity from evolving foreign interference tactics.

---

[11] Hénin, EU DisinfoLab, op. cit., p. 11.

[12] https://www.eeas.europa.eu/eeas/factsheet-rapid-alert-system_en.

The EU has developed several frameworks to combat disinformation, including the EU Cybersecurity Strategy[13] and initiatives through the European Centre of Excellence for Countering Hybrid Threats.[14] These bodies help coordinate responses to foreign interference across EU institutions and Member States, building resilience against cyberattacks and disinformation campaigns targeting elections.[15]

The EU established the East StratCom Task Force,[16] part of the European External Action Service (EEAS), to identify and expose pro-Russian disinformation targeting EU Member States.

The European Parliament has agreed a regulation harmonising political advertising requirements and banning foreign sponsorship of political ads before elections. The regulation includes provisions for clear labelling of political ads, improved access to financing information and the establishment of a public repository for online political ads and related data.[17]

7.9 Tighter Regulations for Digital Influence

The European Commission is currently pushing forward with plans for a new directive, as part of the Defence of Democracy Package[18] modelled after the US Foreign Agents Registration Act (FARA), requiring foreign-funded entities to register and specifically targeting Russian and Chinese influence. This legislation aims to safeguard democracies by imposing transparency obligations on entities seeking to shape public opinion and influence democratic processes. Through enhancing transparency and accountability, such measures seek to mitigate the risk of undue foreign influence on European political systems. Moreover, swift enforcement of regulations on political advertising will help to curb foreign interference. Further sanctions should target individuals and entities involved in Russian FIMI efforts, particularly focusing on those responsible for running disinformation networks like Viktor Medvedchuk and the Voice of Europe.

The Russian 'Doppelganger' operation showed how the abuse of the domain registration system or the European web infrastructure and software can be exploited by hostile actors for the purpose of foreign interference. The EU should

---

[13] https://digital-strategy.ec.europa.eu/en/policies/cybersecurity-strategy.

[14] https://www.hybridcoe.fi/.

[15] Koudelka, Michal, and Petr Fiala, "Czechs Bust Russian Network Paying off European Politicians", Radio Prague International, 28 Mar 2024. https://english.radio.cz/czechs-bust-russian-network-paying-european-politicians-8812632.

[16] https://www.eeas.europa.eu/countering-disinformation/tackling-disinformation-information-work-eeas-strategic-communication-division-and-its-task-forces_und_en?s=2803.

[17] European Parliament, "European Parliament legislative resolution of 27 February 2024 on the proposal for a regulation of the European Parliament and of the Council on the transparency and targeting of political advertising". https://www.europarl.europa.eu/doceo/document/TA-9-2024-0090_EN.html.

[18] https://civic-forum.eu/our-work/defence-of-democracy.

strengthen the verification and legitimacy of EU-registered online domains and companies. It should implement stricter regulations in the domain name industry to protect legitimate entities from being impersonated. It should implement stringent measures for fact-checking content and identifying potential sources of disinformation early. It should ensure appropriate measures so that EU-registered software and infrastructure are not exploited for malicious covert influence operations without facing consequences.

Existing laws, such as the Digital Services Act (DSA) and General Data Protection Regulation (GDPR), should be enforced to their full extent to safeguard citizens. Access to platform data to European researchers (including non-academics from civil society organisations) working for the public interest under Article 40 of the DSA needs to be greatly improved.[19]

We need better transparency with respect to the supported content published in social media. Social media influencers should make it clear when they receive money for their posts. Sponsors should be registered with the social media to know who sponsors what kind of content. This will make it clear when foreign actors (or their proxies) sponsor the distribution of specific content in social media. Better regulation of these sponsors should help with transparency. Attempts to bypass the regulation should have legal consequences. Regulatory bodies and legal authorities must take proactive steps to pursue legal actions and enforce measures against entities spreading false narratives.

Ethical and privacy concerns around the collection and use of social media data remain insufficiently addressed. The absence of clear ethical guidelines can lead to privacy violations, undermining public trust. Robust ethical protocols that align with legal standards like the GDPR must be developed to guide FIMI analysis practices.

7.10 International Cooperation

Effective countermeasures against disinformation campaigns require a multifaceted approach, involving cooperation between governments, private sector entities (especially social media platforms), civil society and the public. Given the rise of state-sponsored disinformation campaigns, particularly from authoritarian countries such as Russia, China and Iran, international collaboration is essential. Governments need to work together to develop coordinated strategies to identify, counter and mitigate the impact of these foreign threats, especially regarding political narratives and international relations. In addition, the interdisciplinary nature of FIMI requires a cross-sectoral collaboration with experts across government, industry, media and academia which will in turn encourage collaboration between fields such as political science, social data analysis, security studies and

[19] Art. 40 concerns providing "access to data to vetted researchers… for the sole purpose of conducting research that contributes to the detection, identification and understanding of systemic risks in the Union".

artificial intelligence. This cross-sectoral and international collaboration should support cross-disciplinary training and joint research initiatives to ensure a holistic understanding of FIMI and the development of interdisciplinary, collaborative data-sharing platforms and tools that could also support knowledge exchange, enabling better integration of technological, societal and geopolitical insights into the study and response to FIMI. These tools should be accessible and available to the public to identify and flag disinformation, including deepfakes and other manipulated content, helping to reduce confusion in the information space.

Governments should establish rapid-response teams trained to debunk FIMI as soon as it emerges. This can be supported by partnerships with fact-checking organisations, as exemplified by initiatives like #UkraineFacts. Strengthening international cooperation to facilitate swift information sharing across borders will help stem the flood of disinformation. Also vital is promoting global partnerships to share best practices on countering FIMI. The DISARM Framework is a good example. The use of international fact-checking databases should be encouraged to ensure swift identification of disinformation across different linguistic and cultural contexts.

European countries should deepen their cooperation in intelligence-sharing mechanisms to swiftly detect and disrupt foreign interference efforts, particularly ahead of elections. They should enhance cooperation with international bodies and third countries to prevent the relocation of disinformation operations to jurisdictions outside the EU's control. This includes coordinating sanctions and other measures to disrupt financial and logistical support for these campaigns.

Governments should strengthen international legal frameworks for prosecuting transnational disinformation campaigns. Enhanced cooperation between nations and the private sector, especially tech companies, is vital to detect, prevent and penalise attackers.

7.11 Gaps in Current Analysis Practices

Analysts face challenges in collaborating effectively due to limited tools for participatory and real-time analysis. Improved collaboration platforms are needed to support the sharing of insights, coordinating efforts on complex cases and ensuring agility in response. Furthermore, inconsistent methodologies and lack of training may result in variability in analysis quality. To address this, standardised methodologies and frameworks are needed to ensure consistency, along with enhanced training programmes.

The absence of version control in analysis workflows makes it difficult to document and manage the evolution of a case or incorporate differing viewpoints. Proper versioning systems are necessary to ensure that analyses are consistently reviewed, updated and accurately documented, which will facilitate collaboration and allow for comprehensive tracking of analytical progress.

There is no standardised approach to categorising or recording data, resulting in isolated analysis efforts that prevent cross-comparison of incidents. This hinders the ability to derive broader insights, especially for long-term campaigns. Establishing unified data formats and taxonomies, like DISARM, is essential for comparative analysis and to uncover trends across FIMI incidents.

Diverse tools and platforms currently in use do not communicate effectively, creating barriers to data sharing and comprehensive analysis. Improved interoperability through standardised APIs or data formats will enable seamless integration between systems, leading to more robust, integrative analyses.

7.12 Sharing Knowledge

EU-funded projects such as ATHENA form clusters with other similar projects to exchange knowledge and leverage impact, but much more could be done to foster a network of projects focused on disinformation in Europe and beyond, in the US, Canada and elsewhere. Good practice should be shared globally to tackle the scourge of disinformation and FIMI.

Collaborating with organisations to expose disinformation enhances the public's understanding of the authenticity and credibility of the information to which they are exposed. By collaborating with fact-checking organisations, and promoting verified information through official channels, stakeholders can identify false narratives as part of a FIMI campaign.

National governments should strengthen monitoring mechanisms, improve transparency and work more closely with fact-checking organisations to mitigate the impact of FIMI. Fostering collaboration between researchers, governments and AI specialists is crucial. Researchers can provide valuable insights into the evolving tactics of disinformation campaigns and the psychological mechanisms that make them effective. Governments can leverage these insights to inform policy and support the development of countermeasures. AI researchers can contribute by developing advanced detection tools and creating innovative solutions for identifying and mitigating the spread of disinformation. By combining their expertise, these stakeholders can create a more comprehensive and effective approach to combating FIMI and safeguarding democratic processes.

A significant deficiency exists in how knowledge and insights are stored and shared. Valuable insights from past analyses are often inaccessible, leading to repeated efforts and missed opportunities to leverage prior work. The need for centralised, easily accessible knowledge repositories—ideally shared among different analysis teams—would allow analysts to search and retrieve data from previous cases efficiently.

To counter future FIMI attacks, stakeholders should invest in and enhance OSINT capabilities, particularly in detecting automated accounts and fake profiles. Analysing and tracing digital footprints, such as fake accounts and bots, OSINT becomes indispensable in countering these threats. Additionally, a coordinated effort between physical surveillance and digital intelligence gathering is essential to not only disrupt the tactics but also to prevent future dissemination of false information. Increased training in these areas for both military and civilian personnel involved in defence against FIMI attacks can further bolster these efforts.

Cybercriminals and governments are creative in their attack strategies, which strengthens the need for the DISARM Framework so that defenders and researchers can identify and compare the tactics and techniques used in disinformation campaigns. Understanding the attack strategies of different players will help in attribution. The development and adoption of comprehensive frameworks such as DISARM should be pursued to standardise the monitoring, analysis, assessment and response to foreign influence. The DISARM Framework should be updated to include tools for measuring the time needed to react to FIMI activities, predict the political consequences of disinformation campaigns and categorise threat actors. State-owned media networks and political influencers should be classified as separate communication tools in the Framework.

7.13 Media Literacy and Public Awareness

The Eurobarometer published in December 2023[20] showed that the main concerns for EU citizens in the context of the elections in Europe were related to people basing their voting decision on disinformation (78%), followed by elections being manipulated through cyberattacks (72%), foreign countries influencing elections covertly (70%) and people being pressured into voting in a particular way (65%).[21]

Fortifying democratic practices necessitates an increase in the public's media literacy through well-funded educational campaigns. EU Member States should promote image and video fact-checking skills to help individuals identify manipulated content and other forms of digital deception. This will help build long-term resilience to disinformation. The widespread use of reverse image search tools[22] to trace the origin of false content has proven valuable and should be widely promoted as a best practice. Disinformation campaigns are becoming more visually persuasive, making it imperative for policymakers to develop media literacy programmes that equip the public with tools to critically assess both textual and visual information.

[20] https://www.europarl.europa.eu/at-your-service/en/be-heard/eurobarometer/plenary-insights-december-2023.

[21] European Commission, "Defence of Democracy—Commission Proposes to Shed Light on Covert Foreign Influence", press release, 12 December 2023. https://ec.europa.eu/commission/presscorner/detail/en/ip_23_6453.

[22] Reverse image search tools are used to verify the authenticity and origin of images. These tools allow users to upload or link to an image and find where it has appeared online, helping to identify whether the image has been reused, manipulated or misrepresented. For example, they can reveal if a photo claiming to show a current event was actually taken in a different location or time. Common tools include Google Reverse Image Search, TinEye and Yandex Image Search.

Educating users about disinformation tactics can help them act as a first line of defence, significantly reducing the spread and impact of false information. Promoting media literacy, especially in the verification of images and videos, will help the public to recognise and question the authenticity of the information they encounter. Children as well as adults will benefit from an education that helps them to critically analyse and question information. Governments and/or civil society organisations (CSOs) should launch campaigns to educate the public on how to critically assess news sources and check for the credibility of information and to critically evaluate motives behind information sources. Moderated public forums, debates and media outlets that purposefully present balanced perspectives on contentious issues could foster critical thinking and decision-making.

Individuals should be encouraged to seek alternative sources and question information in public campaigns. Educational initiatives should enhance the ability to discern manipulative content and empower the public to identify credible sources. These programmes should work in partnership with credible media organisations to provide accurate information and develop strategies for identifying and countering disinformation.

Informing the public about expected FIMI attacks is part of raising public awareness. This has been happening more often since the Russian invasion of Ukraine and especially in advance of the US elections in November 2024.[23] This is a welcome form of pre-bunking, advising the public in advance about an expected attack.

Given the growing complexity of FIMI and the increased reliance on social media and AI, there is a need to improve technological and digital literacy across all sectors and amongst the citizens. These efforts should focus on media literacy, helping citizens recognise and critically assess content, recognise manipulated information and understand the role of AI and algorithms in shaping the information landscape, especially in the context of political and international conflicts. Citizens should enhance their participation in mitigating the negative impact of manipulated information on democratic discourse.

Governments should establish partnerships with reputable media organisations to amplify accurate information. Government agencies, media regulatory bodies and educational institutions should provide journalists with comprehensive training to identify and effectively report misinformation. Collaboration with international journalism associations and experienced media professionals will ensure the training is robust, practical and aligned with global best practices.

[23] "In recent weeks, the intelligence agencies have dramatically stepped up their alerts. Two weeks ago, they warned of post-election violence. Over the last 10 days, they have now issued three warnings about Russian attempts to undermine faith in the election. And Jen Easterly, the director of the Cybersecurity and Infrastructure Security Agency, said her organization would give regular updates Tuesday to inform the public of threats to the election." Barnes, Julian E., and Steven Lee Myers, "Russian and Other Groups May Try to Undermine U.S. Elections After Vote", *The New York Times*, 4 November 2024. https://www.nytimes.com/2024/11/04/us/politics/election-threats-russia.html.

Public awareness campaigns and social cohesion campaigns are needed to build a robust and trustworthy social fibre amongst people.It is crucial to promote media literacy programmes that help people recognise false narratives and misinformation, especially on social platforms along with community-building initiatives for bridging political and social divides, fostering trust and collaboration among diverse groups. Efforts to strengthen social cohesion should focus on building shared identities and encouraging open dialogue to counter polarisation and there should be a long-term strategy focusing on enhancing social unity, resilience and a healthy public discourse.

Combatting FIMI necessitates a comprehensive strategy. Governments and international organisations must work together to share insights and formulate tactics against disinformation. Supporting civil society organisations that advocate for media literacy will also help to educate individuals on how to critically evaluate online information and differentiate trustworthy sources from propaganda.

Promoting transparent and inclusive political dialogue within countries needs to address the root causes of social unrest and reduce vulnerability to external manipulation. By addressing the underlying causes of social unrest, promoting media literacy and holding perpetrators accountable, countries can strengthen their resilience against foreign information manipulation and interference to safeguard their democratic processes.

MIX
Papier aus verantwortungsvollen Quellen
Paper from responsible sources
FSC® C105338

If you have any concerns about our products,
you can contact us on
ProductSafety@springernature.com

In case Publisher is established outside the EU,
the EU authorized representative is:
Springer Nature Customer Service Center GmbH
Europaplatz 3, 69115 Heidelberg, Germany

Printed by Libri Plureos GmbH
in Hamburg, Germany